The
Princeton
Review

PrincetonReview.com

BEST 168
MEDICAL
SCHOOLS

Malaika Stoll
2009 EDITION

Random House, Inc.
New York

The Princeton Review, Inc.
2315 Broadway
New York, NY 10024
E-mail: bookeditor@review.com

ISBN: 978-0-375-42881-4

Printed in the United States of America.

Publisher: Robert Franek
Editors: Adam Davis, Laura Braswell
Account Manager: David Soto
Executive Director, Print Production: Scott Harris
Senior Production Editor: M. Tighe Wall

9 8 7 6 5 4 3 2 1

2009 Edition

Acknowledgments

Special thanks must go to the hundreds of med students and scores of Admissions Officers who have supplied information for this book over the years. This year's edition owes a great debt to the efforts of many: to Adam Davis, Laura Braswell, Adrinda Kelly, M. Tighe Wall, and Scott Harris for their editorial and design talents; to David Soto for heading the data collection efforts; to Ben Zelevansky for his data-pouring wizardry and sense of humor; and to Robert Franek, Publisher, for his enthusiasm.

Contents

Preface

For more than 25 years The Princeton Review has offered preparatory courses and tutoring for standardized tests such as the SAT, MCAT CBT, LSAT, GRE, GMAT, and USMLE. More than 100,000 students took our courses last year, and hundreds of thousands have bought our *Cracking* series test-prep books. At the center of our approach is the desire to help students tear away the anxiety and sense of helplessness that have surrounded these entrance exams for so many years. The Princeton Review has long been an advocate of students' right to be informed consumers, and it works to make sure that information on these tests is readily accessible to all.

In addition to being consumers of entrance exams, students are also consumers of education. Before investing in a graduate degree, they have the right and the need to gather as much information as possible. We hope that this publication will provide students with a viable means of achieving this goal. The *Best 168 Medical Schools* contains the essentials students will need to answer basic and advanced questions regarding their lists of prospective medical schools. The 2009 edition is our most complete medical school handbook to date; it contains 125 accredited allopathic schools in the United States, including Puerto Rico (we've retained a separate profile for the University of Minnesota Medical School—Duluth), 17 accredited allopathic schools in Canada, 20 accredited osteopathic schools, and a section profiling 6 accredited naturopathic schools in the United States and Canada.

When viewing individual schools listed in this year's guide, you will find the union of painstakingly researched school profiles coupled with school-specific statistical data. Each profile has been sent to the medical school for review prior to publication so that we may provide our readers with the most accurate and current information about the programs. The data presented was the most up-to-date available at the time of publication; students should consult the schools' websites for further information.

We hope this book will serve as an important guide as you research, gather, and consider information before embarking on your medical career, and we wish you the best of luck as you pursue your career in medicine. If you have questions, comments, or suggestions, we welcome them. Please give us your insights:

The Princeton Review
Best 168 Medical Schools
2315 Broadway
New York, NY 10024
bookeditor@review.com

We appreciate your input and want to make our books as useful to you as they can be.

Sincerely,
Adam Davis and Laura Braswell
Co-editors
The Princeton Review Books

So Much More Online!

MORE GUIDANCE...

- Find the school that best fits your needs, from part-time options to specialized programs.
- Learn about raising test scores, finding an internship, and planning out your career after you graduate.
- Get the inside scoop of scholarships and financial aid.

MORE INFORMATION...

- Read articles on what it's really like to be in grad school.
- Learn what students have to say in detailed profiles for hundreds of colleges covering everything from administration to student diversity on campus.
- Compare Top 10 ranking lists regarding Quality of Professors, Classroom Experience, Career Prospects, Competitive Students, Quality of Life, and tons more!

MORE GOOD STUFF . . .

- Discover other Princeton Review titles that will help you take your career in a new direction or ace that next big exam.
- Discuss issues with your peers on our discussion board.
- Find answers to any of your grad school questions, and much, much more!

1 How to Use This Book

Although some people describe medical school education as somewhat canned—downplaying the differences between schools—differences do exist. Some differences, like the fact that a family medicine clerkship lasts two weeks at one school and eight at another, might not seem like a big deal, but such details may help convey a school's priorities. The school profile section of this guide will help you to discern such differences, and in doing so, match your interests with the school that can best fulfill them. But don't just use this book to decide where to apply; use it also as a resource to help you decide when to apply—or if you really want to apply at all. The detailed information about course offerings and facilities will help you prepare for interviews. Examine the profiles for descriptions of each program's fundamental academic approach and resources, the student body, and the school's emphasis as evidenced by the path its graduates take. These are all good points to bring up in an interview and will aid your decision of where to attend.

As you review the school profiles, keep the following in mind:

- Just as admissions offices rely too heavily on quantitative measures to evaluate candidates (MCAT CBT and GPAs), applicants probably rely too much on school ranking in deciding where to apply and where to go to school. Often, the criteria for determining a school's ranking have little to do with how well a school will train you or how enjoyable your experience will be (National Institutes of Health research dollars, for example). Thus, you will find no quantitative rankings in this book.

- Our goal is to present accurate and complete descriptions of medical schools. Note that the admissions offices of each medical school had the opportunity to read and edit our write-ups. The data presented in this book was the most up-to-date at the time of publication. In deciding where to apply or where to go, you should consult the schools' websites in addition to using this book as part of your research. Take every opportunity to meet with medical students at the schools in which you are interested. Speak with more than just one student—and with students in different years—at each school.

- In response to managed care and other trends, many medical schools that traditionally focused on research or specialty medicine now claim to focus on primary care. Whether a school really has changed its focus may be partially gleaned from the percentage of graduates entering primary care fields. Note, however, that definitions of primary care vary (some include ob/gyn for example).

- In the Graduates section (under Students), a statistic on what percent of students match within their top one, two, or three residency preferences may appear. Less prestigious schools often have impressive rates. This is due in part because students only rank schools that they have a good chance of getting into (and at which they obtained an invitation to interview). In addition, students at less prestigious schools are less likely to enter highly specialized residency positions that are typically the most competitive. Please note that this stat is often misleading.

- For most schools, we list website addresses—they are often helpful and some include candid student opinions. Try to visit these websites before you make a commitment to apply, to interview, or to attend.

HOW THIS BOOK IS ORGANIZED

The 2009 edition of this book includes 142 U.S. and Canadian accredited allopathic medical schools. You may notice that we no longer list Puerto Rican schools separately from U.S. schools. The AAMC lists them under one umbrella, and so do we. The profile of each school is broken down into five text sections—Overview, Academics, Students, and Admissions. Three categories of hard stats supplement the general data in the allopathic profiles—Student Body, Admissions, and Cost and Aid—listed in the shaded sidebar column. We also created supplementary chapters of lists—including a general overview and admissions requirements—of the 23 accredited osteopathic schools, and of the 6 accredited naturopathic schools.

Here's what you will find in the various text and statistic sections for each school profile.

PROFILE

ACADEMICS

First, we give you a basic look at the academic program—quarter system or semester, pass/fail or honor, and USMLE requirements. Then we break it down in accordance with how your own studies will be broken down—Basic Sciences and Clinical Training—outlining the academic requirements and path of each. Here you will find out how much time you have to spend hunched over a book versus the fun part—hunched over, say, a cadaver. We will often use the term *selective* to describe certain clinical requirements. It means that students have some choice within a specified area: Selective courses are less "free" than an *elective* (which might also have some restrictions).

STUDENTS/CAMPUS LIFE

Discover where your potential classmates call home and who they are—percentage-wise. In the Student Life section, we describe what kind of recreation facilities are available, where you might live, where you might go out. We also include information about the graduates. Who are the grads of this school—primary care physicians, surgeons, public health administrators—and in what type of community do they choose to practice?

ADMISSIONS

The Requirements section details what the school is looking for in its prospective students. Pay special attention to the Suggestions section for some hints about how to impress the school. Then whip out your Palm Pilot—the Process section will tell you the dates you need to know and key stats about who gets interviews (and then who the lucky recipients of the fat envelopes are).

SIDEBAR

The shaded column next to each school listing contains the following information:

STUDENT BODY

Type: Is the school private or public? This is important information that is closely tied to the cost of tuition. In addition, public schools are often open only to state residents.

Enrollment: Total number of students enrolled in the medical school.

% male/female: Gender breakdown based on total enrollment.

% underrepresented minorities: Percentage of African Americans, Native Americans, Mexican Americans, and mainland Puerto Ricans in the total enrollment.

 # applied: The number of people who applied to the school in the most recently reported year, presented as the total number, and the number of out-of-state/province residents who applied.

 # accepted: The number of applicants who were accepted at the school in the most recently reported year. Also broken down in terms of total and out-of-state/province.

 # enrolled (out-of-state): The number of out-of-state applicants who were accepted who actually entered the school as first-year medical students in the most recently reported entering class.

Average age: The average age of the entering class.

FACULTY

Total faculty: The number of faculty employed by the medical school.

% female: Percentage of female faculty members.

% minority: Percentage of underrepresented minorities present on the faculty.

% part-time: Percentage of part-time faculty members.

Student-faculty ratio: The ratio of faculty members to enrolled students.

ADMISSIONS
Overall GPA
Average undergraduate grade point average of the students who matriculated in the most recently reported entering class.

MCAT CBT
Average MCAT CBT scores of the students who matriculated in the most recently reported entering class, broken down into the following areas: Biology, Physics, Verbal, and Essay.

Application Information
Outlines all the dates and facts you need to know:

Regular application: The latest date the school will accept all application materials for regular admission.

Regular notification: The latest date the school will notify prospective students of its decisions concerning regular admission.

Early application: The latest date the school will accept all application materials for the early decision plan.

Early notification: The latest date the school will notify prospective students of its decisions concerning admission to the early decision plan.

Are transfers accepted? Yes or No.

Admissions may be deferred? Yes or No.

Interview required? Yes or No.

Application fee: How much does it cost to apply?

Admissions requirements (required): Required qualifications in order for an applicant to be considered for admission into the school's program.

Admissions requirements (optional): Additional suggested qualifications for applicants—not required for admission.

Overlap schools: The other schools to which applicants are most likely to apply.

COSTS AND AID
Tuition & Fees
Most recent yearly tuition figures available for state residents and nonresidents. The amount of money students can expect to spend on books and fees is listed here as well.

Financial Aid
% students receiving aid: Percentage of medical students at the school receiving some sort of financial aid.

Average grant: The amount of money in grants students receive on average.

Average loan: The amount of money students borrow on average.

Average debt: How much do students owe when they get out?

2 So You Want to Be a Doctor . . .

A GLIMPSE AT MEDICINE IN THE TWENTY-FIRST CENTURY

Do you want to be a doctor? If your answer is yes, use this chapter to prepare yourself for what lies ahead. (This chapter can also prepare you for medical school interviews—you can impress interviewers with your knowledge of current trends in health care!) If you're not yet sure whether medicine is the career for you, this chapter will help you decide. Learn about current issues as well as potential future trends in health care, medicine, and physician practice. The purpose of this chapter is to provide a glimpse of what life will be like for you as a doctor. Although it is impossible to predict the future, research and analysis have allowed us to identify some of the issues that will shape medicine in the coming years.

DECISIONS, DECISIONS . . .

Becoming a doctor requires a real commitment, so your decision to pursue this career path should be an informed one. You should consider information from discussions with medical professionals as well as from books such as this one. Talk to as many doctors as you can. Find out how they spend their days and what they love and don't love about their professions. Think about whether you could fill their shoes and whether you would thrive in doing so. Always consider your source when gathering information. For example, television shows with exciting plots and attractive actors glamorize medicine, whereas newspapers sometimes do the opposite by highlighting negative trends and emphasizing scandals.

While you are fortunate to have hundreds of career options to choose from, having so many choices can be confusing and overwhelming. Don't let indecision paralyze you. Consider taking time off after college to work in medical or nonmedical fields, to travel, or to volunteer before applying to medical school. This type of experience serves the dual purpose of allowing you to assess your interest in medicine and giving you something to write about in your medical school application essays (not to mention that it can be fun and meaningful, depending on what you do). The chapter in this book on nontraditional medical school applicants discusses several alternative paths to medical school. In deciding whether medicine is the career for you, you should also reflect on the paths that you won't be taking. Are you deciding between being a teacher or a doctor? Why not teach for a year or two and then reconsider medical school? The skills you learn teaching will help you explain medical issues to patients if you decide to become a physician.

Perhaps you feel that there are too few rather than too many career possibilities from which to choose. Some people consider medicine, law, and other obvious professions because they just don't know what else is out there. In this situation, there is nothing like spending a couple of years in the real world. This will expose you to various professions and career options. Even working for a temp agency can be beneficial; it can provide exposure to a number of fields and organizations. Learning about other options might confirm your interest in medicine or could lead you in another direction. Either way, it will be a valuable use of your time.

WHAT IT TAKES TO BE A DOCTOR

In some ways, being a doctor in the United States in the twenty-first century is similar to being a doctor in any number of cultures during just about any time period. There are a few traits that are essential, no matter where you are or what century you're in. Consider the following questions:

Do you want to spend your life helping others?

Doctors heal people, save lives, and help others—often through direct, face-to-face interactions. If this is your motivation, you're in good company. However, there are other altruistic careers out there, all of which involve less schooling and less debt than medical school. The desire to help others should be one, but not your only, reason for becoming a doctor.

Do you enjoy working hard?

Medicine is an incredibly challenging field. This was the case a hundred years ago when doctors worked to fight yellow fever, polio, and influenza, and it is the case today as health professionals try to prevent and treat heart disease, cancer, AIDS/HIV, and influenza, while dealing with the constraints of managed care. Consider medicine only if you love challenges and you know you want tremendous challenge in your professional life. As you read through this chapter, think about whether the challenges involved in practicing medicine are the ones that appeal to you. For example, a physician who is 20 years out of medical school is still expected to be familiar with the latest medical developments. One of the challenges of practicing medicine is a commitment to lifelong learning.

Are you interested in science and health issues?

If you enjoyed some aspects of your science courses (few people enjoy all aspects of pre-medical course work) and you find yourself drawn to health issues, there is a good chance that you will enjoy studying and practicing medicine. Although medicine has changed significantly over the years, its roots remain in basic science.

Do you like working with different people?

With the exception of a few fields, medicine involves working with people, many of whom may be very different from you. If science interests you but working with people does not, you may wish to consider a PhD rather than an MD (this choice also involves less debt). You might also look into an MD that allows you to do only research.

WHAT IT'S LIKE TO BE A DOCTOR

What is life like as a doctor in the twenty-first century? Although it varies a great deal depending on specialty, geographic region, employment situation, and so on, we can get a general idea by examining recent data.[1,2]

PATIENT CARE

Most doctors—90 percent—spend their time seeing patients; in fact, they see 20 to 25 patients per day on average. Doctors generally work in one of three situations: solo, as part of a group practice, or as an employee of a hospital or organization. The most common reason people go to the doctor is for some sort of checkup or test. Other common reasons for doctor visits are respiratory (allergies, the flu), gastrointestinal (heart burn, nausea), and psychological (e.g., depression) complaints. An important responsibility of the primary care physician is to identify potentially serious issues during routine examinations. On the other side of the spectrum, a major challenge for doctors with highly specialized training (e.g., oncologists, cardiologists, and surgeons) is to work intensely to save and improve lives. The most common causes of mortality (death) in the United States are listed below.

Top Ten Causes of Mortality in the United States[3]

1. Diseases of the heart (heart disease).

2. Malignant neoplasms (cancer).

3. Cerebrovascular diseases (stroke).

4. Chronic lower respiratory diseases (e.g., emphysema, asthma, bronchitis).

[1] Association of American Medical Colleges. *AAMC Data Book*. Statistical Information Related to Medical Schools and Teaching Hospitals. January 2003. www.aamc.org/data/databook.

[2] The Future of American Medicine. American Medical Association. Council on Long Range Planning and Development. 1994.

[3] National Center for Health Statistics. Deaths: Leading Causes for 2005. www.cdc.gov/nchs.

5. Accidents.

6. Diabetes mellitus (diabetes type 2).

7. Alzheimer's disease.

8. Influenza and pneumonia.

9. Nephritis, nephrotic syndrome, and nephrosis (kidney disease).

10. Septicemia (blood poisoning).

Note that all of the above except Alzheimer's are preventable. Preventive medicine and the interdisciplinary approach are important elements of practicing medicine.

WORKLOAD AND COMPENSATION

On average, doctors work 60 hours per week. Obstetricians work longer hours, 62 per week, while the typical psychiatrist works shorter hours, 49 per week. Although their annual incomes have decreased over the past few years, physicians are still among the highest paid professionals in the country. The following table presents median annual income for nine areas of practice. Incomes listed are after expenses (such as staff and malpractice insurance) but before taxes.

Medical Field	Annual Income
Anesthesiology	$322,000
General/Family Practice	$156,000
Internal Medicine	$166,000
Ob/Gyn	$247,000
Pathology	$223,000
Pediatrics	$161,000
Psychiatry	$180,000
Radiology	$286,000
Surgery	$283,000
All Physicians	$160,000

Source: Medical Group Management Association. *Physician Compensation and Production Report*. 2005.

The figures listed above do not account for residents, who are notoriously underpaid. The national median salary for a resident is about $35,000. In the interest of patient safety, there have been some efforts—at the state and hospital level, and among residents themselves—to limit the number of hours that residents work each week. These efforts have been somewhat successful. However, despite the rules limiting the workweek to 80 hours, many residents continue to work more than 100 hours per week. Why are residents required to work so hard? In part, it's because hospitals depend on residents as a cheap source of labor, since they are paid much less than other physicians and somewhat less than nurses and other health professionals.

PRESTIGE

Almost universally, being a doctor carries prestige. Doctors are generally thought to be smart, well educated, hardworking, caring, and dedicated. Even in this era of managed care and malpractice lawsuits, doctors are well respected. In a recent Harris poll, Americans ranked "doctor" as one at the most prestigious professions/occupations.[4] You should consider the degree to which having a prestigious career is important to you. Other health professions, although perhaps less glamorous, also involve healing and helping others.

TRENDS IN MEDICINE IN THE TWENTY-FIRST CENTURY

Several trends in medicine that began during the past few decades are likely to continue well into the twenty-first century. These trends have implications for you, the aspiring doctor. They will impact the nature of your work, the structure of the organization in which you work, your salary, the relationship you have with patients, and above all, the quality of the health care you deliver.

In the sections that follow, we consider some important trends (we call them the Top 10, with a disclaimer that predicting the future is difficult) affecting medicine in the twenty-first century.

Top 10 List: Trends in Medicine in the Twenty-First Century

1. Development of new technology.

2. Increased health care costs.

3. Evolution of health care delivery and payment systems.

4. Greater reliance on primary and preventive care.

5. More guidelines for patient care.

6. A possible surplus of physicians, at least in certain specialty areas.

[4] The Harris Poll #58. "Firefighters, Doctors and Nurses Top List as 'Most Prestigious Occupations.'" July 26, 2006. www.harrisinteractive.com/harris_poll.

7. Improved gender and ethnic diversity among physicians.

8. An aging patient population.

9. The emergence of new ethical issues.

10. Changes in academic medicine and medical education.

Note that the above list is by no means complete. Also, the trends listed are interrelated and are not necessarily in order of importance.

NEW TECHNOLOGY

Medicine and health care has improved during the past few decades largely because of technological advancement; there are probably even more exciting developments on the horizon. The term *technology* is often used broadly. In the health care arena, it means the development of new drugs, procedures, techniques, and means of communication that, if used correctly, have the potential to improve diagnosis, care, and patient outcomes.

- **Medications and Procedures.** The increase in life expectancy over the past few decades is partially due to improvements in medications and procedures. For example, the death rate due to heart disease is declining because of better drugs (hypertension, heart, and cholesterol medications) and surgical techniques.

- **Laboratory Techniques.** Often, improvements in laboratory tools or techniques lead to important discoveries. For example, better tools allowed the human genome to be mapped.

- **The Internet.** Patients who are Internet users arrive at their doctor's office well informed about their illnesses. On the other hand, the Internet houses a great deal of misinformation. The physician who is Web savvy can guide patients to informative websites and web-based support groups. The Internet is an invaluable tool for research.

- **Telemedicine.** Telemedicine is defined by the American Telemedicine Association as *"the use of medical information exchanged from one site to another via electronic communication for the health and education of the patient or health care provider and for the purpose of improving care."* Sharing of radiographic images and patient information (X rays, MRIs) via computer between physicians is an important current application. In the future, we may see telemedicine bring the expertise of specialists to rural or other remote areas.

- **Other Computer Applications.** Computerized database systems are used for billing and patient records. Some physicians take advantage of software programs made for handheld devices. These can be used for note-taking, reference, or even patient management. Not surprisingly, it is often the younger doctors (and medical students) who are the most comfortable with computer technology. Interest in and understanding of relevant computer applications can give you an advantage when it comes to working with older, more experienced doctors; instead of just learning from them, you will have something to contribute. The key is being able to explain, teach, and pass on your knowledge effectively.

HEALTH CARE COSTS

The United States spends more money per capita on health care than any other country in the world. Some believe that the U.S. offers the best medical care in the world, thereby justifying the high cost. Others note that, according to indicators such as life expectancy and infant mortality, the U.S. lags behind other industrialized countries. In 1960, 6 percent of the U.S. Gross Domestic Product (the sum total of all expenditures, by all people, in a given country) went to health care. In 2000, that figure climbed to 20 percent, meaning that nearly a fifth of the GDP went to health-related goods and services. There are many theories as to what has caused this escalation, two of which are discussed below.

Technology

As discussed above, technological advances usually serve to improve health care and health outcomes. However, technology is often cited as a major cause of rising health care costs. When new tools are developed and advertised, hospitals and physicians may feel pressure to purchase and use them, even if the benefit of the new device is still questionable. Someone ultimately pays for such purchases, and thus we see rising health care costs. The MRI—an imaging device that, for about $2,000, provides pictures of a patient's organs—is often thought to be overused in this country. For example, there are more MRI machines in Orange County, California, than in all of Canada.[5] It is important to remember, however, that technological advances can also serve to reduce costs. By preventing illness and reducing the spread of disease, new vaccines (anti-influenza, for example) lower the cost of treatment for society overall. New surgical instruments and the development of medication in pill form facilitate the use of out-patient procedures instead of expensive hospital stays.

Incentives

Patients are generally far removed from the cost of their care and, therefore, have little incentive to keep costs down. Employers and the government—not patients themselves—foot most of the bill for health care, creating a system of "third-party payers."[6] Some believe that since patients don't pay much for their own health care, they overuse it, thereby driving government and employer health care expenditures up.

[5] "By the Numbers: Health Care Costs." *Scientific American*. April 1999.

[6] The United States relies largely upon an employer-based health care financing system, which means that most people (60 percent) receive health benefits through their work. In other words, employers pay for employees' health care—typically by taking responsibility for paying monthly premiums. Twenty percent of the population receives government health care benefits in the form of Medicare (everyone over 65 is eligible) or Medicaid (eligibility based on financial need).

As a physician, you will undoubtedly feel pressure to keep health care costs down. In many practice settings, doctors are scrutinized on the basis of the cost of the tests and treatments they prescribe. For example, primary care doctors are sometimes encouraged to limit referrals to specialists. All doctors may be monitored for overuse of expensive tests and equipment. Physicians face difficult decisions as they attempt to provide excellent care at a lower cost: if a patient has a slim chance of benefiting from an expensive treatment, should that treatment be employed? The physician must balance the cost of treating with the risk of not treating.

HEALTH CARE DELIVERY SYSTEMS

The push for management of health care costs has led to the growth of managed care. One of the most important trends of the past few decades has been the replacement of simple fee-for-service plans by the growth of the managed care industry.

Fee-for-Service

Before managed care, health care was delivered on a *fee-for-service* basis. Medicare (federally funded health insurance for those over 65 years of age) remains a fee-for-service program. Under a fee-for-service system, doctors and hospitals perform a service (a check-up, an operation, etc.) and charge a fee for the service. Typically, the patient's health insurance company pays the fee for whatever medical service the patient wants or needs. The patient pays the health insurance company a monthly premium or, if the patient has health benefits from his employer, the employer pays the monthly premiums. The insurance company calculates monthly premiums based on how much it pays out to hospitals and doctors each year for all people enrolled in the insurance plan.

Managed Care

Managed care was introduced as a response to rising health care costs, and has succeeded in slowing the rate at which health care costs rise. Thus, the trend toward managed care will probably continue. Although managed care is often thought to be synonymous with Health Maintenance Organizations (HMO), an HMO is, in fact, just one of many systems for managing care.[7]

Managed care usually involves set monthly premiums that are lower than those in fee-for-service plans, and this makes those paying the premiums (usually the employers) happy. How do managed care organizations keep their premiums down? By keeping their financial outlays down. Under managed care, expenditures are typically controlled through several mechanisms:

---

[7] HMOs specify the doctors and hospitals that participants must use. Another example of a managed care organization is a Preferred Provider Organization (PPO). PPOs encourage the use of certain providers ("preferred providers") but will also cover part of the cost of doctors and hospitals outside of the preferred provider network.

- Participants in a managed care plan agree to use doctors and hospitals that are part of the plan, and these providers are either paid yearly salaries or charge reduced fees for services rendered.
- Primary care physicians serve as "gatekeepers" in limiting the use of expensive medical specialists.
- Guidelines/regulations are implemented that attempt to limit the use of expensive tests and equipment in unnecessary situations.
- Inpatient care is reduced, and there is more emphasis on outpatient services (care that does not involve an overnight hospital stay). Associated with the movement toward outpatient care, hospitals are filling fewer of their beds and are seeing a decline in length of stay (LOS) for hospital patients.

Managed care has generated some discontent among some patients and providers in the past. Though public opinion is still far from pleased, managed care companies are making gaining ground, according to a recent study.[8] This is the sixth consecutive year of negative opinion. Over the years the distinction between managed care and health insurance has greatly diminished because most insurance companies (and all the larger ones) now provide HMOs, PPOs, and other managed care services. At times the ratings of managed care have been better than health insurance; sometimes they have been worse. The improvement in the (still very low) public opinion score of managed care companies may result from a decline in all news, and especially unfavorable news, about managed care, as the public debate has focused on Medicare reform. For better or for worse, being a doctor in the twenty-first century is likely to involve practicing in a managed care environment of some form.

The Uninsured

This section on health care delivery and payment would be incomplete without discussing the uninsured. At least 15 percent of people in the United States have no health insurance. The U.S. is unique among industrialized nations in that respect, and it is not exactly something to be proud of. Individuals without health insurance tend to seek medical care—typically through an emergency room—only after a health problem has become really serious. This is obviously bad for the patient, who with early treatment might have avoided serious complications. It is also costly to society, because prevention and early treatment are less expensive than late intervention. Most people—physicians and nonphysicians alike—believe that everyone should have access to health care. However, there is less agreement on how universal access should be achieved and funded. Doctors will need to speak out to assure that this issue is addressed as soon, and as equitably, as possible.

---

[8] "Public Attitudes to Hospitals, Pharmaceuticals, and Managed Care Companies Improve Significantly," May 11, 2005, www.harrisinteractive.com/news.

Primary and Preventive Care

Most observers predict that as managed care grows, primary care physicians will continue to play a very important role, and the demand for primary care doctors will remain relatively high. Primary care physicians may be either MDs, DOs, or NDs (see page 22 for a description of each degree).

Gatekeepers

Before the days of managed care, if a person discovered an odd-looking spot on his skin, he could go directly to a dermatologist and be reimbursed by his insurance company for the visit. An important tenet of managed care has been the requirement that enrollees see a primary care physician prior to visiting a specialist. Family practice, pediatrics, internal medicine, and ob/gyn are typically considered primary care fields. The primary care physician serves as a "gatekeeper," presumably reducing unnecessary visits to expensive specialists.

Without the training of a specialist (a dermatologist in our example above), the primary care physician may not be equipped to judge the seriousness of some conditions. Missing a pre-cancerous skin lesion, for example, may cause hardship for the patient later on. On the other hand, if a primary care doctor refers *all* patients with skin lesions to the dermatologist, the system has failed because each patient required two doctor visits rather than one.

Integrated Approach

A benefit of this emphasis on primary care is that, in theory, patients develop a long-term relationship with their primary care doctor who is better able to understand the social, economic, and community-related issues associated with their health. The primary care doctor presumably has an understanding of all physiologic systems. This comprehensive knowledge facilitates diagnosis or at least allows the physician to make the initial decision about what next steps will lead to diagnosis. Primary care physicians are well-positioned to address behavioral changes, such as exercise programs, that aid in the prevention of disease.

Prevention

Several of the major causes of morbidity (illness) and mortality (death) in the U.S. are preventable. Emphysema, for example, is often the result of heavy smoking. The most common type of diabetes is linked with obesity. We have learned that the spread of HIV can be reduced through educational programs and behavioral interventions. The high death rate in this country due to violent crime is often attributed to the prevalence of handguns, a situation that could be addressed through legislation. Advances in genetics could potentially revolutionize preventive medicine by allowing physicians to identify people who are going to get sick before they show any symptoms of disease.

Prevention is preferable to treatment for the obvious reason that, with prevention, illness is reduced or eliminated altogether. Whether prevention efforts are cost-effective depends upon the disease, its prevalence, and the technology employed. For example, mammography is helpful in detecting breast cancer at a treatable stage and can potentially prevent mortality and reduce the high costs associated with treating end-stage cancer. It is sensible and cost-effective to offer mammograms to women above a certain age. However, it is probably unreasonable to encourage women in their 20s to have annual mammograms because breast cancer at this age is rare and, furthermore, can be difficult to spot on a mammogram from a woman of this age.

GUIDELINES FOR PATIENT CARE

Fundamental to medicine are the doctor-patient relationship, the belief that each patient must be considered individually, and the principle that doctors should be allowed to use their best judgment when providing care. Do these ideals conflict with the recent trend of using guidelines in clinical medicine?

Evidenced-Based Medicine or Cookbook Medicine?

Doctors vary tremendously in their approaches to medicine and disease treatment. This is why, in serious illness, a second opinion is usually recommended. In recent years, there has been increased use of evidenced-based medicine (EBM) in clinical practice. EBM employs *scientific evidence* for the purpose of standardizing and improving patient care. Quantitative indicators such as rate of reduction of disease are typically used to evaluate procedures and treatments. The goal of EBM is to establish guidelines for clinical decision making based on the results of studies, particularly randomized clinical trials (these are generally considered the most accurate type of study).

Some doctors worry that the trend towards EBM de-emphasizes physician judgment, results in strict guidelines for treatment, and amounts to "cookbook medicine." On the other hand, EBM's supporters say that its population-based approach actually complements the one-on-one tradition of medicine by allowing doctors to defend their decisions with data. However, there are many diseases and clinical situations for which the EBM literature fails to provide clear evidence. In some cases, the risks and benefits of a particular therapy may differ depending on the study examined.

Cost Consciousness

Occasionally, guidelines that dictate clinical care are based on cost-cutting objectives rather than on sound medical evidence. Such "guidelines" may compromise patient care. Going back to our mammogram example, an HMO might encourage physicians to recommend mammograms to all women over 50, when research suggests that mammograms are highly beneficial for women in their 40s as well. It is the physician's ethical responsibility to give his patient honest and up-to-date medical advice (in this case, to recommend mammograms after age 40). At the same time, the physician may want to support the cost-cutting goals of his employer. This is the type of conflict that doctors face in the current era of cost-consciousness. There are no easy answers. However, familiarity with medical evidence and the rules of the organization will at least allow you to make informed decisions.

PHYSICIAN SURPLUS OR PHYSICIAN SHORTAGE?

From 1970 to 1990 there was a sharp increase in the number of residency positions in the U.S., largely as a result of government policy encouraging such growth. During the same period, there was a much less dramatic increase in the patient population. Some said that we were training too many doctors and that we would see a surplus. Since 1990, however, the number of residency programs has remained relatively stable, while the patient population has grown (partially as a result of an aging population). The surplus never occured; now some experts predict a shortage.

Whether we have a physician surplus, shortage, or neither, there will always be rural and inner-city areas that are in need of doctors. To combat this problem, federal and state-funded programs offer financial incentives to doctors who agree to work in underserved areas. There is also a shortage of physicians from certain ethnic backgrounds. It is important to have a physician population that represents the population that it serves. Most medical schools attempt to recruit students of ethnic backgrounds that are underrepresented in medicine.

DIVERSITY AMONG PHYSICIANS

Increased diversity among physicians is a positive trend and may result in better patient care.

Women

Approximately 49 percent of entering medical students are women. This is remarkable considering that just 20 years ago, women accounted for about 30 percent of medical students, and in 1960, less than 7 percent of medical students were women. Today, about 25 percent of practicing physicians are women, and this percentage will continue to rise. There are outstanding women physicians in every imaginable medical field. However, women are especially well represented in fields like pediatrics and ob/gyn, and less represented in other fields like surgical subspecialties. Several theories and generalizations have been put forth to help explain why women are attracted to some fields more than others. One such theory is that once there is a critical mass of women within a field, it becomes a more welcoming environment for other women. Also, people tend to be interested in fields that have personal relevance. Finally, many women tend to avoid fields with the very longest residencies (only 10 percent of neurosurgery residents, for example, are women).

Minorities

The medical profession is slowly becoming more ethnically diverse, as increased numbers of non-White medical school graduates enter the work force. This increase in diversity reflects the changing demographics of the U.S. population, better and more widely available educational opportunities, and active minority recruitment on the part of medical schools. If this trend continues, we will someday have a physician work force that is representative of the population at large, including African Americans, Mexican Americans, Puerto Ricans, other Hispanics, Native Americans, and other underrepresented minorities.

AGING POPULATION

In 2020, the median age in the U.S. will be 40 years, up from 36 in 2000 and 30 in 1960. As the population ages, the demand for medical care increases: The average number of doctor visits per year is three for the population at large, but is six for those over 74 years old. The aging of the American population contributes to rising health care costs. Because 99 percent of individuals over 65 are covered by Medicare, government expenditures on health care are expected to rise. The paperwork involved in treating a patient with Medicare is notoriously time consuming.

An older population will cause growth within certain fields, such as geriatrics, internal medicine, orthopedics, and cardiovascular medicine. The incidence of chronic disease, meaning disease that is long-lasting and often incurable, will increase. Thus, physicians will often be called upon to provide palliative care that addresses symptoms when the underlying disease cannot be cured. Physician-researchers will be encouraged to find treatments for conditions that afflict the elderly, such as Alzheimer's Disease.

ETHICAL ISSUES

Physicians have always dealt with important ethical issues related to life and death. As a physician in the twenty-first century, some of your ethical dilemmas are likely to involve the conflict between saving money and saving lives. Consider the following scenario:

> *You are a pediatrician, seeing a patient you have never seen before. The patient is a very ill six-year-old without health insurance. Do you treat her, knowing that you will hear about it later? Or do you send her to the free clinic across town, even though it will entail a long bus ride for the sick girl?*

Ethical issues surrounding end-of-life care will become increasingly relevant because of an older patient population. For example:

> *Your patient is 80 years old and suffers from terminal lung cancer, which has spread to his brain. There are no cures for this man at this stage, so your care has been focused on keeping him comfortable. He can't breathe on his own, is incoherent, and has been more or less motionless in the hospital for one week. His daughter does not want you to remove life support. What do you do?*

The rule of doctor-patient confidentiality can also be the basis for ethical issues. Consider this situation:

> *You have been treating a young man in the hospital for a lung infection. During his hospital stay, he was tested for HIV, and the test results were positive. He is unwilling to discuss the matter, does not want medications that will help his HIV symptoms, and appears to be in denial. Do you have a responsibility to alert the man's wife?*

Unfortunately, some medical schools barely address ethics, leaving you on your own to learn about and think through important ethical issues. A mentor, someone whose opinion you respect, can serve as a resource for sorting out ethical questions. If you feel strongly about a particular issue, you should consider getting involved—through writing, attending conferences, or engaging in dialogue.

CHANGES IN ACADEMIC MEDICINE AND MEDICAL EDUCATION

Most medical schools are directly affiliated with teaching hospitals. Three advantages to this arrangement are the following:

- Medical students have the opportunity for hands-on learning.

- Patients are treated by expert physicians and benefit from the latest technology.

- The academic environment coupled with the clinical facilities provide an ideal setting for research that ultimately pushes medicine forward and improves care.

Academic medical centers throughout the country are having a tough time financially, leading some experts to question their future viability. Although medical school tuition seems incredibly high, it does not cover the actual cost of medical education; academic medical centers have historically depended on income from clinical activities to subsidize medical education, research activities, and management of a teaching hospital. As discussed, the shift toward outpatient medicine has resulted in reduced earnings for hospitals. For academic medical centers, this means less revenue to cover their high costs. As more and more academic medical centers face financial crisis, there will be pressure to cut costs and/or raise revenue significantly. We might see academic medical centers restrict their patients to those who can pay higher fees, or perhaps we'll see an increase in government funding and/or medical school tuition.[9]

In response to these changes in medicine and health care, most medical schools are attempting to revise their curricula. Some of the revisions we see are the following:

- Less time spent in lecture. Educators recognize that in this age of technology and information, there are simply too many facts to learn. Rather than inundate

[9] Keynotes on Health Care. Association of American Medical Colleges. 34 (1) Winter, 2000.

students with a massive amount of information, some medical schools hope to teach students general concepts that will prepare them for a lifetime of learning.

- More clinical problem solving during the first two years. With all that we know and all the treatment options available today, physicians must be thinkers and problem solvers.

- Greater emphasis on health economics, health care management, and public health. Doctors should understand the interdisciplinary nature of health care and the forces that affect medicine.

- Better training in outpatient medicine, with the use of outpatient clinics and doctors' offices for clinical rotations of outpatient facilities.

With the requirement of at least 11 years of post–high school training, becoming a physician takes longer in the U.S. than anywhere else in the world. This amount of required education is costly to society. Some people predict that as a result of financial pressures, the amount of schooling required to become a doctor will be reduced. For the time being, however, you have a long (but exciting) road ahead of you.

CONCLUSION: IS MEDICINE YOUR CALLING?

Whether you will be able to work effectively amidst all these changes depends in part on your flexibility. According to the American Medical Association." The next 10 to 15 years will be a period of substantial change for physicians. Physicians who are flexible, adaptable, and responsive to changing circumstances are likely to prosper during such a period."[10]

Apart from flexibility, what other traits will help you succeed and find job satisfaction as a physician in the twenty-first century?

What It Takes to Be a Doctor in the Twenty-First Century

Compassion—a critical part of healing

Advocacy—for your patients and for those without health care

Leadership—in improving health care at the team, hospital, and policy level

Lifelong learning—there will always be more to know

Interpersonal skills—communication with patients and among providers is key

Negotiation—ability to work around bureaucratic constraints

Grasp—of increasing amounts of medical knowledge and of a health care system in flux

Ask yourself: Is medicine your **calling**?

[10] ibid

3 So You Still Want to Be a Doctor . . .

Congratulations! The good news is that you are on your way to entering one of the most rewarding and respected fields, one of the few altruistic careers that pays a livable wage. The bad news is that, even armed with all the information we can give you and the help of a premed advisor, the application process is still tough. The painful reality is that there are about 40,000 applicants for approximately 18,000 spots. The good news, however, is that if you are persistent and have worked hard for the past several years to make yourself a competitive candidate, you have a good chance of obtaining a certified letter and a career that will keep you challenged and fulfilled for the rest of your life.

WHAT MAKES A COMPETITIVE APPLICANT?

Well, that's the $130,500 question (average debt of current medical school graduates). In 2006, the average matriculated (accepted) medical student had an undergraduate science GPA of 3.57, a non-science GPA of 3.71, and an overall GPA of 3.64; the average matriculated (accepted) medical student had average Medical College Admission Test Computer-Besed Test (MCAT CBT) scores of 9.8 Verbal Reasoning, 10.5 Physical Science, 10.4 Biological Sciences, and a P on the Writing Sample. But while GPA and MCAT CBT scores will play a large role in the admissions decision, they aren't everything. Solid numbers are a good start, but medical schools are also quite interested in who you are, why you want to be a physician, and whether or not you have a clue about what being a doctor is like. Therefore, in addition to strong grades and scores, you will strengthen your application by having volunteer activities listed, some experience in scientific academic research, practice in leadership roles, extracurricular activities, a well-written personal statement, excellent communication skills, and solid recommendation letters. All these application pieces will provide the Admissions Committee with a comprehensive picture of who you are, which is more than mere numbers can convey.

Also, keep in mind that, despite the odds, there are always large numbers of normal, sane people who actually didn't get straight A's or perfect MCAT CBTs who still manage to get into medical school. You can be one of them, and this book can help you to package yourself and to target schools that are likely to appreciate your unique strengths. If you have a hunch that your set of qualifications is not what traditional medical school admissions committees are looking for, consider a few alternate career paths. This book covers allopathic (MD) programs in the United States, Puerto Rico, and Canada (many Canadian schools accept only Canadians), osteopathic (DO) programs, and includes a brand new section on naturopathic (ND) programs. Don't rule out programs or schools in other health fields, such as dental school, nursing school, and physician assistant programs.

ALLOPATHIC MEDICINE

Allopathic schools confer the MD on their graduates, and allopathic training is by far the most widely available and recognized type of medical training. There are 142 accredited MD schools in the U.S., Puerto Rico, and Canada. The Canadian and Puerto Rican medical schools in this book are part of the American Association of Medical Colleges (AAMC). Teaching methodology varies among schools. The *traditional* model consists of two years of basic science followed by clinical rotations. The *systems-based* program is organized around physiologic systems, such as the lung or kidney. The *case-based* model teaches through clinical vignettes. There are also schools offering hybrids of these approaches. Most schools have made a concerted effort to get students together with patients at a much earlier stage in their education—it used to be that medical students might not come in contact with any patients until they'd already been through two years of school. At most schools, the last two years are spent doing clinical rotations. Even if you're sure that your calling in life is plastic surgery, you're going to have to do a pediatrics rotation. Most medical students really enjoy having a chance to delve into the various specialties, and this structure provides an excellent opportunity to learn about the areas you hope to pursue.

Allopathic training will give you the option to practice in any of the medical specialties, and the MD is universally recognized worldwide as a medical degree. For an abundance of information on all aspects of allopathic training and practice, visit the AAMC website (AAMC.org).

OSTEOPATHIC MEDICINE

Osteopathic medicine in the United States got its start in the late 1800s. Its founding father was Dr. Andrew Taylor Still, who established the American School of Osteopathy in Kirksville, Missouri, in 1892. The various regulatory bodies (osteopathic versions of AAMC and the AMA) were well underway by the early 1900s, and are now the American Osteopathic Association (AOA) and the American Association of Colleges of Osteopathic Medicine (AACOM). The DO is only issued in the U.S. Visit the AOA's website at Do-Online.org and the AACOM's website at AACOM.org to find out more about these organizations.

Osteopathic medicine has an interesting history; until fairly recently, its focus on preventive care, communication with the patient, and a holistic approach to health was considered to be somewhat radical. Now, of course, much of what osteopathic medicine has always espoused is rapidly becoming part of all medical training. In addition to a philosophical difference in approach, an important distinction between osteopathic and allopathic training is that osteopaths are taught an additional modality of treatment called manipulation (not to be confused with chiropractic manipulation, which has an entirely different system of education and is not recognized as a fully licensed medical degree). The osteopathic philosophy posits that there is a unity between a living organism's anatomy and physiology. Osteopathic science includes "the behavioral, chemical, physical, spiritual, and biological knowledge related to the establishment and maintenance of health as well as the prevention and alleviation of disease." Osteopathic concepts emphasize the following principles[1]:

1. The human being is a dynamic unit of function.

2. The body possesses self-regulatory mechanisms that are self-healing in nature.

3. Structure and function are interrelated at all levels.

4. Rational treatment is based on these principles.

What this means to the average osteopathic student is that he or she has to learn all of the same science as his or her allopathic counterpart, plus osteopathic diagnosis and treatment, in the same amount of time. Practicing osteopaths have another way of helping their patients that allopaths do not. Osteopaths achieved full-practice rights in 1973, although some states certified osteopaths to practice in all public hospitals as complete physicians and surgeons much earlier.

As you might guess from their philosophy and training, many osteopathic doctors choose to become primary care physicians. Most work in family practice, internal medicine, pediatrics, ob/gyn, and general surgery. In the words of one osteopathic dean, they tend to be generalists first and specialists second. However, there are DOs in just about every area of modern medical practice, from neurological surgery to psychiatry, oncology, and emergency medicine. Although the DO was not traditionally considered a research degree, the DO/PhD combination is becoming more common, and the AOA is becoming much more active in encouraging research activities, particularly in primary care.

At most osteopathic schools, matriculates have undergrad GPAs of about a 3.4 and combined MCAT CBT CBT scores of just under 25. In 2006, there were 9,700 applicants for approximately 3,900 seats. However, osteopathic schools do have a reputation for "looking past the numbers and place a strong emphasis on the whole picture of the candidate." This often makes osteopathic school an attractive choice for nontraditional, older students whose GPAs from their first trek through undergraduate school prove prohibitive in most allopathic programs. If you have a few blemishes on your academic record but a life that suggests you'll make a dedicated physician, you should consider applying to osteopathic schools.

[1] *AOA Yearbook of Osteopathic Physicians.* American Osteopathic Association. Chicago: AOA, 1996. 732.

Most premeds trying to decide whether or not to apply to osteopathic schools worry about what will happen to them after they graduate and apply for a residency. Osteopathic graduates participate along with allopaths and foreign medical graduates (both American and nonresident) in the National Resident Matching Program (NRMP), known as "the Match". DOs can apply for either osteopathic or allopathic residencies, and for that reason, many take both the United State Medical Licensing Examination (USMLE) and the Comprehensive Osteopathic Medical Licensing Examination (COMPLEX), which is a series of exams administered by the National Board of Osteopathic Medical Examiners and is now accepted in all 50 states. The best way to decide which path is right for you is to spend time with MDs and DOs and to talk to them at length about their practices.

NATUROPATHIC PROGRAMS

Students enrolled in a school of naturopathic medicine are conferred the doctor of naturopathic medicine (ND) degree upon graduation. The program in naturopathic medicine consists of two years of classroom instruction in standard medical school sciences and two years of clinical training under the supervision of a licensed ND. Graduates of naturopathic medical school programs are licensed as primary care physicians who can use natural therapies such as nutrition, homeopathy, acupuncture, hydrotherapy, and lifestyle modification to treat disease and combine these therapies with conventional medical treatments when appropriate.

Naturopathic physicians (NDs) take a holistic approach to healing and aim to cure disease by taking advantage of the body's self-regenerative powers and harnessing the restorative power of nature. Like osteopaths, naturopathic physicians endeavor to treat the whole person by taking into account the emotional, genetic, and environmental factors that have influenced their state of health. Unlike osteopaths, however, naturopathic physicians emphasize natural remedies. NDs also differ from allopaths (MDs); rather than limiting treatment to synthetic drugs and invasive procedures, NDs predominantly utilize natural medicines and procedures. Naturopathic physicians work to identify and eliminate the *cause* of disease using six basic principles:

1. Do no harm.

2. Utilize the healing power of nature.

3. Identify and treat the causes.

4. Treat the whole person.

5. Focus on preventive medicine.

6. Practice doctor-as-teacher.

Naturopathic medicine gained major visibility in the U.S. in the late 1800s, when Dr. Benedict Lust opened the nation's first health food stores and helped put the spotlight on diet and nutrition as the primary means to staying healthy. Naturopathic medicine was hugely popular until WWII when rapid advancements in medicine and technology caused it to lose ground to more high-tech forms of treatment, leading to a near-monopoly in health care practices by the chemical and drug industries. Today, a new crop of scientifically focused proponents of naturopathy largely guided by the principles of EBM, have been able to prove that diet and lifestyle have a significant impact on health, placing naturopathic medicine in the spotlight once more.

Students considering a naturopathic medical program should know that the ND license to practice medicine is valid in only 14 U.S. states (including Washington DC, Puerto Rico, the U.S. Virgin Islands), and 4 Canadian provinces, and graduates are subject to passing national licensing exams. However, legal provisions do allow for the practice of naturopathic medicine in several of the unlicensed states. (See AANMC.org for a list of states and provinces.) NDs may also practice in countries outside of the United States, based on requirements specific to each country. Each of the Association of Accredited Naturopathic Medical Colleges (AANMC) schools is accredited by the Council on Naturopathic Medical Education (CNME) and prepares graduates to sit for board examinations with the North American Board of Naturopathic Examiners (NPLEX). Naturopathic medical schools are looking for applicants who are thoroughly committed to the efficacy of natural therapies and are flexible enough to deal with the challenge of formulating personalized treatment plans. Some opportunities for specialization include dermatology and allergies, women's medicine, pediatrics, diabetes and blood pressure treatment, and cancer treatment and research, to name a few. In order to figure out whether an ND career is right for you, talk to other NDs. Compare their experiences with those of the MDs and DOs you know.

FOREIGN MEDICAL SCHOOLS

If you are seriously considering attending a foreign school but want to practice in the U.S., make sure you research the prospective school's USMLE pass rate and residency placement rate. Although foreign schools are much easier to get into, they will put you in just as much debt as U.S. schools, without the same assurance of a career after graduation that will enable you to pay it off.

THE NUMBERS GAME

Because of the sheer volume of applications they have to wade through, admissions officers have to make some initial screening decisions based largely on GPA and MCAT CBT scores—deceptively simple acronyms for the arcane processes they represent.

Your GPA, for the purposes of applying to medical school, consists of your science GPA (biology, chemistry, physics, and math), your non-science GPA (every other class you ever suffered through), and your cumulative GPA. These are calculated for your undergraduate career, any nondegree-seeking postsecondary work, and any degree-seeking postsecondary programs. In other words, you could conceivably have nine GPAs. Each medical school has its own policies for deciding which GPA means the most to them when they're choosing which applicants to interview and/or to matriculate. The average GPA of all applicants (not necessarily accepted) in 2006 was a 3.38 science, a 3.61 non-science, and a 3.48 overall. It is extremely difficult to get into medical school with a cumulative GPA of less than 3.0. Your GPA is the single most important element of your application because it is the best predictor of your academic readiness.

Although community college classes may count as part of your GPA, they may not always be acceptable as prerequisite premedical course work. If you are planning to take some of your core premed courses (biology, chemistry, physics) at a community college, it's an extremely good idea to do some advance planning and call some of the schools that you're interested in to make sure that they have no qualms about community college credit. Similarly, if you took an AP class in high school and then tested out of a core class, such as physics, you may run into trouble when you apply unless you've taken upper-division course work in that subject. Again, it is very much to your advantage to check with a few medical schools and your pre-health advisor to make sure that your academic record doesn't have any holes in it.

Your GPA and MCAT CBT score are interrelated. The MCAT CBT is an immensely important part of your application, but it's not as important as your GPA. As a standardized test, it provides only a snapshot of your academic readiness. Your MCAT CBT score is made up of four separate marks: Verbal Reasoning, Physical Sciences, Biological Sciences, and the Writing sample. Verbal Reasoning and the Science sections are scored from 1 to 15. The Writing portion of the MCAT CBT requires that you write two essays, which generate a single score. This score is reported as a letter J–T, where J is low and T is high. The average score for all applicants on each section in 2006 was 9.0 Verbal, 9.1 Physical Sciences, 9.5 Biological Sciences, and an O on the writing sample.

The Writing sample, added to the MCAT CBT a few years ago in an attempt to ensure the applicant's ability to communicate, is largely ignored by Admissions Committees. Virtually the only time the Writing sample is looked at very carefully is in the case of a disconnected application—a beautifully written personal statement with low Verbal scores and/or a low Writing sample score. Some schools will also consider the Writing score if they are evaluating the English ability of English as a Second Language applicants. This does not mean that you can take a nap during the Writing sample. You should make every effort to answer the questions in a coherent and focused way on the off-chance that the committee decides to closely examine your score.

THE SUM OF YOUR EXPERIENCE

Although your GPA and MCAT CBT score play a large role in your application, Admissions Committees are also looking for several other attributes. They are quite interested in who you are, why you want to be a physician, and whether or not you have a clue about what being a doctor is really like.

Exposure to the Health Care Field

Although students with no discernible exposure to health care still matriculate, the vast majority of successful premeds have some experience, usually volunteer work, in a hospital, clinic, hospice, or other health care setting. Some premeds are qualified enough to find part-time paying positions as emergency medical technicians (EMTs), nurse's aids, or organ and blood bank workers, while other nontraditional applicants may have had full-time careers in health care. Your goal should be to hold a volunteer or paid position for at least six months. Many premedical programs have specific classes you can take that include organized volunteer time as part of their course work—even if you are a returning adult student and not officially registered as premed. You can often get college credit for community-service work in the medical field. Although it may seem difficult to find the time to volunteer, it will make a huge difference as you work on your personal statement and get through your interviews. You will have stories to tell, and you will be able to speak far more effectively about why you want to become a physician.

Leadership Experience and Community Service

Leadership can mean many things, and being a leader, say, within your family, can be as important as being class president. One of the simpler ways to prove your abilities is to join a club or campus organization and get elected to office. You can also lead youth- or religiously affiliated organizations or participate in a variety of community-service organizations such as food banks, literacy programs, and mentor program. The key is to demonstrate sincere commitment and to have some longevity with whatever cause you decide to embrace, so that you can achieve a measure of responsibility. If you are serious about practicing primary care medicine, for example, this is your chance to build your resume and to start proving yourself. Find a clinic that needs a dedicated volunteer, and get your feet wet.

Research

Academic research is quite a bit easier to get involved with than you might think. Research labs are always looking for drones—basically undergrads—to help with the unlovely business of test-tube cleaning and organism counting. With any luck, however, you should be able to find a program in which you will actually conduct experiments and write about the results. If you are considering a career in academic medicine, you should try to get involved in research projects as early in your undergraduate career as you can convince someone to take you. One way to find out about cool research projects is to sit down with a teaching and research assistant over a cup of coffee and ask about the various projects going on in their departments. Alternatively, check out the Science Department websites at your university for information on current research.

HUMANITY

Medical schools are interested in training bright, empathetic, communicative people who have a strong interest in science and a wide-ranging intellect. They are not interested in students with perfect grades who have clearly never done anything else with their lives than try to break the curve in chemistry class. The schools want to graduate physicians who will listen to their patients and be able to effectively use the myriad tools available to heal them. What this means is that there is no magic system that will create an unbroken path into medical school. You can major in art history, modern dance, or biochemistry—it doesn't matter, as long as you take the classes you need to fulfill medical school requirements. You can take a few years off and join the Peace Corps or go straight to med school upon college graduation. Admissions committees will be trying to discern what you have learned from your experiences and how the things you have seen and done nurtured the values that have led you to pursue a medical career.

THE Z FACTOR IN MEDICAL SCHOOL ADMISSIONS

Although many medical schools will claim not to use a formula when it comes to evaluating an applicant, in actuality, almost all employ an initial screening process that weeds out applicants based on a cut-off score. While the formula used to arrive at this score varies from institution to institution, it's sure to involve the following three elements: GPA, MCAT CBT score, and a Z *factor*. The Z factor represents the bonus points an institution will award based on an applicant's ethnicity, participation in varsity athletics, and any other extraordinary activity and/or circumstance that the applicant may have experienced. Keep in mind that each medical school has its own target score. In order to maximize your rating, focus on improving your GPA and MCAT CBT numbers so that you don't have to rely on bonus points awarded for the Z factor to achieve the school's cut-off score.

THE APPLICATION PROCESS

There are many factors to consider when applying to medical schools. The first rule of thumb is to apply broadly and include safety schools where you will most likely be accepted. Besides the obvious clinical and scholastic goals, it is important to look for a school in a location that suits you. Although you may think that you won't see the light of day for four years, you should apply to schools that are in geographic areas that appeal to you and that will provide outlets for your hobbies and interests.

APPLYING TO ALLOPATHIC MEDICAL SCHOOLS

Most allopathic medical schools use the American Medical Colleges Application Service (AMCAS), which is a centralized and standardized application that is handled by the Association of American Medical Colleges (AAMC). In the spring of 2001, the AAMC switched to an entirely web-based AMCAS application. The online application is available directly from AAMC.org. The AMCAS application costs $160 for the first school; the fee is $30 for each additional school. If you have significant financial hardship, you can apply directly to AMCAS for a fee waiver on their services. You will also need to prepare transcript requests for every postsecondary school you ever attended, even if you only took one class there or the credits transferred elsewhere. Undergraduate colleges will send your transcripts to AMCAS, who forwards them to all medical schools to which you are applying. AMCAS begins accepting transcripts on May 2 each year and completed applications on August 1. It will take a couple of weeks for AAMC to process everything, at which point you'll receive a "transmittal notification." You can call and use AAMC's voice mail to check your status (you can reach AAMC on the Web at AAMC.org or by phone at 202-828-0400). At most universities and colleges, your pre-health advisor will help you navigate the AMCAS application, which can be fairly baffling. One of the toughest parts of the application is the personal comments page, where you have exactly one typewritten, single-spaced page to explain your life and to convince them that you should be one of the chosen few. Needless to say, this part of the application takes time and patience—be sure to read through the suggestions and advice for working on it that are included later in this chapter. Please note that the seven public medical schools in Texas have their own application service called TMDSAS (Texas Medical Dental Schools Application Service). In addition, one U.S. allopathic medical school—the University of North Dakota School of Medicine and Health Sciences—does not participate in any application service at all. If you're interested in attending this school, or any of the 17 accredited Canadian medical schools, you'll need to contact each school directly to obtain an application.

When you are choosing which schools to apply to, make sure you check their in-state residency requirements. Although many allopathic schools are private, there are quite a few public schools that receive free money every year from out-of-state applicants they are prohibited from accepting into their programs. It doesn't matter how qualified you are; if you aren't a state resident, you can't get in.

APPLYING TO OSTEOPATHIC SCHOOLS

Osteopathic schools use their own internal system, called AACOMAS, which in many ways works exactly the same way as AMCAS. Both paper and online applications are available from AACOM. You can request an application from their website at AACOM.org, or call 301-968-4190. Like the AMCAS application, AACOMAS takes some time to fill out, so make sure you get started early. It also includes a personal statement, but it's even shorter than AMCAS's—you have only half of a page to explain why you want to be an osteopathic physician. You will also need to get a recommendation from a DO, a fact that takes some applicants by surprise. If you are serious about osteopathic school, search for a mentor DO as early as possible. One of the nice things about AACOMAS is that all osteopathic schools use it—you don't have to worry about tracking down additional applications. Because osteopathic schools are private institutions, they don't have residency requirements (although some may have tuition breaks for residents of particular states). If you are interested in going to an osteopathic school, investigate all of your options and choose one based on your interest in the program and living conditions in the area.

APPLYING TO NATUROPATHIC SCHOOLS

The admission process varies slightly at each of the six AANMC schools. In general, naturopathic medical schools require a bachelor's degree and a base of undergraduate science courses that include physics, biology, and general and organic chemistry for an applicant to be considered. Math and psychology courses may also be specified. Admission into most of the naturopathic medicine programs requires students to have completed three years of premedical training. The duration of an ND program is the same as that of an MD program, with residency period optional. Check with each school you are considering in order to make sure that you've met all prerequisites and that you fully understand the school's application procedures. It is worth noting that the MCAT CBT is not required for admission to a naturopathic medical school.

WHEN TO APPLY TO MEDICAL SCHOOL

Whether you're applying to osteopathic, allopathic, or naturopathic medical schools, you need to apply as early as you can in the process. In general, premedical students begin the application process in the spring semester of their junior year, or approximately a year and a half before they want to enter medical school. The vast majority of medical schools engage in some type of rolling admissions, which means that they read and evaluate applications as the folders arrive. Admissions officers are only human. Even though they make every effort to give the same consideration to applicant number 6,005 as they give to applicant number one, the sheer volume of applications takes its toll on their patience and enthusiasm. In practical terms, this means that if you take the April MCAT CBT and get your applications in by late June, you will have a distinct advantage over someone taking the August test. Even if you turn in your AMCAS or AACOMAS application early, many medical schools will not look closely at your application until they have a copy of your MCAT CBT scores. Each year, students are accepted with August test scores and applications that arrived late in the process. Unfortunately, there are also large numbers of students who are not accepted but would have had a decent chance had they applied earlier. Basically, you should try for every possible advantage. Turning in your application early can certainly help to give you an edge. Also, procrastinators take note: AMCAS is serious about its deadlines. If an application or transcript is late, you'll get it back.

INFORMATION ABOUT THE MCAT CBT

The MCAT CBT is administered by the AAMC and is an admissions requirement for most allopathic and osteopathic medical school programs. More than 60,000 students take the test each year. The test is broken up into four sections: Physical Sciences, Biological Sciences, Verbal Reasoning, and a Writing sample. All of the questions (with the exception of the Writing sample) are multiple-choice.

In 2007, the AAMC adopted a CBT (computer-based test) format for the MCAT and reduced the number of questions on the test by nearly one-third. The test structure, content, and scoring system did not change.

The MCAT CBT, like the old exam, has four components:

1 Scientific Reasoning: The Physical Sciences

2. Verbal Reasoning

3. Writing Sample

4. Scientific Reasoning: The Biological Sciences

The current test is structured as follows:

Test Section	Questions	Time
Tutorial (optional)		5 minutes
Physical Sciences	52	70 minutes
Break (optional)		10 minutes
Verbal Reasoning	40	60 minutes
Break (optional)		10 minutes
Writing Sample	2	60 minutes
Break (optional)		10 minutes
Biological Sciences	52	70 minutes
Survey		5 minutes
Total Test Content Time		4 hours, 20 minutes

You should arrive at the test center at least one half-hour before testing begins. The entire test day is approximately five and a half hours long.

You will receive four scores, one for each component. The Verbal Reasoning component and the two Scientific Reasoning components (Biological and Physical Sciences) are scored on a scale of 1 to 15 in which 1 is low and 15 is high. The Writing sample component is scored on a scale of J to T in which J is low and T is high. With the new CBT format, scores will be released approximately 30 days after you complete the exam.

WHEN TO TAKE THE MCAT CBT

You should try to take the MCAT CBT on one of the April test dates, at least one year prior to the date you wish to begin medical school. Completing the exam earlier will allow you to complete your application early, and the earlier you submit your application, the better. Of course, not all applicants' academic schedules realistically allow them to take the April test. The new MCAT CBT enables greater flexibility in scheduling by providing students with 19 test dates to choose from throughout the year. To register for the MCAT CBT online, visit the AAMC website.

If you have not finished most of the prerequisites for the test—two semesters each of biology, physics, general chemistry, and organic chemistry—you probably should not sit for the exam. If you are determined to try the test without being fully prepared, take advantage of the fact that you can take a practice test at any Princeton Review office. It is much, much better to find out precisely what your current scoring levels are on a practice exam than to have to explain a woefully low score on a later medical school application.

It is possible, although it's certainly not the best idea, to take the last semester of one of the required science courses concurrently with studying for the MCAT CBT. If you find yourself in this situation, it is vitally important to lighten your course load so that you will be able to adequately study for the exam while maintaining good grades in your courses. Thoroughly studying for the MCAT CBT is not a small task.

How to Study for the MCAT CBT

You are correct in assuming that since you're reading a book published by The Princeton Review, we're a little biased as to how we think you should study for the MCAT CBT. The short answer here is that for most people, taking a course to prepare for the MCAT CBT is worth the investment in both time and money. This is simply because MCAT CBT scores are as important as your GPA in terms of admissions criteria. The MCAT CBT is a tedious and wretched business, and having a class full of fellow sufferers at least makes you feel less alone in your pain. A class also forces you to study in a reasonable way, to cover the material effectively, and to get plenty of practice, and the class gives you the resources to fill any gaps in your academic preparation.

There are some people who do not need much preparation for the MCAT CBT, and you'll meet them in medical school. They'll be getting honors designations in all of their classes while maintaining their world rankings as premier ice climbers/Sanskrit poets/ master chefs. Unless you're pretty sure you're one of them (you might qualify if you're reading this while skydiving), you'll need some help with the test.

First, assume that you will be spending about 20 hours a week for several months studying for the MCAT CBT. Although it doesn't test everything you've learned in school, it will feel that way. And, if you're rusty or haven't studied one of the subjects in a while—physics, general chemistry, organic chemistry, and biology—you're going to have to do some in-depth review. At the same time, you have to keep in mind that this is a standardized test, and even though it's one of the better ones available, it still suffers from the same flaws as all other standardized tests, which you can use to your advantage.

The key to doing well on the exam is to know the material and then to know the test. The MCAT CBT consists of four timed sections administered over a period of more than five hours.

The MCAT CBT tests basic sciences—but don't assume that the exam is a science test similar to the kind you have learned to take as an undergraduate. Fundamentally, the MCAT CBT is a verbal test, which is why on average, humanities majors tend to get slightly better scores in all of the sections than any other major. They are seeing a test format that they are used to: passages and questions. Science majors, on the other hand, are generally used to manipulating formulas and answering questions that may have a setup but are not embedded in a long series of paragraphs.

In practice, it is much easier to raise your score if you start with low science numbers but a high verbal score. Unfortunately, most examinees are in exactly the opposite position. This is of real concern because more and more medical schools have come to regard scores that are out of balance as undesirable. They will often look more favorably on a candidate with three 10s than someone with an 8 Verbal and two 12s. In order to change your Verbal score, you will have to practice the type of causal, linear logic that it tests. AAMC releases five previous MCAT CBTs, including one that is free, and a couple of books of practice items (any formal test preparation course should give you reams of additional practice material). If you don't have access to test preparation courses, you will probably find yourself rapidly running out of verbal practice material, although most college bookstores are reasonably well stocked with practice materials relating to the science portions of the MCAT CBT. You can use reading comprehension sections from other graduate-level standardized tests such as the GRE or LSAT to supplement your verbal study, but keep in mind that the passages in these tests were not written to be read under the same time constraints as were the MCAT CBT passages. In addition, you may want to consider using online training materials.

MCAT CBT Score Reporting—Full Disclosure

Gone are the days when prospective med students could choose whether or not to release their MCAT CBT scores to schools before seeing them. The MCAT CBT is, in fact, moving toward a full disclosure policy, whereby scores from any MCAT CBT taken in 2003 or later will automatically be reported as part of the examinee's test history. AMCAS and the medical schools to which you're applying will always receive your MCAT CBT Testing History Report, or THx Report (previously known as the Additional Score Report). If you took the MCAT CBT between 1991 and 2002, those scores will be released unless you request that they not be released. Still, the dates of those tests will appear on the THx Report.

Although you'll no longer have the option to withhold MCAT CBT scores except in the case of older test dates, this isn't necessarily a bad thing. In the past, schools knew when you withheld your scores, and as you might imagine, they could interpret this in many different ways. Although some schools told us that they did not hold it against you if you withheld your scores, others said they were inclined to look negatively on withheld scores and would rather see your entire test history. Problem solved! Seriously though, these issues may still come into play if you choose to withhold test scores from 2002 or earlier.

There are a few perks to the new THx Report online system too: The reports are free, and you can check out your score online much earlier—as soon as it's available to the AAMC.

Check out PrincetonReview.com for more information on the MCAT CBT, including a detailed discussion of changes to the test.

Your Budding Career as a Novelist

If you've ever harbored any fantasies of becoming a writer, now is your chance. If you've ever harbored fantasies of wiping the art of composition from human memory in retaliation for the suffering you endured in your freshman English class, you're going to have to find a way to cope. The personal comments section of the ACOMAS and AMCAS application is your chance to convince the committee that you are more than the sum of your numbers and that you deserve a chance at an interview.

Idea Generators

It is extremely difficult to write about anything important in a page or less, so assume that you will be spending some quality time with your computer. To get started, you can try a couple of different approaches to get your fingers moving:

Clustering

You may remember this from freshman Composition. You probably thought it was silly back then, but it just might save you now. Get a large blank piece of paper, and write down a few words to describe some of the experiences that have led you to pursue medical school. Or jot down some interesting, sad, or memorable experiences and later link them to your interest in medicine. You don't have to write them down in any particular order, just scatter your thoughts across the page. After you have several topics to work with, see if you can spot any patterns. Some of them will probably be interrelated. Next, generate longer descriptions of the words you wrote. For example, try to explain what you mean by "intellectual challenge." Was there a particular class you took? A paper you wrote? After you have some ideas on paper, try pulling them together based on the patterns of relationships you see between the topics. For example, telling a story about helping to clean a wound while volunteering in the ER might be a good way of letting the reader know that compassion is one of your qualities. It is often more effective to let the reader draw conclusions rather than spelling them out. For example, relate how you felt while treating a patient, and let the reader see that you are compassionate. Don't write, "That experience demonstrates my compassion."

Free Writing

This is particularly helpful if you find that you are having trouble figuring out where to start. All you have to do is sit down and force yourself to write about anything that comes into your mind. Don't worry about punctuation or grammar—just write for several pages. Take a break and look back at what you wrote. Most of the time, you'll be surprised to discover the beginnings of an idea. Keep a notepad with you and by your bed. Jot down ideas as they come to you.

Talk, Talk, Talk

One way to avoid writer's block is to talk into a tape recorder or to bribe a friend to write as you speak. Sometimes an empty screen or page can be intimidating. You can get started on your essay by telling your story to a tape recorder, or by having a friend write down what he or she thinks is interesting or important as you explain why you want to go to medical school. Don't expect to have suddenly generated your essay in this way. However, you can generate some material with which to start writing.

Three Basic Approaches

There are many different ways to structure the personal essay, but there are three basic approaches that can be used alone or in combination.

"My History in School"

This essay focuses on college experiences. It works well for people whose grades are fairly high and who want to emphasize their growth during the college years. The essay should be about your development, specialties, and strengths. The best essays usually have specific examples. It helps to have a specific class, professor, paper, or experience that crystallizes your experiences and ties into your goals. One of the benefits of this essay is a built-in chronology and organizational structure.

"My Life History"

In this essay, focus on a few events or main ideas that illustrate the qualities you can bring to medicine. If your whole life clearly leads up to being a physician (even if it might not have seemed that way at the time), this can be a good choice. One of the pitfalls of this structure is that it can let you ramble and lose coherency. Although you need to give a brief overview of your life, you also need focus your paragraphs around individual ideas.

"The Story"

This is often the most effective essay if it's done correctly. Focus on one or two stories that illustrate some of the points listed above. The story essay is the most fun for admissions officers to read, and is the most likely to be coherent and cohesive. You don't have to go overboard with adjectives and turns of phrase to write effective narrative. Just pick a few moments that most clearly define why you want to be a physician.

Key Bragging Points

No matter the subject you plan to focus on, the following are points that you should consider incorporating into the finished essay:

Academic Strength

You can discuss this generally, or with a specific example of a class, an assignment, or a moment in which you enjoyed an intellectual challenge. Medical school will require a lot of hard work. What demonstrates your love of hard work?

Commitment to Ideals

No one expects you to be Mother Teresa, but most good physicians have a streak of empathy and altruism.

Balance

What makes you whole? What balances the hardworking academic powerhouse that you are?

Careful, Complex Thinking

It is very difficult to explain something as complicated as your motivation to be a physician. Most people, when writing about a defining moment in their lives, assume that the audience is right there with them. This is not the case. You have to explain what you think and feel after you describe the event. Don't assume that the Admissions Committee is going to fill in the blanks for you.

Why You Want to Be a Doctor

The question you should ask yourself is why—when many other people who've had similar life/career/academic experiences take one look at the horrendous hours involved in medical training and decide that teaching or counseling would be a perfectly good alternative—you want to be a doctor. For instance, although many physicians decide to be doctors because of an early experience with the illness of a family member, there are far greater numbers of people with the same background who never consider medicine—but would still describe themselves as compassionate and moved to help people. You have to force yourself to ascertain what odd mixture of qualities—intellectual and emotional—have convinced you that going more than $100,000 in debt in the era of HMOs is a good idea.

Reasons, Not Excuses, for Weakness

Do not attempt to cover up or gloss over any deficiency, academic or otherwise. You will earn yourself points by honestly and openly dealing with your less-than-sterling qualities. If you have a couple of low grades or if you had a bad semester, briefly explain what happened, discuss what the experience taught you, and move on.

Good, Clever, Interesting Writing

Translation: Lots and lots and lots of drafts. Everybody has a distinct voice, and you're not going to survive medical school without a sense of humor. Find a way to get both qualities across without resorting to clichés. Prohibited phrases include: Lifelong learning, challenge of a lifetime, healing the mind as well as the body, childlike wonder, frail hands, quiet desperation, and any variations on these overused terms.

Overall Conservative Tone

Shock value doesn't work, despite the tales you might have heard about cartoons and poems. Admissions committees expect you to take the exercise seriously and to treat the process with respect. Humor is fine, but it needs to be subtle.

Show, Don't Tell

One of the traps of the personal statement is to rewrite your resume in prose. Instead of listing your accomplishments, explain what they mean to you and show how they have affected your life. For example, if you really want to practice primary care, it is far more effective for you to explain in detail what motivates you than to simply state your goal.

The Evolution of the Essay

Good essays tend to evolve and often bear very little resemblance to rough drafts. Don't be afraid to start over or to let the essay build on itself. If you write something that doesn't use any of the forms described above but that you feel gets across the points you want to make, then that is the essay you should stick with. Don't force yourself into a mold.

No matter what your essay looks like, however, there are a few general issues that you should think about.

Focus

Your essay must communicate specific points clearly and effectively. This means that every time you write a sentence that could be used in any other essay, you need to cross it out and start over. For example, "I truly enjoy working with people" could be the opening line in an application for fry guy at McDonald's just as easily as it could be a statement about the profound impact you want to have on your patients' health.

Editing

No mistakes. If you are not one of those people who goes around making a pest of themselves by correcting everyone else's grammatical errors, you need to find one. Most colleges and universities have writing centers with free editorial assistance, or you can check the local college paper for teaching assistants who are willing to edit for food. No matter what, make sure someone else reads your essay.

Interest

Everyone has a compelling style, and you need to write until you find yours. You are who you are for a reason; you have to write until that reason becomes apparent to anyone reading the essay.

Relevance

At some point, the reader will need a clear sense of why they should let you into medical school. Don't get so caught up in explaining your inner child that you forget to write about your desire to become a doctor.

Coherence

Make sure your essay fits together. You shouldn't be able to move a paragraph or a sentence when you're finished.

Remember that your entire personality is not going to be reflected in this essay, nor can you entirely offset an otherwise weak application. But this is your big chance to talk to the committee, so make the most of it. Spend the necessary time to draft and rework your essay until it is the best measure of your writing ability and candidacy for medical school.

SECONDARIES AND LETTERS OF RECOMMENDATION

After medical schools receive your application, they will send you what's called a *secondary*. Some schools send all of their applicants a secondary, while others go through an initial cut (usually based totally on GPA and MCAT CBT scores). One of the reasons that schools like to send out secondaries is that they usually charge you about $50 for the privilege of filling them out. Secondaries usually include a variety of essay topics that are slightly more directed than the personal comments in either the ACOMAS or AMCAS. The following are some typical secondary questions:

- What is your favorite novel?

- What are your hobbies?

- Where do you see yourself in 10 years?

- Name a leadership role that you've taken and what it taught you about yourself.

- What has been your greatest academic achievement? What has been your greatest academic failure?

- What type of medicine do you think you might want to practice?

As you can see, most of these essays seem fairly simple, but that doesn't mean you shouldn't spend time thoughtfully filling them out. Many secondaries are quite lengthy, so it's a good idea to fill them out as you get them, unless you've decided for some reason not to continue with your application to the school. If you find that the cost of sending back secondaries rapidly becomes prohibitive, you can call the individual schools and request a fee waiver. If you were eligible for a waiver from AMCAS, for example, you will probably be able to have most of your secondary fees waived.

You should also take care of your letters of recommendation at the secondary stage. If you are a student who is still in school and you have access to pre-health advising, your letters will probably be handled by that office, and at least one of your letters will probably be from the pre-health advisor. Usually, your recommenders will write one letter that the Advising Office will copy and send to your list of schools. If you are a returning adult, you may have to take care of all the requests and letters yourself.

Letters of recommendation for medical school work in much the same way as any other such letters; you will have much better luck if you approach your potential recommender with a copy of your resume, transcript, and personal statement. Try to make an appointment to speak to the person to discuss the various schools to which you are applying—and to make your case. Even if you have been out of school for a while, you should try to get at least one letter from a former professor. Medical schools are interested in your character, your desire to be a physician, your academic preparedness, and your intellectual ability. Although most employers could attest to some of those qualities, you will probably need a letter from a professor that discusses your academic abilities. As an undergrad or in your postbacc program, try to build relationships with faculty members so they can write something meaningful about you. Don't ask for a letter from someone famous unless they know you pretty well. Name-dropping is not considered to be particularly attractive in a prospective medical student.

Although many returning adults feel awkward approaching professors they might not have spoken with in several years, most are pleasantly surprised to discover that for the most part, professors do tend to remember their students, and most are happy to write them letters of recommendation. Both current and former students should also consider asking for letters from doctors with whom they have worked or volunteered— and remember that if you're applying to an osteopathic school, you need a letter from a DO.

Once you discover how painless it really is to get a letter of recommendation, you may be tempted to go into overdrive on the theory that inundating the committee with reams of stationary will force them to recognize your worthiness. Resist this! Do not send more letters than the school asks for. The committee will not read them, and you will not have done yourself any favors. The only time you might consider sending extra letters is if you are placed on hold after an interview and have been working in the meantime with someone who you feel would be able to contribute some additional information about your abilities.

MINORITY RECRUITMENT

Minority status refers to ethnicities that are *underrepresented* in medicine, such as Native Americans, African Americans, Latinos, Native Hawaiians, and some other specific groups. If you are not sure whether you qualify as a minority in this sense, you should contact AMCAS. Many public and private medical schools recognize the value of educating physicians who may choose to work in underserved areas and communities. Some committees look favorably on a candidate with a background that suggests he or she will fill this need. In some cases, this amounts to a preference for candidates with specific ethnic backgrounds—but it is a preference that occurs after a field of equally qualified applicants is generated from the initial pool. Medical schools are simply too competitive to accept candidates who are not up to the intellectual challenge of medicine. This selectivity advantage often extends to people of any ethnicity who come from underserved rural areas and seem inclined to return there to practice medicine.

There is also a type of minority status that AMCAS recognizes that deals only with economic factors and does not take into account ethnicity or country of origin. To be considered a "financially disadvantaged" minority, you need to have been under financial strain for a long period of time, and to have been the recipient of federal aid in the form of AFDC, welfare, food stamps, or other such programs. Your financial situation needs to have had an ongoing and persistent negative effect on your ability to procure education, housing, food, etc. In other words, the average two-job-struggling-to-make-ends-meet college student does not qualify. This minority status is reserved for those who have struggled uphill their entire lives and have somehow managed to make it through undergraduate school. The basic rule of thumb here is: If you are a financially disadvantaged minority, you probably know it. If you're in doubt, you probably aren't.

Medical schools are faced with a problem that is actually a boon for the quality of health care in the United States: They literally have more good applicants than they can take. This means that medical schools can easily fill their classes with students who are academically qualified. Medical schools have the opportunity to select from this pool those students who are most likely to improve underserved communities and to help those with the most need. The AAMC has sought to increase enrollment of underrepresented minorities in recent years. AOA has recently instituted a minority scholarship, the Sherry R. Arnstein Minority Student Award, to boost minority recruitment at osteopathic schools.

WHAT HAPPENS AFTER YOU'VE BEEN ACCEPTED

So you've achieved the impossible, the best-case scenario: multiple acceptances. First, congratulations. Second, it's probably not a good idea to share your good fortune with too many of your premed friends, unless you don't particularly want to keep them, and you've first removed all the sharp objects from the room.

BACK TO REALITY

After the giddiness wears off, you will have to deal with the best problem you will ever have: choosing which school to attend. Remember that you have lots of time to choose the medical school that best fits your goals and lifestyle. You can hang on to your acceptances until May 15, at which point schools will begin dropping your name off of their acceptance lists if you have not committed. Remember, however, that most of your fellow premeds do not share your enviable position. If you are accepted by a school that you know you will not attend, notify them before the deadline so that they can offer the seat to someone else. If you are on the wait list for a school you really want, don't hesitate to write a short note letting the committee know that their school is your first choice.

Factors to Consider

So while you are basking in your acceptance, think seriously about the following factors, but don't selfishly hold onto too many acceptances while you are deliberating:

How much does the school emphasize and reward teaching?

This is a huge concern and often overlooked. Look into how much the school values teaching versus how much they emphasize research. This can be the difference between being taught and being forced to teach yourself. The best way to determine teaching quality is to ask current students for their opinions.

What are community, social life, and support systems like?

Talk to current students to determine the overall community of the school. You'll be there for four years, and you certainly won't be studying all—okay, most, but not all—of the time. Are the students accepting the rigors of med school with a positive attitude or do they waste all of their extra energy complaining? What is the quality of life in general like at this school? Do students study together? Is it a community or commuter lifestyle?

What's the quality of the residents?

The residents are the ones who will be teaching you when you're a med student, so of course you want them to be good. You should presumably be able to approximate the quality of the residents based on the quality of postgraduate training programs (residency programs) at the hospitals affiliated with the school.

How family friendly are the school and its surroundings?

If you're a returning adult student with a family, look into the spouse/partner support services available at the schools you're considering. Getting through medical school will be hard on you and your family, and many places have begun programs that allow spouses/partners to attend special seminars and support groups that acclimate you to the pressures of your chosen educational and career path. Will your partner be able to find work/activities he or she enjoys?

Where will you be living?

Believe it or not, you will occasionally escape to the outside world. Make sure that the activities and hobbies you enjoy are available somewhere in the general vicinity. If you come from one climate and are moving to another, consider how that will affect you. Also, find out how close the clinical facilities are to the school and housing. The closer, the better.

What kind of research opportunities are available?

Some schools are much better equipped than others, and it's not always the high-profile schools that are doing the most cutting-edge research. Different schools have different specialties, and some benefit from affiliated schools of public health, business, or law. Other schools offer paid research opportunities.

Traditional or systems-based?

Teaching methodologies include traditional (two years of science plus two years of rotations), organ-based (learn everything about the liver), case-based (learn science by delving into patient histories), and everything in between. Which method will be best for you? It is difficult to know. It is also likely that other issues are more important for you to consider, such as the school's regard for education, commitment to teaching, and responsiveness to student input and overall academic climate. These issues may prove more important than the curricular grid (i.e., when you take anatomy), in terms of how much you learn and how much you enjoy learning.

What kind of financial aid offer are they making?

Is the offer good for all four years? In comparing offers between schools, consider cost of living differences and variation in the terms of loans.

How much will you owe?

This is the most important financial aid statistic a school can offer because it encompasses tuition, expenses, and financial aid. No matter what kind of financial package you get, you will most likely owe a staggering sum when you graduate, and it all has to be paid back eventually. As an intern and resident, you won't be making much in the way of a salary (about $38,000 to $49,000). Although most physicians eventually achieve a comfortable living (average of $233,000 annual salary in 2006), the practice of medicine is in such a state of flux that it is impossible to predict what kinds of jobs and compensation will be available 10 years from now. A public university education, while perhaps not carrying quite the cachet as a private school, may save you tens of thousands of dollars and relieve some of the stress associated with gargantuan debt.

BEHIND DOOR NUMBER 1 . . . MORE STANDARDIZED TESTS!

Most medical students take the USMLE Step 1 (and/or the first COMLEX—the COMLEX exams go in the same order as the USMLEs) at the end of the second year of medical school. Osteopathic students must pass the USMLE to obtain allopathic residency spots. Step 1 is often used to determine whether or not a student has passed their pre-clinical course work and can continue into their third and fourth years of training. Step 2 is usually taken during the third or fourth year of school during clerkships. At this point, the vast majority of senior U.S. medical students go through the Match in order to obtain residency positions. Very few contract privately for their first year of graduate medical training. Most programs in the Match now use ERAS (Electronic Residency Application Service), which is administered by AAMC, rather than a traditional paper application. Step 3 is usually taken after at least one year of residency (most physicians do at least three years of residency, but still take the test after the first year). The USMLE is written and scored by the National Board of Medical Examiners, which administers Steps 1 and 2. Step 3 is administered by the state. The state confers the license; the USMLE is a prerequisite.

INTERNATIONAL MEDICAL GRADUATES

International medical graduates (IMG) go through a special process to be granted licensure in the United States. Before you can start a residency program, you need to be certified by the Education Commission for Foreign Medical Graduates (ECFMG). To be certified, an IMG must complete the following five steps:

- Take USMLE Steps 1 and 2.

- Send medical credentials and fill out the paperwork necessary to show proof of medical education.

- Take the English test administered by the ECFMG.

- If you don't pass the English test, you can take the Test of English as a Foreign Language instead.

- Take the Clinical Skills Assessment, which is a live standardized patient exam.

After this, contact the board of the state in which you want to practice for the Step 3 requirements (each state determines its own passing score). You can get a residency through the NRMP Match or through a private contract. After passing Step 3 and following any other state guidelines, you are granted a temporary license to practice in that state.

If you are currently in a medical program abroad and are thinking about transferring to a U.S. medical school, you need to contact the school and ask about its transfer policies. In general, it is extremely difficult to transfer into a U.S. medical school.

ANOTHER PRINCETON REVIEW RESOURCE FOR PROSPECTIVE MED STUDENTS

If you're a premed student and want an in-depth, holistic guide to becoming the best possible applicant to med school, check out The Princeton Review's *Planning a Life in Medicine*, available in our online bookstore: PrincetonReview.com/college/bookstore.asp.

HIGH SCHOOL STUDENTS

If you've picked up this book and you're still in high school, you're very much ahead of the game. You can get started on the road to medical school by participating in volunteer activities and researching potential college choices to learn about their premedical training. Remember, you can major in any subject that interests you as long as you complete your premedical courses. Choose a subject you enjoy, and you are more likely to earn good grades and get into medical school. A few schools have special programs that funnel students through their undergraduate education directly into medical school. If you are interested in these programs, you should contact the following schools directly for more information:

Boston University

Brown University

Case Western University

East Tennessee State University

George Washington University

Howard University

Louisiana State University—New Orleans

Louisiana State University—Shreveport

Michigan State University

New York University

Northwestern University

University of Alabama

University of Miami

University of Michigan

University of Missouri—Kansas City

University of Rochester

University of South Alabama

University of Southern California

University of Wisconsin

IMPORTANT CONTACT ORGANIZATIONS

**AMERICAN ASSOCIATION OF COLLEGES OF
OSTEOPATHIC MEDICINE (AACOM)**
5550 Friendship Boulevard
Suite 310
Chevy Chase, MD 20815-7231
301-968-4100
301-968-4101 (fax)
www.aacom.org

**AMERICAN ASSOCIATION OF MEDICAL
COLLEGES (AAMC)**
2450 N Street, Northwest
Washington, DC 20037-1126
202-828-0400
202-828-1125 (fax)
www.aamc.org

ASSOCIATION OF ACCREDITED NATUROPATHIC MEDICAL COLLEGES
4435 Wisconsin Avenue, Northwest Suite 403
Washington, DC 20016
202-237-8150 or 866-538-2267 (toll-free)
202-237-8152 (fax)
www.aanmc.org

AMERICAN OSTEOPATHIC ASSOCIATION (AOA)
142 East Ontario Street
Chicago, IL 60611-2864
800-621-1773
312-202-8200 (fax)
www.osteopathic.org, www.do-online.org

**EDUCATIONAL COMMISSION FOR FOREIGN
MEDICAL GRADUATES**
3624 Market Street
Philadelphia, PA 19104-2685
215-386-5900
215-386-9196 (fax)
www.ecfmg.org

FEDERATION OF STATE MEDICAL BOARDS
400 Fuller Wiser Road
Suite 300
Euless, TX 76039-3855
817-868-4000
817-868-4099 (fax)
www.fsmb.org

NATIONAL BOARD OF MEDICAL EXAMINERS
3750 Market Street
Philadelphia, PA 19104-3102
215-590-9500
215-590-9457 (fax)
www.nbme.org

TEXAS MEDICAL AND DENTAL SCHOOLS APPLICATION SERVICE
702 Colorado, Suite 6400
Austin, TX 78701
512-499-4785
512-499-4786
www.utsystem.edu/tmdsas
(Texas public schools do not use AMCAS)

4 Advice for the "Nontraditional" Applicant

Forty years ago, most medical school applicants shared certain traits. The "traditional" medical school applicant was White, male, and just older than 20. Most likely, he majored in biology or chemistry while in college. Although he knew that medical school would be difficult and that his career would be challenging, he looked forward to choosing from a wide range of medical specialties and being financially secure. As a trained professional, he would possess real skills and expertise and, as a result, could expect to enjoy authority and autonomy.

The past few decades have seen substantial changes in the composition of the medical school applicant pool and in the professional opportunities available to medical school graduates. Based on the previous idea of the traditional medical student, women and minority applicants could be considered "nontraditional," but the term is currently used to describe applicants who are older than most med students. The average age of applicants is 25, but a significant and increasing proportion of applicants are several years older.

Some of these older applicants, always intending to apply to medical school, completed premedical requirements during their years as undergraduates and simply postponed medical school to work, travel, or start a family. Others were unsuccessful at gaining admission directly out of college and are attempting a second or third time. Another group considered medical school in college but did not complete requirements or the application process. Some older applicants never seriously considered medicine until after they graduated college and were involved in another occupation. Whatever the reason for postponing, older applicants now represent a significant proportion of the medical school candidate pool.

Aspiring doctors who did not take the prerequisite science courses in college or did not excel in them face a formidable challenge. These individuals have a minimum of seven years of medical school and residency on the horizon and, in addition, must complete (and do well in) one to two years of basic science courses before even applying to medical school. Nonetheless, thousands of adults, despite the arduous path ahead of them, decide to tackle this challenge. This chapter is intended as a source of information and support for nontraditional applicants at all stages of the application process. It is written by a nontraditional applicant and includes input from others who are or were in the same category. Follow eight nontraditional applicants through the entire process—from decision making, to postbacc training, to MCAT CBT preparation, and acceptance. The group is composed of real individuals[1] coming from a wide range of backgrounds, some elements of which will hopefully resemble aspects of your own situation. When these people decided that medical school was their goal, this is who they were and what they were doing:

- Becky, a 28-year-old who completed two years of college and had worked as a medical assistant for 10 years.

- Pete, a 28-year-old with a law degree who was unhappy in his field.

- Tina, a 27-year-old art history major who was working in a gallery and dating a medical student.

- Bob, a 35-year-old chemistry professor at a small college.

- Mitch, a 30-year-old former Peace Corps volunteer who was working in international development.

- Jacob, a 24-year-old volunteer firefighter. A car accident and subsequent hospitalization kept him from completing organic chemistry while in college. Discouraged, he dropped out of the premedical track.

- Eve, a 42-year-old wife and mother of three who graduated college 20 years ago, and had little experience working outside of the home.

- Donald, an engineering graduate student who decided that he needed more human contact in his work.

[1] Names have been changed.

DECIDING THAT MEDICINE—AND MEDICAL SCHOOL—IS WHAT YOU WANT

Some of these people were absolutely sure about going to medical school. Jacob, for example, had always known. Tina, who was fascinated by what her boyfriend studied in medical school, had a strong hunch. Donald imagined that being a physician would give him what he felt was missing from his career, but he had limited contact with the medical field and had not fully considered other options that would give him more personal interaction.

Being reasonably sure about medicine is important because you will invest time, money, and energy into the medical school preparation and application process. It is also important because admissions officers will look for indications of your commitment. If you are sure of it, your commitment is more likely to come through in your personal statement and your interview.

If you have never worked or volunteered in a medical setting, you should explore opportunities to do so. You might arrange to informally shadow a physician or to volunteer in a hospital that has a formal program. Some volunteers find that they are given more responsibility at a small clinic than they are in a large hospital, so look into clinic programs as well. Explore opportunities to volunteer in overseas medical projects. Of our eight subjects, those who had more than one medically related experience felt that it was beneficial because they were exposed to the variation that exists within the field. Not only are volunteer activities helpful in your decision-making process, but they will become significant resume builders should you decide to apply to medical school. In addition, they are likely to be valuable and, hopefully, enjoyable experiences.

One way to help determine if medicine is the right career for you is to talk to others who have made the choice. Interview as many people as you can. Talk to practicing physicians, residents, medical students, and those involved in academic medicine such as researchers. Find out what they love and hate about their work. Ask questions that will help you put their comments about medicine in perspective. For example, if you come across someone who positively hated medical school and dislikes being a physician, ask him what part of medical school he hated the least. If his favorite part of the experience was the relaxing cruise-ship vacation he took after his first year, he probably could have made a better career choice for himself. His views of medical school may not be an indication of what the experience will be like for you.

If possible, talk to medical students, practicing physicians, and resident physicians who are or were nontraditional. Find out whether they feel that they made the right decision. What were the biggest sacrifices they had to make? Visit the premedical and medical student discussion pages online where many nontraditional applicants and students share their thoughts.

Bob's decision to apply to medical school was influenced by his sister-in-law. She works in medical equipment sales and is five years older than Bob. She encouraged him to follow his dream, saying that she, too, had entertained the idea of becoming a physician when she was 30. She decided against it and at 40 still dreams about doing it today. But with two young children, she feels that it would be too difficult. Bob decided that it would be more painful to spend his life wondering if he should have gone to medical school than to go and—in the worst-case scenario—drop out and return to teaching.

Mitch also found it helpful to talk to people working in totally unrelated fields. He had worked for two years in a clinic in rural Africa and thought that he wanted to become a pediatrician. However, he became discouraged while talking to his friends who were medical students, residents, or newly graduated practicing physicians because it seemed that few people loved everything about what they were doing. Many of his friends warned him of the burden of debt and the prospect of having little free time. One friend told him that in comparison to Mitch's current job, which involved traveling around the world, he would be *bored* in medicine. Mitch then took an informal poll of all his friends who included teachers, writers, business owners, software designers, lawyers, and full-time parents. He found that people in all occupations both love *and* hate certain things about their work.

Although medical students and physicians complain about debt, teachers complain about low salaries, and business owners complain about financial insecurity. All of Mitch's friends in their early 30s complain about working too hard and about the difficulty of balancing their personal and family lives with their careers. Mitch concluded that despite the initial discouragement he got from friends in the medical profession, people in medicine are among the *most* professionally fulfilled. Although medical students and physicians had complaints, they were engaged in their work, and most couldn't imagine a better career. He also noticed that a significant number of nonphysicians he spoke to, although unhappy with their own jobs, still discouraged him from going into medicine. He realized that some of these people had, at one point in their lives, entertained the idea of becoming a doctor. They had successfully talked themselves out of medical school and were sold on all the reasons why *not* to go into medicine. As far as his friend's comment about being bored, Mitch realized that others tended to glamorize his current work because it involved travel. He knew that being a pediatrician would, on a day-to-day basis, be more interesting than the paperwork he dealt with in his current job. Furthermore, he could probably work overseas as a physician if he found himself yearning for travel.

After you follow Mitch's example and grill everyone you know, ask yourself some serious questions. What jobs and experiences have you loved most in your life? Do you foresee medicine providing similar satisfaction? Have you enjoyed some aspects of your medically related work? Do you have the skills it takes to become a physician? To be fulfilled as one? Whether or not to pursue a career in medicine is an important decision that will affect many years of your life. Give yourself time, both for information gathering and personal reflection. Write down your thoughts on what is influencing your decision. Whether or not you decide to go for it, if you carefully weigh the decision now, you will be less likely to doubt it later on.

Resist feeling that because you are older, you should make your decision to enter medical school as quickly as possible. Medical school, internship, and residency require at least seven years to complete. Moreover, medicine is a career of lifelong learning. Start finding things to enjoy about the process of becoming a doctor now. Deciding to go to medical school is part of the process. Try not to stress too much about the decision, and find some satisfaction in your information gathering and self-reflection.

GETTING INTO MEDICAL SCHOOL AS A NONTRADITIONAL APPLICANT

If you are reading this, you have probably decided to move forward with your plan to become an MD, DO, or ND. Hopefully, your level of maturity and your life experience have allowed you to make a well-informed decision that a student just out of college may not be in a position to make. Between 20 percent and 30 percent of applicants in the 24- to 37-year-old age range are admitted to medical school, while approximately 45 percent of 21- to 23-year-olds are admitted. Although these statistics suggest that the odds are against older applicants, age itself is not regarded as a disadvantage, and may in some cases be a plus. Even the most exciting and unique older applicant must have a competitive GPA and MCAT CBT score.

The timing of the admissions process is often an issue for nontraditional applicants. Donald started thinking about medical school midway through his first year of graduate school. We will call this January of Year one. He realized that he had prerequisites to fulfill and that he wouldn't be eligible to enter medical school the following fall, but thought he would be able to matriculate in the fall of Year three. Donald quit his graduate program and entered an intensive premedical curriculum, completing his requirements by January, Year two. He took the MCAT CBT in April, Year two. If Donald had taken premedical courses part-time rather than full-time, he could not have adhered to this schedule. Had he done poorly on the MCAT CBT the first time, he could have been delayed an entire year and postponed entrance until Year four. As a result of the timing of the admissions process, it takes two to four years to matriculate after deciding to pursue medical school. The following are the important dates to remember as you think about timeframe and requirements:

- April: MCAT CBT is given. You should have completed all prerequisite science courses by this date.

- June: AMCAS (preliminary) applications are accepted. Filling out the AMCAS application requires all undergraduate, graduate, and post bacc transcripts (they accept transcripts beginning on March 15, but the completed application isn't accepted until June 1). You will need your own copies, and you will need to have copies sent directly to AMCAS. It is important to submit AMCAS applications as soon as possible because most schools offer rolling admissions.

- August: MCAT CBT is given. Use this test date only if you need to improve your scores from the April test. You will indicate on your AMCAS application whether you intend to take (or retake) the test on this date. If so, many schools will not look at your application until August scores are available (some time in October). The penalty for this delay may very well outweigh your score improvement. Thus, unless you anticipate *significant* score improvement, the August MCAT CBT is not advised.

- August: Medical schools to which AMCAS applications have been submitted begin sending secondary applications. Some schools will review AMCAS applications closely and will send secondary ones to a limited number of applicants. Others send them to everyone who applies through AMCAS. There is usually an additional fee. In some cases, secondary applications require essays or short-answer questions that focus on motivation, personal characteristics, values, and experiences. In other cases, the application is very simple and similar to the AMCAS application. Thus, receiving a secondary application *may* be an indication that a school is interested in you. When you return the application and fee, you demonstrate your interest in the school. Schools often want these back within two to four weeks. You will also need to submit recommendations at this time. Some schools ask for a photo.

- August–May: Based on AMCAS and secondary applications and recommendations, applicants are invited to interview during this period. Some schools conduct all their interviews during one or two months, while others spread them out. Most schools accept 25–50-plus percent of interviewed candidates. Thus, getting an interview is an excellent sign. Most admissions decisions are also made during this period, with the exception of applicants who fall into a "hold" or "wait list" category.

- June–August: Wait listed candidates may be accepted.

ACADEMIC REQUIREMENTS

Most medical schools require or strongly prefer that applicants have a BA or BS degree from a four-year accredited college or university. All medical schools require a minimum level of science preparation that includes approximately one year each of biology, chemistry, organic chemistry, and physics. Some nontraditional candidates meet these requirements by taking night courses while simultaneously working part- or full-time. Others enroll full-time at private or public undergraduate institutions. Some choose to enroll in special *postbaccalaureate premedical* programs (we call them postbacc programs) offered by a surprisingly large number of colleges and universities (see Chapter 10 for a comprehensive listing of postbacc programs). Postbacc programs vary widely in terms of cost, rigor of course work, grading system, percentage of graduates admitted to medical school, structure and flexibility of curriculum, duration, size, and class composition. Unlike medical schools, postbacc programs are neither accredited as such, nor ranked.

Becky needed to complete her BA in addition to fulfilling science prerequisites. When she decided it was time to take a shot at fulfilling her long-time dream of becoming a physician, she lived and worked in California, which has some of the most selective state-affiliated medical schools in the country. Becky decided to move to another state and complete her BA there so that she would be qualified for admission to the state's medical school. Becky enrolled full-time for three years to complete her BA—not all of her previous college credits transferred—and fulfill all her science requirements.

Becky's strategy is interesting and may be advisable for others in similar situations who are prepared to relocate. Before moving across the country, be sure that you understand your new state's criteria for determining residency. In some states, being a full-time student does not ensure resident status. Becky might have saved herself a year of schooling had she looked at more colleges and possibly uncovered schools willing to award her credit for all her previous college work.

Tina graduated from a prestigious college but had taken neither science nor math classes while in school. She was also concerned about her undergraduate GPA, which was 2.9. To make herself a more competitive applicant, she wanted to demonstrate both competence in the sciences and overall improved study skills. Some postbaccalaureate premedical programs are quite structured and involve only the minimum science prerequisites; Tina felt that she needed more than this to make up for her undergrad GPA. One of Tina's options was to apply to a postbacc program that allows participants to take additional courses beyond those in the required scientific disciplines. This type of program tends to be somewhat flexible, allowing students to spend as much time as needed to fulfill requirements and take any additional courses. Students get the opportunity to learn foreign languages, improve writing or math skills, or take courses often recommended—but not required—by medical schools such as biochemistry or statistics. Other postbacc programs apply students' course work toward a master's degree.

Tina decided not to enter an organized postbacc program. Instead, she enrolled full-time as a nondegree candidate at a local, private university. This gave her access to larger course offerings. One of the advantages of postbacc programs is that they are compact, scheduling courses and labs so students may complete all requirements within a year. Tina was less worried about speed and more interested in earning excellent grades. Another important consideration for Tina was letters of recommendation. Medical schools usually prefer that applicants submit a composite letter from their premedical advisor who is typically an administrator or dean, a department head, a specified faculty member, or some type of counselor. The letter discusses the student's qualifications and incorporates comments from his or her premedical professors. Because Tina chose a small school, she had the opportunity to get to know her professors and, presumably, to secure meaningful comments from them. At some colleges, only degree-earning students have full access to premedical and other advisors, but Tina was able to identify one who agreed to write a letter for her. One advantage to true postbacc programs is that the premedical advisors are able to write appropriate letters of recommendation for nontraditional applicants.

Some premedical candidates are highly concerned with getting through the application process quickly and have no interest in prolonging premedical course work. Pete had a 3.7 GPA in college and an excellent record in law school. He had no need to prove himself scholastically, but just wanted to "get the sciences out of the way." He was a good candidate for a highly selective postbacc program. To be admitted to one of these programs, applicants must submit detailed information including personal statements, prior standardized test scores, and several recommendations. Interviews are often required. These programs seek to admit students who will not only complete the course work, but who are likely to be accepted to medical school. Often, the brochures for these programs boast the percentage of graduates who have been admitted into medical school. Although a high acceptance rate is partially a reflection of the quality and resources of the program itself, it also indicates that they accept well-qualified students. In one year, Pete was able to complete all his sciences and study for and take the MCAT CBT.

Pete took advantage of an arrangement between his postbacc program and a medical school, allowing him to enter medical school in the fall following completion of premedical course work. Thus, he avoided an "in between" year generally devoted to the medical school application process. Several selective postbacc programs offer this type of arrangement, affiliation, or linkage with a number of medical schools. In some cases, the medical school and the postbacc program are part of the same university. Many nontraditional candidates are disappointed to discover that top medical schools such as Harvard, University of Pennsylvania, and Columbia do not offer these arrangements with their own university's postbacc program.

Pete took the shortest path possible to medical school. In the fall of 1996, he left the law firm where he was working, and in the fall of 1997, he was beginning medical school. He was happy to skip the long and stressful medical school application process, having been through a similar experience with law school. While ideal for some, Pete's path is neither available nor advisable for everyone. The short, intensive postbacc programs are grueling and may be too fast paced for some people. Graduates of these programs often claim that their postbacc work was more demanding than medical school itself. Although these programs can serve as excellent preparation for medical school, they may discourage people who could have succeeded had they enrolled in a more relaxed program.

Earning acceptance to a postbacc program with affiliated medical schools does not assure your acceptance to medical schools. Postbacc students in these programs usually apply to the affiliated schools, but acceptances are only provisional, and conditional upon securing a minimum GPA and MCAT CBT score. Only a handful of medical schools participate in these linkages, and each school limits the number of positions available through the direct admissions route. Pete chose his postbacc program in part because one of the linked medical schools interested him. If none of the medical schools that allow admission through this route appeal to you, saving one year now is probably not worth spending four years someplace you don't want to be. Generally, medical schools agree to these arrangements as a means of enrolling students who they would otherwise not attract. Thus, if you are accepted as a postbacc student to one of these schools, you are not likely to be accepted to other schools if you apply through the regular admissions process. Another disadvantage to these arrangements is that they are usually binding: if you get in, you must go. If you earn a perfect score on the MCAT CBT, you cannot withdraw and apply to your dream school for the following year. Additionally, you have no opportunity to compare financial aid packages.

While Donald, Tina, Pete, and Becky quit their jobs to enter premedical studies full-time, Mitch, Jacob, and Eve opted for part-time schooling. Eve wanted to ease into school, and decided to take one course at a time. She enrolled in a general chemistry class through the extension office of a local public university. Her children spent summers at camp and with relatives, allowing her to take a compact organic chemistry course during the summer. The following school year, she enrolled in a two-semester biology course, and she took an intensive physics course the next summer. Eve was concerned that her age would hurt her chances of being accepted to medical school. However, had she crammed all of the required science courses into just one year, she would have been only one year younger when she applied to med school, but a whole lot more frustrated and perhaps not as appealing a candidate because her grades could have suffered. In retrospect, Eve's only regret about taking courses on her own is that she missed the camaraderie and support that she might have had in a postbacc program. An advantage to postbacc programs is that you will meet people facing challenges similar to your own.

Most medical schools advise nontraditional applicants to demonstrate success in *recent* course work. Bob had fulfilled all the prerequisites in college about 15 years earlier. Since Bob had a graduate degree in science and remained active in an academic environment, the fact that he completed his prerequisite courses years earlier did not hurt him. His hurdle was the MCAT CBT, for which he reviewed intensely.

The grading systems vary tremendously among undergraduate institutions and postbacc programs. Some material that you learn as a premed, such as the basic biochemical processes, will serve you in medical school. Other topics, like whether your rowboat sinks or rises if you fall into the water, might not. As a premedical student, your goals should be to figure out whether you enjoy studying science, to learn the material for the MCAT CBT, and to get good grades.

Some colleges and universities with postbacc programs assign nontraditional students to regular, undergraduate science courses. You attend lectures, labs, and exams alongside undergraduates and may or may not be graded on the same curve as your younger classmates. Most likely, the mean score of postbacc students is somewhat higher than that of the rest of the class. Undergraduates shouldn't be penalized by your presence since, after all, you already have your BA. Thus, schools with significant numbers of postbacc students are likely to separate them from the undergraduates for grading purposes. Unfortunately, this practice could hurt you because you may be competing with your undergraduate classmates for positions in medical schools. Your cumulative test score of 90 percent put you in the middle of the postbacc curve and earned you a C, while your classmate's 90 percent put him at the front end of the undergraduate curve and earned him an A. Although a letter of recommendation could explain that you did in fact maintain a 90 percent average, a C is still a C.

Some postbacc programs address this issue by setting the postbacc curve higher. The mean score will represent a B grade rather than a C grade. Highly selective postbacc programs usually recognize that all their students were strong in college and will set the mean somewhere in the A-minus or B-plus range. If a college that does not have a formal postbacc program allows you to enroll in science courses, your GPA might be slightly higher because you will be graded with your classmates, many of whom are probably less focused and less serious than you about maintaining excellent grades. Note, however, that many medical schools consider the caliber of undergraduate institutions when evaluating GPAs. This applies to traditional and nontraditional applicants alike.

THE MCAT CBT

The MCAT CBT takes about 4.5 hours and is currently offered 22 times yearly at locations throughout the country. It is composed of four sections. An individual's raw score (number wrong out of number possible) on each section is compared with those of test-takers nationwide and is converted to a scaled score. Many find the experience a test of endurance and concentration as much as a test of knowledge (see page 30 for more information on the MCAT CBT).

Virtually all medical schools require the MCAT CBT. Schools evaluate MCAT CBT scores in different ways. Some have devised formulas that incorporate MCAT CBT results and GPAs and produce numerical scores to assign to candidates. In some cases, if an applicant's score falls above a cutoff, he will receive a secondary application or perhaps be invited to interview. Although certain sections of the MCAT CBT may be weighted more heavily than others by some admissions offices, most schools regard all sections except the essay as equally important. In some formulas, the MCAT CBT and GPA carry roughly equal weight, while in others one is weighted more heavily. A number of schools claim that GPA is more important than MCAT CBT. Although this may be true, consider such statements in light of the recent outcry against standardized tests. A school that admits to using test scores as its primary means of weeding out applicants could be regarded as lazy and discriminatory.

Most schools claim not to use specified formulas or cutoff points and indicate that they might consider an applicant with a very low MCAT CBT score if other aspects of his application are extraordinary. But generally, admissions committees rely heavily on MCAT CBT scores because they are considered a strong indicator of success in the first two years of medical school, and because they are the easiest part of an application to judge. Examining the average MCAT CBT scores of accepted students at a school gives you a rough idea of what score you will need to gain admission there.

The MCAT CBT is important for all applicants but may be especially so for nontraditional applicants. Eve's college grades were 20 years old. Over the years, colleges and universities have made changes and adjustments to grading scales and curricular requirements. Thus, her GPA might not be comparable to that of someone who graduated from the same school in 2005. Furthermore, how she performed in college 20 years ago is probably not a great indicator of how she will fare in medical school today. Grades in postbacc courses are important, but as mentioned earlier, there is wide variation in grading policies among postbacc programs and between regular undergraduate courses and the same courses within postbacc programs. The benefit of the MCAT CBT is that it is standardized, supposedly allowing admissions committees to compare the aptitude of people with different backgrounds.

When preparing for the MCAT CBT, consider that the results of that one day of work are nearly as important as all your other academic achievements. Beyond striving for a sound academic background, most medical school applicants—both traditional and nontraditional—take some sort of MCAT CBT preparation course like the ones offered by The Princeton Review. For some, a test-prep course teaches material never learned, or never absorbed, in class. For others, it relieves some anxiety associated with standardized tests, allowing for an improved performance. For those lacking self-motivation, taking a course is a good way to encourage studying.

Some postbacc programs offer an MCAT CBT review along with premedical courses. Usually, such a review will be much less intensive than a course offered by an outside organization. In Pete's postbacc program, most students enrolled in a private course that met twice weekly for three months prior to the April MCAT CBT. Since the postbacc program itself was so intensive and required many hours per day of studying, the students needed to be pushed to devote time to MCAT CBT preparation. Pete did not take the course because he felt confident that he would enter medical school the following fall through the arrangement he had made with an affiliated medical school. The medical school required Pete to take the MCAT CBT and to score at least a 9 in all subjects. By January of his postbacc year, Pete was scoring 8's or higher in all sections, and reasoned that, by finishing his premedical courses and studying for the MCAT CBT on his own, he could score 9's.

Formal MCAT CBT courses typically include three or four practice, full-length MCAT CBTs. The exams are scored, giving students an idea of their strengths, weaknesses, and overall progress throughout the course. Pete obtained practice MCAT CBTs through the Association of American Medical Colleges (AAMC) and set aside three Saturdays prior to the April exam to take them. For those who do not take a course, it is important to order these practice exams and to be disciplined about taking them.[6] The exams come with tables that allow you to convert your raw score to the scaled score that gives you an accurate idea of how you'll score on an actual MCAT CBT. There are a number of books available that review important MCAT CBT topics and offer tips for taking the exam.

Review books and courses are a good idea for nontraditional and traditional students, although nontraditional students who have been out of the standardized test scene for many years may particularly need the help. For example, when Becky took her first practice exam, she was discouraged because she was barely able to complete half of the questions in the science sections. MCAT CBT questions are not arranged in order of difficulty, and Becky was spending too much time on really tough passages that appeared early in the sections. She improved her score significantly on the science sections just by training herself to skip and go back to difficult passages.

Some nontraditional applicants have an advantage on the verbal section. By just being older, you may have had more time than a college student to read a wide variety of books. Eve loves reading and found the verbal section to be a confidence builder. Becky, who did not read extensively for work or pleasure, found the verbal section very difficult. Donald, who learned English as his second language, studied more for the verbal section than for both science sections combined. Becky improved her verbal score by focusing on concentration skills. One way to do this is to read slightly complicated or technical magazine and journal articles every day for several months before the MCAT CBT. Force yourself to concentrate for an extended period of time each day.

[6] Practice exams are real MCAT CBTs from years past. Visit AAMC.org/students/MCAT.

THE PERSONAL STATEMENT AND INTERVIEW

Health care has changed dramatically in the United States, and some experts argue that physicians in the twenty-first century (see Chapter 2) will have to possess a wider range of skills than was previously considered adequate. Not only must physicians be experts in their respective fields, but it is advantageous to understand the financial, legal, ethical, and political issues surrounding health care provision. Medical schools recognize the need for well-rounded physicians. The schools now offer revised curriculums that include non-science courses, and they admit more and more non-science majors.

As a nontraditional applicant, you have unique experiences and skills. These will help differentiate you from other applicants and can be an important strength. The AMCAS personal statement, essays for secondary applications, and the interview are opportunities for you to shine. Although you are probably tired of being asked why you want to become a doctor, you will have to figure out how to answer the question with sincerity and enthusiasm. As a nontraditional applicant, your motivation for pursuing a career in medicine is an extremely important consideration for Admissions Committees.

Despite recognizing the value of nontraditional students, admissions committees may be skeptical of applicants who are embarking on their second or third career. Essays and interviews are also opportunities for you to address their concerns and doubts about your motivation. In interviews, Donald was often asked what made him so sure he wouldn't drop out of medical school as he had engineering school. The school's concern is that poor judgment with respect to your first career choice may suggest the possibility of poor judgment in your decision to apply to medical school. Or perhaps the worry is that some people are eternally unfulfilled and will therefore be unfulfilled by a career in medicine. Many people believe that if you are good at something, you enjoy it. Thus, not liking your previous job suggests to some that you were bad at it and that you may possess some hidden faults.

All medical school applicants—both traditional and nontraditional—must figure out how to package themselves. Like wrapping a present that is oddly sized, some nontraditional applicants have to be creative in their packaging. Donald's strategy was to maintain a positive attitude. He told interviewers that some of the things that attracted him to engineering, such as the analytic thinking required, also applies to medicine. He asked interviewers whether some of the principles in engineering would translate to physiological issues. He emphasized his excellent academic record, his success in science courses, and his demonstrated willingness to work hard in school. He also stressed how much he enjoyed volunteering at a clinic. He did his best to be personable and talkative, thereby showing off his people skills rather than restating what was written in his essay—that he was switching fields because he wanted to work directly with people.

Tina's story—that she was bored working in an art gallery and envious of her boyfriend's career—would not get her into medical school without clarification. Tina enjoyed certain aspects of her job, such as interacting with artists and clients. She loved much of the art with which she worked, particularly the pieces that were highly expressive and revealed human emotion. On the other hand, she missed a sense of social purpose in her gallery work, and she felt that she wasn't being intellectually challenged. Tina packaged herself as passionate, people-oriented, and interested in helping others. She was good at her job but knew that it would not engage her for life. Through her work, she came to know what she liked and disliked, what fulfilled her and what did not. Unlike children of physicians who are likely to consider medicine as a potential career from an early age, Tina never thought about it as a realistic pursuit until her 20s when her boyfriend entered medical school. Now that she had an idea of what medical school and medicine were like, and now that she knew herself better, she was ready to commit to the career. Because she enjoyed working with people, she envisioned a career in primary care. She believed that as a result of her studies and work in the art world, she had good insight into the mental capacity and emotions of people. She wondered if psychiatry was the field for her.

Packaging Jacob was relatively straightforward. He had a reasonably consistent interest in medicine, demonstrated by earlier premedical courses and more recent firefighting work that involved some emergency medical skills. In Jacob's personal statement, he needed to address the reasons he dropped out of the premedical track in college. Jacob had been hospitalized, and this experience was emotionally difficult for him. Being in a hospital and being around sick and dying people was enough to make him question whether he really could be a physician. When he returned to school, he was less committed to going to medical school and decided to focus on completing his major and general requirements with good grades. After graduation, he fully recovered and had regained his interest in medicine. He took several first aid courses, volunteered in an emergency room, trained to become a fireman, and looked around for postbacc programs. In his essay, Jacob brought up the doubts that he had about becoming a physician, and discussed how he overcame them. Had he glossed over his hospital experience and the fact that he only took one semester of organic chemistry in college, admissions committees may have concluded that he "just couldn't cut it" as a premed. By addressing the situation, he presented himself as someone who matured and grew from a difficult experience.

Some medical schools read the essays and personal statements of all applicants and use them, along with grades and scores, for initial screening. Others only read essays after some applications have been weeded out. If you are filling out applications, you are at the point where you can't do much about your grades or scores. However, you can write an excellent personal statement. Enlist a friend, relative, advisor, or coworker who is well read and writes well to review your statement and make suggestions. Have someone who really knows you read it to be sure that you have conveyed your strengths. On the AMCAS application, exactly one page is provided for an applicant's personal statement. The resume of a nontraditional applicant is probably longer than that of a college senior, and limiting your statement to one page may seem difficult. However, you need not mention all of your accomplishments, experiences, or reasons for pursuing medicine. Choose your most impressive accomplishments, your most meaningful experiences, and your most compelling reasons for pursuing medicine (see page 33 for more advice on how to compose a good essay).

There are countless approaches to writing a personal statement. Becky wrote about learning. By focusing on a concept, she subtly brought up her relevant accomplishments and experiences and explained her motivation for wanting to go to medical school. During her career as a nurse, she learned a tremendous amount from doctors, other nurses, patients, and families. She loved applying her knowledge to her daily work and seeing her work pay off in the people she helped. However, she felt that her formal education did not enable her to really understand disease, treatments, and the healing process. Having worked closely with physicians, she understood that they didn't always know everything. She felt, however, that they had the tools to ask the right questions. Asking and answering questions, addressing problems and solving them, and observing others and analyzing their techniques are among the activities Becky looked forward to in medical school.

Eve concentrated on the doctor-patient relationship, discussing vivid memories of her own pediatrician and comparing the relationship she had with him to that of her children and their current pediatrician. She was able to elaborate on her accomplishment of raising three well-adjusted children, a feat that involved serving as caretaker, healer, friend, manager, teacher, advisor, and so on. Mitch described a few of his work experiences in Africa and Latin America, focusing on the ones that were most directly related to health care issues. He wrote that although he enjoyed working overseas, he felt that he would be able to contribute more as a physician than as a project manager. Jacob's prose included personal accounts of saving peoples' lives as a firefighter and how fulfilling he found that aspect of his work.

The secondary application may have general questions that allow you to elaborate on topics mentioned in the AMCAS essay. Some secondaries contain questions about particular experiences that you may have had, such as research, community service, or employment. Some questions focus on your values and personal experiences. Chapter 7 of this book includes a profile of each allopathic medical school. In the "Application Process" section of each description, we give the percentage of AMCAS applicants who generally receive secondaries. Some schools send secondary applications to a very limited number of applicants, and receiving a secondary from these schools means that you made it through a significant screening.

All schools limit the number of applicants they interview. If you have been invited to interview, it is a sign that you are a competitive applicant and you should be pleased. If you receive several interview invitations, the odds are that you will get into medical school. Nontraditional applicants who have interesting life experiences have an advantage in interviews because there is more to talk about than college courses or summer jobs. In addition, you may have had more experience interviewing for jobs and other educational programs than a college student. Hopefully, this will allow you to be more relaxed during the interview process.

In writing a personal statement, you can edit, rewrite, rethink, and start over. In an interview, you don't have this luxury. Being relaxed is important, but so is being prepared. Interviewers may ask about courses you have taken. Before going into an interview, review your academic transcripts. Which courses were your favorites? Your least favorite? Why? How do your preferences relate to your desire to go to medical school? If there are any particularly low or high grades, be prepared to discuss what went on in those classes. Review your AMCAS and secondary applications. Be sure that you can discuss every experience you have listed or discussed. Think of some sort of interesting, impressive, (tastefully) funny, or meaningful comment for each experience. Be prepared to answer questions about your childhood. What aspect of yourself do you really hate talking about? Be ready to talk about it or figure out a good way to divert the conversation from it. What (of relevance) do you know about and enjoy talking about? Think about ways to introduce this subject into your interview.

Although most interviews are one-on-one, some schools use panels of more than one interviewer. Some schools offer group interviews where you interview alongside other applicants. Interviewers may be faculty members, administrators, medical students, or members of the community. Older applicants may find that interviewing with current students, who could be somewhat younger, is challenging. An important part of being a physician is the ability to communicate and to get along with all types of people in all types of positions. The interview is an opportunity to demonstrate your skills in this area.

There are predictable interview questions, such as, "Why do you want to go to medical school?" Others are much less predictable and may even be surprising or shocking. You may be asked about your strategy for balancing personal/family life and medical school or whether you intend to have children. These questions might seem to be inappropriate, particularly to women. However you choose to answer such questions, it is probably best *not* to get defensive. It is reasonable to have concerns about these issues. Tina found that she got a good response when she turned the questions around and asked the interviewer whether *he* felt being a medical student/resident/physician was stressful on a marriage and what *he* felt about having children while in medical school. For more advice on interviewing techniques, turn to Chapter 6.

CHOOSING YOUR MEDICAL SCHOOL

Due to the intense competition in medical school admissions, most premedical advisors recommend that applicants apply to at least 10 schools. Some applicants, particularly those from states with competitive state-affiliated medical schools and whose grades and test scores are below average, should apply to 30 or more schools. In deciding which and how many schools to apply to, it is valuable to talk to a premedical advisor. They will help you determine how strong your application is.

The average MCAT CBT scores of students at a particular school are an indicator of how difficult it is to get in. Be sure to apply to a few safety schools to which you have a better chance of being admitted. Medical school admission and rejection decisions don't always make sense. Donald was accepted to some of the most prestigious schools in the country, but not to his own state school. This element of chance is one reason it's better to apply to a number of schools and not to set your hopes on a single school.

For legal reasons, most schools claim that "age is not a factor in admissions." One way to evaluate a school's attitude toward nontraditional students is to look at its student body. Are there a significant number of nontraditional students? What is the average age of incoming students, and what is the age range? Typically, a school's student body reflects its applicant pool, and some schools with fewer nontraditional students simply have fewer nontraditional applicants. If a school that interests you has few nontraditional students, you may want to ask why. It is possible that the school is looking to diversify its student population and will be particularly interested in your application. Medical schools that have arrangements with postbacc programs are clearly interested in nontraditional students. You should explore them carefully.

Some people argue that all the medical schools in the United States are very good and that there is no particular reason to aspire toward a "top" school. An important difference between medical school and many other graduate or professional degree programs is that medical training does not end at graduation. Rather, a physician's formal education continues during internship, residency, and possibly into fellowship experiences. In terms of job opportunities, where you do your residency could be more important than where you go to school. While attending a well-reputed school will help in residency placement, doing well at a lesser-known school will also allow you to secure a desirable residency. On the other hand, an advantage to attending a well-reputed school is the comfort of knowing that you don't necessarily have to graduate at the top of the class in order to be competitive after graduation.

For those who want to practice strictly clinical medicine, there are factors to consider that may be as important as, if not more important, than a school's general reputation, which is often based largely on the research associated with the institution. When evaluating the training you will receive, some of the issues to consider are the school's location, the patient population to which students are exposed, the extent to which first-

and second-year students learn clinical medicine, the format of the basic science curriculum,[7] interdisciplinary aspects of the curriculum,[8] the learning resources available to students, the school's role in the community and as a health care provider, the emphasis on primary care, the grading system, and the accessibility of faculty. Even if you are uninterested in a career in medical research, there are educational benefits to becoming involved in research efforts while in medical school, and you may be interested in schools that facilitate faculty/student collaboration and encourage student participation in research.

Rather than focusing on prestige or a published ranking,[9] concentrate on what you want from a school. Among other features, Mitch wanted access to a school of public health so that he could continue working in public and international health issues. Eve looked for schools that devoted significant resources to primary care. Donald looked for more structured programs, while Becky was interested in programs that allowed flexibility. Jacob applied primarily to schools with strong reputations for emergency medicine. Bob hoped to continue teaching part-time or during summers while in school. He looked for schools that would allow this.

Beyond academic features, there are lifestyle issues to consider that may be quite different from those faced by recent college graduates. In college, Mitch enjoyed being part of a cohesive student body at a small, remote, private school. As a 30-year-old who had spent significant time overseas, he wanted to live in a more multicultural environment. He hoped to have a social life that, to some degree, involved people other than his medical school classmates. Most of the schools he applied to were either in urban areas or were closely associated with a larger university. Tina wanted to remain near her boyfriend and decided to limit her applications to schools in the region of the country where he was studying. Because of her family, Eve had location issues as well. As a nontraditional student, you are likely to have more responsibilities and complexities in your life than a recent college graduate. As a result, you may find that lifestyle issues play a more important role in determining where you apply and where you go to school.

The day of your interview affords a rare opportunity to hear firsthand what it is like to be a student at a particular medical school. During the course of the day, you will probably speak with current students, either formally or informally. Ask the students you meet for the names of nontraditional students within the class. If you have a spouse and/or children, ask for the names of students in similar situations. While interviewing, you will be focused on making a good impression and getting in. Later, however, you

---

[7] Some schools use lectures and labs while others have an entirely case-based approach. A number of schools fall somewhere in the middle, incorporating some of each educational methodology. There is no evidence that a particular curriculum is "best." You need to consider your own learning style.

[8] Presumably, nontraditional students bring an interdisciplinary perspective and benefit from this approach.

[9] There is no definitive ranking. *U.S. News & World Report* publishes a yearly report ranking graduate schools. Be sure to understand the methodology used when reading their findings.

might have some choices to make and you may be desperately trying to differentiate one school from the next. Input from current students, particularly those with backgrounds similar to your own, will be invaluable (for more advice on how to choose a school, turn to page 40).

FINANCIAL ISSUES

The cost of a medical education is daunting for traditional and nontraditional students alike. With the exception of those who have accrued savings in former careers, financing medical school as a nontraditional student involves challenges. Nontraditional students often have higher living expenses associated with off-campus housing, dependents, debt, and other financial responsibilities. With few exceptions, financial aid offices will look at your parents' income and assets in determining assistance packages. This applies to all students, regardless of their age and whether they themselves are parents. If you are married, medical schools will expect your spouse to contribute to the extent that he or she can. If your parents and/or spouse are less than thrilled about supporting you in this endeavor, financial questions can translate to personal/emotional issues. Older medical students will have less time in the workforce to pay off educational debt, and it is unclear whether financial aid offices consider this in making awards (for more information on financial issues, turn to Chapter 5).

You should carefully consider the financial implications of going to medical school and try to come up with a strategy for dealing with them. If your heart is set on going, financial issues alone should probably not stop you. When deciding where to apply, add to your list of considerations the average debt of graduating students. Even if this figure is not published, financial aid offices will probably provide it if you ask. Look very closely at your state-affiliated medical school because in-state tuition is typically much less than private school costs. Ask financial aid offices about loan repayment programs. Think about ways to trim your budget, such as living with relatives or giving up your car. The material possessions you forego now, and the loan payments you make in the future, should be weighed against the value of having a truly fulfilling career.

5 Financing Medical School

HOW MUCH IS ALL OF THIS GOING TO COST?

There's no doubt that med school is expensive. The average first-year tuition for a U.S. private medical school is upwards of $34,000, and the average tuition at public schools is upwards of $18,000 for in-state residents. When planning for the cost of attending medical school, however, tuition is only part of the picture. You must also pay for books, equipment, housing, utilities, food, insurance, transportation, and miscellaneous costs. All of these expenses add up quickly; depending on where you attend school, they may equal or exceed the price of tuition and can add up to an additional $18,000. Note that tuition is 30 percent higher during second and third years to cover the cost of year-round education.

The cost of a medical education is daunting, but once in practice, physicians are among the most highly paid professionals. In recent years, the difference in pay across specialties has made it difficult to assess physician pay as an overall average. The many options available to current doctors in the way they practice have further complicated this analysis. While all doctors may look forward to earning a comfortable salary, some will be better compensated than others. For example, in 2005 a typical family practitioner made $156,000, while the average for all specialists was close to $300,000. Although it will be years before today's first-year students make that kind of money, they can assume the financial burden of their education with the confidence that they will one day make enough money to justify the investment.

AND HOW CAN I PAY FOR IT?

Since the medical student of today will be the well-paid physician of tomorrow, medical schools expect the students and their families to be responsible for the cost of their education. Except in cases in which a student has exceptional financial resources, it is essential to rely on outside sources of financial assistance to pay the bill.

FINANCIAL AID PROGRAMS

There are two general types of financial assistance available: loans and scholarships/grants. Loans must be repaid and have varying interest rates, deferment options, and repayment periods. Many subsidized loans will be available to you only if you have documented need, while other funds are available regardless of your financial situation. Most medical students borrow heavily, relying on the prospect of a generous salary once they begin practice. For 2006 med school graduates, the average debt was $149,460 for students from private schools and $119,131 for students from public schools, and by all indications, these amounts will continue to increase. Scholarships and grants are gifts that need not be repaid. They can be awarded on the basis of several factors—financial need, outstanding academic merit, specific criteria such as gender, or a promise of future service—or a combination of those factors. Note that the financial aid offices of the schools you are accepted to should provide you with a package that covers all costs somehow. The question is how much of the package comes from you or your parents or from high-interest loans.

Loans

Anyone with good credit can borrow enough money to finance a medical education. Borrowing is simplified if you take advantage of federal lending programs. Qualifications are as follows:

- American citizenship or permanent U.S. resident status.

- If you are a male 18 years of age or older, you are registered for Selective Service, or you have documentation proving that you are not required to register.

- You have a good credit history, including good standing on prior student loans.

- You are an active, enrolled student in good academic standing.

If you have financial resources that disqualify you for some types of need-based aid, but you meet the above requirements, you are still eligible for federal loans (unsubsidized and private loans). The loans for which you qualify may have higher interest rates and offer less favorable repayment schedules than the subsidized loans that are aimed at those with financial need.

Following is a description of five basic types of loans: federal, state, private, charitable, and institutional.

Federal

Federal loan programs are funded by the federal government or are funded by banks and guaranteed by the federal government. Federal loans, particularly the Stafford Loan, are usually the "first resort" for medical student borrowers. Some federal loans such as Perkins or Stafford subsidized loans are need-based, but some higher-interest loans are available to students or their families regardless of financial circumstance.

State

Students who are residents of the state in which they attend medical school may be eligible for state loan programs. Eligibility is often based on need and may be further tied to specific segments of the population (e.g., minority or disadvantaged students, or students who are interested in practicing family medicine in underserved areas of the state). Individual schools can provide you with information about state loan programs.

Private

Privately funded, commercial loans are available from banks and other financial institutions. It is important to research your options intensely because you will want to fully understand the interest that you will accrue as well as the repayment terms before signing on the dotted line.

Charitable

Charity loans are funded by contributions from foundations, corporations, and associations. A number of private loans are targeted to aid particular segments of the population (e.g., minority or disadvantaged students, women, or students who are interested in practicing family medicine in underserved areas of the state). You may have to investigate to identify all of the charitable loans for which you qualify. The best place to begin your search is in public, undergraduate, and med school libraries. There are also a number of commercial financial aid search services available, but beware— financial aid officers warn that search services sometimes charge hefty fees for information that, in the majority of cases, students can obtain themselves. Private financial aid resources are also available online. Visit the Financial Center at PrincetonReview.com to get information on many of them.

Institutional

The amount of loan money available, and the method by which it is disbursed, varies greatly from one school to another. As part of the shift toward emphasizing primary care, some schools offer assistance to students who are committed to providing primary care after graduation. To find out about the resources available at a particular school, refer to its catalog or contact its Financial Aid Office.

In the chart on pages 70 and 71, we have compiled a table of the most commonly used loan programs. Included in this table is information about the characteristics of each loan. The following characteristics are discussed:

Name: The full name of the loan and the acronym, if applicable, by which it is most commonly known.

Source: Information about the organization that funds and administers each loan.

Eligibility: Whether the loans are need-based. Others are open to people regardless of their financial situation. A few federal and private schools require that a student fit a

TABLE OF LOANS

NAME OF LOAN	SOURCE	ELIGIBILITY	MAXIMUM ALLOCATION
Federal Stafford (Subsidized) Student Loan http://studentaid.ed.gov/students/publications/student_guide/index.html	Federal, administered by participating lender	Demonstrated financial need	$8,500/year. The maximum aggregate total for subsidized loans is $65,500. The maximum aggregate total includes any Stafford loans received for undergraduate study.
Unsubsidized Stafford Student Loan http://studentaid.ed.gov/students/publications/student_guide/index.html	Federal, administered by participating lender	Not need-based	The total Stafford loan limit is $20,500, including Unsubsidized loans and Subsidized loans not to exceed $8,500. The maximum aggregate total of Stafford loans is $138,500, including Unsubsidized loans and Subsidized loans not to exceed $65,500.*
Health Professions Student Loan/Primary Care Loan (HPSL) Contact school for more information	Federal, administered by school	Exceptional financial need; commitment to primary care	For first- and second-year students, the maximum allocation is the cost of attendance (including tuition, educational expenses, and reasonable living expenses). Third- and fourth-year students may receive allocations beyond this amount.
Perkins Loan (formerly NDSL) Contact school for more information	Federal, administered by school	Demonstrated financial need	$6,000/year, with aggregate of $40,000. Aggregate amount includes undergraduate loans.
Alternative Loan Program (ALP) www.aamc.org/programs/medloans	AAMC, administered under MEDLOANS division of AAMC	Not need-based	Cost of attendance minus other aid received. Aggregate: $250,000 (total educational indebtedness from all sources).

*Students pursuing certain health professions and enrolled in programs accredited by the appropriate approved accreditation agency are eligible to receive increased amounts of Unsubsidized Stafford loans. If a student is granted the maximum additional allocation, the maximum aggregate total will be $189,500. This number includes all undergraduate and graduate Subsidized and Unsubsidized Stafford loans. See "Increased Eligibility for Health Professions Students" in the Federal Student Aid Handbook for details and updates.

TABLE OF LOANS (continued)

REPAYMENT AND DEFERRAL OPTIONS	INTEREST RATE	PROS	CONS
10–30 years to repay. Begin repayment 6 months after graduation. Forbearance possible for up to 3 years of residency training.	Variable 4% loan disbursement fee. Capped at *8.25%.	Most common medical school loan. Interest is paid by the government during school. Once you get a loan, later loans are at the same rate.	None
10–30 years to repay. Interest begins to accrue from day loan is disbursed; you can pay the interest or have it capitalized (added to principal). Begin repayment 6 months after graduation. Forbearance possible for up to 3 years of residency training.	Variable 4% loan disbursement fee. Capped at *8.25%.	Not need-based.	Interest is not paid by the government while you're in school.
10 years to repay, beginning 1 year after graduation. Deferrable during residency and under special circumstances.	Fixed, 5%.	Fixed, relatively low interest rate.	Very limited availability.
10 years to repay. Begin repayment 9 months after graduation. Can be deferred for 2 years during residency.	Fixed, 5%.	Fixed, relatively low interest rate.	Low maximum allocation.
Standard: 20 years of interest and principal payments. Alternative: 3 years of interest only and 17 years of interest and principal. Repayment generally begins 3–4 years after graduation, depending on length of residency.	Prime rate plus 1.25%; variable, adjusted monthly. (While in school, prime rate plus 0%. Variable, adjusted monthly.)	High maximum allocation; not need-based.	"Loan of last resort." High interest rate.

*Check http://studentaid.ed.gov/students/publications/student_guide/index.html

specific demographic profile. Note that regardless of your age or how long you have been independent of your parents, their income is considered in calculating your need in almost all cases.

Maximum Allocation: The maximum amount of money you can borrow from any one program. Many medical students find it necessary to borrow from more than one source. Most loans have both maximum yearly and aggregate loan amounts. Amounts you borrowed from the same loan program for your college education are deducted, in some cases, from the aggregate amount you can borrow in medical school.

Repayment and Deferral Options: Information about the repayment period and deferral options for each loan. Important considerations in structuring your educational debt are how long you have to pay back loans and whether principal and/or interest may be deferred until you have completed your education. It is important to remember that, no matter what the source of a loan, the responsibility for keeping track of loan activity is yours.

Interest Rate: Information about the current interest rate of the loan. Fixed-rate loans use the same interest rate throughout the life of the loan. Variable-rate loans base their interest rate on established financial values, usually 91-day Treasury Bills (T-Bills) or the prime lending rate. Since these rates fluctuate greatly, you should check with a bank to find out the exact interest rate.

Pros: Factors that make this an attractive loan source. Attractive features include long repayment terms, deferral policies that waive interest and principal throughout medical school and all or part of residency training, and low, fixed-rate interest.

Cons: Factors that make a particular loan unattractive. Such features include short repayment times, limited deferral options, or variable, high-interest rates.

Scholarships/Grants

Some grant, or gift money, comes with no strings attached; these are nonobligatory scholarships. Although such scholarships may be available on the basis of outstanding academic merit alone, others are based on a combination of merit and need. In fact, all federal, nonobligatory scholarships are based on need and may also require that you fit a particular demographic profile. Scholarship amounts vary, and they are administered by the same groups as loans: federal and state governments, private foundations, and institutions. For more information about private, state, and institutional scholarships, contact the financial aid offices at some of the schools to which you are going to apply, or visit the Scholarships & Aid section of PrincetonReview.com.

Obligatory Scholarships

Some federal scholarships are available to students who agree to practice at the Public

TABLE OF GRANTS

NAME OF GRANT	SOURCE	ELIGIBILITY	SERVICE OF OBLIGATION	AMOUNT OF GRANT
National Health Service Corps (NHSC)	Federal	Need-based; former EFN recipients and students with interest in primary care are preferred.	Two- to four-year contract. Years spent in residency do not count toward fulfilling obligation.	Maximum amount is full tuition and fees plus stipend.
National Medical Fellowship Scholarship (NMF)	Private	First- or second-year underrepresented minority, female, rural, or disadvantaged background with documented financial need.	None	Varies. Awards have ranged from $500–$10,000.
Scholarships for Disadvantaged Students (SDS)	Federal, administered through school	Full-time, financially needy students from disadvantaged backgrounds, enrolled in health professions and nursing programs. U.S. citizens only.	None	Varies; tuition and other educational expenses.
Armed Forces Health Professions Scholarship Program (HPSP)	U.S. Army, U.S. Navy, and U.S. Air Force	Able to serve in military; age restrictions; U.S. citizens only.	One year for every year of support. Years spent in residency do not count toward fulfilling obligation.	Full tuition, "reasonable" fees, and stipend. Student becomes officer in service branch upon matriculation and receives all benefits of rank.

Health Service, at the Veterans Administration, or in the Armed Forces. These scholarships provide full tuition, some or all expenses, and a monthly stipend. Service-based scholarships, which are not based on need, all carry an obligation to serve at least one year for every year of support. The advantage—a "free" medical education—is obvious, but this is not an option to take lightly. Time spent in residency—which is often restricted to only military residencies—does not count toward your service debt, so you may be out of medical school for 7 to 12 years before you're free of your obligation. Some states and counties also offer service-based scholarship programs or tuition remission programs. Despite their lengthy obligations, service-based scholarships are in high demand. To increase your chances of obtaining one, apply as early as possible. Ask the financial aid offices of schools in which you are interested whom to contact locally for more information. There are also loan repayment programs available to which you apply after you have accrued debt and when you are ready to start working in an underserved area.

THE FINANCIAL AID PROCESS

PREPARING TO APPLY

Many students miss out on potential assistance by making some basic, avoidable mistakes. Top financial aid officers supplied the following common errors and their remedies.

Missing Deadlines and Keeping Poor Records

Like your applications for admission, your financial aid applications should be submitted as early as possible. File your income tax forms early and encourage your parents (all med students are considered dependent by med schools, even if they have been independent for years) to do the same. Photocopy all forms that you submit and note the date you send them. File these forms along with any material related to the decisions of the financial aid committees of the schools to which you apply. Keep careful track of deadlines, which are strongly enforced.

Submitting Information to the Wrong Needs Analysis Service

There are several third-party organizations that assist medical schools in determining the financial need of entering and continuing students. Many applicants assume that because they have submitted information to one of the services for one school, they have done everything they need to do for all the schools they are considering. Making this assumption can have serious repercussions. Until the proper service completes the needs analysis, the financial aid office cannot package your financial aid. To avoid making this mistake, check with the financial aid offices of all the schools to which you are applying to see which service they use. Submit the proper materials to the appropriate service. More detailed information on the needs analysis services and their function can be found under Calculating Your Expected Family Contribution.

Having a Poor Credit History

People are often unpleasantly surprised when they see their credit histories. Even relatively minor financial problems, like making a couple of late payments on loans or credit cards, can lower your credit rating. Also, credit bureaus sometimes make mistakes, causing negative, but false, information to show up on your record. Since a bad credit history will make you ineligible for many, if not all, loan programs, it is a good idea to check your credit history before you apply for financial aid. Recent federal legislation has made it possible to get a copy of your credit report free of charge once a year from any of the major credit bureaus. You can visit them online at Equifax.com, Experian.com, or TransUnion.com to obtain a copy of your free report.

Defaulting on Undergraduate Student Loans

If you have not kept up with your student loan payments, you will have a very hard time qualifying for loans, especially those funded by the federal government. Clear up any problems with prior student loans well before applying for additional assistance. If you are still in school and have not yet begun repaying your loans, talk to your undergraduate Financial Aid Officer to clarify repayment and deferral options on your loans. Remember that the burden of keeping track of your loan activity is on you, and that once you start medical school, you must keep the lenders apprised of your whereabouts.

APPLYING FOR AID

Schools' policies may vary somewhat, but they all follow the same general lines. To determine whether you qualify and for how much, schools must first determine how much it will cost for you to attend, and then how much of that cost you and your family can absorb.

HOW SCHOOLS DETERMINE THEIR COST

Each medical school prepares a student budget that reflects the expenses associated with being a first-year medical student. Included in this budget are items such as tuition and fees, books, equipment, housing, utilities, food, insurance, transportation, and personal expenses. To some degree, schools customize expenses if a student has particular needs. For example, projected costs may increase if you live off campus.

CALCULATING YOUR CONTRIBUTION

To determine how much you and your family can contribute, medical schools use a needs analysis service. Refer to the financial aid guidelines of the schools you are considering attending. Some schools use more than one service to calculate need, and many ultimately use their own formulas to determine institutional assistance. To make sure you have all the information required to fill out the forms completely, file your previous year's income tax returns early. Because some federal loan programs and some institutions require parental information even from independent or married students, your parents should also file their income tax forms as early as possible.

On the basis of the information you give them, the needs analysis calculates your financial need by subtracting your expected personal and family contribution from the total student budget furnished by the school. If expenses are higher than the estimated contribution, you show financial need.

Your Tentative Financial Aid Package

Most schools will prepare a financial aid package for accepted students only. Once you have been accepted to a school, be on the lookout for a financial aid package. The package can include loans, scholarships, grants, or a combination of these elements. If financial aid is an important consideration in deciding between schools, be sure that you have estimates from all schools by the applicant decision deadline.

Accepting Your Financial Aid Package

Once you matriculate at a school, the Financial Aid Office will put together your actual financial aid package. In most cases, loans will make up a portion of the package. Remember, loans must be repaid—with interest—and the amount of this debt will affect your lifestyle far beyond medical school and residency. For instance, if you borrow a large sum of money for medical school, you may have trouble later obtaining a loan for a large purchase like a car or a house. You are not required to accept all the aid you are offered, so it is in your best interest to borrow only what you need to meet your expenses.

CUTTING COSTS

Medical schools formulate their student budgets by using average expenses for everything except tuition. By making some adjustments to your lifestyle, it is usually possible to undercut this budget and therefore decrease the amount of money you borrow. Following are some strategies recommended by financial aid professionals to reduce debt.

Books and Equipment

Buy good-quality used textbooks and equipment whenever possible. Selling books and equipment you no longer need is a good way to earn extra cash.

Transportation

Automobile loan payments, insurance premiums, licensing fees, fuel, and maintenance really add up. Evaluate your need for a car before taking one to medical school. If you attend school in a place where public transportation is available or where you can bike or walk to school, leave the car behind. If you must have a car, you can save by raising insurance deductibles and carpooling with fellow students.

Insurance

Most medical schools require you to carry medical and, in some cases, disability insurance. Before you buy into the school's plan, check your existing coverage. If your parents still claim you as a dependent, or if you have a spouse whose medical benefits extend to you, you may already have adequate coverage.

Other Expenses

Millions of Americans find themselves in dire financial straits each year because of revolving credit. Medical students are no exception. If you find that you have trouble avoiding the temptation to pull out the plastic for purchases you can't afford, cut up your cards. Remember, if you can't afford to pay for something with cash or a check, you probably can't afford to charge it either. To keep discretionary expenses from getting out of hand, set up a detailed budget and stick to it. If you've never used a budget before and need help, there are many computer programs that will help you set up a budget, track expenses, and give you reports on how you're doing.

A FINAL WORD

Your Financial Aid Rights

- You have the right to expect that the Financial Aid Office will assist you in obtaining financial aid and information about financial aid opportunities.

- Financial Aid Officers to whom you give information about your/your family's financial profile cannot publicize this information.

- You have the right to accept or decline all or part of the aid offered.

- You have the right to appeal your financial aid package if your financial aid picture changes for the worse. (This does not necessarily mean, however, that the amount of aid will increase.)

- You have the right to examine your financial aid file at any time.

- You are entitled to treatment that does not discriminate on the basis of race, creed, age, handicap, gender, or national origin.

YOUR FINANCIAL AID RESPONSIBILITIES

- You are responsible for meeting the expenses related to attending medical school.

- You are responsible for reading and understanding the conditions and terms of all of the elements in your financial aid package.

- You are responsible for submitting financial aid applications on time.

- You are responsible for obtaining and filling out financial aid forms and supplying accurate and complete information on these forms.

- You are responsible for reporting to your Financial Aid Office any outside scholarships or loans that may affect your amount of need.

- You are responsible for using loan funds to pay tuition.

- You are responsible for repaying all loans.

- You are responsible for notifying all lenders of all changes of address during and after medical school.

- You are responsible for keeping accurate and complete records of all financial aid applications and transactions.

6 The Interview:

Separating the Merely Qualified from the Truly Worthy

Be proud if you're invited to an interview. You've made it through two initial screenings, one before and one after the supplemental application. Usually, this means that the Admissions Committee thinks you're qualified to attend their school. Unfortunately, they also invite a lot of other qualified people, and they don't have space to admit all of you. Therefore, your objective is to convince everyone who interviews you that the school would be a better place with you in it. Easy to say, a little harder to do. It is important to realize that the weight of the interview varies from school to school. At some schools it is the key to admission, while at others it is mainly a formality—more for you than for them.

Because almost everyone has heard horror stories about someone else's interview, most people start to worry about the interview before they even submit their applications. Try to relax. A good interview begins with good preparation. You can start by becoming familiar with the interview process.

WHO CONDUCTS INTERVIEWS?

Different schools have different policies about who conducts the actual interview. In general, schools have a Medical Selection Committee made up of professional admissions or student affairs people and faculty members. Often, especially in more progressive schools, upper-level med students also participate. At some schools, you'll have a couple of separate, one-on-one interviews; at others, you'll be interviewed by a panel. You may be the only applicant in front of a panel (this really seems more like an inquisition), or you may be joined by other candidates.

At many schools, the person or people you speak with become your advocates in the final selection process. When all the interviews in a certain time period are finished and the selection committee meets, these people share their observations about you and sometimes recommend a particular action. The final decision, of course, is up to the entire committee.

WHAT CAN I EXPECT?

Expect some interviews to go well and others to go poorly. In the vast majority of cases, the interviewers are trying to build an honest picture of you beyond the numbers, and most try to reduce stress during the interviews. Despite this, you will probably experience one or two bad interviews with interviewers who have not read your file and therefore seem disinterested, are insecure or awkward themselves, or are simply having a bad day. Keep this in mind as your interview dates approach.

HOW SHOULD I ACT?

The golden rule for interviews is "be yourself." Interviewers have been through all of this before, and they're pretty good at spotting people who are putting on an act or reading from a mental script. What they're trying to find out from this interview is what kind of person you are and how you relate to others. Up until now, you've been only a few sheets of paper, a bunch of numbers, and a (probably horrible) photograph. Now's the time to show them your stuff. But remember: no lying and no BS.

BE PREPARED

You should be ready to answer questions about your motivation to become a physician, your academic background, your extracurricular and leisure activities, your job or research experience, and your views on medical problems and ethical issues. Later in this chapter is a sample of questions that current medical students were asked in their interviews. Some of them are typical; others are truly strange. As you get ready to interview, try to answer some of these questions on your own, and then ask a friend, parent, or professor to grill you. In addition, you may want to audiotape or videotape mock interviews to see how you sound and look. When you choose a guinea pig to be your surrogate interviewer, select someone who will be honest with you about the strengths and weaknesses of your responses. Don't try to memorize answers word for word; canned responses, no matter how valid, are stiff and unconvincing (just look at a video of a presidential debate). It is a good idea, however, to enter an interview with several anecdotes or points in mind. Questions are often open-ended, giving you the chance to direct the conversation toward your strengths and away from your weaknesses.

APPROACH WITH CONFIDENCE

Like dogs, interviewers seem to smell fear. The tone of your interview is often set in the first few seconds, so approach with confidence. Greet your interviewer with a firm handshake and look him or her in the eye. During the interview, be positive. Think of it as a pleasant conversation with someone you'd like to get to know better. A good interview is a dialogue, where there is considerable give and take. Unless your interviewer brings them up, avoid controversial or emotionally charged subjects like abortion. If you're asked your views, state them and move on.

TAKE YOUR TIME

In the course of your interviews, you may be asked scores of questions, some on issues to which you haven't given a great deal of thought. Your interviewers don't expect you to have a ready answer for every one of these questions, but they do expect you to come up with a coherent, well-thought-out response. Many applicants are afraid that if they hesitate, it will seem that they are unprepared. Not so. Good physicians don't rush to a conclusion without considering the facts; rather, they think through a problem before they decide how to act. If a question catches you off guard, take a second to think it through. If it seems ambiguous, don't be afraid to ask for clarification. If you don't know, admit it and ask the interviewer to share the answer. By taking the time to make sure that your response is well conceived and well spoken, you will impress the interviewers as thoughtful and articulate—two characteristics essential in a good doctor.

ASK QUESTIONS

Although the interview is the time for medical schools to find out about you, it is also an excellent opportunity for you to find out more about the school. Before you go to an interview, make sure you've studied the school's information packet and are ready to ask intelligent questions about the program. Search the archives at your undergraduate or public library to see if the school has been in the news and, if so, for what. Remember that most people love to talk about themselves. Ask the interviewer about his work or impressions of the curriculum.

BE ON TIME

Make sure that you get detailed directions before you make the trip and arrive with enough time to park and find the office. If you are invited to interview at several schools in the same geographic region, you might save on travel costs and time by making an interview circuit, visiting several schools on the same trip. This can mean that you have several interviews in the same week or even the same day. Give yourself as much time as possible at each, so that you have time to make the transition, both physically and mentally, from one school to the next. If you can, try to get to each campus early enough to walk around, talk to students, and formulate questions that are specific to the school.

DRESS FOR SUCCESS

Like it or not, looks count. No matter what your usual mode of dress, you should dress conservatively and professionally for your interviews. For men, this means a suit or a blazer and nice pants (and, of course, a tie); for women, a suit, blazer and skirt or dress pants, or a business-style dress is appropriate. Regardless of your gender, pay attention to detail; even the most beautiful suit looks shabby if your shoes are scuffed and worn, and the effect of a great-looking blazer is ruined by a ragged backpack. Polish your shoes, invest in a nice portfolio or case for your papers, and by all means, iron your clothes. If you are generally somewhat less than conservative in your dress, you may want to tone it down: men, replace the big hoop earring with a stud; women, take off the gold glitter polish and paint on clear. After all, you don't want to be asked, as one of the respondents to our survey was, "Why are you dressed the way you are? Why did you come here looking the way you do?"

CONDUCT YOURSELF PROFESSIONALLY

Admissions committees can see from your application that you are smart, accomplished, and highly regarded by your professors. The interview is an opportunity for them to gauge things that are not so easily conveyed on paper. Medical schools are looking for students with maturity, empathy, and superior interpersonal skills. All of these things come through in the interview. In a group setting, where the committee talks with more than one candidate at a time, you will be observed not only when you answer a question, but also when your fellow applicants are speaking. Keep alert, and show interest. After all, you never know what you may learn that you can use in your next interview.

HOW AND WHEN TO FOLLOW UP ON YOUR INTERVIEWS

First, don't forget to send a thank-you note after each set of interviews. You can write several different notes to each of your interviewers, or send just one addressed generally to the interview committee. Don't write a novella in your thank-you note. It's fine to mention a particular question or topic you found interesting during your interview, but you should limit yourself to only a few lines. As you might have guessed, it's a good idea to take a few brief notes, such as the interviewer's names and some of the topics they covered, right after you leave the interview. For the thank-you notes themselves, you can use any nice stationery paper.

If the school is not entirely certain of the strength of your application relative to other candidates after your interviews, you may be placed on a hold list. Don't despair. You made it as far as the interview process, which (except in the case of some public schools who interview every candidate) means that you have survived some of the initial cuts. Sometimes being put on hold simply means that the school has already accepted enough students that month. You can, however, send supplementary information to further support your application. For example, if you have been doing research, volunteer work, or taking classes that didn't appear on your initial application, and if you didn't get a chance to talk about your new activities during the interview, you can write a short—less than one page—letter outlining your recent accomplishments and send it to the school. This shows that you are still working hard to better your chances of acceptance into medical school.

WHAT ARE THEY GOING TO ASK?

The sample interview questions in this section come from various sources. Although the following list of questions is by no means exhaustive, it is a good sampling of questions that were asked in real interviews in the recent past. Get ready, because while some of the questions are pretty standard, others are truly bizarre.

So You Want to Be a Doctor?

Some students are often unprepared for questions like the ones that follow, thinking them so mundane that they wouldn't be asked. However, if you're granted even one interview, you're almost sure to be asked several questions about your motivation and suitability for medical school.

- Why do you want to be a doctor?
- The future of medicine looks bleak. Why do you want to go into it?
- What articles have you read recently that relate to the reasons you want to become a doctor?
- What do you see yourself doing with a medical degree?
- Were you influenced by relatives to pursue a career in medicine?
- Why do you want to attend [name of school]?
- Why should we accept you?
- How are your accomplishments better than those of the other candidates in this interview?
- Evaluate yourself based on the required evaluation of the interviewer.
- Do you think you are motivated enough for medical school?
- When you don't get into medical school, what will you do?
- What career path would you follow if all the medical schools closed today?
- You've taken an odd, nontraditional path to get here. Why are you interested in medicine?
- What disadvantages do you see in being an older student?
- Can you afford to come here?
- How will you finance your medical education?
- Describe what you believe to be the financial rewards of medicine.
- If doctors were paid a teacher's salary, would you still want to be a doctor?

Tell Me a Little Bit About Yourself . . .

Selection committees use the interview as an opportunity to find out what makes you tick. Prepare yourself for personal questions about your character traits, your coping mechanisms, and your life experiences. You may also be asked to comment on your interpersonal relationships. Always be honest.

- What is your worst quality?
- If you could change anything about yourself, what would it be?
- Are you aggressive?
- What makes you a fun person?
- What makes you angry?
- What makes you sad?
- What scares you?
- Do you like sick people?
- Are you afraid of death?
- What are you the most proud of?
- One of the people who wrote a letter of recommendation for you described you as [adjective]. Do you agree with that description?
- Was there a time in your life when you had tremendous responsibility?
- What is the wackiest thing you've ever done?
- What was the biggest mistake you ever made?
- What is the worst thing that has happened to you in the past four years?
- Tell me something you wanted to achieve but did not, or something you've failed at. How did you cope with failure?
- What role has stress played in your life?
- How could you prove to me that you can perform well under stress?
- What do you do to alleviate stress?
- Tell me about your family.
- What role do you play in your family dynamic?
- How is your relationship with your parents?
- What is the physical health of your parents, and how would you handle an illness of theirs while attending school?

- Who is the person in the world to whom you are closest?

- Describe your best friend.

- What does your closest friend think about your relationship with him or her?

- Give one word that a friend would use to describe you.

It's All Academic

Grades, MCAT CBT scores, and courses are fair game for the inquisitive interviewer. You may be asked to explain your performance in a course or to tell what you learned. A hint: To be better prepared for questions of this type, get a copy of your transcript and take a look at it. Look for things that might cause an interviewer to ask a question. Lower-than-normal grades stick out, as do courses with funny names (like Rocks for Jocks). Then again, be honest.

- What do you think of the GPA as a valid method of categorizing students?

- Why were your first-year grades so bad?

- Why do you have so many C grades on your transcript?

- Explain your low math grade.

- Why are your grades high compared to your MCAT CBT scores?

- Do you realize that your MCAT CBT scores aren't anything special?

- Tell me about your research.

- Have you taken any humanities classes, and what papers did you write in them?

- What did you learn in [name of course]? (It's worth noting that some people were asked about normal courses like "Philosophy 101" and others were asked about bizarre courses like "The Art of Murder," "Fairy Tales," and "Play, Games, Toys, and Sports.")

- Who was the author of your biochemistry textbook?

Extra, Extra, Read All About It!

Whatever your extracurricular activities and work experiences, you will most likely be asked how they relate to your commitment to and preparedness for studying medicine. Think about your extracurricular experiences and what you learned about yourself, the medical field, and/or working with people as a result of participating in these activities. If you've been out of school for a while and have worked extensively in another field, be ready for questions about why you decided to change fields. Scientific or medical research experience is a plus, but it can be a real liability if you're not able to discuss it in detail.

- What are your hobbies?

- How does your hobby relate to being a doctor?

- Have you taught yourself to do anything, and if so, what?

- How has working as a [name of job] made you a better candidate for medical school?

- What volunteer work contributed to your commitment to become a doctor?

- What did you do with your job earnings?

MEDICAL ISSUES AND ETHICS: WHERE DO YOU STAND?

Interviewers love to ask students about a medical issue or about an ethical dilemma related to medicine. In general, there are no wrong answers to these questions. You should know the terminology (for example, the difference between euthanasia and euthenics) and be aware of some pros and cons for each of these issues. Since the health care crisis and attendant problems in reforming the health care delivery system have been grabbing headlines, you should be prepared to discuss the issues intelligently. No one expects you to be an expert on this or any other issue, but you should do some research before your interviews. Don't be surprised if an interviewer challenges your view on an issue; usually, he or she is trying to see how well you support your argument.

- What is the greatest problem facing medicine today?

- What do you consider the most important thing medicine has done for humanity?

- What do you think will be the most significant scientific breakthrough in the next 10 years?

- If you could find a cure for AIDS or for cancer, which would you choose and why?

- If you were the U.S. Surgeon General, what is the first thing you would do?

- If you were the health commissioner of [a large city], what would you do?

- What is preventive medicine?

- What is the biggest problem family practitioners face?

- What are your views on euthanasia?

- What do you think about euthenics (not euthanasia)?

- What would you do about the alcoholism problem in this country?

- What do you think about condoms being distributed in high schools?

- What are your views on mandatory HIV testing for doctors and patients?

- Current AIDS education programs aren't working; what should we do?

- Why will organ rationing be the problem of the future in medicine?

- Should people have the right to sell their own organs?

- Do you think it's ethical to take the life of a fetus for a cell line to save the life of a sibling with cancer?

- Should we spend so much time and effort trying to keep premature infants alive?

- If a cure were invented for aging, what repercussions would it have on society in general and the medical profession in particular?

- How do you feel about animal research?

- What role should politics play in medicine?

- Is health care a right or a privilege?

- What is your opinion of socialized medicine?

- How would you organize health care in an ideal world?

- Discuss the health care system of Australia.

- What do you think should be done about patients who can't pay for treatment?

- What is the difference between Medicare and Medicaid?

- What is your opinion of HMOs and PPOs?

- How will you react to the death of your first patient?

- Who would you go to if your mom needed surgery: a surgeon with good hands and a bland personality or a surgeon with not as good hands with a great personality?

- How would you tell your best friend's wife (who is your patient) that she has cancer? What would you do if she then refused to tell her family?

- You have to amputate one of the legs of an eight-year-old child. How would you tell him?

- Would you give a transfusion to a child whose parents were Jehovah's Witnesses?

- If a Hindu, for example, comes in and refuses surgery on the basis of religion, and the surgery is his only hope, what would you do? What if the patient was this man or woman's child?

- If you diagnosed a patient with a terminal illness as having only two months to live and the family and the patient wanted to end the turmoil ("pull the plug"), would you allow it or strongly disagree?

- What would you do if you saw a bleeding child on the side of the road?

- What would you do if you had a female patient who was trying to conceive, and your colleague had that patient's husband, and the husband was HIV positive?

- If one of your colleagues refused to treat a patient with AIDS, how would you address that colleague?

- How would you react if a fellow medical student had AIDS and entered surgery with you?

- Would you let a surgeon with AIDS operate on you?

- Would you treat a white supremacist, and should physicians be forced to treat such a patient?

- If you made a mistake as a physician, how would you handle it?

To Choose or Not to Choose

Abortion is not only a hot political topic, it also seems to be a hot topic for interviews. Some schools are affiliated with hospitals where abortions are performed; some are not. Don't try to guess if the interviewer is hoping you will espouse a particular position; honesty seems the best policy on this issue. If you are asked about your willingness to perform an abortion (as a large number of those we surveyed were), you may want to mention that it is not only your beliefs but also the rules of the hospital or laws of the land that you must consider.

- What should a physician's role be in the politics of abortion?

- What would you do as a physician if you were asked to do something contrary to your stand on abortion?

- Would you perform an abortion for a teenager, and would you tell her parents?

- How would you justify being a Catholic and going to an institution that allows abortion?

Have You Heard the News?

Good doctors are aware of, and involved in, the world around them. You may be asked about current events, even things completely unrelated to medicine. The questions that follow are only examples; in most cases, these events are no longer current. To prepare for questions like these, keep up with what's happening. If you get most of your news from the television or radio, start reading newspapers and news magazines for more in-depth coverage.

- Who is the U.S. Secretary of State?

- What do you think about the political situation in Iraq and surrounding countries?

- Do you think the Israelis beat up on the Palestinians?

PHILOSOPHY 101

From the serious to the silly, questions interviewers ask can make you stop and think. (And for some of these questions, one of the things you might think is, "What does this have to do with med school?")

- What are the top five priorities of society?
- Do you see any parallels between medicine and the priesthood?
- What is Zen Buddhism?
- Explain Hinduism.
- Are you a racist?
- Do you believe that racism still exists?
- How do you feel about affirmative action?
- Would you move to Canada to avoid serving active duty during a military conflict abroad?
- What is your view on censorship in the arts?
- What would you do if you saw a classmate cheating on a test?
- Do you believe in drug legalization?
- Do you believe that volunteerism could help eliminate greed from society's social structure?
- Is altruism ever pure, without some kind of motive?
- Do you believe in life after death?
- What is your opinion about natural law ethics?
- Explain the mind-body problem.
- Are you a vertical or horizontal thinker?
- If you could be any cell in the human body, what would you be?
- If you were to build a human being, what would you include and exclude?
- Define hope.

TRIED AND TRUE

Some questions sound more like pickup lines than med school interview questions. Although none of those surveyed was asked, "What's your sign?" there were plenty of old favorites that you may as well be prepared for.

- Are you a person who thinks a glass is half empty or half full?
- If you could go back in history and meet anyone, who would it be and why?

- If you could talk to someone from the future, what would you ask him or her?

- If a genie were able to grant you three wishes, what would they be?

- If you were stranded on a desert island, what five books would you want?

- If your house was burning down and you could save only one thing, what would
it be?

- If you could be any vegetable, what would you be?

- If you could be any kind of fruit, what would you be?

- If you could be any kind of animal, what would you be?

- What is your favorite color?

- What was the last book you read, and how did it influence your life?

- What was the last good movie you saw?

- Tell me what you see when you look in the mirror.

- What was the most embarrassing moment in your life?

- Who is your hero?

- If you could invite three role models to dinner, who would they be and why, and what would you serve them?

- When you die, what would you like your tombstone to read?

I'll Take "Potpourri" for $500, Alex

The students we surveyed were asked some trivia worthy of "Final Jeopardy." The bad news is that because of the very nature of these questions, you can't prepare for them. The good news is that a simple "I don't know" seemed to satisfy the interviewers. For bonus points, ask for the answer or, as one student did, tell them you'll check and get back to them. He did, and subsequently, he got in.

- What is the largest lobbyist group in the United States?

- Which state first had women's suffrage?

- What language did Abraham (of the Bible) speak?

- When did Iraq become an independent nation?

- How many numbers that contain 9 are there between 1 and 100?

- What is the capital of Vietnam?

- When and how was Pakistan formed?

- Who won the 1969 World Series?

- What is the difference between European and American eighteenth-century poetry?

- Why was the Civil War fought?

- What is the origin of the name "Cincinnati"?

- What do the e's in e.e. cummings' name stand for?

- When and why was the March of Dimes founded?

- When did Istanbul become Istanbul?

- Name the four non-Arabic-speaking countries in the Middle East.

- What was Thomas Aquinas famous for?

- Who was the architect who built the Great Wall of China?

- Where was Millard Filmore born?

- Give a brief history of the Jesuit order.

- Define the Apollonian and the Dionysian as they figure in the philosophy of Nietzsche.

- Who was the head of NATO during World War II?

- What size tippets do you use on your fly lines with a 14X fly?

A COROLLARY: I'LL TAKE "SCIENCE & MEDICINE" FOR $1,000, ALEX

A few interviewees were asked trivia questions that actually related to science and medicine. For the most part, they knew the answers. When they didn't, and the question was obscure, it didn't seem to hurt their chances of getting in. Your undergraduate course work and MCAT CBT review should be preparation enough for a lot of these questions.

- What was the first industrialized country to practice socialized medicine? The second?

- How much does the United States spend each year on medical care?

- How does a lightbulb work?

- Why don't fish die in winter?

- Why does ice float on the top of water?

- How do you make a protein?

- So what is Alzheimer's disease, anyway?

- Where is your hamstring region?

- Tell me what you know about DNA.

- What is the Grignard Reaction?

- What is Poisson's equation?

- Describe protein structure.

- What is PKU?

CAN YOU SAY "INAPPROPRIATE"?

Despite the media attention that issues of gender discrimination and sexual harassment receive, medical school interviewers are still asking questions that, if they were asked in a job interview, would be deemed inappropriate or illegal. These kinds of questions are more common than you would expect. The students who told us they'd been asked these questions (and there were lots of them, mostly female) expressed emotions from confusion to outrage. Still, most admitted to being afraid that they would be rejected if they did anything but reply calmly, and therefore they answered honestly and without additional comment. How you handle a question like this is up to you. At this point, you too might feel that there is too much at stake to make waves, but on the other hand, it is certainly within your rights to ask how the question is relevant or even to politely decline to answer.

- How did you get such a high score in math? I've never seen such a high score from a woman!

- Do you know that you have extraordinarily good looks?

- Why do you want to be a doctor rather than a nurse?

- Will you faint if I take you into surgery?

- Would you feel uncomfortable being alone with a male patient?

- How did taking a nude art class make you feel?

- What would your ideal date be?

- Do you find it hard to find educated black men to date?

- Why don't you like men?

- How does your boyfriend feel about your going to medical school?

- Would having a boyfriend affect your decision in choosing a medical school and career?

- Are you prepared to handle possibly losing your boyfriend/girlfriend over the stress and distance?

- Are you married?

- What kind of person would you like to marry?

- Do you plan to marry while in medical school?

- Why aren't you married?

- How will you deal with being married while in medical school?

- What does your husband do?

- Why did you get divorced?

- Do you plan to remarry?

- Do you expect to have a family? If so, why are you applying to medical school?

- If you become pregnant, what will you do?

- How do you plan to manage a family and a career? After all, you are a woman.

- How would you raise your children if you were a doctor?

- What would you do if you were sexually harassed at any time during school, residency, or your career?

- Are you prepared for the sexual discrimination you will most likely face as a student, resident, intern, and so on?

EXPECT THE UNEXPECTED

Although most of the questions fall into one of the previous categories, some of the questions are just plain off the wall. Some of the following questions were logical from the perspective of the candidates' background, so be prepared to answer questions about the leisure activities you listed on your application or the experiences you related in your essays. Other questions came straight out of left field. These are unlikely to be repeated, but they give you an idea of the kind of things interviewers ask to catch you off balance. If you're asked a question like this, take your time and think it through. If all else fails, remember, it's better to say "I don't know" than to try to baffle 'em with bull. As one of those surveyed said after an unsuccessful attempt at bluffing, "It doesn't work—they've heard it all before."

- What would you do if I dropped unconscious right now?

- What would you say if you smashed your finger with a hammer?

- How tall are you?

- How did you get your hair to do that?

- Is that your natural hair color?

- Why are you dressed the way you are? Why did you come here looking the way you do?

- Do you think that anyone can become a singer?

- Do you know how to play an instrument?

- Who is your favorite classical music composer?

- What's your favorite Beatles album?

- What is your favorite college football team?

- What do you think the chances are that the [team name] will make the playoffs?

- Why are the majority of NBA players black?

- How much can you bench press?

- If you're accepted, will you play on our softball team?

- What was your opinion of the rich, yuppie Greek students on your undergraduate campus?

- How much do you drink?

- Have you ever cheated?

- Have you ever tried an illegal substance?

- Have you ever stolen a car?

- What kind of car do you drive?

- What is your opinion of Charlie Brown?

- Do you prefer the old Star Trek or the new one?

- Why didn't you take Latin?

- Do you dream in Chinese or English?

- Do you know how to surf?

- Are you most like Madonna, Margaret Thatcher, or Mother Teresa, and why?

- What is your favorite card game?

- Do you play bingo?

- Does your mother know where you are?

7 Allopathic Profiles

ALBANY MEDICAL COLLEGE

47 NEW SCOTLAND AVENUE, MAIL CODE 3, ALBANY, NY 12208 • **ADMISSION:** 518-262-5521
FAX: 518-262-5887 • **E-MAIL:** ADMISSIONS@MAIL.AMC.EDU • **WEBSITE:** WWW.AMC.EDU

STUDENT BODY

Type	Private
Enrollment	538
% *male/*female	45/55
% minorities	8
# applied (total/out)	6,833/5,369
# accepted (total/out)	313/215
# enrolled (total/out)	94/65
Average age	26

FACULTY

Total faculty (number)	1,522
% female	24
% minority	7
% part-time	64
Student-faculty ratio	3:1

ADMISSIONS
Average GPA and MCAT Scores

Overall GPA	3.5
MCAT Bio	10.1
MCAT Phys	9.8
MCAT Verbal	9.5
MCAT Essay	P

Application Information

Regular application	11/15
Regular notification	12/1
Are transfers accepted?	No
Admissions may be deferred?	Yes
Interview required?	Yes
Application fee	$100

Academics

Albany Medical College responded to the changing health care needs in the United States by restructuring its curriculum to better address contemporary issues in health care, while simultaneously providing a solid clinical and scientific education. The curriculum focuses specifically on the principles and practices of comprehensive care—health care that addresses the full spectrum of patient needs from medical and preventive to palliative and psychosocial. Grades of honors, excellent, good, marginal, and unsatisfactory are used to evaluate student performance. In the clinical years, narrative assessments of performance are also used as an important evaluation tool. Graduation requirements include passing Step 1 of the USMLE and taking Step 2, including the clinical skills exam.

BASIC SCIENCES: Basic science education is coordinated and integrated in a manner that spans all 4 years of medical school, systematically increasing basic science knowledge within the context of clinical medicine. By teaching within a clinical context, the college offers a learning environment that focuses on developing problem-solving skills. Basic science concepts are divided into themes or modules that are most often organ based. Taught in conjunction with clinical case experience, these modules come together to form the foundation for the clinical education. In the first year, students combine basic science instruction with clinical cases to focus on normal function. In the second year, students further expand their knowledge and focus primarily on abnormal function and the disease state. Students learn clinical skills beginning in their first year by working within small groups and interacting with standardized patients who are trained to simulate actual illness. Students explore legal, ethical, and humanistic concerns in a 4-year module called Health Care and Society. Systems of health care, epidemiology, biostatistics, and the principles of evidence based medicine are concurrently studied in a 4-year module called Evidence Based Health Care. Fundamental knowledge of nutrition also begins in year one and is integrated in all 4 years of the curriculum. Managing information is a key component throughout all thematic modules. The Schaffer Library of Health Sciences houses more than 144,000 volumes, 974 journals in print and 8,500 available on-line, contains 3,900 multimedia programs and has 40 computer stations in the independent learning center. Throughout their medical education, students rely on these resources as well as the support of the library faculty.

CLINICAL TRAINING

An innovative experience, Orientation Clerkship, transitions students from the first 2 years of the curriculum to the clinical and rotation requirements of the final 2 years. This two-week clerkship occurs during the summer prior to year 3. These learning opportunities on standardized patients enable medical students to develop, practice, and enhance their clinical skills and abilities. Students participate in mock preceptor rounds, assess their own clinical skills, and perform basic medical procedures. The third-year required clinical clerkships are a combination of hospital-based experiences to hospital- and ambulatory-based experiences. The third-year required clerkships are Medicine (12 weeks), Surgery (8 weeks), Pediatrics (8 weeks), obstetrics/gynecology (6 weeks), Family Practice (6 weeks), and Psychiatry (6 weeks). Fourth-year rotation requirements are Emergency Medicine (4 weeks), Neuro/Opthomology (4 weeks), Critical Care (4 weeks), and an elective in either Family Practice, Medicine, Surgery, or Pediatrics (4 weeks).

Required rotations take place primarily at Albany Medical Center Hospital, as well as other regional and local community hospitals, community health centers, psychiatric inpatient units, nursing homes, adult homes, and patients' homes. The remainder of fourth year includes electives chosen by the students.

Campus Life

Of students in the 2005 entering class, 11 percent were underrepresented minorities. Geographic representation was as follows: Northeast (66 percent), South (6 percent), Midwest (4 percent), West (22 percent), foreign countries (2 percent). There is usually a wide range of ages within the student body. The average class size is 130.

STUDENT LIFE

The student community is very active both on and off campus. There are about 30 campus clubs and organizations, including a student newspaper, outdoor and athletic clubs, support groups for students with similar backgrounds or situations, and groups focused on community activities. For example, one student organization arranges activities for the medical center's pediatric cancer patients, while another brings AIDS education programs to local schools.

GRADUATES

Graduates gain acceptance into some of the top institutions in the nation. Forty percent of the 2004 graduates entered residency programs in primary care.

Admissions

REQUIREMENTS

Requirements are 6 semester hours each or 9 quarter hours of biology, general chemistry, organic chemistry, and physics each of which must include associated labs. When assessing GPAs, the Admissions Committee considers the intensity of each student's course load as well as his or her undergraduate institution. The MCAT is required of all applicants. For those who have retaken the exam, the best set of scores is considered most important, though all scores should be submitted.

SUGGESTIONS

Community-service and medically related activities are valued. College courses should be varied and demonstrate breadth and depth. There is no preference for New York State residents.

PROCESS

All AMCAS applicants are sent secondary applications. About 25 percent of those completing secondaries are interviewed. Interviews take place from September through April and are conducted by faculty, students, administrators, and local physicians. The interview day also features a group orientation and the opportunity to meet with deans, faculty, and students. Candidates are notified on a rolling basis and are either accepted, rejected, or under consideration. Albany Medical College offers combined-degree programs with Siena College, Union College, and Rensselaer Polytechnic Institute with a special focus on community service, business management, or research, respectively. Interested students should apply during their senior year in high school. The MCAT is waived for students admitted through these joint programs. Students admitted to the programs earn both degrees in 7 or 8 years, depending on the undergraduate institution.

Admissions Requirements (Required)

MCAT scores, science GPA, non-science GPA, letters of recommendation, interview, essays/personal statement

Admissions Requirements (Optional)

State residency, extracurricular activities, exposure to medical profession

COSTS AND AID

Tuition & Fees

Tuition	$41,224
Room and board (off-campus)	$8,500
Cost of books	$1,835
Fees	$30

Financial Aid

% students receiving aid	88
Average grant	$5,942
Average loan	$42,382
Average debt	$161,051

BAYLOR COLLEGE OF MEDICINE

OFFICE OF ADMISSIONS INFORMATION, ONE BAYLOR PLAZA HOUSTON, TX 77030 • ADMISSION: 713-798-4842
FAX: 713-798-5563 • E-MAIL: ADMISSIONS@BCM.EDU • WEBSITE: WWW.BCM.EDU

STUDENT BODY

Type	Private
Enrollment	673
% male/female	52/48
% minorities	19
# applied (total/out)	4,285/2,909
# accepted	285
# enrolled (total/out)	168/39
Average age	23

FACULTY

Total faculty (number)	2,111
% part-time	18
Student-faculty ratio	3:1

ADMISSIONS

Average GPA and MCAT Scores

Overall GPA	3.8

Application Information

Regular application	11/1
Regular notification	Rolling
Early application	6/1
Early notification	10/1
Are transfers accepted?	Yes
Admissions may be deferred?	Yes
Interview required?	Yes
Application fee	$70

Academics

Students enjoy a flexible and balanced curriculum that helps them prepare for whatever career in medicine they choose. This flexibility is enhanced by the opportunity to create individualized schedules in the clinical curriculum, which, due to a 1.5-year pre-clinical curriculum, is 2.5 years. Throughout all 4 years, grading is honors, high pass, pass, marginal pass, and fail. Students must take the USMLE Steps 1 and 2 prior to graduation (but performance does not affect graduation). Most students opt to take Step 1 midway through their third year and Step 2 late in their fourth year. About 10 percent of students each year enter one of several combined-degree programs offered in conjunction with the University of Houston and Rice University. These programs include the MD/PhD, MD/MBA, and MD/JD degrees. Many of the MD/PhD students are funded annually by the NIH MSTP training grant. Other students are supported by private or institutional sources.

PRE-CLINICAL CURRICULUM: The pre-clinical curriculum starts early in August with an integrated course called core concepts. This is followed by a series of interdisciplinary, organ-based modules (e.g., cardiology, respiratory, endocrinology) which are sequenced in order to build on language, vocabulary, and skills. Throughout the 18-month pre-clinical curriculum, students attend lectures and labs in the morning. Most lectures are available online via streaming video for review. Two afternoons a week, students meet in small groups of 8–10 students with a faculty facilitator or in a preceptor's office, leaving the remaining afternoons open for studying. Complementing the basic science focus of the organ-based modules are courses which emphasize problem solving, early clinical experiences, social and behavioral sciences, and ethics. For example, the two afternoon courses, integrated problem solving and patient, physician, and society, help students develop skills in life long learning, use of modern informational technologies, and the basics of patient care. Both faculty and student tutors are available for additional instruction outside of the classroom. State-of-the-art learning resources (print and digital) are available via the Internet, in the Educational Resource Center in the DeBakey Building, or across the street in the Houston Academy of Medicine-Texas Medical Center Library, one of the largest medical libraries in the country. Students also have the opportunity to choose from a wide array of basic science elective experiences (e.g., Compassion and the Art of Medicine, International Health Care, etc.).

CLINICAL TRAINING

Clinical rotations begin in January of the second year. Required clerkships include the following: Medicine (12 weeks), Surgery (12 weeks), Obstetrics/Gynecology (8 weeks), Pediatrics (8 weeks), Psychiatry (8 weeks), Neurology (4 weeks), Family and Community Medicine (4 weeks), and Surgical Subspecialties (4 weeks). Other requirements include 4 weeks of electives and 20 weeks of electives. Throughout the clinical curriculum, students leave their clinical rotation one afternoon a week to engage in one of three unique courses: clinical applications of the biomedical science (year 1), longitudinal ambulatory care experience (year 3), and mechanisms and management of disease (year 4). As part of the third-year longitudinal ambulatory care experience, students visit community agencies that provide important health-related services to families and patients (e.g., hospice, homeless shelters, etc). At the end of the fourth year, students may elect to take a 2-week course in integrated clinical experiences (ICE), which serves as a transition to residency training. Students train in the Baylor Affiliated Teaching Hospitals (with over 5,000 beds total) in the Texas Medical Center complex and at other sites around the city. Elective credits may be earned at institutions throughout the United States as well as overseas. Students with special interest in care of the underserved, geriatrics, international health, medical ethics, or research can complete elective requirements within a "track" organized around the topic. These students receive a special certificate at graduation. In 2005, Baylor adopted a set of core competency graduation goals and began implementation of a competency-based curriculum in which students will have increased opportunity to receive feedback about specific strengths and weaknesses in their knowledge, skills, and attitudes expected by the competency-based residency training programs they will seek to enter after graduation.

Campus Life

Approximately 70 to 80 percent of students are Texas residents. Students in the class that entered in 2005 came from 54 undergraduate institutions around the country. About 23 percent of students are underrepresented minorities, and a wide age range is seen within the student body. The entering class size is 168.

STUDENT LIFE

A 5-day orientation introduces entering students to the school's academic and non-academic resources and promotes a supportive atmosphere from the beginning. First-year students also benefit from peer counseling groups and professional advising. Numerous organizations promote extracurricular, professional, community service, and religious interests, or offer support for minority or other groups of medical students. Some examples include the Family Practice Club, the Texas Medical Association Medical Student Section, and the Baylor Association of Minority Medical Students. An athletic center with exercise equipment and weights, basketball, racquetball, aerobics, and volleyball is available to medical students. Houston is home to almost 2 million people and is a center for commerce, industry, arts, and recreation. A dormitory operated by the Texas Medical Center is located near Baylor, although most medical students opt to live off-campus in nearby residential areas.

GRADUATES

Graduates are successful in securing residencies in all generalist and specialty areas. Baylor also administers postgraduate programs.

Admissions

REQUIREMENTS

Prerequisites are one year in each of the following: biology, general chemistry, English, and organic chemistry. Science courses must include associated labs. The MCAT is required and must be from within the past 5 years. For applicants who have taken the exam on more than one occasion, the most recent set of scores is weighted heavily.

SUGGESTIONS

Approximately 70–75 percent of the positions in each class are reserved for Texas residents, making nonresident positions highly competitive. The April, rather than August, MCAT is recommended. Beyond intellectual ability, Baylor is interested in personal integrity and demonstrated interest in medicine, human compassion, and leadership skills.

PROCESS

Baylor participates in AMCAS. The AMCAS Web-enabled application is available in May preceding the year of anticipated entrance. Approximately 15 percent of applicants are interviewed between September and February. Interviews usually consist of two sessions that are 30 minutes each with a faculty member or medical student. The interview day features a group orientation session, a campus tour, and the opportunity to meet informally with students and faculty members. Of interviewed candidates, about 45 percent are accepted on a rolling basis.

Admissions Requirements (Required)

MCAT scores, science GPA, non-science GPA, letters of recommendation, interview, essays/personal statement

Admissions Requirements (Optional)

State residency, extracurricular activities, exposure to medical profession

COSTS AND AID

Tuition & Fees

In-state tuition	$6,550
Out-of-state tuition	$19,650
Room and board (off-campus)	$13,365
Cost of books	$6,298
Fees	$5,198

Financial Aid

% students receiving aid	81
Average grant	$8,823
Average loan	$21,557
Average debt	$67,679

BOSTON UNIVERSITY
SCHOOL OF MEDICINE

715 ALBANY STREET BOSTON, MA 02118 • ADMISSION: 617-638-4630 • FAX: 617-638-4718
E-MAIL: MEDADMS@BU.EDU • WEBSITE: WWW.BUMC.BU.EDU

Type	Private
Enrollment	674
% male/female	45/55
% minorities	23
# applied (total/out)	11,324/9,980
# accepted (total/out)	489/389
# enrolled (total/out)	168/119
Average age	24

FACULTY

Total faculty	1,162
% female	41
% minority	19
% part-time	20
Student-faculty ratio	1:1

ADMISSIONS
Average GPA and MCAT Scores

Overall GPA	3.72
MCAT Bio	11.44
MCAT Phys	11.11
MCAT Verbal	10.45
MCAT Essay	P

Application Information

Regular application	11/1
Regular notification	Rolling
Early application	8/1
Early notification	10/1
Are transfers accepted?	No
Admissions may be deferred?	No
Interview required?	Yes
Application fee	$100

Academics

Several combined degree programs are offered, including the M.D./M.P.H. and MD/MBA, to which all students accepted into the medical school may apply. Qualified students may pursue a joint M.D./Ph.D. program, earning the doctorate degree in Anatomy, Biochemistry, Biomedical Engineering, Biophysics, Behavioral Neuroscience, Cell Biology, Genetics; Immunology, Microbiology, Molecular Biology, Pathology, Pharmacology, or Physiology. Most students take part in a four-year curriculum of basic and clinical science, leading to the M.D. However, up to ten students each year enter an Alternative Curriculum which spreads out the first year of study into two years, thereby freeing up time for academic or personal interests. Evaluation uses Honors, Pass, and Fail in addition to narrative reports when possible. Passing the USMLE Step 1 is a requirement for promotion to year three.

BASIC SCIENCES: An Integrated Problems course supplements the traditional lecture/lab format of first- and second-year courses. Integrated Problems meets in small groups, and uses an interdisciplinary approach to tackle case studies that relate to subjects discussed in other courses. First-year courses are: Gross Anatomy; Histology; Biochemistry; Physiology; Endocrinology; Neuroscience; Principles of Psychiatry in Medicine; Essentials of Public Health; Immunology; Genetics; and Introduction to Clinical Medicine I (ICM I). ICM I develops an understanding of the doctor-patient relationship and discusses sociocultural issues related to it. Second-year courses are: Pathology; Pharmacology; Microbiology and Infectious Diseases; Biology of Disease I; Biology of Disease II; ICM II; Psychiatry; and Integrated Problems. In ICM II, students learn to conduct patient interviews and physical examinations. A benefit of the ICM continuum is that instruction involves mentorships with practicing physicians, often in primary care settings. Most basic science instruction takes place in the Instructional Building, which has classrooms, administrative offices, and a library with 117,000 volumes and 1,300 periodicals. This building connects to the Housman Research Building, which offers a learning center and a computer room.

CLINICAL TRAINING

Required third-year clerkships are: Family Medicine (6 weeks); Medicine (11 weeks); Surgery (11 weeks); Ob/Gyn (6 weeks); Pediatrics (6 weeks); and Psychiatry (6 weeks). More than half of the fourth year is reserved for electives and many of our students to one or more blocks in International Health. Required fourth-year clerkships are: Home Medicine/Geriatrics (4 weeks); Neurology (4 weeks); Radiology (4 weeks); Primary Care (4 weeks); and a Sub internship (4 weeks). Clinical training takes place at the Boston Medical Center (633 beds), the Veterans Affairs Administration Medical Center (535 beds), and at least eighteen other affiliated hospitals and health care facilities. Several research centers are part of the Medical Center, and also serve as educational facilities for medical students.

Students

Underrepresented minorities account for more than 10 percent of the student body. The average age of entering students is 22, with a very broad range. Although a large number of states and colleges are represented, a significant proportion of students have completed their undergraduate education on the east or west coast.

STUDENT LIFE

Students are involved in a large number of student organizations, both professional and nonprofessional. These activities range from the Creative Arts Society to volunteer efforts like the Domestic Violence Awareness Project or the Outreach Van that provides medical care to the poor and homeless, to interest groups in the various specialties. Housing is convenient to instructional facilities and promotes cohesion among students. Medical students have access to the academic and athletic facilities of the medical campus as well as those on the Charles River Campus, including the student union and several athletic facilities that offer swimming pools, an ice skating rink, dance, and sailing or rowing on the Charles River. As part of the Introduction to Clinical Medicine courses and clinical rotations, medical students travel in and around Boston, giving them a chance to explore diverse neighborhoods and communities.

GRADUATES

In the 2007 graduating class, the most prevalent specialties were Internal Medicine (20 percent), Obstetrics/Gynecology (8 percent), Radiology, Diagnostic (8 percent), Emergency Medicine (7 percent), Surgery-General (7 percent), Pediatrics (6 percent), Anesthesiology (4 percent), Ophthalmology (6 percent), Surgery-Prelim (5 percent).

Admissions

REQUIREMENTS

Prerequisites include one year each of English, Humanities, General Chemistry with lab, Organic Chemistry with lab, Biology with lab and Physics. In evaluating GPA, factors such as the intensity of the undergraduate workload are considered. The MCAT is required and must be taken within four years of the date of matriculation. For applicants who have taken the exam more than once, the committee looks at the best set of scores. Advanced Placement courses and community or junior college courses are discouraged for use in fulfilling prerequisites.

SUGGESTIONS

In addition to requirements, college-level mathematics (Calculus or Statistics), Biochemistry and Genetics are recommended, as is a broad background in the Humanities and Social Sciences. Applicants are encouraged to take a Spring MCAT. For applicants who have been out of college for a period of time some recent coursework in the biological or physical sciences is advised.

PROCESS

BUSM uses a limited secondary application and applicants are invited to provide any additional materials that they believe might be helpful to the Committee on Admissions. About 10 percent of the approximately 11,000 AMCAS applicants are invited to interview, with interviews held between October and February. The interview day consists of an introductory session with the Associate Dean for Admissions, a session with staff from the Offices of Student Affairs, Minority Affairs, Registrar, and Financial Services, lunch with first- and second-year students and a tour of the facilities with third- and fourth-year students. The interview consists of a one-hour session with a faculty member who is on the Admissions Committee. With only 115 positions available for applicants to the four-year program, admission is very competitive. There are several alternate paths to gaining admission. A seven-year program, leading to a BA/MD degree is offered in conjunction with BU's undergraduate college. The MMEDIC program at BU offers an integrated curriculum composed of liberal arts and medical school courses, enabling pre-selected students to fulfill portions of the requirements of the medical school curriculum. The ENGMEDIC program at BU offers a joint, early selection program for the training of biomedical engineers interested in becoming physicians. The Early Medical School Selection Program was developed with a consortium of historically black undergraduate institutions and colleges with large Hispanic populations to provide an early and more gradual transition into the medical school curriculum beginning with the summer after the second year of undergraduate study.

Admissions Requirements (Required)

MCAT scores, Science GPA, Non-science GPA, Letters of recommendation, Interview, Essays/personal statement, Extracurricular activities, Exposure to medical profession

COSTS AND AID

Tuition & Fees

Tuition	$42,734
Room and board	$11,933
Cost of books	$2,235
Fees	$500

Financial Aid

% students receiving aid	83.4
Average debt	$161,147

BROWN UNIVERSITY
THE WARREN ALPERT MEDICAL SCHOOL

97 WATERMAN STREET, BOX G-A213 PROVIDENCE, RI 02912 • **ADMISSION:** 401-863-2149 • **FAX:** 401-863-2660
E-MAIL: MEDSCHOOL_ADMISSIONS@BROWN.EDU • **WEBSITE:** MED.BROWN.EDU

STUDENT BODY

Type	Private
Enrollment	372
% male/female	44/56
% minorities	16
# applied (total/out)	6,016/4,927
# accepted (total/out)	208/197
# enrolled (total/out)	95/88
Average age	24

FACULTY

Total faculty	2,305
% female	37
% minority	15
% part-time	65
Student-faculty ratio	7:1

ADMISSIONS
Average GPA and MCAT Scores

Overall GPA	3.66
MCAT Bio	12
MCAT Phys	11.6
MCAT Verbal	10.8
MCAT Essay	Q

Application Information

Regular application	11/1
Regular notification	Rolling
Are transfers accepted?	Yes
Admissions may be deferred?	Yes
Interview required?	Yes
Application fee	$95

Academics

The Warren Alpert Medical School of Brown University continues to update and revise its medical curriculum. This curriculum renewal aims to achieve several goals: the integration of science content between disciplines, the integration of science content with clinical medicine through the new but fully implemented Doctoring course, and the promotion of scholarship and opportunities for creativity in the medical curriculum. The later is being pursued through a Scholarly Concentrations Program that was implemented for the MD Class of 2010. This program allows students to pursue academic and career goals both within and beyond the traditional areas of medical education. Students are encouraged to develop independent study options either at Brown or sites in the US or overseas. The Warren Alpert Medical School admits about half of its students through the Program in Liberal Medical Education (PLME), an eight-year BA/MD combined degree program. Most of the remainder are admitted through the standard premedical route.

BASIC SCIENCES: Principles of patient care and the social and behavioral aspects of medicine are integrated into the basic science curriculum. The first two years are organized into semesters. During year one, students participate in two courses: Integrated Medical Sciences (IMS) and Doctoring. IMS sections include the Scientific Foundations of Medicine, Histology, Anatomy, and Pathology. During the spring semester, the IMS sections include Brain Sciences, Integrated Endocrine Sciences and Microbiology/Infectious Diseases, which again are coordinated with the content of Doctoring. The basic science courses are taught primarily through lectures and labs but also utilizing small-group teaching and clinical correlations. The Integrated Pathophysiology/Pharmacology course provides the structure for year two, which is organized around organ systems or concepts. Epidemiology for the Practice of Medicine and Doctoring II round out the second-year curriculum. Preclinical instruction takes place primarily in the Biomedical Building on the main Brown campus. The Science Library is fully computerized, with access to 250 online database systems. Medical students have access to all of Brown's academic facilities, including the main library, housing two million volumes.

CLINICAL TRAINING Patient contact begins in the first year with Doctoring, a two-year clinical skills course. In each semester of Doctoring, students spend one half-day per week at a community site with a physician-mentor, where theoretical concepts are applied to a real-world setting. Formal clinical training, consisting of required core rotations and electives, occupies years three and four. In total, 50 weeks are devoted to core clerkships and 30 weeks to electives. Clinical training takes place at eight affiliated teaching hospitals in the Providence area: Bradley Hospital; Butler Hospital; The Miriam Hospital; Memorial Hospital of Rhode Island; Rhode Island Hospital; Hasbro Children's Hospital; V.A. Medical Center; and Women and Infants Hospital. Noteworthy areas of clinical care and research include Child/Adolescent Medicine, Psychiatric Care, International Health, Cancer, AIDS/HIV, Artificial Organs, and Diabetes Treatment and Management. Evaluation of clinical performance uses an Honors/Satisfactory/No Credit scale supplemented by narratives. Students are required to take the USMLE Steps 1 and Step 2 (CK and CS) prior to graduation.

Students

The medical student body is a heterogenous group admitted through several routes. The range of matriculants; ages is 19-38 years, resulting in an active enrollment with diverse life experiences. About 55 percent of medical students participate in a community-based activity before graduation, while more than 80 percent of the graduates collaborate on a research project with a faculty sponsor. The American Medical Student Association (AMSA) chapter has a long tradition of service and advocacy; three Brown students have been served as president of the national organization during the past 30 years.

STUDENT LIFE

Medical students have full access to the school's recreational activities and facilities. Brown University has over 200 student clubs and organizations that unite students. Although most students choose to live off campus, residence halls and housing co-ops are available.

GRADUATES

In recent years, approximately 16 percent of graduates entered residency programs at hospitals affiliated with Brown. About 44 percent of each class enters primary care residencies.

Admissions

REQUIREMENTS

Students admitted to Alpert Medical School must attain competence in the sciences basic to medicine and sufficient to provide adequate preparation for medical school. Applicants are expected to demonstrate competence by successfully completing courses in the following areas of study: Biology (at least one course); Chemistry (two courses in general inorganic chemistry and one course in organic chemistry); Physics (a two-course sequence for coverage of topics in mechanics, heat, electricity, optics, and radiation physics); and Social and Behavioral Sciences (at least two courses, preferably in anthropology, sociology, psychology, economics, or political science). All applicants are selected on the basis of academic achievement, faculty evaluations, evidence of maturity, motivation, leadership, integrity, and compassion. In order to be eligible for consideration, candidates generally must present a minimum cumulative grade point average of 3.00 (on a 4.00 scale) in courses taken as a matriculated student at an undergraduate college. Applicants who have attended graduate school generally must achieve a cumulative grade point average of 3.00 (on a 4.00 scale) in courses taken in graduate school. In addition, applicants must have completed the requirements for a baccalaureate degree prior to matriculation into medical school.

SUGGESTIONS

Admission to Brown's Alpert Medical School is now available to a greater number of applicants through the AMCAS application administered by the AAMC.

PROCESS

Brown accepts applications from qualified graduates of any college or university as part of the standard admissions route. Those interested in applying for the standard route of admission must file an application with the American Medical College Application Service (AMCAS) by November 1 and submit a secondary application with required documents before December 15. The PLME application is part of the undergraduate application package. Students attending schools that are part of the EIP program in Rhode Island should contact their premedical advisers for application procedures. Those interested in applying to the MD/PhD Program require approval before submitting an AMCAS application before October 15 and the Brown secondary application before November 15; notification of admissions decisions are made before February 15. Interviews are required of most applicant groups.

Admissions Requirements (Required)

MCAT scores, Science GPA, Non-science GPA, Letters of recommendation, Interview, Essays/personal statement, Exposure to medical profession

Admissions Requirements (Optional)

State residency, Extracurricular activities

Overlap Schools

Boston University, Columbia University, Cornell University, Dartmouth College, Harvard University, New York University, Tufts University, University of Chicago—Pritzller.

COSTS AND AID
Tuition & Fees

Tuition	$38,000
Room and board	$14,800
Cost of books	$2,000
Fees	$3,184

Financial Aid

% students receiving aid	74
Average grant	$19,974
Average loan	$34,473
Average debt	$95,480

CASE WESTERN RESERVE UNIVERSITY
SCHOOL OF MEDICINE

ASSOCIATE DEAN OF ADMISSIONS, 10900 EUCLID AVENUE CLEVELAND, OH 44106 • ADMISSION: 216-368-2000
FAX: 216-368-4621 • E-MAIL: AXH65@CASE.EDU • WEBSITE: HTTP://CASEMED.CASE.EDU

STUDENT BODY

Type	Private
Enrollment	631
% male/female	54/46
% minorities	12
# applied (total/out)	5,295/4,267
# accepted (total/out)	462/376
# enrolled (total/out)	170/124
Average age	23

FACULTY

Total faculty (number)	1,729

ADMISSIONS
Average GPA and MCAT scores

Overall GPA	3.74
MCAT Bio	12
MCAT Phys	12
MCAT Verbal	11
MCAT Essay	Q

Application Information

Regular application	11/1
Regular notification	Rolling
Are transfers accepted?	No
Admissions may be deferred?	Yes
Interview required?	Yes
Application fee	$85

Academics

The curriculum is decidedly nontraditional, combining several approaches to learning and two distinct paths, each of which provides flexibility. All students participate in the Core Academic Program (CAP), which incorporates the Core Physician Development Program (CPDP), a case-based system. Patient Based Learning (PBL) is introduced in year 1, required clerkships in year 3, and the Flexible Program allows students to participate in pre-clinical and clinical electives throughout the 4 years. Students who elect the Primary Care Tract (PCT) have enhanced clinical opportunities early in the program and direct contact with primary care providers throughout medical school. Joint MD/PhD programs are offered in physiology, engineering, and biophysics and in 13 divisions of biomedical sciences including nutritional sciences and environmental health. Approximately 10 students in each class are admitted as MD/PhD candidates. A BA/MD is offered in conjunction with the undergraduate college, and approximately 10 students matriculate as part of this yearly program.

BASIC SCIENCES: During the first year, students are presented Cellular and Developmental Biology, Integrated Human Physiology, and the Cellular Basis of Disease by faculty teaching teams representing both basic science and clinical departments. Each course lasts 2 months and is followed by an exam. For the remainder of the first year and for the duration of year 2, students cover basic sciences through study of the individual organ systems, and students retain the information with the help the case-study approach. With this integrated approach to learning, students attend class, and student note-taking collectives are not emphasized. Afternoons are generally free from scheduled courses, allowing for elective study or research. Computer facilities support classroom learning, and computers loaded with first- and second-year course material are available in the MicroComputer Lab. The Health Center Library houses 150,000 volumes. Grading is pass/fail. Students choose their own academic advisors and have a great deal of control over their own courses of study. The USMLE Steps 1 and 2 are required for graduation.

CLINICAL TRAINING

Students have ample opportunity for clinical training outside of traditional clerkships. Most students begin their clinical responsibilities during the first year when they are assigned to either a pregnant woman in the Family Clinic or a patient in the geriatric care program. For 2 years the student follows the patient and his or her development. Second-year students learn physical diagnosis and history-taking under the supervision of physician preceptors. In the third year, required rotations include Family Medicine, Medicine, Neuroscience, Obstetrics/Gynecology, Pediatrics, Psychiatry, and Surgery. Fourth year is devoted to clinical electives. Training takes place at affiliated teaching hospitals including the University Hospitals of Cleveland, Metro-Health Medical Center, Saint Luke's, VA Cleveland, Mount Sinai Medical Center, and the Henry Ford Health System. Some training takes place in clinics rather than in a traditional hospital setting. The patient population represents urban Cleveland and rural Ohio. The Primary Care Tract is a relatively new mechanism for encouraging and training primary care physicians that promotes ongoing student-physician mentorships and intensive primary-care clinical training. Grading during years 3 and 4 is pass/fail/honors.

Campus Life

Case Western is partially supported by the State of Ohio and gives preference to in-state residents, which is reflected in its matriculates. Sixty percent of students are Ohio residents. The student body is slightly more mature than average and is particularly diverse in terms of experience and background. Class size is about 135.

STUDENT LIFE

Although campus residence halls are available, most students choose to live off campus and most rely on cars for transportation to and from school. University-sponsored, married-student housing is unavailable. Student groups are involved in both community and social activities. The structure of the academic program allows time for extracurricular activities, and students participate in both university and community events.

GRADUATES

Of the 140 graduates of a recent class, 52 went on to residency programs in Cleveland; 5 remained in Ohio. The rest went to Pennsylvania (8), Washington (8), and other states (13), New York (7), California (7), Michigan (6), Illinois (5), Maryland (5), Georgia (4), and Texas (4). Specialties were family medicine (22), surgery (17), pediatrics (13), radiology (7), obstetrics/gynecology (9), orthopedic surgery (5), psychiatry (5), emergency medicine (4), anesthesiology (3), neurology (3), Ophthalmology (3), pathology (3), urology (2), transitional (2), neurosurgery (2), physical medicine (1), and plastic surgery (1).

Admissions

REQUIREMENTS

Requirements include 1 year of biology; 1 year of physics; and 2 years of chemistry, which should include cover both organic and inorganic. In addition, students should demonstrate writing ability through course work. Recent academic performance is more heavily weighted, and although many older students are admitted, most have taken some relevant courses within the past 2 years. The MCAT is required, and the most recent set of scores is considered. Due to the rolling admissions process, applicants are encouraged to submit materials as soon as possible.

SUGGESTIONS

Case offers no further recommendations for college courses and accepts students of all undergraduate majors.

PROCESS

About half of those submitting AMCAS applications receive a secondary. Secondaries should be completed promptly and are due by December 15 at the latest. Less than one-third of those completing secondaries are interviewed, with interviews held from September to March. Students have a one-on-one interview with a faculty member that generally lasts one hour. Those interviewed are notified shortly afterward of their status (accept, reject, or wait list). The wait list is not ranked. About half of the students who are accepted decline the offer, freeing up spaces for wait listed applicants. Wait listed candidates may submit additional material and should indicate if Case Western is their top choice. All Case Western undergraduates are invited to interview at the medical school.

Admissions Requirements (Required)

MCAT scores, science GPA, non-science GPA, letters of recommendation, interview, essay/personal statement, extracurricular activities, exposure to medical profession

Admissions Requirement (Optional)

State residency

Overlap Schools

Cornell University, Duke University, The University of Chicago, University of Michigan, University of Pennsylvania, Washington University in St. Louis.

COSTS AND AID

Tuition & Fees

Tuition	$39,727
Fees	$380

Financial Aid

Average debt	$135,565

COLUMBIA UNIVERSITY
COLLEGE OF PHYSICIANS AND SURGEONS

ADMISSIONS OFFICE, 630 WEST 168TH STREET, PO BOX 41, NEW YORK, NY 10032 • ADMISSION: 212-305-3595
FAX: 212-305-3601 • E-MAIL: PSADMISSIONS@COLUMBIA.EDU • WEBSITE: CUMC.COLUMBIA.EDU/DEPT/PS

STUDENT BODY

Type	Private
Enrollment	624
# applied (total/out)	4,595/3,808
# accepted (total/out)	274/215
# enrolled (total/out)	155/111

ADMISSIONS
Average GPA and MCAT scores

Overall GPA	3.78
MCAT Bio	12.1
MCAT Phys	12.1
MCAT Verbal	11.2
MCAT Essay	Q

Application Information

Regular application	11/15
Regular notification	3/1
Are transfers accepted?	Yes
Admissions may be deferred?	Yes
Interview required?	Yes
Application fee	$75

Academics

The Columbia curriculum is multidisciplinary and integrated. It focuses on not only understanding the science, skills, and techniques of medicine, but also appreciating the art and ethics involved. Several joint-degree programs such as the MD/MPH and MD/MBA are offered in conjunction with other schools and departments at Columbia. Qualified students interested in careers in scientific research may pursue a combined MD/PhD, earning the doctorate in fields such as anatomy, biochemistry, biophysics, cell biology, genetics, immunology, microbiology, molecular biology, neuroscience, pathology, pharmacology, and physiology. Medical students are evaluated with an honors/pass/fail system. Successful completion of Steps 1 and 2 of the USMLE are required for graduation.

BASIC SCIENCES: The first 2 years provides information and experiences essential for all physicians. The majority of instruction is conducted in lectures and lab, but small-group teaching is increasingly emphasized. Students spend approximately 25 hours per week in scheduled activity. The first year (42 weeks) includes Clinical Practice, Gross Anatomy, Neural Science, and an integrated course that covers biochemistry, cell biology, Genetics, human development, and Physiology. The majority of the second year (40 weeks) is devoted to a multidisciplinary course that examines the basic concepts of immunology, microbiology, pathology, and pharmacology. Physical diagnosis, basic psychiatry, and clinical practice are also taught. Columbia has extensive laboratory, informational, and computer facilities that enhance classroom learning. The Augustus C. Long Health Sciences Library houses nearly 450,000 volumes and is one of the largest medical center libraries in the nation.

CLINICAL TRAINING

In the third year, students complete required rotations in the following: Medicine (10 weeks), Surgery (5 weeks), Pediatrics (5 weeks), Obstetrics/Gynecology (5 weeks), Primary Care (5 weeks), Psychiatry (5 weeks), Neurology (5 weeks), Anesthesiology (2 weeks), Orthopedics (2 weeks), Urology (2 weeks), Otolaryngology (1 week), and Ophthalmology (1 week). The fourth year consists of 1- and 2-month-long electives drawn from a large number of offerings and student-designed experiences. There are extensive opportunities for clinical electives abroad. Each student is also required to complete a back-to-basic science elective. These include 1-month seminars in advanced pathophysiology, clinical pharmacology, or clinical pathology. Rotations are conducted at various medical centers and hospitals throughout the metropolitan area. Columbia-Presbyterian Medical Center, Harlem Hospital Center, Roosevelt Hospital, St. Luke's Hospital, and other institutions combine for a comprehensive clinical experience.

Campus Life

Columbia attracts an extremely diverse, nationally represented student body. About 10 percent of students are underrepresented minorities. There is a wide age range among incoming students, with significant numbers of students in their late 20s and 30s.

STUDENT LIFE

Despite the rigorous schedule, student life abounds at Columbia. Medical students have access to the recreational and athletic facilities of Columbia University and to university-sponsored cultural events. The P&S Club, the oldest student organization of its kind at any medical school in America, provides a variety of extracurricular activities. Students have opportunities in the fine arts, athletics, and service-oriented projects. In addition, Manhattan offers unparalleled access to museums, concerts, and every imaginable type of dining. Most students live in on-campus housing, which helps make New York affordable. Both residential halls and apartments buildings are available. Newly accepted married students are guaranteed married-student housing.

GRADUATES

Graduates gain acceptance to the most competitive residency programs in the nation. A Columbia education allows students to emphasize academic medicine, research, or primary care.

Admissions

REQUIREMENTS

One year each of biology, English, chemistry, organic chemistry, and physics are required for admission along with the MCAT. For those students who have taken the MCAT more than once, the most recent scores are weighed most heavily. Thus, there is no advantage in withholding scores. Columbia does not admit students on a rolling basis. Therefore, submitting MCAT scores from the fall of the admission year does not place applicants at a disadvantage.

SUGGESTIONS

The Admissions Committee is interested in the depth and breadth of an applicant's extracurricular experiences. Community service, artistic activities, athletics, and medically related experiences are all valuable. It is valuable to denote that Columbia is an applicant's first choice for medical school, particularly for those who have been placed on the wait list.

PROCESS

Columbia is a participant in the AMCAS application. All applicants are invited to fill out the P&S secondary application, which can be accessed through the Columbia website. Between Labor Day and early March, approximately 25 percent of applicants are invited for an interview. The interview day consists of one session with a faculty member who is a member of the Admissions Committee. Applicants also have lunch and tour the facilities with a current medical student. About 15 percent of interviewed applicants are accepted, with notification occurring in early March. A wait list is also created at this time. Wait listed applicants may send additional information to update their files.

Admissions Requirements (Required)

MCAT scores, science GPA, non-science GPA, letters of recommendation, interview, essay/personal statement, extracurricular activities, exposure to medical profession

Admissions Requirement (Optional)

State residency

Overlap School

Harvard University.

COSTS AND AID
Tuition & Fees

Tuition	$40,270
Room and board (on-campus)	$11,430
Cost of books	$1,750
Fees	$3,430

CORNELL UNIVERSITY
JOAN AND SANFORD I. WEILL MEDICAL COLLEGE

OFFICE OF ADMISSIONS, 445 EAST 69TH STREET NEW YORK, NY 10021 • ADMISSION: 212-746-1067
FAX: 212-746-8052 • E-MAIL: CUMC-ADMISSIONS@MED.CORNELL.EDU • WEBSITE: WWW.MED.CORNELL.EDU

STUDENT BODY

Type	Private
Enrollment	405
% male/female	50/50
# applied (total/out)	5,235/4,168
# accepted (total/out)	273/168
# enrolled (total/out)	101/67
Average age	24

FACULTY

Total faculty (number)	2,340

ADMISSIONS
Average GPA and MCAT scores

Overall GPA	3.72
MCAT Bio	11.8
MCAT Phys	11.6
MCAT Verbal	10.8
MCAT Essay	Q

Application Information

Regular application	10/15
Regular notification	3/10
Early application	8/1
Early notification	10/1
Are transfers accepted?	Yes
Admissions may be deferred?	Yes
Interview required?	Yes
Application fee	$75

Academics

A revised curriculum strives to limit the time students spend in lectures, thereby promoting independent and interactive learning and research. The curriculum integrates basic and clinical sciences, utilizes problem-based learning (PBL), includes principles of public health, and encourages student research efforts. Joint MD/PhD programs can be pursued in conjunction with the Weill Graduate School of Medical Sciences, Rockefeller University, and the Sloan-Kettering Institute in the following fields: biochemistry, cell biology, immunology, microbiology, molecular biology and genetics; and molecular pharmacology, neuroscience, and physiology. Fifteen students per year may enter joint programs.

BASIC SCIENCES: The curriculum was completely revised in 1996 and has been both highly successful and widely emulated. The first and second years of study consist of 5 basic science courses and Medicine, Patients, and Society. In the first year, the basic science courses are Host Defenses, Human Structure and Function, and Molecules to Cells and Genetics. In the second year, they are Basis of Disease and Brain and Mind. The core basic science courses are sequential, integrated, interdisciplinary block courses that employ PBL in small groups. PBL emphasizes active learning and requires the student first to identify issues needed to solve a medical problem, then seek out the information needed to solve the problem, and finally to reconvene in small groups with the faculty to apply the information learned. There are few lectures, and they emphasize the conceptual framework of a field. Anatomic dissection and experimental laboratories complete the learning experience. The course Medicine, Patients, and Society approaches the doctor-patient relationship from both conceptual and practical perspectives. For 1 day each week throughout each year, students spend the morning in seminar and the afternoon in physicians offices. Areas treated include biostatistics, clinical epidemiology, human behavior in illness, medical ethics, medical interviewing, physical diagnosis, and public health. Thus, students learn these vital topics in patient-centered contexts. The evaluation system uses an honors/pass/fail scale.

CLINICAL TRAINING

Upon completion of the second year, students take 3 introductory clinical courses: Anesthesia, Clinical Pharmacology, and the Introductory Clerkship. The third year is dedicated to clinical learning and emphasizes the core clerkships, including Medicine, Neurology, Obstetrics/Gynecology, Pediatrics, Primary Care, Psychiatry, and Surgery. In these courses, students are assigned to clinical inpatient and outpatient services at New York-Presbyterian Medical Center and throughout the network of clinical affiliates. Clinical affiliates include the Hospital for Special Surgery, a leader in the fields of orthopedics, rheumatology, and sports medicine; Memorial Sloan-Kettering Cancer Center, one of the premier facilities in the world devoted to the study and treatment of cancer; The New York Methodist Hospital; and others throughout the city. Students are integral members of the health care team and actively care for patients, under the supervision of the faculty. The fourth year centers on completion of clinical requirements, a sub intern-ship, and electives. While electives can be taken at anytime in the third or fourth year, most students focus on 3 major types of electives in the fourth year: clinical electives, often in subspecialty areas; research; and international electives. Each year up to half of the fourth-year class spends time abroad, typically in Cornell-funded programs that combine clinical care and research in the Third World: South America, the Caribbean, Africa, and Asia. In the month before graduation, 8 weeks of advanced basic science allow students to study leading-edge biomedical science in depth.

Campus Life

In a typical class, students graduated from over 40 different undergraduate institutions and came from over 25 different states. The class size is 101.

STUDENT LIFE

Despite the urban environment, students are cohesive and student life is apparent around the Medical College. Ninety-five percent of students live within 3 blocks of cam-pus, generally in college-owned dorms or apartments. The rent is subsidized and com-petitive for New York. In the residence halls, there are athletic facilities for student use. Student organizations, including those that support women and minority students, are active. Parks, including Central Park, are accessible, as are countless museums, theaters, shops, and restaurants. Students do not own cars.

GRADUATES

Graduates gain acceptance to the nation's top residency programs. Many stay in New York City for postgraduate training.

Admissions

REQUIREMENTS

Weill/Cornell requires 24 semester credit hours in science courses, including 2 semesters each of biology, general chemistry, organic chemistry, and physics. In addition, 6 semes-ter hours of English are required. The science GPA is given considerable weight. The MCAT is required and is used to assist the Admissions Committee in assessing the GPAs of applicants who typically come from a wide range of undergraduate backgrounds.

SUGGESTIONS

Beyond required courses, Weill/Cornell recommends 1–2 additional upper-division biol-ogy courses for non-science majors. For students who graduated college several years ago, recent science course work is suggested. The Medical College is interested in the extracurricular activities of applicants, particularly if they demonstrate commitment and dedication. Some exposure to the field of medicine is also desirable. Biomedical research is recommended.

PROCESS

All AMCAS applicants receive secondary applications. About 13 percent of applicants who complete secondaries are invited to interview, and about 30 percent of those who interview are offered a place in the first-year class. Interviews are held from October through February and consist of two 30-minute sessions, each with a member of the Admissions Committee. Decisions are announced by March 15. For a wait listed candi-date, submitting supplemental material can serve to strengthen his or her application and is also helpful in that it indicates interest in attending Weill/Cornell.

Admissions Requirements (Required)

MCAT scores, science GPA, non-science GPA, letters of recommen-dation, interview, essay/personal statement, extracurricular activities, exposure to medical profession, secondary application

COSTS AND AID

Tuition & Fees

Tuition	$33,775
Room and board (on-campus)	$10,400
Cost of books	$1,800
Fees	$1,350

Financial Aid

% students receiving aid	83

CREIGHTON UNIVERSITY
SCHOOL OF MEDICINE

OFFICE OF MEDICAL ADMISSIONS, 2500 CALIFORNIA PLAZA OMAHA, NORTHEAST 68178 • ADMISSION: 402-280-2799
FAX: 402-280-1241 • E-MAIL: MEDSCHADM@CREIGHTON.EDU • WEBSITE: WWW2.CREIGHTON.EDU/MEDSCHOOL

STUDENT BODY

Type	Private
Enrollment	498
% male/female	53/47
% minorities	16
# applied (total/out)	4,884/4,688
# accepted (total/out)	305/279
# enrolled (total/out)	126/112
Average age	23

FACULTY

Total faculty (number)	295
% female	23
% part-time	7
Student-faculty ratio	1:1

ADMISSIONS
Average GPA and MCAT scores

Overall GPA	3.67
MCAT Bio	10.2
MCAT Phys	9.7
MCAT Verbal	9.8
MCAT Essay	P

Application Information

Regular application	11/1
Regular notification	Rolling
Early application	
	8/1 (AMCAS Application)
	9/1 (Supplemental Application)
Early notification	10/1
Are transfers accepted?	Yes
Admissions may be deferred?	Yes
Interview required?	Yes
Application fee	$75

Academics

The educational program is divided into 4 years based on: biomedical fundamentals, organ- and disease-based concepts, clinical clerkships, and elective clinical experiences. Students may apply to PhD programs in several areas of biomedical science, medical microbiology, or pharmacology and pursue the degree jointly with the MD. The grading system at Creighton uses an honors/pass/fail scale supplemented with written, narrative evaluations. Students are not ranked against their peers.

BASIC SCIENCES: In some cases, basic sciences are taught using the traditional lecture/lab format, and in others, small groups and case-based learning is used. First- and second-year students are in scheduled sessions of some sort for about 25 hours per week. First-year courses, comprising the first unit, are Anatomy, Ethics in Medicine, Evidence-Based Medicine, Host Defense, Human Development in Medicine, Interviewing and Physical Exam, Microbiology, Molecular and Cell Biology, Neuroscience, and Pharmacology. Many students use the summer between years 1 and 2 for funded research projects. The second component, organized by organ-and disease-based concepts, occurs during year 2. Concepts or systems include cardiovascular, endocrinology reproductive, gastrointestinal, infectious disease, multisystems, muscular/skeletal, psychiatry, renal-urinary hematology/oncology, and respiratory courses. Throughout year 2, students take Psychological and Social Dimensions of Medical Practice, in which they are exposed to health policy, public health, medical ethics, and behavioral science issues. During years 1 and 2, students also participate in clinical activities related to the patient physical and examination. Tutoring and review sessions for the USMLE Step 1 are provided. Creighton's Bio-Information Center houses 200,000 books and maintains extensive multimedia resources, computer teaching laboratories, and computerized literature search facilities. Passing the USMLE Step 1 is a requirement for progression to year 3. Students at Creighton benefit from the new on-site computer testing facility for administration of their exams, which is 1 of 8 in the nation.

CLINICAL TRAINING

Second-year students take part in a Longitudinal Care clerkship, which demands a half-day per week. This allows students to develop longer-term relationships with mentors and patients. Third-year, core clerkships are Inpatient General Medicine (8 weeks), Obstetrics/Gynecology (8 weeks), Primary Care (8 weeks, encompassing Internal Medicine and Family Medicine), Pediatrics (8 weeks), Psychiatry (8 weeks), and Surgery (8 weeks). Fourth-year guidelines require that students select 1 Critical Care elective, 1 Neurology clerkship, 1 Primary Care sub internship, 1 Surgery elective and participate in Senior Colloquium. The remaining 28 weeks are reserved for residency interviewing and electives. CUMC (which houses 404 beds) is the primary teaching hospital. Other sites for clinical training include Omaha Children's Hospital, Omaha Veterans Medical Center, and Bergen Mercy Medical Center. During the summer, Creighton students have the opportunity to gain clinical experience through volunteer efforts in medical settings in the Dominican Republic or in communities closer to home.

Campus Life

Among the 126 students in a recent class, California, Minnesota, and Nebraska accounted for 40 percent of the students' home states, though 30 states were represented. Seventy colleges were represented, with about 17 percent of the class having graduated from Creighton—either with an undergraduate or graduate degree. About 74 percent of the students were science majors. The age range was 20–34, with an average age of 23. Of the entire class, 50 percent are women, 9 percent are members of underrepresented minority groups (mostly Hispanic and African American), and 6 percent have at least 1 parent who is an MD alumnus/alumna of Creighton.

STUDENT LIFE

The student body is cohesive and supportive, as evidenced by a student-published Wellness Chronicle in which students offer tips and share experiences on issues such as exercise, nutrition, mental health, relationships, and spirituality. Through clubs, organizations, and extensive volunteer opportunities, students associate with one another outside of the academic setting. The School of Medicine is part of the main campus of Creighton, allowing medical students to take advantage of programs and facilities of the greater university and to interact with students from other programs. The Physical Fitness Center, the Student Center, and graduate student housing are all convenient to the School of Medicine. Omaha is a comfortable, friendly, and inexpensive city, allowing students to meet their own lifestyle needs. Affordable off-campus housing is widely available.

GRADUATES

Our students have gained entrance into virtually all available specialty areas and prestigious programs throughout the United States. Over the last 3 years, an average of 52 percent of the graduates enter primary care specialties, defined as family practice, internal medicine, or pediatrics. This is well above the national average of 48 percent. Creighton alumni are found in every state, but are more numerous in the Midwest and Western regions.

Admissions

REQUIREMENTS

Requirements are biology (8 semester hours), chemistry (8 hours), English (6 hours), organic chemistry (8 hours), and physics (8 hours). The MCAT is required, and scores must be from within the past 3 years. For applicants who have retaken the exam, the best set of scores is considered.

SUGGESTIONS

No particular courses or majors are recommended beyond requirements, but advanced courses, including biochemistry and/or molecular biology, are a plus. Studying overseas is encouraged, as are volunteer and community activities that demonstrate motivation and character.

PROCESS

All AMCAS applicants receive a secondary application, and about 15 percent of those returning secondaries are invited to interview. Interviews are held from September through the spring and consist of one 30-minute session with a faculty or alumnus member of the Admissions Committee and 1 session with a medical student who is usually a committee member. A tour of the campus and lunch with current medical students are also provided. About half of the interviewed candidates are initially offered a place in the class, with notification occurring on a rolling basis. Wait listed candidates may send supplementary information, such as grades and updates on extracurricular activities to strengthen their applications.

Admissions Requirements (Required)

MCAT scores, science GPA, non-science GPA, letters of recommendation, interview, essay/personal statement, extracurricular activities, exposure to medical profession, volunteer and/or service experience

Admissions Requirement (Optional)

State residency

Overlap Schools

Georgetown University, Loyola University—Chicago, Medical College of Wisconsin, Saint Louis University, University of Iowa, University of Minnesota, University of Nebraska—Omaha.

COSTS AND AID

Tuition & Fees

Tuition	$39,208
Room and board	$13,500
Cost of books	$3,010
Fees	$760

Financial Aid

% students receiving aid	94
Average grant	$20,000
Average loan	$61,828
Average debt	$155,871

DALHOUSIE UNIVERSITY
FACULTY OF MEDICINE

5849 UNIVERSITY AVENUE, HALIFAX, NOVA SCOTIA, CANADA B3H 4H7 • ADMISSION: 902-494-1874
FAX: 902-494-6369 • E-MAIL: MEDICINE.ADMISSIONS@DAL.CA • WEBSITE: WWW.MEDICINE.DAL.CA

STUDENT BODY

Type	Public
Enrollment	91
% male/female	37/63
% minorities	37
# applied	581
# accepted	91
# enrolled	91

FACULTY

Total faculty (number)	1,311
% female	30
% part-time	32

ADMISSIONS
Average GPA and MCAT Scores

Overall GPA	3.5
MCAT Bio	10.0
MCAT Phys	10.0
MCAT Verbal	9.0
MCAT Essay	0

Application Information

Regular application	10/31
Regular notification	3/1
Are transfers accepted?	No
Admissions may be deferred?	No
Interview required?	Yes
Application fee	$70

Academics

The progressive Case-Oriented Problem-Stimulated (COPS) curriculum prepares students for the pressures and problems facing physicians today. The COPS curriculum uses real-life patient cases and is based on a tutorial system that emphasizes group learning, contextual learning, communication skills, and clinical interaction with patients. In addition to the MD curriculum, programs leading to master's and PhD degrees are offered. Some students opt for a combined-degree program, earning both an MD and a graduate degree in a biomedical or related field.

BASIC SCIENCES: In their first 2 years, students are organized into small groups and build their basic science knowledge by examining matter relevant to patient cases. Faculty/staff tutors guide the group's learning process. Students also choose specific areas of medicine for an elective period and begin to acquire clinical skills in the first month of school. The first academic period lasts 40 weeks and covers the following subjects: embryology and reproduction; human body; metabolism and function; pathology, immunology, and Microbiology; Genetics; Pharmacology; and clinical epidemiology and critical thinking. During the second academic period, students learn brain and behavior; skin, glands, and blood; respiratory and cardiovascular; genitourinary, gastrointestinal, and musculoskeletal; and population health, community service, and critical thinking. Throughout the first and second years, students have ongoing patient contact through the patient-doctor unit and have the opportunity to take elective courses. Teaching, research, and administration take place within two buildings, the Sir Charles Tupper Medical Building and the Clinical Research Center. The patient-doctor sessions are organized within the hospitals and pair the students with a clinical preceptor each week. Additionally, students attend the Learning Resource Centre weekly where they participate in small groups in hands-on skills and procedures such as casting, blood gases, tubes and wires. Each student also completes case practice sessions that support each unit and use simulated patients. The students gain exposure to pediatrics, psychiatry, and various disciplines of medicine. The Kellogg Health Sciences Library houses more than 150,000 books and journals. The library is fully computerized and provides links to other libraries on campus.

CLINICAL TRAINING

The clerkship is organized into two phases, each of which has a central theme. All clerks will begin in an introduction to clerkship unit for 1 month in which clinical skills, procedures, history-taking, and physical-taking skills will be reviewed for all students. Phase 1 includes medicine, surgery, obstetrics and gynecology, pediatrics, family medicine, emergency medicine and psychiatry. Each unit will be accountable for integrating objectives from other disciplines and ambulatory and community experiences will be expected. Phase 2 begins with elective rotations offering the clerks maximum choice or remediation depending on their performance. In the final unit, continuing and preventive care, clerks are required to complete 3-week rotations in long term care and care of the elderly and again have an opportunity for a choice of rotations. Clerks will be evaluated frequently to receive feedback on their progress to guide self-directed learning. The major teaching hospitals are within walking distance of the school. They include a 202-bed pediatric hospital, a 254-bed obstetrics hospital, a psychiatric hospital, a rehabilitation center, and 2 large tertiary care adult hospitals. Other affiliated hospitals, clinics, and outpatient facilities also provide important training sites for medical students.

Campus Life

Each entering class has 90 students. In a recent class, 81 students were from the maritime provinces and 9 were from nonmaritime regions. At least 50 percent of students are women.

STUDENT LIFE

Although the academic workload is heavy, students are encouraged to pursue nonacademic interests. All students belong to the Dalhousie Medical School Society (DMSS), which promotes the interests of medical undergraduates. The DMSS organizes social and sporting events and raises money to support various nonprofit organizations. Through the student advisory, students have access to informal counseling, activities, and organized discussions that are coordinated and sponsored by other students. Dalhousie offers a variety of housing options on campus, including residencies, singles rooms, and shared apartments. Outside of the campus, the city of Halifax offers a wide variety of entertainment, leisure, and shopping activities.

GRADUATES

Many graduates choose to enter postgraduate training at Dalhousie. Areas of training include family practice, numerous surgical and medical specialties, and laboratory medicine.

Admissions

REQUIREMENTS

The MCAT is required, and scores cannot be more than 5 years old. A baccalaureate degree is required for entrance to Dalhousie medicine. There are no absolute prerequisite courses, though a minimal science background is advisable for success on the MCAT. Maritime applicants (those from Nova Scotia, New Brunswick, and Prince Edward Island) should have a minimum academic average of a B-plus, while nonmaritime applicants should have at least an A average.

SUGGESTIONS

Applicants from nonmaritime provinces and countries other than Canada should be exceptionally qualified. In addition to place of residence and academic credentials, the Admissions Committee reviews recommendations, results of personal interviews, and the applicant's extracurricular interests and activities.

PROCESS

For applications and details on the admissions cycle, view the website at www.medicine.dal.ca or contact the Admissions Office at the phone number and/or address above. Applications are available online only, beginning September 1 of each year.

Admissions Requirements (Required)

MCAT scores, non-science GPA, letters of recommendation, interview, essays/personal statement, extracurricular activities, exposure to medical profession, official school transcripts

Admissions Requirements (Optional)

Science GPA, state residency

Overlap Schools

Memorial University Newfoundland.

COSTS AND AID

Tuition & Fees

In-state tuition	$12,806
Out-of-state tuition	$18,446
Cost of books	$2,000
Fees	$674

Financial Aid

Average grant	$4,000
Average loan	$12,000

DARTMOUTH COLLEGE
DARTMOUTH MEDICAL SCHOOL

THREE ROPE FERRY ROAD HANOVER, NH 03755-1404 • ADMISSION: 603-650-1505
FAX: 603-650-1560 • E-MAIL: DMS.ADMISSIONS@DARTMOUTH.EDU • WEBSITE: WWW.DMS.DARTMOUTH.EDU

STUDENT BODY	
Type	Private
Enrollment	316
% male/female	53/47
% minorities	22
# applied (total/out)	5,310/5,237
# accepted (total/out)	233/225
# enrolled (total/out)	73/68
Average age	24

FACULTY	
Total faculty (number)	2,045

ADMISSIONS
Average GPA and MCAT scores

Overall GPA	3.7
MCAT Bio	11.59
MCAT Phys	11.27
MCAT Verbal	10.57
MCAT Essay	P

Application Information

Regular application	11/1
Regular notification	Rolling
Are transfers accepted?	Yes
Admissions may be deferred?	Yes
Interview required?	Yes
Application fee	$85

Academics

Dartmouth Medical School (DMS), founded in 1797, is the nation's fourth oldest. Well-known for its commitment to teaching, excellence in clinical care, and strong sense of col-legiality, DMS is also an important research institution. In the past decade, annual research grants and contracts awarded to DMS increased by more than 100 percent. Annual grant support today totals over $137 million. The innovative New Directions curriculum integrates study of the basic and clinical sciences throughout the 4 years of medical school. Dartmouth combines small-group discussions, problem-based learning, independent study, and traditional classroom presentations in the right mix to supply focus and support without hindering individual learning and creativity. DMS is a small school, with a national student body, where opportunities for collaboration with the faculty abound. The medical school is located on the campus of Dartmouth College in Hanover, New Hampshire, one of the nation's classic college towns. DMS students are well traveled, with the opportunity to participate in clinical clerkships and electives around the country and throughout the world.

BASIC SCIENCES: Structured class time in both years 1 and 2 totals approximately 20 hours per week. During the three 13-week terms of year 1, students focus on the human organism's physical and psychosocial functioning. They gain a strong basic science grounding through course work in Human Gross Anatomy and Embryology, Immunology, Microbiology, Microscopic Anatomy, Neuroscience, Pathology, and Physiology. The year also includes an integrated course called The Biochemical and Genetic Basis of Medicine. Topics in Biostatistics and Epidemiology are introduced, as well as Biochemistry and Metabolism. The major component of year 2 is an interdisci-plinary pathophysiology course called The Scientific Basis of Medicine. Principles of Medical Pharmacology is another important second-year course.

CLINICAL TRAINING

Clinical training begins at the start of the first year when students are paired with a faculty preceptor in the On Doctoring course. On Doctoring continues through year 2. The Dartmouth-Hitchcock Medical Center was recently identified by Solucient, a leading health care data company, as one of America's top 16 major teaching hospitals. A second major training facility, the White River Junction Veterans Affairs Hospital, was awarded the Robert W. Carey Quality Achievement Award, the Department of Veterans Affairs' highest quality award, 3 years in a row. System wide, the Dartmouth-Hitchcock Clinic conducted almost 1.7 million patient visits last year. In addition to other teaching sites in New England, students can complete clinical clerkships in Dartmouth-affiliated teaching hospitals in Alaska, Arizona, California, Florida, and New Mexico. Fellowships from the Dartmouth International Health Group have made it possible for DMS students to explore health care opportunities throughout the world.

Campus Life

DMS is located on the campus of Dartmouth College, an Ivy League institution with an international student body and reputation. DMS students participate fully in the life of the institution and have access to the facilities, events, activities, and society that are part of the academic community. Students may enjoy national performing arts groups, professional theater, and high-quality films at Dartmouth's Hopkins Center. The Hood Museum of Art, the Berry Sports Center, Thompson Arena, and Alumni Gymnasium are other focal points of interest. Dartmouth's athletic facilities include a ski area, golf course, horse farm, boathouses, and approximately 5,000 acres on Mt. Moosilauke. Many medical students volunteer in the community through such organizations as Planned Parenthood, the Good Neighbor Health Clinic, HEART (Health Education and Rescue Training), and the DMS Dermatones, a singing ensemble. There are several medical interest groups at the medical school. On-campus housing is available, though the majority of students live off-campus.

STUDENT LIFE

Student life at DMS is marked by a strong sense of community and collaborative spirit. In an entering class of approximately 78 individuals, over 50 different undergraduate institutions are represented along with every region of the country and several foreign countries. Students of color and or international backgrounds comprise 40 percent of the most recent entering class. Although medical education is demanding, DMS students do not typically view medical school as 4 years set aside. The environment is rich in opportunities for intellectual and personal growth.

GRADUATES

Graduates are successful in securing residencies in all fields at locations across the country. The Dartmouth-Hitchcock Medical Center sponsors 41 ACGME accredited residency and fellowship training programs.

Admissions

REQUIREMENTS

One year (8 semester hours) each of general biology, general chemistry, organic chemistry, and physics, along with half a year of calculus, are required. Facility in written and spoken English is also required. MCAT results are strongly recommended and must be no more than 3 years old.

SUGGESTIONS

Biochemistry is a recommended course, though it is not required. In addition to scientific acumen, applicants should demonstrate motivation and interest in their chosen major, which need not be science. Relevant research, medical experience, social service, and other co-curricular activities are important evidence of commitment.

PROCESS

All AMCAS applicants to DMS receive a secondary application that must be completed by January 2, 2008. Approximately 700 applicants are invited to interview from a pool of over 5,500 candidates. Interviews occur from September to March and take place on the Dartmouth campus. Dual degree applicants (MD/PhD, MD/MBA, MD/MPH) also interview at Dartmouth. About 30 percent of those interviewed are admitted. A small number are placed on the wait list.

Admissions Requirements (Required)

Science GPA, non-science GPA, letters of recommendation, interview, essay/personal statement

Admissions Requirements (Optional)

MCAT scores, extracurricular activities, exposure to medical profession

COSTS AND AID
Tuition & Fees

Tuition	$40,120
Room and board	$9,750
Cost of books	$2,500
Fees	$840

Financial Aid

% students receiving aid	85
Average grant	$26,131
Average loan	$29,123
Average debt	$113,347

DREXEL UNIVERSITY
COLLEGE OF MEDICINE

2900 QUEEN LANE PHILADELPHIA, PA 19129 • ADMISSION: 215-991-8202 • FAX: 215-991-8225
E-MAIL: MEDADMIS@DREXEL.EDU • WEBSITE: WWW.DREXELMED.EDU

STUDENT BODY

Type	Private
Enrollment	1,081
% male/female	50/50
% minorities	8
# applied (total/out)	8,073/7,283
# accepted (total/out)	711/483
# enrolled (total/out)	280/187
Average age	23

FACULTY

Total faculty	629
% female	39
% minority	8
% part-time	10

ADMISSIONS
Average GPA and MCAT Scores

Overall GPA	3.51
MCAT Bio	11
MCAT Phys	10
MCAT Verbal	10
MCAT Essay	P

Application Information

Regular application	12/15
Regular notification	10/15
Early application	8/1
Early notification	10/1
Are transfers accepted?	Yes
Admissions may be deferred?	Yes
Interview required?	Yes
Application fee	$75

Academics

With its dedication to academic and clinical excellence and a historic commitment to diversity, the Drexel University College of Medicine has earned national recognition as an institution that provides innovation in medical education. Medical students are trained to consider each patient's case and needs in a comprehensive, integrated manner, taking into account more factors than the presenting physiological condition. First-year students are introduced within their first few weeks to clinical experience and community service. Standardized patients and model examination rooms are some of the methods used to enhance clinical instruction. Students also spend time in offices of primary care physicians, thereby gaining firsthand experience with patient care. Students learn to think like physicians from their first days on campus. Students can gain research experience through the Summer Research Fellowship Program in the laboratory of a participating mentor. Combined MD/MPH and MD/MBA programs are available, as are MD/PhD programs through which students may earn graduate degrees in bioengineering; microbiology and immunology; molecular and cell biology and genetics; molecular pathobiology; neuroscience; pharmacology and physiology; and biochemistry. The Medical Humanities Scholars Program allows students who are particularly interested in the humanistic elements of medicine to graduate with the designation of Humanities Scholar. The Women's Health Education Program incorporates women's health into all aspects of medical education. Medical students are evaluated using the grades of Honors/Highly Satisfactory/Satisfactory/Unsatisfactory. Passing Step 1 of the USMLE is required for promotion to year 3, and passing Step 2 (CS and CK) of the USMLE is required for graduation.

BASIC SCIENCES: College of Medicine students choose between two innovative academic curricula for their first two years of study. Interdisciplinary Foundations of Medicine (IFM), integrates the basic science courses and presents them through clinical symptom-based modules. Students learn in lectures, labs, and small group settings. The Program for Integrated Learning (PIL), a problem-based curriculum, teaches the basic sciences primarily in small groups, and is supervised and facilitated by faculty. Laboratories and resource sessions complement the case studies.

CLINICAL TRAINING Required rotations, most of which are completed in the third year, are medicine (12 weeks), surgery (12 weeks), pediatrics (6 weeks), ob/gyn (6 weeks), psychiatry (6 weeks), neurology (4 weeks), an internal medicine sub internship (4 weeks), and family medicine (6 weeks); neurology and a medical sub-internship in the fourth year; and a unique Pathway System in the fourth year for career planning and advising. Drexel University College of Medicine has many affiliated hospitals to accommodate students who wish to work in large tertiary care hospitals and those who prefer small community hospitals. Our academic campuses include leading hospitals in Pennsylvania, New Jersey, and Delaware. A sampling of our clinical sites includes: Hahnemann University Hospital, St. Christopher's Hospital for Children, Allegheny General Hospital, Saint Peter's University Hospital, Friends Hospital, Lehigh Valley Hospital, York Hospital, Monmouth Medical Center, and Pinnacle Health.

Students

Eight percent of students are underrepresented minorities, 50 percent are women, and at least 25 percent of students are nontraditional, having pursued other interests or careers in between college and medical school.

STUDENT LIFE

Despite the relatively large class size, students are a cohesive group and are supportive of each other. Drexel University College of Medicine offers a variety of clubs and activities that are both academically and socially oriented. Many students are involved in community outreach activities in local public schools, health clinics, and rehabilitation centers. Students have access to a new on-site fitness center at the College of Medicine. Philadelphia, a diverse and interesting city with a large student population, is replete with history, culture, sports, clubs, and restaurants. For additional attractions, New York City and other urban areas can be easily reached by train or car. Affordable and attractive housing surrounds the Queen Lane campus.

GRADUATES

Drexel graduates do very well in the residency matching program, both in primary care and in more specialized fields. Matches for the past two years can be viewed on the school's website.

Admissions

REQUIREMENTS

Applicants are required to have two semesters each of biology, English, general chemistry, organic chemistry, and physics. Science courses must include associated labs. The MCAT is required, and scores must be from within the past three years. For applicants who have retaken the exam, the most recent set of scores is weighted most heavily.

SUGGESTIONS

Beyond prerequisites, recommended courses include ethics, history, philosophy, psychology, and other social science and humanities courses. An advanced course in molecular biology or genetics is strongly encouraged. Drexel University College of Medicine seeks highly qualified and motivated students who demonstrate the desire, intelligence, integrity, and emotional maturity to become excellent physicians. The College encourages nontraditional applicants and is committed to a diverse student body. Students who have demonstrated a commitment to the service of others are given strong consideration. In accordance with this institution's historic commitments, women, students interested in careers as generalist physicians, those who come from Pennsylvania, non-traditional students, and those who come from populations that are underrepresented in medicine are particularly encouraged to apply. Applicants must be U.S. citizens or permanent residents.

PROCESS

All AMCAS applicants receive secondary applications. Of those returning secondaries, about 20 percent are interviewed between September and April. The interview typically consists of two sessions, one with a faculty member or administrator, which is open file, and one with a student, which is closed file. Of interviewed candidates, about half are accepted on a rolling basis. Wait-listed candidates may send transcripts or other material to update their files. An alternate route to admissions is through BA/MD and BS/MD (3+4) programs in conjunction with Lehigh, Drexel, and Villanova Universities, and Rosemont College. We also have early assurance programs with Monmouth University, Muhlenberg College, Kean University, Robert Morris University, Allegheny College, Ursinus College, and West Chester University for students interested in 4+4 programs. For highly qualified post-baccalaureate students at participating institutions, a provisional acceptance to Drexel University College of Medicine may be granted, contingent on successful completion of the premedical curriculum. Post-baccalaureate programs through which this type of arrangement is possible are offered at Drexel University, Bryn Mawr College, Columbia University, Goucher College, University of Pennsylvania, Scripps College, and West Chester University.

Admissions Requirements (Required)

MCAT scores, Science GPA, Non-science GPA, Letters of recommendation, Interview, Essays/personal statement

Admissions Requirements (Optional)

State residency, Extracurricular activities, Exposure to medical profession, Research

Overlap Schools

Georgetown University, New York Medical College, Penn State University, Temple University, Thomas Jefferson University, UMDNJ, Yeshiva University.

COSTS AND AID

Tuition & Fees

Tuition	$38,800
Room and board	$14,840
Cost of books	$13,195
Fees	$1,170

Financial Aid

% students receiving aid	61
Average grant	$10,690
Average loan	$43,000
Average debt	$182,684

DUKE UNIVERSITY
SCHOOL OF MEDICINE

COMMITTEE ON ADMISSIONS, PO BOX 3710, DUMC, DURHAM, NC 27710 • **ADMISSION:** 919-684-2985
FAX: 919-684-8893 • **E-MAIL:** MEDADM@MC.DUKE.EDU • **WEBSITE:** HTTP://MEDSCHOOL.DUKE.EDU

Academics

By condensing the basic sciences into the first year and scheduling required clinical clerk-ships for the second year, Duke allows medical students additional opportunities for research, clinical, or other enriching experiences during their third year. Those who are particularly interested in research may apply for joint MD/PhD programs in fields such as anatomy, biochemistry, biomedical engineering, cell biology, genetics, immunology, microbiology, molecular biology, neuroscience, pathology, pharmacology, and physiolo-gy. Other joint-degree programs are the MD/JD, MD/MBA, MD/MPH, MD/MPP, and the Medical Historian Program, which leads to an MD and either an MA or PhD in his-tory. In most courses, medical students are evaluated by the grades pass with honors/pass/incomplete/fail. The USMLE is not required for graduation, though most students opt to take it, and virtually all pass each section with scores in the 90th per-centile or higher.

BASIC SCIENCES: A new introduction to critical care course meets weekly during the first and second years and integrates clinical and basic science concepts. Each week dur-ing the first year, practice alternates between the classroom, where students meet in small groups, and the clinics, so that shortly after lessons are learned, they are applied. Computers are issued to all students to be used in the practice course for informational and instructional purposes. Also, part of the course is an intensive 3-week preparation for year II segment, which prepares students for clinical rotations. Other first-year courses, taught primarily in a lecture/lab format, are organized into five blocks, so that no more than three subjects are tackled at a time. Courses are Biochemistry, Cell Biology, Genetics, Gross Anatomy, Microanatomy, Physiology, Neurobiology, Microbiology, Immunology, Pathology I, Pharmacology, and Pathology II. In total, first-year students are in class or scheduled sessions for approximately 30 hours per week. Classes are held in buildings central to the medical complex. The Medical Center Library houses 276,000 books, including a renowned medical history collection. The Medical Library Education Center has electronic classroom and multimedia areas. Basic science concepts are reinforced dur-ing clinical rotations in the second year.

CLINICAL TRAINING

Preparation for and exposure to clinical medicine begins during the first year, as part of the introduction to critical care course. The year-long preparation for clinical clerkships provides students with significant experience in clinical settings before the beginning of their formal clerkships in year 2. Clerkship requirements are fulfilled in the second year. They are: Medicine (8 weeks), Obstetrics/Gynecology (8 weeks), Pediatrics (8 weeks), Psychiatry (6 weeks), Cost-Effective Care (2 weeks), Surgery (8 weeks), and Family Medicine (8 weeks), or neurology and family medicine (4 weeks each). Clinical training takes place at Duke Hospital (1,124 beds), Durham Veterans Affairs Medical Center (455 beds), Lenox Baker Children's Hospital, Durham Regional Hospital (451 beds), and at multiple affiliated hospitals and clinics. The third year is spent in research as part of an independent scholarship project, which may be in behavioral neuroscience, biomedical engineering, biometry, biophysics, cancer biology, cardiovascular studies, cell and regu-latory biology, epidemiology health services and health policy, immunology, infectious diseases, neurobiology, ophthalmology and visual studies, and pathology. Third-year students may design a year of mentored research at Duke or at approved extramural sites (e.g., NIH) or students may begin the dual degree curricula. During their fourth year, students complete clinical training through elective clerkships. There are more than 150 electives offered at Duke. In addition, students may spend up to 2 months in rotations at other institutions.

Campus Life

In the most recent class, 22 percent of the students are underrepresented minorities, most of whom are African American. Women account for 49 percent of the class, and the average age is 22, with an age range of 19–42. Forty-three undergraduate institutions are represented, the top six being Duke, Harvard, North Carolina State, Johns Hopkins, UNC at Chapel Hill, and Yale. Twenty-eight states are represented, and the top five are North Carolina, California, New York, Ohio, and Virginia. Class size is 100.

STUDENT LIFE

Students, faculty, and administrators come together for events that promote a sense of community, congeniality, and friendship within the medical school. For example, the Dean hosts five Dean's Desserts for medical students to interact with teaching, research, and clinical faculty during the year. Organizations based on volunteer work, professional goals, or extracurricular interests are numerous. Medical students have access to all of Duke's athletic and recreational facilities. Durham is popular with students, offering parks, shopping districts, restaurants, and museums. Mountains and beaches are just a few hours away. Convenient campus-owned apartments, some of which have athletic facilities, are available on a limited basis. Social events sponsored by various medical school-based organizations provide opportunities for students to interact together. A fitness facility located with the major hospital complex for medical students and house staff only has recently opened.

GRADUATES

Graduates enter top residency programs in primary and specialty fields. Most students get their top choice for residency appointment.

Admissions

REQUIREMENTS

Prerequisites are one year each of English, inorganic chemistry, organic chemistry, physics, biology, and calculus. The MCAT is required, and scores must be from within the past 4 years. If the exam has been taken on multiple occasions, the most recent set of scores is generally considered. For those who have taken time off after college, science work must have been completed not more than 7 years before matriculation at Duke.

SUGGESTIONS

An introductory course in biochemistry is recommended. The character, motivation, and dedication of applicants is considered along with academic merits. Extracurricular activities, particularly those that are medically related, community service, volunteer experience, research exposure, and work experience are all considered in admission.

PROCESS

About 60 percent of AMCAS applicants receive secondary applications. Of those returning secondaries, about 30 percent are interviewed. Interviews are conducted from September through February, and consist of 2 half-hour sessions with members of the Admissions Committee. On interview day, students also receive a campus tour, and have the opportunity to eat lunch and speak with students. About one-third of interviewees will be considered for admission.

Admissions Requirements (Required)
MCAT scores, science GPA, non-science GPA, letters of recommendation, interview, essays/personal statement, extracurricular activities, exposure to medical profession

Admissions Requirements (Optional)
State residency

Overlap Schools
Harvard University, Johns Hopkins University, Stanford University, University of Pennsylvania, Washington University.

COSTS AND AID
Tuition & Fees

Tuition	$36,880
Room and board (off-campus)	$15,240
Cost of books	$2,480
Fees	$2,844

Financial Aid

% students receiving aid	85
Average grant	$21,110
Average loan	$24,500
Average debt	$75,272

EAST CAROLINA UNIVERSITY
BRODY SCHOOL OF MEDICINE

BRODY SCHOOL OF MEDICINE, 600 MOYE BLVD., BRODY 2N-49 GREENVILLE, NC 27834 • ADMISSION: 252-744-2202
FAX: 252-744-1926 • E-MAIL: SOMADMISSIONS@ECU.EDU • WEBSITE: WWW.ECU.EDU/BSOMADMISSIONS

STUDENT BODY

Type	Public
Enrollment	293
% male/female	52/48
% minorities	22
# applied	815
# accepted (total/out)	105/0
# enrolled (total/out)	73/0
Average age	25

ADMISSIONS
Average GPA and MCAT Scores

Overall GPA	3.5
MCAT Bio	9
MCAT Phys	9
MCAT Verbal	9
MCAT Essay	P

Application Information

Regular application	11/15
Regular notification	Rolling
Early application	8/1
Early notification	10/1
Are transfers accepted?	Yes
Admissions may be deferred?	No
Interview required?	Yes
Application fee	$60

Academics

All first- and second-year students are paired with community physician mentors, and have the opportunity for ongoing patient contact and exposure to primary health care settings. Grading uses A, B, C, and F. In addition, Honors may be awarded in some instances. Passing the USMLE Step 1 is a requirement for promotion to year three, and passing the USMLE Step 2 is a requirement for graduation. Joint Ph.D./M.D. programs can be arranged on a case-by-case basis.

BASIC SCIENCES: During the first two years, students spend about 28 hours per week in classes, most of which are taught in a lecture/lab format. Small group discussions, problem-based learning, and an introduction to clinical medicine are also part of the basic science curriculum. First-year courses are Microbiology and Immunology; Biochemistry; Behavioral Science; Primary Care Preceptorship; Genetics; Gross Anatomy; Histology; Embryology; Neurobiology; Ethical and Social Issues in Medicine; Physiology; and Clinical Skills I. Second-year courses are Introduction to Medicine; Primary Care Preceptorship; Psychopathology and Human Sexuality; Introduction to Child Development; Pathogenic Microbiology; Pathology; Pharmacology; Ethical Social Issues in Medicine; Clinical Skills II and Clinical Aspects of Lifestyle Abuse, which addresses behavioral aspects of health maintenance both for patients and physicians. The Academic Support and Enrichment Center assists students in a variety of ways, including enrichment sessions and tutorials. Most classes take place in the Brody Medical Sciences Building, a modern facility that has classrooms with computer and video technology, large laboratories, auditoriums, and a clinical Outpatient Center. The presence of a clinical facility in this classroom structure suggests the importance of integrating basic and clinical sciences at East Carolina. Another building used frequently by first- and second-year students is the W.E. Laupus Health Sciences Library, which has 52,900 volumes and 1,550 subscriptions in addition to computer and audiovisual learning aids.

CLINICAL TRAINING

Required clerkships are Family Medicine (8 weeks); Internal Medicine (8 weeks); Ob/Gyn (8 weeks); Pediatrics (8 weeks); Psychiatry (8 weeks); and Surgery (8 weeks). At least 10 of these 48 weeks are spent in an ambulatory setting. Fourth-year students make selections from specified categories: Primary Care Experiences (2 months); Surgical Selectives (1 month); Medicine Selectives (1 month); Transition to Residency (1 month); and Electives (4 months). Clinical training takes place at sites throughout Eastern North Carolina, with the cooperation of the School's extended faculty members, some of whom practice in remote, rural areas. Training also takes place at: the Developmental Evaluation Clinic; Eastern Carolina Family Practice Center; Pitt County Memorial Hospital (731 beds); specialized research institutes; and at rural affiliated hospitals throughout the state.

Students

Virtually all students are North Carolina residents, many of whom attended college outside of the state. More than 20 percent of students are underrepresented minorities, mostly African Americans. Almost half of entering students have taken some time off between undergraduate and medical school. In a recent entering class, the mean age at matriculation was 26. Class size is 73.

STUDENT LIFE

The University has an active student union, and facilities such as student lounges, theaters, concert halls, museums, and an athletic center. Medical students are integrated into the greater campus community, but also have a cohesive social life among themselves. Medical student groups are organized around volunteer efforts, professional interests, support groups, and religious affiliations, among other themes. Examples are the Generalist Physicians in Training Interest Group, the Medical Student Council, Peer Counseling, the Christian Medical/Dental Fellowship, and the Greenville Community Shelter Clinic. Greenville is known for its gentle climate and low cost of living, both assets for medical students. There are plenty of housing options, both on and off campus, for married or single students.

GRADUATES

Over half of the medical school graduates typically enter primary care fields. There are at least 12 residency programs and several fellowship programs offered at Pitt County Memorial Hospital, with the majority of positions in Internal Medicine, Family Medicine, and Emergency Medicine.

Admissions

REQUIREMENTS

One year each of Physics, Biology, General Chemistry, Organic Chemistry, and English are all required. Laboratories are required with all science courses. The MCAT is required and must be no more than three years old. For those who have retaken the exam, the most recent set of scores is generally considered. State residency is a requirement for admission.

SUGGESTIONS

Beyond required courses, students are advised to take Humanities, Statistics, and Social Science courses, and an additional year of English. Taking classes that are part of the medical school curriculum is not recommended. Extracurricular activities that involve exposure to the medical practice are important. The Admissions Committee looks for applicants who are likely to contribute to meeting the health care needs of North Carolina.

PROCESS

All AMCAS applicants who are state residents are sent secondary applications. About 60 percent of those returning secondaries are interviewed, with interviews taking place between August and April. The interview consists of two 30- to 60-minute sessions with faculty or student members of the committee. On interview day, applicants have an opportunity to meet with students and to tour the campus. About 15 percent of interviewed candidates are accepted, while others are rejected or wait-listed. Candidates awaiting a decision may send additional information to enhance their files.

Admissions Requirements (Required)

MCAT scores, Science GPA, Non-science GPA, Letters of recommendation, Interview, State residency, Essays/personal statement, Extracurricular activities, Exposure to medical profession

COSTS AND AID

Tuition & Fees

In-stateTuition	$7,130
Out-of-state Tuition	$32,120
Room and board (off-campus)	$11,019
Cost of books	$6,125
Fees	$1,936

Financial Aid

% students receiving aid	91
Average grant	$2,500
Average loan	$25,254
Average debt	$77,656

EAST TENNESSEE STATE UNIVERSITY
JAMES H. QUILLEN COLLEGE OF MEDICINE

JAMES H. QUILLEN COLLEGE OF MEDICINE, PO BOX 70580, JOHNSON CITY, TN 37614-1708 • **ADMISSION:** 423-439-2033
FAX: 423-439-2110 • **E-MAIL:** SACOM@ETSU.EDU • **WEBSITE:** COM.ETSU.EDU

STUDENT BODY

Type	Public
# applied (total/out)	1,225/739
# accepted	140
# enrolled (out-of-state)	7

FACULTY

Student-faculty ratio	1:1

ADMISSIONS
Application Information

Regular application	11/15
Regular notification	7/1
Early application	6/1–8/1
Early notification	10/1
Are transfers accepted?	Yes
Admissions may be deferred?	Yes
Interview required?	Yes
Application fee	$50

Academics

Quillen College of Medicine offers the following degrees of study: Doctor of Medicine, Master of Science, and Doctor of Philosophy. Most students earn an MD in 4 years, through either the traditional track or the rural primary care track (RPCT). Quillen admits a medical class of 60 each fall. Quillen's major educational emphasis is primary care and rural medicine. The Biomedical Science Graduate Program offers study leading to the Doctor of Philosophy and Master of Science in Biomedical Science. The purpose of the program is to prepare students for careers in research and education in the life sciences. Students receive their degrees in biomedical science with a concentration in one of the following five areas of basic science: anatomy and cell biology, biochemistry and molecular biology, microbiology, pharmacology, and physiology.

BASIC SCIENCES: With the exception of clinical work, basic science courses are taught primarily in a lecture/lab format. Students are in scheduled sessions for about 24 hours per week. First-year courses for all students are Anatomy, Biochemistry, Biostatistics and Epidemiology, Communication Skills for Health Professionals, Cell and Tissue Biology, Physiology, Geriatrics, Behavorial Science and Lifespan Development, and Human Development Biology and Genetics. Traditional students also take case-oriented learning, while RPCT students take Introduction to Rural Health, Rural and Community Health, and Health Assessment/Examination. Patient contact begins in case-oriented learning for traditional track students and as part of weekly visits to rural health providers for RPCT students. The second-year curriculum for all students is Geriatrics, Neuroscience, Microbiology, Immunology, Pathology, Pharmacology, Practicing Medicine, and Psychiatry. Traditional track students take Clinical Skills and Clinical Preceptorship while RPCT students take Rural Health Needs, Health Assessment, and Patient/Client Assessment. Instructional facilities are located in a newly constructed, multimillion-dollar basic sciences building on the grounds of the Mountain Home Veterans Affairs facility. The medical library, also located on the same databases, has almost 100,000 volumes, several online medical databases, educational software programs, computerized access to the university library system, computers for student use, and rooms for audiovisual study, reading, and conferences. Evaluation uses an A–F grading system. Students must pass Step 1 of the USMLE for promotion to the third year.

CLINICAL TRAINING

Third-year required rotations for traditional track students are Family Medicine (8 weeks), Obstetrics/Gynecology (8 weeks), Pediatrics (8 weeks), Psychiatry (8 weeks), Internal Medicine (8 weeks), and Surgery (8 weeks). RPCT students take part in shorter rotations in the same specialties, and are required to complete a 16-week primary care clerkship in a rural area. During the fourth year, all students complete a minimum of 16 weeks of electives. RPCT students have additional rural, primary care requirements, and traditional tract students must take Internal Medicine and Senior Surgery. Clinical training takes place in the following three cities: Bristol, Kingsport, and Johnson City, and in neighboring rural towns. Affiliated hospitals are The Johnson City Medical Center, VA Medical Center, Woodridge Psychiatric Hospital, Johnson City Specialty Hospital, Northside Hospital, The Holston Valley Hospital, Indian Path Medical Center, Bristol Regional Medical Center, and Hawkins County Hospital. In total, these hospitals provide 3,000 patient beds. Evaluation uses an A–F grading system, and the USMLE Step 2 is required for graduation.

Campus Life

Almost all students are from Tennessee or the immediately surrounding areas. Most students went to college in Tennessee, although undergraduate institutions from around the country are represented in the medical student body. About 15 percent of students are underrepresented minorities, most of them African American. Class size is 60.

STUDENT LIFE

Medical students take advantage of the extracurricular opportunities at ETSU, such as its theater, films, intramural sports, and athletic and recreational facilities. They are active in a wide variety of special interest and service organizations. Housing options include campus housing as well as a selection of apartments, townhouses, condominiums, and houses for rent or sale. As an urban area, Johnson City offers many services and attractions.

GRADUATES

More than 60 percent of Quillen graduates pursue careers in primary care medicine and 22 percent practice in rural settings. Quillen provides a strong background in both the art and science of medicine, and graduates who wish to pursue advanced training in specialty areas have a high degree of success getting into residency programs of their choice.

Admissions

REQUIREMENTS

Applicants must complete chemistry (8 semester hours), organic chemistry (8 hours), physics (8 hours), biology (8 hours), and communication skills (9 hours). An additional 49 hours of course work is required. The MCAT is required and should be no more than 2 years old. The April MCAT is advised as the August exam will delay application processing.

SUGGESTIONS

Other recommended courses are comparative vertebrate anatomy, histology, mammalian anatomy, advanced mathematics, statistics, biochemistry, microbiology, public speaking, history, economics, philosophy, psychology, social science, and foreign languages. For those who have been out of school for a significant period of time, recent course work is helpful. The Admissions Committee looks for traits and experiences that are consistent with primary care practice. Admissions is particularly competitive for out-of-state residents, and with the exception of applicants from the contiguous Appalachian region who are interested in primary care, out-of-state applicants must have extremely strong qualifications to be considered.

PROCESS

About one-third of AMCAS applicants are sent secondary applications. Of those submitting secondaries, the majority of Tennessee residents and about 10 percent of out-of-state residents are invited to interview between September and March. Applicants receive two interviews with faculty, medical students, administrators, or community members, which last 1 hour. Of interviewed candidates, about 40 percent of Tennessee residents and 15 percent of out-of-state residents are accepted on a rolling basis. Others are either rejected or wait listed. Generally, only a few students are accepted from the wait list.

Admissions Requirements (Required)

MCAT scores, science GPA, non-science GPA, letters of recommendation, interview, state residency, essay/personal statement, extracurricular activities, exposure to medical profession

COSTS AND AID

Tuition & Fees

In-state tuition	$19,034
Out-of-state tuition	$38,798
Room and board (off-campus)	$12,000
Cost of books	$1,360
Fees	$847

Financial Aid

% students receiving aid	91
Average grant	$8,000
Average loan	$28,000
Average debt	$94,000

EASTERN VIRGINIA MEDICAL SCHOOL

OFFICE OF ADMISSIONS, 700 WEST OLNEY ROAD, NORFOLK, VA 23507-1607• ADMISSION: 757-446-5812
FAX: 757-446-5896 • E-MAIL: NANEZKF@EVMS.EDU • WEBSITE: WWW.EVMS.EDU

STUDENT BODY

Type	Public
Enrollment	441
% male/female	50/50
% minorities	12
# applied (total/out)	4,239/3,554
# accepted (total/out)	275/93
# enrolled (total/out)	110/36

ADMISSIONS
Average GPA and MCAT Scores

Overall GPA	3.4
MCAT Bio	10.3
MCAT Phys	9.8
MCAT Verbal	10.2

Application Information

Regular application	11/15
Early application	6/1–8/1
Early notification	10/1
Are transfers accepted?	Yes
Admissions may be deferred?	Yes
Interview required?	Yes
Application fee	$90

Academics

The curriculum is designed to help students master both the science of medicine and the art of clinical problem solving. A combined MD/PhD program is available for qualified students, leading to the doctorate degree in one of the biomedical science fields. For medical students interested in medical research, summer research projects are available. Medical students are evaluated with honors, high pass, pass, and fail.

BASIC SCIENCES: The first 2 years are devoted to basic sciences that are fundamental to the practice of medicine. Students also learn the clinical skills of physical diagnosis and interviewing. Throughout the first 2 years, students are in class or other scheduled sessions for about 25 hours per week. Lectures, labs, and small-group discussions are the instructional modalities used. First-year courses are the following: Biochemistry, Gross Anatomy, Histology, Human Development, Introduction to the Patient/Longitudinal Generalist Mentorship, Medical Ethics, Medical Molecular and Cellular Biology, Neuroscience, Physiology, The Doctor, and The Patient. Second-year courses are the following: Biostatistics, Epidemiology, Introduction to the Patient/Longitudinal Mentorship, Medical Ethics, Microbiology/Immunology, Pathology, Pathophysiology, Pharmacology, and Psychopathology.

CLINICAL TRAINING

Required third-year clerkships are Family Medicine (6 weeks), Internal Medicine (12 weeks), Obstetrics/Gynecology (8 weeks), Pediatrics (8 weeks), Psychiatry (6 weeks), and Surgery (8 weeks). Fourth-year required clerkships include 4 weeks of Surgical Specialties, 2 weeks of Geriatrics, 1 week of Substance Abuse, and 25 weeks of electives, which may be selected from basic science and clinical offerings. For clinical training, students have access to a wide range of facilities including the East Coast's largest naval hospital, full-service community hospitals, interdisciplinary primary care centers, one of the largest Level I shock trauma centers in the state, private hospitals, a prestigious children's hospital, and clinics built for the medically underserved.

Campus Life

At least 70 percent of students are Virginia residents. The student body has a number of older or nontraditional students, and the average age of incoming students is often over 25. Underrepresented minorities account for approximately 7 percent of the student body. Class size is 110.

STUDENT LIFE

EVMS supports students' non-academic lives and puts significant resources into the well-being of its students. Each fall, students and faculty members convene at a nearby resort for the orientation retreat sponsored by the school's Human Values in Medicine Program. The retreat provides a relaxed and informal atmosphere and allows incoming students the chance to interact before classes begin. Throughout the year, students are involved in a number of organizations and events, including ongoing community-service projects and a monthly Friday-night social hour. In general, the school's location in the Hampton Roads area is ideal for medical students, offering urban conveniences, the friendliness of a small town, and the attractions of a beach community. Most medical students live in the section of Norfolk near the medical school known as Ghent, a beautiful neighborhood of tree-lined streets and Victorian houses. EVMS also owns and operates an apartment complex near the school that offers housing for both married and single students. Washington, DC, with its many attractions and recreational opportunities, is only a 4-hour drive away.

GRADUATES

From 20 percent to 25 percent of graduates are accepted into one of the many residency programs sponsored by the Eastern Virginia Graduate School. Other graduating students are successful in securing residency positions at institutions throughout the state and at locations around the country.

Admissions

REQUIREMENTS

Required courses are 1 year each of biology, chemistry, organic chemistry, and physics, all with associated labs. Applicants are expected to have a B or better in these courses. The MCAT is required, and scores should be from no more than 2 years prior to the date of application. For applicants who have retaken the exam, the best set of scores is weighed most heavily. Thus, there is no advantage in withholding scores.

SUGGESTIONS

In addition to academic transcripts, an applicant's experiences and background are examined. Personal characteristics are evaluated during the interviews, and honesty and spontaneity are considered essential qualities. Interviewers are interested in an applicant's concept of a physician's role, motivation, sensitivity to the needs of others, and communication skills.

PROCESS

After an initial screening of academic credentials, state residency, and other factors, about 50 percent of AMCAS applicants are sent secondary applications. A slightly larger percentage of state-resident applicants are asked to submit secondaries. Of those returning secondaries, about one-third are interviewed between September and March. Interviews consist of one session with a small panel of faculty members and medical students. On interview day, candidates also have the opportunity to meet with current students, tour the campus, and attend group information presentations. About one-third of interviewed candidates are accepted on a rolling basis. Alternate paths to admission are possible for students at schools that have special arrangements with EVMS. These are Old Dominion University, The College of William & Mary, Norfolk State University, Hampton University, Hampden-Sydney College, Saint Paul's College, Virginia State University, and Virginia Union University.

Admissions Requirements (Required)

MCAT scores, science GPA, non-science GPA, letters of recommendation, interview, extracurricular activities, exposure to medical profession

Admissions Requirements (Optional)

State residency, essays/personal statement

COSTS AND AID
Tuition & Fees

In-state tuition	$21,546
Out-of-state tuition	$39,828
Cost of books	$1,500
Fees	$1,566

Financial Aid

% students receiving aid	90

EMORY UNIVERSITY
SCHOOL OF MEDICINE

1648 PIERCE DRIVE NE SUITE 231 ATLANTA, GA 30322-4510 • **ADMISSION:** 404-727-5660 • **FAX:** 404-727-5456
E-MAIL: MEDADMISS@EMORY.EDU • **WEBSITE:** WWW.MED.EMORY.EDU

STUDENT BODY

Type	Private
Enrollment	480
% male/female	50/50
% minorities	18
# applied (total/out)	4,109/3,696
# accepted (total/out)	344/275
# enrolled (total/out)	132/92
Average age	23

FACULTY

Total faculty	2,053
% female	36
% minority	12
% part-time	9

ADMISSIONS
Average GPA and MCAT Scores

Overall GPA	3.7
MCAT Bio	11.9
MCAT Phys	11.6
MCAT Verbal	10.9
MCAT Essay	Q

Application Information

Regular application	10/15
Regular notification	Rolling
Are transfers accepted?	Yes
Admissions may be deferred?	Yes
Interview required?	Yes
Application fee	$100

Academics

In 2007, Emory School of Medicine opened a new Medical Education Building and began a new curriculum. The new 162,000 square-foot environmentally "green" Medical Education building incorporates the historic facades of the school's original Anatomy and Physiology Buildings. The new curriculum reflects the extraordinary advances taking place in biomedical science; meets the needs of an ever-changing local and global healthcare environment; takes advantage of the unique educational resources in Atlanta; and respects the intellectually-gifted and highly-motivated students who choose to come to Emory. The new curriculum stresses early clinical exposure, an interweaving of basic and clinical science, close faculty-student interactions, and a discovery phase.

CLINICAL TRAINING

The Foundations Phase begins with a four-month section on the "Healthy Human," a section designed around the human life cycle and emphasizing healthy human activities: Development, Neural Function (including cognition), Exercise, Nutrition, and Aging. Basic science concepts including cell biology, genetics, biochemistry, physiology, embryology, histology, reproduction, and human development are covered during the Healthy Human section. By beginning with the "Healthy Human" approach, the curriculum emphasizes: 1) the important role that behavior plays in health and disease; 2) that the approach to the patient must include consideration of the community, environment, family, and the "whole" of the person; and 3) the importance of healthy human activities, such as exercise, nutrition, procreation, and cognition/creativity as foundational to human well-being.

The Healthy Human is followed by Prologue II, a section designed to prepare students for the Human Disease Section. Prologue II introduces the principles of microbiology, pathology, immunology, and pharmacology. The Human Disease section consists of organ block sections. Human Anatomy, including cadaveric dissection, is completed during the first five months of the Human Disease Section, and where possible, will correlate with the organ system being taught. The organ system blocks begin each week with a simulated or real case presentation. Each student attends a primary care clinic one half day every other week. Normal human function is taught simultaneously with the disease process where appropriate. Clinical cases drive the week's learning objectives, including social topics such as cultural competency, addiction, homelessness, etc.

The Foundations Phase and Step I of the USMLE are completed within 19 months, allowing students to begin the Applications Phase during the middle of Year 2. Students complete the Applications Phase in the middle of Year 3, at which time an individual student may move directly into five months of Discovery, or may choose to take clinical electives in sub-specialty fields.

The Applications Phase includes "clerkship" training in the core clinical areas of medicine, including Internal Medicine, Surgery, Obstetrics/Gynecology, Pediatrics, Psychiatry and Neurology. During the Applications Phase, one-week inter-sessions prior to each block of clinical rotations highlight basic science knowledge, clinical skills, and ethics. During clinical rotations, students operate as full members of a medical care team. While core clinical knowledge is learned, patient-directed learning is emphasized. This patient-directed learning is the best preparation for the engaged life of a practicing, inquisitive physician/learner.

The mandatory Discovery Phase is new for Emory but coincides with an enormous growth in research at the University level. The Discovery Phase may be spent in any field, but must be related to medicine, closely mentored, and result in a final product approved by the mentor. The time period for this phase may be extended to 9 months by using elective months available during the Translations Phase. Alternatively, students may choose to spend an extra year in research, either at Emory (tuition-free) or at another institution (e.g. CDC or NIH). While it is anticipated that most students will spend their Discovery Phase in a basic science lab or on a clinical science or public health project, students may also choose to spend this time in matters of the medical humanities, medical anthropology, medical sociology, etc.

The Translation Phase includes four required rotations: Intensive Care Unit (ICU); Emergency Medicine; a Senior Clerkship in Medicine, Surgery, or Pediatrics; and a Capstone Course. The ICU month reinforces essential basic science concepts and ethical precepts. The Capstone month occurs the final month as an Emory medical student and will include team training, standardized patient cases, instruction in the art of clinical teaching for "soon-to-be" residents, and important didactic material relevant to medical-legal, ethical, and communication issues.

Students

STUDENT LIFE

Emory School of Medicine is located on the main campus of Emory University. Therefore, medical students have access to the organizations, events, and facilities of the medical, other professional graduate, and undergraduate schools. Students frequent the athletic center and are active participants in intramural sports. Medical students organize community service projects and participate in local and national medical student organizations, which serve to integrate students into the greater community and often provide additional clinical exposure. Atlanta is an excellent city for students since it is affordable and offers many cultural, recreational, and entertainment opportunities. While many choose to live off campus, where apartments and houses are plentiful and affordable, others choose to live in the new Clairmont Campus residential community. Located within walking distance to the main campus, it includes modern luxury apartments, recreational areas, a student center, dining facilities, and much more. Georgia's climate is conducive to year round outdoor recreation, including hiking, cycling, climbing, mountain biking, and many other activities.

Admissions

REQUIREMENTS

In addition to the traditional requirements of one year each of Biology, Chemistry, Physics, and Organic Chemistry, Emory also requires six semester hours of English and 18 semester hours of Humanities and Behavioral/Social Science course work. The MCAT is required. For applicants who have retaken the exam, the best set of scores is typically weighted most heavily. Emory operates a rolling admissions process, making it beneficial for the applicant to submit MCAT scores and application material early in the summer.

SUGGESTIONS

In addition to required courses, Genetics and Biochemistry are both strongly recommended. It is also important that students have patient contact in a clinical setting and show genuine interests outside of medicine. Research experiences, volunteerism, and evidence of professionalism are also highly valued.

PROCESS

All verified AMCAS applicants are sent a supplemental application. Of the supplemental applications received, approximately 750 are invited to interview between October and February. Emory conducts group interviews that involve three applicants and two faculty members and a current medical student. An additional one-on-one interview is conducted with a faculty member. On interview day, candidates meet the Dean of Admissions, tour the campus and affiliated clinical locations, and meet Emory medical students and faculty. Following the interview, accepted students are notified on a monthly basis. Students placed on the alternate list are encouraged to submit new information to update their files.

Admissions Requirements (Required)

MCAT scores, Science GPA, Non-science GPA, Letters of recommendation, Interview, Essays/personal statement, Extracurricular activities, Exposure to medical profession, Emory Supplemental Application

Admissions Requirements (Optional)

State residency

Overlap Schools

Duke University, Harvard University, The University of Chicago, University of Michigan—Ann Arbor, University of Pennsylvania, Vanderbilt University, Washington University in St. Louis (Olin).

COSTS AND AID

Tuition & Fees

Tuition	$40,700
Room and board (off-campus)	$22,414
Cost of books	$3,146
Fees	$676

Financial Aid

% students receiving aid	86
Average grant	$25,164
Average loan	$32,547
Average debt	$120,321

FLORIDA STATE UNIVERSITY
COLLEGE OF MEDICINE

1115 WEST CALL STREET TALLAHASSEE, FL 32306-4300 • **ADMISSION:** (850) 644-7904 • **FAX:** (850) 645-2846
E-MAIL: MEDADMISSIONS@MED.FSU.EDU • **WEBSITE:** MED.FSU.EDU

STUDENT BODY

Type	Public
Enrollment	358
% male/female	40/60
% minorities	34
# applied (total/out)	981/0
# accepted (total/out)	229/0
# enrolled (total/out)	120/0
Average age	22

FACULTY

Total faculty	1,349
% female	23
% minority	18
% part-time	93
Student-faculty ratio	1:1

ADMISSIONS
Average GPA and MCAT Scores

Overall GPA	3.62
MCAT Bio	9.61
MCAT Phys	9.09
MCAT Verbal	9.38
MCAT Essay	O

Application Information

Regular application	12/1
Regular notification	4/15
Early application	8/1
Early notification	10/1
Are transfers accepted?	No
Admissions may be deferred?	Yes
Interview required?	Yes
Application fee	$0

Academics

The FSU College of Medicine is truly a 21st century medical school. Created in June of 2000 by the Florida Legislature, it is the first new medical school to open in the United States since 1982, and as such it is charting a new course for medical education.

BASIC SCIENCES: The basic science component of the training program takes place on the FSU campus and is integrated into the culture and value system of the liberal arts university. The curriculum is based on a biopsychosocial foundation that balances biomedicine, medical humanities, and social sciences. Basic science faculty responsible for the first two years of the medical education program are chosen to provide a diverse range of background and experience across all specialties. Some faculty are responsible for research and are valued contributors to medical education for first- and second-year students. The majority of the basic science faculty are positioned to make medical education their primary focus, producing a climate of innovative teaching methods and individual attention rarely found in medical education in the United States today. In this faculty-scholar model, highly skilled faculty present a well-structured continuum of education in biomedical, behavioral, and clinical sciences utilizing problem-based and small-group learning experiences.

CLINICAL TRAINING Clinical training begins in the first week with introduction to working with standardized patients in a state-of-the-art Clinical Learning Center. Numerous opportunities to work with community physicians in Tallahassee and at area health clinics also are available during the first two years. From a clinical training standpoint, students especially reap the rewards of the College of Medicine's community-based model during the third and fourth years. All clinical training from that point takes place on the front lines of the health care delivery system throughout Florida. The emphasis is on ambulatory care settings such as hospitals, physicians' clinics, HMOs, and chronic care facilities in rural, urban, and suburban areas. Because the College of Medicine partners with existing medical facilities and practitioners throughout the state rather than operating a teaching hospital, students have the opportunity to learn under the direct supervision of physicians throughout Florida. More than 1,300 of the state's top physicians, carefully chosen for their ability to provide high quality and personalized educational experiences, are part of the College of Medicine faculty. Community campuses are located in Daytona Beach, Ft. Pierce, Orlando, Pensascola, Sarasota, and Tallahassee.

Students

In partnership with Florida communities, the FSU College of Medicine is creating a new model of medical education and research that uses interdisciplinary teams and emerging technologies. Building upon the FSU Program in Medical Sciences, a first-year medical school program begun in 1971, the college's educational program is designed to produce compassionate physicians who will practice patient-centered medicine and who are prepared to practice in a rapidly changing health care environment. FSU trains the physicians of tomorrow in such a way that they will become lifelong learners equipped to teach themselves what they need to know in an era of tremendous innovation in knowledge management and information technology.

STUDENT LIFE

The Florida State University College of Medicine carefully selects students who are outstanding academically and are committed to the college's mission of service to Florida's medically underserved populations. FSU medical students come from all over Florida and are culturally diverse. Many come from small towns and rural areas, but the state's major metropolitan areas are also well represented. A number of students are older than average for medical school and bring a broad range of professional and life experiences, while others come straight out of undergraduate programs. Most are active in student organizations, community service projects, and medical outreach programs.

GRADUATES

Including the Class of 2008, 59 percent of the College of Medicine's 169 graduates (covering four graduating classes) have matched in primary care residency programs (family medicine, internal medicine, pediatrics and obstetrics/gynecology). College of Medicine graduates also have matched with leading residency programs in specialties ranging from general and orthopaedic surgery to radiology, dermatology and plastic surgery. Nearly half of our graduates are in residency in Florida.

Admissions

REQUIREMENTS

Applications are accepted through the AMCAS and invited applicants submit a secondary application before being invited for a personal interview at the main campus in Tallahassee. The College of Medicine accepts 120 students a year and, as an early-start program, classes begin in June.

Applicants should meet academic standards predictive of success in medical school through academic grade point average and MCAT (Medical College Aptitude Test) score. An applicant's MCAT score should be dated no more than three years prior to the beginning of the year of the application cycle. If an applicant is currently enrolled in a degree program, the program must be completed and final transcripts provided to the College of Medicine Admissions Office prior to the beginning of classes. Non-U.S. citizens must possess a permanent resident visa. Applicants are assessed on their qualifications without discrimination in regard to gender, sexual orientation, color, age, disability, race, religion, veteran status, or national origin. Applicants may begin to certify and submit their AMCAS application beginning June 1. The deadline for submitting applications to AMCAS is December 1.

PROCESS

We seek students who have demonstrated a commitment of service to others and we encourage applications from traditional and nontraditional students, as well as students from rural, inner-city, or other medically underserved areas. An applicant should have completed prerequisite courses in English, biology, chemistry, organic chemistry, physics, and biochemistry. While grades and test scores are important, a great deal of emphasis is placed on finding students committed to service and to the ideals of compassionate medical care. Personal interviews, conducted between September and March, provide an excellent opportunity for applicants to exhibit the personal qualities such as motivation, sensitivity to the needs of others, oral communication skills, and maturity that the College of Medicine is looking for. In addition, personal attributes such as compassion and altruism are, in the view of the admissions committee, essential to the art of good medical practice and are of special interest in the selection process.

Admissions Requirements (Required)

MCAT scores, Science GPA, Nonscience GPA, Letters of recommendation, Interview, State residency, Essays/personal statement, Extracurricular activities, Exposure to medical profession

Overlap Schools

University of Florida, University of Miami, University of South Florida.

COSTS AND AID

Tuition & Fees

In-state Tuition	$19,332
Out-of-state Tuition	$52,160
Room and board (off-campus)	$15,910
Cost of books	$2,320
Fees	$770

Financial Aid

% students receiving aid	86
Average grant	$3,525
Average loan	$33,988
Average debt	$114,543

THE GEORGE WASHINGTON UNIVERSITY
SCHOOL OF MEDICINE AND HEALTH SCIENCES

OFFICE OF ADMISSIONS; 2300 I STREET, NW, ROSS HALL 716 WASHINGTON, DC 20037 • ADMISSION: 202-994-3506
FAX: 202-994-1753 • E-MAIL: MEDADMIT@GWU.EDU • WEBSITE: WWW.GWUMC.EDU/EDU/ADMIS

STUDENT BODY

Type	Private
Enrollment	699
# applied	10,213
# accepted	302
# enrolled (total/out)	177/174
Average age	24

ADMISSIONS
Average GPA and MCAT scores

Overall GPA	3.57
MCAT Bio	9.97
MCAT Phys	9.6
MCAT Verbal	9.32
MCAT Essay	P

Application Information

Regular application	12/1
Regular notification	Rolling
Early application	6/1
Early notification	9/1
Are transfers accepted?	Yes
Admissions may be deferred?	Yes
Interview required?	Yes
Application fee	$125

Academics

The George Washington University School of Medicine and Health Sciences is located in the heart of Washington, DC. Within the larger mission of the university, the vision of The George Washington University Medical Center is to be a preeminent academic health institution, dedicated to improving the health and well-being of our local community, our country, and beyond. The Medical Center works to achieve this goal through commitment to excellence and innovation in education and to research that expands the frontiers of science and knowledge.

BASIC SCIENCES: The George Washington University MD curriculum prepares well-trained physicians to complete residencies in primary care or specialized areas of concentration. Our medical school also stresses education through cooperation and collaboration rather than competition and emphasizes working with groups of colleagues and coworkers. Courses in anatomy, biochemistry, immunology, microbiology, neurobiology, and physiology constitute the first year study. The second-year curriculum focuses on abnormal human biology through courses in pathology, pharmacology, and an interdisciplinary, organ-system course titled Introduction to Clinical Medicine.

CLINICAL TRAINING

The School of Medicine curriculum contains a unique course titled The Practice of Medicine (POM). This revolutionary course, spanning all 4 years, allows students to begin clinical training during their first year of medical school while at the same time learning the traditional basic sciences. During POM, students learn about the doctor-patient relationship, essential communication skills, basic clinical assessment skills of interviewing and physical examination, professionalism, ethics, and many issues of the medicine-society interface.

The GW Clinical Learning and Simulation Skills (CLASS) Center is housed on the sixth floor of the GW Hospital. Dedicated to education and research, the center features cutting edge technology in a setting that is among the most innovative in the nation. It is in this setting that students gain the comprehensive clinical exposure, feedback, and evaluation they need to become both technically adept and humane caregivers for their patients. This hands-on experience proves invaluable in preparation for the USMLE Step 2 Clinical Skills.

Campus Life

The Fall 2007 entering class hailed from 29 different states plus D.C., spanning the United States from Oregon to Florida and matriculation from 90 different undergraduate institutions. Forty-nine percent of incoming students were non-science majors, and 19 percent held various graduate degrees. Last year's entering class ranged in age from 20-49 years old.

STUDENT LIFE

The GW campus is nestled in the Foggy Bottom area of Washington, DC, and is within walking distance of the White House and many other governmental, historical, and cultural landmarks. The campus is accessible by subway; the Foggy Bottom/GWU metro stop sits immediately outside the School of Medicine. A new Student Opportunity Office provides a wealth of resources and coordinates the new track programs. A state-of-the-art Health and Wellness Center, also 2 blocks from Ross Hall, is an 188,000-square-foot facility that hosts a wide variety of fitness and instructional classes; walk-in recreation; and sport club, intramural, and wellness programs and services.

GRADUATES

The GW SMHS maintains a national reputation for placing qualified graduates into quality residency programs. Many students choose to continue their postgraduate work at GW and be a part of our new state-of-the-art hospital. In fact, of the graduating class of 2008, 20 members remained at GW to complete their residencies. Some of the institutions at which the members of the class of 2008 were placed include Yale University, Mt. Sinai Hospital, and the Mayo Clinic. The following list indicates some of the specialties and/or programs that were most highly matched by GW graduates: medicine, pediatrics, radiology, emergency medicine, obstetrics/gynecology, and psychiatry.

Admissions

REQUIREMENTS

Applicants must have completed a minimum of 90 semester hours at an accredited American or Canadian college or university prior to matriculation. Applicants must be U.S. or Canadian citizens or U.S. permanent residents.

Applicants must have completed 6 credits of English as well as 6 credits of lecture and 2 credits of lab in each of the following sciences at an accredited American or Canadian college or university prior to matriculation: biology (botany or biochemistry courses do not fulfill this requirement), general chemistry, organic chemistry, and physics. Last year's entering class averaged an overall GPA of 3.57 and a science GPA of 3.48. The MCAT is required and should be no more than 3 years old from the year of medical school matriculation.

SUGGESTIONS

We strongly urge you to complete your file as early as possible.

PROCESS

Once the Admissions Office receives an AMCAS application, the secondary application is sent to the applicant. GW requires up to 5 letters of recommendation (2 from science faculty and 1 from someone familiar with your personal traits), but prefers a pre-medical advisory committee letter if available. It will take 4-5 weeks to process your application and letters of recommendation after we have received them. The application process is very competitive, as there are over 10,000 applicants for approximately 175 seats. Interviews and acceptances are offered on a rolling admissions basis. Please note the following deadlines: The AMCAS application is due December 1. The GW secondary application is due January 1 (postmarked), and letters of recommendation are due January 1 (postmarked). Each year the Admissions Office offers approximately 1,000 interviews to selected applicants. These interviews are blind (the interviewers do not read the applicant's file prior to the interview). Although we only offer interviews from September to March, acceptances into the class may be offered anytime after October 15 until early August. All final decisions will be mailed to applicants.

Admissions Requirements (Required)

MCAT scores, science GPA, non-science GPA, letters of recommendation, interview, essay/personal statement, extracurricular activities, exposure to medical profession

Admissions Requirement (Optional)

State residency

COSTS AND AID

Tuition & Fees

Tuition	$45,892
Room and board	$16,425
Cost of books	$934
Fees	$375

Financial Aid

% students receiving aid	83
Average grant	$12,638
Average debt	$185,700

GEORGETOWN UNIVERSITY
SCHOOL OF MEDICINE

OFFICE OF ADMISSIONS, BOX 571421, WASHINGTON, DC 20057 • ADMISSION: 202-687-1154
E-MAIL: MEDICALADMISSIONS@GEORGETOWN.EDU • WEBSITE: HTTP://SOM.GEORGETOWN.EDU

STUDENT BODY	
Type	Private
Enrollment	779
% male/female	50/50
% minorities	10
# applied	11,237

ADMISSIONS
Average GPA and MCAT Scores

Overall GPA	3.6

Application Information

Regular application	10/30
Regular notification	10/15
Are transfers accepted?	Yes
Interview required?	Yes
Application fee	$130

Academics

While most students earn their MD through a 4-year program, some extend their studies more than 5 years to take part in year-long research projects between their second and third years. Others participate in combined-degree programs leading to the MD and the PhD in biochemistry, bioethics, biophysics, cell biology, molecular biology, microbiology and immunology, pathology, pharmacology, physiology, neuroscience, tumor biology, or other disciplines. The proximity of the National Institutes of Health facilitates student involvement in important research projects, either during summers or year-long periods. Medical students are evaluated with grades of honors/high pass/pass/fail, with the exception of elective courses, which are usually taken as satisfactory/unsatisfactory. Passing Step 1 of the USMLE is a requirement for promotion to year 3, and passing Step 2 is a graduation requirement.

BASIC SCIENCES: The first 2 years focus on basic science instruction but incorporate interdisciplinary courses; principles of patient care; problem-based learning modules; and ethical, social, economic, and religious aspects of health care as well. Lectures, labs, and small-group discussions are the teaching methods used, with students in scheduled sessions for about 22 hours per week. A student-run note-taking service assists with the volume of material presented during the first 2 years. First-year courses are ambulatory care, Biochemistry, biostatistics and epidemiology, Embryology, endocrinology, Gross Anatomy, introduction to health care, introduction to the patient, medical data and reasoning, microscopic Anatomy, Neurobiology, and Physiology. Second-year courses are ambulatory care, clinical problem solving, Microbiology and Immunology, Pathology, Pharmacology, Physical Diagnosis, and psychiatry. Also during the second year, 2 hours each week are reserved for elective courses, some of which may be taken at Georgetown's main campus. Basic science instruction takes place in several science/research buildings that are part of the medical center complex. The Dahlgren Memorial Library houses over 177,000 volumes and subscribes to over 1,800 journals. Within the library is the Biomedical Academic Computer Center (BACC), with a variety of audiovisual, computer, and educational services. Students have access to the Internet, e-mail, medical software, and databases.

CLINICAL TRAINING

Third-year required rotations are Medicine (12 weeks), Surgery (12 weeks), Pediatrics (6 weeks), Obstetrics/Gynecology (6 weeks), Neurology (4 weeks), Psychiatry (4 weeks), and Family Medicine (4 weeks). Fourth-year requirements are Medicine (6 weeks), Surgery (6 weeks), Emergency Medicine (4 weeks), selectives (20 weeks), and electives (20 weeks). Medical students train at the Georgetown University Hospital (407 beds) and at nine other affiliated federal and community hospitals in the Washington, DC metropolitan area. Electives may be taken abroad through Georgetown's International Programs or through individually arranged clerkships. Examples of possible training sites are the Bahamas, Colombia, and the Dominican Republic.

Campus Life

Virtually all states are represented in the student body. Among students in the entering class, 49 percent majored in biological sciences, 24 percent in physical sciences, 18 percent in social sciences, and 9 percent in various humanities or other disciplines. Approximately 11 percent of students are underrepresented minorities. Class size is 194.

STUDENT LIFE

Though Georgetown is a Jesuit institution, the school encourages students of all denominations to express their spirituality. In addition to religious organizations, student groups focused on professional interests and community service are active. Outside of the classroom, students socialize at organized events and informally in common areas such as the new Student Lounge in the Pre-clinical Science Building. Medical students take advantage of the Yates Memorial Field House, which is conveniently located behind the library. It has a pool, track, squash and tennis courts, a fitness center, and other athletic facilities. At the Leavey Center, students enjoy performing arts, shops, services, and restaurants. Washington, DC has vast cultural and recreational opportunities. Admission to the Smithsonian museums is free, restaurants abound, Rock Creek Park offers running and biking trails, and the city's attractions are all accessible on the metro system. A free shuttle between the medical center and nearby metro stations is provided. Baltimore, Philadelphia, and New York are easily reached by train, and the Appalachian Mountains and the Atlantic coast are within a few hours drive. All students live off campus, within walking or biking distance of campus.

GRADUATES

Graduates are successful in securing residency positions at institutions throughout the country.

Admissions

REQUIREMENTS

Prerequisites are 1 year each of biology, chemistry, English, math, organic chemistry, and physics. One semester of biochemistry may be substituted for 1 semester of organic chemistry. Science courses should include associated labs. The MCAT is required, and scores must be from within the past 3 years.

SUGGESTIONS

Recommended courses include biochemistry, computer science, cellular physiology, genetics, embryology, biostatistics, physical chemistry, and quantitative analysis. Applications are not processed until MCAT scores are received. The Admissions Committee considers character, maturity, and motivation along with academic achievement.

PROCESS

All AMCAS applicants are sent secondary applications. Of those returning secondaries, about 15 percent are interviewed between September and May. Interviews consist of one session with a faculty member or senior medical student. Also on interview day, candidates have lunch with medical students, tour the campus, and attend informational meetings. About 20 percent of interviewees are accepted. Notification begins after October 15 and continues on a rolling basis. A few highly qualified Georgetown undergraduates may be accepted to the School of Medicine during their sophomore year without MCAT scores.

Admissions Requirements (Required)

MCAT scores, science GPA, non-science GPA, letters of recommendation, interview, state residency, extracurricular activities, exposure to medical profession, Essays/personal statement

COSTS AND AID

Tuition & Fees

Tuition	$41,356
Room and board (on-campus)	$14,440
Cost of books	$1,516
Fees	$3,088

Financial Aid

% students receiving aid	87

HARVARD UNIVERSITY
HARVARD MEDICAL SCHOOL

OFFICE OF ADMISSIONS, 306 GORDON HALL, 25 SHATTUCK STREET, BOSTON, MA 02115 • ADMISSION: 617-432-1550
FAX: 617-432-3307 • E-MAIL: ADMISSIONS_OFFICE@HMS.HARVARD.EDU • WEBSITE: WWW.HMS.HARVARD.EDU

STUDENT BODY	
Type	Private
Enrollment	739
% male/female	50/50
% minorities	21
# applied	5,950
# accepted	220
# enrolled	165
Average age	23

FACULTY	
Total faculty (number)	11,049

ADMISSIONS
Average GPA and MCAT Scores

Overall GPA	3.81
MCAT Bio	12.08
MCAT Phys	11.87
MCAT Verbal	11.14
MCAT Essay	Q

Application Information

Regular application	10/15
Regular notification	3/15
Are transfers accepted?	No
Admissions may be deferred?	Yes
Interview required?	Yes
Application fee	$85

Academics

Two distinct programs are available at Harvard: the New Pathway and the Health Science and Technology (HST) Program. All entering students are assigned to one of five societies, organizational units used both to structure academic activities and to facilitate interaction among students and between faculty and students. Joint-degree opportunities include the MSTP, other MD/PhD programs designed in collaboration with science and non-science graduate departments, the combined MD/MPH, an accelerated 5-year MD-MBA program, and an MD/MPP with the Kennedy School of Government. More than half of the students take at least 5 years to complete their education to take full advantage of scholastic and research opportunities, some of which are actually off campus and perhaps overseas.

BASIC SCIENCES: Students in the first year of the New Pathway concentrate on biomedical and social sciences. The year is divided into six sections: Chemistry and Biology of the Cell, Genetics, The Human Body, Immunology, Physiology, and Pharmacology. Students are also introduced to clinical medicine in their first year. Year 2 has four segments: Human Nervous System, Human Systems I, Human Systems II, and Pathology. Concepts of behavioral and community health are integrated into the basic science studies. During the first 2 years, lectures are enhanced with tutorials and labs, but learning also takes place outside of the classroom environment. Students are responsible for addressing specific clinical challenges through independent and small-group research and analysis. Participants in HST also manage their own learning but pose questions to answer through research rather than answering questions that arise through case presentations. During the fall semester of year 1, HST students take the following: Cellular and Molecular Immunology, Functional Human Anatomy, Genetics, Human Pathology, and Molecular Biology. During the spring semester, students take Endocrinology; Cardiovascular, Renal, and Respiratory Pathophysiology; and Research. Electives in social and clinical medicine are taken throughout the year. During year 2, students take Gastroenterology, Microbial Pathogenesis, Neuroscience, Reproductive Biology, and Research during the first semester and Clinical Medicine, Hematology, Pharmacology, and Psychopathology during the second semester. HST students complete a thesis as part of their requirements. Computers, loaded with curriculum-related software and linked with online data sources, are considered an important information management tool and are accessible in the Educational Center, the library, and the residence hall. The Countway Library of Medicine has one of the largest biomedical collections in the country. Grading is satisfactory/unsatisfactory for all courses. Passing Step 1 of the USMLE is required prior to graduation.

CLINICAL TRAINING

Patient contact begins in year 1, when students learn to take histories and become familiar with basic elements of the physical exam. Formal clinical instruction begins in year 3, when HST and New Pathway students join for required clerkships. These are Medicine (4 months), Women's and Children's Health (3 months), Surgery (3 months), Neurology (1 month), Psychiatry (1 month), and Radiology (1 month). Throughout years 3 and 4, students take part in ongoing, part-time primary care training. Year 4 is composed mostly of electives, which can be clinical and/or research oriented. Elective credit may be earned from several departments at Harvard University or from MIT. Clinical training takes place at Harvard-affiliated hospitals, which are Beth Israel Medical Center, Brigham and

Women's Hospital, Cambridge Health Alliance, The Center for Blood Research, The Children's Hospital Boston, Dana-Farber Cancer Institute, The Forsyth Institute, Harvard Pilgrim Health Care, Joslin Diabetes Center, Judge Baker Children's Center, Massachusetts Eye and Ear, Massachusetts General, Massachusetts Mental Health Center, McLean Hospital, Mount Auburn Hospital, Schepens Eye Research, Spaulding Rehab Hospital, and the Veterans Affairs Boston Healthcare System. Evaluation of student performance in clinical settings uses a high honors/honors/satisfactory/unsatisfactory scale. Narrative comments accompany these marks. In addition to formal rotations, students can gain experience in clinical environments through volunteer activities such as the Family Van and the Health Care for the Homeless projects, which provides preventive and curative care to community health centers and underserved populations. Students must pass the USMLE Step 2 to graduate.

Campus Life

About 47 percent of students were science majors in college. About 20 percent of the members of a typical class are underrepresented minorities, and about 35 percent took significant time off between college and medical school. Students are from all around the country and around 9 percent international. Class size is 165, of which 30 are HST and 135 are New Pathway participants.

STUDENT LIFE

The compact class schedule allows students to take part in activities of the medical school, the greater university, and the city of Boston. About 50 percent of medical students live in Vanderbilt Hall, a renovated building adjacent to the medical school. Married students live either off campus or in university-owned apartments. Students are active in organizations focused on topics ranging from support for various minority groups, to abortion rights, to soccer.

GRADUATES

Approximately half of each graduating class remains at Harvard for their residencies. The University of California at San Francisco also appears to be a popular choice. Of the graduating class, the most common specialty choices were internal medicine (24 percent), pediatrics (10 percent), general surgery (8 percent), and orthopedic surgery (3 percent).

Admissions

REQUIREMENTS

Requirements include one year of biology with lab, college-level calculus, expository writing, and physics with lab. 2 years of chemistry are required, both of which should involve laboratory experience. For New Pathway applicants, at least 16 additional credit hours in non-science courses are required. For HST applicants, calculus through differential equations and calculus-based physics are required. The quality of an applicant's undergraduate institution is assessed in evaluating his or her GPA. The MCAT is required, and all scores are considered.

SUGGESTIONS

Unlike many schools with rolling admissions, decisions at Harvard are made after all interviews are complete. Thus, applicants submitting scores from the August MCAT are not penalized. There is no preference for particular undergraduate majors, but demonstration of academic excellence is expected. In addition, most successful applicants have impressive professional, volunteer, community-service, or other extracurricular achievements.

PROCESS

Harvard participates in AMCAS, and in the past, about 18 percent of applicants were interviewed. Interviews take place from September through February and consist of two sessions that last one hour each with a member of the Admissions Committee. Decisions are made in late February, and all applicants are notified in mid-March. A wait list is established at that time, but usually only a handful of candidates are ultimately accepted from the list.

Admissions Requirements (Required)

MCAT scores, science GPA, non-science GPA, letters of recommendation, interview, essays/personal statement, exposure to medical profession

Admissions Requirements (Optional)

Community service, research experience

COSTS AND AID

Tuition & Fees

Tuition	$37,200
Room and board	
(on-campus)	$11,005
(off-campus)	$12,000
Cost of books	$2,241
Fees	$1,863

Financial Aid

% students receiving aid	74
Average grant	$23,000
Average loan	$28,700
Average debt	$97,390

HOWARD UNIVERSITY

COLLEGE OF MEDICINE

ADMISSIONS OFFICE, 520 WEST STREET, NORTHWEST, WASHINGTON, DC 20059 • ADMISSION: 202-806-6270
FAX: 202-806-7934 • E-MAIL: SHUMPHREY@HOWARD.EDU • WEBSITE: WWW.MED.HOWARD.EDU

STUDENT BODY

Type	Private
Enrollment	454
% male/female	51/49
% minorities	59
# applied (total/out)	4,940/4,592
# accepted (total/out)	368/283
# enrolled	
(total/out-of-state)	138/118

ADMISSIONS

Application Information

Regular application	12/15
Regular notification	10/15
	until filled
Are transfers accepted?	No
Admissions may be deferred?	Yes
Interview required?	Yes
Application fee	$45

Academics

Although most students earn their MD in 4 years, some are given permission to complete requirements over a 5-year period. The College of Medicine and the Graduate School of Arts and Sciences offer a joint MD/PhD program. The following departments award the PhD: Anatomy, Biochemistry, Biology, Chemistry, Genetics, Microbiology, Pharmacology, and Physiology.

BASIC SCIENCES: Basic sciences are presented primarily in a lecture/lab format. Students are in scheduled classes from 25 to 30 hours per week. First-year courses are Anatomy; Biochemistry; Histology; Microbiology; Immunology; Neuroscience; Physiology; Psychiatry; Introduction to Patient Care, in which students visit clinics and interact with physicians; and Introduction to Psychodynamic Thinking, which discusses healthy and pathological mental mechanisms. Second-year courses are the following: Genetics, Epidemiology, Immunology, Microbiology, Pathology, Pathophysiology, Pharmacology, Physical Diagnosis, Physiology, and Psychopathology. Grading is honors/satisfactory/unsatisfactory, and academic support services such as workshops, tutorials, and summer sessions are available. The USMLE Step 1 is required for promotion to the third year. Instruction takes place in the Seeley G. Mudd Building, which features auditoriums, laboratories, audiovisual, and computer-assisted study areas. The Health Sciences Library has 260,000 volumes and journals, video equipment, and a computer linkage with the National Library of Medicine.

CLINICAL TRAINING

Patient contact begins in the first year in introduction to patient care. Throughout medical school, students have the opportunity to gain clinical experience by volunteering and participating in community outreach programs. Others gain research experience through work at NIH or other prominent institutions. Formal clinical training begins in year 3 (or year 4 for those in a 5-year course of study), with the following required clerkships: Medicine (12 weeks), Surgery (8 weeks), Obstetrics/Gynecology (8 weeks), Pediatrics (8 weeks), Psychiatry (6 weeks), Rehabilitation and Neurological Disease (4 weeks), and Family Practice (4 weeks). For 2 hours per week, during one semester, third-year students attend lectures on ethical and legal issues in health care. Senior-year requirements are medicine (4 weeks) and surgery (4 weeks). In addition, students take 20–24 weeks of electives in 4-week blocks. Evaluation of clinical performance uses honors/satisfactory/unsatisfactory grading, and the USMLE Step 2 is required for graduation. Clinical training takes place largely at Howard University Hospital (300 beds). Other sites used are Howard University Cancer Center, Center for Sickle Cell Disease, Walter Reed Army and National Naval Medical Centers, DC General Hospital, St. Elizabeth's Hospital, VA Medical Center, Providence Hospital, Greater Southeast Community Hospital, Prince George's Hospital Center, Washington Hospital Center, and National Rehabilitation Hospital.

Campus Life

About 60 percent of the students are African American, and about 10 percent are from African or Caribbean countries. An average of 30 states and several foreign countries are usually represented. From 10 percent to 20 percent of the students in each entering class attended Howard for undergraduate premedical studies. About 20 percent of entrants are considered nontraditional, having taken time off between college and medical school and participated in some sort of postbaccalaureate premedical program. Class size is 110.

STUDENT LIFE

Medical students enjoy both an active campus life and involvement in the greater community. They may participate in Howard University activities, such as its radio and television stations, intramural athletic teams and events, conferences, and social or special-interest clubs. Washington, DC is a center for cultural, academic, recreational, and, obviously political activities. In addition to being an international city, DC has a strong local, predominantly African American community that is highly diverse. The College of Medicine is part of Howard's downtown campus, which is metro accessible and convenient to lively neighborhoods and interesting parts of the city such as the White House and Smithsonian Museums. Housing for graduate students is available in modern, university-owned apartments. However, most students live off campus and either walk or take public transportation to school.

GRADUATES

About 25 percent of African American physicians practicing in the United States are Howard alumni. Howard graduates secure postgraduate positions at institutions all over the country. Significant numbers enter one of the 16 residency programs at Howard University Hospital or at DC General Hospital, where they are also supervised by Howard faculty.

Admissions

REQUIREMENTS

Requirements are the following: biology (8 hours), chemistry (8 hours), organic chemistry (8 hours), physics (8 hours), college math (6 hours), and English (6 hours). The MCAT is required and must have been taken within the past 3 years.

SUGGESTIONS

Beyond required courses, biochemistry, cell biology, and developmental biology or embryology are recommended. For students who have taken time off after college, recent course work is helpful. The Admissions Committee values activities that demonstrate an interest in working with underserved communities.

PROCESS

All AMCAS applicants receive secondary applications. Of those submitting secondaries, about 10 percent are interviewed with faculty or administrators. Others are rejected, advised to retake the MCAT, or put in a hold category and considered for interview later in the year. Of those interviewed, 70 percent are accepted on a rolling basis, and the rest are either rejected or wait listed. Wait listed candidates may submit supplementary information and grades. A limited number of high school seniors are accepted into a combined BS/MD program organized with Howard's College of Arts and Sciences that allows students to earn both degrees in a 6-year period. Through an early entrance program, a few students nationwide may be admitted to the College of Medicine after their college junior year.

Admissions Requirements (Required)

MCAT scores, science GPA, non-science GPA, letters of recommendation, interview, state residency, extracurricular activities, exposure to medical profession

Admissions Requirements (Optional)

Essays/personal statement

COSTS AND AID

Tuition & Fees

Tuition	$24,055
Fees	$1,636
Cost of books	$1,240
Room and board	$11,663

Financial Aid

% students receiving aid	85
Average debt	$63,000

INDIANA UNIVERSITY
SCHOOL OF MEDICINE

MEDICAL SCHOOL ADMISSIONS OFFICE, FESLER HALL 213, 1120 S. INDIANAPOLIS, IN 46202 **ADMISSION:** 317-274-3772
FAX: 317-278-0211 • **E-MAIL:** INMEDADM@IUPUI.EDU • **WEBSITE:** WWW.MEDICINE.IU.EDU/

STUDENT BODY

Type	Public
Enrollment	1,173
% male/female	57/43
% minorities	12
# applied (total/out)	3,490/2,796
# accepted (total/out)	471/163
# enrolled (total/out)	294/42
Average age	23

FACULTY

Total faculty	1,303
% female	48
% minority	3
% part-time	5

ADMISSIONS
Average GPA and MCAT Scores

Overall GPA	3.73
MCAT Bio	10.3
MCAT Phys	10
MCAT Verbal	9.9
MCAT Essay	P

Application Information

Regular application	12/15
Regular notification	10/15
Early application	6/1–8/1
Early notification	10/1
Are transfers accepted?	Yes
Admissions may be deferred?	Yes
Interview required?	Yes
Application fee	$50

Academics

The School of Medicine in Indianapolis is part of the Indiana University (IU) Medical Center, which includes schools of Nursing, Dentistry, and Allied Health Sciences. The Medical Center complex occupies 85 acres and is situated one mile from downtown Indianapolis. In conjunction with the University Graduate School, The School of Medicine offers selected students an opportunity to pursue the M.S. or Ph.D. degrees along with an M.D. Through this program, degrees may be earned in Anatomy, Biochemistry, Biophysics, Genetics, Neurobiology, Microbiology, Pathology, Pharmacology, Physiology, Toxicology, and in Humanities and Social Studies disciplines.

BASIC SCIENCES: First-year students select one of the following nine locations for their preclinical studies: IU Bloomington; IU Indianapolis; Lafayette Center at Purdue; University of Notre Dame; Ball State University; Indiana State University; University of Evansville; Indiana University Northwest; and Fort Wayne Center for Medical Education at Purdue. While the curriculum is essentially the same at each campus, the methods of instruction may differ, with some programs relying more or less on case-based learning. At all schools, the "core" basic science courses are complemented by early clinical correlations. Throughout the first two years, scheduled classes account for 26-28 hours per week. At the Indianapolis campus, 80 percent of class time is devoted to lectures and labs, and 20 percent is used for small-group discussions. First-year courses are the following: Anatomy; Histology; Biochemistry; Physiology; Microbiology; Evidence-Based Medicine; Immunology; Patient/Doctor Relationship; and Concepts of Health and Disease, which teaches students how to apply basic science concepts to clinical problems. Year two courses are: Biostatistics; Pharmacology; Pathology; Clinical Medicine; Medical Genetics; and Neurobiology. With the exception of Clinical Medicine, during which students join medical teams in hospitals, second-year courses use lectures and labs as instructional techniques. The Medical Center offers all modern learning tools, including computers and audiovisual equipment. The Ruth Lilly Medical Library (200,000 volumes) is located in the Medical Research Building in Indianapolis and serves the Schools of Medicine and Nursing. All campuses have affiliated library systems, and all libraries are electronically linked. The libraries have access to 400 databases and online informational resources. Evaluation uses an Honors/High Pass/Pass/Fail system. Passing the USMLE Step 1 is a requirement for promotion to year three.

CLINICAL TRAINING

All students spend their third year at the Medical Center in Indianapolis, rotating through 11 hospitals in the Indianapolis area. The patient population is drawn from both urban and rural areas. Year three is largely composed of required rotations which are the following: Medicine (12 weeks); Surgery (8 weeks); Pediatrics (8 weeks); Ob/Gyn (6 weeks); Psychiatry (6 weeks); and Family Medicine (4 weeks). Required fourth-year clerkships are Surgical Subspecialties (8 weeks), Neurology (4 weeks), and Radiology (4 weeks). Year four is mostly dedicated to elective study, which may be pursued off campus, around the country, or overseas. Evaluation of clinical performance uses an Honors/High Pass/Pass/Fail system, augmented by narratives. Honors students generally take part in departmental research activities. Passing the USMLE Step 2 is a requirement for graduation.

Students

Typically, 95 percent of an entering class are Indiana residents. About 6 percent are underrepresented minorities, most of whom are African Americans. Approximately 5 percent of students are older than 30 at the time of matriculation.

STUDENT LIFE

Students are given a voice in school administration and curriculum development through an elected Student Government. Though student life differs from one campus to another, in general medical students benefit from the social and cultural offerings of a large university system. There is a wide range of lifestyles among students, with some living on campus in residence halls or apartments and others living off campus, perhaps with their families. Medical students have access to all campus recreational facilities and events.

GRADUATES

Slightly less than half of the 2000 graduating class entered residency programs in Indiana. Other popular locations for post-graduate training were Michigan, Ohio, and Illinois. The most common specialty choices were Family Medicine (16 percent of the class); Internal Medicine (11 percent); Pediatrics (11 percent); Surgery (10 percent); Radiology (9 percent); Ob/Gyn (8 percent); and Emergency Medicine (7 percent); and Anesthesia (7 percent). About 60 percent of graduates entered fields considered to be primary care.

Admissions

REQUIREMENTS

Required undergraduate courses are one year each of the following: Chemistry, Organic Chemistry, Biology, and Physics. All courses must include labs. Beyond GPA, the quality of an applicant's undergraduate course load is considered rather than the quantity of extra course hours. The MCAT is required, and must be no more than four years old. If an applicant has retaken the MCAT, the most recent score is considered.

SUGGESTIONS

Undergraduate coursework in Social Sciences and Humanities is important. For applicants who have taken significant time off after college, some recent coursework is useful. The April, rather than August MCAT is strongly recommended. Among out-of-state applicants, those with strong qualifications and some sort of ties to the state are the most likely to be admitted. The School aims to admit candidates who are likely to choose careers in primary care.

PROCESS

Almost all Indiana residents receive a secondary application, and about 93 percent of those returning secondaries are interviewed. Among out-of-state applicants, only highly qualified candidates are sent secondary applications, and about 10 percent are invited to interview. Interviews take place on Wednesdays, from September through February and are scheduled in the order in which completed applications are received. Interviews consist of a one-hour session with a team of faculty members. Notification occurs on a monthly basis, beginning in October. Applicants are either accepted, rejected, or deferred and re-evaluated later in the year. In the spring, a wait-list is established. Wait-listed candidates may submit supplementary material if it adds new information to his or her file.

Admissions Requirements (Required)

MCAT scores, Science GPA, Non-science GPA, Letters of recommendation, Interview, State residency, Essays/personal statement, Extracurricular activities, Exposure to medical profession

Overlap Schools

The University of Chicago, University of Illinois at Chicago, University of Michigan.

COSTS AND AID

Tuition & Fees

In-state Tuition	$25,140
Out-of-state Tuition	$42,130
Room and board	$10,394
Cost of books	$3,900
Fees	$755

JOHNS HOPKINS UNIVERSITY
SCHOOL OF MEDICINE

733 NORTH BROADWAY, SUITE G-49, BALTIMORE, MD 21205 • ADMISSION: 410-955-3182
FAX: 410-955-7494 • E-MAIL: SOMADMISS@JHMI.EDU • WEBSITE: WWW.HOPKINSMEDICINE.ORG

STUDENT BODY

Type	Private
Enrollment	482
% male/female	52/48
% minorities	16
# applied (total/out)	4,149/3,850
# accepted (total/out)	258/241
# enrolled (total/out)	120/110
Average age	23

ADMISSIONS
Average GPA and MCAT scores

Overall GPA	3.85
MCAT Bio	11.93
MCAT Phys	11.86
MCAT Verbal	11.07
MCAT Essay	Q

Application Information

Regular application	10/15
Regular notification	Rolling
Early application	7/1–8/15
Early notification	10/1
Are transfers accepted?	No
Admissions may be deferred?	Yes
Interview required?	Yes
Application fee	$75

Academics

In 1992 Hopkins implemented a revised curriculum that introduced case-based learning, exposure to clinical settings during the first year, and a physicians and society (P&S) course, which integrates social, economic, and ethical perspectives into the 4-year basic and clinical science curriculum. Studies leading to both an MD and a PhD or MA/MS are possible in the following fields: biochemistry, cellular and molecular biology, biological chemistry, biomedical engineering, biophysics, biophysics/molecular biophysics, cell biology and Anatomy, cellular and molecular medicine, genetics, history of medicine, history of science, medicine and technology, human genetics and molecular biology, immunology, medical and biological illustration, neuroscience, pharmacology, molecular sciences, physiology, and public health. The combined MD/MPH is particularly popular, which is not surprising given the excellent reputation of the School of Public Health.

BASIC SCIENCES: The first year is organized into the following 4 blocks, all 10 weeks in length: Molecules and Cells (block 1), Anatomy and Developmental Biology (block 2), Neuroscience and Clinical Epidemiology (block 3), and Organ Systems (block 4). The P&S course is year-long as is Introduction to Clinical Medicine, in which students spend 2 days a month working with a private physician. During the first year, classes end at 1:00 P.M. 4 days a week, giving students ample time to study. Many students take on research projects during the summer between their first and second years. Second-year students study pathology, pathophysiology, and pharmacology, which are offered as yearlong courses. All three courses are integrated and are organized around organ systems. Lectures, discussion, case-study, and labs are all important components of the basic science curriculum. With relatively few hours of scheduled lectures, students generally attend classes and do not rely on student note-taking cooperatives. Grading is honors/high pass/pass/fail. Faculty members, assigned to incoming students, both advise and monitor their progress. The Welch Medical Library and its three affiliated sites own over 380,000 books and subscribe to about 3,000 journals. It provides resources that support instruction, such as extensive database and Internet tools. The USMLE is not used for grading or promotional purposes.

CLINICAL TRAINING

Facilities for clinical training include the Johns Hopkins Hospital complex, which is comprised of numerous affiliates, is housed in 37 buildings, and contains over 1,100 beds. In addition to serving the urban population of Baltimore and the surrounding areas, Johns Hopkins Hospitals attract patients from around the country and the world. Students are exposed to patient care at renowned institutions such as the Wilmer Eye Institute, Adolf Meyer Center for Psychiatry, Brady Urological Institute, Clayton Heart Center, Meyerhoff Center for Digestive Diseases, the Children's Center, Oncology Center, Halsted Surgical Service, and Osler Medical Service. Students are also encouraged to pursue clinical experiences away from Hopkins and a significant number do so overseas. With faculty input, students determine the order of their required clerkships and electives. Requirements are the following: Medicine (9 weeks), Surgery (9 weeks), Pediatrics (9 weeks), Psychiatry (4 weeks), Neurology (4 weeks), Obstetrics/Gynecology (6 weeks), Emergency Medicine (4 weeks), Ambulatory Internal Medicine (3 weeks), and Opthalmology (1 week). Clinical instruction is generally carried out in small groups, and individual initiative is encouraged. Grading is honors/high pass/pass/fail for both required and elective courses. Through its subsidiaries, the Johns Hopkins Health Systems provides statewide health care services to individuals and health-plan participants. This integration into managed care operations, coupled with large federal research grants, suggest that the institution is financially stable.

Campus Life

The diversity of the student body reflects the school's national reputation. A typical class has students from 35 different states and 70 or more colleges. As is the case with most top schools, half the entrants are women. Efforts are made to recruit ethnic minorities, and approximately 15 percent of the student body are from underrepresented minorities groups. Class size is limited to 120.

STUDENT LIFE

For some, social life revolves around school, where students spend a great deal of time. Others, particularly those from the area or with families, have lives outside of the medical school. Housing is available for single students or for married students living alone, in Reed Hall dorms adjacent to campus. However, most choose to live in apartments off campus. For those accustomed to New York or Washington, DC, the housing situation in Baltimore is good. The Housing Office assists students in their apartment searches. Recreational facilities, including a full-size gym, are free to medical students and are located next to Reed Hall. Several medical societies exist, including a Women's Medical Alumni Association, which provides support for women students and physicians. There is also a Student National Medical Association, which is active in both campus and community minority affairs.

GRADUATES

Graduates of Hopkins have their pick of residency programs, even those graduating with GPAs that are at the lower end of their class. About 50 percent of graduates enter primary care specialties; 20 percent ultimately enter academic medicine or work primarily in research.

Admissions

REQUIREMENTS

In addition to the typical requirement of 1 year each of biology, chemistry, organic chemistry, physics, and 1 year of calculus (or 1 semester of calculus and 1 semester of statistics), 24 semester hours of humanities and social sciences combined are required. Advanced placement credits accepted by the applicant's undergraduate institution may be submitted in lieu of taking the required courses for calculus, chemistry, and physics. Johns Hopkins does participate in AMCAS. The online secondary application may be accessed at any time after June 1, once the applicant has received an AAMC ID number but before the December 1 deadline.

SUGGESTIONS

Hopkins is concerned with both the academic and personal records of applicants and notes that intellectual progress through college is important. Extracurricular activities need not be medically related but should demonstrate humanistic values and perseverance.

PROCESS

About 15 percent of applicants are invited for interviews, which occur between September and March, and about 29 percent of those interviewed are accepted on a rolling basis. Applicants are interviewed by Admissions Committee members, and regional interviews may be arranged for applicants living a distance from Baltimore. At Admissions Committee meetings, decisions are made to admit, reject, or wait list applicants. In April, wait listed candidates are notified of their position on the list.

Admissions Requirements (Required)

MCAT scores, science GPA, non-science GPA, letters of recommendation, interview, essay/personal statement

Admissions Requirements (Optional)

State residency, extracurricular activities, exposure to medical profession

Overlap Schools

Columbia University, Harvard University, Mayo Clinic College of Medicine, University of California—Hastings, University of Michigan, University of Pennsylvania, Yale University.

COSTS AND AID

Tuition & Fees

Tuition	$33,200
Room and board	
(on-campus)	$10,829
(off-campus)	$14,849
Cost of books	$2,222
Fees	$1,850

Financial Aid

% students receiving aid	80
Average grant	$25,447
Average loan	$23,321
Average debt	$75,589

LOMA LINDA UNIVERSITY
SCHOOL OF MEDICINE

LOMA LINDA UNIVERSITY SCHOOL OF MEDICINE LOMA LINDA, CA 92350 • **ADMISSION:** 909-558-1100
FAX: 909-824-4146 • **E-MAIL:** ADMISSIONS.SM.APP@LLU.EDU • **WEBSITE:** WWW.LLU.EDU/LLU/MEDICINE

STUDENT BODY

Type	Private
Enrollment	661
% male/female	59/41
% minorities	6
# applied (total/out)	3,990/2,083

ADMISSIONS

Application Information

Regular application	11/1
Regular notification	12/15
Early application	6/1–8/1
Early notification	10/1
Are transfers accepted?	No
Admissions may be deferred?	Yes
Interview required?	No
Application fee	$55

Academics

Joint-degree programs are offered to qualified students. Along with the MD, students may earn an MS or PhD degree in fields such as anatomy, biochemistry, genetics, immunology, microbiology, neuroscience, molecular biology, pharmacology, and physiology. Examinations and other methods of evaluation are given percentile scores, but the courses are graded as pass or fail. Passing the USMLE Step 1 is a requirement for promotion to the third year.

BASIC SCIENCES: Although Loma Linda's curriculum covers the basic science topics typical of most medical schools, its religious affiliation adds another dimension. In addition to learning about human biology, the nature of disease, and the appropriate treatment for disease, first- and second-year students participate in a course called Whole Person Formation, which emphasizes biblical, ethical, and relational aspects of the practice of medicine. Patient contact occurs during the first year in Physical Diagnosis and interviewing. Other first-year courses are Biochemistry/Molecular Biology, Cell Structure and Function, Gross Anatomy and Embryology, Human Behavior, Information Sciences and Population-based Medicine, Medical Applications of the Basic Sciences, and Neuroscience. Second-year courses are Human Behavior, Microbiology, Pathology, Physiology, Pathophysiology and Applied Physical Diagnosis, and Pharmacology. First- and second-year instruction takes place in facilities located on the Loma Linda campus and close to the medical center, giving students access to university resources and clinical activities. Computers are available in a comprehensive computer lab and are used for instruction and research.

CLINICAL TRAINING

Third-year required rotations are Orientation to Clinical Medicine/Preventive Medicine (4 weeks), Family Medicine (4 weeks), Obstetrics/Gynecology (6 weeks), Internal Medicine (12 weeks), Pediatrics (8 weeks), Psychiatry (6 weeks), and Surgery (12 weeks). Half of the fourth year is reserved entirely for basic science and clinical electives, and half of the year is split between required clerkships and selectives. Required clerkships are sub internship selectives (8 weeks, selected from Family Medicine, Internal Medicine, Obstetrics/Gynecology, Pediatrics, and Surgery), Intensive Care Unit (4 weeks), Neurology (4 weeks), Ambulatory Care (4 weeks), and electives (16–22 weeks). Training takes place primarily at Loma Linda University Medical Center (500 beds), the Jerry L. Pettis Memorial Veterans Hospital, Riverside General Hospital, and the White Memorial Medical Center in Los Angeles. Other affiliated sites are San Bernardino County General Hospital, Kaiser Foundation Hospital, and Glendale Adventist Medical Center.

Campus Life

Most students are members of the Seventh-Day Adventist Church. About 6 percent of students are underrepresented minorities, most of whom are African American. Generally, there is a wide age range among incoming students, with the average at about 24. Class size is 189.

STUDENT LIFE

For the most part, student life revolves around the medical school and the immediate community. When in need of a change of scenery, Los Angeles and beautiful Southern California beaches are a short drive. Perhaps as a result of a shared religious background, students are cohesive. Alcohol is not a part of the social life, as it is prohibited in the Seventh-Day Adventist Church. Beyond extracurricular activities sponsored by the medical school, students are welcome to participate in university-wide events and organizations. Medical students have access to the university's athletic facilities, and are active in intramural sports. Students live both on and off campus, and virtually all students own cars.

GRADUATES

Graduates are successful in securing residencies in all specialty fields. Loma Linda Medical Center is a popular destination for postgraduate training, offering about 25 residency programs.

Admissions

REQUIREMENTS

Prerequisite course work is 8 semester hours each of biology, general chemistry, organic chemistry, and physics. Applicants should have met the English and religion requirements of their respective undergraduate institution. The MCAT is required, and scores should be no more than 3 years old. For applicants who have taken the test more than once, all sets of scores are considered.

SUGGESTIONS

Courses in the humanities and social sciences are recommended, and applicants are urged to take the April, rather than August, MCAT. For applicants who have taken time off after college, recent course work is important. Some involvement in health care delivery is valued by the Admissions Committee. Preference is given to qualified applicants who are members of the Seventh-Day Adventist Church. However, others who demonstrate a commitment to Christian principles are also considered favorably.

PROCESS

All AMCAS applicants are sent secondary applications. Of those returning secondaries, about 10 percent are invited to interview between November and March. Interviews consist of 1 or 2 hour-long sessions with faculty, students, and/or administrators. On interview day, lunch, a campus tour, and the opportunity to meet with current students are all provided. About 40 percent of interviewed candidates are accepted on a rolling basis, while others are rejected or wait listed. Wait listed candidates may send updated transcripts.

Admissions Requirements (Required)

MCAT scores, science GPA, non-science GPA, letters of recommendation, state residency, extracurricular activities, exposure to medical profession

Admissions Requirements (Optional)

Interview, essays/personal statement

COSTS AND AID
Tuition & Fees

Tuition	$32,994
Fees	$736

LOUISIANA STATE UNIVERSITY
SCHOOL OF MEDICINE IN NEW ORLEANS

OFFICE OF ADMISSIONS, 1901 PERDIDO STREET, PO BOX P3-4, NEW ORLEANS, LA 70112 • ADMISSION: 504-568-6262
FAX: 504-568-7701 • E-MAIL: MS-ADMISSIONS@LSUHSC.EDU • WEBSITE: WWW.MEDSCHOOL.LSUHSC.EDU/ADMISSIONS

STUDENT BODY

Type	Public
Enrollment	712
% male/female	50/50
% minorities	15
# applied	1,179

ADMISSIONS
Average GPA and MCAT Scores

Overall GPA	3.7
MCAT Bio	9.5
MCAT Phys	9.0
MCAT Verbal	9.0
MCAT Essay	P

Application Information

Regular application	11/15
Regular notification	Rolling
Early application	9/1
Early notification	10/1
Are transfers accepted?	Yes
Admissions may be deferred?	Yes
Interview required?	Yes
Application fee	$50

Academics

The course of instruction leading to the MD extends over a 4-year period. A revised first-and second-year curriculum was introduced and changes in the third- and fourth-year clinical curriculum were implemented. An honors program, which involves independent research and challenges the exceptional student, is open to those who excel during their first semester of medical school. For highly qualified students interested in careers in research, a combined MD/PhD program is available. Medical students are graded with honors/high pass/pass/fail. All students are required to pass Step 1 of the USMLE following completion of year 2, and fourth-year students must pass Step 2 of the exam.

BASIC SCIENCES: Although most instruction uses a lecture format, small-group discussions and tutorials are also part of the curriculum. First-year courses are Anatomy, Biochemistry, Cell Biology and Microanatomy, Clinical Correlation, Human Prenatal Development, Introduction to Clinical Medicine, Neuroscience, Medicine, Medical Ethics, Physiology, Psychiatry, and Social Issues in Medicine. Electives are offered in Community Service, Geriatrics, Health Promotion and Wellness, and Problem-based Learning. Second-year courses are Clinical Pathology, Immunology and Parasitology, Introduction to Clinical Medicine, Microbiology, Pathology, and Pharmacology. Basic sciences are taught in a modern building that is part of the medical center complex. Important educational resources are maintained by the LSU Division of Learning Resources, which provides audiovisual and classroom services to the downtown campus of the LSU Health Sciences Center. The medical library in New Orleans has a total of about 188,000 volumes, nearly 4,000 audiovisual titles, and approximately 2,000 periodicals. The library is fully computerized and houses individual computers that are equipped with educational software programs.

CLINICAL TRAINING

The third and fourth years are devoted primarily to clinical rotations. Lectures, conferences, and small-group discussions supplement the hands-on clinical training. Year 3 consists of 8.5 days of ophthalmology course work in addition to rotations in Medicine (12 weeks), General Surgery (8 weeks), Pediatrics (8 weeks), Obstetrics/Gynecology (6 weeks), Psychiatry (6 weeks), Family Medicine (4 weeks), Otolaryngology (2 weeks), and Urology (2 weeks). The final year consists of 36 weeks divided into nine 4-week blocks, which include an acting internship, ambulatory care, general medicine, neural sciences, and special topics. The special-topics block includes drug and alcohol abuse, financial planning, geriatrics, human sexuality, nutrition, and office management. The remainder of the year may include electives either in basic or clinical sciences with 4 weeks allowed for vacation. Most training takes place at LSU-affiliated hospitals including Charity Hospital, which has a total of 2,200 beds. Elective requirements may be fulfilled at any accredited medical school or teaching hospital in the United States or Canada. With approval, electives may also be taken at foreign institutions.

Campus Life

All students are Louisiana residents. Approximately 15 percent of students are underrepresented minorities, most of whom are African American. The average age of entering students is about 23, and there are usually a number of students in their late 20s and 30s. Class size is 165.

STUDENT LIFE

Some medical students are active in the student government, which works closely with the faculty and the administration on a range of important issues. Others are involved in the student publication or in any number of professional clubs, honor societies, recreational groups, and community-service projects. Extracurricular opportunities in New Orleans abound. The restaurants, music scene, historic and cultural sights, and annual festivals and events are world renowned. Some students opt to live in the school's residence hall, which has its own student center. Others live off campus where housing is generally reasonably priced.

GRADUATES

The school assists and advises graduating students in obtaining suitable appointments in hospitals. LSU—New Orleans offers a comprehensive graduate medical education program in more than 20 specialty fields.

Admissions

REQUIREMENTS

Louisiana residency is a requirement. Prerequisite courses are 8 semester hours each of biology, chemistry, organic chemistry, and physics, all with associated labs. Strength in both written and spoken English is required. The MCAT is required, and scores should be from within the past 3 years. For applicants who have taken the exam more than once, the most recent set of scores is weighed most heavily.

SUGGESTIONS

A well-rounded undergraduate experience with course work in English, humanities, math, and social sciences is advised. Community service or medically related work or volunteer activities are valued.

PROCESS

All AMCAS applicants who are Louisiana residents are sent secondary applications. Of those returning secondaries, about 50 percent are invited to interview between October and April. The interview consists of 2 or 3 one-on-one sessions, each with a faculty member, student, or administrator. On interview day, candidates also have the opportunity to meet with students, tour the campus, and have lunch. About 60 percent of interviewed candidates are accepted on a rolling basis. Wait listed candidates may send additional information to update their files.

Admissions Requirements (Required)

MCAT scores, science GPA, nonscience GPA, letters of recommendation, interview, state residency, extracurricular activities, exposure to medical profession

Admissions Requirements (Optional)

Essays/personal statement

COSTS AND AID
Tuition & Fees

In-state tuition	$11,534
Out-of-state tuition	$25,682
Fees	$1,427

LOUISIANA STATE UNIVERSITY
SCHOOL OF MEDICINE IN SHREVEPORT

ADMISSIONS OFFICE, 1501 KINGS HIGHWAY, PO BOX 33932, SHREVEPORT, LA 71130-3932 • **ADMISSION:** 318-675-5190
FAX: 318-675-5244 • **E-MAIL:** SHVADM@LSUHSC.EDU • **WEBSITE:** WWW.LSUHSC.EDU

STUDENT BODY

Type	Public
Enrollment	391
% male/female	67/33
% minorities	5
# applied (total/out)	1,046/272
# accepted (total/out)	27/0

ADMISSIONS

Application Information

Regular application	11/15
Regular notification	10/15
	until filled
Early application	6/1–8/1
Early notification	10/1
Are transfers accepted?	Yes
Admissions may be deferred?	Yes
Interview required?	No
Application fee	$50

Academics

The first 2 years are devoted to basic medical sciences with orientation to clinical applications. The second 2 years are devoted to clinical training and are spent primarily in hospitals and clinics. In addition to the MD degree, advanced studies leading to the MD/PhD are possible. The doctorate may be earned in anatomy, biochemistry, microbiology, pharmacology, and physiology. All medical students are encouraged to take advantage of the many research opportunities available during summers and year-round. Special funds are provided for this purpose, and medical students who complete prescribed research activities are awarded diplomas with the special designation Honors Research Participant. During summer terms, the school offers opportunities for rural, clinical electives. Medical students are evaluated with an A–F scale, with the exception of elective courses, which are pass/fail. Passing both steps of the USMLE is a graduation requirement.

BASIC SCIENCES: During the first year, students are in lectures, small-group seminars, labs, or other scheduled sessions for about 25 hours per week. Courses are Biochemistry and Molecular Biology, Biometry, CPR, Ethics, Family Medicine and Comprehensive Care, Histology, Human Anatomy, Human Embryology, Introduction to Computer-aided Learning, Library Science, Medical Genetics, Medical Neuroscience, Physiology and Biophysics, Psychiatry, and Radiology. The second year is increasingly clinically oriented. Students are in class or other scheduled sessions for about 35 hours per week. Courses are Clinical Diagnosis, Clinical Neurology, Clinical Pathology, Clinical-Pathological Conference, Family Medicine and Comprehensive Care, Microbiology, Pathology, Perspectives in Medicine, Pharmacology, Psychiatry, and Radiology. A note-taking service, organized by and for students, assists with learning and retaining material. Computer-assisted instruction is a critical component of the basic science education, and all entering students are required to own a computer.

CLINICAL TRAINING

An unusual longitudinal clerkship called comprehensive care spans both the third and fourth years. In it, students work together and serve as the primary caregivers in a functioning clinic. Other third-year required rotations are Family Medicine (8 weeks), Medicine (8 weeks), Obstetrics/Gynecology (8 weeks), Surgery (4 weeks), Pediatrics (4 weeks), Psychiatry (4 weeks), and Surgery Subspecialties (3 weeks). A minimum of 16 weeks during the fourth year are reserved for electives. Required clerkships are medicine (6 weeks), surgery (3 weeks), pediatrics (3 weeks), and neuroscience (3 weeks). Most training takes place at the LSU Hospital (650 beds), the Shreveport Veterans' Administration Hospital, and the Comprehensive Care Clinic.

Campus Life

All students are Louisiana residents. About 5 percent of students are underrepresented minorities. There is a wide age range among entering students, including those in their late 20s or 30s. Class size is 100.

STUDENT LIFE

Outside of class, LSU offers medical students a rich campus life. The university offers more than 60 student organizations in addition to intramural sports, performing arts events, visiting speakers, and social activities. The university center has dining facilities, a lounge, student activity rooms, and a bookstore, among other student services. Generally, it serves as a meeting place for students. The Health and Physical Education Building houses an indoor swimming pool; handball and racquetball courts; basketball; tennis, volleyball, and badminton courts; a dance studio; and fitness and weight training rooms. Shreveport is a historic Southern city with a population of more than 370,000. Museums, art galleries, parks, gardens, restaurants, bars, and shopping areas are some of its many attractions. The cities of Baton Rouge and New Orleans are easily accessible. Houston, Memphis, Little Rock, and Jackson are also within driving distance. Most medical students live off campus.

GRADUATES

An increasing proportion of graduates are entering primary care fields. The majority of graduates return to Louisiana to practice.

Admissions

REQUIREMENTS

Admission to the School of Medicine is limited to Louisiana residents. Requirements are 1 year each of biology, chemistry, English, organic chemistry, and physics. All science courses must include laboratory work. The MCAT is required, and scores should be from within 3 years of application. For applicants who have taken the exam more than once, the most recent set of scores is generally weighed most heavily.

SUGGESTIONS

Once prerequisites are fulfilled, prospective applicants are encouraged to pursue their own interests and to develop their own special talents in gaining a broad educational background. In making admissions decisions, a candidate's motivation as well as his/her intellectual ability and preparation are assessed. Applicants must show potential of developing into mature, sensitive physicians who will inspire and deserve trust and confidence.

PROCESS

All AMCAS applicants who are Louisiana residents are sent secondary applications. Of those returning secondaries, about 30 percent are invited to interview between September and March. Interviews are given by members of the Admissions Committee, which is composed of Medical School faculty from the basic and clinical sciences as well as physicians from the community at large. The interview is used to assess personal traits and also allows candidates to see the facilities and to meet current students. Approximately 90 percent of interviewed candidates are accepted on a rolling basis. Others are rejected or wait listed.

Admissions Requirements (Required)

MCAT scores, science GPA, non-science GPA, letters of recommendation, state residency, extracurricular activities, exposure to medical profession

Admissions Requirements (Optional)

Interview, essays/personal statement

COSTS AND AID

Tuition & Fees

In-state tuition	$9,777
Out-of-state tuition	$23,295
Fees	$830

Financial Aid

% students receiving aid	81

LOYOLA UNIVERSITY—CHICAGO
STRITCH SCHOOL OF MEDICINE

2160 SOUTH FIRST AVENUE MAYWOOD, IL 60153 • ADMISSION: 708-216-3229 • FAX: 708-216-9160
E-MAIL: SSOM-ADMISSIONS@LUMC.EDU • WEBSITE: WWW.MEDDEAN.LUMC.EDU

STUDENT BODY

Type	Private
Enrollment	559
% male/female	49/51
% minorities	22
# applied (total/out)	5,434/4,455
# accepted (total/out)	269/163
# enrolled (total/out)	146/76
Average age	23

FACULTY

Total faculty	1,442
% female	30
% minority	24
% part-time	55
Student-faculty ratio	2:1

ADMISSIONS
Average GPA and MCAT Scores

Overall GPA	3.64
MCAT Bio	10.4
MCAT Phys	9.9
MCAT Verbal	9.6
MCAT Essay	P

Application Information

Regular application	11/15
Regular notification	10/15
Are transfers accepted?	Yes
Admissions may be deferred?	Yes
Interview required?	Yes
Application fee	$70

Academics

Students follow a four-year curriculum leading to the M.D. degree. A dual degree M.D./Ph.D. program accepts up to three students each year. In this program, a doctorate degree may be earned in anatomy, biochemistry, cell biology, immunology, microbiology, molecular biology, neuroscience, pathology, pharmacology, or physiology. Evaluation of student performance uses Honors/High Pass/Pass/Fail. Students must pass USMLE Step 1 and USMLE Step 2 in order to graduate.

BASIC SCIENCES: Stritch's curriculum relies on small-group sessions and problem-based learning as much as it does on traditional lectures and labs. Students are in class or other scheduled sessions for approximately 25 hours per week, discussing behavioral science and humanistic perspectives along with basic science concepts. First-year courses are: host defense, molecular cell biology and genetics; structure of the human body; function of the human body; and Patient Centered Medicine I, a two-year continuum that begins with the medical interview and later covers the physical diagnosis, health promotion, medical ethics, healthcare finance, and legal issues in medicine. As part of the course, each student participates in special mentoring programs, participating on hospital rounds with a primary care physician and chaplain. Second-year courses are: neuroscience; mechanisms of human disease; pharmacology and therapeutics; behavioral development, and Patient Centered Medicine II. During years 2, 3, and 4, medical humanities and ethics grand rounds take place. The Stritch facility includes classrooms of many different sizes to accommodate different instructional modalities, labs, video equipment, computer laboratories, lounges, study areas, and other spaces. The Health Sciences Library houses 133,565 print serial volumes, and provides access to approximately 824 additional electronic subscriptions. Our virtual science labs are second to none and include Virtual Vince (human patient simulator), Harvey (cardiopulmmonary patient simulator), Sim-Man, Sim-Woman and Sim-Baby.

CLINICAL TRAINING

Required third-year rotations are family medicine (6 weeks); internal medicine (12 weeks); ob/gyn (6 weeks); pediatrics (6 weeks); psychiatry (6 weeks); and surgery (12 weeks). During the fourth year, requirements are neurology (4 weeks); medical humanities (1 week); subinternships (8 weeks); and 26 weeks of electives. Clinical facilities include: Hines Veterans Affairs Hospital; Loyola University Hospital and Loyola Outpatient Center; Cardinal Bernardin Cancer Center; and a variety of community hospitals. Elective credits can be earned at other academic or clinical institutions.

Students

STUDENT LIFE

At Loyola, there is a very strong indentity among each class. Class officers, including social chairs, promote numerous group activities, from small study groups to class specific events to all-school social events. In order to help promote the interaction among classes, students from all classes are assigned to one of three communities. Each student has a wardrobe locker and mailbox within the community and shared study space along with a lounge area and kitchenette. Students also get to know one another through an active student government and almost 30 registered student organizations, which include professional, academic, social, and religious-based groups. Each organization has a faculty adviser, who in turn helps the student leaders and student members to direct their own organization. During the first two years, most preclinical courses end early enough to allow time for self-directed learning and extracurricular pursuits. Many students use this time to volunteer for public clinics, homeless shelters, senior centers, hospital-based pediatrics, school and reading programs, and to present educational health-related topics at various local schools. On and off-campus events and programs also are sponsored by University Ministry. To help round out the physical well-being of the students, there is a 62,000-square-foot Health and Fitness Center adjacent to the medical school. The center features various cardio equipment, a state-of-the-art aerobic/exercise studio, free weights and variable resistance equipment, basketball and volleyball court, aquatics area, elevated running track, racquetball courts, and spa and massage services. Off-campus activities are plentiful, as Chicago is easily accessible from the medical center. All students live off-campus and most within the western suburbs of Chicago.

GRADUATES

Graduates are successful in securing residency positions nationwide in primary care and specialized fields. About 56 percent of graduates remain in the Midwest, 20 percent go to the western United States, 17 percent to the east, and 6 percent to the south.

Admissions

REQUIREMENTS

Applicants must be U.S. citizens or hold a permanent resident visa. Prerequisites are one year each of biology, chemistry, organic chemistry, and physics, all with associated labs. One semester of biochemistry may be substituted for a semester of organic chemistry. The MCAT is required and scores should be from within four years of anticipated entrance to medical school.

Students are advised to take the MCAT in the spring and repeat the exam no later than August of the year of application if their scores are not close to the national average.

SUGGESTIONS

Although state residents are given some preference, there are no positions reserved for them. Some recent coursework is important for nontraditional applicants who have been out of school for a period of time. Qualities that are sought in applicants are maturity, integrity, the ability to work with diverse populations, dedication to community service, and an awareness of the environment surrounding health care provision.

PROCESS

All applicants who meet minimum qualifications receive secondary applications. Of those returning secondaries, about 12 percent are interviewed between September and April. Interviews consist of two one-hour sessions each with a faculty member administrator or Student Committee on Admissions member. On interview day, candidates also have lunch with current medical students and tour the campus. Among interviewed candidates, about 50 percent are accepted on a rolling basis, with notification beginning in October. Wait-listed candidates, or those in a hold category, may send additional information to update their files and indicate interest in Loyola.

Admissions Requirements (Required)

MCAT scores, Science GPA, Non-science GPA, Letters of recommendation, Interview, Essays/personal statement, Extracurricular activities, Exposure to medical profession, Baccalaureate Degree

Admissions Requirements (Optional)

State residency

COSTS AND AID

Tuition & Fees

Tuition	$36,600
Room and board (on-campus)	$0
Room and board (off-campus)	$13,688
Cost of books	$3,544
Fees	$1,108

Financial Aid

% students receiving aid	95
Average grant	$10,608
Average loan	$46,567
Average debt	$169,042

MARSHALL UNIVERSITY
JOAN C. EDWARDS SCHOOL OF MEDICINE

OFFICE OF ADMISSIONS, 1600 MEDICAL CENTER DRIVE, HUNTINGTON, WV 25701 • **ADMISSION:** 800-544-8514
FAX: 304-691-1744 • **E-MAIL:** WARREN@MARSHALL.EDU • **WEBSITE:** WWW.MUSOM.MARSHALL.EDU

STUDENT BODY

Type	Public
Enrollment	227
% male/female	60/40
% minorities	17
# applied (total/out)	1,573/1,375
# accepted (total/out)	123/27
# enrolled (total/out)	64/16
Average age	25

FACULTY

Total faculty (number)	239
% female	29
% minority	16
% part-time	17
Student-faculty ratio	1:1

ADMISSIONS
Average GPA and MCAT Scores

Overall GPA	3.5
MCAT Bio	8.9
MCAT Phys	8.5
MCAT Verbal	9.1
MCAT Essay	0

Application Information

Regular application	12/1
Regular notification	10/15
Are transfers accepted?	Yes
Admissions may be deferred?	Yes
Interview required?	Yes
Application fee (resident)	$50
Application fee (nonresident)	$100

Academics

The academic curriculum is influenced by the needs of rural providers and the community's and the state's priorities. It is geared toward achieving greater retention of West Virginia trained physicians in underserved communities. Although most students complete a 4-year course of study leading to the MD degree, qualified students interested in research may concurrently pursue an MS or PhD in biomedical sciences. Evaluation of student performance uses an A–F scale. Passing Step 1 of the USMLE is required for promotion to year 3, and passing Step 2 is a graduation requirement.

BASIC SCIENCES: Basic science is taught primarily by using a lecture/lab format, although some time is spent in small-group discussions and clinical settings. Students are in scheduled sessions for about 25 hours per week. First-year courses are Gross Anatomy and Embryology, Behavioral Medicine, Biochemistry, Human Sexuality, Introduction to Patient Care, Medical Cell and Molecular Biology, Medical Ethics, Microanatomy and Ultrastructure, Neuroscience, and Physiology. Second-year courses are Community Medicine, Genetics, Introduction to Clinical Medicine, Immunology, Introduction to Patient Care, Microbiology, Pathology, Pharmacology, Physical Diagnosis, Psychopathology, and Medical Ethics. The medical education building where basic sciences are taught is self-contained, with a library and other educational resources.

CLINICAL TRAINING

Third-year students participate in required third-year clerkships. These are Medicine (8 weeks), Obstetrics/Gynecology (8 weeks), Psychiatry (8 weeks), Surgery (8 weeks), Pediatrics (8 weeks), Family Practice (8 weeks), and Clinical Orientation (1 week). During the fourth year, required rotations are Medicine (4 weeks), Surgery (4 weeks), Emergency Medicine (4 weeks), and Senior Symposium (1 week). A full 23 weeks are reserved for elective study. During the third and fourth years, a total of 2 months must be taken in a rural area. Affiliated clinical teaching sites are numerous and include Cabell Huntington Hospital (300 beds), St. Mary's Hospital (440 beds), and the Veterans Affairs Medical Center (80 beds).

Campus Life

Among entering students in a recent class, 37 percent graduated from Marshall's undergraduate college. A total of 32 other undergraduate institutions were represented in the class. Forty-eight percent majored in biology, 14 percent in chemistry, and the remainder in other disciplines. The average age of incoming students is about 25, with an age range of 20–45. About 17 percent are minorities, mostly Asians. Class size is 70.

STUDENT LIFE

The small class size at Marshall contributes to a supportive and friendly environment. Students are active in chapters of national organizations, and in groups like the Christian Medical Association, American Medical Women's Association, and the American Medical Student Association. Huntington is a small city, offering the amenities and resources that students need while providing easy access to rural areas. For more recreational and cultural opportunities, the larger cities of Pittsburgh and Cincinnati are each about a 4-hour drive away. Medical students have access to the athletic and recreational facilities of the main university and take part in university-wide events. University-administered housing options include university dormitories and units suitable for families. Off-campus housing is also affordable and readily available.

GRADUATES

Two-thirds of graduates enter primary care fields, which include family medicine, internal medicine, pediatrics, and obstetrics/gynecology. Graduates are successful in securing residencies inside and outside of West Virginia.

Admissions

REQUIREMENTS

Prerequisites are 8 semester hours each of biology, chemistry, organic chemistry, and physics. Six semester hours each of social or behavioral science and English are also required. An applicant's GPA is evaluated with consideration given to the academic institution and the rigor of courses taken. The MCAT is required and scores must be from within 3 years of matriculation. For applicants who have retaken the exam, the latest set of scores is weighed most heavily.

SUGGESTIONS

As a state school, Marshall gives preference to West Virginia residents. A number of positions in each year's class are reserved for well-qualified residents of states that border West Virginia, and for candidates with strong ties to the state. The spring, rather than fall, MCAT is recommended. In addition to the academic record, Marshall considers personal qualities such as judgment, responsibility, altruism, integrity, and sensitivity important. Strong communication skills are valued.

PROCESS

All West Virginia AMCAS applicants receive secondary applications. Almost all West Virginia residents are interviewed, while only about 4 percent of out-of-state applicants are interviewed. Interviews take place between September and February and consist of two 30-minute sessions with members of the Admissions Committee. Acceptances are issued on a rolling basis. Wait listed candidates may send information to update their files as the year progresses.

Admissions Requirements (Required)

MCAT scores, science GPA, non-science GPA, letters of recommendation, interview, extracurricular activities

Admissions Requirements (Optional)

State residency, essays/personal statement, exposure to medical profession

Overlap Schools

West Virginia University.

COSTS AND AID

Tuition & Fees

In-state tuition	$15,062
Out-of-state tuition	$39,154
Room and board (off-campus)	$15,120
Cost of books	$2,000
In-state fees	$578
Out-of-state fees	$1,530

Financial Aid

% students receiving aid	96
Average grant	$6,093
Average loan	$33,396
Average debt	$132,857

MAYO CLINIC COLLEGE OF MEDICINE
MAYO MEDICAL SCHOOL

MAYO MEDICAL SCHOOL, 200 FIRST STREET, SW, ROCHESTER, MN 55905 • ADMISSION: 507-284-3671
FAX: 507-284-2634 • E-MAIL: MEDSCHOOLADMISSIONS@MAYO.EDU • WEBSITE: WWW.MAYO.EDU/MMS

STUDENT BODY

Type	Private
Enrollment	166
% male/female	51/49
% minorities	13
# applied (total/out)	2,464/266
# accepted (total/out)	59/46
# enrolled (total/out)	42/25
Average age	26

FACULTY

Total faculty (number)	460
Student-faculty ratio	1:1

ADMISSIONS
Average GPA and MCAT Scores

Overall GPA	3.81
MCAT Bio	11.4
MCAT Phys	11.1
MCAT Verbal	10.6
MCAT Essay	Q

Application Information

Regular application	11/1
Regular notification	Rolling
Early application	8/1
Early notification	10/1
Are transfers accepted?	No
Admissions may be deferred?	Yes
Interview required?	Yes
Application fee	$85

Academics

Each year, 34 students begin a 4 year curriculum, leading to the MD degree, and six students pursue a joint MD/PhD program in connection with the Mayo Graduate School. Through this program, a PhD may be obtained in biochemistry, biomedical engineering, cell biology and genetics, immunology, molecular neuroscience, molecular pharmacology and experimental therapeutics, tumor biology, and virology and gene therapy. Two students with DDS degrees are admitted each year for training toward careers in oral and maxillofacial surgery. Students also have opportunities to obtain MD-MPH and MD-JD degrees. Educational experiences are grouped into themes, which include basic science foundations, clinical experiences, leadership, physician and society, and pharmacology and therapeutics. Evaluation of student performance in the pre-clinical years uses pass/pass with remediation/fail; evaluation in the clinical years uses honors/high pass/pass/pass with remediation/fail. Successful completion of the USMLE Step 1, Step 2 Clinical Knowledge, and Step 2 Clinical Skills Examinations are required for graduation.

BASIC SCIENCES: Prior to arriving at Mayo Medical School, all first-year students are assigned to a faculty mentor, who is selected based on student interests. During the first 3 weeks of medical school, the mentor facilitates initial clinical experiences for incoming medical students and continues to be a resource for students throughout their 4 years of training. The basic and clinical sciences are heavily integrated throughout the entire 4-year curriculum. During the first 3 weeks, students are introduced to the role of the physician as a member of a health care team. The early part of year 1 focuses on the scientific foundations of medicine, which include molecular biology, genetics, gross and microscopic anatomy, immunology, cell biology, and pathology. The clinical component of year 1 focuses on the basic history and physical examination. Early exposure to bioethics, medical jurisprudence, medical economics, complementary-integrative medicine, and diversity are provided. After completing basic principles of pharmacology and therapeutics, the second year is organized into organ system blocks: fluids, brain and nervous system, circulation, oxygenation, nutrition/digestion, immunity/blood, endocrine, and musculoskeletal system. These organ system blocks integrate normal structure, normal function, and pathophysiology. Clinical experiences in year 2 include clinical integration, a series of clinical experiences which are directly related to the didactic material being covered in each block and Advanced Doctoring, a multidisciplinary course which prepares students to conduct a comprehensive history and physical exam on real and simulated patients. Approximately 20 weeks in the first 2 years are allocated for selectives, during which students are free to shadow clinicians, pursue career exploration, participate in service learning or volunteer activities both within the community and abroad.

CLINICAL TRAINING

The third year is divided into 3-week blocks. During year 3, students generally do core clinical rotations in Surgery (6 weeks), Medicine (6 weeks), Pediatrics (6 weeks), Obstetrics /Gynecology (6 weeks), Psychiatry (3 weeks), Family Medicine (3 weeks), and Neurology (3 weeks). Students spend one quarter working with a faculty member on a basic science or clinical research project. Students have an opportunity to present their findings at local or national meetings; over 80 percent of students have at least 1 publication prior to graduation. There are two "didactic" blocks in year 3, which provide time for students to prepare for internships, prepare for the residency application process, and to revisit basic science topics likely to transform medicine during the next 30 years. Students have opportunities to pursue training at Mayo Clinic Rochester, Mayo Clinic Jacksonville, or Mayo Clinic Arizona. During the fourth year, students normally pursue clerkships in Emergency Medicine, a sub internship in medicine and/or pediatrics, and electives in medicine, pediatrics, and surgery.

Campus Life

The student body consists of about 170 students from more than 40 states. About 15 percent of a typical class are underrepresented minorities. Class size is 42.

STUDENT LIFE

The small class size facilitates cohesion among students. Mitchell Student Center, in addition to housing the Learning Resource Center, provides an area for relaxation and communal study. Students are involved in medically related organizations and societies, community-service projects, and groups organized around athletic and cultural interests. Students also play an important role in the school's administration, participating in governing committees. Rochester's population is 93,000, offering concerts, theater, museums, golf courses, and parks, among other recreational opportunities. All students live off campus.

GRADUATES

In a class of recent graduates, 43 percent entered residencies in primary care. Specialties selected by more than one student were pediatrics (14 percent) anesthesiology (7 percent), internal medicine (12 percent), family medicine (17 percent), obstetrics/gynecology (5 percent), orthopedic surgery (10 percent), emergency medicine (7 percent), neurosurgery (5 percent), and ENT (5 percent).

Admissions

REQUIREMENTS

Prerequisites are biochemistry (1 course), biology with lab (1 year), chemistry with lab (1 year), organic chemistry with lab (1 year), and physics with lab (1 year). The MCAT is required and must be no more than 3 years old.

SUGGESTIONS

Mayo is interested in undergraduate course work that demonstrates both aptitude in science and breadth of knowledge in social science and humanities. Substantial experience in community service and leadership are also very important considerations. Additionally, Mayo is committed to matriculating a diverse student body that includes students from racial and ethnic backgrounds, which are underrepresented in medicine.

PROCESS

A supplementary essay from various racial, ethnic, and socioeconomic backgrounds is required. About 20 percent of AMCAS applicants are asked to submit letters of recommendation. About 50 percent of those screened applicants are invited to an on-campus interview. The interviews are scheduled between September and March. Applicants have two interviews about 30–45 minutes with faculty, students, community members, or administrators. Of interviewed applicants, about 20 percent are accepted on a rolling basis. Others are rejected or wait listed. Additional material from wait listed candidates is not encouraged.

Admissions Requirements (Required)

MCAT scores, science GPA, non-science GPA, letters of recommendation, interview, essays/personal statement, extracurricular activities, telephone interview

Admissions Requirements (Optional)

State residency, exposure to medical profession

Overlap Schools

The University of Iowa, University of California—Irvine, University of California—Los Angeles, University of California—San Diego, University of Florida, University of Minnesota, University of Wisconsin—Madison.

COSTS AND AID

Tuition & Fees

Tuition	$27,700
Room and board (off-campus)	$16,115
Cost of books	$1,950
Fees	$2,000

Financial Aid

% students receiving aid	100
Average grant	$22,600
Average loan	$22,500
Average debt	$84,700

McGill University

Faculty of Medicine

3655 Sir William Osler Promenade, Suite 602, Montreal, QC H3G 1Y6 • **Admission:** 514-398-3517
Fax: 514-398-4631 • **E-mail:** ADMISSIONS.MED@MCGILL.CA • **Website:** WWW.MEDICINE.MCGILL.CA/ADMISSIONS

STUDENT BODY	
Type	Public
Enrollment	674
% male/female	45/55
# applied	1,179
# accepted	243
# enrolled (total/out)	176/16
Average age	22

FACULTY	
Total faculty (number)	2,377
% female	41

ADMISSIONS
Average GPA and MCAT scores

Overall GPA	3.76
MCAT Bio	12
MCAT Phys	11
MCAT Verbal	10
MCAT Essay	P

Application Information

Regular application	11/15
Regular notification	3/31
Early application	None
Early notification	1/15
Are transfers accepted?	No
Admissions may be deferred?	Yes
Interview required?	Yes
Application fee	$80

Academics

The Faculty of Medicine offers a 4-year undergraduate medical curriculum leading to an MD, CM degree. Joint programs of MD/MBA and MD/PhD are also offered. All programs are fully accredited by the LCME. The curriculum objectives correspond to the Faculty of Medicine mission and aim to equip the student to meet the most stringent standards of medical practice and professionalism to ensure career-long excellence in whole-person care. Upon completion of the program, the graduate will be able to function responsibly, in a supervised clinical setting, at the level of an "undifferentiated" physician.

The program's curriculum structure emphasizes the fundamental sciences and scientific methodology as pillars of medical knowledge. It provides traditional lectures and small-group teaching, as well as laboratory and computer teaching.

The curriculum consists of 4 components: Basis of Medicine, Introduction to Clinical Medicine, Core Clerkships, and Senior Clerkships. In addition to the medical sciences, a Physicianship Program focuses on the two roles of the physician—that of a healer and that of a professional—program are present in each component. A longitudinal Physician Apprenticeship course is part of all 4 years.

CLINICAL TRAINING

McGill medical students have access to a new, state-of-the-art Medical Simulation Centre facility to experience hands-on training in a controlled, simulated teaching environment. Teaching hospitals include the McGill University Health Centre (MUHC: Montreal General Hospital, Montreal Children's Hospital, Montreal Neurological Hospital, Royal Victoria Hospital, Montreal Chest Hospital), Sir Mortimer B. Davis Jewish General Hospital, Douglas Hospital, and Saint Mary's Hospital. Training also takes place at a number of affiliated hospitals and other clinical care centers.

Campus Life

Each entering class has about 172 students, with reservations for 9 students from the United States or other international applicants. The student body is among the most culturally diverse, and is approximately 55 percent women.

STUDENT LIFE

McGill is a large and active campus that offers social and recreational activities to a diverse student body. In addition, the city of Montreal itself is an interesting and exciting place for students to live. McGill offers three residence styles suited to your needs (including one women's residence), which are located on the main campus and are open to medical students. Information concerning apartments or flats located in the vicinity of the campus can be obtained from the Off-Campus Housing Office.

Admissions

REQUIREMENTS

The Faculty of Medicine offers a 4 year undergraduate medical curriculum. A premed (MED-P) program is available to Québec residents following an approved curriculum in the Québec Collegial system. The faculty does not accept transfers, part-time medical studies, or award advanced standing. Deferrals and leaves of absence may be granted on academic grounds. An MD/PhD program is offered for students interested in a research career in academic medicine. For students interested in both medicine and management, the faculties of medicine and management offer a five-year program leading to an MD/MBA degree. The language of instruction is English with option to submit papers and exams in French. Requirements include the following: Applicants must have received an undergraduate degree or be in the final year of a course of study at a recognized college or university leading to an undergraduate degree with at least 120 academic credits. Prerequisites include 1 year with laboratory work in each of general biology, general chemistry, and physics; and 1 semester with laboratory work in organic chemistry. The MCAT is required and applicants must have taken the exam no later than August 2004.

SUGGESTIONS

In addition to prerequisite science courses, some course work in biochemistry or molecular biology is strongly recommended. Applicants to the 4 year program should have undergraduate GPA of 3.5 or better and a total of 30 or more in the MCAT scores. In a recent entering class, the average GPA was a 3.75 and the average overall MCAT score was 31.10.

PROCESS

The deadline for receipt of applications to the regular MD/CM program is January 15 for Quebec residents and November 15 for all others. Applicants with strong academic qualifications submit an application that includes an autobiographical letter used to assess personal qualities and achievements. Selection for interview is based on grades, MCAT scores, letters of reference, and autobiographical letter. Once interviews have been completed, all the components of the application are considered in making admissions decisions. Residents of Quebec will be notified after May 1. Nonresidents will be notified as soon as possible after March 31.

Admissions Requirements (Required)

MCAT scores, science GPA, non-science GPA, letters of recommendation, interview, essay/personal statement, extracurricular activities, exposure to medical profession

Admissions Requirement (Optional)

State residency

Overlap Schools

Johns Hopkins University, Stanford University, Université Laval, University of British Columbia, University of Montreal, University of Sherbrooke, University of Toronto.

COSTS AND AID
Tuition & Fees

In-state tuition	$3,565
Out-of-state tuition	$24,846
Cost of books	$850

McMaster University

Undergraduate Medical Programme

1200 Main Street, Room: 1M7 Hamilton, ON L8N 3Z5 • Admission: 905-525-9140
Fax: 905-546-0349 • E-mail: MDADMIT@MCMASTER.CA • Website: WWW.FHS.MCMASTER.CA

STUDENT BODY

Type	Public
# applied	3,732
# accepted	193
# enrolled	138
Average age	26

ADMISSIONS

Average GPA and MCAT Scores

Overall GPA	3.8

Application Information

Regular application	10/1
Regular notification	5/31
Are transfers accepted?	No
Admissions may be deferred?	Yes
Interview required?	Yes

Academics

The 3-year program in medicine uses a problem-based approach to learning that emphasizes skills, knowledge, critical thinking, independent study, professional behavior, and lifelong learning. The components have been organized in sequential units with early exposure to patients and case management. Flexibility is ensured to allow for the variety of student backgrounds and career goals. In addition to required units, electives form an integral part of the curriculum. Full-time elective blocks, ongoing horizontal electives, and special enrichment electives are all important components of the medical education. The 3-year program (130 weeks of instruction) uses an approach to learning that will apply throughout the physician's career. Flexibility is ensured to allow for the variety of student backgrounds and career goals. The graduates of McMaster's Undergraduate Medical Programme will have developed the knowledge, ability, and attitudes necessary to qualify for further education in any medical career. The general goals for students in the program include the following: the development of competency in problem-based learning and in problem solving; the development of the personal characteristics and attitudes compatible with effective health care; the development of clinical and communication skills; and the development of the skills to be a lifelong, self-directed learner. To achieve the objectives of the Undergraduate Medical Programme, students are presented with a series of health care problems and questions requiring the understanding of principles and data collection. Much of the students' learning occurs within the setting of the small-group tutorial. Faculty members serve as tutors/facilitators or as sources of expert knowledge. The Undergraduate Medical Programme is arranged as a 4-unit preclerkship sequence followed by a clerkship; there are additional elective opportunities, both in block periods (totaling 27 weeks) and horizontal electives taken concurrently with ongoing units. Unit 1 is a 12-week introduction to concepts and information from 3 of the following knowledge perspectives: behavior, biology, and population. In addition, a major theme of the entire curriculum, the life cycle, is developed as a perspective and anchors the 3 sub units of Unit 1 including early development, maturation, and aging units 2 and 3 are 14 weeks. Unit 4 is 13-week units organized on the basis of organ systems, in which biomedical and health care problems are analyzed in depth. The clerkship emphasizes the clinical application of concepts learned in the earlier units and consists of experience in inpatient and ambulatory settings. These concepts include family medicine, internal medicine, obstetrics/gynecology, pediatrics, psychiatry, and surgery. Unit 6, which follows the clerkship, is an interactive unit in which students will tackle issues derived from societal expectations of a practicing physician.

Campus Life

Each entering class has 138 students. In a recent entering class, 130 were from Ontario, and 8 were from the rest of Canada. About one-third of the class is over 25, with an age range of 19–49.

STUDENT LIFE

The teaching methodology and general approach at McMaster fosters student interaction, which carries over outside of the classroom. Medical students take part in extracurricular activities including clubs, athletics, and community service. Off-campus housing is available.

GRADUATES

Postgraduate programs are offered at McMaster in anesthesia, community medicine, critical care, emergency medicine, family medicine, internal medicine, laboratory medicine, obstetrics/gynecology, pediatrics, psychiatry, radiology, and surgery.

Admissions

REQUIREMENTS

At the time of entrance, students must have completed a minimum of 3 years (30 full credits) of undergraduate work. Two years (20 full credits) must be above the year 1 level of courses. Only degree credit courses taken at an accredited university are considered. Applicants must have achieved an overall simple average of at least a 3.0 on a 4.0 scale in their academic work at the time of application. There are no specific prerequisite courses, and the MCAT is not required. Students granted admission must be proficient in spoken and written English. All students are required to have obtained a current certificate in Basic Cardiac Life Support prior to registration in the medical program.

SUGGESTIONS

Priority is given to residents of Ontario and then to applicants from the rest of Canada. International students may choose to apply through this applicant pool.

PROCESS

The application and transcript deadline for submission to OMSAS is October 15. Approximately 400 applicants are invited for interviews at McMaster in March or April. All applicants are notified in writing on the last day of May as to the results of their application.

Admissions Requirements (Required)

Science GPA, non-science GPA, letters of recommendation, interview, extracurricular activities

Admissions Requirements (Optional)

MCAT scores, state residency, essays/personal statement, exposure to medical profession

Overlap Schools

University of Ottawa.

COSTS AND AID

Tuition & Fees

In-state tuition $4,422

MEDICAL COLLEGE OF GEORGIA
SCHOOL OF MEDICINE

OFFICE OF ADMISSIONS, AA-2040, AUGUSTA, GA 30912 • ADMISSION: 706-721-3186
FAX: 706-721-0959 • E-MAIL: SCLMED.STDADMIN@MAIL.MCG.EDU • WEBSITE: WWW.MCG.EDU

STUDENT BODY

Type	Public
Enrollment	734
# applied (total/out)	1,917/941
# accepted (total/out)	270/6
# enrolled (total/out)	190/5

FACULTY

Total faculty (number)	612
% female	22
% minority	23
% part-time	22

ADMISSIONS
Average GPA and MCAT scores

Overall GPA	3.65
MCAT Bio	10.33
MCAT Phys	9.67
MCAT Verbal	9.92

Application Information

Regular application	11/1
Regular notification	5/1
Early application	6/1–8/1
Early notification	10/1
Are transfers accepted?	Yes
Admissions may be deferred?	Yes
Interview required?	Yes
Application fee	$0

Academics

The school emphasizes early patient contact, uses problem-based learning, and strives to educate physicians who will help meet the health care needs of Georgians. Students and applicants interested in earning both an MD and a PhD may apply to combined-degree programs arranged with the School of Graduate Studies or with departments of the University of Georgia, Georgia Institute of Technology, or Georgia State University. Areas of doctorate study include, but are not limited to, anatomy, biochemistry, biomedical engineering, biophysics, cell biology, genetics, immunology, microbiology, molecular biology, neuroscience, pharmacology, and physiology.

BASIC SCIENCES: During the 2 pre-clinical years, students acquire the building blocks of basic science that underlie medical practice and the skills required for clinical decision-making and patient interaction. The modular content of the curriculum is taught in lectures, labs with integrated clinical conferences, and small-group activities. In the first semester of year 1, the Introductory Molecular Cell Biology module provides a foundation for the basic sciences and is followed by the Cellular and Systems Structures module to introduce students to gross anatomy, histology, and development. In the second semester, biochemistry and physiology are taught in the Cellular and Systems Processes module while the Brain and Behavior module gives students an understanding of the interplay between psychiatry and neuroscience. Offered concurrently with the basic science modules, the year-long Essentials of Clinical Medicine emphasizes family, cultural, and population aspects of health care, communication skills, and information retrieval and analysis, health promotion/disease prevention, ethics, history-taking with children and adults, and a community project. The Essentials of Clinical Medicine is a 2-year sequence that emphasizes skills needed for success in the third year. In year 2, Essentials of Clinical Medicine addresses interviewing and physical examination, common medical problems, and interdisciplinary topics such as ethics, nutrition, and the impact of behavior on health while highlighting principles of patient care for each stage of life. Cellular and Systems Disease States is a year-long module running in parallel so the students are exposed to the topics of medical Microbiology, pathology, and pharmacology as the issues related to patient care throughout the stages of life. Teaching strategies, including interactive small groups, preceptor relationships, and lectures are linked to course objectives. On average, students are in scheduled activities for 26 hours per week during the first 2 years. Classes are held in the modern research and education building and the medical student resource area, which includes small group rooms with computers and Internet access. Each student is advised to purchase a computer capable of using relevant educational software. The Greenblatt Library maintains more than 1,800 current journal subscriptions and provides access to many external databases. Audiovisual learning aids are used in class and are available to the library. Grading is A–F with a C constituting a passing grade. Passing the USMLE Step 1 is a requirement for promotion to the third year.

CLINICAL TRAINING

Patient contact begins during year 1 in the Essentials Clinical Medicine course, which extends through year 2. Year 3 consists of required core clerkships: Internal Medicine (12 weeks), Surgery (8 weeks), Pediatrics (6 weeks), Family Medicine (6 weeks), Obstetrics/Gynecology (6 weeks), Psychiatry (6 weeks), and Neurology (4 weeks). Core clerkships take place at the Medical College of Georgia Hospitals and Clinics, the Children's Medical Center, various affiliated hospitals, and community-based teaching sites throughout the state. Students may rotate to affiliated community hospitals for part of the core curriculum. During year 4, students must complete 4-week rotations in critical care, emergency medicine, and an acting internship in family medicine, gynecology, medicine, pediatrics, and surgery or obstetrics. The remainder of the fourth year is for elective study, which can include both clinical and research courses. Evaluation during the clinical years is based on assessment of knowledge, clinical skills, and professional behavior, and uses an A–F scale. Passing the USMLE Step 2 is a requirement for graduation.

Campus Life

At least 95 percent of students are Georgia residents. Underrepresented minorities account for about 6 percent of the student body. About one-fourth of each class took time off after college, and there is a wide range of prior experiences within the student body. Class size is 180.

STUDENT LIFE

The campus is close to downtown Augusta, the second-largest metropolitan area in Georgia. Augusta offers a wide range of activities including museums, theater, restaurants, music, shopping, water skiing, sailing, tennis, and golf. Students are cohesive, brought together by popular on-campus housing and student groups. Students are involved in organizations focused on professional, social, athletic, and community-service activities. Many on-campus housing options are available, including residency halls, 1- or 2-bedroom apartments, and family housing.

GRADUATES

In the past, the majority of graduates have selected specialized fields. As part of their generalist initiative, the Medical College encourages students to explore primary care. The goal of the initiative is for at least half of the graduates to enter residencies in family practice, internal medicine, or pediatrics. Students may remain at the Medical College of Georgia for their postgraduate study while others enter programs elsewhere in the state and the nation.

Admissions

REQUIREMENTS

Undergraduate preparation must include biology with lab (1 year), English (1 year), inorganic chemistry with lab (1 year), organic chemistry with lab (1 semester), physics with lab (1 year), additional upper-level chemistry (1 semester). Transcripts should have grades; pass/fail courses are not advised. The MCAT is required and must be no more than 3 years old.

SUGGESTIONS

The April, rather than August, MCAT is strongly advised. For students who have taken time off after college, recent course work is recommended. Experiences that involve patient contact is valuable. In addition to academic strength and general personal qualities, the Admissions Committee looks for an individual's potential for meeting the health care needs of Georgia.

PROCESS

All Georgia residents who submit AMCAS application are sent secondary applications, while only selected out-of-state residents receive secondaries. About half of in-state residents and less than 5 percent of out of state residents are interviewed. Interviews consist of 2 sessions that are a half-hour each with faculty, administrators, or students. One interview is done by a member of the Admissions Committee and the other interview is done by a faculty member who is not a member of the Admissions Commitee. Interviews take place from October through March. Notification is rolling for regular admissions. After enough offers have been made to fill the class, an alternate list is established from which about 40–50 candidates are usually admitted.

Admissions Requirements (Required)

MCAT scores, science GPA, non-science GPA, letters of recommendation, interview, state residency, essay/personal statement, extracurricular activities, exposure to medical profession, completion of secondary application

COSTS AND AID
Tuition & Fees

In-state tuition	$12,350
Out-of-state tuition	$30,976
Cost of books	$923

MEDICAL COLLEGE OF WISCONSIN

OFFICE OF ADMISSIONS, 8701 WATERTOWN PLANK ROAD MILWAUKEE, WI 53226 • ADMISSION: 414-456-8246
FAX: 414-456-6505 • E-MAIL: WWW.MEDSCHOOL@MCW.EDU • WEBSITE: WWW.MCW.EDU

STUDENT BODY

Type	Private
Enrollment	795
% male/female	52/48
% minorities	10
# applied (total/out)	6,665/6,053
# accepted (total/out)	453/311
# enrolled (total/out)	204/119
Average age	23

FACULTY

Total faculty	1,100
Student-faculty ratio	0:1

ADMISSIONS
Average GPA and MCAT Scores

Overall GPA	3.77
MCAT Bio	10
MCAT Phys	10
MCAT Verbal	9.7
MCAT Essay	P

Application Information

Regular application	11/1
Regular notification	10/15
Early application	8/1 & 9/1
Early notification	10/1
Are transfers accepted?	Yes
Admissions may be deferred?	Yes
Interview required?	Yes
Application fee	$70

Academics

The curriculum at the Medical College of Wisconsin leading to a Doctor of Medicine degree consists of a four-year traditional program with two years of preclinical coursework followed by two years of clinical rotations. The preclinical coursework represents a combination of basic science courses plus a substantial amount of work in the Clinical Continuum which represents interactive, experiential, and clinically relevant opportunities to develop the skills and identity of a physician. The Clinical Continuum coursework is taken in both the first and second years of the curriculum. An Extended Curriculum allows students to complete their first-year coursework over a two-year period leading to graduation in five years. This program enables students to pursue research, employment or other activities that may match their interests. Medical students are encouraged to participate in summer research programs following the completion of their first-year coursework and many choose to complete a rigorous research program that leads to an additional Honors designation. Qualified students may enter a combined M.D./Ph.D. degree program through the Medical Scientists Training Program (MSTP). The Graduate School of Biomedical Sciences offers additional degrees that include Ph.D., M.S., M.A., and M.P.H., and joint-degree programs. The Graduate School offers programs in Bioethics, Biochemistry, Biophysics, Biostatistics, Cell and Developmental Biology, Epidemiology, Functional Imaging, Microbiology and Molecular Genetics, Pharmacology and Toxicology, Physiology, and Public Health. To earn the M.D. degree, students must successfully complete all of their coursework which is evaluated on a five-interval grading system. In addition, the students must successfully pass the Step 1 exam of the USMLE in order to be promoted to the fourth year of the curriculum and pass the USMLE Step 2CK in order to graduate. They must take the Step 2CS exam. They must also pass an end-of-third-year OSCE exam in order to meet graduation requirements.

BASIC SCIENCES: Basic sciences are taught during the first two years of the curriculum. The learning activities consist of a mix of traditional curriculum formats (lectures, labs, dissection, and discussion groups) and newer educational methods including computer aided instruction (CAI), problem-based learning (PBL), and independent study options. First-year courses include Biochemistry, Clinical Human Anatomy, Human Development, Cell and Tissue Biology, Integrated Medical Neurosciences, and Physiology. Second-year courses include a yearlong Pathology course, Foundations in Clinical Psychiatry, Microbiology, and Pharmacology. Support services for medical students include individual and group advising and tutorials. Educational facilities include the Medical Education Building that provides a variety of learning settings and contains two large modern auditoriums, the newly renovated Computer Aided Instruction laboratory, Multi-Use Teaching Spaces, and the recently completed state-of-the-art Standardized Teaching and Resource Center containing a center for assessment of history-taking and physical examination skills using standardized patients and simulation centers housing advanced human simulators. The Health Research Center contains an auditorium with state-of-the-art communication technology, small-group teaching spaces, teleconferencing room with satellite capabilities, and research laboratories. The MCW Libraries houses a collection of 250, 000 volumes and subscribes to print and electronic medical journals, offering a comprehensive network of electronic databases and resources.

CLINICAL TRAINING

Exposure to the clinical environment begins shortly after entering medical school during the Clinical Continuum. This two-year long course consists of Introduction to Patient Care, Medical Interviewing, Foundation of Human Behavior, Medical Information Management and the Mentor course which are all taken in the first year. In the second year, Medical Ethics and Palliative Care, Clinical Examination and Reasoning, and Health Policy are taken. Third-year rotations include Internal Medicine (2 months), Surgery (2 months), Pediatrics (2 months), Obstetrics and Gynecology (1 and 1/2 months), Psychiatry (1 month), Neurology (1/2 month), Clinical Procedures Rotation (1 month), Family Medicine (1 month), and one month of vacation, but most students choose to take an elective instead of the vacation. The fourth year consists of 4 months of required rotations that include Internal Medicine, Medically-Oriented Sub-Internship, Surgery-Oriented Sub-Internship, and an Integrated Selective. Five elective rotations may be chosen by the student, some of which may be taken as away rotations or international rotations. The Medical College of Wisconsin is the academic center of the Milwaukee Regional Medical Center campus that includes Froedtert Hospital, Children's Hospital of Wisconsin, Curative Rehabilitation Center, Milwaukee County Mental Health Complex, the Blood Center of Southeastern Wisconsin Research Institute, and the Eye Institute. MCW is affiliated with numerous hospitals and clinics in and around Milwaukee and with rural care centers in other parts of the state.

Students

MCW is the 8th largest medical school and the largest free standing medical school in the country. With grants totaling more then $125 milllion dollars, the College had 3,000 research projects in progess in 2005. As a free-standing institution, MCW attracts and enrolls students from across the country each year in its class of 204 students. Located on the Milwaukee Regional Medical Center Campus, the Medical College is able to provide all clinical clerkships and rotations at this location or in the metropolitan area.

STUDENT LIFE

Student organizations focus on professional and leadership development, community service, and recreational pursuits. The College is involved in over 30 community service activities, including a student-run clinic for the uninsured, an AIDS interventions center, and health education programs in local schools. Organized social events include parties, dinners and ongoing activities such as intramural sports. Along with the College's fitness center, these activities allow students to relax, socialize or exercise between or after class. Located in a suburb seven miles west of downtown Milwaukee, students live and go to school in a safe comfortable environment. At the same time they are also within easy access of the cultural, social and sporting events offered in the metropolitan

GRADUATES

MCW students consistently perform at or better then the national average on the USLME. This coupled with the school's reputation for providing excellent clinical training results in an excellent placement record for graduates.

Admissions
REQUIREMENTS

Eligibility requirements to apply include: Candidates must have completed or are in the process of completing 90 or more undergraduate graded credits, including the prerequisites, at an accredited college/university in the United States or Canada. The MCAT is required and must have been taken no more then three years prior to matriculation. Prerequisites include eight semester hours, two of which must be labs, in biology, inorganic chemistry, and organic chemistry, eight semester hours of physics, four of college algebra, and six of English. With the exception of organic chemistry, AP credit is accepted for prerequisites.

Admissions Requirements (Required)

MCAT scores, Science GPA, Non-science GPA, Letters of recommendation, Interview, Essays/personal statement, Extracurricular activities, Exposure to medical profession

Admissions Requirements (Optional)

State residency

COSTS AND AID
Tuition & Fees

Tuition	$34,538
Room and board (off-campus)	$7,500
Cost of books	$1,641
Fees	$45

Financial Aid

% students receiving aid	95
Average grant	$8,808
Average loan	$38,516
Average debt	$143,784

MEDICAL UNIVERSITY OF SOUTH CAROLINA
COLLEGE OF MEDICINE

96 JONATHAN LUCAS STREET, SUITE 601, MSC 617 CHARLESTON, SC 29425 • ADMISSION: 843-792-2055
FAX: 843-792-4262 • E-MAIL: TAYLORWL@MUSC.EDU • WEBSITE: WWW.MUSC.EDU/COM1/MED_STU_EDU/MEDSTUEDU.HTM

STUDENT BODY

Type	Public
Enrollment	584
% male/female	55/45
% minorities	14
# applied (total/out)	1,746/1,324
# accepted (total/out)	179/5
# enrolled (total/out)	135/2
Average age	26

FACULTY

Total faculty	612
% female	32
% minority	13
Student-faculty ratio	2:1

ADMISSIONS
Average GPA and MCAT Scores

Overall GPA	3.6
MCAT Bio	9.4
MCAT Phys	9.8
MCAT Verbal	9.8
MCAT Essay	Q

Application Information

Regular application	12/1
Regular notification	Rolling
Early application	6/1–8/1
Early notification	10/1
Are transfers accepted?	Yes
Admissions may be deferred?	Yes
Interview required?	Yes
Application fee	$55

Academics

The goal of the College of Medicine is to produce caring and competent physicians capable of succeeding in their postgraduate career. The four-year program, which leads to an M.D. degree, is divided into two years of preclinical instruction which consists of education in the basic sciences and an introduction into clinical medicine, followed by years of clinical science education. The curriculum during the first two years addresses four major objectives: provision of basic science concepts, acquisition of problem-solving strategies, development of skills which permit the performance of an adequate history and physical examination, and an introduction to the role of the physician in society. Throughout, emphasis is placed on small group instruction. The curriculum was changed in fall, 1999, to expand and improve opportunities for independent, self-directed learning. As a result, students are being exposed earlier to clinical skills.

CLINICAL TRAINING

The junior year consists of eight clinical core clerkships. The clinical core consists of eight weeks each of internal medicine, obstetrics/gynecology, pediatrics, and surgery, as well as four weeks each of family medicine, psychiatry, Dean's Rural Primary Care, and neurology. During the clerkships, emphasis is placed on the development of clinical, interpersonal, and professional competence. In addition, students participate in the Foundations in Clinical Medicine course. This course is designed to integrate basic and clinical sciences utilizing small group discussions and patient case scenarios. During the senior year, students take a minimum of eight four-week rotations. The student is required to take a clinical externship and one month each of surgery, psychiatry, and internal medicine. The remaining four blocks are elective and, depending upon previous academic performance, can be taken at approved sites throughout the state or country. A complete listing of elective courses may be found in the Catalog of Electives at www.musc.edu/comelectives/index.html. In addition, students are required to complete and satisfactorily pass the Clinical Practice Exam (CPX).

Students

Over 95 percent of students are South Carolina residents. About 15 percent are under-represented minorities, most of whom are African American. The average age of incoming students is typically around 25, and usually at least 10 percent of entering classes are over 30 years old. Class size is 135.

STUDENT LIFE

During orientation, incoming students are assigned to groups composed of first- and second-year students and a faculty member. The groups serve as informational resources for both academic and nonacademic matters. Also during the first week of school, the Activities Fair is held and introduces various student activities, groups, and events. Organizations that are popular with medical students include chapters of national medical fraternities, professionally oriented interest groups, and groups focused on health care-related community service. Intramural sports are also popular. The Harper Student Center (HSC) houses student service offices, a student lounge, and a comprehensive fitness center with indoor and outdoor tracks, rooftop tennis courts, and a swimming pool, among other features. HSC is also a gathering site for students, offering happy hours and other social events. Beyond the campus, Charleston is a city known for its beauty and charm. Students enjoy the nearby beaches and other outdoor attractions. All students live off campus.

GRADUATES

Graduates are successful in securing residencies in all medical fields, with a significant number entering Family Medicine. MUSC itself offers over 20 post-graduate training programs. More than 95 percent pass USMLE Step 2.

Admissions

REQUIREMENTS

No prerequisites are specified. An applicant's GPA is evaluated with consideration given to the undergraduate institution attended and the difficulty of the course load. The MCAT is required, and scores must be from within the past five years. For applicants who have taken the exam on multiple occasions, the best set of scores is used.

SUGGESTIONS

South Carolina residents are given strong preference. The MCAT requirement suggests that applicants should have a basic science background. However, breadth of course-work, including courses in the Humanities and Social Sciences, is also valued. Since the best set of MCAT scores is used, withholding scores has no advantage. Extracurricular activities, specifically those that are medically, community-service, or research-related are important. During the interview, noncognitive traits such as emotional stability, integrity, honesty, and enthusiasm are evaluated.

PROCESS

All applicants are asked to submit secondary applications. Of those returning secondaries, about 65 percent of state residents, and 3 percent of out-of-state residents are interviewed if they are academically qualified. Interviews are conducted from September through March, and consist of three sessions each with a faculty member or MUSC alumni. About one-third of interviewees are accepted on a rolling basis. Others are rejected or wait-listed.

Admissions Requirements (Required)

MCAT scores, Science GPA, Non-science GPA, Letters of recommendation, Interview, Essays/personal statement, Extracurricular activities, Exposure to medical profession, Preference is given to SC residents

Admissions Requirements (Optional)

State residency

Overlap Schools

Duke University, Emory University, University of South Carolina.

COSTS AND AID
Tuition & Fees

In-state Tuition	$6,654
Out-of-state Tuition	$21,380
Room and board (off-campus)	$9,830
Cost of books	$3,890
In-state Fees	$16,137
Out-of-state Fees	$41,067

Financial Aid

% students receiving aid	81
Average grant	$2,000
Average loan	$25,865
Average debt	$92,883

MEHARRY MEDICAL COLLEGE
SCHOOL OF MEDICINE

1005 DR. D.B. TODD JR. BOULEVARD NASHVILLE, TN 37208-3599 • ADMISSION: 615-327-6223
FAX: 615-327-6228 • E-MAIL: ADMISSIONS@MMC.EDU • WEBSITE: WWW.MMC.EDU

STUDENT BODY

Type	Private
Enrollment	380
% male/female	44/56
% minorities	65
# applied (total/out)	4,500/3,595
# accepted (total/out)	189/165
# enrolled (total/out)	96/82
Average age	26

FACULTY

Total faculty	184
% female	0
% minority	0
% part-time	0
Student-faculty ratio	2:1

ADMISSIONS
Application Information

Regular application	12/15
Regular notification	10/15
Early application	6/1–8/1
Early notification	10/1
Are transfers accepted?	Yes
Admissions may be deferred?	Yes
Interview required?	Yes
Application fee	$60

Academics

Meharry benefits from its proximity to Fisk University and Tennessee State University. The three schools share certain facilities and together provide an active academic community. Most medical students at Meharry complete their studies in four years, although some extend their first year over a longer period of time and complete medical training in five years. A combined M.D./Ph.D. program is offered in Biochemistry, Biomedical Science, Microbiology, Pharmacology, and Physiology. Grades are A, B, C, and F. All medical students must pass Step 1 of the USMLE in order to be promoted to year three, and Step 2 in order to graduate.

BASIC SCIENCES: First-year courses are Anatomy, Biochemistry, Physiology, and Introduction to Clinical Medicine I. Students are in class or other scheduled sessions for 20-25 hours per week. Most instruction uses a lecture format, supplemented by labs and small-group discussions. Second-year courses are Microbiology, General and Clinical Pathology, Behavioral Sciences, Genetics, Pharmacology, and Introduction to Clinical Medicine II. During the second year, students are in class for about 30 hours per week, a significant proportion of which is devoted to small-group discussions. The Teaching and Learning Resource Center is located in the Student Center, serves as a comprehensive academic support unit, and provides tutoring and board review, among other services. The Library, holding over 50,000 volumes and 1,000 journals, is located in the same complex.

CLINICAL TRAINING

Third-year required rotations are Medicine (12 weeks); Surgery (12 weeks); Pediatrics (8 weeks); Ob/Gyn (8 weeks); Family and Preventive Medicine (8 weeks); and Psychiatry (4 weeks). Fourth-year subinternships are Medicine (4 weeks); Surgery (4 weeks); Family and Preventive Medicine (4 weeks); Radiology (4 weeks); and Psychiatry (4 weeks). Twelve weeks are reserved for electives. Major teaching hospitals are Metropolitan Nashville General Hospital, Alvin C. York Veterans Administration Medical Center, and Blanchefield Army Community Hospital. Other affiliated health care institutions are Centennial Medical Center, Vanderbilt Medical Center, Middle Tennessee Mental Health Hospital, and numerous clinics and health centers throughout the state. All students complete an ambulatory rotation in an underserved area.

Students

About 70 percent of students are African American. Students come from around the country, with about 20 percent of students from Tennessee. Class size is 80.

STUDENT LIFE

Students are supportive and cooperative, usually opting to study together in groups. There are a large number of student organizations, including honor societies, medical fraternities, support groups such as the Meharry Wives Club, groups focused on professional interests, such as the Family Practice Club, and societies focused on a common religion or ethnicity. The Daniel T. Rolfe Student Center accommodates student activities and organizations and provides a focal point for extracurricular life. Many students are involved in community activities, such as serving as mentors for high school students. Medical students interact with other Meharry students and also with peers at nearby universities. Nashville offers restaurants, nightlife, outdoor activities, and a generally student-friendly atmosphere. On-campus housing options are residence halls and apartment complexes with both one- and two-bedroom units.

GRADUATES

The College of Medicine has graduated more than 5,000 African American physicians, almost half of the total number of African American physicians who studied and who practice in the United States. About three-quarters of graduates go on to work in medically underserved rural and inner-city areas. Some graduates enter residency programs at Meharry, which has a total of 30 post-graduate positions in Family Practice, Internal Medicine, Occupational Medicine, Preventive Medicine, and Psychiatry.

Admissions

REQUIREMENTS

Required coursework is eight semesters hours each of Biology, General Chemistry, Organic Chemistry, and Physics, all with associated labs. Six semester hours of English are also required. The MCAT is required, and scores should be from within the past three years. The April, rather than August, MCAT is strongly advised. For applicants who have taken the exam on multiple occasions, all sets of scores are considered.

SUGGESTIONS

Special consideration is given to underrepresented minority students and students from disadvantaged backgrounds. Meharry is interested in applicants who are dedicated to improving health care for the underserved. In addition to academic credentials, medically related or community service activities are viewed as important.

PROCESS

All qualified AMCAS applicants are sent secondary applications. Of those returning secondaries, about 10 percent are interviewed between September and May. Interviews consist of two sessions, each with a faculty member, administrator, or current medical student. On interview day, applicants also have the opportunity to meet informally with students. About one-third of interviewed candidates are accepted on a rolling basis. Others are rejected or placed on a wait-list. Wait-listed candidates may send additional information if it serves to update their files.

Admissions Requirements (Required)

MCAT scores, Science GPA, Non-science GPA, Letters of recommendation, Interview, Essays/personal statement, Extracurricular activities, Exposure to medical profession

Admissions Requirements (Optional)

State residency

COSTS AND AID

Tuition & Fees

Tuition	$27,957
Room and board (on-campus)	$11,813
Cost of books	$1,185
Fees	$1,435

Financial Aid

% students receiving aid	79
Average grant	$1,000
Average loan	$28,893
Average debt	$125,339

MEMORIAL UNIVERSITY NEWFOUNDLAND
FACULTY OF MEDICINE

ROOM 1751, HEALTH SCIENCES CENTER, ST. JOHN'S, NF A1B 3V6 • **ADMISSION:** 709-777-6615
FAX: 709-777-8422 • **E-MAIL:** MUNMED@MUN.CA • **WEBSITE:** WWW.MED.MUN.CA/ADMISSIONS

STUDENT BODY

Type	Public
Enrollment	244
% male/female	48/52
# applied	648
# accepted	77
# enrolled	60

FACULTY

Total faculty (number)	186
% female	31
% part-time	60

ADMISSIONS
Average GPA and MCAT Scores

Overall GPA	3.7
MCAT Bio	9.0
MCAT Phys	9.0
MCAT Verbal	9.0
MCAT Essay	0

Application Information

Regular application	11/15
Regular notification	3/1
Are transfers accepted?	No
Admissions may be deferred?	Yes
Interview required?	Yes
Application fee	$75

Academics

Each of the first 2 years is organized into 3 terms. Although the emphasis of the course work is on basic science, clinical medicine is also introduced. During the second 2 years, students perform clerkships in affiliated hospitals that provide both undergraduate and graduate medical education. In addition to the 4-year MD, MS, and PhD degree programs are also open to qualified students. Areas of academic strength include cardiovascular sciences including epidemiology, community medicine, endocrinology and metabolism, gastroenterology, human genetics, immunology, molecular biology, and neurosciences.

BASIC SCIENCES: An important component of the first year is basic science of medicine. This course introduces students to the biology of the normal human and integrates anatomy, biochemistry, physiology, immunology, cell biology, genetics, microbiology, nutrition, pharmacology, pathology. Teaching methods include lectures, small group sessions, laboratories, seminars, and open discussions. Students have the opportunity to initiate basic science research, which can be pursued throughout medical school. First-year students also take integrated study of disease, which teaches pathology and Pharmacology through the study of diseases of the major organ systems. In Clinical Skills, students are first introduced to the medical interview and techniques of counseling. The physical exam and important ethical issues are also part of the course. Community Medicine is a unique course, which focuses on the contextual aspects of disease and introduces behavioral sciences, biostatistics, community nutrition, environmental and occupational health, epidemiology, preventive medicine, and social and organizational factors in health. The course includes visits to community-based hospitals and clinics. All courses continue in the second year, building on principles learned during the first year. On average, pre-clinical students are in class or other scheduled sessions for 23 hours per week.

CLINICAL TRAINING

Year 3 is a 12-month duration beginning in September and continuing to the following fall. It is composed of the core clerkships and some electives. Core clerkships, typically 8 weeks in length, are Internal Medicine, Obstetrics/Gynecology, Psychiatry, Pediatrics, and Surgery. A 4-week rural family medicine rotation is also required. The fourth year consists of electives and selectives, some of which may be completed at institutions other than those affiliated with the university. Teaching hospitals include General Hospital (531 beds), Grace General Hospital, Dr. Charles A Janeway Child Health Centre, St. Clare's Mercy Hospital, Waterford Hospital, and a number of institutions that are not under the Health Care Corporation of St. Johns.

Campus Life

The school's class size is relatively small at 60 students. The male/female ratio within the student body is about 50/50.

STUDENT LIFE

On-campus housing is available for both single and married students. In addition, the university provides assistance in locating off-campus housing. Medical students benefit from an active Counseling Center, child care services, learning enhancement programs, a Career Planning Office, and a Student Health Service. The Student's Union promotes artistic, educational, charitable, and social activities, and the graduate student union provides common areas for social and other activities. Medical students have access to the services and resources of the greater university.

GRADUATES

A significant proportion of graduates enter residencies at affiliated hospitals in areas such as anesthesia, internal medicine, neurology, obstetrics/gynecology, orthopedics, anatomic pathology, general pathology, pediatrics, psychiatry, radiology, and surgery. Most graduates enter clinical medicine, often in primary care fields.

Admissions

REQUIREMENTS

To be eligible for admission, a bachelor's degree is required in almost all circumstances. Requirements include 2 courses in English. The MCAT is also required, and must be taken prior to the application deadline, which is normally November 15. Transcripts and letters of reference must be submitted by November 29. Interviews are required of some candidates. The majority of places in each class are reserved for applicants who are residents of Newfoundland and Labrador. There are a limited number of places available for applicants from New Brunswick, from other Canadian provinces, and non-Canadians. Non-Canadians pay higher fees.

SUGGESTIONS

There are approximately 650 applications received for 60 places each year. Therefore, competition is high. Material submitted after the stated deadlines will not be considered. Academic achievement, MCAT scores, work or other experiences, and personal traits are all reviewed in admissions decisions. Though age itself is not used as a basis for selection, time away from academic studies may be taken into consideration.

PROCESS

Requests for applications should be directed to the address above. Applications are accepted until November 15 in the year preceding anticipated matriculation. Decisions are made in the spring. Notification of the committee's decision will be made to candidates by letter from the Admissions Committee. Applicants have 14 days in which to confirm acceptance.

Admissions Requirements (Required)

MCAT scores, letters of recommendation, interview, essays/personal statement, extracurricular activities

Admissions Requirements (Optional)

Science GPA, non-science GPA, state residency, exposure to medical profession

COSTS AND AID

Tuition & Fees

In-state tuition	$6,250
Out-of-state tuition	$30,000
Room and board (off-campus)	$9,000
Cost of books	$1,593
In-state fees	$457
Out-of-state fees	$645

Financial Aid

% students receiving aid	90
Average grant	$800
Average debt	$150,000

MERCER UNIVERSITY
SCHOOL OF MEDICINE

1550 COLLEGE STREET, MACON, GA 31207 • ADMISSION: 478-301-2542
FAX: 478-301-2547 • E-MAIL: FAUST_EK@MERCER.EDU • WEBSITE: HTTP://MEDICINE.MERCER.EDU

STUDENT BODY	
Type	Private
Enrollment	221
% male/female	54/46
% minorities	4
# applied	738
# enrolled (total)	60
Average age	23

ADMISSIONS	
Average GPA and MCAT scores	
Overall GPA	3.61
MCAT Bio	9.27
MCAT Phys	8.33
MCAT Verbal	9.18
MCAT Essay	N

Application Information	
Regular application	11/1
Regular notification	Rolling
Early application	6/1–8/1
Early notification	10/1
Are transfers accepted?	Yes
Admissions may be deferred?	Yes
Interview required?	Yes
Application fee	$50

Academics

Each entering student is assigned to a faculty advisor who assists with the transition to medical school, with strategies for pre-clinical studies, and later with decisions involved in elective and specialty selection. Almost all students complete the MD curriculum in 4 years. Evaluation uses satisfactory/unsatisfactory during the first 2 years, and honors/satisfactory/unsatisfactory during the third and fourth years. Self and peer evaluations are also used in some situations. Passing both steps of the USMLE is a requirement for graduation.

BASIC SCIENCES: Basic sciences are presented during the first 2 years as part of the Biomedical Problems Program, which uses case-based instructional techniques and computer-assisted, self-directed study. The curriculum is organized around physiological systems or "phases," which are biology of reproduction, brain and behavior, cardiology, cells and metabolism, gastrointestinal, genetics and development, hematology, host defense, infectious disease, musculoskeletal, neurology, pulmonology, and renal endocrinology. Issues related to medical ethics are also discussed in the context of case studies. Community science is another important part of the first 2 years. Courses included in this category are Clinical Biostatistics, Community Epidemiology, Managed Care and Physician Workforce, Rural Preceptorship, and Research Design and the Medical Literature. Clinical training begins during the first year, when students learn interviewing and examination skills by working with simulated patients. Actual patient contact occurs through the Community Office Practice Program (COPP) in which students work directly with community physicians. Most basic science instruction takes place in the Medical Education Building, which, in addition to classrooms, houses the Medical Library; Mercer Health Systems, which provides clinical services; the Health Education Center; and the school's administrative offices. This physical arrangement, with basic science and clinical facilities in the same building, guarantees first- and second-year students an integrated educational experience. The library has over 90,000 volumes, 2,500 audiovisuals, and 850 current subscriptions. The Learning Resource Center offers computers and labs.

CLINICAL TRAINING

Third-year required rotations are Internal Medicine (12 weeks), Surgery (8 weeks), Pediatrics (8 weeks), Obstetrics/Gynecology (6 weeks), Family Medicine (8 weeks), and Psychiatry (6 weeks). During the fourth year, students choose among fields within surgical subspecialities (4 weeks). They also complete clerkships in community science (4 weeks), substance abuse (2 weeks), and critical care (2 weeks). The remainder of the year is reserved for elective study. The primary teaching hospitals are the Medical Center of Central Georgia in Macon (503 beds) and the Memorial Health University Medical Center in Savannah (503 beds). Other major affiliates are Floyd Medical Center in Rome, Phoebe Putney Memorial Hospital in Albany, and the Medical Center in Columbus. Training also takes place outside of major hospitals, at sites such as community hospitals, clinics, and physicians' offices throughout the state.

Campus Life

All students are Georgia residents. About 4 percent are underrepresented minorities. The average age of incoming students is around 24, and at least 20 percent of a typical entering class took significant time off between college and medical school.

STUDENT LIFE

Medical students have access to the facilities of the greater university. These include cafeterias, athletic facilities, and recreational centers. Medical students also have their own student center, which has a snack bar and functions as a meeting place. Students may join chapters of national medical student organizations, including those that focus on the needs of women and minority medical students. Affordable accommodations are also available in and around Macon. The Office of Admissions and Student Affairs helps students find suitable housing.

GRADUATES

Most graduates enter residency programs in Georgia and go on to practice in primary care fields within the state.

Admissions

REQUIREMENTS

Only residents of Georgia are accepted. Required course work is 1 year each of biology, physics, chemistry, organic chemistry, and biochemistry. The MCAT is required and scores must be no more than 2 years old.

SUGGESTIONS

In addition to required preparatory courses, biochemistry is recommended. The April MCAT is strongly advised, as files are not reviewed until MCAT scores are available. The Admissions Committee is interested in students who are strongly motivated to work with underserved populations and in rural areas. For applicants who have taken time off after college, some recent course work is important.

PROCESS

Secondary applications are sent to AMCAS applicants who meet minimum requirements. Typically, about 70 percent of Georgia residents who apply receive secondary applications. Of those returning secondaries, about 20 percent are invited to interview. Interviews take place between October and March, and consist of two sessions with faculty. About one-third of interviewees are accepted. All decisions are made before March 15, at which point a wait list is formed.

Admissions Requirements (Required)

MCAT scores, science GPA, non-science GPA, letters of recommendation, interview, state residency, essay/personal statement, extracurricular activities, exposure to medical profession, practice vision statement

COSTS AND AID
Tuition & Fees

Tuition	$34,932
Room and board (off-campus)	$13,190
Cost of books	$2,900
Fees	$200

Financial Aid

% students receiving aid	94
Average grant	$5,734
Average loan	$27,619
Average debt	$147,265

MICHIGAN STATE UNIVERSITY
COLLEGE OF HUMAN MEDICINE

A-239 Life Sciences East, Lansing, MI 48824 • **Admission:** 517-353-9620
Fax: 517-432-0021 • **E-mail:** MDadmissions@msu.edu • **Website:** MDadmissions.msu.edu

STUDENT BODY

Type	Public
Enrollment	459
% male/female	44/56
% minorities	34
# applied (total/out)	3,941/2,926
# accepted (total/out)	192/48
# enrolled (total/out)	106/19
Average age	25

FACULTY

Total faculty (number)	625
% part-time	3

ADMISSIONS
Average GPA and MCAT scores

Overall GPA	3.51
MCAT Bio	9.8
MCAT Phys	9.2
MCAT Verbal	9.1
MCAT Essay	0

Application Information

Regular application	11/15
Regular notification	Rolling
Early application	8/1
Early notification	10/1
Are transfers accepted?	Yes
Admissions may be deferred?	Yes
Interview required?	Yes
Application fee	$60

Academics

The 4-year curriculum is modern and highly innovative. All students begin study at MSU on the East Lansing campus. Fifty students move to Grand Rapids for years 2, 3, and 4. The remainder complete year 2 in East Lansing before moving to a clinical community campus for years 3 and 4. The community locations are in Flint, Kalamazoo, Lansing, Marquette, and Saginaw. Special clinical programs include the Rural Physician Program and Leadership in Medicine for the Underserved. Along its focus on primary care, the College of Human Medicine welcomes students seeking a dual degree. Fields in which graduate degrees may be earned include the following: biochemistry/molecular biology, bioethics/humanities/society, epidemiology, health communication, microbiology/molecular genetics, pharmacology/toxicology, and physiology. Medical students are evaluated with a modified pass/no pass system.

BASIC SCIENCES: In addition to mastering basic science concepts, first-year students address the doctor/patient relationship in Clinical Skills. A unique mentor program assigns small groups of students to a preceptor, allowing the groups to explore patient care and the complex roles of the physician. Students accompany their mentor for hospital rounds and patient visits. The course Integrative Clinical Correlations, taught by basic science faculty members and clinicians, develops problem-solving skills and allows students to apply basic science concepts to clinical case studies. Other first-year courses are the following: Biochemistry, Biostatistics and Epidemiology, Cell Biology and Physiology, Clinical Skills, Gross Anatomy, Human Development and Behavior in Society, Neuroscience, Molecular Biology and Genetics, Microbiology and Immunology, Pathology, Pharmacology, and Radiology. The second year is organized around body systems and general disease categories. These are the following: cardiovascular, digestive, disorders of development and behavior, hematopoietic/neoplasia, infectious diseases, major mental disorders, metabolic endocrine reproductive, neurological/musculoskeletal, pulmonary, urinary tract. In the social context of clinical decisions, students take part in a series of small-group seminars dealing with the concepts of medical ethics; epidemiology; biostatistics; critical reasoning; humanities; and social, economic, and organizational issues in medicine. The primary mode of instruction during the second year is small-group discussions/tutorials. Students are in scheduled sessions for fewer than 20 hours per week, allowing ample time for individual and group study. Academic facilities include the Echt Computer Lab, which offers computer-based instructional programs and audiovisual aids, a 24 hour exclusive and comprehensive Student Learning Center, and MSU's main library.

CLINICAL TRAINING

Most clerkship requirements are fulfilled during the third year and the early part of year 4. Students move to one of six communities during the summer of their third year. They then rotate through 8 weeks of each of the following: Family Practice, Internal Medicine, Obstetrics/Gynecology, Pediatrics, Psychiatry, and Surgery. Four weeks of advanced medicine and advanced surgery are also required. Throughout the period in which students complete required clerkships, students also participate in a core competency seminar, which requires 2 hours per week and provides a forum for discussion of interdisciplinary topics important to the care and health management of patients. A total of 20 weeks are reserved for elective experiences. Students may rotate to other communities in the state, to hospitals and academic centers in other states, and to clinical sites overseas.

Campus Life

At least 80 percent of students are Michigan residents. Class size is 156. In a recent class, the average age of incoming students was 25.

STUDENT LIFE

Pre-clinical students enjoy the activities, facilities, resources, and social life of a Big Ten university. Medical students are also involved in the greater community, volunteering at clinics and as health educators in schools. Professionally focused and special-interest organizations are numerous, as are athletic opportunities such as intramural sports. A variety of campus-owned housing options are available. Some single students live in a graduate/professional student residence hall. Apartments of all sizes are also available, accommodating single and married students, and students with larger families. Students are assigned to a clinical community. Students may note a preferred community and those with special needs are given priority.

GRADUATES

Students typically score above the national average on the USMLE, contributing to their success in securing top-choice residency positions. A recent 3 year average of residency choices are in the following: family practice (27 percent), internal medicine (15 percent), surgery (13 percent), pediatrics (15 percent), obstetrics/gynecology (10 percent), psychiatry (3 percent), and other programs (17 percent). About 50 percent of graduates remained in Michigan for residency programs.

Admissions

REQUIREMENTS

Students are required to complete a baccalaureate degree at an accredited undergraduate institution in the U.S. or Canada. Prerequisites are one year of biology, chemistry, organic chemistry, and physics, all with associated labs. One year in English and social science, one upper-level biology course, and college algebra or statistics and probability are also required. The MCAT is required, and scores must be no more than 4 years old. For applicants who have retaken the exam, the most recent set of scores is used. Applicants should be United States or Canadian citizens, hold a permanent resident visa, or have asylum in the United States.

SUGGESTIONS

Though Michigan residents are given preference, about 20 percent of the positions in an entering class are available to highly qualified nonresident applicants. With a strong history on training primary-care and community-oriented physicians, MSU seeks to train physicians of all specialties who may address an unmet need for medical care in underserved areas or with underserved populations. Applicants should have medical/clinical experience. Important personal traits are excellent interpersonal communication skills, leadership, social responsibility, and compassion.

PROCESS

All applicants have an opportunity to complete a secondary application. Of those returning secondaries, about one-third are interviewed. Interviews are conducted on Thursdays and Fridays, from September through March. Interviews consist of 2 sessions, one with a faculty member and one with a current medical student. On interview day, candidates attend informational sessions and have lunch with medical students. About one-third of interviewees are accepted on a rolling basis.

Admissions Requirements (Required)

MCAT scores; science GPA; non-science GPA; letters of recommendation; interview; essay/personal statement; extracurricular activities; exposure to medical profession; U.S. resident, U.S. permanent resident visa, or Canadian

Admissions Requirement (Optional)

State residency

Overlap Schools

University of Michigan, Wayne State University.

COSTS AND AID

Tuition & Fees

In-state tuition	$23,802
Out-of-state tuition	$53,802
Room and board	$12,168
Cost of books	$3,400
Fees	$1,742

Financial Aid

% students receiving aid	93
Average grant	$3,500
Average loan	$26,000
Average debt	$130,000

MOREHOUSE COLLEGE
SCHOOL OF MEDICINE

ADMISSIONS AND STUDENT AFFAIRS, 720 WESTVIEW DRIVE, SOUTHWEST, ATLANTA, GA 30310
ADMISSION: 404-752-1650 • FAX: 404-752-1512 • E-MAIL: SROAF@MSM.EDU • WEBSITE: WWW.MSM.EDU

STUDENT BODY

Type	Private
Enrollment	210
% male/female	40/60
% minorities	86
# applied (total/out)	2,973/2,579
# accepted (total/out)	143/80
# enrolled (total/out)	53/20
Average age	24

FACULTY

Total faculty (number)	260
% female	43
% minority	85
% part-time	14
Student-faculty ratio	1:1

ADMISSIONS
Application Information

Regular application	12/1
Regular notification	11/1
Early application	6/1–8/1
Early notification	10/1
Are transfers accepted?	Yes
Admissions may be deferred?	Yes
Interview required?	Yes
Application fee	$50

Academics

Most students follow a 4-year curriculum leading to a MD, although some pursue joint-degree programs of MD/MPH or MD/PhD. To be considered for these programs, applications must be submitted to the appropriate graduate department at the time of application to medical school. Medical students are evaluated on an A–F scale. Passing the USMLE Step 1 is a requirement for promotion to year 3, and passing Step 2 is a requirement for graduation.

BASIC SCIENCES: Instruction uses a lecture/lab format, and students are in class or laboratories for about 30 hours per week. First-year courses are Fundamentals of Medicine I, Human Morphology, Medical Biochemistry, Community Health, Medical Physiology, Neurobiology, and a weekly preceptorship with a community physician. Second-year courses are Fundamentals of Medicine II, Pathology, Pathophysiology, Microbiology and Immunology, Nutrition, and Pharmacology. During the second year, students learn patient interview and examination techniques. Instruction takes place in the Basic Medical Sciences Building, which contains classrooms, laboratories, and administrative offices in the adjacent Medical Education Building.

CLINICAL TRAINING

Third- and fourth-year required clerkships are Psychiatry (7 weeks), Internal Medicine (2 months), Pediatrics (2 months), Obstetrics/Gynecology (2 months), Surgery (2 months), Family Medicine (1 month), Ambulatory Medicine (1 month and a year-long Fundamentals of Medicine III series), Maternal Child Health (1 month), and Rural Primary Care (1 month). Five months are reserved for electives. Third-year rotations take place primarily at Grady Memorial Hospital (1,000 beds), a full-service facility for indigent patients that, for training purposes, is shared with Emory University. A portion of elective credit may be earned at accredited medical schools other than Morehouse and at a wide range of clinical institutions.

Campus Life

Approximately 67 percent of students are African American. About 51 percent of students are from Georgia, while others are from a wide geographic area. Class size is 52.

STUDENT LIFE

Community service is an important part of student life, and virtually all students are involved in some sort of volunteer activity while in medical school. Students are cohesive both in and out of the classroom. A demonstration of cooperation between students is the large percentage of students who are in study groups. Students participate in local chapters of national medical school organizations and in student groups focused on professional interests. Atlanta is the cultural, financial, and industrial hub of the Southeastern United States and offers a wide range of activities and attractions including arts, sports, recreation, dining, and entertainment. The city is accessible by public transportation. Although there is no school-owned housing, students are able to locate affordable housing off campus.

GRADUATES

Graduates are successful in securing residencies in prestigious programs nationwide. Approximately 75 percent of graduates enter primary care fields, one of the highest percentages among medical schools. Most go on to work with underserved populations, either in inner cities or in rural areas.

Admissions

REQUIREMENTS

Prerequisites are biology (1 year), general chemistry (1 year), organic chemistry (1 year), physics (1 year), college-level math (1 year), and English (1 year). All science courses must include associated labs. Grades are assessed with consideration given to academic improvement, balance and depth of academic program, difficulty of courses taken, and overall achievement. The MCAT is required, and scores must be from within the past 2 years. Applicants who have taken the exam on multiple occasions are not penalized, but the most recent set of scores is weighed most heavily.

SUGGESTIONS

Of the 52 spots in a class, at least 20 are reserved for Georgia residents. Thus, competition for out-of-state residents can be intense. For all applicants, the April, rather than August, MCAT is advised. Beyond academic achievement, the committee is interested in extracurricular activities, research projects and experiences, and evidence of pursuing interests and talents in depth. Compassion, honesty, motivation, and perseverance are qualities that are considered important to the practice of medicine.

PROCESS

About 80 percent of AMCAS applicants are sent secondary applications. Of those returning secondaries, about 8 percent are invited to interview between October and March. Of Georgia residents, about 25 percent are invited to interview. Interviews generally consist of one 30-minute session with a faculty member. On interview day, candidates receive a campus tour, group orientation sessions, lunch, and the opportunity to meet with current medical students. About 10–20 percent of interviewees are accepted, with notification beginning in December. Wait listed candidates may send supplementary material to update or strengthen their files.

Admissions Requirements (Required)

MCAT scores, science GPA, non-science GPA, letters of recommendation, interview, essay/personal statement, extracurricular activities, exposure to medical profession

Admissions Requirement (Optional)

State residency

COSTS AND AID

Tuition & Fees

Tuition	$26,000
Room and board	$12,470
Cost of books	$11,087
Fees	$6,252

Financial Aid

% students receiving aid	93
Average grant	$11,148
Average loan	$38,817
Average debt	$136,335

NEW YORK MEDICAL COLLEGE

OFFICE OF ADMISSIONS, ADMINISTRATION BUILDING VALHALLA, NY 10595 • ADMISSION: 914-594-4507
FAX: 914-594-4976 • E-MAIL: MDADMIT@NYMC.EDU • WEBSITE: WWW.NYMC.EDU

STUDENT BODY

Type	Private
Enrollment	774
% male/female	49/51
% minorities	4
# applied (total/out)	7,559/6,047
# accepted (total/out)	736/512
# enrolled (total/out)	194/134
Average age	24

FACULTY

Total faculty (number)	3,018
% female	30
% minority	32
% part-time	1

ADMISSIONS

Average GPA and MCAT scores

Overall GPA	3.52
MCAT Bio	10.4
MCAT Phys	10
MCAT Verbal	9.4
MCAT Essay	Q

Application Information

Regular application	12/15
Regular notification	Rolling
Early application	8/1
Early notification	10/1
Are transfers accepted?	Yes
Admissions may be deferred?	Yes
Interview required?	Yes
Application fee	$100

Academics

Students have an opportunity to earn joint-degrees, combining the MD with an MPH, which is of great value considering the increased awareness of public health issues, or a PhD in the basic medical sciences. Grading is on an honors/high pass/pass/fail scale. Passing Step 1 and 2 of the USMLE is a graduation requirement. In recent years, the pass rate has been at or near 100 percent.

BASIC SCIENCES: The curriculum of the first 2 years, though focused on the basic sciences, maintains a consistent clinical orientation. The program has been revised to bring clinical relevance and small group teaching into all courses. The first 2 years focus on developing a thorough understanding of the sciences basic to clinical medicine. The core of the first-year curriculum—Anatomy, Behavioral Science, Biochemistry, Histology, Neural Science, and Physiology—supplemented by clinical case correlations and courses in epidemiology and biostatistics. The second-year curriculum, with its strong focus on pathology/pathophysiology, emphasizes small group discussion, problem-based learning, and self-study, with only 25 percent of class time spent in large lectures. Clinical Skills Training, Medical Microbiology, and Pharmacology prepare students for the clerkship experience of the next 2 years.

CLINICAL TRAINING

While immersed in the basic science curriculum, all first-year students have ongoing, direct patient contact, working in the office of a primary care physician. This one-on-one placement gives students clinical exposure and a personal mentor relationship. This preceptorship experience continues throughout the second year. Third-year clinical clerkships are the following: Family Medicine (4 weeks), Medicine (12 weeks), Neurology (4 weeks), Obstetrics/Gynecology (6 weeks), Pediatrics (8 weeks), Psychiatry (6 weeks), and Surgery (8 weeks). The school's location in the suburban New York area and large hospital network afford clinical-training opportunities in demographically and clinically diverse settings. About half of the third-year class moves into New York City for their clinical years. The following are the students' fourth-year requirements: Ambulatory Surgical subspecialties (4 weeks), Anesthesiology/Rehabilitation Medicine (2 weeks), Geriatrics or Chronic Care Pediatrics (4 weeks), and Medicine or Pediatrics sub internship (4 weeks). The 18 weeks of electives can be taken anywhere. About 15–20 students take international electives each year.

Campus Life

The school's student body is generally representative of the demographic diversity of the country. The first-year class size is 190 students; in recent years, it has been equally divided by gender, with the proportion of females increasing incrementally. About half come from public colleges and universities.

STUDENT LIFE

Most first- and second-year students live on campus in attractive, unfurnished garden apartments or furnished suite-style apartment shares in a suburban setting that encourages a sense of community. Students gather for pick-up football, soccer, and basketball games outdoors when the weather permits. New York Medical College has an arrangement with Fordham University to allow our students to use recreational facilities at Fordham's Marymount campus in Tarrytown, about 10 minutes away. The facilities include cardio and weight rooms, locker and shower rooms, a pool for lap swimming, and a gymnasium for basketball. Students can participate in more than 40 clubs and organizations groups focused on professional, cultural, social, educational, and athletic interests. These include The Arrhythmias, an a cappella singing group; a chamber music club; and other cultural groups. Project Sunshine works to better the lives of children in hospitals, and AMSA, AMA, AMWA, and SMNA—student chapters of major professional organizations—offer students an opportunity to represent the school at regional and national student conferences.

GRADUATES

The School of Medicine encourages students to aim high in applying for residency matches. While a large number of students are choosing to match in primary care disciplines, there are equally impressive matches in highly competitive specialty programs. Matches for the current year can be viewed on the school's website. Some 12,000 alumni are supported by alumni association chapters in major cities. Alumni can track university announcements of upcoming events on the website, and a special alumni section allows them to post news and read about other alumni. Alumni can also keep current on their classmates' activities via the university magazine, *Chironian*, which is mailed to all alumni and is also available for viewing on the website.

Admissions

REQUIREMENTS

All applicants must have taken the MCAT within the last 3 years and must have completed or have in progress the following prerequisites: 2 semesters of biology, chemistry, organic chemistry, and physics. Each of these must have been completed with lab work. Two semesters of English are also required. The most recent MCAT scores are given greatest weight. While most students have majored in the sciences, the school encourages those with strong humanities backgrounds and the necessary science requirements to apply.

SUGGESTIONS

In addition to purely academic factors, we look for students who show clear evidence through their activities of strong motivation toward medicine and a sense of dedication to the service of others. Personal qualities of character and personality are evaluated from letters of recommendation, from the personal statement and the interview. New York Medical College does not deny admission to any applicant on the basis of race, color, creed, religion, national or ethnic origin, age, sex, sexual orientation, or disability.

PROCESS

All AMCAS applicants are requested to complete an online secondary application. After the completed secondary application and all letters of recommendation have been processed, the applicant's file is reviewed for consideration. Interviews are by invitation and are conducted on campus. We generally interview from October through April, and decisions are made on a rolling basis.

Admissions Requirements (Required)

MCAT scores, science GPA, non-science GPA, letters of recommendation, interview, essay/personal statement, extracurricular activities, exposure to medical profession

COSTS AND AID
Tuition & Fees

Tuition	$38,500
Room and board	
(on-campus)	$13,306
(off-campus)	$17,538
Cost of books	$2,028
Fees	$3,270

Financial Aid

% students receiving aid	90
Average grant	$20,000
Average loan	$45,000
Average debt	$166,000

NEW YORK UNIVERSITY
MOUNT SINAI SCHOOL OF MEDICINE

ANNENBERG 5-04A, BOX 1002, ONE GUSTAVE L. LEVY PL. NEW YORK, NY 10029-6574 • ADMISSION: 212-241-6696
FAX: 212-828-4135 • E-MAIL: ADMISSIONS@MSSM.EDU • WEBSITE: WWW.MSSM.EDU/BULLETIN

STUDENT BODY

Type	Private
Enrollment	505
% male/female	45/55
% minorities	35
# applied (total/out)	4,770/2,936
# accepted (total/out)	349/225
# enrolled (total/out)	140/98
Average age	24

FACULTY

Total faculty	1,922
% female	36
% minority	25
% part-time	13
Student-faculty ratio	4:1

ADMISSIONS
Average GPA and MCAT Scores

Overall GPA	3.64
MCAT Bio	11.4
MCAT Phys	10.7
MCAT Verbal	11.7
MCAT Essay	Q

Application Information

Regular application	11/1
Regular notification	Rolling
Early application	8/1
Early notification	10/1
Are transfers accepted?	Yes
Admissions may be deferred?	Yes
Interview required?	Yes
Application fee	$105

Academics

Mount Sinai's approach to medical education emphasizes cooperative rather than competitive learning to prepare students for the lifelong learning that is essential for the modern medical career. Group study, small classes and, for the past 30 years, a Pass/Fail grading system for the first- and second-year students contribute to this emphasis. The majority of the students' time in the first two (preclinical) years is focused on the core biomedical knowledge and the basic skills of the doctor-patient relationship. Through direct patient contact during the third and fourth (clinical) years in inpatient and ambulatory settings, students develop the skills necessary for the practice of medicine. We offer the following joint degree programs: M.S./M.D., M.D/M.P.H., M.D./M.B.A. In addition, eight to ten students each year pursue an MSTP-sponsored Ph.D. degree along with the M.D. in conjunction with the Mount Sinai Graduate School of Biological Sciences. The Ph.D. may be earned in Biochemistry, Biomathematical Sciences, Cell Biology and Anatomy, Genetics, Immunobiology, Microbiology, Molecular Biology, Neuroscience, Pharmacology, or Physiology/Biophysics. Evaluation of student performance uses Pass/Fail for the preclinical courses and Honor/High Pass/Pass/Fail for clinical training. Students must pass Step 1 of the USMLE for promotion to year three, and Step 2 in order to graduate.

BASIC SCIENCES: Basic sciences are taught through a combination of lectures, small-group discussions, labs, and clinical correlates. Lecture time is kept to two hours per day and students typically have three mornings or afternoons per week study time. Beginning on Day One, The Art and Science of Medicine, taught in both the first and second years, introduces students to the skills needed to care for patients. Throughout both years the emphasis is on case-based learning. Integrated with every course are numerous means for providing clinical relevance for the basic science being studied. Topics-such as ethics, radiology, and palliative care-that overlap many areas are incorporated into the curriculum of all four years through Courses Without Walls. First-year courses are Genetics, First Aid, Embryology, Molecules and Cells, Histology and Physiology, and Pathogenesis and Host Defense Mechanisms. The year ends with an integrative core that focuses on translational topics, allowing students to work with faculty from the bench to the bedside on a selected and structured topic. Extensive study of Mechanisms of Disease and Therapy is the major focus of the second year. This sequence of courses addresses each of the major pathophysiology topics essential to the practice of medicine. Organs and systems covered include respiratory, cardiovascular, renal/genitourinary, breast, skin, gynecologic, hematologic, endocrine, and musculoskelatal. A section on Brain and Behavior encompasses both psychopathology and neurology and at the end of the year the focus shifts to epidemiology and biostatistics.

CLINICAL TRAINING

The curriculum in the third year is composed of four 12-week modules of clinical clerkships. The modules are Pediatrics, Obstetrics, Nursery, and Gynecology; Medicine and Geriatrics; Surgery and Psychiatry; and Neurology, Anesthesia and Family Practice. Four weeks of electives are also offered in the third year. As in the first two years, an integrated case-based curriculum enriches the learning opportunities throughout the year. The fourth year begins with a four-week preparation period for Step 2 of the USMLE followed by an emergency rotation and a subinternship in medicine. A clinical Translational

Fellowship combines the clinical practice of medicine with the relevant basic science. A four-week required Post-Match Integrated Selective addresses issues essential for students to explore before going on to residency. A significant portion of clinical training takes place at The Mount Sinai Hospital, which includes the 625-bed Guggenheim Pavilion and a Primary Care Building with an expansive ambulatory care program. Affiliated teaching facilities include, but are not limited to, Bronx Veterans Affairs Medical Center (561 beds), Elmhurst Hospital Center (Queens, 526 beds), Englewood Hospital and Medical Center (New Jersey, 520 beds), North General Hospital (Central and East Harlem), and Maimonedes Medical Center.

Students

The class entering in 2005 came from 46 different undergraduate institutions and pursued 54 undergraduate majors. Underrepresented minorities accounted for 21 percent of the students. The average age of incoming students was 23.

STUDENT LIFE

Mount Sinai provides a healthy environment and encourages the development of lifelong healthy habits. Cultural diversity is respected and supported, both in and out of the classroom. Students are active in a wide range of school-related organizations, particularly those focused on community service activities, and New York City is a rich source of extracurricular life. The Recreation Office provides discounted tickets to theater, movies, sporting events, and concerts. The Aron Residence Hall offers over 600 furnished suites for single students. It is conveniently located, and features a fitness center, among other amenities. School-owned housing for couples is also available.

GRADUATES

Among those who graduated in 2005, 21 percent entered Internal Medicine, 8 percent entered Pediatrics, 19 percent entered Surgical Specialties, and 5 percent entered Ob/Gyn. The remainder entered a broad range of other post-graduate programs.

Admissions

REQUIREMENTS

Prerequisites are one year each of General Chemistry, Organic Chemistry, Biology, college-level Math, English, and Physics. The MCAT is required, and scores from 2000 onward are acceptable.

SUGGESTIONS

Students who have taken significant time off after college should have some recent coursework. No particular extracurricular activities are specified, although successful applicants usually have some community service, research, or medically related experience.

PROCESS

All AMCAS applicants receive secondary applications. Of those returning secondaries, about 17 percent are interviewed. Interviews are conducted from September through March, and consist of two half-hour sessions, either with two faculty members or a faculty member and a medical student. Candidates are notified of the committee's decision with two to six weeks after the interview. Wait-listed candidates may send supplementary material to update their files. An early assurance program admits a limited number of sophomores with admission contingent upon completing undergraduate requirements.

Admissions Requirements (Required)

MCAT scores, Science GPA, Non-science GPA, Letters of recommendation, Interview, Essays/personal statement, Extracurricular activities, Exposure to medical profession

Admissions Requirements (Optional)

State residency

COSTS AND AID
Tuition & Fees

Tuition	$33,250
Room and board (on-campus)	$13,800
Cost of books	$1,220
Fees	$3,800

New York University

School of Medicine

550 First Avenue, New York, NY 10016 • Admission: 212-263-5290
Fax: 212-263-0720 • E-mail: ADMISSIONS@MED.NYU.EDU • Website: WWW.MED.NYU.EDU

STUDENT BODY

Type	Private
Enrollment	711
% male/female	50/50
% minorities	12
# applied (total/out)	7,423/6,019
# accepted (total/out)	467/335
# enrolled (total/out)	160/99
Average age	24

FACULTY

Total faculty (number)	1,344
% female	33
% minority	4
% part-time	22

ADMISSIONS

Average GPA and MCAT scores

Overall GPA	3.77
MCAT Bio	11.2
MCAT Phys	11.24
MCAT Verbal	10.25
MCAT Essay	Q

Application Information

Regular application	10/15
Regular notification	3/1
Are transfers accepted?	No
Admissions may be deferred?	Yes
Interview required?	Yes
Application fee	$100

Academics

The goal of the curriculum is to train physician-scholars who will approach the profession of medicine with intellectual rigor and who also understand the humanistic and ethical aspects of the field. Selected students may pursue a curriculum leading to both MD and PhD degrees. The PhD degree is earned in a basic medical science field. The honors program permits students who are following the standard 4-year MD curriculum to supplement formal class work with summer research or ongoing projects and to receive credit. The work of the first two years is reported as pass/fail. The work of each required clinical clerkship is reported as honors/high pass/pass/fail.

BASIC SCIENCES: The School of Medicine's basic science curriculum is organized into interdisciplinary modules. Year 1 begins with Morphological and Development Basis of Medicine, covering anatomy and embryology, and Molecular Basis of Medicine, which encompasses molecular biology, genetics and biochemistry. The spring semester includes the Cellular Basis of Medicine Module (both cell biology and immunology), and Foundations for Medicine, a series of modules covering the histology and physiology of basics tissues and organs, as well as neuroscience and behavior. Throughout the first and second year, students take Skills and Science of Doctoring. In first year, this includes a preceptorship in the office of a practicing physician and serves to integrate basic science concepts with clinical applications.

The second year begins with the Host Defense module, covering general pathology, general pharmacology, microbiology and parasitology. Students then take a series of Mechanisms of Disease modules integrating pathophysiology, pharmacology, and systemic pathology in the study of human organ systems. The second-year Skills and Science of Doctoring module includes Physical Diagnosis, the Physician Patient and Society unit, and Epidemiology, Biostatistic and Preventive Medicine.

During the first 2 years, class time is divided between lectures and small-group discussions. Laboratory work and computer-assisted instruction enhance learning. In total, first- and second-year students are in class or other scheduled sessions for about 20 hours per week. The division of academic computing has resulted in increased integration of bioinformatics into the curriculum. Each of the courses has a web page, and students can access all course materials, including lecture slides and recordings, through the Web. Instruction takes place in the Medical Science Building and adjacent facilities, which provide laboratory space, lecture halls, rooms for small-group discussions and conferences. The Frederick L. Ehrman Medical Library occupies 3 stories in the Medical Science Building, contains a computer lab, and has areas that are open to students 24 hours a day. Its collection includes over 160,000 volumes and 2,000 current serial titles.

CLINICAL TRAINING

Students in the third year curriculum have a choice between 2 types of schedules. Each schedule contains the following required third year clerkships: Medicine (8 weeks), Surgery (8 weeks), Pediatrics (8 weeks), Obstetrics/Gynecology (6 weeks), Psychiatry (6 weeks) and Neurology (4 weeks). One schedule also includes the required core clerkship Ambulatory Care Medicine (4 weeks), and an elective period (4 weeks). The other third-year schedule contains all the required cores excluding Ambulatory Care Medicine and 8 weeks of elective time. In the fourth year, students must take Ambulatory Care if they did not take it as a third year as well as Critical Care (4 weeks), and Advanced Medicine (4 weeks). The remainder of the year is reserved for elective study. Clinical training takes place at Bellevue Hospital Center and New York University Medicine Center Complex and at affiliated institutions. A port of electives may be taken at other hospitals in the United States or abroad.

Campus Life

Approximately 40 percent of students are New York residents. Though the majority of students are in their early 20s, each class has several nontraditional students who pursued careers or other activities between college and medical school. Class size is 160.

STUDENT LIFE

NYU School of Medicine (SoM) is located in one of the most vibrant and centrally located neighborhoods in New York City. The area's many resources are easily accessible to NYU's campus, so that our students are presented with a vast array of cultural, social, and recreational opportunities. By way of the NYU SoM student ticket office, students are able to take advantage of the city's many cultural events and performances at discount prices. The NYU SoM is easily accessible to other parts of the city. Midtown and Union Square are within walking distance, and other popular neighborhoods are only a short subway ride away. The SoM operates housing facilities for students, assuring that all NYU medical students can afford convenient and comfortable housing. Both residence halls and apartments are available.

GRADUATES

Of the 2007 graduates, the most prevalent fields for postgraduate training were the following: internal medicine (20 percent), pediatrics (10 percent), emergency medicine (7 percent), general surgery (6 percent), psychiatry (6percent), ophthalmology (5 percent), and diagnostic radiology (5percent). Most graduates enter residency programs at top institutions nationwide.

Admissions

REQUIREMENTS

Prerequisites are 6 semester hours each. They include the following: English, biology, general chemistry, organic chemistry, and physics. All science courses must include lab work. The MCAT is required and must be taken no more than 3 years prior to application. For applicants who have taken the exam more than once, the best set of scores is considered.

SUGGESTIONS

Biochemistry is strongly recommended. Other recommended courses are calculus, embryology, genetics, quantitative and physical chemistry, and Spanish if the applicant intends to practice in New York City. Experience in health care, research, and community service are considered valuable.

PROCESS

NYU Medical School participates in the AMCAS program. About 15 percent of applicants are invited to interview between September and January. Interviews consist of one session with a faculty member. On the day of the interview, the applicants tour the campus and have lunch with current students. About 40 percent of interviewed candidates are accepted, with notification occurring by early March. Others are either wait listed or rejected. Wait listed candidates can be selected for admission up until the first day of class in August.

Admissions Requirements (Required)

MCAT scores, science GPA, non-science GPA, letters of recommendation, interview, essay/personal statement, extracurricular activities, exposure to medical profession

Overlap Schools

Columbia University, Cornell University, Harvard University, Johns Hopkins University, State University of New York—Stony Brook University, University of Medicine and Dentistry of New Jersey, University of Pennsylvania.

COSTS AND AID

Tuition & Fees

Tuition	$36,079
Room and board	$10,000
Cost of books	$1,200
Fees	$7,850

Financial Aid

% students receiving aid	69
Average grant	$9,960
Average loan	$37,000
Average debt	$128,000

NORTHEASTERN OHIO UNIVERSITIES COLLEGE OF MEDICINE

PO BOX 95, ROOTSTOWN, OH 44272-0095 • ADMISSION: 330-325-6270
FAX: 330-325-8372 • E-MAIL: ADMISSION@NEOUCOM.EDU • WEBSITE: WWW.NEOUCOM.EDU

STUDENT BODY

Type	Public
Enrollment	430
% male/female	46/54
% minorities	6
# applied (total/out)	1,402/524
# accepted (total/out)	254/20
# enrolled (total/out)	102/7
Average age	22

FACULTY

Total faculty (number)	1,905
% female	19
% minority	15
% part-time	86

ADMISSIONS
Average GPA and MCAT Scores

Overall GPA	3.66
MCAT Bio	9.0
MCAT Phys	9.1
MCAT Verbal	9.3
MCAT Essay	P

Application Information

Regular application	11/1
Regular notification	3/21
Early application	6/1–8/1
Early notification	10/1
Are transfers accepted?	Yes
Admissions may be deferred?	No
Interview required?	Yes
Application fee	$30

Academics

While most students participate in the 6 or 7 year BS/MD program, about 15–25 students each year enter the 4 year MD program. A combined MD/PhD program is offered in collaboration with either Kent State or the University of Akron, leading to the doctorate degree in biomedical engineering or a number of medically related science fields. A summer fellowship program provides a stipend to selected medical students who undertake research or clinical education projects related to community health. Medical students are evaluated with marks of honors, satisfactory, conditional-unsatisfactory, or unsatisfactory for most courses. Passing the USMLE Step 1 is a requirement for promotion to year 3, and passing Step 2 is a requirement for graduation.

BASIC SCIENCES: Basic sciences are taught primarily in a lecture/lab format, although some courses also utilize small-group discussions and tutorials. On average, students are in class or other scheduled sessions for 32 hours per week. First-year courses are Behavioral Science, Biochemistry and Molecular Pathology, Developmental Medicine, Human Anatomy/Embryology, Infectious Diseases, Introduction to Physical Exam and Ambulatory Care Experience, Immunobiology, Microscopic Anatomy, Medical Neuroscience, Physiology, and Problem-based Learning. Second-year courses are Infectious Disease 2, Introduction to Clinical Medicine (ICM), M2 Ambulatory Care Experience, Pharmacology, Principles of Medical Sciences, Radiology, and Systemic Pathology. The ICM course focuses on clinical problems, fundamental doctor-patient communication skills, the physical examination, and clinical evaluation. NEOUCOM's approach to instruction in this transitional year allows for extensive clinical exposure and patient contact. As part of ICM, students spend time each week in family practice centers. Students benefit from academic support and counseling services offered by the Office of Academic Affairs. The Oliver Ocasek Regional Medical Information Center, on the Rootstown campus, houses more than 91,000 books and journals in addition to computerized information systems. The center is electronically linked to libraries in the teaching hospitals and consortium universities.

CLINICAL TRAINING

Third-year required rotations are Internal Medicine (10 weeks), Surgery (10 weeks), General Pediatrics (8 weeks), Obstetrics/Gynecology (8 weeks), Psychiatry (6 weeks), and Family Medicine (6 weeks). During the fourth year, additional requirements are Primary Care Preceptorship (4 weeks), Medical Humanities (4 weeks), Community Medicine clerkship (4 weeks), and 20 weeks of electives. Training takes place at the following affiliated hospitals: Lodi Community Hospital, Wadsworth-Rittman Hospital, Akron General Medical Center, Barberton Citizens Hospital, Children's Hospital Medical Center, Edwin Shaw Hospital, Summa Health System, Robinson Memorial Hospital, Hillside Rehabilitation Hospital, Trumbull Memorial Hospital, St. Elizabeth Health Center, Western Reserve Care System, Salem Community Hospital, Aultman Hospital, Massillon Psychiatric Center, and Columbia Mercy Medical Center. In addition, students train at community-based centers that are part of the Area Health Education Center Program.

Campus Life

Approximately 95 percent of students are Ohio residents. About 105 students in each class are admitted through the BS/MD program, and up to 25 are admitted through the traditional route. Although most entering students are in their early twenties, there are a few older or nontraditional students in each class. Underrepresented minorities account for about 4 percent of the student body.

STUDENT LIFE

Rootstown is a small town located about 15 miles east of Akron. On the medical school campus are recreation and exercise centers, student lounges, a picnic area, and tennis, basketball, and volleyball courts. Student groups include chapters of national medical student organizations, groups focused on professional interests, student-to-student support groups, and a recreation club. On-campus housing, including residence halls and apartments, is available on all three campuses.

GRADUATES

NEOUCOM graduates usually score well above the national average on the USMLE. Of the 1,350 graduates currently in residency or practice, 55 percent have remained in Ohio. About half of graduates enter primary care fields.

Admissions

REQUIREMENTS

Prerequisites are 1 year each of organic chemistry and physics, although success on the MCAT probably requires preparation in biology and general chemistry as well. The MCAT is required, and scores must be no more than 2 years old. For applicants who have retaken the exam, the most recent set of scores is considered. Thus, there is no advantage to withholding scores.

SUGGESTIONS

Ohio residents are given strong preference in the admissions process, and slight preference is given to graduates of consortium schools. Highly qualified applicants are encouraged to apply to the early decision program. Beyond requirements, recommended course work includes biochemistry, calculus, community health, embryology, general biology, general chemistry, humanities, Microbiology, molecular biology, physiology, psychology, sociology, and statistics. For applicants who have taken time off after college, some recent course work is advised.

PROCESS

High school students interested in the combined BS/MD program apply to NEUOCOM in the fall of senior year and complete a condensed undergraduate experience at Kent State, University of Akron, or Youngstown State before arriving at the Rootstown campus. As a result of attrition from this program, a limited number of seats are available for college graduates interested in the 4 year MD program. These applicants must apply through AMCAS. About 30 percent of AMCAS applicants are sent secondary applications. Of those returning secondaries, about 40 percent are interviewed between November and March. On interview day, candidates receive one interview with a panel of members of the Admissions Committee, a tour of the campus, lunch with current students, and a group informational session. Of interviewed candidates, about 10 percent are accepted on a rolling basis. Wait listed candidates may update their files with transcripts.

Admissions Requirements (Required)

MCAT scores, science GPA, non-science GPA, letters of recommendation, interview, essays/personal statement

Admissions Requirements (Optional)

State residency, extracurricular activities, exposure to medical profession

COSTS AND AID
Tuition & Fees

In-state tuition	$25,288
Out-of-state tuition	$50,576
Room and board (off-campus)	$15,000
Cost of books	$1,250
Fees	$1,720

Financial Aid

% students receiving aid	95
Average grant	$2,350
Average loan	$15,000
Average debt	$80,916

NORTHWESTERN UNIVERSITY
FEINBERG SCHOOL OF MEDICINE

ADMISSIONS OFFICE, 1ST FLOOR, ROOM 606, 303 EAST CHICAGO AVENUE, CHICAGO, IL 60611-3008 • **ADMISSION:** 312-503-8206
FAX: 312-503-0550 • **E-MAIL:** MED-ADMISSIONS@NORTHWESTERN.EDU • **WEBSITE:** MED-ADMISSIONS.NORTHWESTERN.EDU

STUDENT BODY

Type	Private
Enrollment	695
% male/female	50/50
% minorities	12
# applied	6,753
# accepted (total/out)	438/384
# enrolled (total/out)	174/125
Average age	23

FACULTY

Total faculty (number)	3,256
% female	37
% minority	4
% part-time	43
Student-faculty ratio	5:1

ADMISSIONS
Average GPA and MCAT Scores

Overall GPA	3.71
MCAT Bio	11.6
MCAT Phys	11.3
MCAT Verbal	10.7
MCAT Essay	Q

Application Information

Regular application	10/15
Regular notification	12/15
Are transfers accepted?	Yes
Admissions may be deferred?	Yes
Interview required?	Yes
Application fee	$75

Academics

The Feinberg medical curriculum retains the best aspects of traditional medical education and incorporates innovative, interactive methods designed for the independent adult learner. The curriculum is designed to cultivate leaders who will effect change in their communities and in the profession. Approximately 20 percent enter joint-degree programs. The MD/MPH (Masters in Public Health), MD/MA (Masters in Medical Humanities and Bioethics) and MD/MS (Masters in Health Care Quality and Patient Safety) can be completed in 4 years. The MD/MBA, offered in conjunction with the Kellogg School of Management, requires 5 years. The Medical Scientist Training Program leading to both MD and PhD degrees requires a minimum of 7 years. Many other students conduct research during the summer after the first year; this can lead to ongoing research involvement in the Research Thesis Program. A number of students also undertake extended research opportunities during an additional year at Feinberg or in extramural programs. International academic and clinical opportunities are provided through a network of over a dozen partner institutions around the world.

BASIC SCIENCES: The first- and second-year curriculum is composed of 4 major courses, each presented in a series of discreet, topically focused units. Each course and nearly every unit is interdisciplinary and draws faculty from a number of departments. There is one integrated course in the basic medical sciences in each of the first 2 years, involving approximately 10 hours of lecture per week, complemented by problem-based learning sessions, laboratories, and small-group discussions and tutorials. Structure-Function, the first-year course, begins with a review of cell and molecular biology, genetics, and signal transduction, then addresses gross and microscopic anatomy, biochemistry, and physiology in a consecutive sequence of organ systems. The second year basic science course, Scientific Basis of Medicine, begins with an overview of immunology, microbiology, and infectious diseases and then details the pathology, pathophysiology, and pharmacology specific to each organ system. The Medical Decision-Making course occupies 3 short blocks of time: The initial week of the first year, 1 week later in the first year, and the final portion of the second year. This innovative course allows students to develop the knowledge and skills in information management, epidemiology and biostatistics, and clinical problem solving essential to the contemporary practice of medicine. The fourth major course, Patient, Physician and Society, is devoted to the development of clinical skills and professional perspectives and provides each student the opportunity to develop mentoring relationships with a variety of faculty preceptors. The class is divided into 4 colleges, each led by an experienced clinician. Colleges meet 2 afternoons per week throughout the first 2 years, and continue to meet on a regular basis through the third and fourth years (see below). One afternoon offers learning experiences centered around clinical skills development and the provision of an integrated biopsychosocial perspective on illness and patient care. The second afternoon's course sequence addresses medical ethics and humanities, public health, and health policy. Activities in both afternoon tracks incorporate health promotion and disease prevention as a guiding principle of the practice of medicine.

CLINICAL TRAINING

The third year consists of 49 weeks of required clerkships. Students gain experience in medicine (12 weeks), Surgery (12 weeks), Pediatrics (6 weeks), Obstetrics/Gynecology (6 weeks), Psychiatry (4 weeks), Neurology (4 weeks), and Primary Care (4 weeks). A 1 week introduction to clinical clerkships provides orientation to the clerkship environment. During the fourth year, students complete a 4 week acting internship in medicine or pediatrics, 4 weeks in emergency medicine, 4 weeks in intensive care, and 2 weeks in physical medicine and rehabilitation. Most clinical rotations are conducted within a consortium of major clinical affiliates, known as the McGaw Medical Center, that also sponsors one of the largest graduate medical education (residency) programs in the country. These clinical affiliates include Northwestern Memorial Hospital, Children's Memorial Hospital, the Rehabilitation Institute of Chicago, Evanston Northwestern Healthcare, and VA Chicago Health care System. The remainder of the fourth year is elective, and many students use this opportunity to explore extramural and international experiences.

Campus Life

The 175 students in Feinberg's entering class typically represent 60 or more undergraduate institutions, more than 30 states, and several foreign countries. Approximately half the students are female. Over the last few years, about a fourth of each class has been made up of students with at least 1 year of experience in another field between undergraduate school and medical school matriculation. Admission deferments of one year are routinely available, and a special arrangement with Teach for America allows students accepted into that program to defer admission for 2 years. Within each class of about 175 students, 10 to 12 are admitted through the Medical Scientist Training Program (MD/PhD), and 30–35 are from the Honors Program in Medical Education (HPME), a combined BA/MD program through Northwestern University.

STUDENT LIFE

Northwestern students spend less time in class than students at many other schools, and more time in outside preparation and independent learning. Students are encouraged to pursue supplemental academic interests, community-service endeavors, and other activities. The school's location is an important asset. Chicago is one of the most vibrant and diverse cities in the world, offering students a variety of community-service learning activities as well as access to world-class museums, theaters, restaurants and other attractions. About half the medical students live within walking distance of the school and Northwestern Memorial Hospital. Others live in a variety of neighborhoods throughout the city, and take advantage of Chicago's excellent public transportation system.

GRADUATES

Northwestern graduates are accepted to competitive residencies throughout the nation. Today there are more than 12,000 medical school alumni living in the United States and around the world. Northwestern alumni are particularly well represented in academic medicine.

Admissions

REQUIREMENTS

There are no specific course requirements, but a full year each of modern biology, organic chemistry, inorganic chemistry, general physics, and English are recommended. The MCAT is required, with scores no more than 3 years old at the time of application. A minimum of 3 years of college (135 quarter hours/90 semester hours) is required for admission; a bachelor's degree is preferred.

SUGGESTIONS

The Feinberg School seeks applicants who have demonstrated academic excellence, leadership qualities, intellectual curiosity, and personal maturity. Applicants should be liberally educated men and women who have studied a discipline in some depth beyond the conventional premedical courses. The school has a particular interest in students with promise as physician-scholars. Experience in research and evidence of commitment to medicine as a service profession are positive factors in selection.

PROCESS

All qualified AMCAS registrants applying to Feinberg are sent a supplemental application. Of those returning the supplemental, about 10 percent are interviewed between October and February. The medical school uses a combined interview approach, with both individual and panel interview. The individual interview is conducted by a member of the Dean's Administration or Committee on Admissions, and a panel of 3 to 4 candidates is interviewed by three members of the Interview Committee (usually 2 faculty and 1 medical student).

Admissions Requirements (Required)

MCAT scores, science GPA, non-science GPA, letters of recommendation, interview, essays/personal statement

Overlap Schools

Case Western Reserve University, New York University—Mount Sinai School of Medicine, New York University—School of Medicine, The University of Chicago, University of Michigan—Ann Arbor, University of Pittsburgh, Vanderbilt University, Washington University.

COSTS AND AID

Tuition & Fees

Tuition	$38,614
Room and board (on-campus)	$12,078
Cost of books	$2,577
Fees	$0

Financial Aid

% students receiving aid	76
Average grant	$29,736
Average loan	$36,057
Average debt	$100,014

THE OHIO STATE UNIVERSITY
COLLEGE OF MEDICINE

155 D MEILING HALL, 370 WEST 9TH AVENUE COLUMBUS, OH 43210 • **ADMISSION:** 614-292-7137
FAX: 614-247-7959 • **E-MAIL:** MEDICINE@OSU.EDU • **WEBSITE:** MEDICINE.OSU.EDU

STUDENT BODY

Type	Public
Enrollment	832
% male/female	62/38
% minorities	30
# applied (total/out)	4,141/3,071
# accepted (total/out)	370/202
# enrolled (total/out)	211/96
Average age	23

FACULTY

Total faculty (number)	3,041
% female	32
% minority	14
% part-time	35
Student-faculty ratio	3:1

ADMISSIONS
Average GPA and MCAT scores

Overall GPA	3.72
MCAT Bio	11.13
MCAT Phys	10.99
MCAT Verbal	10.36
MCAT Essay	P

Application Information

Regular application	11/1
Regular notification	10/15
Early application	8/1
Early notification	10/1
Are transfers accepted?	Yes
Admissions may be deferred?	Yes
Interview required?	Yes
Application fee	$60

Academics

All students begin with a 14-week course in Human Anatomy, embryology, and histology. This includes cadaver dissection, cross-sectional anatomy, multimedia for self-directed learning, imaging technology, and clinical correlation's. Students also initiate their study of the Medical Humanities and Behavioral Sciences during this period. After the conclusion of the first 14-week academic experience, students enter one of two pre-clinical pathways: integrated or independent study. Also, the Patient-Centered Medicine and Physician Development courses take place weekly, combining lectures, small-group learning, and clinical exposure in the community. Passage of Step 1 of the USMLE is required for progression to year three. A hallmark of Ohio State's M.D. curriculum is the opportunity for students to select experiences that fit with their individual learning styles and long-term career goals. The curriculum provides a variety of analytical and managerial skills specifically designed to be applicable in the health services setting.

BASIC SCIENCES: Joint-degree programs include four options. The Medical Scientist Program (MSP), a 7-year combined M.D./Ph.D. degree for highly qualified and motivated students who have excellent academic backgrounds, motivation for a career in academic medicine, and a commitment to or demonstrated aptitude for a research career. The Master of Public Health (M.P.H.), a combined 5-year program allows students to simultaneously earn the M.D. and M.P.H. degrees, with instruction in Epidemiology/Biometrics, Environmental Health Sciences, Health Services Management/Policy, and Health Promotion. The Master of Health Administration (M.H.A.) is a joint 5-year program that allows students to simultaneously earn the M.D. and M.H.A. degrees. The Master of Business Administration (M.B.A.) is a 5-year degree program designed to prepare future physicians to meet the challenges of business administration and financial issues in the practice of medicine in physician offices, hospitals, and health care systems. The Doctor of Medicine/Juris Doctor (M.D./J.D.) combined six-year degree program has been designed to prepare future physicians to meet the challenges of legal issues in physician offices, hospitals, comprehensive medical centers, and health-care related industries.

CLINICAL TRAINING

Clinical rotations begin with the Introduction to Clinical Medicine (ICM). The goal of this clerkship is to enable students to better use their major and elective experiences to become excellent physicians. The third-year required clerkships include: ambulatory, internal medicine, pediatrics, surgery, Ob/Gyn, psychiatry, neurology, and one elective. Curriculum in the fourth year includes four selective experiences called the Differentiation of Care Selectives (DOCS), covering the undifferentiated patient, chronic care, sub-internship in internal medicine, and a sub-internship in surgical care. There is a great amount of flexability in the fourth year with four months of elective rotations and three months of vacation. Passage of Step 2 CK and Step 2 CS of the USMLE is required for graduation.

Students

The class profile for 2006 reflects a class size of 211 entering students, with 55 percent from Ohio, 45 percent women, and 15 percent underrepresented minority students. The average GPA was 3.72 with an MCAT average of 11 in the subscores.

STUDENT LIFE

There are over 40 medical student organizations. Medical students have access to all of the resources and facilities of the University including the Recreation and Physical Activity Center which contains 25,000 square feet of fitness space. Campus and city bus transportation is free with the presentation of student ID. Computerized housing opportunities are available free of charge through the Off-Campus Student Services. University graduate residence halls and family housing are also available.

GRADUATES

PGY-1 Match Results for 2006 reflect 41 percent of the graduating class plan to enter primary care residencies, and 47 percent matched with Ohio residency programs.

Admissions

REQUIREMENTS

One year of Biology with labs, Chemistry, Organic Chemistry with labs, and Physics are required. Also recommended are courses in Biochemistry and Molecular Genetics. To receive consideration for the current application cycle, applicants must submit the AMCAS application, Ohio state Secondary application, MCAT scores, and reference letters. All applicants are required to take the MCAT within three yeas of their application. The last month to take the MCAT is September for the year prior to intended matriculation. Although the MCAT is offered in January, first-time takers scores will be received too late for consideration for that year's entering class. Consideration will be given to applicants who have interview dates and elect to repeat the January test in an effort to improve previous scores.

SUGGESTIONS

The Admissions Committee evaluates candidates according to competitive standards. Applicants are judged on the basis of academic performance as well as personal qualities such as integrity, leadership, and interpersonal skills. Clinically related experiences, as well as physician shadowing, community service, leadership roles, and research positions are encouraged.

PROCESS

Applications are initiated through AMCAS. Secondary applications are available upon receipt of the AMCAS application. Between 650 and 700 on-campus interviews are conducted from mid-September to mid-March. Interviewing applicants participate in a morning program, have an opportunity to interact with current medical students, and have a tour of the medical center.

Admissions Requirements (Required)

AMCAS and secondary applications, clinical experience with physician shadowing, research, volunteer service

Admissions Requirement (Optional)

State residency

COSTS AND AID

Tuition & Fees

In-stateTuition	$22,833
Out-of-state Tuition	$35,644
Room and board	$13,560
Cost of books	$4,134
Fees	$573

Financial Aid

% students receiving aid	89
Average grant	$9,563
Average loan	$37,379
Average debt	$127,405

OREGON HEALTH AND SCIENCE UNIVERSITY
SCHOOL OF MEDICINE

OFFICE OF EDUCATION AND STUDENT AFFAIRS, L102, 3181 SOUTHWEST, PORTLAND, OR 97201
ADMISSION: 503-494-2998 FAX: 503-494-3400 • E-MAIL: MDADMISS@OHSU.EDU • WEBSITE: WWW.OHSU.EDU

STUDENT BODY	
Type	Public
Enrollment	452
% male/female	52/48
% minorities	14
# applied (total/out)	3,601/3,292
# accepted (total/out)	184/110
# enrolled (total/out)	112/44
Average age	25

FACULTY	
Total faculty (number)	1,066
% female	40
% minority	3
% part-time	4
Student-faculty ratio	4:1

ADMISSIONS
Average GPA and MCAT Scores

Overall GPA	3.6
MCAT Bio	10.16
MCAT Phys	10.2
MCAT Verbal	10.15
MCAT Essay	P

Application Information

Regular application	10/15
Regular notification	Rolling
Are transfers accepted?	Yes
Admissions may be deferred?	No
Interview required?	Yes
Application fee	$75

Academics

Although most students complete a 4-year MD curriculum, others follow alternative courses of study, including joint-degree programs. The 5-year MD/MPH degree program is offered by the School of Medicine's Department of Public Health and Preventive Medicine in conjunction with appropriate departments at Oregon State University and Portland State University. Generally, students indicate their interest in this program when they apply to the School of Medicine. First-year medical students may pursue an epidemiological and biostatistical track, which also serves as preparation for careers in public health. The joint-degree program is the MD/PhD in the following fields: biochemistry and molecular biology, cell biology and anatomy, molecular and medical genetics, medical psychology, molecular microbiology and immunology, neuroscience, and pharmacology and physiology. Grades are honors/near honors/satisfactory/marginal/fail. Step 1 and Step 2 of the USMLE are a requirement for graduation.

BASIC SCIENCES: Students spend 2 hours per day in lecture. An additional 2 hours each day are used for small-group sessions and/or laboratory activities. One afternoon each week is devoted to principles of clinical medicine in which students work one-on-one with physicians and an additional afternoon studying issues related to public health, behavioral sciences, history-taking and learning physical diagnosis skills. First-year courses are Anatomy, Embryology, and Imaging; Biological Basis of Disease; Cell Structure and Function; Systems Process and Homeostasis; and Principles of Clinical Medicine, which continues into the second year. The second year is organized around organ systems and physiological concepts, which include blood, circulation, neuroscience and behavior, metabolism, and human development and life cycle. The first 2 years are spent largely in the Basic Sciences and Education Buildings, which have facilities for lectures, discussions, computer learning, and laboratories. The library contains more than 150,000 volumes and 2,500 periodicals.

CLINICAL TRAINING

Required third-year rotations are Medicine (12 weeks), Primary Care (6 weeks), Obstetrics/Gynecology (6 weeks), Child Health (6 weeks), Psychiatry (6 weeks), Family Medicine (6 weeks), Surgery (6 weeks), and Transition to Clerkship (1 week). During the fourth year, students fulfill advanced clerkship requirements in medicine, surgery, child health, and neurology (4 weeks each) in addition to selectives and electives. The fourth year culminates in Transition to Physician, a week-long experience. Clinical training takes place at the University Hospital and Clinics and at affiliated institutions, which include Doernbecher Children's Hospital and Portland's Veterans Affairs Medical Center. The School of Medicine's research touches all realms of modern medical sciences. Some investigate the causes and treatments of learning disorders, addiction, heart disease, stroke, cancer, infertility, movement disorders, and emotional disorders. Others work at the molecular and cellular levels to unravel the most basic aspects of human health.

Campus Life

About 6 percent of students at OHSU are from underrepresented minority backgrounds. The average age of incoming students is around 25. Class size is 96.

STUDENT LIFE

Portland is an ideal location for students, offering the comforts of a medium-size city and proximity to spectacular outdoor destinations. Close to campus are parks and other places to run, walk, or bike ride. A bit further are mountains for hiking and skiing. For an urban area, Portland is relatively affordable and safe. On-campus activities are also popular with medical students. The newly renovated fitness and sports center includes a full weight room, racquetball and squash courts, aerobics classes, swimming pools, and a spa. The Office of Multicultural Affairs supports students of ethnic and international backgrounds with supplemental counseling services, recreational activities, workshops, and classes. Numerous clubs and organizations bring students together around professional or extracurricular interests. Although student housing is available on a limited basis in the residence hall, most opt to live off campus.

GRADUATES

Graduates are successful in securing residency positions at prestigious institutions all over the country. However, most enter programs in the Western United States. More than half enter primary care residencies.

Admissions

REQUIREMENTS

Prerequisites are chemistry/organic chemistry (2 years), biology (1 year), physics (1 year), English (1 year), humanities (1 year), social science (1 year), and college-level math (1 semester). GPAs from all 4-year undergraduate institutions are evaluated equally, although factors such as the breadth of education, rigor of major, GPA trends, course load, and extracurricular activities are considered. The MCAT is required and scores must be from within 3 years of the year of matriculation.

SUGGESTIONS

Preference is given to Oregon, WICHE-certified residents of Montana and Wyoming, MD/PhD and MD/MPH candidates, and nonresident applicants with superior achievements in academics and other related experiences. The School of Medicine Admissions Committee fully recognizes the importance of diversity in its student body and in the physician workforce in providing for effective delivery of health care. Accordingly, the OHSU School of Medicine strongly encourages applications from persons from all socioeconomic, racial, ethnic, religious, and educational backgrounds and persons from groups underrepresented in medicine. The committee adheres to a policy of equal opportunity and nondiscrimination on the basis of sex, age, race, ethnic origin, religion, or sexual orientation.

PROCESS

About half of AMCAS applicants receive secondaries, and about 40 percent of candidates in this group are interviewed. Interviews consist of two 30-minute sessions with members of the faculty or Admissions Committee. Interviewees are invited to lunch with medical students and are given a tour of the campus. Approximately 20 percent of interviewees are accepted on a rolling basis. Wait listed candidates are ranked and have a fairly good chance of being accepted later in the spring.

Admissions Requirements (Required)

MCAT scores, science GPA, non-science GPA, letters of recommendation, interview, essays/personal statement, extracurricular activities, exposure to medical profession

Admissions Requirements (Optional)

State residency. Preference is given to Oregon residents

Overlap Schools

Stanford University.

COSTS AND AID

Tuition & Fees

In-state tuition	$25,068
Out-of-state tuition	$35,466
Cost of books	$2,800
Fees	$3,255

Financial Aid

% students receiving aid	90
Average grant	$2,000
Average loan	$30,000
Average debt	$112,000

PENNSYLVANIA STATE UNIVERSITY
COLLEGE OF MEDICINE

OFFICE OF STUDENT AFFAIRS, PO BOX 850, HERSHEY, PA 17033 • ADMISSION: 717-531-8755
FAX: 717-531-6225 • E-MAIL: HMCSAFF@PSU.EDU • WEBSITE: WWW.HMC.PSU.EDU/COLLEGE

STUDENT BODY	
Type	Private
Enrollment	423
% male/female	50/50
% minorities	13
# applied (total/out)	6,615/5,509
# enrolled (out-of-state)	135
Average age	23

FACULTY	
Total faculty (number)	155
% female	18
% minority	23

ADMISSIONS

Average GPA and MCAT

GPA	3.65
MCAT Bio	10.05
MCAT Phys	9.51
MCAT Verbal	9.06
MCAT Writing	P

Application Information

Regular application	11/15
Regular notification	Until filled
Early application	6/1–8/1
Early notification	10/1
Are transfers accepted?	Yes
Admissions may be deferred?	Yes
Interview required?	No
Application fee	$40

Academics

Pennsylvania State was one of the first medical schools in the country to institute departments of humanities and behavioral science and to incorporate these perspectives into the basic science and clinical education programs. The College of Medicine was also among the first to develop a separate Family and Community Medicine Department. A combined MD/PhD program is offered, allowing students to earn the doctorate degree in biochemistry, biomedical engineering, cell biology, genetics, immunology, microbiology, molecular biology, pharmacology, and physiology. There are also numerous opportunities to pursue discrete research projects as electives or during summers. Grading designations are honors, high pass, pass, and fail. Students must pass USMLE Step 1 after the pre-clinical years, and Step 2 to graduate.

BASIC SCIENCES: During the first and second years, students are in class or other scheduled sessions for approximately 23 hours per week. This schedule gives students the opportunity for independent and collaborative study. Clinical problems are used as a means of applying and correlating the basic science information that is presented in lectures or discussions. Labs and computer-assisted learning are also important parts of the curriculum. First-year courses are Biological Basis of Disease; Cellular and Molecular Basis of Medical Practice; Humanistic Aspects of Medicine; Physicians, Patients and Society, which touches on the psychological, social, ethical, and legal; and Structural Basis of Medical Practice. Second-year courses are Immunology, Issues in Medical Practice, Introduction to Medicine III and IV, Microbiology, Pathology, Pharmacology, Physical Diagnosis, and Psychiatry. Instruction takes place in the Medical Sciences Building, which houses classrooms and laboratories. The Harrell Library is open 24 hours a day and holds approximately 125,000 volumes, 2,000 periodicals, and modern computer and audiovisual resources.

CLINICAL TRAINING

Third-year required clerkships are Internal Medicine (8 weeks), selectives (8 weeks), Surgery (8 weeks), Pediatrics (6 weeks), Obstetrics/Gynecology (6 weeks), Psychiatry (4 weeks), Family and Community Medicine (4 weeks), and Primary Care (4 weeks). The fourth year is devoted to electives and selectives, which are chosen from clinical or research departments. An overseas elective program allows a number of fourth-year students to fulfill elective requirements at clinical sites in Asia, Africa, and Latin America. Generally, clinical training takes place at the University Hospital (463 beds), Children's Hospital, the Rehabilitation Center, and at other hospitals and clinics affiliated through an organized health network called Alliance Health. Additional facilities on campus are a sports medicine center, the General Clinical Research Center, an animal research center, and a trauma center.

Campus Life

About 40 percent of students are Pennsylvania residents. More than 25 percent of students are underrepresented minorities, a tribute to the school's commitment to recruiting a diverse student body. The average age of incoming students is 23, with a wide age range. Class size is 110.

STUDENT LIFE

Educational facilities, clinical teaching sites, campus housing, and recreational centers are within walking distance of one another. The College of Medicine is an attractive campus, occupying 550 acres. Hershey provides a comfortable, student-friendly community that is relatively safe. As a tourist destination, Hershey offers a variety of dining and entertainment possibilities. Medical students are involved in organizations such as honor societies, professional interest groups, local chapters of national organizations, and groups focused on community service or recreational pursuits. When in need of urban distractions, the state capital, Harrisburg, is 12 miles away, and both Philadelphia and Pittsburgh are easily accessible. On-campus housing options include 1-, 2-, and 3-bedroom apartments.

GRADUATES

Graduates are successful at securing residencies nationwide. Pennsylvania State emphasizes primary care and encourages students to consider postgraduate training programs in primary care fields.

Admissions

REQUIREMENTS

Prerequisites are 1 year each of biology, chemistry, college-level math, organic chemistry, physics. All science courses should have associated labs. One semester each of social sciences and humanities is also required. The MCAT is required, and scores must be no more than 2 years old. For applicants who have taken the exam on multiple occasions, all sets of scores are considered.

SUGGESTIONS

Beyond requirements, course work in anthropology, calculus, genetics, psychology, sociology, and statistics is recommended. The April, rather than August, MCAT is strongly advised. Health care related experience is valued, as are interpersonal and communication skills. State residency is not a consideration in the application process.

PROCESS

All AMCAS applicants are sent secondary applications. About 10 percent of those returning secondaries are interviewed between September and March. Interviews consist of 2 or 3 sessions each with a faculty member. On interview day, candidates also tour the campus and have lunch with current medical students. About one-third of interviewees are accepted on a rolling basis. Another group is wait listed. Wait listed candidates are not encouraged to send supplementary material.

Admissions Requirements (Required)

MCAT scores, essays/personal statement, extracurricular activities, exposure to medical profession

Admissions Requirements (Optional)

Science GPA, non-science GPA, letters of recommendation, interview, state residency

COSTS AND AID
Tuition & Fees

In-state tuition	$30,744
Out-of-state tuition	$42,742
Room and board (on-campus)	$6,144
Cost of books	$1,205
Fees	$448

Financial Aid

% students receiving aid	91
Average grant	$10,248
Average loan	$23,500
Average debt	$98,061

PONCE SCHOOL OF MEDICINE

PO Box 7004, Ponce, PR 00732 • Admission: 787-840-2575
Fax: 787-842-0461 • E-mail: ADMISSIONS@PSM.EDU • Website: WWW.PSM.EDU

STUDENT BODY

Type	Private
# applied (total/out)	1,274/927
# accepted (total/out)	174/40
# enrolled (total/out)	63/23

ADMISSIONS
Average GPA and MCAT Scores

Overall GPA	3.25
MCAT Bio	7
MCAT Phys	7.0
MCAT Verbal	8
MCAT Essay	M

Application Information

Regular application	12/15
Regular notification	Rolling
Early application	8/1
Early notification	10/5
Are transfers accepted?	Yes
Admissions may be deferred?	No
Interview required?	Yes
Application fee	$100

Academics

The primary goal of the Ponce School of Medicine is to provide quality medical education to bilingual students, with an emphasis on primary care and family medicine. The curriculum includes a strong emphasis on basic sciences, enabling students to get the most out of their clinical training. Longitudinal programs in preventive medicine and medical ethics are integrated into the 4-year curriculum.

BASIC SCIENCES: Basic sciences are taught during the first 2 years. First-year courses include the following: Behavioral Science, Biochemistry, Bioethics, Cellular Biology and Histology, General Pathology, Gross Anatomy Imaging and Embryology, Human Genetics, Microbiology and Immunology, Neuroscience, Physiology, and a year-long session devoted to clinical correlation. Second-year courses are Bioethics, Family and Community Medicine, Infectious Diseases, Introduction to Clinical Medicine, Pathophysiology, Pathology, Pharmacology, and Psychiatry. Instructional methods include computer-assisted learning, lectures, labs, and problem-based learning. Standardized patients are used for teaching and evaluation of basic clinical skills. During the first 2 years, students are in class or other scheduled sessions for about 30 hours per week. Students must pass Step I of the USMLE for promotion to year 3.

CLINICAL TRAINING

The third year begins in July with 2 weeks of a course called Introduction to Hospital Life. Following this orientation, students begin required clerkships. These are: Internal Medicine (10 weeks), Surgery (10 weeks), Pediatrics (10 weeks), Obstetrics/Gynecology (5 weeks), Psychiatry (5 weeks), and Family Medicine (5 weeks). The third year also includes a dean's hour, which emphasizes bioethics, health economics, law, literature, and medical humanities. In the fourth year, students participate in a required clerkship in medicine (4 weeks); a sub internship (medicine, obstetrics/gynecology, pediatrics, or family medicine); a clerkship in emergency medicine (4 weeks); and a primary care selective (4 weeks). Students are also required to complete 16 weeks of elective rotations, of which 5 weeks may be completed at sites other than Ponce. USMLE Step II must be passed prior to graduation.

Campus Life

STUDENT LIFE

The relatively small class size of 60 students encourages communication among students and faculty. The school's location is an asset, offering a pleasant environment for living and studying.

Admissions

REQUIREMENTS

Required undergraduate course work includes 8 semester credits in biology, general chemistry, organized chemistry, and physics in addition to 6 credits in advanced math and Spanish. Twelve credits in both behavioral sciences and English are also required. Behavioral science includes anthropology, economics, political sciences, psychology, and sociology. Applicants must have a minimum overall grade point average of 2.7 and an average of 2.5 in science courses. The MCAT is required, and scores should be from within one year of application. Applicants should have at least the mean on all sections of the MCAT.

SUGGESTIONS

In evaluating applicants, the Admissions Committee considers academic achievements, MCAT scores, interview reports, letters of recommendation, and other supplementary information. Preference is given to residents of Puerto Rico.

PROCESS

Ponce takes part in the AMCAS application process. The deadline for submission to AMCAS is December 15. Secondary applications are sent to all qualified applicants, and interviews are conducted throughout the spring.

Admissions Requirements (Required)

MCAT scores, science GPA, non-science GPA, letters of recommendation, interview, essays/personal statement

Admissions Requirements (Optional)

State residency, extracurricular activities, exposure to medical profession

COSTS AND AID

Tuition & Fees

In-state tuition	$19,051.77
Out-of-state tuition	$28,850.37
Fees	$2,625

Financial Aid

Average grant	$8,000
Average loan	$38.000
Average debt	$129,750

QUEEN'S UNIVERSITY
SCHOOL OF MEDICINE

68 BARRIE STREET, KINGSTON, ON K7L 3N6 • ADMISSION: 613-533-2542
FAX: 613-533-6190 • E-MAIL: JEB8@POST.QUEENSU.CA • WEBSITE: HTTP://MEDS.QUEENSU.CA

STUDENT BODY	
Type	Public
Enrollment	100
% male/female	52/48
% minorities	2
# applied	1,388
# accepted	175
# enrolled	100

ADMISSIONS
Average GPA and MCAT Scores

Overall GPA	3.6
MCAT Bio	11
MCAT Phys	11.11
MCAT Verbal	10.84
MCAT Essay	P

Application Information

Regular application	10/1
Regular notification	5/31
Are transfers accepted?	No
Admissions may be deferred?	Yes
Interview required?	Yes
Application fee	$250

Academics

Most students follow a 4-year curriculum leading to an MD degree. Masters and doctoral degree programs are also offered in biochemistry, biostatistics, environmental and occupational health, epidemiology, general community health, health-care systems, pathology, and preventive medicine. Although there are no formally structured combined programs, superior students may be permitted the flexibility to work toward an MSc or a PhD concurrently with the MD. Grading uses an honors/pass/fail system.

BASIC SCIENCES: Most basic science instruction takes place during the first 3 years. First-year course starts with Phase I, Introduction to the Sciences Relevant to Medicine, an introduction to the fundamental language and concepts of medical science, and Communication/Clinical Skills. Phase IIA includes Allergy and Immunology, Clinical Skills, Dermatology/Musculoskeletal Systems, Haematology and Oncology, and Microbiology and Infectious Diseases. Second-year courses are Clinical Skills, Genitourinary/Cardiovascular/Respirology, and Psychiatry/Neuroscience/Ophthalmology/ENT. In addition, 8 weeks are left open for an elective. Third year courses are Clinical Skills, Endocrine/Metabolism/Reproduction, and Gastrointestinal. In addition to problem-based learning, teaching methods include lectures, seminars, small-group discussions, laboratory experience, and computer-based instruction. Basic science instruction takes place primarily at Botterell Hall, which also houses administrative offices and Bracken Library. The Clinical Learning center is an important educational facility within the Faculty of Health Sciences specifically designed for the teaching, learning, and evaluation of important clinical skills, and is used during both pre-clinical and clinical years. The Health Sciences Library subscribes to approximately 844 serials, and its total collection consists of 156,000 volumes. In the library is the Multimedia Learning Centre, which offers both video- and computer-assisted instruction.

CLINICAL TRAINING

Clerkships begin in January of the third year. They are: Medicine (12 weeks), Surgery (8 weeks), Psychiatry (6 weeks), Obstetrics/Gynecology (6 weeks), Pediatrics (6 weeks), Family Medicine (4 weeks), Geriatrics (2 weeks), and Emergency Medicine (2 weeks). Four weeks of selectives and 12 weeks of electives are also required. Clerkships takes place at a number of affiliated hospitals, including Kingston General Hospital, Hotel Dieu Hospital, St. Mary's of the Lake Hospital, Kingston Psychiatric Hospital, and Ongwanada Hospital. The provision of health care services in Kingston is presently being restructured and will change over the next few years.

Campus Life

Each class has 90 students, about 50 of whom are typically from the province of Ontario. The student body is approximately 50 percent women.

STUDENT LIFE

Medical students enjoy the recreational, cultural, social activities of the greater university, and the city of Kingston. On-campus attractions include museums, concert halls, cinema, and an observatory. Student services include a child care resource center, a foundation supporting women, comprehensive health services, an international center, a physical education center, and a student center. The university provides accommodations in single and double occupancy rooms for approximately 300 graduate students. In addition, the Apartment and Housing Office manages university-owned rentals in the area.

Admissions

REQUIREMENTS

In order to apply, students must have completed 3 years of full-time study at a university. In addition, 1 year each of biological sciences, physical sciences, and humanities/social sciences are required. The MCAT is required. To be eligible for admission, applicants must be Canadian citizens, Canadian permanent residents, or children of Queen's University alumni.

SUGGESTIONS

The Admissions Committee looks for both academic abilities, such as commitment, achievement, critical thinking, and self-directed learning, and personal characteristics such as communication skills, creativity, and sensitivity. No preference is given to a particular undergraduate program of studies, and college students seeking admission are encouraged to pursue studies in their area of interest.

PROCESS

Applicants seeking further information about admission should contact the School of Medicine. Applications are made through the following: Ontario Medical Schools' Application Service, 70 Research Lane, Guelph, Ontario N1G 5E2. The deadline is October 15. The first admissions cutoff is based on the cumulative converted grade point average, and the second is made on the basis of MCAT scores. Those applicants who qualify are interviewed. Applicants are then ranked according to evaluation of letters of reference, autobiographic sketch, and interview results.

Admissions Requirements (Required)

MCAT scores, science GPA, non-science GPA, letters of recommendation, interview, essays/personal statement, extracurricular activities

Overlap Schools

McMaster University, University of Ottawa, University of Toronto, University of Western Ontario.

COSTS AND AID

Tuition & Fees

Tuition $13,500

ROSALIND FRANKLIN UNIVERSITY OF MEDICINE AND SCIENCE

OFFICE OF ADMISSIONS, 3333 GREEN BAY ROAD NORTH, CHICAGO, IL 60064 • ADMISSION: 847-578-3204
FAX: 847-578-3284 • E-MAIL: CMS.ADMISSIONS@ROSALINDFRANKLIN.EDU • WEBSITE: WWW.ROSALINDFRANKLIN.EDU

STUDENT BODY

Type	Private
Enrollment	750
% male/female	57/43
% minorities	6
# applied (total/out)	7,210/6,203
# accepted (total/out)	438/313
# enrolled (total/out)	184/112
Average age	23

FACULTY

Total faculty (number)	674
% female	27
% part-time	44
Student-faculty ratio	1:1

ADMISSIONS

Average GPA and MCAT scores

Overall GPA	3.45
MCAT Bio	10.2
MCAT Phys	10
MCAT Verbal	9
MCAT Essay	P

Application Information

Regular application	11/1
Regular notification	10/15
Early application	7/1–9/1
Early notification	10/1
Are transfers accepted?	Yes
Admissions may be deferred?	Yes
Interview required?	Yes
Application fee	$95

Academics

Founded in 1912, Rosalind Franklin University of Medicine and Science has been dedicated to excellence in medical education for nearly a century. The school has educated thousands of professionals with recognized innovation in health education, excellence in the creation of knowledge, and scientific discovery focused on prediction and prevention of disease, outstanding clinical programs, and compassionate community service. Major hospital affiliates include Advocate Lutheran General Hospital, John H. Stroger Jr., Hospital of Cook County, Mount Sinai Hospital and Medical Center, and the North Chicago Veterans Affairs Medical Center (NCVAMC). The university's clinical campus consists of the NCVAMC and The Clinics at Rosalind Franklin University.

BASIC SCIENCES: Rosalind Franklin University of Medicine and Science curriculum offers a strong grounding in the sciences basic to medicine along with assuring competency in skills necessary for the practice of medicine. The curriculum features a unique interprofessional approach with interaction among a broad range of health professional students and practitioners. The curriculum is a mix of lectures, labs, small group discussions, team-based learning, and opportunities for peer to peer learning. Our educational information system, Desire to Learn (D2L), provides 24-hour-a-day access to learning materials. Topic integration across courses and a unique interprofessional teams course are the hallmark of the M1 curriculum.

CLINICAL TRAINING

Students have early clinical experiences in our state of the art evaluation and education center, as well as opportunities to connect with physician preceptors. The required junior clinical clerkships include Ambulatory Care, Family Medicine, Medcore, Medicine, Neurology and Emergency Medicine, Obstetrics/Gynecology, Psychiatry, Pediatrics, and Surgery. The senior requirements include 4 weeks in a medicine or pediatrics sub internship, plus 32 weeks of approved electives (14 of which must be intramural). The elective period gives students an opportunity, through both intramural and extramural experiences, to explore and strengthen their personal career interests.

Campus Life

Rosalind Franklin University of Medicine and Science is situated in the northern suburbs of Chicago, with easy access to downtown Chicago and the surrounding areas by car or public transportation. The university's main campus comprises a four-story Basic Sciences Building and a newly constructed Health Sciences Building. State-of-the-art facilities include a recently completed $10 million research wing expansion, multimedia classrooms and gross anatomy laboratory, and an Education and Evaluation Center for physical examination skills training. Recreation facilities include an exercise room, game room, and the Student Union (home to the University Bookstore, Union Café, and dedicated e-mail stations). Underrepresented minorities, mostly African American students, account for about 8 percent of the student body. Of the class entering in 2005, 20.5 percent were in-state residents. The entering class size in 2005 was 185.

STUDENT LIFE

Most first- and second-year students live in the vicinity of campus and drive to school. On-campus housing is available at Rosalind Franklin University. Each of the university's 3 apartment buildings has 5 floors and consists of 60 one- and two-bedroom apartments. Individual apartments feature a variety of amenities, such as kitchen appliances, fully networked Internet connectivity, and washer/dryer hookups. Each apartment building also includes study and lounge areas, shared laundry facilities on every floor, and individual storage units. Often, third- and fourth-year students elect to live in Chicago, where they are closer to clinical training sites. Public transportation from downtown Chicago to campus facilitates such living arrangements. Chicago is one of the largest and most culturally rich cities in the country, providing a wealth of entertainment, museums, theater, restaurants, nightlife, indoor and outdoor athletic activities, and spectator sporting events. The city provides distraction for medical students when they need it. Students have a voice in school administrative affairs through the university student council and through participation on various boards and committees. Rosalind Franklin University has chapters of most national medical student associations and has special interest clubs and organizations based on recreational activities, professional interests, and ethnic/social background.

GRADUATES

Of the 2005 graduating class, the most popular specialty choices were internal medicine (22.7 percent), pediatrics (10.2 percent), emergency medicine (9.7 percent), family practice (9.1 percent), anesthesia (6.8 percent), general surgery (5.7 percent), obstetrics/gynecology (5.1 percent), and orthopedics (5.1 percent).

Admissions

REQUIREMENTS

One year of biology, chemistry, organic chemistry, and physics, all with labs, are required. The MCAT is required and must be no more than 3 years old at time of matriculation. For multiple exams, the most recent set of scores are used.

SUGGESTIONS

In addition to requirements, courses in math, social sciences, English, and the arts are recommended. A solid preparation in science, accompanied by a broad background in the liberal arts, is recommended. The Admissions Committee also puts strong emphasis on other non-academic factors, such as an applicant's motivation, character, personality, experience, and achievements.

PROCESS

In addition to the AMCAS, a secondary application is required. Interviews take place from October through May and consist of 2 sessions with faculty, administrators, and/or medical students. Notification of acceptance begins in November and is an ongoing process until the class is filled. Candidates awaiting a decision may submit supplemental information about course work, activities, or new MCAT scores.

Admissions Requirements (Required)

MCAT scores, science GPA, non-science GPA, letters of recommendation, interview, essay/personal statement, exposure to medical profession, 1 year of each of the following with a lab: biology, physics, organic chemistry, inorganic chemistry

Admissions Requirements (Optional)

State residency, extracurricular activities

Overlap Schools

Loyola University—Chicago, New York Medical College, Rush Medical College of Rush University, University of Illinois at Chicago.

COSTS AND AID

Tuition & Fees

Tuition	$36,740
Room and board	$16,000
Cost of books	$1,730
Fees	$160

Financial Aid

% students receiving aid	84
Average grant	$6,521
Average loan	$41,581
Average debt	$169,863

RUSH UNIVERSITY
RUSH MEDICAL COLLEGE

OFFICE OF ADMISSIONS, 524 AAC, 600 SOUTH PAULINA, CHICAGO, IL 60612 • ADMISSION: 312-942-6915
FAX: 312-942-2333 • E-MAIL: RMC_ADMISSIONS@RUSH.EDU • WEBSITE: WWW.RUSHU.RUSH.EDU/MEDCOL

STUDENT BODY

Type	Private
# applied	5,406
# accepted	262
# enrolled (total/out)	128/25
Average age	23

ADMISSIONS
Average GPA and MCAT Scores

Overall GPA	3.6
MCAT Bio	10
MCAT Phys	10
MCAT Verbal	10
MCAT Essay	Q

Application Information

Regular application	11/1
Regular notification	Rolling
Early application	NA
Early notification	NA
Are transfers accepted?	No
Admissions may be deferred?	Yes
Interview required?	Yes
Application fee	$70

Academics

Rush provides a firm background in the science of medicine and a balanced introduction to the practice of clinical medicine in a four-year curriculum designed to provide educational flexibility. The faculty have created an environment that fosters commitments to competent and compassionate patient care and to attitudes of inquiry and life-long learning. USMLE Step 1 and USMLE Step 2 Clinical Skills (CS) and Clinical Knowledge (CK) are required. A passing score on the USMLE Step 1 is required for promotion to year 3.

BASIC SCIENCES: The first year exposes students to the vocabulary and fundamental concepts upon which clinical medicine is based. The courses are taught by discipline and utilize lecture, lab, small groups, and workshops. The second year centers on the causes and effects of disease and therapeutics. The pathophysiology course utilizes a case-based approach during its workshops. Students also participate in clinical skills courses, which include the Primary Care Preceptorship, Interviewing and Communication, and Physical Diagnosis.

CLINICAL TRAINING

The third and fourth years provide students with training in clinical skills, diagnosis, and patient management in a variety of clinical settings. The third year is comprised of required core clerkships: Internal Medicine (12 weeks), Surgery (8 weeks), Pediatrics (8 weeks), Obstetrics & Gynecology (6 weeks), Family Medicine (4 weeks), and Psychiatry (4 weeks). Neurology (4 weeks) may be taken in the third or fourth year. In the fourth year, students participate in a four-week subinternship (family medicine, internal medicine, pediatrics, or surgery) and pursue areas of special interest. Students complete the majority of their required clinical rotations at Rush University Medical Center or the John H. Stroger, Jr. Hospital of Cook County.

Campus Life

Rush Medical College is located on the near west side of Chicago. The John H. Stroger, Jr. Hospital of Cook County, a major teaching affiliate, is two blocks away. The community is thriving and culturally diverse, with easy access by public transportation.

STUDENT LIFE

Rush seeks to attract students who will promote an environment of tolerance, respect and compassion, and who will make the student body more representative of the national population and more informed about the social problems affecting the delivery of health care. Student housing is available in the Center Court Garden Apartments, located one block from campus. The Rush Community Service Initiatives Program creates a network of community programs that matches students' interest and initiative with the social and healthcare needs of Chicago's underserved population. Students have the opportunity to participate in clinical and non-clinical programs.

GRADUATES

In 2008, Rush medical students matched in 19 distinct specialties at 66 institutions in 27 different states across the nation.

Admissions

REQUIREMENTS

Prerequisites are 8 semester hours each of inorganic chemistry, organic chemistry, biology, and physics. The MCAT is required. For the entering class of 2009, scores must be dated January 2007 or later.

SUGGESTIONS

The Committee on Admissions considers both the academic and non-academic qualifications of applicants in making its decisions and places strong emphasis on the applicant's humanistic concerns, unique experiences and demonstrated motivation for a career in medicine. All applicants are invited to complete the supplemental application and submit letters of recommendation. The Committee looks for objective evidence that the applicant will be able to handle the academic demands of the curriculum. We look at the selected community, health-related or social service activities as a measure of how an applicant pursues their values, engages in activities that move them outside of their usual boundaries and expands their horizons. Academic achievement, letters of recommendation, MCAT performance, health care experience and interviews are considered in the final evaluation of all applicants. Only U.S. citizens or permanent residents are considered for admission.

PROCESS

All AMCAS applicants are invited to complete a Supplemental Application. Approximately 400 applicants will be invited for on-campus interviews between September and March. The interview day consists of two 40-minute interviews, tours of the clinical and academic facilities, and the opportunity to meet with current students. Each year 128 students matriculate; approximately 70 to 75 percent of the entering class are in-state residents.

Admissions Requirements (Required)

MCAT scores, science GPA, non-science GPA, letters of recommendation, interview, state residency, essays/personal statement, extracurricular activities, exposure to medical profession

COSTS AND AID

Tuition & Fees

Tuition	$44,900
Cost of books	$1,400
Fees	$0

Financial Aid

% students receiving aid	90

SAINT LOUIS UNIVERSITY
SCHOOL OF MEDICINE

COMMITTEE ON ADMISSIONS, 1402 S. GRAND BLVD., M226 ST. LOUIS, MO 63104 • ADMISSION: 314-977-9870
FAX: 314-977-9825 • E-MAIL: SLUMD@SLU.EDU • WEBSITE: MEDSCHOOL.SLU.EDU

STUDENT BODY

Type	Private
Enrollment	668
% male/female	57/43
% minorities	27
# applied (total/out)	5,062/4,732
# accepted (total/out)	593/517
# enrolled (total/out)	179/144

FACULTY

Total faculty	537
% female	32
% minority	22
% part-time	8
Student-faculty ratio	35:1

ADMISSIONS
Average GPA and MCAT Scores

Overall GPA	3.72
MCAT Bio	10.69
MCAT Phys	10.29
MCAT Verbal	10.24
MCAT Essay	P

Application Information

Regular application	12/15
Regular notification	10/15
Early application	6/1–8/1
Early notification	10/1
Are transfers accepted?	Yes
Admissions may be deferred?	Yes
Interview required?	Yes
Application fee	$100

Academics

The medical curriculum is continually evolving to respond to the rapid changes in the health care field and to reflect national trends in medical education. Current students enjoy a program of study that uses a block schedule and human organ systems-based learning and emphasizes small-group and independent study. SLU offers several options for students interested in research. Qualified students may enter an M.D./Ph.D. program, allowing them to complete both degrees within 6-7 years. The doctorate is offered in Anatomy, Health Care Ethics, Biochemistry, Cell Biology, Genetics, Immunology, Microbiology, Molecular Biology, Neuroscience, Pathology, Pharmacology, and Physiology. Students interested in summer or elective research experiences may graduate in four years, earning an M.D. with distinction in research. Medical students are evaluated with Honors, Pass, or Fail throughout all four years. Passing the USMLE Step 1 is a requirement for promotion to year three, and passing Step 2 CK and taking Step 2 CS is a requirement for graduation.

BASIC SCIENCES: The first and second years each consist of 36 weeks of instruction, which includes laboratories, demonstrations, discussion groups, didactic lecture sessions, and preceptorships at clinical sites. Students are in class or other scheduled sessions for about 20 hours per week, providing ample time for self-directed learning. First-year courses are Human Anatomy; Cell Biology; Metabolism; Microbes and Host Responses; Introduction to Pathology; Molecular Biology and Genetics; Principles of Pharmacology; Health Information Resources; and Patient, Physician, and Society Series 1, which covers topics such as Normal Development, Epidemiology and Biostatistics, Applied Clinical Skills, and Health Care Ethics. Second-year courses are Nervous System; Hematopoietic and Lymphatic Systems; Cardiovascular System; Respiratory System; Renal-Urinary System; Gastrointestinal System; Bone Skin and Joint; Endocrine and Reporductive Systems; and Patient, Physician, and Society 2, which includes Applied Clinical Skills 2 and electives. An important resource for students is the Learning Resources Center, which houses the Health Sciences Center Library, anesthesiology lab, and the Clinical Skills Center, where diagnostic and treatment skills are taught.

CLINICAL TRAINING

The third year consists of core clerkships in most basic medical fields. These are Surgical Subspecialties (4 weeks); Internal Medicine (12 weeks); Surgery (8 weeks); Ob/Gyn (6 weeks); Pediatrics (8 weeks); Family Medicine (6 weeks); Psychiatry (6 weeks); and Neurology (4 weeks). The fourth year is flexible, allowing students to pursue elective opportunities in both clinical and research areas. A minimum of 36 weeks of instruction must be completed. Required rotations are in Intramural Floor Service (4 weeks) and Surgery Subspecialty Selective (4 weeks). Training is conducted at the St. Louis University Hospital, a 365-bed tertiary care facility. It is also a Level I trauma center. Other affiliated institutions include the Cardinal Glennon Children's Hospital, the Anheuser-Busch Eye Institute, David P. Wohl Mental Health Institute, St. Elizabeth's Hospital, St. John's Mercy Medical Center, St. Mary's Hospital, Bethesda Cancer Research Ceneter, and the St. Louis Veterans Affairs Medical Center. A portion of electives may be taken at other academic and clinical institutions.

Students

Students come from all regions of the country. About 10 percent of students are underrepresented minorities and about 30 percent are nontraditional, having pursued other careers or interests between college and medical school.

STUDENT LIFE

SLU students can pursue their health-related interests by taking part in research forums or by participating in the School's many organizations. The campus ministry is particularly strong. Those who need a break from academic and career pursuits can take advantage of the resources of the main campus, including the award-winning Simon Recreational Center or the well-subscribed intramural sports program. St. Louis also offers a wide variety of extracurricular activities. Tower Grove Park and the Missouri Botanical Gardens are a few blocks from the Medical School. Nearby Forest Park, one of the nation's largest metropolitan parks, is the home of the St. Louis Zoo, the Art Museum, and the Science Center. St. Louis also has its own opera, theater, and ballet, in addition to professional baseball, football, and hockey teams. Although the school has some housing facilities, most medical students choose to live off campus, where housing is affordable and comfortable.

GRADUATES

About 42 percent of graduates enter primary care residencies. Our students are competitive applicants for specialty and surgical fields as well.

Admissions

REQUIREMENTS

Requirements are one year each of Chemistry, Biology, Organic Chemistry, and Physics. A laboratory is required for all science coursework. In addition, 6 semester hours of English and 12 hours of Humanities or Behavioral Science are expected. The MCAT is required. For applicants who have taken the exam more than once, the best set of scores is considered.

SUGGESTIONS

Students should apply early in the application cycle as interviews and acceptances are given on a rolling basis. Both hospital and research experience is highly valuable. Activities that demonstrate a commitment to serving others is also useful.

PROCESS

All AMCAS applicants receive secondary applications. Of the approximately 4,200 students who return secondaries, about 23 percent are interviewed on a rolling basis. Interviews are one hour in length and are conducted by a faculty member. The remainder of the interview day includes a tour of the campus, group informational sessions, and lunch with current students. Applicants are notified of committee decisions in 6 to 8 weeks of the interview and are either accepted, rejected, or put into a hold category. Approximately 45 percent of the interviewed group is accepted. For wait-listed applicants, additional grades or new MCAT scores are useful supplementary information.

Admissions Requirements (Required)

MCAT scores, Science GPA, Non-science GPA, Letters of recommendation, Interview, Essays/personal statement

Admissions Requirements (Optional)

State residency, Extracurricular activities, Exposure to medical profession, Exposure to research, volunteer experience

Overlap Schools

Creighton University, Ohio University, University of Illinois at Chicago, University of Minnesota, University of Missouri—Columbia, University of Southern California, Washington University in St. Louis (Olin).

COSTS AND AID
Tuition & Fees

Tuition	$42,140
Room and board (off-campus)	$11,988
Cost of books	$1,040
Fees	$643

Financial Aid

% students receiving aid	83
Average grant	$7,778
Average loan	$48,330
Average debt	$156,722

SOUTHERN ILLINOIS UNIVERSITY
SCHOOL OF MEDICINE

PO Box 19624 SPRINGFIELD, IL 62794-9624 • **ADMISSION:** 217-545-6013
FAX: 217-545-5538 • **E-MAIL:** ADMISSIONS@SIUMED.EDU • **WEBSITE:** WWW.SIUMED.EDU

STUDENT BODY

Type	Public
Enrollment	289
% male/female	47/53
% minorities	14
# applied (total/out)	1,034/57
# accepted (total/out)	158/2
# enrolled (total/out)	72/2
Average age	23

FACULTY

Total faculty (number)	336
% female	37
% minority	19
% part-time	6
Student-faculty ratio	1:1

ADMISSIONS
Average GPA and MCAT scores

Overall GPA	3.53
MCAT Bio	9.14
MCAT Phys	8.57
MCAT Verbal	9.36
MCAT Essay	0

Application Information

Regular application	11/15
Regular notification	10/15
Are transfers accepted?	Yes
Admissions may be deferred?	Yes
Interview required?	Yes
Application fee	$50

Academics

SIU offers a case-based, small group-oriented curriculum with an abundance of patient contact and early clinical exposure. In cooperation with the SIU School of Law, an MD/JD joint-degree program is also offered. Medical students are evaluated on a pass/fail scale and with an honors system. Students must pass the USMLE Step 1 to graduate.

BASIC SCIENCES: The instructional format not only emphasizes small group instruction, self-directed study, and a case-based approach, but also it incorporates lectures and an organ system organizational scheme. Courses covered in the first year are Cardiovascular, Endocrine, Gastrointestinal, Renal, Reproductive, Respiratory, and Sensorimotor Systems and Behavior. In Carbondale, basic science instruction takes place in Lindegren Hall. Early clinical experiences are offered at Memorial Hospital in Carbondale (151 beds), the Carbondale Clinic, offices of local physicians, and at the Veterans Affairs Hospital (171 beds). In Springfield, the medical instructional facility contains lecture halls, classrooms, labs, and a teaching museum. A 4-year doctoring curriculum (which covers topics such as physicians' conduct and attitudes, Clinical Skills development, and medical humanities issues) begins immediately. Both simulated and real patients are used. Courses covered in the second year include Circulation, Infection and Host Diseases, Neuromuscular Medicine and Behavior, Neoplasia, Population Health, and Preventative Medicine. Computer-assisted instruction is used as a learning aid, and computers are available in the student computer lab and at other sites. The Morris Library at Carbondale houses more than 100,000 volumes, while the Medical Instruction Facility in Springfield contains 113,000.

CLINICAL TRAINING

The required multidisciplinary rotations in students' third year are Internal Medicine, Surgery, Family and Community Medicine, Psychiatry, Obstetrics/Gynecology, and Pediatrics. Four weeks of electives, which may include Emergency Medicine, Radiology, and Anesthesiology, are allowed in the third year. The doctoring curriculum continues during this year. At the conclusion of the third year, students must pass an examination that evaluates their skills in assessing and managing patient problems. During the fourth year, students complete 1 additional required clerkship: Neurology (4 weeks). Thirty-one weeks are reserved for elective studies. Clinical training sites include Memorial Medical Center (580 beds), St. John's Hospital and Pavilion (715 beds), and the clinics and offices of faculty and community physicians. Electives may be taken off campus, and SIU has an institutional agreement with overseas universities—including locations in Germany and the Netherlands—that facilitates training overseas.

Campus Life

All regular MD students are Illinois residents. The average age of incoming students is 24. Underrepresented minorities account for 14 percent of the student body. The class size is 72 students.

STUDENT LIFE

On-campus recreational facilities at Carbondale include a complete fitness room, swimming pools, racquetball courts, and a student center. Taking part in intramural sports and attending intercollegiate sporting events are popular extracurricular activities for medical students. St. Louis, with the amenities of a large city, is a 2-hour drive away. The surrounding area features a state park and the Shawnee National Forest, where the students can hike, bike, camp, canoe, or enjoy the beach. In Springfield, medical students enjoy membership at a local fitness center. Lake Springfield offers fishing, swimming, boating, and sailing. Parks, golf courses, and cultural and historical sites are other local attractions. All students live off campus in both Carbondale and Springfield.

GRADUATES

Among the 2006 graduating class, the most prevalent fields for postgraduate training were internal medicine (16 percent), pediatrics (15 percent), and emergency medicine (11 percent), family medicine (21 percent), general surgery (7 percent), and obstetrics/gynecology. Students generally score around the national mean on the USMLE Part 1 and above the mean on Part 2, making them well positioned for securing residency positions.

Admissions

REQUIREMENTS

To do well on the MCAT, students should have taken at least 1 year each of biology, chemistry, English, math (which should have included some statistics), organic chemistry, and physics. The MCAT is required, and scores must be no more than 2 years old. For applicants who have taken the exam on multiple occasions, the most recent set of scores is considered.

SUGGESTIONS

As a state school, preference is given to applicants from Central and Southern Illinois who are interested in practicing in the region. Applicants are expected to have a good foundation in the natural sciences, social sciences, and humanities in addition to sound English skills. The Admissions Committee looks beyond scholastic achievement for evidence of responsibility, integrity, compassion, motivation, interest in medicine, community service, and sound interpersonal skills. The Medical Education Preparatory Program (MEDPREP) is a non-degree postbaccalaureate program that assists disadvantaged students with meeting the requirements for medical schools throughout the country.

PROCESS

About one-quarter of the applicants are interviewed. Interviews are conducted between August and March and consist of 2 sessions with individual faculty and/or administrators. About 30 percent of interviewed candidates are accepted on a batch basis. Others are rejected or wait listed. Wait listed candidates may send supplemental material to update their files.

Admissions Requirements (Required)

MCAT scores, science GPA, non-science GPA, letters of recommendation, interview, state residency, essay/personal statement, extracurricular activities, volunteer/employment experience

Admissions Requirement (Optional)

Exposure to medical profession

Overlap School

University of Illinois—Chicago.

COSTS AND AID

Tuition & Fees

In-state tuition	$20,144
Out-of-state tuition	$54,936
Room and board (off-campus)	$6,956
Cost of books	$5,650
In-state fees	$2,140
Out-of-state fees	$1,673

Financial Aid

% students receiving aid	20
Average grant	$13,681
Average loan	$29,338
Average debt	$28,736

St. George's University*
School of Medicine

Admissions Office, One East Main Street, Bay Shore, NY 11706-8399 • Admission: 800-899-6337
Fax: 631-665-5590 • E-mail: SGUINFO@SGU.EDU • Website: WWW.SGU.EDU

STUDENT BODY

Type	Private
Enrollment	2,485
% male/female	56/44
# applied	1,780
# enrolled	347
Average age	25

FACULTY

Total faculty (number)	158
% part-time	31

ADMISSIONS
Average GPA and MCAT Scores

Overall GPA	3.35
MCAT Bio	9
MCAT Phys	9
MCAT Verbal	8

Application Information

Regular application	Rolling
Regular notification	Rolling
Interview required?	Yes
Application fee	$75

Academics

Founded as an independent school of medicine in Grenada over 28 years ago, St. George's University has evolved into a top international center of education, offering medical, premedical, veterinary, and preveterinary programs. The School of Medicine also offers advanced research degrees in the biomedical sciences, a Master of Public Health, and a variety of combined-degree programs.

Over 5,500 physicians have graduated from the School of Medicine and are practicing medicine in over 35 countries and every state in the United States. They practice in virtually every specialty and subspecialty, and in positions in academic medicine, as well as public health and institutional practice. Students' scores on standardized tests over the years attest to the academic excellence of our curriculum. St. George's University has a 5-year average pass rate of 90 percent for first time USMLE Step I examinees, far exceeding the 62 percent average pass rate of all non-U.S. schools during the same period.

State Education Departments across the United States and various Government Councils around the world have conducted site visits and extensive evaluations of our medical program, and St. George's University has received a favorable review each time, meeting or exceeding all standards.

BASIC SCIENCES: The first 2 years of study concentrate on the traditional basic science disciplines and the curriculum incorporates small-group discussions designed for problem-based learning, lectures and laboratory experiences. Clinical Skills are introduced into the first term and enhanced by hospital visits to the Kato Memorial Hospital in St. Vincent during terms 5 and 6, emphasizing integration of basic science into the clinical experience.

CLINICAL TRAINING

St. George's offers a highly integrated system of affiliated hospitals and Clinical Centers in the United States, all of whose core rotations have ACGME-approved residency training programs running concurrently. The program in the United Kingdom is similar to that in the United States, providing students with clinical opportunities at over 50 affiliated hospitals in the U.S. and U.K. Although clinical training may be completed in one country, students may combine clinical experiences in the United States and the United Kingdom for a more international experience.

Campus Life

Over the last 10 years, over 52 new buildings have been beautifully blended into the Caribbean environment on the True Blue campus in Grenada. The brand-new administrative, residential, academic, and scientific buildings include a 45,000-square-foot fully electronic library; gross anatomy laboratory; Microbiology, pathology, and histology laboratories with extensive microscopic and gross preparations collections and an up-to-date array of audiovisual and computerized materials in all subjects.

The student center is home to 2 restaurants, a fully equipped weight room, and exercise facilities. After classes and on weekends students can also be found on the new sports fields and basketball courts, participating in many sporting activities and team sports. There is on-campus housing. In addition, there are numerous choices for living off-campus which can be accessed by the university bus system.

From the first contact with the university, the welfare of each student is carefully considered and safeguarded. Financial counselors stay closely involved with students through the course of their study and beyond, to ensure their financial health; the Dean of Students Office monitors and supports students in academic progress as well as non-academic activities and concerns, and Department of Educational Services provides course work tutorials, workshops in study, test-taking, and time-management skills.

Additionally, Counseling Service offers both formal clinical and peer counseling services. Throughout clinicals and after graduation the Office of Career Guidance advises students and graduates in specialty selection, residency application processes, and CV development. The university also supports programs and opportunities for spouses and dependents through our SOs Club (Significant Others) which sponsors a regular series of events and gatherings, developing a close camaraderie among club members.

STUDENT LIFE

Students attend their basic science years on our campuses in Grenada and the neighboring island of St. Vincent. The inhabitants of both islands are English speaking, and all course work is delivered in English. Students have options of taking clinical rotations in the U.S. and/or in the U.K. The community at St. George's University gathers there from all 4 corners of the world—it is extremely diverse. Over 90 nations are represented in the student population and over 25 student organizations are organized around various interests—cultural, religious, avocational, and community service.

Students participate in many types of sporting activities and team sports such as basketball, tennis, flag football, soccer, cricket, badminton, volleyball, street hockey, lacrosse, and softball to name a few. Water sports include sailing, boating, swimming, snorkeling, and scuba diving. Aerobics, fitness, and martial arts classes are held regularly.

Admissions

REQUIREMENTS

Applicants are advised that the Board of Admissions requires an academic indicator within the 3 years prior to making application. MCAT scores must be from within the 3 years prior to application and may be used as a recent academic indicator.

A bachelor's degree from an accredited university is required. In rare instances, an unusually well-qualified applicant is considered for admission with only 3 years of postsecondary education completed toward a bachelor's degree. (Please see the website for additional information about course work required prior to admissions.) All North American applicants must submit MCAT scores. If English is not the applicant's principal language, he/she must submit an official record of a score of at least 600 from the Test of English as a Foreign Language (TOEFL).

PROCESS

The Office of Admissions will acknowledge receipt of a candidate's application within 2 weeks. A candidate will be informed of any required supporting documents missing at that time. Within one month after receipt of all application materials, a candidate will receive notice that the application is complete and is being reviewed to determine whether an interview will be granted. Candidates are advised that being granted an interview is no guarantee of acceptance; the interview itself plays a significant part in the decision by the Board of Admissions.

For information or to speak to an Admissions Counselor, interested students can call 800-899-6337 or visit www.sgu.edu.

Admissions Requirements (Required)

MCAT scores, science GPA, non-science GPA, letters of recommendation, interview, essays/personal statement, extracurricular activities

Admissions Requirements (Optional)

State residency, exposure to medical profession

COSTS AND AID
Tuition & Fees

Tuition $29,837

* INTERNATIONAL MEDICAL SCHOOL

NOT ACCREDITED BY AAMC

STANFORD UNIVERSITY
SCHOOL OF MEDICINE

OFFICE OF MD ADMISSIONS, 251 CAMPUS DR., MSOB XC301 STANFORD, CA 94305-5404 • ADMISSION: 650-723-6861
FAX: 650-725-7855 • E-MAIL: MDADMISSIONS@STANFORD.EDU • WEBSITE: WWW.MED.STANFORD.EDU

STUDENT BODY

Type	Private
Enrollment	463
% male/female	51/49
% minorities	22
# applied (total/out)	5,999/3,796
# accepted (total/out)	175/116
# enrolled (total/out)	86/51
Average age	24

FACULTY

Total faculty (number)	710
% female	33
% minority	5

ADMISSIONS
Average GPA and MCAT scores

Overall GPA	3.7
MCAT Bio	12.03
MCAT Phys	11.84
MCAT Verbal	10.48
MCAT Essay	Q

Application Information

Regular application	10/15
Regular notification	Rolling
Early application	6/1–8/1
Early notification	10/1
Are transfers accepted?	Yes
Admissions may be deferred?	Yes
Interview required?	Yes
Application fee	$85

Academics

Generally, about 60 percent of Stanford students receive their MD in 5 rather than 4 years, which allows for individual research and elective study. In addition to the MD, departmental dual degrees include a PhD in biochemistry, developmental biology, genetics, microbiology and immunology, molecular and cellular physiology, chemical and systems biology, and structural biology. Interdepartmental joint-degrees are also possible and include an MS in biomechanical engineering and health services research, an MS and PhD in epidemiology and medical information dciences, and a PhD in biophysics, cancer biology, immunology, and neuroscience. There are about 6–8 Medical Scientist Training Program (MSTP) slots available. In addition to formal degree programs, students may take electives in nonmedical departments. Through the Medical Student Scholars Fellowship Program and other programs, students enjoy a range of research opportunities, most of which are remunerated.

BASIC SCIENCES: The Stanford curriculum melds a strong introduction to basic science and clinical experience with in-depth study and independent research through scholarly concentrations. In the first 5 quarters, in-depth instruction in basic science and the pathophysiology of disease runs in parallel with clinical skills instruction and the introduction to patient care in the Practice of Medicine course sequence. The Practice of Medicine sequence is held on 2 afternoons per week, using a combination of small and large group instructional formats. Topic areas include clinical skills (history-taking and physical examination), medical ethics, biostatistics and epidemiology, health care systems, clinical psychiatry, and other aspects of the practice of medicine in society. In quarters 1 and 2, the Foundations of Medicine courses include Anatomy (taught through a traditional cadaver lab), Cells to Tissues, Genetics, Development and Disease Mechanisms, Immunology, Molecular Biology, and Overview of the Nervous System. Wednesdays remain unscheduled throughout the first 6 quarters so that students may engage in electives and course work for their scholarly concentration. Quarter 3 initiates the integrated Human Health and Disease course sequence using a modular organ-system based approach with instruction in Histology, Infectious Disease, Pathology, Pharmacology, and Physiology. Instruction in the Practice of Medicine continues at the same time over the first 5 quarters, culminating in quarter 6 with a 4-week intensive course that prepares students for clinical clerkships. In conjunction with their MD studies, students also participate in course work and complete a project in a scholarly concentration. The Stanford curriculum is structured to encourage students to engage in individual or group study, elective course work, research, and other opportunities for professional growth, with many students electing to extend their studies for an additional year. Grading is on a pass/fail basis. Step 1 of the USMLE must be passed no later than 1 year prior to graduation, with 2 months available for study between quarter 6 and the beginning of clinical clerkships. Step 2 must be passed prior to graduation.

CLINICAL TRAINING

Patient contact begins in the fall quarter of the first year, and there are opportunities for clinical experiences during the first 2 years. Third- and fourth-year clerkships take place at the major affiliated teaching hospitals, which include Stanford Hospital (613 beds), the Lucile Salter Packard Children's Hospital (264 beds), Santa Clara Valley Medical Center (524 beds), the Palo Alto Veterans Affairs Hospital (900 beds), and Kaiser Permanente (327 beds). These facilities serve both rural and urban populations with diverse needs. Students complete 15.5 months of clinical clerkships, including 12.5 months of required core clerkships in General Medicine, General Surgery, Pediatrics, Obstetrics/Gynecology, Psychiatry, Family Medicine, Ambulatory Internal Medicine, Neurology, and Critical Care. Two months are spent training in areas related to required clerkships through selectives, in which students choose from Fundamentals of Clinical Care and Sub internship. The final month is designated as an elective clerkship.

Campus Life

Stanford students are often characterized as being less cutthroat than those attending other top-ranked schools, perhaps because the flexible curriculum encourages students to focus beyond the classroom. Special effort is made to recruit students from under-represented minority backgrounds, and student organizations support these and other student groups. With 86 students per class, Stanford is relatively small.

STUDENT LIFE

The campus and the surrounding area offer excellent sports and other outdoor activities. San Francisco is 35 minutes to the north, San Jose is 20 minutes south, and Oakland is 45 minutes northeast. All are accessible by public transportation—train and subway. Numerous on-campus housing options exist, including family housing, apartments, dormitories, and co-ops.

GRADUATES

Stanford offers excellent residency programs, and many graduates opt for postgraduate training at Stanford. Perhaps as a result of the teaching and research experience students gain while in school, many go into academic medicine. Increasingly, graduates are entering primary care fields.

Admissions

REQUIREMENTS

Applicants should have completed course work in the following areas: biology with a lab (1 year), chemistry/organic chemistry with labs (2 years), and physics with lab (1 year). MCAT scores must be no more than 3 years old. The most recent set of scores is used.

SUGGESTIONS

Course work in behavioral sciences, biochemistry, and calculus are recommended, as is knowledge of a second language. No preference is given to California residents or Stanford undergraduates. Successful applicants generally have significant medical, health-related, research, or community service experience.

PROCESS

Secondary applications are sent out on a rolling basis. Interviews involve 2 semi-structured, 60-minute sessions, 1 with a faculty member and 1 with a medical student. Of the interviewed candidates, about one-third are accepted, one-third are rejected, and one-third are put on a wait list, with responses given within 4–6 weeks of the interview. During the past few years, 0–15 applicants were eventually accepted off the wait list.

Admissions Requirements (Required)

MCAT scores, science GPA, non-science GPA, letters of recommendation, interview, essay/personal statement, extracurricular activities, exposure to medical profession

Admissions Requirement (Optional)

State residency

Overlap Schools

Harvard University, University of California—San Francisco.

COSTS AND AID

Tuition & Fees

Tuition	$39,840
Room and board (on-campus)	$15,549
Room and board (off-campus)	$20,732
Cost of books	$1,590

Financial Aid

% students receiving aid	82
Average grant	$32,426
Average loan	$15,037
Average debt	$70,235

STATE UNIVERSITY OF NEW YORK—DOWNSTATE MEDICAL CENTER

OFFICE OF ADMISSIONS, 450 CLARKSON AVENUE, PO BOX 60M, BROOKLYN, NY 11203 • ADMISSION: 718-270-2446
FAX: 718-270-7592 • E-MAIL: ADMISSIONS@DOWNSTATE.EDU • WEBSITE: WWW.HSCBKLYN.EDU

STUDENT BODY

Type	Public
Enrollment	757
% male/female	50/50
% minorities	15
# applied (total/out)	3,505/1,159
# enrolled	185
Average age	24

ADMISSIONS

Application Information

Regular application	12/15
Regular notification	10/15
	until filled
Early application	6/1–8/1
Early notification	10/1
Are transfers accepted?	No
Admissions may be deferred?	Yes
Interview required?	No
Application fee	$65

Academics

The curriculum emphasizes the development of clinical reasoning and problem-solving skills. It integrates basic and clinical sciences and exposes students from the first year to patient care. Each student spends 1 afternoon biweekly in a physician's private office or clinic; the practicing physician serves as the student's clinical mentor for the entire year. Students are also encouraged to participate in research. Opportunities are available throughout the 4 years of medical school. Those who make a significant research contribution are eligible to graduate with distinction in research. A MD/PhD program is open in one of 2 modern biomedical science areas, neuroscience, or molecular and cell biology. Medical students are evaluated with an honors/high pass/pass/fail system. Students must pass Step 1 of the USMLE to be promoted to year 3. Students are encouraged to take Step 2 prior to graduation, but it is not a requirement.

BASIC SCIENCES: Basic science courses have been integrated into topics or blocks. Each block is taught using a combination of traditional lectures, case-based, small-group sessions, laboratories, conferences, and a weekly clinical experience. First-year topics are blood/hematopoiesis/lymphoid, cardiovascular system, endocrine and reproduction systems, gastrointestinal system/intermediary metabolism, genes to cells, head and neck, musculoskeletal system, neuroscience, renal/urinary system, respiratory system, and skin and connective tissue. The current second-year curriculum includes courses in Microbiology and Immunology, Nutrition, Pathology, Pathophysiology, Pharmacology, Preparation for Clinical Medicine, Preventive Medicine, and Psychopathology. With the exception of the last 2, each course runs throughout the full academic year, with each discipline presenting material related to specific organ systems. The Office of Academic Development promotes students' academic success through seminars, workshops, and individual tutoring. The Health Science Education Building holds 2 floors of study carrels, which serve as home base to students during the first 2 years. In the same building is the Medical Research Library, one of the largest medical school libraries in the country, and a 500-seat auditorium. A Learning Resource Center has 90 computer work stations loaded with an array of medical applications.

CLINICAL TRAINING

The current clerkships are Medicine (10 weeks), Surgery (8 weeks), Pediatrics (6 weeks), Obstetrics/Gynecology (6 weeks), Psychiatry (6 weeks), Neurology (4 weeks), and Anesthesia (2 weeks). Also included are Primary Care, a sub internship (4 weeks), and at least 20 weeks of electives. Training takes place at a number of major affiliates, University Hospital, and Kings County Hospital. Electives can be completed at those institutions or at extramural hospitals or medical centers.

Campus Life

This year's first-year class is 185 students from more than 60 individual colleges. About 93 percent are New York State residents. Approximately 13 percent of students are underrepresented minorities.

STUDENT LIFE

All entering students are assigned a clinical faculty mentor who provides guidance and support throughout the first year. The focal point for recreational, social, and cultural activities on campus is the Student Center, which has lounges, a piano room, an athletic center, a swimming pool, squash courts, and a spa. Student organizations focus on professional, ethnic, service related, social, and recreational interests, and also provide support for groups of students. For example, the Daniel Hale Williams Society, named for a prominent Black physician, is a voice for minority students on campus and also brings students together to participate in educational, social, and service-related goals. Brooklyn is a culturally rich, active community that provides an exciting extracurricular life for medical students. Manhattan is easily accessible on the subway. On-campus housing options are single or shared studios or dormitory rooms. Students who live off campus often reside in the nearby neighborhood of Park Slope.

GRADUATES

SUNY—Downstate graduates perform above the national average in terms of securing residency positions at top institutions nationwide. Alumni hold faculty positions at universities such as Harvard, Case Western, Stanford, Yale, Johns Hopkins, Columbia, Cornell, and the University of Pennsylvania, among other prestigious institutions. Forty percent of 2002 graduating students entered residency programs in primary care. More than 69 percent of graduates chose to stay within New York State.

Admissions

REQUIREMENTS

Fifteen positions in each class are reserved for students in a BA/MD program organized with Brooklyn College. Five positions are reserved for early-assurance applicants from Queens College and the College of Staten Island. New York residents are given strong preference for the remaining spots. Prerequisites are 8 semester credits each of biology, chemistry, organic chemistry, and physics, all with associated labs. Six semester hours of English are also required. The MCAT is required and scores must be from within 3 years of the date of anticipated enrollment. Component scores for each MCAT series are looked at individually.

SUGGESTIONS

In addition to required courses, 1 year each of biochemistry, college-level math, and another advanced science are recommended. Medically related experience and demonstrated commitment to social service and community outreach activities are important factors in admission.

PROCESS

All AMCAS applicants are sent secondary applications. About 20 percent of those returning secondaries are interviewed between September and April. Interviews consist of one session for 1 hour with a faculty member. On interview day, candidates also have a group orientation session, lunch with current students, and a campus tour. Of interviewed candidates, about 40 percent are accepted on a rolling basis. Wait listed candidates are not encouraged to send supplementary information.

Admissions Requirements (Required)

MCAT scores, science GPA, non-science GPA, letters of recommendation, state residency, extracurricular activities, exposure to medical profession

Admissions Requirements (Optional)

Interview, essays/personal statement

COSTS AND AID

Tuition & Fees

In-state tuition	$18,800
Out-of-state tuition	$33,500
Fees	$450

Financial Aid

Average debt	$59,906

STATE UNIVERSITY OF NEW YORK—STONY BROOK UNIVERSITY
SCHOOL OF MEDICINE

COMMITTEE ON ADMISSIONS, LEVEL 4, RM 147, HEALTH SCIENCES, STONY BROOK, NY 11794 • **ADMISSION:** 631-444-2113
FAX: 631-444-6032 • **E-MAIL:** SOMADMISSIONS@STONYBROOK.EDU • **WEBSITE:** WWW.HSC.SUNYSB.EDU/SOM/

STUDENT BODY

Type	Public
Enrollment	447
% male/female	53/47
% minorities	14
# applied (total/out)	1,934/876
# accepted (total/out)	263/125
# enrolled (total/out)	101/2
Average age	24

FACULTY

Total faculty (number)	574
% female	35
% part-time	13

ADMISSIONS
Average GPA and MCAT Scores

Overall GPA	3.6
MCAT Bio	11.0
MCAT Phys	12.0
MCAT Verbal	10.0
MCAT Essay	Q

Application Information

Regular application	12/15
Regular notification	10/15
Early application	6/1–8/1
Early notification	10/1
Are transfers accepted?	Yes
Admissions may be deferred?	Yes
Interview required?	Yes
Application fee	$75

Academics

Most students earn the MD degree in 4 years. Students who engage in relevant projects or course work may be eligible for the MD with recognition in research, the MD with recognition in primary care, or the MD with recognition in humanities. A combined MD/PhD program is offered as part of the MSTP. The doctorate degree may be earned in anatomy, biochemistry, biomedical engineering, cell biology, genetics, immunology, microbiology, molecular biology, neuroscience, pathology, pharmacology, and physiology. Medical students are evaluated with honors/pass/fail and must take Step 1 and 2 of the USMLE to graduate.

The curriculum of the School of Medicine provides the opportunity for extensive training in the basic medical sciences and teaching in the clinical disciplines of medicine. The curriculum requires the acquisition and utilization of a variety of skills in basic and clinical sciences. The official grading system is honors/pass/fail. The first 2 years are devoted to basic sciences and the integrated Foundations of Medicine course. This latter course teaches medical ethics, patient assessment skills, preventative medicine, human behaviour, and nutrition. The second year focuses on an organ system-based pathophysiology and therapeutics course. Third-year students complete core clerkships in Medicine Pediatrics, Family Medicine, Obstetrics/Gynecology, Psychiatry, and Surgery. One month of elective time is available. Fourth-year students are offered selectives and electives. Core clerkships are completed at University Hospital or one of three teaching affiliates. Electives can be completed at other sites.

USMLE, Step 1: Required. Students must record a passing score for promotion.

USMLE, Step 2: Required. Students must record a passing total score to graduate.

Campus Life

Typically, 90–95 percent of students are New York residents. About 15 percent are underrepresented minorities. There is a wide age range among students, and at least 5–10 students in each class are in their thirties. Class size is 100.

STUDENT LIFE

Stony Brook is located on the North Shore of Long Island, just more than a 1 hour train ride from Manhattan. Students enjoy both the comfort of their school's suburban location and its proximity to the city. The campus offers a vast sports complex, and the immediate area offers bike trails, beaches, and parks. The Stony Brook Union is the campus center for hundreds of activities, including eating, socializing, watching TV, taking art and other noncredit classes, playing billiards and table tennis, and shopping. It is also the home of student organizations, student government, and informational services. On-campus child care is available to students. University-owned housing includes residence halls and several apartment complexes with units of all sizes. Most students own cars, which are particularly important during the clinical years.

GRADUATES

Among 2006 graduates, the most prevalent fields for residencies were medicine (30 percent), anesthesiology (14 percent), pediatrics (12 percent), emergency medicine (10 percent), and surgery (2 percent). About 15 percent entered programs at university-affiliated hospitals.

Admissions

REQUIREMENTS

Academic prerequisites are 1 year each of biology, chemistry, English, organic chemistry, and physics. Science courses must include associated labs. The MCAT is required, and scores must be no more than 5 years old. For applicants who have taken the exam more than once, the best scores are considered. Thus, there is no advantage in withholding scores.

SUGGESTIONS

Applicants who have taken significant time off after college should have some recent course work. For all applicants, some medically related experience is important, and patient contact is particularly valued.

PROCESS

All AMCAS applicants receive secondary applications. About 25 percent of those returning secondaries are interviewed between September and March. Interviews consist of one session with a member of the Admissions Committee in addition to a group orientation session, tour, and the opportunity to meet with current medical students. About 40 percent of interviewed candidates are accepted, with notification occurring on a rolling basis. An alternate admissions path is through the BA/MD scholars for the medicine program, which admits a limited number of high school students via the Honors College into an 8 year combined program. In addition, 7 postbaccalaureate programs, including Bryn Mawr, Goucher, Stony Brook, NYU, Queens, Hunter, and Columbia have admission arrangements with Stony Brook through a linkage program.

Admissions Requirements (Required)

MCAT scores, science GPA, non-science GPA, letters of recommendation, interview, essays/personal statement, extracurricular activities, exposure to medical profession

Admissions Requirements (Optional)

State residency

Overlap Schools

Brown University, Columbia University, Cornell University, New York University, SUNY Downstate Medical Center, SUNY Upstate Medical University, Yale University.

COSTS AND AID

Tuition & Fees

In-state tuition	$18,800
Out-of-state tuition	$33,500
Room and board (off-campus)	$21,350
Cost of books	$1,500
Fees	$983

Financial Aid

% students receiving aid	84
Average grant	$6,300
Average loan	$37,300
Average debt	$120,000

STATE UNIVERSITY OF NEW YORK—UNIVERSITY AT BUFFALO
SCHOOL OF MEDICINE AND BIOMEDICAL SCIENCES

131 BEB BUFFALO, NY 14214-3013 • **ADMISSION:** 716-829-3466
FAX: 716-829-3849 • **E-MAIL:** JJROSSO@BUFFALO.EDU • **WEBSITE:** WWW.SMBS.BUFFALO.EDU

STUDENT BODY

Type	Public
Enrollment	567
% male/female	46/54
% minorities	7
# applied (total/out)	3,839/1,506
# accepted (total/out)	379/87
# enrolled (total/out)	136/26
Average age	23
Student-faculty ratio	1:1

ADMISSIONS
Average GPA and MCAT scores

Overall GPA	3.62
MCAT Bio	10.1
MCAT Phys	10.3
MCAT Verbal	10.1
MCAT Essay	P

Application Information

Regular application	11/15
Regular notification	10/15
Early application	8/1 or 8/31
Early notification	10/1
Are transfers accepted?	No
Admissions may be deferred?	Yes
Interview required?	Yes
Application fee	$65

Academics

In addition to the MD, the School of Medicine and Biomedical Sciences awards the PhD, MA, MS, and the combined MD/PhD. There are 4 MSTP-sponsored MD/PhD positions available each year. Departments awarding graduate degrees include anatomy, biochemistry, biophysics, cell biology, genetics, immunology, microbiology, molecular biology, neuroscience, pathology, pharmacology, and physiology. A new joint-degree program, leading to the MD/MBA began in 1997. Evaluation of medical students is based on an honors/high satisfactory/satisfactory/unsatisfactory scale. Passing the USMLE Step 1 is required before matriculants can enter their third year.

BASIC SCIENCES: Basic sciences are taught through a combination of lectures, labs, small group sessions, problem-based learning, and clinical experiences. On average, students are in class or scheduled sessions for about 20 hours per week. The required first-year courses are Biochemistry; Clinical Practice of Medicine, which provides early patient-contact experiences; Embryology; Gross Anatomy; Histology; Human Behavior; Neuroscience; Medical Genetics; Physiology; Scientific Basis of Medicine; and Social and Preventive Medicine. Second-year courses include the continuation of Clinical Practice of Medicine, Genetics, Hematology, Human Behavior, Microbiology, Pathology, Pharmacology, Scientific Basis of Medicine, and Social and Preventive Medicine. Summer externships that allow up to 60 first- and second-year medical students to shadow primary care physicians are available with stipends. Stipends are also available on a limited basis for summer research projects. The Health Sciences Library features a media resources center with approximately 2,000 multimedia items; a history of medicine collection with 12,000 volumes; and a comprehensive general medicine/scientific book and journal collection.

CLINICAL TRAINING

Third-year required rotations are Internal Medicine (8 weeks), Surgery (8 weeks), Obstetrics/Gynecology (6 weeks), Pediatrics (6 weeks), Psychiatry (6 weeks), Family Medicine (6 weeks), and two elective courses. The Family Medicine clerkship includes 6 sessions in a community-based family physician's office, 2 sessions in a problem-based learning format, 1 session focusing on a community project, and 1 session devoted to independent learning. During the third year, students also choose a week-long seminar from diverse selective offerings. Fourth-year requirements are 4 weeks each of Neurology, Medicine, and Surgery and 4 weeks of an ambulatory experience. Fourth-year electives are also available. Training takes place at the Buffalo General Hospital, Children's Hospital of Buffalo, Erie County Medical Center, Mercy Hospital, Millard Fillmore Health System, Sisters of Charity Hospital, Roswell Park Cancer Institute, and the Buffalo VA Medical Center. The Community Academic Practice Program identifies community-based sites for clinical training. With faculty approval, up to 16 weeks of electives may be taken at other academic institutions.

Campus Life

All but 25 or 26 students in each class are New York residents. About 20 percent of entering students are over 25 years old. Approximately 5 percent of students are underrepresented minorities. The class size is 135.

STUDENT LIFE

The first year begins with a relaxed orientation week that allows students to get acquainted with one another and their new surroundings. Several student centers serve as focal points for student life on campus. The Student Union houses more than 75 clubs and organizations in addition to recreational facilities, dining areas, and a theater. The Oasis Recreation Center features pool tables, music, and a TV room. The Harriman Student Activities Center is an alternate student union, and the Creative Craft Center provides ongoing craft programs and courses. The Living Well Center (LWC) is dedicated to improving students' overall health and wellness. It offers a range of services to students, including counseling, health education, fitness assessments, seminars on personal health issues, relaxation services such as massage, and special events with outside speakers. For medical students, the LWC also provides opportunities for volunteer work in areas related to preventive medicine. Buffalo is an affordable and student-friendly community. Residence halls and graduate student apartments are available close to campus.

GRADUATES

Among graduates in a recent class, the most prevalent specialty fields were internal medicine (27 percent), pediatrics (28 percent), family practice (4 percent), obstetrics/gynecology (4 percent), surgery (32 percent), and emergency medicine (8 percent). Approximately half of the graduates entered residency programs in New York State.

Admissions

REQUIREMENTS

Prerequisite course work includes biology (2 semesters), chemistry (4 semesters, including 2 of organic chemistry), English (2 semesters), and physics (2 semesters). The MCAT is required, and scores are not accepted if they were obtained prior to 2005. For applicants who have taken the exam on multiple occasions, the best set of scores is generally considered. Thus, there is no advantage in withholding scores.

SUGGESTIONS

In addition to science requirements, 2 years of course work in social sciences and 1 year in the humanities are advised. For applicants who have taken time off after college, some recent course work is recommended. Medical-related experience is important.

PROCESS

All AMCAS applicants are sent secondary applications. Between 600 and 650 applicants are interviewed from September through May. These candidates are selected from a pool of about 4,000, meaning that about 15 percent of the applicants make it to the interview stage. Interviews consist of 2 sessions each with a faculty member or medical student. On interview day, there are also group informational sessions, a campus tour, and the opportunity to have lunch with current medical students. The first acceptance letters are mailed in October, with subsequent batches of letters sent at 4–6-week intervals throughout the year. Approximately 30 percent of interviewees are accepted initially. Others are rejected or placed on a wait list. Supplementary material from wait listed candidates is not encouraged. Usually 60 percent of interviewees are eventually offered an acceptance before orientation begins.

Admissions Requirements (Required)

MCAT scores, science GPA, letters of recommendation, interview, essay/personal statement

Admissions Requirements (Optional)

Non-science GPA, state residency, extracurricular activities, exposure to medical profession

Overlap Schools

State University of New York Upstate Medical University, University of Rochester.

COSTS AND AID

Tuition & Fees

In-state tuition	$18,800
Out-of-state tuition	$36,900
Room and board (off-campus)	$8,000
Cost of books	$3,500
Fees	$1,115

Financial Aid

% students receiving aid	85
Average grant	$3,000
Average loan	$35,000

STATE UNIVERSITY OF NEW YORK—UPSTATE MEDICAL UNIVERSITY
COLLEGE OF MEDICINE

OFFICE OF STUDENT ADMISSIONS, 766 IRVING AVENUE SYRACUSE, NY 13210 • ADMISSION: 315-464-4570
FAX: 315-464-8867 • E-MAIL: ADMISS@UPSTATE.EDU • WEBSITE: WWW.UPSTATE.EDU

STUDENT BODY

Type	Public
Enrollment	623
% male/female	54/46
% minorities	10
# applied (total/out)	4,508/2,921
# accepted (total/out)	395/214
# enrolled (total/out)	160/82
Average age	25

FACULTY

Total faculty	645
% part-time	31
Student-faculty ratio	1:1

ADMISSIONS
Average GPA and MCAT Scores

Overall GPA	3.63
MCAT Bio	10.4
MCAT Phys	10.4
MCAT Verbal	9.6
MCAT Essay	P

Application Information

Regular application	12/1
Regular notification	5/1
Early application	8/1
Early notification	10/1
Are transfers accepted?	Yes
Admissions may be deferred?	Yes
Interview required?	Yes
Application fee	$100

Academics

The College of Medicine curriculum integrates the basic and clinical sciences-with basic science courses teaching the clinical implications of the material-and provides clinical experience starting in the first semester.

All courses are aligned by organ systems. For example, in the first year, students learn the structure and function of the brain in February, the heart in March, and the lungs in April. Similarly, the second year aligns the pharmacology, microbiology, and pathology of each organ system.

The curriculum also addresses the humanistic aspects of medicine, including its ethical, legal and social implications. Throughout their four years at Upstate, students acquire the knowledge, skills, and attitudes necessary to become competent, caring physicians.

All College of Medicine students spend their first two years on the Upstate campus in Syracuse. At the start of the third year, one-quarter of the class moves to the Binghamton Clinical Campus. The rest of the class remains in Syracuse, and completes clinical education at University Hospital and its clinical affiliates. Students learn the same skills at both campuses, but the ambiance is different.

Much of the clinical training in Syracuse takes place in a tertiary care setting, the special focus of a university hospital. In Binghamton, most of the training occurs in a community-based setting that is more akin to the environment in which most physicians will practice later on. Applicants indicate their campus preference within two weeks of the admissions interview, and are assigned to a clinical campus upon acceptance to the College of Medicine.

Students

80 percent of students are New York residents, however admissions decisions are merit-based and state of residency is not a factor considered when making a decision on an application. Applications from non-NY state residents are welcome. About 12 percent of students are underrepresented minorities, and about 15 percent took some significant time off between college and medical school. Class size is 160.

STUDENT LIFE

A large part of college life takes place outside the classroom, and Upstate is no exception. We offer 45 student clubs and organizations including ballroom dancing and student government, special events and athletic programs.

The Campus Activities Governing Board schedules social, cultural, and recreational programs for students including first-run movies on weekends, a guest lecture series, comedy hours, weekend getaways, and discount tickets to local sports and cultural events. The Campus Activities Building (CAB), located next door to our residence hall, has a computer lounge, snack bar, bookstore, TV lounge, pool, sauna, gym, squash and racquetball courts, treadmills, step machines, Nautilus, tennis courts, billiards, ping-pong, and more. Our intramural sports program runs men's, women's and/or co-ed leagues in basketball, volleyball, softball, football, racquetball, and soccer.

Syracuse is a medium-size city surrounded by countryside. It is a one-hour drive to Lake Ontario's beaches, and four hours to New York City. The Binghamton campus is conveniently situated about three hours from New York City, Philadelphia, and Buffalo. Modern residence halls at the Syracuse campus provide dormitory rooms, studios, and one-bedroom apartments for single and married students. Off campus housing is readily available for students choosing to attend the Binghampton campus during their last two years of study.

GRADUATES

Graduates are successful in securing residencies in all fields.

Admissions

REQUIREMENTS

Prerequisites are General Chemistry (6-8 semester hours); Organic Chemistry (6-8 hours); General Biology (6-8 hours); General Physics (6-8 hours); and English (6 hours, at least 3 of which must be composition).

SUGGESTIONS

Academic work in the Humanities and Social Sciences is considered equally as important as science coursework.

PROCESS

All applicants are sent secondary applications. Of those returning secondaries, about 20 percent are invited to interview between September and March. Interviews consist of two sessions each with faculty members, administrators, students, or alumni. About 20 percent of interviewed candidates are accepted on a rolling basis, while others may be admitted later in the year.

Admissions Requirements (Required)

MCAT scores, Science GPA, Non-science GPA, Letters of recommendation, Interview, Essays/personal statement, Extracurricular activities, Exposure to medical profession

Admissions Requirements (Optional)

State residency

Overlap Schools

State University of New York—University at Buffalo, State University of New York—Stony Brook University

COSTS AND AID

Tuition & Fees

In-state Tuition	$18,800
Out-of-state Tuition	$33,500
Room and board (on-campus)	$10,450
Cost of books	$2,000
Fees	$2,050

Financial Aid

% students receiving aid	80
Average grant	$6,205
Average loan	$31,736
Average debt	$120,442

TEMPLE UNIVERSITY
SCHOOL OF MEDICINE

3340 NORTH BROAD STREET , SFC SUITE 305 PHILADELPHIA, PA 19140 • ADMISSION: 215-707-3656
FAX: 215-707-6932 • E-MAIL: MEDADMISSIONS@TEMPLE.EDU • WEBSITE: WWW.TEMPLE.EDU/MEDICINE

STUDENT BODY

Type	Private
Enrollment	707
% male/female	53/47
% minorities	16
# applied (total/out)	9,890/8,666
# accepted (total/out)	539/352
# enrolled (total/out)	178/101
Average age	23

FACULTY

Total faculty	525
% female	29
% minority	26
% part-time	14
Student-faculty ratio	2:1

ADMISSIONS
Average GPA and MCAT Scores

Overall GPA	3.64
MCAT Bio	11
MCAT Phys	10
MCAT Verbal	10
MCAT Essay	P

Application Information

Regular application	12/15
Regular notification	10/15
Early application	8/1
Early notification	10/1
Are transfers accepted?	No
Admissions may be deferred?	Yes
Interview required?	Yes
Application fee	$70

Academics

The academic program has options that appeal to all students, be they interested in research and/or intensive clinical training. Summer research projects in both basic and clinical sciences are encouraged and are often funded. Qualified students may pursue an MPH or PhD concurrently with an MD. PhD degrees may be obtained in the following fields: Anatomy, Biochemistry, Immunology, Microbiology, Molecular Biology, Pathology, Pharmacology, and Physiology. Temple's system of student evaluation uses Honors/High Pass/Pass/Fail. A grade of Pass or higher is required for promotion, and passing both steps of the USMLE and an internally administered Objective Structured Clinical Examination are graduation requirements.

BASIC SCIENCES: During the first two years, students are assigned to basic science faculty advisers who are available to discuss academic matters as well as personal issues. Students are in class for about 25 hours per week, with about half of scheduled sessions utilizing a lecture format. Other instructional methods include small-group discussions, labs, patient simulators, and interactive clinical training. All formal classes are held in the morning, with afternoon hours used for workshops and the Doctoring course. The curriculum was modified in August 2006 to a hybrid systems-based curriculum. First-year blocks are: Anatomy, Elements of Bioscience, Biological Systems 1 and 2, Neuroscience, and Basic Principles of Immunology, Pathology and Pharmacology. Doctoring 1 and a choice of electives runs throughout the year. Second-year blocks are: Microbiology of Infectious Diseases, Diseases of the Cardiovascular System, Respiratory System, Bone and Muscle, Gastrointestinal System, Nervous System, Renal System, Endocrine System, Hematology-Oncology and Integrated Cased-based Topics. Doctoring 2 and a choice of electives run concurrently. Students are evaluated based on a series of internal exams, National Board-style exams, and standardized patient exams. The current library system includes clinical and research journals and texts; an electronic reference/information center; a microcomputer learning center; and access to online Internet informational services. A new academic building is being constructed and will open in late Spring 2009.

CLINICAL TRAINING

Students are introduced to clinic medicine in the first two years, in our Doctoring course, in which students learn to take a medical history, perform a physical examination, and receive training in medical ethics and professionalism. Clinical skills are learned through use of patient simulators, standardized patients, and real patient encounters. In the third year, students are assigned to a clinical faculty adviser who assists with decisions about clinical electives and post-graduate training. Third-year required rotations are Internal Medicine (12 weeks); Ob/Gyn (6 weeks); Pediatrics (6 weeks); Family Medicine (6 weeks); Psychiatry (6 weeks); Surgery (8 weeks); Radiology (4 weeks); Intensive Care and Anesthesiology (4 weeks). During the fourth year, 20 weeks of electives are required, in addition to clerkships in Emergency Medicine (4 weeks) and Neurology (4 weeks), and two subinternships (total of 8 weeks); one in a surgical subject, and one in either Internal Medicine, Pediatrics, Surgery, Family Medicine, Obstetrics-Gynecology or Psychiatry. Training takes place at the Temple University Hospital, St. Christopher's Hospital for Children, and affiliated hospitals including the Crozer Chester Medical Center, Scranton Mercy Hospital, the Western PA Medical Center, the Fox Chase Cancer Center, the Reading Hospital and Medical Center, Abington Memorial Hospital, St. Luke's Hospital, Mercy Hospital, Geisinger Medical Center, Lehigh Valley Hospital, and

Moss Rehabilitation Hospital. Students may circulate to several hospitals or choose to take all their required clinical rotations at one of our clinical campuses: Western PA Medical Center, Geisinger Medical Center, St. Luke's Hospital or Crozer Chester Medical Center.

Students

Approximately 50 percent of students are Pennsylvania residents. About 17 percent of students in a typical class are underrepresented minorities. In particular, Temple has a strong contingent of African American and Latino students. Class size is 180, but will be expanding with the opening of the new medical school building in 2009.

STUDENT LIFE

Temple students benefit from rich extracurricular offerings both on and off campus. Both Temple Medical School and the main Temple campus have comprehensive athletic and recreational facilities. Medical students are active in school governance, and are members of the Curriculum, Financial Affairs, and Admissions Committees. A special support program is designed primarily for groups underrepresented in medicine, but is open to all students. There are numerous student organizations that range from community outreach to political advocacy to specialty interest groups. Philadelphia is a historically and culturally rich city. It is also a very student-friendly city, where medical students in particular abound. Most students live off campus.

GRADUATES

About half of Temple's graduates enter residency programs in Pennsylvania. Among students who graduated in 2006, the most prevalent specialty choices were Internal Medicine (35 percent); Surgery (9 percent); Transitional (9 percent); Pediatrics (8 percent); Emergency Medicine (6 percent); Family Medicine (6 percent); Orthopedics (4 percent); Psychiatry (4 percent) and Ob/Gyn (3 percent).

Admissions

REQUIREMENTS

One year each of biology, chemistry, organic chemistry, and physics are required as well as 6 semester hours of humanities. The MCAT is required, and scores must be no more than three years old.

SUGGESTIONS

As a state-related school, Temple strongly considers Pennsylvania residents, although a significant number of out-of-state applicants are admitted. For applicants who have been out of school for a period of time, recent coursework is important. The spring, rather than August/September, MCAT is advised. Medically related and community-service activities are valued, and the Admissions Committee is serious about selecting students who will make supportive class members and caring physicians.

PROCESS

All "complete" applications are reviewed by a member of the Admissions Committee. There is no absolute cutoff for MCAT scores and GPAs. All applicants are sent secondary application material, and about 20 percent of those completing their application are invited to interview. Interviews take place between September and April and consist of a half-hour long session with a faculty member. On interview day, applicants meet with the Admissions Director, a representative of the Office of Student Financial Services, and take the campus tour and have lunch with second-year medical students. About one-third of interviewees are accepted, with notification occurring on a rolling basis. Admission may also be gained through programs with post-baccalaureate, pre-medical programs at Temple, Goucher, Duquesne, Bryn Mawr, Columbia, Scripps, West Chester and the University of Pennsylvania. Early assurance linkages are available with Duquesne, Washington and Jefferson, and Widener. Uniquely qualified high school students may apply for the BA/MD programs with Duquesne, Washington and Jefferson, and Widener.

Admissions Requirements (Required)

MCAT scores, Science GPA, Non-science GPA, Letters of recommendation, Interview, Essays/personal statement, Extracurricular activities, Exposure to medical profession, 6 s.h. Humanities

Overlap Schools

Boston University, New York University, Thomas Jefferson University, University of Maryland—College Park, University of Pennsylvania, University of Pittsburgh, Yeshiva University.

COSTS AND AID

Tuition & Fees

Tuition	$37,828
Room and board (on-campus)	$0
Room and board (off-campus)	$16,453
Cost of books	$1,598
Fees	$728

Financial Aid

% students receiving aid	88
Average grant	$11,005
Average loan	$42,745
Average debt	$150,614

Texas A&M University System Health Science Center
College of Medicine

159 Joe H. Reynolds MB, College Station, TX 77843 • Admission: 979-845-7743
Fax: 979-845-5533 • E-mail: ADMISSIONS@MEDICINE.TAMHSC.EDU • Website: WWW.MEDICINE.TAMHSC.EDU

STUDENT BODY

Type	Public
Enrollment	414
% male/female	51/49
% minorities	16
# applied (total/out)	3,061/406
# accepted (total/out)	353/16
# enrolled (total/out)	139/10
Average age	24

FACULTY

Total faculty (number)	1,172
% female	21
% minority	20
% part-time	11
Student-faculty ratio	1:2.5

ADMISSIONS
Average GPA and MCAT Scores

Overall GPA	3.67
MCAT Bio	10
MCAT Phys	10
MCAT Verbal	9.6
MCAT Essay	Q

Application Information

Regular application	10/01
Regular notification	11/15
Are transfers accepted?	Yes*
Admissions may be deferred?	Yes
Interview required?	Yes
Application fee	$50

*Admission is on a competitive basis and considers only applicants in good standing from LCME accredited medical schools in the U.S. and Canada and who have extraordinary personal reasons for wishing to transfer. The number admitted depends on the availability of places, faculty, and facilities. There is no specific number of places set aside for advanced standing candidates.

Academics

Students may pursue a MD degree or a joint M.D./Ph.D. in conjunction with graduate departments of the Health Science Center in the following fields: Biochemistry and Structured Biology, Cell and Molecular Biology, Neuroscience, Microbial and Molecular Pathogens, Pharmacology and Experimental Therapeutics and Systems and Translational Biology. Clinical instruction is integrated into the basic science curriculum, as are sessions that emphasize the social and ethical aspects of medicine.

BASIC SCIENCEs: The first year is organized into blocks distributed over 36 weeks. Year one, consists of the following: Gross Anatomy and Embryology (14 weeks); Biochemistry and Genetics (18 weeks); Human Organ Systems: Cardiovascular, Respiratory, Renal, and Endocrinology/Reproduction (15-weeks); Neuroscience (7-weeks). Year 1 is taught at both the Colleges Station and Temple campuses, and instruction in the basic sciences and organ systems is integrated with clinical correlation experiences and instruction in behavioral sciences, working with patients, physical diagnosis, humanities in medicine, community medicine, leadership in medicine, evidence-based medicine and epidemiology. Year two like year one is similarly organized into blocks over 36 weeks, covering a Basic Science Block comprised of Medical Microbiology/Immunology, Pathology /Laboratory Medicine and Medical Pharmacology/Toxicology (12-weeks); and, Human Organ Systems. Tutoring is available to all students, and is conducted by professors and qualified students. Study facilities include two Learning Resources Units (College Station and Temple). Computer labs at each facility give students access to E-mail and the internet. Group study rooms and individual study carrels are also available. Evaluation of performance during years one and two uses an A-F scale. Passing the USMLE Step 1 is required for promotion to year three. The passing rate for Texas A&M Medical Students exceeds the national average.

CLINICAL TRAINING

Patient contact begins in year one, in Working with Patients and continues through year two, in the preceptorship for Primary Care program. Early informal patient contact is possible for those who engage in certain community service or volunteer activities. During the third and fourth years, students receive clinical training in several different patient settings: Scott & White

Memorial Hospital and Clinic, the Central Texas Veterans Health Care System, Carl R. Darnall Army Medical Center at Fort Hood, Brazos Family Medicine Residency, College Station Medical Center, St Joseph's Health System, Driscoll Children's Hospital, the CHRISTUS Spohn Health System in Corpus Christi, Texas, and the John Peter Smith Health Network in Fort Worth, Texas, Scott & White Hospital University Medical Campus, Round Rock, Texas, Seaton Medical Center, Round Rock, Texas, St. David's Round Rock Medical Center, Round Rock, Texas and the Lone Star Circle of Care, Round Rock, Texas. Year three begins with a week-long orientation, followed by 48 weeks of required rotations: Family Medicine (6 weeks); Ob/Gyn (6 weeks); Pediatrics (6 weeks); Psychiatry (6 weeks); Internal Medicine (12 weeks); and, Surgery (12 weeks). Year four consists of 27 weeks of electives plus four required clerkships: Neurology (4 weeks); Alcohol and Drug Dependence (2 weeks); Becoming a Clinician (2 weeks); and, an Acting Internship (4 weeks). During year three, students are evaluated by using an A-F scale. During year four, most rotations are evaluated with Pass/Fail. Passing the USMLE Step 2 is required for graduation.

Campus Life

The vast majority of students are from Texas. About 16 percent of students are underrepresented minorities, most of whom are Mexican American and African American. About 77 percent of the student body were science majors of some type as undergraduates.

STUDENT LIFE

Within the College of Medicine are many opportunities for students to express themselves and to demonstrate a variety of talents and interests far beyond classrooms and laboratories. This added dimension to a challenging academic regimen plays a vital role in the development of well-rounded individuals.

Community service has always been a priority for students at the College of Medicine. Each class chooses to support different human service organizations throughout the year, thereby focusing their energy and enthusiasm on a variety of cases within the community, state and beyond.

GRADUATES

As a result of the comprehensive educational and clinical opportunities available from the College of Medicine and its affiliated institutions, our medical students continue to enter a broad spectrum of excellent residency programs across the state and nation. Approximately 41% enter primary care residency training programs (Family Practice, Internal Medicine and Pediatrics) throughout the state and country.

Of those students that graduated between 2003 and 2005, the following residencies were the most popular: Internal Medicine (17% of graduates); Pediatrics (12% of graduates); Surgery (12% of graduates); Family Practice (10%).

Admissions

REQUIREMENTS

Admission to the College of Medicine is highly competitive, and considers for enrollment only individuals who have earned a baccalaureate degree or completed at least 90 semester credit hours (or equivalent quarter hours) of their undergraduate course work at a fully accredited college or university in the United States. By state mandate, enrollment of individuals who are residents of states other than Texas may not exceed 10 percent. Academic ability, grades in college courses and performance on the MCAT are important selection criteria. Equally important are interpersonal and communication skills, maturity, motivation, and compassion. Careful consideration is given to other factors such as dedication to service, disadvantaged circumstances, socioeconomic background, race/ethnicity, faculty support, primary care interest and/or service in a rural/underserved area. Knowledge of and experiences in the medical profession are important. Admission is open to qualified individuals regardless of race, color, religion, gender, age, national origin or disability. Applicants are invited for personal interviews based upon their competiveness in the review process. Each year 170 entering students are enrolled. Most entering students complete a baccalaureate degree before enrolling.

PROCESS

Approximately 27 percent of Texas applicants are interviewed, and 21 percent of those interviewed matriculate to the class. About 12 percent of out-of-state residents are interviewed, and only a few are accepted each year. Interview sessions typically are scheduled from August to December, and applicants are assigned to either College Station or Temple for their interviews. Each applicant is given two 30-minute interviews with admissions committee members, medical student committee members and faculty or administrator guest interviewers. The College of Medicine tenders acceptances on a rolling basis between November 15 and December 31. A match will be conducted on February 1 to fill any remaining positions. The College of Medicine participates in the Texas Medical Schools Matching Program employed by the Texas Medical and Dental Schools Application Service. A ranked wait list is established on February 15. The Texas Medical and Dental Schools Application Service (TMDSAS) processes all applications. Application materials may be obtained after May 1 online at http://dpweb1.dp.utexas.edu/mdac/.

Admissions Requirements (Required)

MCAT scores, science GPA, non-science GPA, letters of recommendation, interview, state residency, essays/personal statement, extracurricular activities, exposure to medical profession, non-health related community service

Admissions Requirements (Optional)

Extracurricular activities, exposure to medical profession

Overlap Schools

Rush Medical College of Rush University, Texas Tech University, University of Texas.

COSTS AND AID

Tuition & Fees

In-state tuition	$7,750
Out-of-state tuition	$19,650
Room and board (off-campus)	$12,160
Cost of books	$4,300
Fees	$1,262

Financial Aid

% students receiving aid	93
Average grant	$1,000
Average loan	$25,641
Average debt	$102,982

TEXAS TECH UNIVERSITY
HEALTH SCIENCES CENTER SCHOOL OF MEDICINE

3601 FOURTH STREET, 2B116 LUBBOCK, TX 79430 • ADMISSION: 806-743-2297
FAX: 806-743-2725 • E-MAIL: MICHELLE.KOVACH@TTUHSC.EDU • WEBSITE: WWW.TTUHSC.EDU/SOM/ADMISSIONS

STUDENT BODY

Type	Public
Enrollment	550
male/female	243/307
%underrepresented minorities	84
# applied	3,038
# accepted	300
# enrolled	140
Average age	24

FACULTY

Total faculty (number)	527
% female	29
% minority	31
% part-time	9
Student-faculty ratio	1:1

ADMISSIONS
Average GPA and MCAT Scores

Overall GPA	3.65
MCAT	30

Application Information

Regular application	12/1
Regular notification	Rolling
Early application	8/1
Early notification	9/15
Are transfers accepted?	Yes
Admissions may be deferred?	Yes
Interview required?	Yes
Application fee	$50

Academics

Most students complete a 4-year curriculum designed to prepare physicians with a broad base of medical knowledge and sound analytic and problem-solving skills. It is organized in two stages: basic science and clinical training. Some students devote an additional year to research and earn an MD degree in five years. Others are involved in summer research projects. Qualified students interested in biomedical research or academic medicine can earn a PhD along with the MD degree. To address the needs of a rapidly changing health care system, students can participate in an MD/MBA joint-degree program in which both degrees are earned in four years. Medical students are graded on a pass/ fail system. First-year courses are Clinical Oriented Anatomy, Biology of Cell and Tissues, Structure and Function of Major Organ Systems and Host Defense. Second year courses include General Principles and Integrated Neurosciences, Multisystem Disorders and Cancer, Systems Disorders I, Systems Disorders II and Life Span Issues. We have moved to the block system and each of these classes is 12 weeks long. Students take one class at a time. There is also an Early Clinical Experience block that runs the duration o f years I&II that allows students direct patient contact, helping them to be more prepared for clinical rotations.

CLINICAL TRAINING

Third-year required rotations are Internal Medicine, Surgery, Pediatrics, Family Medicine, Ob/Gyn, and Psychiatry. Each rotation is 8 weeks long.

Fourth-year requirements are Neurology (4 weeks), selectives (8 weeks), a sub internship (4 weeks), and 16 weeks of electives. After successful completion of years 1 and 2, approximately 35 students go on to Amarillo for clinical training, 35 stay in Lubbock, and 50 go to El Paso. Amarillo, El Paso, and Lubbock all serve both urban and rural populations. Multiple clinical affiliations of each site provide a wealth of training opportunities for students. El Paso serves an urban border population of more than 700,000 and provides a unique multicultural educational opportunity. Training sites include Thomason Hospital and other community and military facilities. In Lubbock, students benefit from recreational and cultural opportunities available on the Texas Tech University campus of the main university. The primary teaching hospital is University Covenant Health-Lakeside. Other affiliated hospitals include Mary of the Plains Hospital, Charter Plains Hospital, and the Veterans Administration Outpatient Clinics. Amarillo provides exposure to medicine primarily from a private hospital perspective. Teaching hospitals include Northwest Texas Health Care System, Baptist St. Anthony Health Care System, and Veterans Administration Hospital. In total, Texas Tech affiliates provide almost 3,000 teaching beds.

Campus Life

During their first two years, students benefit from the resources of the Health Science Center and from being adjacent to Texas Tech University, a major undergraduate institution. Medical students are supportive of one another, as demonstrated by a student-initiated, peer-tutoring program. First and second-year students are often involved in community service projects, which provide early clinical exposure. Student life during the third and fourth years varies according to location.

GRADUATES

Approximately 21 percent of graduates enter Texas Tech residency programs, which operate on all four campuses. Others are successful in obtaining positions throughout Texas and at institutions in other regions of the country. Eighty-one percent of graduates matched with one of their top three residency choices.

Admissions

REQUIREMENTS

Requirements are biology (12 semester hours), biology lab (2 semester hours), general-chemistry with lab (8 semester hours), organic chemistry with lab (8 semester hours), physics with lab (8 semester hours), English (6 semester hours), and statistics (3 semester hours). All prerequisite courses require a grade of C or better. The MCAT is required and must be taken within the past five years. For applicants who have taken the exam more than once, the highest set of scores is weighed most heavily, but all scores must be reported. Texas residents and residents of neighboring counties in New Mexico and Oklahoma, which comprise the service areas of the school, are given preference in admission.

SUGGESTIONS

In addition to high intellectual ability and a record of strong academic achievement, the Admissions Committee looks for qualities and traits such as compassion, motivation, communication skills, maturity, and personal integrity.

PROCESS

Texas Tech does not participate in AMCAS. Texas Tech participates with six other state-supported medical schools in the Texas Medical and Dental Application Service (TMDAS). A single application is sent to the TMDAS for processing and then is forwarded to any or all of the participating schools as requested by the applicant. A secondary application is also required by Texas Tech. Both applications will be available via the Internet. In addition, application forms may be requested from Texas Medical and Dental Application Service, 702 Colorado Street, Suite 6400, Austin, TX 78701. About 38 percent of applicants are interviewed between September and January. Interviews consist of two sessions, each with an Admissions Committee/faculty member. On interview day, applicants tour the campus, attend group information sessions, meet current students, and have the opportunity to attend classes. Notification begins on October 15 and continues until the class is filled.

Admissions Requirements (Required)

MCAT scores, science GPA, non-science GPA, letters of recommendation, interview, essays/personal statement, extracurricular activities, exposure to medical profession

Admissions Requirements (Optional)

State residency

COSTS AND AID
Tuition & Fees

In-state tuition	$11,314
Out-of-state tuition	$24,414
Room, board, and fees (off-campus)	$32,306
Cost of books	$2,271

Financial Aid

% students receiving aid	88
Average debt	$140,000

THOMAS JEFFERSON UNIVERSITY

JEFFERSON MEDICAL COLLEGE

1015 WALNUT STREET, ROOM 110 PHILADELPHIA, PA 19107 • **ADMISSION:** 215-955-6983
FAX: 215-955-5151 • **E-MAIL:** JMC.ADMISSIONS@JEFFERSON.EDU • **WEBSITE:** WWW.JEFFERSON.EDU/JMC

STUDENT BODY

Type	Private
Enrollment	999
% male/female	50/50
% minorities	9
# applied (total/out)	8,897/7,820
# accepted (total/out)	521/380
# enrolled (total/out)	259/172
Average age	23

FACULTY

Total faculty	2,570
% female	25
% minority	21
% part-time	1
Student-faculty ratio	2:1

ADMISSIONS

Average GPA and MCAT Scores

Overall GPA	3.62
MCAT Bio	10.6
MCAT Phys	10.3
MCAT Verbal	10.3
MCAT Essay	Q

Application Information

Regular application	11/15
Regular notification	Rolling
Early application	6/1–8/1
Early notification	10/1
Are transfers accepted?	Yes
Admissions may be deferred?	Yes
Interview required?	Yes
Application fee	$80

Academics

Along with basic science and clinical training, Jefferson's curriculum emphasizes the social and public health issues related to medicine. Students with solid science backgrounds may pursue an MD and a PhD in one of the departments of the College of Graduate Studies. These include Biochemistry and Molecular Biology, Genetics, Immunology and Microbial Pathogenesis, Molecular Cell Biology, Molecular Pharmacology and Structural Biology, Neuroscience, Physiology, and Tissue Engineering and Regenerative Medicine. An MD/MBA joint-degree is offered in conjunction with Widener University in Chester, Pennsylvania, as is a combined MD/Master's in Hospital Administration. A 5-year program is available in which Jefferson students have the opportunity to earn an MPH at Johns Hopkins School of Hygiene and Public Health while earning their MD degree at Jefferson Medical College. This program is offered to students with special interests such as community health and in recognition of the increasing importance of population medicine. Pennsylvania State University and Jefferson Medical College allow students to pursue a combined BS/MD program, which grants both degrees in a 6- or 7-year period. Jefferson has special arrangements with the University of Pennsylvania's, Bryn Mawr's, and Columbia University's postbaccalaureate programs through which highly qualified students may be admitted to Jefferson prior to completion of their premedical requirements.

BASIC SCIENCES: During the year, Jefferson students focus on the structure and function of the human organisim in its physical and psychosocial context. Course work in the basic sciences of Biochemistry, Cell Biology, Genetics, Human Gross Anatomy, Microscopic Anatomy, Neuroscience, and Physiology provides first-year sturdents with a strong basic science grounding. Practice-related topics such as Ethics, Evidence-Based Medicine, Health Policy, and Medical Information are also introduced during the first year. Clinical course work focuses on Behavioral Science Principles, the History-Taking, the Human Developmental Trajectory, Medical Interviewing, and Patient-Doctor Relationship. This curricula provides students with both a behavioral science foundation and a clinical framework; it establishes an educational bridge between lay perspectives and the realities of medical practice. In addition to increasing emphasis on the study of bedside skills, the curriculum shifts in the second year to the study of pathophysiology and disease. After an introductory block of general pathology and general pharmacology, the subjects of clinical medicine, immunology, microbiology, pathology, physical diagnosis, and systems-based pharmacology are presented as an interdisciplinary curriculum. The curriculum includes small group sessions focusing on the problem-solving evidence-based medicine and service-based learning. Grades are an honors/pass/fail scale. Pre-clinical studies take place in the central medical college building complex, which includes labs and lecture halls. The Scott Library includes 200,000 print volumes, a learning resources center, and computer labs in addition to videos, slides, and supplemental learning materials. MEDLINE and other electronic data systems are available, as well as more than 500 electronic journals and books. The Rector Clinical Skill Center occupies more than 9,000 square feet and houses a 14-room standardized patient suite and classrooms for high-tech simulators.

CLINICAL TRAINING

Patient contact officially begins in year 1, with Introduction to Clinical Medicine. There are also ongoing opportunities for medical students interested in volunteer clinical experience or clinical research through summer programs and part-time jobs. Formally, the clinical portion of the curriculum begins in year 3 with required rotations. These are Family Medicine (6 weeks), Surgery (12 weeks), Internal Medicine (12 weeks), Pediatrics (6 weeks), Psychiatry and Human Behavior (6 weeks), and Obstetrics/Gynecology (6 weeks). Phase II of clinical rotations are selectives in which students choose specialties within broadly defined categories. Twelve weeks are also designated as purely elective. Training sites include Albert Einstein Medical Center, Bryn Mawr Hospital (383 beds), Bryn Mawr Rehabilitation Hospital, Christiana Care Medical Center, DuPont Hospital for Children, Geisinger Medical Center (in Danville, Pennsylvania, providing rural exposure), Lankenau Hospital (475 beds), Latrobe Hospital (280 beds and specializing in family medicine), Magee Rehabilitation Hospital, Mercy Hospital (in Pittsburgh), Wills Eye Hospital, and West Jersey Health System.

Campus Life

About 30 states are represented by the students within a class, mostly states in the eastern part of the country. About 40 percent of the students are Pennsylvania state residents. Applicants underrepresented in medicine make up about 9 percent of each class. Class size is 255. Approximately 20 percent of each class is 25 years or older at matriculation. In recent years, about 5 percent of matriculates have held advanced degrees.

STUDENT LIFE

Numerous professional, athletic, and cultural student organizations exist on campus. Beyond campus, the city of Philadelphia provides ample recreational and cultural possibilities, and New York is just over an hour away. On-campus housing options include residence halls and apartments of all sizes; housing is guaranteed to first-year students. With Jefferson's central and urban location, a car is unnecessary during the first 2 years of study.

GRADUATES

More than 70 percent of Jefferson graduates enter residency programs at university-affiliated hospitals around the nation. Jefferson graduates do very well in the residency-matching program, both in primary care and in more specialized fields.

Admissions

REQUIREMENTS

Required course work includes 1 year each of biology with a lab, chemistry with a lab, organic chemistry with a lab, and physics with a lab.

SUGGESTIONS

Applicants should demonstrate problem-solving capabilities, success in a range of subjects, and some in-depth knowledge of 1 or a few subjects. Strong writing skills are also valued. Experience in a medical or research environment is important. Delaware residents are given preference, as are applicants from programs that have special arrangements with Jefferson. Applicants are advised to submit all materials in a timely fashion.

PROCESS

On receipt of the verified AMCAS application, Jefferson will send, via e-mail, notification of receipt. Also included will be instructions for completing the Jefferson Medical College online secondary application with online payment capability. The Committee on Admissions will begin reviewing the application when all of the following supplementary materials have been received: the Jefferson Medical College secondary application form, the non-refundable $80 application fee, MCAT scores, and the required letters of recommendation. Interviews are conducted from September through March, and about 10 percent of the applicant pool is eventually interviewed. Interviews are approximately 30–45 minutes in length and are conducted by a member of the faculty or administration. Admissions are rolling. About 50 percent of those who interview are accepted. Others are either rejected or wait listed. When places become available later in the cycle, wait listed applicants will be notified and offered positions. Indicating interest in Jefferson may help the prospects of wait listed candidates.

Admissions Requirements (Required)

MCAT scores, Science GPA, Nonscience GPA, Letters of recommendation, Interview, Essays/personal statement, Extracurricular activities, Exposure to medical profession, secondary application

Admissions Requirements (Optional)

State residency

COSTS AND AID
Tuition & Fees

Tuition	$40,701
Room and board (on-campus)	$15,609
Cost of books	$6,758
Fees	$400

TUFTS UNIVERSITY
SCHOOL OF MEDICINE

OFFICE OF ADMISSIONS, 136 HARRISON AVENUE, STEARNS 1, BOSTON, MA 02111 • ADMISSION: 617-636-6571
E-MAIL: SGP@COR.CDM.NEMC. • WEBSITE: WWW.TUFTS.EDU/MED

STUDENT BODY

Type	Private
Enrollment	695
% male/female	54/46
% minorities	11
# applied (total/out)	8,277/8,336
# accepted	473
# enrolled (total/out)	168/113

ADMISSIONS
Average GPA and MCAT Scores

Overall GPA	3.5
MCAT Bio	10.5
MCAT Phys	10.3
MCAT Verbal	9.9

Application Information

Regular application	11/1
Regular notification	Rolling
Early application	8/1
Early notification	10/1
Are transfers accepted?	Yes
Interview required?	Yes
Application fee	$95

Academics

The majority of students follow a 4-year curriculum leading to the MD degree. Students with an interest in public health have the opportunity to earn an MPH along with their MD. This combined MD/MPH program may be completed in 4 years. Other combined-degree programs include the 4-year MD/MBA in health management in partnership with Brandeis University and Northeastern University; the MD/PhD in conjunction with the Sackler School of Graduate Biomedical Sciences; and the BS in engineering and combined MS/MD in an engineering degree program, a collaborative effort of the Tufts College of Engineering and the Tufts University School of Medicine. The doctorate may be earned in the following fields: anatomy, biochemistry, biophysics, cell biology, genetics, immunology, microbiology, molecular biology, neuroscience, pathology, pharmacology, and physiology. Each year, 4 funded MD/PhD positions are available. A primary care preceptorship program allows students with a particular interest in primary care to experience early patient contact.

BASIC SCIENCES: In addition to required courses, first- and second-year students choose among pre-clinical selectives. These are graded as pass/fail and allow students to explore their interests early on in the program. A new Principles and Practice of Medicine Program (PPM) was developed to enhance the first- and second-year curriculum. PPM integrates basic science topics with interdisciplinary subjects such as computer literacy, ethics, health care economics, information management, and negotiation/team building skills. PPM also introduces important clinical techniques such as the patient interview, examination, and physical diagnosis. First-year courses are the following: Biochemistry, Cell Biology, Epidemiology Biostatistics, Genetics, Gross Anatomy, Hematology, Histology, Immunology, Molecular Biology, Physiology, Pre-clinical Selectives, Problem-based Learning, and PPM. Second-year courses are the following: Addiction Medicine, Microbiology, Neuroscience, Pathology, Pathophysiology/Infectious Disease, Pharmacology, Pre-clinical Selectives, Problem-based Learning, Psychopathology, and PPM, which focuses on clinical skills and serves as an important transition to third-year clerkships. During the first and second years, instruction involves lectures, labs, and small-group sessions. As an important learning aid, Tufts Health Sciences Library developed the Health Sciences Database. It contains the full text of many syllabi, lecture slides, reserve slide collections, lecture recordings, and other multimedia and resource materials.

CLINICAL TRAINING

Third-year required clerkships are the following: Medicine (12 weeks), Surgery (12 weeks), Obstetrics/Gynecology (6 weeks), Pediatrics (6 weeks), and Psychiatry (6 weeks). About 4-weeks are available for elective study during the third year. Fourth-year requirements are a 4-week primary care clerkship and a 4-week neurology elective. At least 32 weeks of electives are also required, 20 of which must be completed at Tufts facilities. Twelve weeks of electives may be taken at other academic and clinical institutions. Some students fulfill a portion of elective requirements overseas.

Campus Life

In last year's entering class, about 28 percent of students were Massachusetts residents, and about 14 percent of students went to Tufts as undergraduates. Another 28 percent of students were California residents, and 10 percent were New York residents. Approximately 30 percent of students were at least 23 years old, and 15 percent were 25 or older. Women accounted for 46 percent of the class, and underrepresented minorities accounted for about 11 percent.

STUDENT LIFE

Medical students at Tufts are generally cohesive and supportive of one another. Some students are involved in clubs or in local chapters of national medical student organizations. Off campus, students enjoy the offerings of Boston, a city filled with students, bookstores, coffee shops, restaurants, parks, and cultural activities. Residence facilities are available on a limited basis in Posner Hall, located close to the medical school campus. Students who live off campus generally share apartments in neighborhoods that are convenient to the school.

GRADUATES

Graduates are successful in securing residency positions at institutions in all regions of the country. Tufts prepares graduates for careers in both primary care and specialty areas.

Admissions

REQUIREMENTS

Requirements are 8 semester credits of biology, chemistry, organic chemistry, and physics all with associated labs. Applicants must possess the ability to speak and write English correctly. The MCAT is required, and scores should be from within the past 3 years. For applicants who have taken the exam on multiple occasions, the best scores are used.

SUGGESTIONS

In addition to prerequisite courses, recommended course work includes biochemistry, calculus, computer science, English, and statistics. The selection of candidates for admissions is based not only on performance in the required premedical courses but also on the applicant's entire academic record and extracurricular experiences.

PROCESS

All AMCAS applicants are sent secondary applications. Of those returning completed applications, about 12 percent are invited to interview between November and March. Interviews consist of 2 sessions, each with a faculty member, school administrator, or senior medical student. On interview day, applicants also attend informational sessions and a reception with current medical students. Approximately half of interviewed candidates are accepted. Notification occurs on a rolling basis and is completed by May. Wait listed candidates are generally not encouraged to send additional information.

Admissions Requirements (Required)

MCAT scores, science GPA, non-science GPA, letters of recommendation, interview, state residency, extracurricular activities, exposure to medical profession

Admissions Requirements (Optional)

Essays/personal statement

COSTS AND AID
Tuition & Fees

Tuition	$44,735
Room and board (on-campus)	$9,864
Cost of books	$1,500
Fees	$575

Financial Aid

% students receiving aid	75
Average grant	$6,867
Average loan	$24,383

TULANE UNIVERSITY
SCHOOL OF MEDICINE

OFFICE OF ADMISSIONS, 1430 TULANE AVENUE, SL67 NEW ORLEANS, LA 70112 • ADMISSION: 504-988-5187
FAX: 504-988-6462 • E-MAIL: MEDSCH@TMCPOP.TMC.TULANE.EDU • WEBSITE: WWW.MCL.TULANE.EDU

STUDENT BODY

Type	Private
Enrollment	653
% male/female	43/57
% minorities	7
# applied (total/out)	6,800/6,109
# accepted (total/out)	341/265
# enrolled (total/out)	175/139
Average age	25

FACULTY

Total faculty	1,597
% female	37
% minority	12
% part-time	70
Student-faculty ratio	2:1

ADMISSIONS
Average GPA and MCAT Scores

Overall GPA	3.4
MCAT Bio	11
MCAT Phys	10
MCAT Verbal	10
MCAT Essay	P

Application Information

Regular application	1/15
Regular notification	10/15
Early application	6/1–8/1
Early notification	10/1
Are transfers accepted?	Yes
Admissions may be deferred?	Yes
Interview required?	Yes
Application fee	$95

Academics

The School of Medicine is one part of the Tulane University Health Sciences Center. In addition to the School of Medicine, the Health Sciences Center includes the School of Public Health and Tropical Medicine, and the Primate Research Center. The following programs and centers of excellence are located within the Health Sciences Center: Center for Gene Therapy, Center for Infectious Diseases, Hayward Genetics Center, Hypertension and Renal Center, Center for Bioenvironmental Research at Tulane and Xavier University, DePaul-Tulane Behavioral Health Center, Tulane Cancer Center, Tulane Center for Abdominal Transplant, the Tulane Institute of Sports Medicine, Tulane-Xavier National Women's Center, and Tulane Cardiovascular Center of Excellence.

BASIC SCIENCES: First-year courses include anatomy, histology, neuroscience, physiology, and biochemistry, taught in an integrated fashion. Multimedia lectures, problem-based learning sessions, small group discussions, laboratories and clinical correlations are all employed by these first year courses. An emphasis is placed upon the clinical application of the basic science material. The second year takes a systems-oriented approach that integrates pharmacology, pathology, microbiology, immunology, pathophysiology, and physical diagnosis. During the second semester of the first year and throughout the entire second year, students choose from an extensive offering of both basic and clinical science electives, including many research opportunities. Each year, many students will use some of their elective time to take courses in the School of Public Health and Tropical Medicine; approximately 40 to 45 students each year graduate with the M.D. and the M.P.H. degrees, having earned both degrees over a four-year period. Combined degree programs are also available for students wishing to obtain M.B.A., M.S., or J.D. degrees. Basic science instruction takes place in both the Medical School Building and a newly renovated facility located two blocks away, which are both central to the research and clinical facilities. Computers are used as learning aids and research tools; a Computing Center serves the needs of the campus. The Rudolph Matas Library houses 130,000 volumes and receives 1,200 periodicals. The grading scale is Pass/Fail for the first two years and Honors/High Pass/Pass/Conditional/Fail for the clinical years. Students are required to pass USMLE Step 1 prior to entering the fourth year and are required to pass both USMLE Step 2 CK and 2CS in order to graduate.

CLINICAL TRAINING

During the first two years, clinical training is integrated with the basic science curriculum, with patient contact beginning immediately in year one through the Foundations in Medicine program. During these two years, students work with actual patients in hospitals near the school (the Tulane University Hospital, University Hospital, and Ochsner Medical Center), with patient simulators, and with surrogate, or standardized, patients. Students are also required to participate in community service activities that often involves direct patient care. Formal clinical training begins with the third and fourth years which are constructed as a 20-month clinical continuum, with students choosing the order of rotations depending on their own personal career goals. Required rotations include: Internal Medicine, Obstetrics and Gynecology, Pediatrics, Psychiatry, Neurology, Family Medicine, and Surgery. Students are also required to do a four-week Ambulatory Internal Medicine clerkship focusing on the undifferentiated patient, and a two-week Outpatient Surgery rotation. Additionally, students complete a four-week subinternship in ward management, in addition to two weeks of Radiology, and Emergency Medicine. Clinical students also have five elective months, which may include rotations taking place in locations either domestically or internationally. Established international rotations are available in Africa, South and Central America, and Asia. A formal exchange program exists with organizations in Sweden, Germany, and Japan.

Students

Students of the class of 2007 entering class represented 36 states and 3 countries. Of a class of 175 students, 36 came from the state of Louisiana, 28 from California, 14 from New York, and 8 from Texas. They received their undergraduate training at 77 different colleges and/or universities, with 26 earning the bachelor's degree from Tulane University. The average age of the class was 24, with a range of 21 to 39. About 14 percent of the class is from an underrepresented minority population.

STUDENT LIFE

Students are very much involved in life both on- and off-campus. Medical school extracurricular groups dedicated to student social life include MedArt, Music & Medicine, the Tulane Chorale, and Students Against Right Brain Atrophy. Organizations based upon academics, specialty interests, religion, hobbies, ethnicity, and athletics bring medical students together around shared interests. An expansive support program is available for students experiencing problems, be those of an academic or personal nature. The medical school is within walking distance of the world-famous French Quarter and Superdome, and New Orleans has many parks and areas suitable for fishing, biking, running, tennis, and other outdoor activities, which are possible year-round. Of course the New Orleans cuisine and music scene is unparalleled in the United States. A housing facility, located adjacent to the Tulane University Health Sciences Center, makes over 250 apartments available to medical students, although most students choose to live off-campus, where houses and apartments are affordable and attractive. At the uptown, or university campus a large athletic facility, which includes an indoor track, two swimming pools, basketball and handball courts, and a very large selection of exercise equipment, is available for medical student use.

GRADUATES

Of the 2007 graduating class, the most popular residencies were Internal Medicine, Surgery, Pediatrics, Family Practice and Psychiatry. Approximately 35 percent of the class entered specialties considered to be primary care. Graduates from the class of 2007 will be pursuing residency training in 32 different states, with 27 staying in the state of Louisiana. Other popular states for residency training were Texas, California, Washington, Pennsylvania, Massachusetts, and Maryland.

Admissions

REQUIREMENTS

All students must have completed the following prerequisites prior to matriculation: English (six semester hours); general chemistry (six semester hours); organic chemistry (six semester hours); physics (six semester hours); and biology (six semester hours). While an undergraduate degree is not required, it is preferred. All required sciences courses must include a laboratory. The MCAT is required and should be no more than three years old; if the MCAT is taken more than once, the best set of scores is considered.

SUGGESTIONS

It is strongly required that applicants take the MCAT prior to September 1st in the year in which they intend to apply to medical school. Tulane's admission policy has no preference for any particular major; about one-third of the student body majored in a discipline other than science. While volunteer work in a hospital is useful, Tulane is more interested in seeing that applicants have an established history of providing service to a community, be it the college campus, church, or hometown, rather than a one-time exposure to a clinical environment. Activities that demonstrate strong interpersonal skills and/or evidence of self-discipline are valued, as are leadership positions.

Admissions Requirements (Required)

MCAT scores, Science GPA, Non-science GPA, Letters of recommendation, Interview, Essays/personal statement, Extracurricular activities, Exposure to medical profession

Admissions Requirements (Optional)

State residency

Overlap Schools

Baylor College of Medicine, Duke University, Emory University, The University of North Carolina at Chapel Hill, University of Alabama at Birmingham, University of Florida, Vanderbilt University.

COSTS AND AID
Tuition & Fees

Tuition	$42,000
Room and board (on-campus)	$10,000
Room and board (off-campus)	$8,000
Cost of books	$1,000
Fees	$3,080

Financial Aid

% students receiving aid	84
Average grant	$10,000
Average loan	$51,378
Average debt	$175,598

Uniformed Services University of the Health Sciences
F. Edward Hebert School of Medicine

4301 Jones Bridge Road, Room A1041 Bethesda, MD 20814 • Admission: 301-295-3101 • Fax: 301-295-3545
E-mail: ADMISSIONS@USUHS.MIL • Website: WWW.USUHS.MIL

STUDENT BODY

Type	Public
Enrollment	670
% male/female	70/30
% minorities	6
# applied	1,908
# accepted	280
# enrolled	170
Average age	24

FACULTY

Total faculty	2,104
% female	22
% minority	9
% part-time	87
Student-faculty ratio	4:1

ADMISSIONS
Average GPA and MCAT Scores

Overall GPA	3.51
MCAT Bio	10
MCAT Phys	9.5
MCAT Verbal	9.8
MCAT Essay	P

Application Information

Regular application	11/15
Regular notification	Rolling
Are transfers accepted?	No
Admissions may be deferred?	Yes
Interview required?	Yes
Application fee	$0

Academics

BASIC SCIENCES: Lectures and labs are the primary means of instruction during the first two years, and students are in scheduled sessions for about 25 hours per week. In addition to a solid grounding in the basic sciences, students receive interdisciplinary instruction that includes sociological, historical, ethical, and legal perspectives on medicine. First-year courses are Biochemistry; Fundamentals of Epidemology and Biometrics; Clinical Head, Neck, and Functional Neuroscience; Human Context in Health Care; Introduction to Clinical Medicine I; Introduction to Structure and Function; Medical Psychology; Medical History; Military Studies; Military Medical Field Studies-Summer; Structure and Function of Organ Systems; and Physiology II. During the summer following the first academic year, students take part in a hands-on field experience that serves as an introduction to military operations. Students who have a background in this area use the summer for research or other activities. Second-year courses are Ethical, Legal, and Social Aspects of Medical Care; Human Behavior; Introduction to Clinical Medicine II and III; Diagnostic Parasitology and Medical Zoology; Introduction to Clinical Reasoning; Microbiology and Infectious Diseases; Military Studies II; Pathology; Pharmacology; Preventive Medicine; and Radiographic Interpretation. Instruction takes place on the grounds of the National Naval Medical Center, in Bethesda, Maryland. Educational resources include the Multidisciplinary Laboratories and the Anatomical Teaching Laboratories, both of which are open 24 hours a day. The Learning Resource Center serves as the library, and has 120,000 volumes, journals, slides, videotapes, CDs, microcomputer programs, and online informational programs.

CLINICAL TRAINING

Third-year required clerkships are Family Practice (6 weeks); Medicine (12 weeks); Ob/Gyn (6 weeks); Pediatrics (6 weeks); Psychiatry (6 weeks); and Surgery (12 weeks). During the fourth year, 20 weeks are reserved for clinical electives or research. Required fourth-year clerkships are Military Contingency Medicine; Military Emergency Medicine; Military Preventive Medicine; Neurology; and a Subinternship. The main teaching hospitals are Walter Reed Army Medical Centers and National Naval Medical Center, which are all in the Washington, D.C., area, and the Wilford Hall USAF Medical Center, and Brooke Army Medical Center, in San Antonio, Texas. In total, these hospitals provide over 3,000 beds. Electives may be fulfilled at clinical sites nationwide and overseas.

Students

In a recent class, 60 percent had no prior military experience. Others have backgrounds in service academies, ROTC activities, as active and prior duty officers and enlisted service members, and as Reservists. Students are from all over the country, and represent a large number of undergraduate institutions. The most prevalent undergraduate majors were Biology (34 percent); Biochemistry (10 percent); Chemistry (13 percent). About 6 percent of students are underrepresented minorities. The average age of entering students is about 24. Class size is 171.

STUDENT LIFE

USUHS student groups include chapters of national organizations in addition to organizations focused on professional or service-oriented goals. These organizations are devoted to activities such as journalism, providing support to women medical students or spouses of medical students, and recreational pursuits. The school sponsors intramural athletic programs for men and women, and offers comprehensive athletic facilities. Nearby military posts and bases provide recreational and social activities for students and their families. Washington, D.C., with its museums, sites, parks, events, and diverse population, is an important resource and enriches the lives of medical students. All students live off campus, most in the immediate vicinity of the school or in Metro-accessible areas.

GRADUATES

Graduates must select residency programs at military hospitals, and often enter programs at the hospitals where they performed clerkships. Residencies vary in length, depending on the medical specialty. The residency period does not fulfill the seven-year commitment involved in attending USUHS. The military branch in which a graduate will serve is determined when he or she enters the School of Medicine and reflects both the student's preference and the needs of the organization.

Admissions

REQUIREMENTS

Applicants must be citizens of the United States; be at least 18 years old at the time of matriculation (but no older than 30 as of June 30) in the year of admission; however, an applicant who has commissioned active duty time in the Armed Services may exceed the age limitation by a period equal to the time served on active duty provided the applicant has not become 36 years of age in the year of admission. If a civilian or military member exceeds the age limit, an age waiver may be requested. In addition, meet military regulations related to physical health; possess a baccalaureate degree by June 15 in the year of admissions; and fulfill academic prerequisites. These are one year each of Biology, Physics, General Chemistry, and Organic Chemistry with lab.

One year of English Composition and/or Literature and one semester of Calculus are required. The MCAT is required, and scores must be from within three years of desired matriculation. For applicants who have retaken the exam, the best set of scores is used.

SUGGESTIONS

A broad undergraduate background, with courses in History, Philosophy, Literature, Economics, Political Science, Foreign Languages, Sociology, and Psychology is considered valuable. Applicants must be dedicated both to the medical profession and to the idea of serving the country.

PROCESS

All applicants are sent secondary applications and about 25 percent are invited to interview. Interviews take place between September and February and consist of two 30-minute sessions with practicing physicians. About one-half of interviewees are accepted, with notification occurring on a rolling basis. Wait-listed candidates may send supplementary material to enhance their files.

Admissions Requirements (Required)

MCAT scores, Science GPA, Non-science GPA, Letters of recommendation, Interview, Essays/personal statement, Exposure to medical profession

Admissions Requirements (Optional)

State residency, Extracurricular activities

COSTS AND AID

Tuition & Fees

Tuition	$0
Cost of books	$0
Fees	$0

Financial Aid

% students receiving aid	100
Average grant	$0
Average loan	$0
Average debt	$0

UNIVERSIDAD CENTRAL DE CARIBE

UNIVERSIDAD CENTRAL DEL CARIBE, CALL BOX 60-327, BAYAMON, PR 00960-6032 • ADMISSION: 787-798-3001 EXT. 2403
FAX: 787-269-7550 • E-MAIL: ICORDERO@UCCARIBE.EDU • WEBSITE: WWW.UCCARIBE.EDU

STUDENT BODY

Type	Private
Enrollment	240
% male/female	49/51
% minorities	5
# applied (total/out)	806/592
# accepted (total/out)	126/24
# enrolled (total/out)	64/14
Average age	22

FACULTY

Total faculty (number)	332
% female	52
% minority	12
% part-time	31
Student-faculty ratio	1:1

ADMISSIONS

Average GPA and MCAT Scores

Overall GPA	3.31
MCAT Bio	7.75
MCAT Phys	6.84
MCAT Verbal	6.47
MCAT Essay	M

Application Information

Regular application	12/15
Regular notification	2/15
Are transfers accepted?	Yes
Admissions may be deferred?	No
Interview required?	Yes
Application fee	$50

Academics

The mission of the School of Medicine is to develop competent physicians with an outstanding preparation within a humanistic and holistic framework. A guiding principle of our mission is to ensure that our graduates possess a strong sense of professionalism and commitment to social duties and service to Puerto Rico and Hispanic communities throughout the United States mainland. The curriculum emphasizes techniques and values related to the provision of primary medical care. The first 2 years primarily teach basic medical sciences with a strong introduction to the clinical sciences through a longitudinal primary care preceptorship, human behavior, and Clinical Skills. The second 2 years are devoted to clinical rotations and to continuing interdisciplinary instruction.

BASIC SCIENCES: Basic sciences are taught primarily through lectures. Labs and small-group sessions are also utilized. First-year courses consist of Behavioral Sciences, Bioethics and Humanities in Medicine I, Histology, Human Gross Anatomy, Introduction to Clinical Skills, LPCP I, Neurosciences, Physiology, and Problem-based Learning I. Second-year courses are Bioethics and Humanities in Medicine II, Clinical Skills, LPCP II, Microbiology and Immunology, Pathology, Pathophysiology, Physiopathology, Pharmacology, Problem-based learning II, and Psychopathology. Most instruction during the first 2 years takes place in the new Biomedical Sciences Building, which also houses laboratories and research facilities.

CLINICAL TRAINING

Clinical clerkships begin in the third year. These are comprised of Internal Medicine (10 weeks), Family Medicine (6 weeks), Surgery (10 weeks), Pediatrics (6 weeks), Psychiatry (6 weeks), Obstetrics/Gynecology (6 weeks), and Radiology/Emergency Medicine (2 weeks). Major teaching hospitals are the Dr. Ramon Ruiz Arnau University Hospital, San Pablo Hospital, First Hospital Panamericano, San Jorge Children's Hospital, San Juan Veterans Administration Hospital, and the San Juan City Hospital.

Campus Life

Around 52 percent of students are women. Virtually all students are from underrepresented minority groups.

STUDENT LIFE

To help students acclimate to medical school, an orientation is given to the entering first-year class. This also serves as an opportunity for students to interact with one other and with faculty members and administrators. Students are encouraged to develop an interest in culture and the arts. With this in mind, the Dean of Student Affairs sponsors an extracurricular activities program for medical students. Counseling services are aimed at helping students take advantage of the extensive educational opportunities at the medical school. A comprehensive health plan is offered to all medical students. Housing facilities are available through individual arrangements in areas adjacent to the medical school and the University Hospital.

GRADUATES

The Medical School has graduated about 1,832 physicians who serve the Commonwealth of Puerto Rico and Hispanic communities in the United States.

Admissions

REQUIREMENTS

Applicants must demonstrate proficiency in both Spanish and English. This is essential, as lectures are conducted in the language preferred by the respective professor, most often Spanish. In addition, Spanish is necessary for all clinical work. Applicants must complete a minimum of 90 credits at an institution of higher education. A baccalaureate degree is highly recommended. Required premedical courses are English (12 credit hours), behavioral sciences and social sciences (12 credit hours), general biology (8 credit hours), general chemistry (8 credit hours), organic chemistry (8 credit hours), physics (8 credit hours), college-level math (6 credit hours), and Spanish (6 credit hours). The MCAT is required. Official exam results from within the past 2 years must be submitted to the School of Medicine.

PROCESS

The Universidad Central del Caribe School of Medicine participates in the American Medical College Application Service (AMCAS). All applicants must file an AMCAS application. In addition, applicants should contact the School of Medicine for additional application materials and a processing fee, photograph (optional), an essay, and a Certificate of Police Record. After applications, MCAT scores and transcripts are given an initial review. Applicants who are under consideration will be invited for personal interviews with members of the faculty.

Admissions Requirements (Required)

MCAT scores, science GPA, non-science GPA, letters of recommendation, interview, essays/personal statement

Admissions Requirements (Optional)

State residency, extracurricular activities, exposure to medical profession

Overlap Schools

University of Puerto Rico.

COSTS AND AID

Tuition & Fees

Tuition (in-state)	$20,000
Tuition (out-of-state)	$27,000
Room and board (on-campus)	$6,000
Cost of books	$1,800
Fees	$4,890

Financial Aid

% students receiving aid	94
Average grant	$38,500
Average loan	$38,500
Average debt	$132,000

Université Laval
Faculté de Médecine

Pavillon Vandry, U. Laval Ste Foy, QC G1K 7P4 • **Admission:** 418-656-2131
Fax: 418-656-2733 • **E-mail:** GUY.LABRECQUE@FMED.ULAVAL.CA • **Website:** WWW.FMED.ULAVAL.CA

STUDENT BODY	
Type	Public
# applied (total/out)	1,508/123
# accepted	208
Average age	20

FACULTY	
Total faculty (number)	208
% female	74

ADMISSIONS

Application Information

Regular application	3/1
Regular notification	5/15
Are transfers accepted?	No
Admissions may be deferred?	No
Interview required?	Yes
Application fee	$30

Academics

Laval offers a 4-year curriculum leading to the MD degree. In addition, academic programs are available in a number of health and medical science fields including community health, epidemiology, molecular biology, occupational health and safety, and physiology. Research is an important part of the academic experience at Laval, and students are encouraged to pursue research during summers and throughout the academic year.

BASIC SCIENCES: The first 2 years involve basic science instruction and opportunities for addressing clinical problems. The first year includes such courses as Biochemistry, Histology-Pathology, Introduction to Problems, Microbiology-Immunology, Physiology, and Pharmacology. During the second part of the first year, instruction is organized around anatomical systems and medical concepts. These are cardiovascular system, microbiology/infectious disease, physiological/sociological, respiratory system, and uronephrology. Introduction to Problems continues during the second semester. Students also study endocrinology, growth/development, and obstetrics/gynecology during their first year. Year 2 subjects are ENT, gastroenterology, hematology, locomotor system, medical ethics, nervous system, ophthalmology, preventive medicine, problem discussion, psychopathology, skin, and the art of interviewing. Laval's library system is an important academic resource for students, holding millions of volumes and periodicals.

CLINICAL TRAINING

Years 3 and 4 are devoted to clinical rotations. Required clerkships are Medicine (8 weeks), Surgery (8 weeks), Pediatrics (8 weeks), Psychiatry (8 weeks), Obstetrics/Gynecology (8 weeks), Introduction to Clinical Medicine (5 weeks), Preventive Medicine (4 weeks), Geriatrics/Rehabilitation Medicine (4 weeks), Family Practice (4 weeks), and Emergency Medicine (4 weeks). In addition, up to 20 weeks are open for various clinical and basic science electives. Training takes place at a number of affiliated hospitals including Centre Hospitalier de l'Université Laval, Hôpital Laval, Hôpital de l'Enfant-Jesus, Hôtel-Dieu de Levis, Hôtel-Dieu de Quebec, Hôpital du Saint-Sacrement and Hôpital Saint-Francois d'Assie.

Campus Life

Each entering class at the Faculty of Medicine is comprised of about 112 students. Typically, all but a few are from within the province of Quebec. Students from other provinces must be French speakers. Within the student body are a limited number of international, French-speaking students. Women make up about 60 percent of the students.

STUDENT LIFE

Laval supports medical students both inside and outside the classroom. Programs offered include orientation and counseling services, religious organizations, career placement services, social and athletic organizations, childcare, and attractive, low-cost student housing. The Laval campus is situated in an urban environment.

GRADUATES

Graduates of Laval Faculty of Medicine enter both clinical and academic medicine. The teaching hospitals affiliated with Laval offer many programs for graduate medical training.

Admissions

REQUIREMENTS

Generally, all applicants must have completed at least 2 years of college to be considered for admission. Required undergraduate courses are biology (8 semester hours), general chemistry (8 semester hours), organic chemistry (8 semester hours), general physics (2 hours), and mathematics including calculus (2 hours). In addition, some course work in French, humanities, and social sciences is required. Fluency in French is a requirement for admission.

SUGGESTIONS

Priority is given to residents of the province of Quebec. Candidates are evaluated on the basis of academic achievement, interpersonal skills, experience, and personal characteristics. Although 2 years of college is the minimum requirement, additional schooling serves to strengthen applications.

PROCESS

Applications are coordinated in part by the organization of Quebec Colleges and Universities. For entrance in the fall, the application deadline is March 1. In addition to a written application, interviews are an important part of the selection process. Generally, about 10–15 percent of applicants are accepted in a given year.

THE UNIVERSITY OF ALABAMA AT BIRMINGHAM
SCHOOL OF MEDICINE

MEDICAL STUDENT SERVICES, VH 100, 1530 THIRD AVENUE SOUTH, BIRMINGHAM, AL 35294-0019
ADMISSION: 205-934-2433 FAX: 205-934-8740 • E-MAIL: MEDSCHOOL@UAB.EDU • WEBSITE: WWW.UAB.EDU/UASOM

STUDENT BODY

Type	Public
Enrollment	685
% male/female	59/41
% minorities	22
# applied (total/out)	1,734/1,298
# accepted (total/out)	213/33
# enrolled (total/out)	160/16
Average age	23

FACULTY

Total faculty (number)	1,113
% female	29
% minority	21
% part-time	4
Student-faculty ratio	2:1

ADMISSIONS
Average GPA and MCAT Scores

Overall GPA	3.72
MCAT Bio	10.4
MCAT Phys	10.1
MCAT Verbal	9.8
MCAT Essay	P

Application Information

Regular application	11/1
Regular notification	11/15
Early application	8/1
Early notification	10/1
Are transfers accepted?	Yes
Admissions may be deferred?	Yes
Interview required?	Yes
Application fee	$70

Academics

Basic sciences are taught during the first 2 years, primarily through lectures and small group case studies. Clinical techniques are introduced early and are often taught in small groups. The curriculum is particularly rich in relevant humanities and social sciences courses such as ethics and behavioral sciences. Joint graduate/MD degrees are offered in many fields, notably the MPH/MD combination. About 8 students a year are accepted into joint MD/PhD programs as MSTP candidates. A combined undergraduate/medical school program is offered at The University of Alabama at Birmingham to which high school seniors who are Alabama residents may apply.

BASIC SCIENCES: First-year students take the following courses: Behavioral Sciences, Biochemistry, Gross Anatomy, Human Sexuality, Medical Ethics, Medical Cell and Tissue Biology, Physiology, Pharmacology, Neurosciences, and Nutrition. Throughout the first year, students participate in a course called Introduction to Clinical Medicine, which addresses doctor/patient interaction including professionalism, history-taking, and physical examinations. During the fall of year 2, Pharmacology continues and Microbiology/Immunology is introduced. Pathology is a year-long course, taken throughout year 2. Introduction to clinical medicine continues in year 2, focusing on physical diagnosis. The Lister Hill Library at the Birmingham campus houses 240,000 volumes and uses computer online search services. Pre-clinical performance is evaluated on a pass/fail by quartile scale. The USMLE Step 1 is required following completion of the pre-clinical studies and before promotion to the third year.

CLINICAL TRAINING

Clinical training begins well before the required clerkships of the third year. In addition to the introductory clinical course work of the first 2 years, some students are involved in community programs, which provide patient exposure to public health programs, such as the AIDS Care Team and other projects aimed at young or homeless populations. The final 2 years are essentially combined, with required clerkships and acting internships filling all of the third year and part of the fourth year. Students choose a primary campus for clerkships prior to acceptance. Each campus has unique strengths. Required clerkships are Family Medicine, Medicine, Neurology, Obstetrics/Gynecology, Pediatrics, Psychiatry, Rural Medicine, and Surgery. Each campus is affiliated with several teaching hospitals, and rotations take students to a variety of learning environments ranging from large Veterans Affairs Hospitals to small, rural clinics. For required rotations, grading is pass/fail by quartile and for electives. The School of Medicine established a Medical Student Enrichment Program, which encourages and facilitates overseas clinical experience. In addition to providing elective opportunities to medical school seniors, medical students may apply to the program or placements during the summer between their first and second years. The USMLE Step 2 is required for graduation.

Campus Life

About 75 percent of the matriculates majored in a scientific field during their undergraduate studies. The school seeks a diverse student body to reflect the diverse health care needs of the state of Alabama. The school has special programs to promote both clinical and basic science research as well as address unmet health care needs of the State of Alabama.

STUDENT LIFE

Outside of class, students are often involved in recreational and volunteer activities. Some are active in student organizations such as national medical groups. The Student Government Association consists of elected members of each class. The Birmingham campus, with its many departments, provides a community beyond that of medical students alone. Most students choose to live off campus where housing is ample and relatively affordable. Most students have cars.

GRADUATES

Primary care residencies are popular among graduates. Although graduates are competitive for residencies nationwide, a significant number enter residency programs in Alabama, at university-affiliated hospitals, or other locations in the state.

Admissions

REQUIREMENTS

Undergraduate requirements are biology or zoology (8 semester hours), chemistry with lab (8 semester hours), organic chemistry with lab (8 semester hours), physics with lab (8 semester hours), math (6 semester hours), and English (6 semester hours). Academic work accomplished overseas may be acceptable, depending on the institution and the course. A minimum total MCAT score, not more than 2 years old at the time of application, is required. The spring MCAT is strongly recommended. The AMCAS application is required.

SUGGESTIONS

The Admissions Committee values experience with patient care and exposure to health care environments. The University of Alabama School of Medicine welcomes nontraditional applicants. Alabama residents are given significant preference in the admissions process.

PROCESS

All qualified Alabama AMCAS applicants, and approximately one-third of out-of-state applicants, receive a secondary application. Generally, about 70 percent of in-state applicants are interviewed. About 2–10 percent of out-of-state applicants are interviewed. In 2005, about 66 percent of the in-state applicants interviewed were accepted, while about 44 percent of the out-of-state applicants interviewed were accepted. Notification begins in October, and the class is generally filled by April. Interviews consist of three 30-minute sessions with faculty members.

Admissions Requirements (Required)

MCAT scores, science GPA, non-science GPA, letters of recommendation, interview, essays/personal statement, extracurricular activities, exposure to medical profession

Admissions Requirements (Optional)

State residency

Overlap Schools

Emory University, University of South Alabama, Vanderbilt University.

COSTS AND AID
Tuition & Fees

In-state tuition	$12,161
Out-of-state tuition	$36,483
Room and board (off-campus)	$11,868
Cost of books	$2,200
Fees	$3,065

Financial Aid

% students receiving aid	80
Average grant	$6,528
Average loan	$12,593
Average debt	$90,742

UNIVERSITY OF ALBERTA
FACULTY OF MEDICINE AND DENTISTRY

2-45 MEDICAL SCIENCES BUILDING, EDMONTON, AB T6G 2H7 • ADMISSION: 780-492-6350
FAX: 780-492-7303 • E-MAIL: DEAN@MED.UALBERTA.CA • WEBSITE: WWW.MED.UALBERTA.CA

STUDENT BODY	
Type	Public
# applied	1,095

ADMISSIONS	
Average GPA and MCAT scores	
MCAT Bio	10.8
MCAT Phys	11.3
MCAT Verbal	9.7
Application Information	
Regular application	1/31
Admissions may be deferred?	Yes
Interview required?	Yes
Application fee	$60

Academics

Alberta's curriculum reflects the school's emphasis on clinical care and research. The pre-clinical curriculum has been revised and is largely centered on organ systems. It is multidisciplinary, including both biological and social science perspectives. Although basic sciences are the focus of study during the first 2 years, courses are taught with clinical applications in mind. The second 2 years integrate classroom and hospital-based instruction. While most medical students earn an MD degree in 4 years, qualified students may pursue joint-degrees such as the MD/PhD or MD/MPH in a longer period of study.

BASIC SCIENCES: Basic sciences are taught in a variety of forums, including lectures, small-group discussions, laboratories, problem-based learning, independent study, and computer-based instruction. The academic period begins in August, covers 35 weeks, and includes such courses as Cardiology, Renal, and Pulmonary; Endocrine and Metabolism; Immunity, Infection, and Inflammation; Introduction to Medicine; and Practice of Medicine (Part I). On average, students are in class or other scheduled sessions for about 25 hours per week. The second academic period also begins in August and includes Gastroenterology, Musculoskeletal, Neurosciences, Oncology, Practice of Medicine (Part II), and Reproduction and Urology, in addition to a systems-based curriculum. Systems studied are cardiovascular, endocrinology, gastrointestinal, hematology, medical ethics, nephrology, ophthalmology, pediatrics, pulmonary, surgery, and urology. Basic science instruction takes place mainly at the medical sciences building and uses the resources of the John W. Scott Health Sciences Library. Medical students may use all university libraries and computer facilities. All enrolled students have access to free online service.

CLINICAL TRAINING

The third and fourth academic periods primarily teach clinical skills and consist of classroom instruction, required rotations, electives, and selectives. Required clerkships are Surgery (10 weeks), Medicine (10 weeks), Obstetrics/Gynecology (8 weeks), Pediatrics (8 weeks), Psychiatry (8 weeks), Rural Family Medicine (4 weeks), Radiology (2 weeks), Anesthesia (2 weeks), and Geriatrics (2 weeks). Selectives include 2 weeks in internal medicine and 2 weeks in surgery. Training takes place at the University of Alberta hospitals, the Royal Alexandra Hospital, Edmonton General Hospital, Misericordia Hospital, Alberta Hospital, Glenrose Hospital, Cross Cancer Institute, and Grey Nuns Hospital. A certain number of electives may be taken at nonaffiliated institutions.

Campus Life

STUDENT LIFE

Campus housing is available, although most students opt to live off campus in the surrounding area. The students' union provides a registry informing students of available housing. Medical students participate in clubs, events, and recreational activities geared toward medical students and the student body in general. Counseling and other support services are available to students, as are groups focused on special interests and minority groups. Edmonton is a mid-size city, offering plenty of restaurants, shops, parks, theaters, sporting events, and outdoor activities. Although public transportation is available, most medical students own cars.

GRADUATES

Graduates enter both clinical medicine and research-oriented careers.

Admissions

REQUIREMENTS

Only Canadian applications are accepted. All applicants should have completed at least 60 units of university course work (approximately 2 years of full-time studies). Requirements are 6 units each of biology, English, general chemistry, organic chemistry, and physics along with 3 units each of statistics and biochemistry. The MCAT is required and scores are valid for 3 years after the exam is taken. In addition to an application form, an autobiographical essay, and 2 letters of reference are required.

SUGGESTIONS

Residency is an important consideration in admissions decisions. For admissions purposes, a resident of Alberta is defined as a Canadian citizen or permanent resident who has lived in the Province of Alberta or Yukon or Northwest Territories for at least 1 continuous year immediately prior to the date of intended matriculation. At least 85 percent of available positions in an entering class are reserved for Alberta residents. The remaining 15 percent are available to other Canadians. Typically, successful applicants have completed 4 years of university with a grade point average of 7.0 on the University of Alberta's 9 point grading system. An MCAT score of less than 7 in any category is not accepted.

PROCESS

Requests for applications should be directed to the address above. Applications are accepted between July 1 and November 1 in the year preceding anticipated matriculation. The essay and reference letters must be received by January 15, and transcripts must be submitted by January 15. Interviews are conducted between February and March, and admissions decisions are made between May and July. Applicants who feel that they may merit special consideration (because of studies in a nontraditional area or unusual pattern) should write to the Admissions Officer outlining their situation and goals. All native (Aboriginal) students who are interested in medical studies are encouraged to contact the coordinator at the Native Health Care Careers Program in care of the above address.

Admissions Requirement (Required)

Interview

COSTS AND AID

Tuition & Fees

In-state tuition	$6,066
Cost of books	$900
Fees	$6,000

UNIVERSITY OF ARIZONA
COLLEGE OF MEDICINE

ADMISSIONS OFFICE, ROOM 2106, PO BOX 245075, TUCSON, AZ 85724 • ADMISSION: 520-626-6214
FAX: 520-626-4884 • E-MAIL: ADMISSIONS@MEDICINE.ARIZONA.EDU • WEBSITE: WWW.MEDICINE.ARIZONA.EDU

STUDENT BODY	
Type	Public
Enrollment	406
% male/female	52/48
% minorities	15
# applied (total/out)	608/71
# accepted	51

ADMISSIONS

Application Information

Regular application	11/1
Regular notification	1/30
	until filled
Are transfers accepted?	No
Admissions may be deferred?	Yes
Interview required?	Yes
Application fee	$75

Academics

Students may apply to joint PhD/MD programs in the following: anatomy, biochemistry, cell biology, genetics, immunology, microbiology, molecular biology, neuroscience, pharmacology, and physiology. Combined studies in other fields are possible as well, including a collaborative program with Arizona State University, Northern Arizona University, and the College of Medicine at the University of Arizona. This program focuses on the health needs of underserved communities and leads to a MPH along with the MD. Through this and other venues, medical students at the University of Arizona take advantage of the resources of the academic and medical institutions throughout the state.

BASIC SCIENCES: The basic sciences are taught in the Basic Science Building of the Tucson campus. Traditional lectures with labs are the primary mode of instruction, occupying about 24 hours per week. Alternative teaching methods, including small-group and case-based learning, account for the remaining 6 hours per week of structured classroom time. First-year courses are Anatomy, Biochemistry, Histology and Cell Biology, Medical and Molecular Genetics, Neuroscience, Physiology, Preparation for Clinical Medicine, and Social and Behavioral Science. During year 2, students take Microbiology, Pathology, Pharmacology, Preparation for Clinical Medicine, and Social and Behavioral Science. In the course preparation for clinical medicine, students focus on clinical problem-solving and learn patient evaluation skills. This course links basic science principles with clinical applications. Computers, located in the Learning Resource Center, supplement lectures and are an important component of the basic science education. The Arizona Health Science Library houses nearly 200,000 volumes, operates extensive online database and informational services, and is connected electronically to the library system of the greater university. To accommodate the study schedules of all students, the library is open 24 hours a day. Students are evaluated with an honors/pass/fail scale. The USMLE Step 1 is required upon completion of basic science course work.

CLINICAL TRAINING

Patient contact begins during year 1 in preparation for clinical medicine. Throughout the 4 years, there are opportunities for clinical exposure through volunteer and outreach programs. In addition, clinical research is often community-based and gives medical students a chance to help others while they learn. The Commitment to Underserved People (CUP) is a program through which many medical students volunteer. In CUP, students are involved in health education for, and supervised treatment of, people in underserved communities. The formal clinical curriculum begins in year 3, when students rotate through the following clerkships: Medicine (12 weeks), Pediatrics (6 weeks), Family Medicine (6 weeks), Obstetrics/Gynecology (6 weeks), Psychiatry (6 weeks), Surgery (6 weeks), Specialty Surgery (3 weeks), and Neurology (3 weeks). Year 4 is composed of electives, many of which can be taken at alternate locations throughout the state. Clinical facilities in Tucson are the University Medical Center, the University Outpatient Clinic, the Children's Research Center, and the Arizona Cancer Center. The hospitals serve managed care participants, and the medical school seeks to respond to the ongoing changes in the economics of health care, as seen in the public health/health policy components of medical school training. Evaluation of clinical performance is honors/pass/fail. Passing the USMLE Step 2 is a requirement for graduation.

Campus Life

Students are either Arizona residents, or are from western states that do not have their own medical schools. Generally, about 15 percent of the student body are underrepresented minorities, most of whom are of Mexican American descent. Older students comprise about one-third of each class. A wide range of undergraduate institutions and majors are represented in a typical class. Class size is 100.

STUDENT LIFE

With access to both the campus community of more than 36,000 students and a medium-sized urban community, students have active social lives. Recreational facilities are extensive at the university. The Medical School's emphasis on community involvement promotes extracurricular activities that are medically related. Student clubs also provide mechanisms for support and social interaction. The Chicano/Latino Club is linked to similar organizations at California universities, providing a larger network for those involved. On-campus housing options include apartments and dorms. Most students, however, opt to live off campus.

GRADUATES

At least 60 percent of graduates enter primary care fields, which include family medicine, internal medicine, obstetrics/gynecology, and pediatrics. About 50 percent of graduates enter residency programs within the state.

Admissions

REQUIREMENTS

Applicants should have completed 1 year of each of the following subjects: biology, chemistry, English, organic chemistry, physics. In addition, at least 30 hours of upper-division course work as part of the undergraduate record is required. For older applicants, recent science course work is necessary. The MCAT is required, and only the best scores are considered, suggesting that applicants should not withhold scores. Together, the MCAT and college record are used for initial screening.

SUGGESTIONS

Hands-on clinical experience is important, as are other activities that demonstrate an applicant's commitment to community service. The Admissions Committee is interested in applicants whose undergraduate records include significant course work in the humanities and social sciences. Applicants are advised to take the April rather than August MCAT.

PROCESS

All AMCAS applicants receive secondary applications, and virtually all who meet residency requirements are interviewed. Interviews are conducted from September through March and consist of 3 short meetings with faculty members and one longer session with a practicing clinician from the area. About one-fourth of those who interview are accepted, with notifications occurring on a rolling basis. A ranked wait list is established, but those who find themselves on this list are not encouraged to send additional information.

Admissions Requirements (Required)

MCAT scores, science GPA, non-science GPA, letters of recommendation, interview, state residency, extracurricular activities, exposure to medical profession

Admissions Requirements (Optional)

Essays/personal statement

COSTS AND AID
Tuition & Fees

In-state tuition	$15,786
Fees	$170

Financial Aid

% students receiving aid	87

UNIVERSITY OF ARKANSAS FOR MEDICAL SCIENCES

COLLEGE OF MEDICINE

4301 WEST MARKHAM STREET, SLOT 551, LITTLE ROCK, AR 72205-7199 • ADMISSION: 501-686-5354
FAX: 501-686-5873 • E-MAIL: SOUTHTOMG@UAMS.EDU • WEBSITE: WWW.UAMS.EDU/COM

STUDENT BODY

Type	Public
Enrollment	576
% male/female	56/44
% minorities	10
# applied (total/out)	675/343
# accepted (total/out)	171/6
# enrolled (total/out)	140/2
Average age	24

ADMISSIONS

Average GPA and MCAT Scores

Overall GPA	3.6
MCAT Bio	9.0
MCAT Phys	9.0
MCAT Verbal	9.0
MCAT Essay	O

Application Information

Regular application	11/1
Regular notification	2/15
Are transfers accepted?	Yes
Admissions may be deferred?	Yes
Interview required?	Yes
Application fee	$100

Academics

The College of Medicine, along with the schools of Nursing, Pharmacy, Public Health, Health Related Professions, and Graduate Studies, comprise the University of Arkansas for Medical Sciences, 1 of 6 campuses of the University of Arkansas system. Most students complete the MD curriculum in 4 years, but a few students each year take part in joint MD/PhD or MD/MPH, and MD/MBA programs. Joint-degrees can be pursued in the following fields: anatomy, biochemistry, immunology, microbiology, neuroscience, pharmacology, and physiology.

BASIC SCIENCES: Throughout year 1, students learn skills related to patient care in Introduction to Clinical Medicine. Fall semester courses are Cell Biology, Genetics, Gross Anatomy, and Microscopic Anatomy. Spring semester courses are Biochemistry, Neuroscience, and Physiology. In the fall semester of year 2, students take Behavioral Sciences, Medical Ethics, Microbiology, and Pathophysiology I. In the spring, classes are Introduction to Clinical Medicine II, Pathophysiology II, and Pharmacology. Scheduled class time accounts for about 20 hours per week, most of which is devoted to lecture and lab. Alternately, for perhaps 2 hours per week, small groups are used as the instructional format. Grading uses an A–F scale. Passing the USMLE Step 1 is a requirement for promotion to year 3, and USMLE 2 for graduation. Basic-science teaching facilities, including libraries and labs, are part of the medical complex, which includes the main hospitals as well as residence halls.

CLINICAL TRAINING

Patient contact begins in year 1, in Introduction to Clinical Medicine. The third year consists of required clerkships in the following: internal medicine (12 weeks), Surgery (8 weeks), Obstetrics/Gynecology (6 weeks), Psychiatry (6 weeks), Pediatrics (8 weeks), Specialties (4 weeks), Family Medicine (4 weeks), and Geriatrics (unspecified). During year 4, students choose among primary care selectives (8 weeks) and specialties clerkships (4 weeks). The remainder of the year is designated as elective study, some of which may be taken off campus, out of state, or overseas. Training takes place primarily at the University Hospital (400 beds), located in the Medical Center complex. Other training sites are the Arkansas Children's Hospital (the sixth largest children's hospital in the country) and two Veterans Affairs Hospitals (500 and 2,000 beds). In addition, outreach training sites in small communities around the state provide exposure to rural medicine. The primary care clerkships involve rotations to these sites, located in El Dorado, Fayetteville, Fort Smith, Jonesboro, Pine Bluff, and Texarkana. Specialized research institutes in Little Rock include The Child Study Center, The Ambulatory Care Center, The Arkansas Cancer Research Center, and the Jones Eye Institute. Evaluation of clinical progress in required clerkships uses an A–F scale, and electives are graded as pass/fail. Students must pass the USMLE Step 2 as a requirement for graduation.

Campus Life

Virtually all students are Arkansas residents. About 70 percent of students earned under-graduate degrees in Arkansas. Approximately 79 percent of incoming students in a recent class had undergraduate majors in science disciplines. Classes include a significant number of older students, including some who were older than 50 at the time of admission. Class size is 150.

STUDENT LIFE

Little Rock is a small but lively city, with indoor and outdoor recreational activities. Students take part in volunteer and community activities. Many single first- and second-year students live on campus in residence halls. Most juniors and seniors and married students live off campus.

GRADUATES

Many graduates enter postgraduate programs in Arkansas. Programs in about 20 specialty areas are offered at university-affiliated hospitals in Little Rock. In addition, a number of family practice residencies are available at rural locations around the state. At least half of the graduates of the School of Medicine enter primary-care fields.

Admissions

REQUIREMENTS

Within each class, 70 percent of students must be equally divided from among the 4 congressional districts in the state. The College of Medicine is allowed to admit a few out-of-state applicants each year but only if they do not displace Arkansas residents with equal qualifications. Out-of-state applicants should be highly qualified and have close ties to Arkansas. Students must have successfully completed the following prior to matriculation: biology (1 year), chemistry (1 year), organic chemistry (1 year), physics (1 year), English (1 year), and math (1 year) or through calculus I. The MCAT is required, and scores must be no more than 3 years old. Scores from all sections of the MCAT, including the writing sample, are considered.

SUGGESTIONS

Other courses deemed helpful are anthropology, biochemistry, botany, calculus, composition, embryology, genetics, histology, history, human ecology, literature, logic, physical chemistry, psychology, sociology, speech, statistics, and zoology. For students who graduated from college several years ago, some recent course work is useful. All medically related extracurricular activities are valued.

PROCESS

All AMCAS applicants are asked to submit secondary applications. All Arkansas residents and highly qualified out-of-state residents are interviewed, with interviews taking place between October and January. Team interviews consist of a 1-hour session with faculty. All applicants are notified by February 15. A ranked wait list is established, and about 25 students from the list are usually admitted. Wait listed candidates who commit to practicing in underserved areas of Arkansas may improve their chances of admission.

Admissions Requirements (Required)

MCAT scores, science GPA, non-science GPA, letters of recommendation, interview, state residency, essays/personal statement, extracurricular activities, exposure to medical profession

COSTS AND AID
Tuition & Fees

In-state tuition	$14,792
Out-of-state tuition	$29,584
Cost of books	$773

Financial Aid

Average grant	$3,000
Average loan	$25,000
Average debt	$88,000

University of British Columbia
Faculty of Medicine

317-2194 Health Sciences Mall, British Columbia, BC V6T 1Z3 • **Admission:** 604-822-2421
Fax: 604-822-6061 • **E-mail:** ADMISSIONS.MD@UBC.CA • **Website:** WWW.MED.UBC.CA

STUDENT BODY	
Type	Public
Enrollment	256
# applied (total/out)	1,800/550
Average age	25

ADMISSIONS
Average GPA and MCAT Scores

MCAT Bio	10.9
MCAT Phys	10.3
MCAT Verbal	9.3
MCAT Essay	P

Application Information

Regular application	09/1
Regular notification	5/15
Are transfers accepted?	Yes
Admissions may be deferred?	
	Yes (exceptional)
Application fee	$105/$155

Academics

The four-year leading to the M.D. degree is integrated and comprehensive, designed to take advantage of the vast resources of the Faculty of Medicine. A new case-based curriculum that emphasizes problem solving and lifelong learning was introduced during the Fall of 1998. In addition to the M.D. program, graduate programs leading to Masters, Doctorate, and combined degrees are available.

BASIC SCIENCES: Basic sciences are taught along with introductory clinical concepts during the first two years. First-year courses include Introductory Clinical Skills and Systems 1; Doctor/Dentist; Patient & Society; Family Practice Continuum; Principles of Human Biology; Host Defenses and Infection; Cardiovascular Systems; Pulmonary; and Fluids, Electrolytes & Renal. Second-year courses include Clinical Skills and Systems II; Doctor/Dentist, Patient & Society; Family Practice Continuum; Blood and Lymphatic; Musculoskeletal and Locomotor; GI/Nutrition; Metabolism and Endocrine; Integument; Brain and Behavior and Reproduction; And Growth and Development. Basic sciences are taught primarily through small group forums, through lectures, computer-based instruction and labs also utilized.

CLINICAL TRAINING

The third academic period begins with courses in Health Care Epidemiology, Radiology, and Therapeutics. Following these three courses, students enter a sequence of required clerkships. These are: Orientation (4 weeks), Anesthesia (2 weeks), Dermatology (1 week), Emergency Medicine (4 weeks), Medicine (10 weeks), Ob/Gyn (8 weeks), Ophthalmology (1 week), Orthopedics (2 weeks), Pediatrics (8 weeks), Psychiatry (8 weeks), and Surgery (8 weeks). Six weeks are left open for electives during the third academic period. Sixteen weeks are left open for electives during the fourth academic period. A portion of electives may be completed at sites outside of the network of affiliated institutions including the University Hospital, St. Paul's Hospital, British Columbia Children's Hospital, Vancouver General Hospital, British Columbia Women's Hospital and Health Center, British Columbia Cancer Center Agency, G.F.Strong Rehabilitation Center, and the Canadian Arthritis and Rheumatism Society Center.

Campus Life

Each entering class has about 256 students, distributed in 3 sites: Vancouver/Fraser, Victoria and Prince George. Approximately 50 percent of students are women. Typically, all but a few of students in each class are from British Columbia.

STUDENT LIFE

Beyond a rich, academic life, medical students enjoy the resources, facilities, and surroundings of the Health Science Center, the University of British Columbia, and the city of Vancouver. The Faculty of Medicine and greater university offer a wide range of support services including counseling, special interest clubs and organizations, resources for minorities and international students, and day care. There are ample opportunities for athletic, social, and recreational activities on campus. Students also enjoy the cultural and recreational aspects of Vancouver.

GRADUATES

A significant number of graduates enter residency programs at hospitals affiliated with the University of British Columbia. Though most graduates enter clinical medicine, others successfully pursue research and academic medicine.

Admissions

REQUIREMENTS

Applicants should have successfully completed a minimum of 90 credits or the equivalent of three years of full-time course work in any degree program at an accredited university. A minimum of 70 percent academic average is required and all undergraduate courses are included in this average. Prerequisites are one year each of university-level Biology, Biochemistry, Chemistry, Organic Chemistry, and English Literature and Composition. The MCAT is required. The exam should be taken no later than August of the year of application.

SUGGESTIONS

There is no preferred program of study for preparation for medical school. Often, due to the large number of applicants, the competitive average for successful applicants is much higher than 70 percent. MCAT scores of a recently admitted class averaged about 10. In addition to excellent academic qualifications, admission decisions are based on the applicant's personal characteristics, such as motivation and integrity. Last year, 1,800 applications were recieved for 256 positions.

COSTS AND AID	
Tuition & Fees	
In-state tuition	$4,000
Cost of books	$1,200
Fees	$256

UNIVERSITY OF CALGARY
FACULTY OF MEDICINE

3330 HOSPITAL DRIVE NORTHWEST, ALBERTA, T2N 4N1 • ADMISSION: 403-220-4262
WEBSITE: WWW.MED.UCALGARY.CA/ADMISSIONS

STUDENT BODY

Type	Public
Enrollment	234
% male/female	48/52
# applied (total/out)	1,314/784
Average age	25

ADMISSIONS
Average GPA and MCAT Scores

Overall GPA	3.5
MCAT Bio	10.67
MCAT Phys	10.48
MCAT Verbal	9.77
MCAT Essay	Q

Application Information

Regular application	11/15
Regular notification	5/14
Are transfers accepted?	Yes
Admissions may be deferred?	Yes
Interview required?	Yes
Application fee	$65

Academics

Medical students follow an intensive, 11-month curriculum for a period of 3 years. Learning is based in part on clinical case presentations. In addition to the standard MD course of study, programs are offered in conjunction with the Faculty of Graduate Studies in Biomedical and Health Sciences with the objective of training clinician-scientists for academic medical research and those who will design, manage, and implement health care delivery programs. MD/PhD and MD/MSc are available in Biochemistry and molecular biology, cardiovascular/respiratory sciences, community health sciences, gastrointestinal sciences, medical science, Microbiology and Infectious Diseases, and Neuroscience.

BASIC SCIENCES: First-year courses are based on organ systems and are taught primarily through lectures and small-group discussions. Subjects are blood, cardiovascular, endocrine metabolic, integrative, medical skills program, musculoskeletal and skin, principles of medicine, renal-electrolyte, and respiratory. The second academic period begins in July. Subjects are gastrointestinal, human development, medical skills program, Neuroscience, reproduction, and the mind. Throughout the first and second years, students also take part in independent research projects. Courses are taught in the Calgary Health Sciences Center, about 1.5 km from the main campus of the University of Calgary. The medical library is fully computerized, receives more than 1,000 serials, and houses approximately 130,000 books. It serves medical and nursing students as well as the greater university and the medical community. Other important facilities include the Medical Learning Resource Center, which houses instructional tools geared toward learning anatomical systems, and the Medical Skills Center for improving clinical skills and techniques.

CLINICAL TRAINING

Required clerkships are Internal Medicine (12 weeks), Surgery (8 weeks), Obstetrics/Gynecology (6 weeks), Pediatrics (6 weeks), Psychiatry (6 weeks), Family Medicine (4 weeks), and Anesthesia (2 weeks). Ten weeks are available for clinical electives. Training takes place primarily at the facilities of the Foothills Hospital, the Peter Lougheed Center, the Alberta Children's Hospital, and the Rockyview Hospital. In addition, the University of Calgary Medical Clinic allows medical students to learn about outpatient service delivery, preventative programs, and travel medicine.

Campus Life

While medical students are primarily Canadian, the student body at the University of Calgary includes several hundred international students. Within the Faculty of Medicine, women compromise about 50 percent of students. The majority of medical students are from within the province of Alberta.

STUDENT LIFE

Student life is enhanced by campus activities, the resources of the community and city of Calgary, and the wide range of outdoor activities available. Nearby national parks, such as Banff and Jasper, offer skiing and hiking. The region also has vibrant wildlife and areas for fishing, swimming, and canoeing. In addition to its academic facilities, the Health Sciences Center includes a medical bookstore, exercise room, student lounge, cafeteria, and mall area. Medical students also have access to the resources of the greater university, including complete athletic and recreational facilities, intramural sports programs, outdoor programs, arts, and theater. The University Student Union organizes events and activities and operates a bookstore, cafe, and bar, along with other services. On-campus housing is available for single and married students. An off-campus registry is managed by the student union.

GRADUATES

Though most graduates enter postgraduate training that leads to careers in clinical medicine, some go on to pursue research and academic medicine. Increasingly, graduates are entering primary care fields.

Admissions

REQUIREMENTS

Students must have completed at least two full years of university education before being considered for admission. The minimum grade requirement for a Canadian citizen or landed immigrant resident of Alberta is an average of 3.0/4.0, which translates to a grade of B or at least 78 percent for each year of study. The minimum grade point average required of Canadians from other provinces is 3.5/4.0. The MCAT is required, and applicants should have at least an average score of 8. In addition to transcripts and a completed application form, three letters of reference are required.

SUGGESTIONS

Although the faculty has no prescribed prerequisites, 1 year of each of the following subjects is strongly recommended: biology, biochemistry, calculus, English, general chemistry, organic chemistry, physics, physiology, and pyschology/sociology. Presently, spaces for international students are limited to those students who come from institutions and/or countries with which the Faculty of Medicine at the University of Calgary has a formal, contractional agreement. All international students must sign an acknowledgment that the MD program would not lead to an opportunity for postgraduate training through the Canadian Resident Matching Service.

PROCESS

The application is available at www.med.ucalgary.ca/admissions. It requires information about all university courses taken, MCAT test dates/results, employment history, extracurricular activities, and an essay. The completed application is due November 15. The deadline for receipt of the three letters of reference, all official transcripts, and official MCAT scores is January 4. Applicants will be notified by March 15 whether or not they will be invited for an interview. In a recent year, there were 1,300 applicants for 100 positions.

Admissions Requirements (Required)

Interview

COSTS AND AID

Tuition & Fees

In-state tuition	$6,519
Out-of-state tuition	$30,000
Cost of books	$1,200
Fees	$333

UNIVERSITY OF CALIFORNIA—DAVIS

SCHOOL OF MEDICINE

4610 X ST. SUITE 1202, SACRAMENTO, CA 95826 • ADMISSION: 916-734-4800
FAX: 916-734-4050 • E-MAIL: MEDADMSINFO@UCDAVIS.EDU • WEBSITE: WWW.UCDMC.UCDAVIS.EDU

STUDENT BODY	
Type	Public
Enrollment	416
% male/female	43/57
% minorities	17.3
# applied (total/out)	4,861/1,080
# accepted (total/out)	229/12
# enrolled (total/out)	105/4
Average age	24

FACULTY	
Total faculty (number)	694
% female	29
% part-time	17
Student-faculty ratio	1:1

ADMISSIONS	
Average GPA and MCAT scores	
Overall GPA	3.62
MCAT Bio	11
MCAT Phys	11
MCAT Verbal	10
MCAT Essay	P

Application Information	
Regular application	10/1
Regular notification	10/15
Are transfers accepted?	Yes
Admissions may be deferred?	Yes
Interview required?	Yes
Application fee	$0

Academics

The School of Medicine is well-integrated into the UC Davis campus and benefits from the academic programs of the university. About 10 percent of each class extend their first 2 years in three, extend their fourth year, or take time off from the standard curriculum at some point. This "Enrichment Option" allows students to pursue research or attend to other academic and personal goals. Joint-degree programs organized in conjunction with graduate departments at UC Davis lead to an MBA, MA, or PhD along with the MD degree. In addition, the MPH degree may be earned through the School of Medicine's Department of Public Health Sciences or at UC Berkeley School of Public Health. Those interested in careers as physician-scientists may apply for programs leading to doctorates in the following fields: biochemistry, biomedical engineering, cell biology, genetics, immunology, molecular biology, neuroscience, pathology, pharmacology, physiology and in the humanities or social sciences. All 4 years of medical school will take place on the Sacramento Medical campus in a new Medical Education Center.

BASIC SCIENCES: The first basic science block (August through December) coordinates Anatomy, Physiology, Cell Biology, and Biochemistry, and approaches the topic of cell biology systematically for the first time. Organ systems are studied together, including gross and microanatomy and function is integrated with structure. These courses will continue to be administered by basic science departments.

The second block features two new concurrent integrated basic and clinical science courses. In Metabolism, Endocrinology and Reproduction, the various topics progress in a logical, integrated manner from normal function to disease models. In Microbiology-Immunology-Pathology-Host Defense, the emphasis will be on how immunologic processes mediate response to infection and autoimmune disease and how the body responds to injury.

Year 2 starts with a summer block that combines Neurobiology, Clinical Neurosciences, Neuropathology, and Neuropharmacology courses. The close temporal proximity of lectures in these areas will help students better appreciate how breakdowns in the normal structure and function of the nervous system cause disease and how these diseases can be treated. The remainder of year 2 places courses in better order to facilitate integration and learning. For example, cardiology/pulmonary/renal are concurrent and hematology, and oncology are placed together.

An earlier start to the school year (August) allows an earlier start to the clinical clerkships (May of the second year). This will increase the number of 8-week blocks in the third year from 6 to 7 (the 6 required third year clerkships will not change). The additional block will enable students to take subspecialty clerkships (important for "early match" specialties) or other electives during their third year. The integrated 3 year doctoring curriculum will continue to run alongside the above courses and link to the concurrent basic science and pathophysiology content.

CLINICAL TRAINING

Third-year required clerkships are Surgery (8 weeks), Medicine (8 weeks), Pediatrics (8 weeks), Obstetrics/Gynecology (8 weeks), Psychiatry (8 weeks), and Primary Care Plus (8 weeks), which includes 4 weeks in a family-practice setting and introduces primary care components of certain specialties. Required clerkships take place at UC Davis Medical Center in Sacramento (578 beds), Kaiser Permanente Hospital, David Grant

Hospital (Travis Air Force Base), Sutter Hospital, Highland General (Oakland), and at community physician sites. Other clinical facilities include a new Shriners Hospital opened on the Sacramento campus to provide care to children with orthopedic and other disorders, an expanded hospital, the Ellison Ambulatory Care Center, and the establishment of the Mather Veterans Affairs Hospital. Among these sites, students serve a diverse patient population. Selectives may be taken at any LCME-accredited medical school. Overseas clinical activities may be taken as elective programs organized by the Departments of Family Practice and Public Health Sciences, and through individual student efforts. Students must take and pass the USMLE Step 2 in order to graduate.

Campus Life

All but a few students in each class are California residents. There is also significant diversity in the age of incoming students, the average being 25 or 26. Class size is 105.

STUDENT LIFE

As stated earlier, the School of Medicine in Davis moved to the new Medical Education Center located on the Sacramento Medical Center campus. The classrooms, lecture halls, library, and student resource facilities will be found in the new facility. All medical students will continue to have access to recreational facilities, housing, intramural sports program, and activities offering support and social opportunities to students in Davis. Students are encouraged to reside in Sacramento close to the medical center and nearby communities.

GRADUATES

Close to 50 percent of graduates enter primary care fields. The UC Davis Health System has at least 20 residency programs. Davis graduates are successful at obtaining residency position in prestigious programs all over the country.

Admissions

REQUIREMENTS

The following courses must be completed prior to matriculation: English (1 year), biology with lab (1 year), upper-division biology (no lab required; can be satisfied with course work in genetics, biochemistry, molecular or cellular biology), general chemistry with lab (1 year), organic chemistry with lab (1 year), physics with lab (1 year) and college level math—calculus and/or statistics (1 year). The MCAT is required and should have been taken within the past 36 months. For those who have repeated the MCAT, the most recent scores are considered.

SUGGESTIONS

Additional helpful courses are biochemistry, genetics, and molecular/cellular biologgy. For students who have been out of school for a period of time, some recent course work is recommended. While no activities or qualities are specified, successful applicants demonstrate interpersonal skills, leadership potential, and the ability to work with diverse populations.

PROCESS

About 2,000 applicants, or roughly 50 percent of AMCAS applicants, receive secondaries. Secondary applications must be returned within a month; 400–500 applicants are interviewed, with interviews held from October through April. Interviews consist of two 1-hour sessions with faculty members and/or medical students. About one-third of those interviewed are accepted on a rolling basis. Others are rejected or put on a wait list that is split into thirds, depending on the candidate's prospect for admission. Wait listed candidates are not advised to send supplementary material.

Admissions Requirements (Required)

MCAT scores, science GPA, non-science GPA, letters of recommendation, interview, essay/personal statement, extracurricular activities, exposure to medical profession, strong leadership background, community service

Admissions Requirement (Optional)

State residency

Overlap Schools

University of California—Hastings, University of California—Irvine, University of California—Los Angeles, University of California—San Diego, University of Southern California.

COSTS AND AID

Tuition & Fees

Tuition (in-state)	$0
Tuition (out-of-state)	$12,245
Room and board (off-campus)	$11,394
Cost of books	$2,303
Fees	$24,299

Financial Aid

% students receiving aid	93
Average grant	$8,807
Average loan	$33,193
Average debt	$106,322

UNIVERSITY OF CALIFORNIA—IRVINE
COLLEGE OF MEDICINE

MEDICAL EDUCATION BUILDING 802, ROOM 100, IRVINE, CA 92697-4089 • ADMISSION: 949-824-5388
FAX: 949-824-2485 • E-MAIL: MEDADMIT@UCI.EDU • WEBSITE: WWW.UCIHS.UCI.EDU/ADMISSIONS

STUDENT BODY

Type	Public
Enrollment	408
% male/female	52/48
% minorities	32
# applied (total/out)	3,993/627
# accepted (total/out)	279/2
# enrolled (total)	104
Average age	23

ADMISSIONS
Average GPA and MCAT scores

Overall GPA	3.7
MCAT Bio	11
MCAT Phys	11
MCAT Verbal	10
MCAT Essay	Q

Application Information

Regular application	11/1
Regular notification	Rolling
Are transfers accepted?	No
Admissions may be deferred?	Yes
Interview required?	Yes
Application fee	$60

Academics

For those that meet the requirements, six students each year are accepted into the Medical Scientist Training Program (MSTP), leading to a combined MD/PhD degree. The PhD can be earned in a number of fields, including all of the biological sciences, engineering sciences, information and computer sciences, and physical sciences. For those who meet requirements, a joint MBA/MD program can be pursued in conjunction with UCI's Graduate School of Management. Most students follow a 4 year curriculum, throughout which a course called Patient-Doctor integrates clinical, social, and basic science concepts.

BASIC SCIENCES: For the duration of 2 years, the course Patient-Doctor gives students an opportunity for interaction with real patients in a clinical setting and with simulated patients in a closely monitored learning environment. During the first year, students also take Anatomy and Embryology, Biochemistry, Histology, Immunology, Medical Genetics, Medical Neurosciences, Molecular Cell Biology, and Physiology/Pathophysiology. All are taught primarily in a lecture/lab format. The Patient-Doctor course continues throughout year 2, by placing students in clinical service experiences within community physician offices. During the second-year students also take Clinical Pathology, General and Systematic, Medical Microbiology, Medical Pharmacology, Pathology, and Topics in Medicine, tutorial programs, academic monitoring, and study-skills workshops promote student success in the basic sciences. The Medical Center Library (MCL) is located at the UCI Medical Center and meets the research, education, and patient care needs of the Medical Center staff and the UCI College of Medicine. The College of Medicine is fully computerized with an internal electronic informational network. Students are evaluated with honors/pass/fail.

CLINICAL TRAINING

Patient contact begins during the first year when students participate in the patient, doctor, and society course and the Patient-Doctor course. Standardized patients and surrogate patients are employed throughout the 4 years to enhance interactive experience. During the fourth year, the Patient-Doctor course continues, teaching students to apply basic science concepts to clinical situations. Required clerkships begin in year 3 and include the following: Inpatient and Ambulatory Medicine (12 weeks), Obstetrics/Gynecology (8 weeks), Surgery (8 weeks), Psychiatry (6 weeks), Family Medicine (4 weeks), and Pediatrics (4 weeks). Year 4 rotations are Intensive Care unit (4 weeks), Neuroscience (4 weeks), Emergency Medicine (2 weeks), Radiology (2 weeks), a musculoskeletal elective (2 weeks), and Substance Abuse (2 weeks). The primary training sites are UCI Medical Center in the City of Orange, which includes several specialized clinical and research centers; the Veterans Administration Medical Center in Long Beach; and the College of Medicine's affiliated hospitals and clinics. Affiliates are located in Orange, Los Angeles, and San Bernardino counties, serving both rural and urban communities. During the clinical years, narrative evaluations supplement the honors/pass/fail grading system. Passing the USMLE Step 1 and Step 2 is a requirement for graduation.

Campus Life

On and off campus, medical students can find a wide variety of recreational and extracurricular activities to help keep overall balance in their lives and discover new outlets for fitness and fun.

STUDENT LIFE

UCI has many student-interest groups, including those that provide support to minority students and to students with children. Other groups are geared toward volunteer and community activities. Medical students have access to a wide variety of resources at UCI, including cultural events, intramural athletics, and all facilities. On-campus, graduate-student housing is affordable, comfortable, and allows medical students to interact with students from other departments. Apartments, residence halls, and residential communities that feature living spaces of all sizes are available. The city of Irvine and surrounding communities, such as Newport Beach, provide recreational opportunities and attractive housing options.

GRADUATES

A large proportion of graduates enter postgraduate programs at UCI, which has one of the nation's largest residency programs in primary care disciplines and internal medicine. Most graduates enter programs in California, but seniors have been successful in obtaining residencies all over the country.

Admissions

REQUIREMENTS

The following must be completed prior to matriculation: General chemistry (2 semesters), organic chemistry (2 semesters), physics (2 semesters), biology (3 semesters, with a minimum of 1 upper-division biology class), biochemistry (1 semester), and calculus (1 semester). The MCAT is required, and scores should be no more than 3 years old. For those who have retaken the exam, the most recent set of scores is considered.

SUGGESTIONS

No specific major is required. In addition to the requirements for admission the following classes are also recommended: Molecular biology, cell biology, genetics, psychology, Spanish, and vertebrate embryology.

PROCESS

The UCI College of Medicine seeks to admit students who are highly qualified to be trained in the practice of medicine and whose backgrounds, talents, and experiences contribute to a diverse student body. The Admissions Committee carefully reviews all applicants whose undergraduate record and scores on the MCAT indicate that they will be able to handle the rigorous curriculum of medical school. Careful consideration is given to applicants from disadvantaged backgrounds (i.e., disadvantaged through social, cultural, and/or economic conditions). In addition to scholastic achievement, attributes deemed desirable in prospective students include leadership ability and participation in extracurricular activities, such as exposure to clinical medicine and/or medically related research, as well as community service. Preference is given to California residents and applicants who are either U.S. citizens or permanent residents. The College of Medicine does not accept transfer students.

Information provided by the AMCAS application is used for the preliminary screening. Based on decisions reached by the Admissions Committee, applicants may be sent a secondary application. A limited number of applicants (approximately 500) are invited to be interviewed. The Admissions Committee reviews the academic records, letters of recommendation, and the results of personal interviews before making its final selections.

Admissions Requirements (Required)

MCAT scores, science GPA, non-science GPA, letters of recommendation, interview, essay/personal statement

Admissions Requirements (Optional)

State residency, extracurricular activities, exposure to medical profession, community service, research

COSTS AND AID

Tuition & Fees

In-state tuition	$0
Out-of-state tuition	$12,245
Room and board (on-campus)	$11,472
Room and board (off-campus)	$19,233
Cost of books	$2,902
Fees	$23,445.50

Financial Aid

% students receiving aid	90

UNIVERSITY OF CALIFORNIA—LOS ANGELES
DAVID GEFFEN SCHOOL OF MEDICINE AT UCLA

CENTER FOR HEALTH SCIENCES, LOS ANGELES, CA 90095-1720 • **ADMISSION:** 310-825-6081
FAX: 310-825-6081 • **E-MAIL:** SOMADMISS@MEDNET.UCLA.EDU • **WEBSITE:** WWW.MEDSTUDENT.UCLA.EDU

STUDENT BODY	
Type	Public
Enrollment	674
% male/female	58/42
% minorities	30
# applied	5,046
# enrolled	121

ADMISSIONS	
Application Information	
Regular application	11/1
Regular notification	1/15
Are transfers accepted?	Yes
Interview required?	Yes
Application fee	$40

Academics

Each year, 10 students are admitted to an extended curriculum program, which spreads the first 2 years of the standard curriculum over 3 years, creating opportunities for special projects or supplemental instruction. In each class, as many as 24 students who are interested in practicing in underserved communities spend their first 2 years at UCLA School of Medicine, and then complete clinical requirements at Drew University facilities. Drew University is a predominantly African American medical institution. Several joint-degree programs are offered to medical students, including an MD/MPH with the School of Public Health, an MD/MBA with the School of Management, and an MSTP-sponsored MD/PhD. All entering students are required to purchase a computer because both the basic science and clinical curriculum emphasize its applications.

BASIC SCIENCES: During the first 2 years, students are in scheduled sessions for about 26 hours per week. In addition to required courses, selectives give students an opportunity to explore topics of interest such as health care reform, addiction, and AIDS. First-year courses include the following: Anatomy, Basic Neurology, Biological Chemistry, Biomathematics, Clinical Applications of Basic Sciences (CABS), Doctoring I, Microanatomy and Cell Biology, Organ System Physiology, Topics in Physiology. Doctoring I is the beginning of the doctoring curriculum, which uses a case-based approach and addresses the interdisciplinary issues that pertain to practicing medicine. In this course, the cultural, ethical, legal, economic, and social perspectives on medicine are considered. In CABS, students participate in community-based, health education, or health care projects and learn to apply basic science concepts to real-life clinical problems. Year 2 courses are the following: Doctoring II; Genetics; Microbiology; Pathology; Pathophysiology; Psychopathology; Pharmacology; and Clinical Fundamentals, which covers physical diagnosis and takes place largely at clinical sites. Both university-sponsored and student-initiated study and tutorial groups are available. Most classes are taught in the Health Sciences Building, a large structure on the UCLA campus in Westwood. The Biomedical Library is nearby and serves faculty, students, and the community with a collection of 500,000 volumes and 6,000 current journals. Grading is pass/fail, with written citations for outstanding achievement. Promotion to year 3 requires a passing score on the USMLE Step 1.

CLINICAL TRAINING

Outside of traditional clerkships, students gain experience with patients in doctoring and through extensive volunteer opportunities. Some students identify volunteer opportunities with the assistance of the Community Service Compendium, a list of community outreach sites. Formal clinical training takes place during the third and fourth years, which are treated as a continuum. Fifty-seven weeks of the third and fourth years are reserved for the following required rotations: Medicine (12 weeks), Surgery (12 weeks), Pediatrics (6 weeks), Obstetrics/Gynecology (6 weeks), Psychiatry (6 weeks), Family Medicine (6 weeks), Radiology (4 weeks), Neurology (2 weeks), and Ophthalmology (2 weeks). Clerkships take place primarily at the University Hospital (517 beds). Other affiliated sites are Harbor General (800 beds), Cedars-Sinai, Kaiser Sunset, Kaiser West LA, Kern Medical Center (Bakersfield), King/Drew Medical Center, Olive View-UCLA Medical Center (Sylmar), Sepulveda Veterans Affairs, St. Mary Medical Center (Long Beach), and West LA Veterans Affairs Medical Center. Doctoring III is taken throughout the years, occupying students for one full day every other week. This segment of the course takes students to community-based medical sites and uses a small-group format to discuss various patient problems. Twenty-seven weeks remain for electives. Some of the elective requirement may be fulfilled around the country or overseas. Grading is pass/fail supplemented with written evaluations. The USMLE Step 2 is required for graduation.

Campus Life

The students reflect the multicultural population of Los Angeles, with underrepresented minorities accounting for one-third of the student body. In entering classes, the average age is 22, and there are usually no more than a few students over 28 years old. Eighty-five percent of the students are California residents. Class size is 145.

STUDENT LIFE

In addition to the beaches and beautiful weather of Southern California and Los Angeles, the UCLA campus itself offers excellent athletic facilities and plenty of entertainment. Student-led groups and activities within the medical school are numerous, ranging from the Iranian/American Medical Organization to the Salvation Army Outreach Clinic. The medical school also sponsors activities that encourage cohesion between faculty and students. Although residence halls and married-student housing are available, most medical students opt to live off campus.

GRADUATES

Graduates are well-prepared for careers in primary care, more specialized clinical fields, and research. About half of the graduates enter primary care fields, which is roughly the current national average. Many enter residencies at UCLA or affiliated hospitals.

Admissions

REQUIREMENTS

Admissions requirements are chemistry (2 years, including inorganic and organic); English (1 year); college math (1 year, includes calculus and statistics); physics (1 year); and biology (1 year). Science courses must have associated labs, and AP credits are not counted. The MCAT is required, and scores must be no more than 3 years old. Generally, if a student has retaken the exam, the best set of scores is used.

SUGGESTIONS

Courses in humanities and social sciences, as well as Spanish and computer skills are highly recommended. Undergraduate courses that overlap with those in the medical school curriculum, such as anatomy, are not recommended. For applicants who graduated college several years ago, recent course work is expected. The April, rather than August, MCAT is advised. Extracurricular activities that are medically related, or that involve research or patient contact, are useful. UCLA is unusual among state-affiliated medical schools in California in that it welcomes applications from well-qualified, out-of-state residents.

PROCESS

Typically, 55 percent of AMCAS applicants are asked to submit supplementary information. Of those returning secondaries, about 20 percent are invited for interviews. Interviews take place from November through May and consist of 1 or 2 sessions with faculty members and/or medical students. Notification begins in January and continues until enough offers have been made to fill the class. About 25 percent of interviewees are accepted, and another group is wait listed. Wait listed candidates may send additional information about academic or extracurricular achievements. The UCLA/UC Riverside Biomedical Sciences Program allows 24 admitted students to obtain both the BS and MD degrees in 7 years. In this program, students enter UCLA School of Medicine after completing 3 years of undergraduate preparation at UC Riverside.

Admissions Requirements (Required)

MCAT scores, science GPA, non-science GPA, letters of recommendation, interview, state residency, extracurricular activities, exposure to medical profession

Admissions Requirements (Optional)

Essays/personal statement

COSTS AND AID
Tuition & Fees

In-state tuition	$12,245
Out-of-state tuition	$27,418
Room and board (on-campus)	$14,000
Room and board (off-campus)	$4,620
Cost of books	$4,360
Fees	$22,024

UNIVERSITY OF CALIFORNIA—SAN DIEGO
SCHOOL OF MEDICINE

9500 GILMAN DRIVE, MC 0621 LA JOLLA, CA 92093-0621 • **ADMISSION:** 858-534-3880
FAX: 858-534-5282 • **E-MAIL:** SOMADMISSIONS@UCSD.EDU • **WEBSITE:** WWW.MEDED.UCSD.EDU/ADMISSIONS

STUDENT BODY	
Type	Public
Enrollment	503
% male/female	51/49
% minorities	18
# applied (total/out)	5,238/1,858
# accepted (total/out)	290/37
# enrolled (total/out)	122/12
Average age	23

ADMISSIONS
Average GPA and MCAT scores

Overall GPA	3.73
MCAT Bio	11.5
MCAT Phys	11.7
MCAT Verbal	10.5
MCAT Essay	Q

Application Information

Regular application	11/1
Regular notification	10/15
Are transfers accepted?	No
Admissions may be deferred?	Yes
Interview required?	Yes
Application fee	$60

Academics

In addition to fulfilling course requirements, students must complete an Independent Study Project to graduate. These projects allow students to explore and define their own interests and collaborate with faculty members who share these interests. The medical school benefits from the resources of other parts of UCSD. Joint MD/PhD programs are possible with UCSD graduate departments in biochemistry, biomedical engineering; biophysics, cell biology, genetics, immunology, microbiology, molecular biology, neuroscience, pathology, pharmacology, and physiology. Normally, these degrees are MSTP sponsored. Students can earn an MPH in conjunction with nearby San Diego State University Graduate School of Public Health.

BASIC SCIENCES: The first 2 years are organized into quarters. Electives are an important supplement to basic science requirements and account for about 20 percent of scheduled course time. During the fall quarter of year 1, Biochemistry and Cell Biology are the principal endeavors. This lecture course is referred to as a block, which means that the material is covered intensely during 1 or 2 quarters. Students also begin a sequence in social and behavioral sciences, taught mostly through small group sessions. Winter-quarter courses are Introduction to Clinical Medicine, which continues throughout the basic science curriculum and prepares students for third-year rotations; Pharmacology; and Physiology. The spring-quarter courses are Endocrinology, Metabolism, Neurology, Pharmacology, and Reproductive Biology, all of which are taught primarily through lectures. Year 2 begins with Anatomy, Biostatistics, Histology, and a social/Behavioral Science course on Health Care Systems. Winter quarter consists of Human Disease, Hematology, and Psychopathology,. The second-year, spring-quarter curriculum consists of Human Disease, Lab Medicine, and Neurology. During the basic science years, there are, on average, 34 scheduled hours per week. Instruction takes place in the modern Basic Science Building, which is adjacent to the Biomedical Library (which houses 100,000 volumes). Computers with access to online informational services and curricular programs are available for student use in the library and in the school's learning resource center. Grading uses an honors/pass/fail system. The USMLE Step 1 is required for promotion to year 3.

CLINICAL TRAINING

Supervised patient contact begins in January of year 1, in Introduction to Clinical Medicine. The physical examination is taught in conjunction with the study of individual organ systems in the first year and, together with the history, refined in the second basic science year. In addition, a simulated patient program provides students the opportunity to improve their history-taking and physical-examination skills, as well as to obtain feedback from faculty mentors and view videotapes of their patient interaction. Required third-year rotations are Medicine (12 weeks), Neurology (4weeks), Obstetrics/Gynecology (6 weeks), Pediatrics (8 weeks), Psychiatry (6 weeks), Surgery (12 weeks), and Primary Care (1 afternoon per week, all year). Students design their fourth-year curricula by selecting courses from within broad subject areas. Twelve weeks are selected from Direct Patient Care clerkships: 4 weeks of a primary care experience, 4 weeks of inpatient training, and 4 weeks of outpatient training. An additional 12 weeks of pure elective, clinical clerkships are also required. Clinical training takes place at large hospitals and small clinics, including UCSD Medical Centers (577 beds), Veterans Affairs Hospital (606 beds), Navy Hospital (750 beds), Children's Hospital (154 beds), Kaiser

Foundation Hospital (1,285 beds), Sharp Memorial Community Hospital (1,415 beds), Clinica De Salubridad de Campesinos, and the U.S. Public Health Service Outpatient Clinic. Electives may be taken from the various departments of UCSD or may be carried out in conjunction with community organizations. Most students take advantage of additional clinical training opportunities through volunteer work, some of which takes them across the border in Mexico. The USMLE Step 2 is required for graduation. UCSD students do exceptionally well on both parts of the USMLE.

Campus Life

Students are predominantly Californians. There is a wide age range among students, and it is very common for them to have taken a year or so off after college for research or other activities. About 60 percent of incoming students in a recent class were science majors. The class size is 122.

STUDENT LIFE

On-campus housing is convenient, attractive, and popular with students. Modern apartments of all sizes are available for single and married students and for those who have children or pets. Some students rely on bicycles or shuttle buses, while others own cars. UCSD's location affords many recreational possibilities. Year-round outdoor activities include swimming, surfing, biking, sailing, rollerblading, running, and walking. Other attractions include the San Diego Symphony, the San Diego Zoo, and the Padres professional baseball team. Medical student organizations and events also contribute to students' extracurricular lives.

GRADUATES

Of the graduating class of 2006, the most popular fields for postgraduate training were internal medicine (38 graduates), pediatrics (15 graduates), emergency medicine (9 graduates), anesthesiology (8 graduates), psychiatry (8 graduates), obstetrics/gynecology (8 graduates), radiology (7 graduates), family medicine (6 graduates), ophthalmology (6 graduates), general surgery (4 graduates), pathology (4 graduates), orthopaedic surgery (4 graduates), and dermatology (3 graduates). Students also matched into neurology, urology, otolaryngology, and plastic surgery. Many entered programs in San Diego, Oakland, San Jose, Los Angeles, and other California locations.

Admissions

REQUIREMENTS

One year of biology, chemistry, math, organic chemistry, and physics are required. Strong written and spoken English is a requirement, and the ability to communicate in a second language is preferred. The rigor of an applicant's undergraduate institution is considered in assessing GPA. The MCAT is required, and taking the spring exam is advised.

SUGGESTIONS

Breadth of academic experience is important. Extracurricular activities are also important, particularly those that involve some sort of medical exposure, community involvement, or leadership.

PROCESS

About 40 percent of applicants receive a secondary application. Of those returning secondaries, between 550–600 are interviewed. Interviews take place from October through early April and consist of two 1-hour sessions with faculty members. Following interviews, candidates are accepted, rejected, or put on hold for later notification. About half of those interviewed are eventually accepted. An extensive wait list is established.

Admissions Requirements (Required)

MCAT scores, science GPA, non-science GPA, letters of recommendation, interview, essay/personal statement

Admissions Requirements (Optional)

State residency, extracurricular activities, exposure to medical profession

Overlap Schools

Stanford University, University of California—Davis, University of California—Irvine, University of California—Los Angeles, University of California—San Francisco.

COSTS AND AID
Tuition & Fees

In-state tuition	$0
Out-of-state tuition	$12,245
Room and board (on-campus)	$7,776
Room and board (off-campus)	$11,412
Cost of books	$2,055
Fees	$22,415

Financial Aid

% students receiving aid	93
Average grant	$16,275
Average loan	$21,634
Average debt	$79,562

UNIVERSITY OF CALIFORNIA—SAN FRANCISCO

SCHOOL OF MEDICINE

SCHOOL OF MEDICINE ADMISSIONS, C-200, PO BOX 0408, SAN FRANCISCO, CA 94143-0408 • **ADMISSION:** 415-476-4044
FAX: 415-476-5490 • **E-MAIL:** ADMISSIONS@MEDSCH.UCSF.EDU • **WEBSITE:**WWW.MEDSCHOOL.UCSF.EDU/ADMISSIONS

STUDENT BODY

Type	Public
Enrollment	600
% male/female	44/56
% minorities	21
# applied (total/out)	5,298/2,520
# accepted (total/out)	257/73
# enrolled (total/out)	141/24
Average age	24

FACULTY

Total faculty (number)	1,663
% female	35
% minority	19
% part-time	4
Student-faculty ratio	2:1

ADMISSIONS
Average GPA and MCAT scores

Overall GPA	3.79
MCAT Bio	11.7
MCAT Phys	11.5
MCAT Verbal	10.6
MCAT Essay	P

Application Information

Regular application	11/1
Regular notification	Rolling
Are transfers accepted?	No
Admissions may be deferred?	Yes
Interview required?	Yes
Application fee	$60

Academics

The standard curriculum for the MD degree may be completed in 4 years. However, approximately 40 percent of UCSF students remain in school for additional time to pursue advanced studies in research or a scholarly project, international health, or additional clinical rotations. Students may spend 1 year in the Certificate in Biomedical Research Program, giving them time to complete a substantial research project and to earn the MD with thesis degree. UCSF has a joint-MD/MPH degree program with UC Berkeley that allows up to 10 students per year to spend 2 semesters in Berkeley earning a master's degree from the School of Public Health. In addition, each year 12 students are admitted to the UCSF/UC Berkeley Joint Medical Program in which they complete the pre-clinical, problem-based curriculum and fulfill requirements for a master's of science degree in either public health or health and medical sciences. Upon completion, they transfer to UCSF to complete the third and fourth years. Up to 12 students enter the Medical Science Training Program (MSTP) joint PhD/MD program yearly. Participants may earn a PhD from the following UCSF programs: biochemistry, biophysics, cancer biology, cell biology, chemistry, developmental biology, endocrinology, genetics, immunology, neuroscience, stem cell biology, vascular and cardiac biology, virology and medical anthropology.

BASIC SCIENCES: The first 2 years form the essential core, and they are organized into 8 block courses, each about 8 weeks long. These courses deal with major themes and draw together a range of interdisciplinary topics. The first-year courses are Brain, Mind, and Behavior; Cancer; Major Organ Systems; and Prologue. In the second year, students take Infection, Inflammation, and Immunity; Life Cycle; Metabolism; and Consolidation Cases. Essential core lectures, labs, and small-group sessions account for about 20 hours a week, and they integrate subjects from the basic, social, and clinical sciences. All courses include supplementary resources on a web-based system that forms the e-curriculum. The essential core comprises a course called Foundations of Patient Care, which offers students exposure to the clinical setting. This course also allows students to explore issues of professional development, ethics, and doctor-patient interaction.

CLINICAL TRAINING

Patient contact begins during year 1 in foundations of patient care and in the week-long immersion in the hospital wards called the clinical interlude. Clinical elements are wholly integrated into the basic science curriculum, allowing for a smooth transition into the third year. Likewise, the clinical years include segments of classroom instruction that focus on basic and social science concepts. For example, the third year includes three intersessions, which occur between clerkship rotations and offer lectures and small-group discussions of basic science connections to the clinical experiences, ethics, evidence-based medicine, and health policy. Required third-year core clerkships are Medicine (8 weeks), Neurology and Psychiatry (8 weeks), Family and Community Medicine (6 weeks), Obstetrics/Gynecology (6 weeks), Pediatrics (6 weeks), Surgery (8 weeks), Anesthesia (2 weeks), and Surgical Subspecialties (2 weeks). Teaching sites are primarily in San Francisco, Oakland, and Fresno and include the California Pacific Medical Center, Children's Hospital, Kaiser Foundation Hospitals, San Francisco City Clinics, San Francisco General Hospital, Veterans Affairs Medical Centers in San Francisco and Fresno, UCSF Medical Center including Mount Zion Hospital, University Medical Center-Fresno, and Langley Porter Neuropsychiatric Institute. Year 4 is primarily elective study, which may entail international work or research in addition to traditional advanced clinical rotations. Evaluation of students during years 3 and 4 includes an honors/pass/fail system enhanced with narrative comments. Outside of clerk-ships, students gain clinical experience through volunteer work and community service at any number of UCSF-affiliated projects.

Campus Life

Twenty percent of the students are out-of-state residents. More than half are nonwhite, and approximately 17 percent are underrepresented minorities, mostly African and Hispanic Americans. Virtually all undergraduate majors are represented in the student body. Class size is 141.

STUDENT LIFE

University-owned housing appropriate for both married and single students is available. Many students take part in community programs, which provide not only an opportunity to contribute but also a chance for student-student and student-faculty interaction in an extracurricular setting. Students have access to school athletic facilities and to many local outdoor activities, including running in Golden Gate Park, surfing at Ocean Beach, mountain biking in Marin County, and skiing around Lake Tahoe, 3 hours away by car.

GRADUATES

Of the graduating class of 2005, the following specialties were selected by the indicated number of students: Family practice (8), internal medicine (23), internal medicine/primary care (10), pediatrics (19), emergency medicine (20), anesthesiology (12), psychiatry (10), obstetrics/gynecology (8), surgery (7), ophthalmology (5), pathology (4), radiation oncology (4), orthopedic surgery (3), neurology (3), otolaryngology (3), radiology (3), dermatology (2), neurosurgery (1), physical medicine (1), urology (2), and other (2). In total, 41 percent entered residencies in fields classified as primary care. See http://medschool.ucsf.edu/medstudents/resources/match/summary _table.html for details.

Admissions

REQUIREMENTS

To be considered for admission, applicants must complete the following courses by June of the year they expect to matriculate: general chemistry with lab (3 quarters, equal to 1 year); organic chemistry (2 quarters); physics and biology (equal to 1 year). Applications are welcome from candidates who have taken time off between college and applying to medical school. The MCAT is required, and the spring MCAT is strongly advised. For those who retake the test, the most recent scores are considered. MCAT scores must be no more than 3 years old. California residents are given preference.

SUGGESTIONS

Beyond requirements, applicants should have taken college-level math, English, and humanities courses. Upper-division biology is also recommended. All extracurricular activities that reveal an applicant's interests and demonstrate his/her commitment strengthen the application. Some exposure to medical issues or to patient care is also valuable.

PROCESS

GPA, MCATs, residency, and the AMCAS application are used to screen for secondary applications. The secondary application is straightforward and does not require additional essays for the MD program. Applicants have 3 weeks from the date of receipt of the secondary application to return the secondary and have their letters of recommendation sent. Letters of recommendation sent prior to receipt of the secondary will be destroyed. About 30 percent of applicants receive a secondary application and about one-third of those returning secondaries are invited to interview. There is also a hold category, which indicates that while the applicant is not in the top group, he/she may be interviewed as the year progresses. Interviews take place between September and March, and consist of two 1 hour blind sessions each with a faculty member or one faculty member and one student. After offers have been made to fill the class, some remaining candidates are placed on a ranked wait list and may be offered a spot as late as August, depending on accepted students' matriculation rate.

Admissions Requirements (Required)

MCAT scores, science GPA, letters of recommendation, interview, essay/personal statement

Admissions Requirements (Optional)

Non-science GPA, state residency, extracurricular activities, exposure to medical profession

Overlap Schools

Harvard University, Stanford University.

COSTS AND AID
Tuition & Fees

In-state tuition	$0
Out-of-state tuition	$12,245
Room and board (off-campus)	$18,447
Cost of books	$1,890
Fees	$22,854

Financial Aid

% students receiving aid	89
Average grant	$8,358
Average loan	$18,592
Average debt	$67,911

University of Chicago
Pritzker School of Medicine

Office of Medical Education BSLC 104W, 924 E. 57th St. Chicago, IL 60637-5416 • Admission: 773-702-1937
Fax: 773-834-5412 • E-mail: PRITZKERADMISSIONS@BSD.UCHICAGO.EDU • Website: PRITZKER.BSD.UCHICAGO.EDU

STUDENT BODY

Type	Private
Enrollment	441
% male/female	50/50
% minorities	17
# applied (total/out)	4,895/4,219
# accepted (total/out)	301/252
# enrolled (total/out)	112/81
Average age	24

FACULTY

Total faculty	982
% female	32
% minority	24
% part-time	6
Student-faculty ratio	2:1

ADMISSIONS
Average GPA and MCAT Scores

Overall GPA	3.76
MCAT Bio	11.9
MCAT Phys	11.8
MCAT Verbal	11
MCAT Essay	Q

Application Information

Regular application	10/15
Regular notification	Rolling
Early application	8/1
Early notification	10/1
Are transfers accepted?	Yes
Admissions may be deferred?	Yes
Interview required?	Yes
Application fee	$75

Academics

Pritzker offers a curriculum best characterized as "modified traditional." Although most preclinical topics are presented in lectures, case-based methods and clinical exposure supplement lectures. For example, as students study particular parts in Anatomy, they view afflictions of that body part in a clinical setting. About 24 percent of the students in each class earn a graduate degree in addition to the M.D. degree. Some of these students are M.S.T.P. participants; others are privately funded M.D./Ph.D. students, and still others earn a J.D. or an M.B.A. along with the M.D. Pritzker students are well prepared by the curriculum as evidenced by their strong board exam performances.

BASIC SCIENCES: Chicago follows a quarter system. First-year students will begin their curriculum in August, studying Human Morphology I and II and participating in the Health Care Disparities series. Autumn quarter, first-year medical students study Biochemistry; Cell and Organ Physiology; and Clinical Skills 1A, which introduces students to the patient interview. During the winter, first-year students study Molecular and Cell Biochemistry, Organ Physiology and Endocrinology, Doctor/Patient Relationship, and Clinical Skills, which covers social issues related to medicine (social context, medical ethics). Spring curriculum includes Neurobiology, Medical Genetics, Nutrition, and Epidemiology and Clinical Investigation as well as an opportunity for elective study. Second-year, fall-quarter curriculum includes: Cell Pathology & Immunology, Microbiology, Pharmacology, and Human Behavior in Health and Illness. Winter quarter includes: Clinical Pathophysiology and Therapeutics and Clinical Skills 2A, called Physical Diagnosis. The final quarter of preclinical studies includes Clinical Pathophysiology and Therapeutics, more clinical skills, Review of Basic Sciences and Electives. Most students use a student-run note-taking co-op in which each participating student is responsible for providing notes on a lecture assigned to him or her. First- and second-year students spend their time in the Biological Sciences Learning Center, which is both a center for instruction and research. Classrooms are equipped with audio/video technology, and excellent computer-based learning tools are available. The Knapp Center is a medical research facility with modern laboratory space. The Crerar Library has one of the largest science collections in the country and houses almost one million volumes. Grading is Pass/Fail although students receive graded feedback on exams. Tutoring is available for students who are in danger of failure. Passage of the USMLE is not required for promotion graduation although most students choose to take Step 1 after year two.

CLINICAL TRAINING

Students are introduced to clinical techniques and experiences during their first quarter at Pritzker, with Clinical Skills 1A. Year three is composed of a series of clerkships with short breaks between rotations. Clerkships take place at the University of Chicago Medical Center and the Comer Children's Hospital. These hospitals serve a broad community, and students learn to treat a diverse patient population. Students rotate through the following departments: Internal Medicine (3 months); Ob/Gyn (1.5 months); Psychiatry (1.5 month); Surgery (3 months); Pediatrics (2 months); and Family Medicine (1 month). During the fourth year, students choose "selectives" from the following categories: Inpatient/Subinternship, Scientific Basis of Medical Practice, Neurology, and Anesthesia. The fourth year is also an opportunity for students to pursue individual research projects or to study overseas. The University of Chicago Medical Center has expanded significantly during the past decade, suggesting a strong patient base and economic situation. Evaluation of clinical performance uses marks of Honors, High Pass,

Pass, Low Pass, and Fail. Though the USMLE II is not required for graduation, it may be substituted for a comprehensive exam, which is otherwise required.

Students

Pritzker attracts a student body that is very diverse, in every sense of the word. Underrepresented minorities have accounted for about 15–20 percent of the student body, and women about 50 percent. Class size is 88. The unique feature of the Pritzker School of Medicine is its integration into the rest of the University of Chicago. It is geographically, administratively, and programmatically integrated. As a consequence it attracts students and faculty who have broader scholarly interests and who see the entire University as a resource for their academic goals. Over 24 percent of Pritzker's graduates leave with two degrees and Pritzker is among the top schools in training faculty for academic medicine. Pritzker students obtain additional degrees in business, law, biological sciences, physical sciences, social sciences, humanities, and public health.

STUDENT LIFE

The University of Chicago is located in Chicago's Hyde Park neighborhood, a diverse and interesting community. Students are active in curriculum development and have representatives on important administrative councils. Student volunteer organizations are involved in projects such as organizing and implementing health education into public schools. Medical students take part in university-wide activities such as intramural sports. Many students also take national leadership in organizations such as SNMA and AMSA.

GRADUATES

During the past five years, the residency programs that attracted the most Pritzker graduates were: University of Chicago Hospitals; UCSF; University of Michigan; Mass General; University of Washington; University of Penn; Brigham and Women's Boston; McGaw Medical Center; Beth Israel, Boston; Barnes Hospital, Washington University; and UCLA. The following specialties were the most popular within the 2007 graduating class: Internal Medicine (24); General Surgery (13); Pediatrics (13); Emergency Medicine (5); Orthopedic Surgery (4); Internal Medicine/Pediatrics (4); Psychiatry (4); Anesthesia (3); Family Practice (3); OB/Gyn (3). About 20 percent of Pritzker graduates ultimately serve as faculty members at universities.

Admissions

REQUIREMENTS

One year of lecture plus lab is required in: Biology, General Chemistry, Organic Chemistry, and Physics. Biochemistry with lab may be substituted for one semester or quarter of organic chemistry. For applicants who graduated from college more than three years prior, recent science coursework is important. The MCAT is required and should be no more than three years old.

SUGGESTIONS

Biochemistry is strongly recommended, as is significant coursework in social sciences and humanities. The Admissions Committee is interested in what factors motivated applicants to pursue medicine and is also concerned with demonstrated problem-solving skills, leadership, experience with persons different from themselves, and experience in research.

PROCESS

Secondary applications are available to all AMCAS applicants and should be completed as soon as possible, no later than December 1. About 15 percent of applicants returning secondaries are interviewed, with interviews held between September and February. Interviewees participate in three one-on-one sessions with faculty members, admissions staff, and medical students. Of those interviewed, about two-fifths are accepted on a rolling basis. Other interviewees will be "Continued" in the process and will be re-evaluated each time the committee meets. Continued candidates are encouraged to submit information that will strengthen their application and will indicate their interest in the school. A wait-list will be created in early May.

Admissions Requirements (Required)
MCAT scores, Science GPA, Non-science GPA, Letters of recommendation, Interview, Essays/personal statement, Extracurricular activities, Exposure to medical profession

Admissions Requirements (Optional)
State residency, Research

Overlap Schools
Columbia University, Cornell University, Harvard University, Stanford University, University of Michigan—Ann Arbor, Washington University in St. Louis (Olin), Yale University.

COSTS AND AID

Tuition & Fees

Tuition	$37,293
Room and board (on-campus)	$0
Room and board (off-campus)	$16,267
Cost of books	$1,419
Fees	$913

Financial Aid

% students receiving aid	87

UNIVERSITY OF CINCINNATI
COLLEGE OF MEDICINE

OFFICE OF ADMISSIONS, P.O. BOX 670552 CINCINNATI, OH 45267-0552 • ADMISSION: 513-558-7314
FAX: 513-558-1165 • E-MAIL: COMADMIS@UCMAIL.UC.EDU • WEBSITE: WWW.MED.UC.EDU

STUDENT BODY	
Type	Public
Enrollment	634
% male/female	57/43
% minorities	8
# applied (total/out)	4,237/3,052
# accepted (total/out)	347/104
# enrolled (total/out)	161/40
Average age	22

FACULTY	
Total faculty	1,421
% female	31
% minority	16
% part-time	8

ADMISSIONS
Average GPA and MCAT Scores

Overall GPA	3.67
MCAT Bio	10.98
MCAT Phys	10.59
MCAT Verbal	10.09

Application Information

Regular application	11/15
Regular notification	Rolling
Early application	6/1–8/1
Early notification	10/1
Are transfers accepted?	Yes
Admissions may be deferred?	Yes
Interview required?	Yes
Application fee	$25

Academics

Most students follow a four-year curriculum leading to the M.D. degree. There is also a combined M.D./M.B.A. program with a five-year curriculum and one year master degrees in Epidemiology, Clinical Research and Public Health. Up to six positions a year are available in a combined M.D./Ph.D. program, an NIH-funded Physician Scientist Training Program (PSTP), which has a seven- to eight-year curriculum. The Ph.D. may be earned in one of the following disciplines: Cell and Cancer Biology; Molecular and Developmental Biology; Environmental Health Sciences (includes clinical/genetic epidemiology); Molecular, Cellular, and Biochemical Pharmacology; Systems Biology and Physiology; Molecular Genetics, Biochemistry, and Microbiology; Neuroscience; Pathobiology and Molecular Medicine, Biomedical Engineering and Immunobiology. Medical students interested in shorter-term research projects may pursue them during the summer or as electives. Course grades are Honors/High Pass/Pass/Fail. Passing the USMLE Step 1 is a requirement for advancing to year three and passing Step 2 is a requirement for graduation.

BASIC SCIENCES: During the first and second years, courses are integrated around content blocks that foster critical thinking skills and problem solving. In both years, a major effort is made to limit lecture and laboratory time, to use more small group activities, and to ensure sufficient daily free time for active, independent learning. First-year classes are Gross Anatomy, Microscopic Anatomy, Biochemistry, Physiology, and Brain and Behavior I. Clinical Foundations of Medical Practice, also in the first year, includes interviewing, history taking, and basic physical examination skills as well as ethics, biopsychosocial issues, human sexuality, and death and loss, and provides each student with a one-on-one clinical experience in a physician's practice. Second-year courses are Pathology, Microbiology, Pharmacology, Brain and Behavior II, and Clinical Foundations of Medical Practice II, which expands physical diagnosis and clinical skills training. An average of 20 contact hours per week and ample study time before each exam allow time for self-directed learning, group study, volunteering, and other activities in the basic science years. There continues to be a concerted effort to vertically integrate content blocks between the basic science and clinical science years. The Office of Student Affairs Academic Support Programs provides tutoring services, academic counseling and training, and preparation seminars for the USMLE Step 1. Preclinical instruction takes place in the Medical Sciences Building, which is central to the Medical Center. Academic IT & Libraries (AIT&L), also in the building, has a wealth of health sciences information resources. To supplement a long history of providing broad and deep collections of books and journals, collaborations with the other libraries at the University of Cincinnati (UC) and AIT&L's participation in OhioLINK have accelerated access to electronic resources far beyond what a single library could provide.

CLINICAL TRAINING

Third-year required clerkships are Internal Medicine (8 weeks); Surgery (8 weeks); Pediatrics (8 weeks); Obstetrics/Gynecology (8 weeks); Psychiatry (6 weeks); Family Medicine (4 weeks); Radiology (2 weeks); and two Specialty electives (2 weeks each). During the fourth year, students complete an eight-week Internal Medicine acting internship, a four-week Neuroscience selective, and 24 weeks of electives, some of which must be in outpatient care. Most clinical training takes place at University Hospital, Veterans Administration Medical Center, Children's Hospital Medical Center, the Christ Hospital, the Good Samaritan Hospital, and the Jewish Hospital. Half of the elective credits may be earned at other institutions in the area, around the country, or abroad. One organized overseas program is the International Health Elective, which involves hands-on clinical experience in a UC clinic in Honduras or other international clinics.

Students

Among students in the 2007 entering class, 75 percent were Ohio residents, 7 percent were minorities, and 11 percent were 26 years of age or older at the time of application. Five percent of the class had earned a master's degree. Seventy three percent of students were science majors, and a total of 59 undergraduate institutions were represented. The 2007 entering class size was 161.

STUDENT LIFE

Medical students enjoy a cooperative and supportive environment. There are over 50 student organizations, clubs, and service groups available: Medical students have access to a UC Fitness Center and other campus athletic and recreational facilities. Cincinnati offers many attractions including theaters, restaurants and bars, museums, parks, bookstores, and professional sporting events. University-owned apartments for single and married students are available on a limited basis.

GRADUATES

Of those who graduated in 2007, 32 percent entered residency programs in Cincinnati, 18 percent entered programs elsewhere in Ohio, and the remainder were successful in securing positions nationwide. The most prevalent fields for post-graduate study were Internal Medicine (all types, 14.1 percent); Pediatrics (14.1 percent); Anesthesia (10 percent); Surgery (9.2 percent); Emergency Medicine (8.5 percent); Family Medicine (9.2 percent); Orthopaedics (4.9 percent); and Radiology (5.6 percent).

Admissions

REQUIREMENTS

The MCAT is required, and scores should be from within the past three years. (For example, if you are applying for the 2009 entering class, you must submit scores from the 2008, 2007, or 2006 administration.) Ohio residents are given preference. Although no courses are specified, applicants are expected to have the knowledge usually gained in a one-year lecture and laboratory course in Biology, General Chemistry, Organic Chemistry, Physics, and Math. Applicants are expected to have an undergraduate preparation that provides insight into behavioral, social, and cultural issues. Academically, applicants are evaluated based on the following: GPA; MCAT scores; and undergrad, graduate, and post-bacc achievement. Personal qualities are strongly considered and applicants should demonstrate motivation, maturity, coping skills, leadership abilities, interpersonal skills, sensitivity and tolerance, and good communication skills.

PROCESS

All applicants must submit an AMCAS application and complete the UC On-line Secondary Application available at www.med.uc.edu. Approximately 650 applicants are invited to interview. Interviewees attend an informational program, eat lunch, and tour the College with current students. Initial notification of the Committee's decision occurs on a monthly basis, beginning on October 15th until March 15th. After that time, students are accepted from the alternate list as openings occur until the class is filled. Additional Programs: The University of Cincinnati's College of Medicine has two early assurance programs for those students who know they want to pursue a career in medicine: the Dual Admissions Program and a ROSE Program. While the Dual Admissions Program selects from exceptional high school seniors, the Research, Observation, Service & Education Program (ROSE) selects from current high-achieving college sophomores. Students interested in the Dual Admissions Program or ROSE Program should contact the University of Cincinnati's College of Medicine Division of Student Affairs & Recruitment at 513-558-5581 or by visiting our website at www.med.uc.edu. The University of Cincinnati College of Medicine and College of Business Administration have partnered to develop a joint M.D./M.B.A. degree program. Students should apply for the program after their first year of medical school.

Admissions Requirements (Required)

MCAT scores, Science GPA, Non-science GPA, Letters of recommendation, Interview, Essays/personal statement

Admissions Requirements (Optional)

Extracurricular activities, Exposure to medical profession, Optional experiences are strongly encouraged

COSTS AND AID

Tuition & Fees

In-state Tuition	$25,722
Out-of-state Tuition	$44,889
Fees	$1,188

UNIVERSITY OF COLORADO
SCHOOL OF MEDICINE

MEDICAL SCHOOL ADMISSIONS, MAIL STOP C-297, PO BOX 5508 AURORA, CO 80045 • ADMISSION: 303-724-8025
FAX: 303-724-8028 • E-MAIL: SOMADMIN@UCHSC.EDU • WEBSITE: WWW.UCHSC.EDU/SOM/ADMISSIONS

STUDENT BODY

Type	Public
Enrollment	588
% male/female	50/50
% minorities	11
# applied (total/out)	2,984/2,381
# accepted (total/out)	277/118
# enrolled (total/out)	156/32
Average age	25

FACULTY

Total faculty	1,900
% part-time	0
Student-faculty ratio	0:1

ADMISSIONS
Average GPA and MCAT Scores

Overall GPA	3.72
MCAT Bio	11
MCAT Phys	11
MCAT Verbal	10.8
MCAT Essay	Q

Application Information

Regular application	11/1
Regular notification	Rolling
Are transfers accepted?	Yes
Admissions may be deferred?	Yes
Interview required?	Yes
Application fee	$100

Academics

The School of Medicine is part of the University of Colorado Health Sciences Center, which includes schools of Dentistry, Nursing, Pharmacy, and Graduate Studies. A combined M.D./Ph.D. degree through the M.S.T.P. is possible in the following fields: Biochemistry, Biophysics, Cell Biology, Immunology, Molecular Biology, Microbiology, Pharmacology, and Physiology.

BASIC SCIENCES: The first two years are organized into quarters. Throughout year one, Microanatomy, Physiology, and Foundations of Doctoring are studied. Foundations of Doctoring, which establishes one-on-one mentoring relationships between students and local practicing physicians, is the first of three segments that together constitute the curricular element of the Generalist Initiative. In addition, during the fall, students take Biochemistry and Human Anatomy. Year one, winter-quarter courses are Genetics and Neurobiology. Spring courses are Biochemistry and Nutrition, Embryology, and Ethics. Year-long courses during year two are the following: Pathology, Pharmacology, Human Behavior, and Foundations of Doctoring. Immunology and Microbiology are also taken in the fall, and Neuroscience, Pathophysiology, and Epidemiology are taken in the winter. Students spend about 28 hours per week in a structured-learning environment. About 40 percent of this time is devoted to lecture, and another 40 percent to lab. Small-group sessions are also employed as an instructional technique. Academic tutoring and counseling are available to students through a student advocacy program. Grading is Honors/Pass/Fail. Students must pass the USMLE Step 1 to begin the clinical years.

CLINICAL TRAINING

Patient contact begins in year one, when students work closely with practicing physicians and gradually gain independent responsibility. Third-year, required clerkships consist of Medicine (12 weeks); Surgery (6 weeks); Family Medicine (6 weeks); Ob/Gyn (6 weeks); Neurology (4 weeks); Pediatrics (6 weeks); and Psychiatry (6 weeks). One afternoon each week is dedicated to the continuing primary care experience as the third segment of the Foundations of Doctoring sequence. During year four, students select from Surgical Specialties (6 weeks, including one week each of Anesthesiology, Ophthalmology, Orthopedics, Otolaryngology, and Urology) and from a wide range of general electives. Most clerkships take place at University Hospital; VA Medical Center; Denver Health Medical Center; Children's Hospital; and the National Jewish Center for Immunology and Respiratory Medicine. Electives and some required clerkships may be fulfilled at community hospitals and clinics around the state, or under the supervision of affiliated private physicians in the area. Denver is a rapidly growing city with a population of over two million. It is an international tourist destination, making the patient population more diverse than that associated with medical schools in other predominantly rural states. Evaluation during the clinical years uses an Honors/Pass/Fail system enhanced with narratives from professors. There are opportunities for clinical experiences outside of traditional rotations, generally through outreach activities and volunteer work. Students may volunteer at clinics that provide care to Denver's homeless population or may spend time working with low-income children in need of care. The Medical Student International Program is popular, granting students credit for up to four months of overseas study or work. Passing the USMLE Step 2 is required for graduation.

Students

At least 85 percent of students are Colorado residents. Science and nonscience majors are equally represented. Of the 2001 entering class, 15 percent are underrepresented minorities, most of whom are Hispanic Americans. With a mean age of 26 for entering students, there is clearly a wide age range within the student body. Class size is 132.

STUDENT LIFE

Denver is a comfortable, affordable, and student-friendly place to live. It is less than an hour from perhaps the best skiing in the country. During the summer, the hiking, swimming, climbing, and mountain biking are all outstanding. Single students live off campus in apartments and shared houses. Married students can find affordable family housing in various Denver neighborhoods. On-campus activities include student-run organizations and events having either a professional or social focus. The Office of Diversity provides support for minority students.

GRADUATES

The most popular residency programs of the 2001 graduating class were Internal Medicine (29 students); Family Medicine (21); Surgery (9); Pediatrics (13); Emergency Medicine (4); Anesthesiology (15); Ob/Gyn (4); and Orthopedics (6). More than half of the graduates entered primary care fields. Graduates often stay in Denver for training. Other states popular for post-graduate training are Texas, Minnesota, and California.

Admissions

REQUIREMENTS

Required courses are College Mathematics (6 hours); Biology with lab (8 semester hours); Chemistry with lab (8 hours); Organic Chemistry with lab (8 hours); Physics with lab (8 hours); English Literature and English Composition or Creative Writing (9 hours). Applicants must demonstrate mathematics competency at least through college level trigonometry, either with college courses or placement test results. The MCAT is required and, if retaken, the best scores are used.

SUGGESTIONS

In addition to required courses, a course in Biochemistry is recommended. For applicants who have been out of school for a significant period of time, recent coursework is suggested. Personal qualities are valued a great deal, as are extracurricular activities that involve medical research or health-related experience. As part of the Generalist Initiative, applicants from rural backgrounds are encouraged to apply.

PROCESS

All AMCAS applicants receive secondary applications. Of Colorado residents completing secondaries, 75 percent are interviewed. Less than 20 percent of out-of-state applicants are interviewed. Interviews take place on campus from September through April and consist of two sessions, each with a member of the Admissions Committee. The Admissions Committee is made up of students, faculty, and community physicians. Notification occurs on a rolling basis. About one-quarter of Colorado residents who interview are accepted, and about one-tenth of out-of-state interviewees are accepted. A wait-list is established, from which 20-40 students are usually taken. Wait-listed candidates are not encouraged to send supplementary material.

Admissions Requirements (Required)

MCAT scores, Science GPA, Nonscience GPA, Letters of recommendation, Interview, State residency, Essays/personal statement, Extracurricular activities, Exposure to medical profession

COSTS AND AID

Tuition & Fees

In-state Tuition	$23,641
Out-of-state Tuition	$47,014
Room and board (off-campus)	$18,000
Cost of books	$2,230
Fees	$1,300

Financial Aid

% students receiving aid	94
Average grant	$5,000
Average loan	$28,000
Average debt	$92,000

UNIVERSITY OF CONNECTICUT
SCHOOL OF MEDICINE

MEDICAL STUDENT AFFAIRS, 263 FARMINGTON AVENUE, RM AG-062, FARMINGTON, CT 06030-1905
ADMISSION: 860-679-3874 • FAX: 860-679-1282 • E-MAIL: SANFORD@NSO1.UCHC.EDU • WEBSITE: WWW.UCHC.EDU

STUDENT BODY

Type	Public
Enrollment	318
% male/female	37/63
% minorities	33
# applied (total/out)	2,699/2,324
# accepted (total/out)	170/71
# enrolled (total/out)	80/13
Average age	24

FACULTY

Total faculty (number)	539
% female	34
% minority	4
% part-time	20
Student-faculty ratio	1:1

ADMISSIONS
Average GPA and MCAT scores

Overall GPA	3.65
MCAT Bio	11
MCAT Phys	9.9
MCAT Verbal	9.9
MCAT Essay	Q

Application Information

Regular application	12/15
Regular notification	10/15
Early application	6/1–8/1
Early notification	10/1
Are transfers accepted?	Yes
Admissions may be deferred?	Yes
Interview required?	Yes
Application fee	$75

Academics

In addition to the required courses, about 75 percent of students take part in a research project while in school. Grading is strictly pass/fail, based on the notion that each student is at the top of the class with regard to some important feature or skill or ability. A combined-degree program, leading to both an MD and a PhD is pursued by about five students each year in conjunction with the following graduate programs: Cell biology, cellular and molecular pharmacology, craniofacial and oral biology, genetics and developmental biology, immunology, molecular biology and biochemistry, neuroscience, and skeletal. It is also possible for medical students to earn a MPH or MBA from the University of Connecticut's graduate program.

BASIC SCIENCES: The first 2 years cover the basic sciences, introduce clinical studies, and integrate behavioral and social aspects of medicine and health care. Instruction uses lectures, labs, case conferences, and problem-based learning. First-year courses are Human Systems, which is composed of human biology; Organ Systems I (neuroscience and anatomy of the head and neck); Organ Systems II (cardiovascular, respiratory and renal systems, anatomy of the thorax, and abdomen); and Organ System III (gastrointestinal, endocrine and reproductive, genetics, and anatomy of the pelvis); electives; correlated medical problem solving; and Principles of Clinical Medicine, which teaches history-taking, the physical examination, and general concepts related to clinical care. Second-year courses are Human Development and Health, which encompasses ethical, social, and legal issues; Mechanisms of Disease, which includes concepts related to pathology; Pharmacology; Infectious Disease; Homeostasis; Oncology; Metabolism; Nervous System; Reproductive System; and Skin, Connective Tissue, and Joints; correlated medical problem solving; and Clinical Medicine. Facilities include modern lecture halls, classrooms for small-group discussions, the Lyman Maynard Stowe Library, and computer resources. Passing the USMLE Step 1 is a requirement for promotion to year 3.

CLINICAL TRAINING

The third year is organized into two segments, one that involves clinical training in ambulatory settings, and the other that takes place in hospitals. The ambulatory experience is composed of the following clerkships: General Internal Medicine (7 weeks), Family Medicine (7 weeks), Pediatrics (5 weeks), Obstetrics/Gynecology (4 weeks), Subspecialties (3 weeks), and Psychiatry (2 weeks). The hospital, or inpatient, segment includes rotations in Medicine (4 weeks); Surgery (4 weeks); Pediatrics (2 weeks); Psychiatry (2 weeks); Obstetrics (2 weeks); and Beginning to End (2 weeks), in which students follow patients from their admittance to each diagnosis/service area that they visit in the hospital. The fourth year includes 20 weeks of electives, which may be taken at local or distant sites. Other fourth-year requirements are advanced inpatient experience (4 weeks); critical care experience (4 weeks); emergency/urgent experience (4 weeks); and selectives, in which students choose from rotations in research, community health, or education-related fields. Each student is paired with a faculty member of his or her choice to assist in scheduling electives and in selecting postgraduate training programs. Clinical training takes place at the University Hospital (232 beds) and at about 10 affiliated hospitals in the area. Some students gain clinical experience overseas by participating in projects in Latin America, Asia, or Africa. Passing the USMLE Step 2 is a requirement for graduation.

Campus Life

Underrepresented minorities, mostly African American, comprise about 15 percent of the student body. The average age of incoming students is typically about 24, with ages ranging from 21 to late 30s. About 80 percent of the students are Connecticut residents, and about 10 percent graduated from the University of Connecticut undergraduate college. Approximately 80 percent of students majored in a scientific discipline in college. Class size is about 80. Dental students participate in the basic sciences classes.

STUDENT LIFE

Life outside the classroom includes theater, concerts, and restaurants in Hartford; organized team sports on campus; and numerous clubs and groups related to professional or extracurricular interests. The Department of Health Career Opportunities provides support services throughout the academic year to minority medical students. Community-service activities, such as volunteering at homeless shelters, bring students together around important projects. Facilities such as golf courses, ski slopes, and public parks are accessible to the campus. On-campus housing is not available. Students live off campus in communities surrounding the university.

GRADUATES

Of the class that graduated in 2004, the breakdown of the most prevalent specialty choices was internal medicine (22 percent), emergency medicine (13 percent), pediatrics (10 percent), and obstetrics/gynecology (9 percent). About 24 percent of graduates entered residency programs at the University of Connecticut Health Center. Other popular destinations were Massachusetts, New York, North Carolina, and California.

Admissions

REQUIREMENTS

Requirements are 1 year of biology, chemistry, organic chemistry, physics. The MCAT is required and should be no more than 3 years old.

SUGGESTIONS

A broad and in-depth liberal arts education that includes art, English, foreign language, history, literature, math, and political science is advised. The Admissions Committee looks very seriously at the non-academic traits of applicants, such as their character and motivation.

PROCESS

All AMCAS applicants are sent secondary applications. About 60 percent of Connecticut applicants, and about 9 percent of out-of-state applicants are interviewed. Interviews are held from August through April and consist of two 1-hour sessions with faculty, administrators, or students. Lunch and a campus tour with medical students are provided. Some candidates are accepted shortly after their interview, while others are notified later in the year. A wait list is established in the spring. Wait listed candidates may send supplementary information, such as transcripts.

Admissions Requirements (Required)

MCAT scores, science GPA, non-science GPA, letters of recommendation, interview, essay/personal statement, extracurricular activities, exposure to medical profession

Admissions Requirement (Optional)

State residency

COSTS AND AID

Tuition & Fees

In-state tuition	$18,250
Out-of-state tuition	$41,525
Room and board (off-campus)	$20,000
Cost of books	$2,200
Fees	$7,670

Financial Aid

% students receiving aid	98
Average grant	$15,000
Average loan	$27,000
Average debt	$94,000

UNIVERSITY OF FLORIDA
COLLEGE OF MEDICINE

PO Box 100216, J. HILLIS MILLER HEALTH CENTER, 1600 SOUTHWEST ARCHER ROAD, GAINESVILLE, FL 32610-0216
ADMISSION: 352-392-4569 • FAX: 352-846-0622 • E-MAIL: ADMISSIONS@MAIL.MED.UFL.EDU • WEBSITE: WWW.MED.UFL.EDU

STUDENT BODY

Type	Public
Enrollment	458
% male/female	49/51
% minorities	16
# applied (total/out)	20,079/874
# accepted (total)	197
# enrolled (total/out)	120/135
Average age	22

FACULTY

Total faculty (number)	1,020
% part-time	2

ADMISSIONS
Average GPA and MCAT Scores

Overall GPA	3.7
MCAT Bio	10.77
MCAT Phys	10.59
MCAT Verbal	9.89
MCAT Essay	P

Application Information

Regular application	12/1
Regular notification	Rolling
Are transfers accepted?	Yes
Admissions may be deferred?	Yes
Interview required?	Yes
Application fee	$30

Academics

Students may pursue their own interests with specialized institutes and centers, such as the Health Policy Institute, the Center for Mammalian Genetics, and the Brain and Cancer Institutes. Students with an interest in public health are encouraged to pursue the MPH degree in conjunction with other academic institutions. Grading uses an A–F scale, and a ranking system. Both steps of the USMLE are required for graduation.

BASIC SCIENCES: Instructional methods include lectures, labs, and small-group sessions that together occupy 25 hours per week or less. First-year basic science courses are Anatomy, Biochemistry, Cell and Tissue Biology, Genetics, Neuroscience, Physiology, and Radiology. Integrated into basic sciences are behavioral sciences, ethical issues, and clinical training. Examples of first-year courses in these areas are Essentials of Patient Care, Keeping Families Healthy, Human Behavior, and the preceptor program. Second-year courses are Clinical Diagnosis, Clinical Radiology, Microbiology, Oncology, Pathology, Pharmacology, Physical Diagnosis, Public Health, and Social and Ethical Issues in Medical Practice. Classrooms, labs, and the library are in one complex. A satellite library also operates in Jacksonville.

CLINICAL TRAINING

Required third-year rotations are Interdisciplinary Generalist Clerkships (10 weeks), Medicine (8 weeks), Surgery (8 weeks), Pediatrics (8 weeks), Psychiatry (6 weeks), Obstetrics/Gynecology (6 weeks), and Neurology (2 weeks). Fourth-year clerkships are Advanced Surgery (4 weeks); Advanced Medicine, Pediatrics, or Family Medicine (4 weeks); Clinical Pharmacology (4 weeks); and electives (28 weeks). The primary teaching hospitals are Shands Hospital (576 beds), the Gainesville Veterans Affairs Medical Center (403 beds), and the University Medical Center (528 beds). Training also takes place at outpatient clinics in nearby communities and at clinical research facilities. Educational affiliations have been established in Tallahassee, Pensacola, Jacksonville, Leesburg, Broward County, and Orlando. With approval, up to 3 months of elective credits may be earned at other institutions around the country and overseas. Outside of formal rotations, students gain clinical experience through outreach projects such as camps for sick children and care for the homeless.

Campus Life

About 99 percent of the students are Florida residents. Underrepresented minorities account for 11 percent of the student body, and students who have taken time off after college make up at least one-fourth of each entering class. Class size is 120.

STUDENT LIFE

Popular extracurricular activities include viewing intercollegiate sports, taking part in outdoor activities made possible by the year-round temperate climate, and occasionally going out at night to restaurants, clubs, and theaters. The university has an active student union with a theater, pool tables, a bowling alley, and a cafeteria. Athletic facilities, including a student gym, are expansive and are well-used by medical students. Outside of the classroom, students get to know each other through involvement with organizations and projects. A few examples of the numerous medical student organizations are Physicians for Social Responsibility, the Christian Medical and Dental Group, and the Family Practice Student Organization. Service projects such as the School of Medicine Outreach to Rural Students (SMORS) and the Equal Access Clinic improve students' interactive skills and give them the opportunity to contribute to their community. There are numerous groups that devote time each year on medical missions to underserved countries.

GRADUATES

There are about 6,500 graduates of the College of Medicine, a number of whom are renowned for important contributions made in their respective fields. At University of Florida–affiliated hospitals there are 56 postgraduate programs. Many of the positions in these programs are filled by graduates of the College of Medicine.

Admissions

REQUIREMENTS

Requirements are biology (8 hours), physics (8 hours), chemistry (8 hours), organic chemistry (4 hours), and biochemistry (4 hours). The MCAT is required and scores must be no more than 3 years old from the date of expected matriculation. Generally, the best set of scores is looked at most closely.

SUGGESTIONS

Early submission, preferably by June, of the AMCAS application is advised. No undergraduate major is preferred, and science and non-science majors are considered equally. Course work in biochemistry, genetics, and microbiology, and statistics is useful. Although there is no math requirement, there is an assumption that math up through calculus was taken as an undergraduate prerequisite for chemistry. Extracurricular activities, non-medically related community service, and health care experience and research are important as well.

PROCESS

Typically, the college receives 2,000 AMCAS applications for 120 available spaces. About 1,000 of the AMCAS applicants receive secondary applications, and about 300 of those returning secondaries are invited to interview. Interviews are held on Fridays from September through March and consist of two sessions with faculty members. On interview day, candidates also receive lunch and tours. Interview notification occurs on a rolling basis. After their interview, applicants are either accepted, rejected, or put on hold for a later decision. In April, an alternate list is established. Additional material, and updates, may be submitted by wait listed candidates. There are the two following routes of admission to the College of Medicine: Junior honors (12 places) and regular admissions (120 places). To apply for the Junior Honors Program, students apply directly to the College of Medicine during their sophomore year of college. If accepted to the program, they complete a special series of seminars at the University of Florida during their junior year and begin medical school after the completion of their junior year. For Junior Honors, call 352-392-4569.

UNIVERSITY OF HAWAII
JOHN A. BURNS SCHOOL OF MEDICINE (JABSOM)

651 ILALO STREET, HONOLULU, HI 96813 • ADMISSION: 808-692-1000
FAX: 808-692-1251 • E-MAIL: MNISHIKI@HAWAII.EDU • WEBSITE: HTTP://JABSOM.HAWAII.EDU

STUDENT BODY

Type	Public
Enrollment	260
% male/female	40/60
% minorities	17
# applied (total/out)	1,629/1,363
# enrolled	62
Average age	24

FACULTY

Total faculty (number)	458
% female	23
% minority	15
% part-time	51
Student-faculty ratio	1:1

ADMISSIONS
Average GPA and MCAT Scores

Overall GPA	3.6
MCAT Bio	10.0
MCAT Phys	10.0
MCAT Verbal	9.0
MCAT Essay	O

Application Information

Regular application	11/1
Regular notification	10/15
Early application	6/1–8/1
Early notification	10/1
Are transfers accepted?	Yes
Admissions may be deferred?	Yes
Interview required?	Yes
Application fee	$50

Academics

The School of Medicine, along with the Schools of Nursing and Social Work, comprise the College of Health Sciences and Social Welfare. JABSOM offers an MD program.

BASIC SCIENCES: Throughout the first 2 years, instruction is entirely case-based and emphasizes self-directed learning and early clinical training. Other subjects are organized into units, each occupying 12 to 14 weeks. Unit 1 courses are Health and Illness and Introduction to Problem-based Learning. Unit 2 focuses on cardiovascular, renal problems, and respiratory. Unit 3 is hematology, endocrine, and gastrointestinal problems. During the summer following year 1, students take part in a primary care precept, which entails working with local physicians. Unit 4 is locomoter, neurologic, and behavioral problems. Unit 5 is life cycle problems in obstetrics/gynecology, pediatrics, adolescents, and geriatrics. The final three months of year 2 are used for a basic science review in preparation for the USMLE Step 1, which is required for promotion to year 3. Scheduled classes during the first 2 years occupy about 20 hours per week, providing ample time for independent, self-directed study. Grading is pass/fail, and students are not ranked. The Medical Education Building, where basic sciences are taught, is equipped with laboratories, audiovisual computer centers, classrooms, a library, and areas for group study and tutorials. The University Library System has the largest collection of information and research materials in the state and includes the Hamilton Library (85,000 volumes), which serves the School of Medicine.

CLINICAL TRAINING

Pre-clinical training instruction in the various basic science disciplines is integrated into the problem-based learning experience as well as provided through a basic science foundation lecture and laboratory series.

In spring 2005, the medical school moved to a new campus near the heart of Honolulu. This new campus provides new classrooms and study space, a biomedical sciences library, a modern educational simulation center, and a standardized patient learning and testing center. The campus includes new research laboratories that will serve as the anchor for a biotechnology park.

Clinical: Most students enter block rotations, referred to as Unit 6B. For these students, third-year clerkships are Internal Medicine (11 weeks), Surgery (7 weeks), Family Medicine (7 weeks), Obstetrics/Gynecology (7 weeks), Pediatrics (7 weeks), and Psychiatry (7 weeks). Two weeks during year 3 are reserved for an elective. As an alternative to the standard block system, Unit 6L is a longitudinal clerkship that provides selected students an opportunity to spend half of their year in a community-based, integrated ambulatory care experience, and half of their year in hospital-based mini-blocks. Year 4, Unit 7, is reserved for electives with the exception of two required rotations in emergency medicine (4 weeks). The final month of the 4 year curriculum is for a senior seminar series, which provides an in-depth review of important topics designed specifically to help prepare graduates for their transition to residency training. Grading is honors/credit/no credit during the third year, and pass/fail during the fourth year. Students must pass the USMLE Steps 1 and 2 to graduate. Training takes place at many sites including The Queen's Medical Center, Kapiiolani Medical Center for Women and Children, St. Francis Medical Center, Tripler Army Medical Center, Hilo Family Medical Center, Hilo Medical Center, Kuakini Medical Center, Shriners Hospital, Kaiser Medical Center, Wahiawa General Hospital, Waiianae Coast Health Center, Kalihi-Palama Health Center, and the Rehabilitation Hospital of the Pacific.

Campus Life

Hawaii's multiethnic population is reflected in the student body, made up of men and women of Caucasian, Chinese, Korean, Japanese, Hawaiian, Filipino, Samoan, Micronesian, and other ancestries. Class size is 62. Graduate residency programs in Hawaii include the following specialties: Family practice, internal medicine, obstetrics/gynecology, orthopedics, pathology, pediatrics, psychiatry, surgery, and transitional. Forty percent of graduates are in the military service, and 1 percent are in full-time academic positions.

STUDENT LIFE

Although the School of Medicine is relatively small and intimate, the University of Hawaii at Manoa enrolls approximately 17,000 students. Medical students take part in campus activities but are integrated into the greater community of the city of Honolulu and the island of Oahu. Almost all students live off campus. Honolulu is a city with a population of about 1 million. It is a major tourist center, offering beautiful beaches in addition to many cultural, recreational, and outdoor activities.

GRADUATES

Residency programs in Hawaii are popular with graduates and include the following specialties: Family practice, internal medicine, obstetrics/gynecology, orthopedics, pathology, pediatrics, psychiatry, surgery, and transitional.

Admissions

REQUIREMENTS

The initial screening of applicants selects those who have close ties to Hawaii and who are most likely to practice in Hawaii and in the Pacific upon completion of postgraduate study. An exception is made for applicants from Wyoming and Montana, states without medical schools that belong to WICHE (Western Interstate Commission on Higher Education). Undergraduate course requirements are physics (8 units), biology (12-semester units, including at least 4 of cell and molecular biology), chemistry (4 units), and biochemistry (3 units). All courses except biochemistry must include laboratory experience. The MCAT is required and must be no more than 3 years old. If the MCAT has been taken more than once, the most recent set of scores is used.

SUGGESTIONS

Additional courses in biological and social science are advised, such as Anatomy, Embryology, genetics, immunology, microbiology, physiology, psychology, and sociology. Previous medical experience is important, as are personal qualities that suggest the applicant will become a humanistic physician. For those who have been out of school for a significant period of time, recent course work is recommended. Each year, a post-baccalaureate program selects 10 students who are promising students for medical school. If these students complete successfully the year-long premedical training, they are offered a position in the subsequent incoming class of medical students.

PROCESS

Annually, about 15–20 percent of applicants are interviewed. Interviews are conducted from October through March and consist of two sessions with faculty members, practicing physicians, fourth-year medical students, or members of the community. Of those interviewed, about 9 percent of in-state applicants and 10 percent of out-of-state residents are accepted. Most applicants are notified of the committee's decision in late April, though a few highly qualified applicants may hear earlier. A wait list is established at this time. Wait listed candidates are not advised to send supplementary information.

Admissions Requirements (Required)

MCAT scores, science GPA, non-science GPA, letters of recommendation, interview, essays/personal statement

Admissions Requirements (Optional)

State residency, extracurricular activities, exposure to medical profession

COSTS AND AID

Tuition & Fees

In-state tuition	$18,446
Out-of-state tuition	$35,064
Cost of books	$2,128
Fees	$192

Financial Aid

Average grant	$6,545
Average loan	$12,561

University of Illinois at Chicago
UIC College of Medicine

808 South Wood Street, Room 165 CME, M/C 783 Chicago, IL 60612 • Admission: 312-996-5635
Fax: 312-996-6693 • E-mail: MEDADMIT@UIC.EDU • Website: WWW.MEDICINE.UIC.EDU

STUDENT BODY

Type	Public
Enrollment	1,242
% male/female	59/41
% minorities	21
# applied (total/out)	2,376/1,248
# accepted (total/out)	574/203
# enrolled (total/out)	324/83
Average age	23

ADMISSIONS
Average GPA and MCAT scores

Overall GPA	3.57
MCAT Bio	10
MCAT Phys	10
MCAT Verbal	10
MCAT Essay	Q

Application Information

Regular application	11/15
Regular notification	6/1
Early application	6/1–8/1
Early notification	10/1
Are transfers accepted?	Yes
Admissions may be deferred?	Yes
Interview required?	Yes
Application fee	$70

Academics

Students participate in one of the following two educational tracks: 175 students complete all 4 years in Chicago, while 125 spend their first year in Urbana-Champaign. After the first year in Urbana-Champaign, 50 students each complete years 2, 3, and 4 in Peoria or Rockford. The remaining 25 students in Urbana-Champaign participate in the Medical Scholars Program.

BASIC SCIENCES: The first and second years include Behavioral Science, Biochemistry, Genetics, Histology, Immunology, Microbiology, Neuroscience, Pathology, Pathophysiology, Pharmacology, Physiology, and the Principles of Anatomy. All students participate in a clinical medicine course. Lectures and labs are the predominant instructional modality.

CLINICAL TRAINING

Patient contact begins in the first year when students are assigned individual physician preceptors. Students sharpen their skills in diagnosis and treatment through problem-solving sessions. In the third and fourth years, students focus on patient care with a series of clerkships supplemented by conferences and lectures. The 25 affiliated facilities range from rural ambulatory health care centers to major metropolitan hospitals. The diverse clinical experiences prepare UIC graduates to succeed within the nation's ever-changing health care system. Required clerkships include Family Medicine, Internal Medicine, Obstetrics/Gynecology, Pediatrics, Psychiatry, and Surgery. The elective phase provides students with the opportunity to identify special interest areas and to select educational experiences most relevant to their goals. The objective of the MD/PhD program is to train students for careers in academic medicine and research. The Medical Scholars Program (MSP), located on the Urbana-Champaign campus, permits students to integrate medicine with graduate studies in both science and non-science fields. The Independent Study Program (ISP) allows students to design their own academic programs with advice from faculty. ISP students complete an in-depth study, usually involving the basic sciences or clinical medicine. The ISP program is offered on the Chicago, Peoria, and Rockford campuses. The Rural Medical Education Program (RMED) and Rural Illinois Medical Student Assistance Program (RIMSAP) recruit students who commit to practice in medically underserved areas of Illinois.

Campus Life

UIC is one of the most ethnically diverse medical schools in the country. Students are assigned to a faculty member who serves as an advisor. The advisor's major role is to be available to the student throughout his or her medical education for academic and personal counseling. Research interests are widely diversified and range from basic molecular biology to patient-related clinical research.

STUDENT LIFE

Students in Chicago enjoy living in one of the country's most exciting cities. In Urbana-Champaign, students benefit from a large and exciting university community. Rockford and Peoria are midsize cities, offering all students basic urban amenities. Campus housing in Chicago includes three residence halls near the college. In Urbana-Champaign, university-certified housing includes campus and private residence halls and university apartments for family housing. In Peoria and Rockford housing is easily accessible and reasonable.

GRADUATES

UIC students undertake career specialization and training in all disciplines. Most graduates who participate in the National Residency Matching Program receive one of their top three residency choices.

Admissions

REQUIREMENTS

Only those applicants who indicate plans to obtain a baccalaureate degree prior to enrollment will be considered for admission. Major fields may be in behavioral, biological, humanities, or physical sciences. All applicants must complete: two semesters of introductory biology or the equivalent with laboratory; two semesters of general inorganic chemistry or the equivalent with laboratory; two semesters of organic chemistry with laboratory (introductory biochemistry may substitute for one semester of organic chemistry); and two semesters of general physics or the equivalent. All applicants are expected to complete three semesters of social science courses with an emphasis in the behavioral sciences. In addition, candidates are expected to take at least one of the following courses: Advanced-Level Biology, Biochemistry, Comparative Vertebrate Anatomy, Mammalian Histology, Molecular Genetics, and Physiology. All applicants must take the MCAT no later than the fall of the year prior to enrollment and no more than 3 years prior to application. All applicants must complete an application to the AMCAS no later than December 31 of the year prior to enrollment. All applicants must be U.S. citizens or possess a permanent resident immigrant visa at the time of application through AMCAS. On receipt of the AMCAS application, eligible applicants will be sent a UIC Supplemental Application. Materials must be postmarked by February 15 of the year prior to enrollment. A minimum of three academic letters of recommendation or one composite recommendation from a pre-professional committee must be postmarked by February 15 of the year prior to enrollment. If you are currently enrolled in a graduate or professional school, one of your three letters of recommendation must be from a faculty member at your graduate or professional school. It is advisable that letters of recommendation be sent from the institution at which the applicant had been most recently enrolled and must be completed on official university or business letterhead. Personal letters of recommendation are not acceptable.

SUGGESTIONS

At least 90 percent of UIC students are Illinois residents. Although Illinois residents are given preference, positions are open to highly qualified nonresidents. In addition to academic strength, experience, and background are considered important factors in admissions decisions.

PROCESS

About one-third of AMCAS applicants are sent a UIC Supplementary Application. Of those returning supplementals, the most highly qualified are invited to interview between September and April. The interview is a requirement and will be arranged by the Office of Medical College Admissions. Interviews are granted by invitation only. Interviews are held on all four campuses, and the interview location does not determine the campus where matriculants may attend. The interview consists of one panel interview session. Candidates have the opportunity to meet faculty members and students, receive financial aid information, tour the campus, and learn more about the College of Medicine. Interviewed candidates are accepted on a batch system. Students not immediately accepted may be put on an alternate list.

Admissions Requirements (Required)

MCAT scores, science GPA, non-science GPA, letters of recommendation, interview, state residency, essay/personal statement

Admissions Requirements (Optional)

Extracurricular activities, exposure to medical profession

Overlap Schools

Loyola University—Chicago, Northwestern University, Rush Medical College of Rush University, Southern Illinois University, The University of Chicago.

COSTS AND AID

Tuition & Fees

In-state tuition	$25,208
Out-of-state tuition	$53,262
Cost of books	$1,280
Fees	$1,574

UNIVERSITY OF IOWA
ROY J. AND LUCILLE A. CARVER COLLEGE OF MEDICINE

100 MEDICINE ADMINISTRATION BUILDING IOWA CITY, IA 52242 • ADMISSION: 319-335-8052 • FAX: 319-335-8049
E-MAIL: MEDICAL-ADMISSION@UIOWA.EDU • WEBSITE: WWW.MEDICINE.UIOWA.EDU/OSAC/ADMISSIONS/

STUDENT BODY

Type	Public
Enrollment	576
% male/female	53/47
% minorities	22
# applied (total/out)	2,956/2,635
# accepted (total/out)	305/176
# enrolled (total/out)	148/49
Average age	23

ADMISSIONS
Average GPA and MCAT Scores

Overall GPA	3.72
MCAT Bio	11
MCAT Phys	10.4
MCAT Verbal	10.2
MCAT Essay	P

Application Information

Regular application	11/1
Regular notification	Rolling
Early application	8/1
Early notification	10/1
Are transfers accepted?	No
Admissions may be deferred?	Yes
Interview required?	Yes
Application fee	$60

Academics

Most students at Iowa follow a four-year course of study, leading to the M.D. About 5 percent of students are M.S.T.P. participants, earning a Ph.D. concurrently with the M.D. The doctorate degree may be earned in Anatomy, Biochemistry, Microbiology, Pharmacology, and Physiology and Biophysics, among other fields. Other joint-degree programs, such as those leading to a master's degree along with the M.D., are also possible. Medical students are evaluated with near Honors/Pass/Fail for all courses except electives, which are Pass/Fail. Although the first two years are primarily devoted to basic sciences, introductory clinical training is also an important part of the curriculum. The second two years are devoted to clinical rotations.

BASIC SCIENCES: First-year courses are the following: Biochemistry; Cell Biology; Medical Genetics; Gross Anatomy; Structure and Functions of Human Organ Systems; Neuroscience; Immunology; and Foundations of Clinical Practice, which continues through the second year. This course covers topics ranging from biomedical ethics and problem-based learning to behavioral medicine, human sexuality, continuity of care, and important clinical techniques such as history-taking, the physical examination, and the doctor-patient relationship. The course Structure and Functions of Human Organ Systems covers principles of Histology and Physiology and is organized around body/organ systems. After completing their first year, many students spend the summer working and learning in an Iowa community hospital or conducting medical research projects. Second-year courses are: Principles of Infectious Diseases; Foundations of Clinical Practice; Pharmacology; Pathology. Throughout the first two years, students are in lectures, discussions, labs, or tutorials for about 23 hours per week. Basic sciences are taught in the Medical Education and Research Faculty and the Bowen Science Building. The Hardin Library holds over 200,000 volumes and nearly 3,000 periodicals and is used by students, faculty, and the medical community for research and studying. It also has a multimedia computer classroom and computer-based informational resources.

CLINICAL TRAINING

Third- and fourth-year required core clerkships are the following: Community-Based Primary Care (6 weeks); Family Practice (3 weeks); Internal Medicine (Inpatient - 6 weeks); Internal Medicine (Ambulatory - 3 weeks); Ob/Gyn (6 weeks); Pediatrics (6 weeks); and Surgery (6 weeks). Subspecialty clerkships are Neurology (4 weeks); Psychiatry (4 weeks); two weeks of each of the following: Anesthesia; Dermatology; Ophthalmology; Orthopedics; Otolaryngology; Radiology; Urology; Electrocardiography and Laboratory Medicine. Two advanced clerkships and at least 12 weeks of electives are also required. Clinical training takes place at the University Hospital (800 beds), the Veterans Affairs Hospital (440 beds), and various sites within the state.

Students

Each entering class has 148 students. About 70 percent of students are Iowa residents. Generally, about 30 undergraduate majors are represented in a class. Approximately 16 percent of students are underrepresented minorities. The majority of students entered medical school one year after college graduation. The Medical Education and Research facility opened for classes in the Fall of 2001. It also houses four learning communities to which each student is assigned.

STUDENT LIFE

Medical students are active in student organizations ranging from groups that support minorities to professional interest groups to a medical school singing group. The Learning communities also sponsor activities that encourage peer-to-peer support and mentoring. Each community is staffed by a faculty director, professional and support staff with leadership provided by the elected student representatives. As part of the greater University of Iowa, medical students enjoy its facilities, resources, and sponsored events, such as Big Ten athletics. The UI campus is central to Iowa City and is convenient to restaurants, clubs, theaters, shopping areas, and parks. Though the city has a population of 60,000 people, it is relatively safe and has the feeling of a friendly small town. Just outside of the city are lakes, hiking areas, and other outdoor attractions. Urban centers such as Chicago, St. Louis, Minneapolis, Omaha, and Kansas City are within a five-hour drive. On-campus housing options include coed medical fraternities with both single and double rooms, and university-owned family housing. Off-campus, reasonably priced apartments are available.

GRADUATES

Graduates are successful in entering residency programs of their choice. Iowa itself offers post-graduate training programs in about 15 fields.

Admissions

REQUIREMENTS

Prerequisites are one year each of Physics, Chemistry, Organic Chemistry, General Biology, one semester of Advanced Biology, and college-level Math or Statistics. All science courses should include laboratory instruction. The MCAT is required, and scores must be from exams no earlier than April 2002 and no later than September 2008 for the 2008 entering class. All sets of scores are evaluated.

SUGGESTIONS

Though preference is given to Iowa residents, well-qualified nonresidents are also considered. Nonscience majors might benefit from additional science courses beyond requirements; specifically, biochemistry, genetics, and an anatomy course. Computer literacy, the ability to write well, strong verbal skills, and general decision-making capabilities are some of the skills sought in applicants. Also important are an applicant's personal characteristics, which are evaluated with the help of letters of reference and interviews. Some medically related experience is important.

PROCESS

Iowa participates in the AMCAS process. Most who apply through AMCAS are sent secondary applications. About one-third of Iowa residents who apply are accepted. Of the nonresident applicant pool, about 6 percent are accepted. Applicants are notified on a rolling basis and are either accepted, rejected, or wait-listed. Wait-listed candidates are not encouraged to send additional information.

Admissions Requirements (Required)

MCAT scores, Science GPA, Non-science GPA, Letters of recommendation, Interview, Essays/personal statement

Admissions Requirements (Optional)

State residency, Extracurricular activities, Exposure to medical profession

COSTS AND AID

Tuition & Fees

In-state Tuition	$25,094
Out-of-state Tuition	$41,124

Financial Aid

Average grant	$11,694
Average loan	$28,094
Average debt	$120,171

UNIVERSITY OF KANSAS
SCHOOL OF MEDICINE

3901 RAINBOW BOULEVARD, 3040 MURPHY BUILDING, MAIL STOP 1049, KANSAS CITY, KS 66160 • ADMISSION: 913-588-5245
FAX: 913-588-5259 • E-MAIL: PREMEDINFO@KUMC.EDU • WEBSITE: WWW.KUMC.EDU/SOM/SOM.HTML

STUDENT BODY

Type	Public
Enrollment	700
% male/female	55/45
% minorities	14
# applied (total/out)	1,585/1,168
# accepted (total/out)	229/60
# enrolled (total/out)	175/33
Average age	24

FACULTY

Total faculty (number)	658
% female	46
% minority	29
% part-time	18
Student-faculty ratio	1:1

ADMISSIONS
Average GPA and MCAT Scores

Overall GPA	3.66
MCAT Bio	9.8
MCAT Phys	9.2
MCAT Verbal	9.6
MCAT Essay	Q

Application Information

Regular application	10/15
Regular notification	3/31
Early application	7/1
	(recommended)
Early notification	10/1
Are transfers accepted?	Yes
Admissions may be deferred?	Yes
Interview required?	Yes

Academics

In comparison to many medical schools, clinical training at the University of Kansas emphasizes rural and primary health care. Joint-MD/PhD degrees are offered in the following fields: anatomy and cell biology, biochemistry and molecular biology, microbiology, molecular genetics and toxicology, pathology and oncology, pharmacology, and physiology. A joint-MD/MPH is also offered.

BASIC SCIENCES: The first two years, taught in Kansas City, consist of 13 sequential modules organized around central themes. Students spend a maximum of 15 hours per week in class lectures. During the remainder of the week, they use problem-based learning, small- group discussions, election procedure simulators, and clinic skills labs to reinforce lecture materials and develop clinical proficiency. Students are evaluated using the following descriptions: superior/high satisfactory/satisfactory/low satisfactory/unsatisfactory. These marks are translated into numeric scores to determine class rank. The USMLE is required upon completion of year 2. The Dykes Library of the Health Sciences supports the educational and research demands of medical students, faculty, and the public. It contains 150,000 books and offers online informational services. In addition, the Clendening History of Medicine Library has one of the top five collections of rare medical books in the country.

CLINICAL TRAINING

Patient contact begins in year 1, when students take part in biweekly sessions with practicing physicians. Required clinical clerkships are Medicine (8 weeks), Neuropsychiatry (8 weeks), General Surgery (8 weeks), Ambulatory Medicine/Geriatrics (6 weeks), Family Medicine (6 weeks), Obstetrics/Gynecology (6 weeks), and Pediatrics (6 weeks). Year 4 is filled primarily with electives, from which there are many to choose including preventive medicine and the history of medicine. Clinical training takes place both at the University of Kansas Hospital (464 beds), which houses nearly all the diagnostic and treatment facilities of the Medical Center and at hospitals in Wichita. Included at the Medical Center in Kansas City are the Kansas Cancer Institute, the Burnett Burn Center, the Smith Mental Retardation Center, the Center on Aging, and the Center on Environmental and Occupational Health. Patients are drawn from Kansas, Missouri, Oklahoma, Arkansas, and Nebraska. The grading scale is the same for performance in clinical rotations as it for basic science courses. In addition to formal rotations, students gain clinical experience through volunteer activities, like the Jay Doc Clinic and the Mobile Medical Unit, which brings basic prevention and care to communities in need. Many students devote free summers to volunteer in medically related activities.

Campus Life

About 90 percent of a typical class are Kansas residents, and most students have liberal arts backgrounds. In recent years, about 13 percent of the student body have been underrepresented minorities, mostly African and Hispanic Americans. Usually, almost a quarter of matriculants in a given year are older than 25 years of age. Class size is 175.

STUDENT LIFE

Medical students from all four classes are organized into academic societies, which bring students together around academic and extracurricular activities. The Kirmayer Fitness Center is a modern facility open to all medical students. Numerous organized activities enrich the lives of medical students. Activities such as Rural Health Weekend provide opportunities for interaction with practicing physicians throughout the state. Organizations such as the Community Outreach Project provide opportunities for community service. All students live off campus.

GRADUATES

About 50 percent of graduates enter primary care fields. Graduates are successful in obtaining residency positions throughout the country. The medical school sponsors events and scholarships that encourage students and residents to consider practicing in Kansas.

Admissions

REQUIREMENTS

Required college courses are 1 year of biology with lab, chemistry with lab, organic chemistry with lab, physics with lab, 1 year of English, and 1 semester of college-level mathematics. A bachelor's degree is required. Evaluation of GPA is irrespective of where course work was completed. The MCAT is required, with the two most recent sets of scores considered. The August MCAT is acceptable.

SUGGESTIONS

Experience in a health care setting is valued, and the breadth of an applicant's undergraduate course work is important. Demonstrated interests in rural and primary care medicine are pluses. Out-of-state residents should have particularly strong qualifications. A few students each year are accepted from the University of Kansas Post-baccalaureate Program and through the Scholars in Primary Care Program.

PROCESS

All Kansas residents are sent secondary applications, while only about 10 percent of out-of-state applicants receive them. About 75 percent of Kansas residents and about 5 percent of out-of-state applicants are interviewed. Interviews are conducted in Kansas City from October through March and consist of one or two sessions each with one or two members of the interview panel. Approximately one-half of those interviewed are offered positions in the class and are notified on a rolling basis after the interview. The wait list is short, and wait listed candidates are not encouraged to send supplementary material.

Admissions Requirements (Required)

MCAT scores, science GPA, non-science GPA, letters of recommendation, interview, essays/personal statement, extracurricular activities, exposure to medical profession, secondary app, prerequisite courses, and bachelor's degree

Admissions Requirements (Optional)

State residency

COSTS AND AID

Tuition & Fees

In-state tuition	$18,920
Out-of-state tuition	$34,674
Room and board (off-campus)	$9,018
Cost of books	$3,120
Fees	$438

Financial Aid

% students receiving aid	85
Average grant	$2,500
Average loan	$27,500
Average debt	$90,600

UNIVERSITY OF KENTUCKY
COLLEGE OF MEDICINE

MN118 UKMC, 800 ROSE STREET LEXINGTON, KY 40536-0298 • ADMISSION: 859-323-6161 • FAX: 859-257-3633
E-MAIL: KYMEDAP@UKY.EDU • WEBSITE: WWW.COMED.UKY.EDU/MEDICINE

STUDENT BODY

Type	Public
Enrollment	400
% male/female	57/43
% minorities	6
# applied (total/out)	2,129/1,704
# enrolled (total/out)	103/23
Average age	23

FACULTY

Student-faculty ratio	1:1

ADMISSIONS
Average GPA and MCAT Scores

Overall GPA	3.69
MCAT Bio	10.1
MCAT Phys	9.9
MCAT Verbal	10.4
MCAT Essay	P

Application Information

Regular application	11/1
Regular notification	Rolling
Early application	6/1–8/1
Early notification	10/1
Are transfers accepted?	Yes
Admissions may be deferred?	Yes
Interview required?	Yes
Application fee	$50

Academics

The curriculum includes early patient contact and teaches lifelong learning skills, ethics, and computer-assisted learning along with traditional basic science and clinical techniques. The goal of the medical education program is to focus on principles and the organization of factual bodies of knowledge rather than on unconnected detail. Although most students complete a four-year curriculum, a few students each year enter a combined M.D./Ph.D. program. The doctorate may be earned in Anatomy, Biochemistry, Biophysics, Cell Biology, Genetics, Immunology, Microbiology, Molecular Biology, Neuroscience, Pharmacology, or Physiology. Combined M.D./M.P.H and M.D./M.B.A. programs are also available. Medical students are evaluated with letter grades and, in some cases, with Pass/Fail. Passing Step 1 of the USMLE is a requirement for promotion to year three, and passing Step 2 is a graduation requirement.

BASIC SCIENCES: During the first and second years, students are in class or other scheduled sessions for about 24 hours per week. Lectures and tutorials are the primary instructional methods. Laboratories, hands-on clinical work, and conferences are also important parts of the curriculum. The first year is devoted to basic sciences and interdisciplinary perspectives. The year is organized into blocks, each of which contains one or two courses. First-year courses are Patients, Physicians, and Society; Introduction to the Medical Profession; Human Structure/Gross Anatomy; Human Structure/Histology; Healthy Human; Cellular Structure and Function/Biochemistry; Cellular Structure and Function/Genetics; Neuroscience; and Human Function. The second year is focused on the disease process and is also broken into blocks. These are Patients, Physicians, and Society II; Introduction to the Medical Profession II; Immunity, Infection, and Disease; and Mechanisms of Disease and Treatment, which covers Pathology and Pharmacology. Students spend most of their first two years in the Medical Science Building, which houses classrooms and laboratories. Computers are important educational tools, and all incoming students are required to have their own computers. The College of Medicine has a nationally recognized program of academic computing in medical education, which provides a wide variety of services to enhance student learning. These educational support services are offered in facilities located in the College of Medicine, the Chandler Medical Center, and in the Area Health Education Centers. The library, which contains more than 150,000 volumes, is also an important resource.

CLINICAL TRAINING

Third-year required clerkships are: Women's Maternal and Child Health (12 weeks); Clinical Neuroscience (8 weeks); Principles Of Primary Care (12 weeks); and Medical and Surgical Care (16 weeks). The fourth year is comprised of a one-month acting internship selected from medical specialties (family practice, internal medicine, pediatric, neurology, psychiatry, rehabilitation medicine), a one-month acting internship selected from surgical specialties (general, subspecialty, ob/gyn), a one-month emergency medicine clerkship, one month of a clinical pharmacology and anesthesiology clerkship, and one month of a primary care or rural medicine selective. In addition, 8 weeks of electives are required. Training takes place primarily at the University of Kentucky Hospital (473 beds), although a number of affiliated hospitals and clinics are also used.

Students

Approximately 90 percent of students are Kentucky residents. About 6 percent of students are underrepresented minorities, most of whom are African American. Generally, about 25 percent of students in each class are nontraditional, having pursued other careers or interests in between college and medical school.

STUDENT LIFE

Medical students enjoy extracurricular activities associated with the main university such as attending UK basketball games. Student groups provide additional extracurricular activities, including opportunities for involvement in community service projects. They also serve as a means of interacting outside of class. Women in Science and Medicine is a group, comprised primarily of faculty and administrators, focused on improving all aspects of life for women in medicine. Lexington is an attractive and safe city with affordable housing.

GRADUATES

Graduates enter residency programs all over the United States in both primary care and specialty fields. The University of Kentucky has post-graduate training programs in more than 20 fields.

Admissions

REQUIREMENTS

One year each of Biology, General Chemistry, Organic Chemistry, Physics, and English are required. All science courses should include associated labs. The MCAT is required, and scores should be from within the past two years. For applicants who have taken the exam more than once, the most recent set of scores is weighed most heavily.

SUGGESTIONS

In addition to academic qualifications, UK seeks students who have the character, personality, values, and motivation for human service. Individual initiative and good judgment are important traits. Some medically related experience is important.

PROCESS

All AMCAS applicants who are Kentucky residents are sent secondary applications. Highly qualified nonresidents are also sent secondaries. About 50 percent of applicants who return secondary applications are invited to interview between September and March. On interview day, candidates also tour the campus, attend group informational sessions, and have the opportunity to meet informally with current students. About 45 percent of interviewed candidates are accepted on a rolling basis. Others are rejected or wait-listed. Wait-listed candidates may send additional information to update their files. The admissions process is rolling and the class is typically full by January so early completion of both the primary and the secondary application is strongly recommended.

Admissions Requirements (Required)

MCAT scores, Science GPA, Non-science GPA, Letters of recommendation, Interview, Exposure to medical profession

Admissions Requirements (Optional)

State residency, Essays/personal statement, Extracurricular activities

Overlap Schools

University of Cincinnati, University of Louisville.

COSTS AND AID

Tuition & Fees

In-state Tuition	$26,600
Out-of-state Tuition	$49,670
Room and board (off-campus)	$12,370
Cost of books	$2,475
Fees	$1,000

Financial Aid

% students receiving aid	94
Average grant	$8,573
Average loan	$30,766
Average debt	$107,110

UNIVERSITY OF LOUISVILLE
SCHOOL OF MEDICINE

ABELL ADMINISTRATION CTR., RM. 413, 323 E. CHESTNUT ST. LOUISVILLE, KY 40202 • **ADMISSION:** 502-852-5193
FAX: 502-852-0302 • **E-MAIL:** MEDADM@LOUISVILLE.EDU • **WEBSITE:** LOUISVILLE.EDU

STUDENT BODY

Type	Public
Enrollment	598
% male/female	59/41
% minorities	7
# applied (total/out)	2,179/1,762
# accepted (total/out)	247/62
# enrolled (total/out)	148/29
Average age	23

FACULTY

Total faculty	795
% female	30
% minority	24
% part-time	8

ADMISSIONS
Average GPA and MCAT Scores

Overall GPA	3.65
MCAT Bio	9.94
MCAT Phys	9.52
MCAT Verbal	9.74
MCAT Essay	0

Application Information

Regular application	10/15
Regular notification	Rolling
Early application	6/1–8/1
Early notification	10/1
Are transfers accepted?	Yes
Admissions may be deferred?	Yes
Interview required?	Yes
Application fee	$75

Academics

Although most students complete a four-year program leading to the M.D., a few earn a combined M.D./Ph.D., which typically demands about seven years. Summer research scholarships allow first- and second-year students to participate in research projects alongside faculty mentors. Throughout all four years, students work closely with faculty advisers who assist with decisions related to academic and professional goals. Medical students are evaluated as Pass/Fail/Honors in both basic science and clinical courses. Passing Step 1 of the USMLE is a requirement for promotion to year three, and passing Step 2 is a requirement for graduation.

BASIC SCIENCES: The Core Curriculum extends over the four-year course of study and provides each student with the general education and training considered essential to all physicians. It stresses understanding concepts and general principles instead of superficial details. It provides opportunities for correlations among the sciences so that information learned in one subject reinforces ideas and builds upon concepts developed in another subject. Incorporating clinical correlations into the first two years demonstrates how knowledge of the basic sciences applies directly to solving clinical problems. The Preclinical Curriculum consists of 11 basic science courses, the two-year Introduction to Clinical Medicine course and the two-year Interdisciplinary Clinical Cases component (a small group activity that emphasizes integration of basic sciences and clinical sciences). The Preclinical Elective Program allows each student to customize his or her education in terms of learning experiences. Students are able to design a medical education program that best meets their needs, abilities, and goals. Students also are permitted to take courses as electives in divisions of the University of Louisville other than the School of Medicine, class schedule permitting. In addition to the courses listed, students with a research interest are permitted to participate in an approved research activity for credit. Elective courses constitute an integral part of the student's total program in medical school. Second-year students take two credit hours of elective courses.

CLINICAL TRAINING

Third-year required rotations are Internal Medicine Clerkship (10 weeks); Family Medicine & Community Medicine Clerkship (6 weeks); Psychiatry Clerkship (6 weeks); Basic Surgery Clerkship (8 weeks); Pediatrics Clerkship (8 weeks); OB/GYN Clerkship (8 weeks). Fourth-year requirements are Inpatient General Medicine (4 weeks); Inpatient General Surgery (4 weeks); Neurology Clerkship (4 weeks); AHEC Rural/Urban rotations in specified disciplines/specialties (4 weeks); Ambulatory Rotation or Longitudinal Ambulatory Rotation (Selectives) (4 weeks); Perioperative Medicine Clerkship (2 weeks); Electives (14 weeks); Transition to Residency Week (1 week).

Students

In the entering class of 2007, 120 of 148 students were Kentucky residents. African Americans represented 7 percent of the class, and students older than 27 years old represented 9 percent of the class.

STUDENT LIFE

Students profit from the school's location in the center of Louisville. Louisville is the largest city in Kentucky, offering cultural and recreational activities such as orchestra, theater, ballet, opera, numerous restaurants and bars, and shopping areas. Louisville is the home of the Kentucky Derby. There is a university-owned Medical Dental Dormitory and Apartment Building, which is two blocks from both the School of Medicine and the university hospital. In this residential complex, there are apartments of all sizes as well as dorm rooms. Also available are varieties of housing options within 10 miles of the Health Science Campus ranging from apartments, lofts, and condominiums to historic houses in Old Louisville.

GRADUATES

A large proportion of practicing physicians in Kentucky are Louisville School of Medicine graduates. At Louisville itself, at least 17 post-graduate training programs are offered.

Admissions

REQUIREMENTS

Requirements are two semesters each of Biology, Chemistry, Organic Chemistry, Physics, and one semester of Calculus or two semesters of other college-level Math. All science courses must include lab work. Two semesters of English is also required. The MCAT is required, and scores should be no more than two years old. For applicants who have retaken the exam, the most recent set of scores is considered. Thus, there is no advantage in withholding scores.

SUGGESTIONS

Approximately 80 percent of positions in each class are reserved for Kentucky residents, making out-of-state admission very competitive. Pre-medical students should develop a strong background in the Humanities, Philosophy, and the Arts. Communication and reading abilities are also important. The Committee values volunteer work, medically related experience, and evidence of strong interpersonal skills

PROCESS

All qualified Kentucky residents and highly qualified nonresidents who submit AMCAS applications are sent secondaries. Of those returning secondary applications, about one-half of Kentucky applicants are invited to interview between September and February. Ten percent of nonresidents are invited to interview. On interview day, candidates receive two 30-minute interview sessions each with a faculty member, administrator, or medical student. In addition, interviewees have a guided campus tour, lunch, and the opportunity to meet informally with current students. About 40 percent of interviewed candidates are accepted on a rolling basis. Wait-listed candidates may send information to update their files in the spring.

Admissions Requirements (Required)

MCAT scores, Science GPA, Non-science GPA, Letters of recommendation, Interview, State residency, Essays/personal statement, Extracurricular activities, Exposure to medical profession

Overlap Schools

University of Kentucky.

COSTS AND AID
Tuition & Fees

In-state Tuition	$22,474
Out-of-state Tuition	$42,820
Room and board (off-campus)	$7,150
Cost of books	$2,332
Fees	$675

UNIVERSITY OF MANITOBA

270-727 McDermot Avenue, Winnipeg, MB R3E 0W3 • Admission: 204-789-3499
Fax: 204-789-3929 • E-mail: REGISTRAR_MED@UMANITOBA.CA • Website: WWW.UMANITOBA.CA/MEDICINE

STUDENT BODY

Type	Public
Enrollment	373
% male/female	53/47
% minorities	5
# applied (total/out)	815/539
# accepted (total/out)	153/48
# enrolled (total/out)	101/8
Average age	24

ADMISSIONS
Average GPA and MCAT scores

Overall GPA	4.03
MCAT Bio	10
MCAT Phys	10
MCAT Verbal	10
MCAT Essay	Q

Application Information

Regular application	10/8
Regular notification	5/15
Are transfers accepted?	Yes
Admissions may be deferred?	Yes
Interview required?	Yes
Application fee	$90

Academics

Medical students complete a 4-year curriculum leading to the MD degree. Classes during the first 2 years are largely systems-based. Small groups are the predominant format for instruction, although lectures, labs, computer-based learning, and early clinical exposure are also important educational tools. The second 2 years are spent in clinical clerkships.

BASIC SCIENCES: Medicine I and Medicine II consist of five mandatory programs: cognitive, clinical skills, medical humanities and laboratory medicine, problem solving, plus the voluntary stress management program. The cognitive component is delivered in a variety of formats, including assigned self-study periods (A), small-group tutorials (T), traditional didactic lectures (L), small-group activities in entire class format (T1), lab practicals (LP) or demonstrations (LD), and computer-simulated labs. The problem solving program attempts to integrate and reiterate important concepts presented during the cognitive component but emphasizes a symptom-based approach to your medical education. The clinical skills program, which includes communication, history-taking and physical examination skills; the medical humanities program, which includes human values, medical ethics, and medical history; and the lab medicine program are integrated with the cognitive program as much as possible. In addition, there will be periods of unstructured, independent, self-directed learning time (SD) for the most part left blank in the weekly schedule.

CLINICAL TRAINING

Rotation through all major clinical disciplines takes place in more than a 48-week period and these are supplemented by elective periods of the students' choice. Periods are spent in family/community medicine, internal medicine, medicine and surgery selective, obstetrics/gynecology, pediatrics, psychiatry, surgery, and in a multiple clerkship rotation of anesthesia, emergency, ophthalmology, otolaryngology, and a community health sciences project. The setting for this experience includes wards and outpatient facilities of the hospitals or doctors' offices. The primary responsibility of the clerks in each of the eight 6-week rotations is the care of patients under the supervision of postgraduate students and faculty. Formal teaching of the pertinent knowledge, skills, attitudes, and behavior to the discipline is provided during the clerkships.

Campus Life

In the entering class of 2005, approximately 50 percent of students were women. The average age of incoming students was 24 years. All students have bachelor's degrees.

STUDENT LIFE

Students are active in a number of areas, including organizing a program to help inner-city youth, coordinating an annual Medical Art Show, developing Codes of Professional Integrity, and carrying out an annual food bank drive.

Admissions

REQUIREMENTS

Applicants must have or be eligible to receive their bachelor's degree prior to admission from a university recognized by the University of Manitoba. Applicants must have completed a full course of English or French and a full course of biochemistry at the university level and received a grade of C or higher. Two full courses in humanities/social sciences are also required. The MCAT is required and should be taken within the past 3 years but no later than August of the year of application. Students usually prepare for the MCAT by taking university courses in biology, organic and physical chemistry, and physics.

SUGGESTIONS

Enrollment is restricted to Canadian citizens or permanent residents. Priority is given to residents of Manitoba. The most successful applicants have grade point averages between 3.8 and 4.2 on a 4.5 scale and at least an 8 on each scored section of the MCAT. In addition to academic and intellectual credentials, the Admissions Committee selects applicants who demonstrate social skills, maturity, and a sense of responsibility. The Admissions Committee selects 100 students for admission out of about 800 applicants. Typically, about nine places are offered to applicants from outside Manitoba.

PROCESS

For application materials, contact the faculty at the following e-mail: admissions@umanitoba.ca or call: 204-474-8805. Applicants who meet scholastic and MCAT requirements will be invited to interview and submit a personal statement. About 250 applicants are interviewed, and from this group the class is selected in early June. There is a special consideration category for some Manitoba residents who fall into one of the following three groups: Those who are sponsored by faculty-approved agencies, those who are from native populations of Manitoba, and those who have been employed for 2 or more years in the areas of health, social welfare, or health education.

Admissions Requirements (Required)

MCAT scores, science GPA, letters of recommendation, interview, essay/personal statement, extracurricular activities, Canadian citizen or permanent resident

Admissions Requirements (Optional)

Non-science GPA, state residency, exposure to medical profession

COSTS AND AID

Tuition & Fees

Tuition	$7,595
Room and board (on-campus)	$6,000
Room and board (off-campus)	$10,000
Cost of books	$4,000

Financial Aid

% students receiving aid	35
Average grant	$750
Average loan	$10,615
Average debt	$46,000

University of Maryland
School of Medicine

Committee on Admissions, Suite 190, 685 W. Baltimore St. Baltimore, MD 21201-1559 • Admission: 410-706-7478
Fax: 410-706-0467 • E-mail: MFOXWELL@SOM.UMARYLAND.EDU • Website: WWW.MEDSCHOOL.UMARYLAND.EDU

STUDENT BODY

Type	Public
Enrollment	621
% male/female	40/60
% minorities	40
# applied (total/out)	4,166/3,395
# accepted (total/out)	314/114
# enrolled (total/out)	160/35
Average age	24

FACULTY

Total faculty (number)	2,600
% female	45
% minority	8
% part-time	8
Student-faculty ratio	2:1

ADMISSIONS
Average GPA and MCAT scores

Overall GPA	3.66
MCAT Bio	10.5
MCAT Phys	10
MCAT Verbal	10.1
MCAT Essay	P

Application Information

Regular application	11/7
Regular notification	Rolling
Early application	8/1
Early notification	10/1
Are transfers accepted?	Yes
Admissions may be deferred?	Yes
Interview required?	Yes
Application fee	$70

Academics

Maryland's dynamic curriculum emphasizes independent and small group learning, informatics, and the integration of basic and clinical science knowledge to produce outstanding clinicians and researchers. The traditional degree program takes students 4 years to complete. However, in selected cases, with permission of the dean, students may be granted extra time to complete the degree requirements. For students interested in a research career, the medical school offers a combined MD/PhD program in which the doctorate degree is offered in numerous disciplines such as biochemistry, biomedical engineering, genetics, molecular biology, neuroscience, and pharmacology. Grading is A–F. Students not only must sit for Step 1 of the USMLE before beginning clinical training, but also they must pass Step 1 within 3 attempts.

BASIC SCIENCES: The basic science curriculum is divided into integrated blocks and uses interdisciplinary teaching with both basic and clinical science instructors. Lectures and labs are limited to 4 hours per day; small group and independent study are emphasized. Course work during the first year lasts 37 weeks and is organized into the following blocks: Cell and Molecular Biology, Functional Systems, Informatics, Neuroscience, Principles of Human Development, and Structure and Development. Introduction to Clinical Medicine runs concurrently throughout the year, covering the doctor-patient relationship, medical ethics, population medicine, and problem-based learning. The second year is particularly rigorous. Students learn pathophysiology and therapeutics by organ system and are trained in conducting a physical diagnosis in the Introduction to Clinical Medicine course. Computers, not microscopes, are the laboratory tool of choice at Maryland. The multidisciplinary laboratories have the latest in educational technology and seat clusters of 10–12 students for small group and laboratory teaching. The recently renovated library is among the largest and most accessible medical libraries in the United States, with at least 240,000 volumes and is fully connected to the information superhighway. The Office of Student Affairs closely monitors students and provides support services. In addition, a prematriculation summer program allows entrants to review premedical course work and preview first-year material.

CLINICAL TRAINING

Year 3 consists of 7 required rotations in Family Medicine (4 weeks), Medicine (12 weeks), Surgery (12 weeks), Pediatrics (6 weeks), Psychiatry (4 weeks), Obstetrics/Gynecology (6 weeks), and Neurology (4 weeks). The senior year includes a mandatory Area Health Education Center experience (8 weeks), 2 sub internships (8 weeks), and 16 weeks of elective rotations. The majority of training takes place at university hospital, a 747-bed tertiary care center adjacent to the medical school. Rotations are also spent at the Baltimore Veterans Affairs Medical Center, Mercy Hospital, and other community hospitals. In total, 1,400 patient beds are used for teaching. One of the most unique electives is a rotation through the R Adams Cowley Shock Trauma Center. Shock Trauma was the first trauma center in America and continues to be a model for the rest of the nation.

Campus Life

The majority of students are Maryland residents, but the medical school attracts and accepts a significant number of out-of-state applicants. In a typical class, approximately 38 of the 150 students are from out-of-state. The student body is highly diverse, with about 20 percent of students from underrepresented minority backgrounds. More than half of our students are women. Increasingly, older students are making up a higher percentage of incoming classes. At least one-third of incoming classes took time off between college and medical school.

STUDENT LIFE

An extensive orientation program allows entering students to get to know fellow classmates, upperclassmen, and faculty advisors. Almost half of the incoming class attends. Other organized events, such as pot-luck suppers, community activities, and meetings of student organizations all serve to bring students together. Baltimore is a lively city, with interesting neighborhoods and real character. The harbor, the commercial district (Fells Point), the Orioles baseball stadium, Ravens football stadium, and other attractions are accessible to the campus. The university offers athletic facilities and housing in the form of dorms. Most students find affordable, private apartments off campus. While the surrounding area has undergone a renaissance in recent years, safety remains a concern, as in most large cities.

GRADUATES

Over half of each year's graduates enter one of the primary care fields. Graduates, however, are competitive candidates for the entire range of specialties.

Admissions

REQUIREMENTS

Maryland requires 1 year each of biology, English, general chemistry, organic chemistry, and physics as prerequisite courses. A grade of C or better is mandatory in each course. While the MCAT is also required, there is no set formula for determining competitive scores. Students with a wide range of scores are accepted each year. In addition, Maryland considers the best scores for those applicants who retake the exam.

SUGGESTIONS

Maryland gives clinical experience with direct patient exposure considerable weight. Research experience and service activity are also highly valued. Letters of recommendation are very important in the selection process.

PROCESS

Maryland uses the AMCAS application. Secondary applications are sent to all applicants. Of those who complete the secondary application, approximately 25 percent are interviewed beginning in October. The interview day consists of a faculty interview, a medical student interview, a casual lunch with students, and a tour of the campus. Interviewed applicants normally receive a decision within a month after the interview. Half of those interviewed are accepted, and the other half are either rejected or wait listed.

Admissions Requirements (Required)

MCAT scores, science GPA, non-science GPA, letters of recommendation, interview, essay/personal statement, extracurricular activities, exposure to medical profession, community service

Overlap Schools

Johns Hopkins University, Pennsylvania State University, Thomas Jefferson University, University of Pennsylvania, University of Pittsburgh, University of Virginia, Virginia Commonwealth University.

COSTS AND AID

Tuition & Fees

In-state tuition	$20,905
Out-of-state tuition	$39,140
Room and board (on-campus)	$12,925
Room and board (off-campus)	$18,490
Cost of books	$850
Fees	$1,071

Financial Aid

% students receiving aid	90
Average grant	$6,800
Average loan	$32,605
Average debt	$112,440

University of Massachusetts

Medical School

Associate Dean for Admissions, 55 Lake Avenue North Worcester, MA 01655 • Admission: 508-856-2323
Fax: 506-856-3629 • E-mail: Admissions@umassmed.edu • Website: www.umassmed.edu/som/admissions/

STUDENT BODY	
Type	Public
Enrollment	425
% male/female	49/51
% minorities	7
# applied (total/out)	802/0
# accepted (total/out)	183/6
# enrolled (total/out)	103/3
Average age	24

FACULTY	
Total faculty	2,488

ADMISSIONS	
Average GPA and MCAT Scores	
Overall GPA	3.59
MCAT Phys	10.46

Application Information	
Regular application	11/1
Regular notification	10/15
Early application	6/1–8/1
Early notification	10/1
Are transfers accepted?	Yes
Admissions may be deferred?	Yes
Interview required?	Yes
Application fee	$100

Academics

The four-year program emphasizes varied educational modalities, lifelong learning, communication skills, and a generalist approach that prepares students for all medical career paths. Ethical issues are an important aspect of the education, demonstrated by the existence of an active Office of Ethics. Yearlong and summer research fellowships are available, as is a joint M.D./Ph.D. program. The doctorate degree may be earned in Biomedical Sciences, Biochemistry and Molecular Biology, Cell Biology, Cellular and Molecular Physiology, Immunology and Virology, Molecular Genetics, Microbiology, Neuroscience, and Pharmacology and Molecular Toxicology. A combined M.D./M.P.H. degree program is also offered. For preclinical courses, grades are Honors, Near Honors, Satisfactory, Marginal, Unsatisfactory, or Incomplete, with the exception of a few courses that are taken as Credit/No Credit. During the clinical years, ratings are Outstanding, Above Expected Performance, Expected Performance, Below Expected Performance, and Failure.

BASIC SCIENCES: First-year courses are Biochemistry/Metabolism; The Gene; Human Anatomy; Cells and Tissues; Systems I; Physiology; Immunology; Mind, Brain and Behavior I; Physician, Patient and Society (PPS); and Longitudinal Preceptor Program (LPP). PPS and LPP together introduce students to medical interviewing, physician-patient relationships, physical diagnosis, medical reasoning and decision analyses, population-based medicine, ethics, epidemiology, medical informatics, and preventive medicine. Systems I covers several body/organ systems: Hematology; Cardiovascular; Respiratory; Renal and Acid/Base; Endocrine Regulation; GI/Nutrition; and Reproduction. Second-year courses focus on the biology of disease. They are General Pathology; Neoplasia; General Pharmacology; Microbiology; Mind, Brain and Behavior II; Systems II; and a continuation of PPS and LPP. In Systems II, Dermatology, Musculoskeletal/Renal, and "Pumps, Wind and Water" are among the body systems studied. Basic sciences are taught in a wing of the School's central complex. A new Learning Center houses amphitheaters, flexible classrooms, and a video conference facility. The Lamar Soutter Library holds over 239,000 volumes, subscribes to 1,500 journals, and provides access to online search and database tools. The Library Computer Area contains personal computers and workstations for computer-assisted instruction, interactive programs, and educational databases.

CLINICAL TRAINING

Third-year required rotations are Medicine (12 weeks); Surgery (12 weeks); Family and Community Medicine (6 weeks); Ob/Gyn (6 weeks); Pediatrics (6 weeks); and Psychiatry (6 weeks). Fourth-year requirements are Neurology (4 weeks), a Subinternship in Medicine (4 weeks), and 24 weeks of elective study. Clinical training takes place at the UMass hospital (388 beds), a comprehensive facility with general and specialty services. Clinical specialties include: Cancer Center; Level I Trauma Center; Kidney-Pancreas transplantation; Children's Medical Center; Center of Stone Disease; advanced laser technology; Cardiovascular Center; Breast Center; AIDS programs; burn unit; and public sector psychiatry. UMass benefits from affiliations with hospitals in and around the Worcester area: Memorial Health Care (319 beds); Saint Vincent Hospital; and Berkshire Medical Center (330 beds).

Students

All students are Massachusetts residents. The average age of incoming students is 25, and at least half of students took some time off after college. About 60 percent of students were science majors as undergraduates. Approximately 7 percent of students are under-represented minorities. Class size is 100.

STUDENT LIFE

Recreational and athletic facilities are conveniently located in the lower level of the basic science building. Facilities include a lounge with a TV, pool and ping-pong tables, study areas, and an exercise and weight room. Students are involved in organizations focused on community service, recreational interests, and professional pursuits. Worcester is a city of nearly 200,000, offering a full range of services and activities. Students live off campus, most choosing to live in the local community. Some students rely on public transportation, while others use cars.

GRADUATES

Among 1997 graduates, the most popular fields for post-graduate training were Internal Medicine (28 percent); Family Practice (25 percent); Pediatrics (15 percent); Emergency Medicine (7 percent); Ob/Gyn (4 percent); and Surgery (5 percent). A significant proportion entered residency programs in Massachusetts.

Admissions

REQUIREMENTS

Massachusetts residency is a requirement. Prerequisites are one year each of Biology, General Chemistry, Organic Chemistry, Physics, and English. All science courses should include associated labs. The MCAT is required, and scores should be from within the past two years. For applicants who have taken the exam on multiple occasions, the best scores are weighed most heavily. Thus, withholding scores is not advantageous.

SUGGESTIONS

Applications should be submitted as early as possible. In addition to requirements, coursework in Computer Science; Calculus; Statistics; Sociology; and Psychology is advised. For applicants who have been out of college for a significant period of time, some recent coursework is important. Medically related experiences or research may strengthen an application.

PROCESS

All in-state AMCAS applicants are sent secondary applications. Of those returning secondaries, about half are interviewed between October and March. Interviews consist of two 30-minute sessions with faculty members and/or medical students. On interview day, candidates also have a group information session and campus tour. Approximately one-third of interviewees are accepted on a rolling basis. Wait-listed candidates may send supplementary information if it serves to update their files.

Admissions Requirements (Required)

MCAT scores, Science GPA, Non-science GPA, Letters of recommendation, Interview, Essays/personal statement, Extracurricular activities, Exposure to medical profession

Admissions Requirements (Optional)

State residency

COSTS AND AID

Tuition & Fees

In-state Tuition	$8,352
Cost of books	$725
Fees	$5,736

Financial Aid

% students receiving aid	75
Average debt	$70,068

UNIVERSITY OF MEDICINE AND DENTISTRY OF NEW JERSEY
NEW JERSEY MEDICAL SCHOOL

185 SOUTH ORANGE AVENUE, MEDICAL SCIENCE BUILDING, RM C-653, NEWARK, NJ 07103 • ADMISSION: 973-972-4631
FAX: 973-972-7986 • E-MAIL: NJMSADMISS@UMDNJ.EDU • WEBSITE: WWW.NJMS.UMDNJ.EDU

STUDENT BODY

Type	Public
Enrollment	695
% male/female	51/49
% minorities	32
# applied	4,331
# accepted	170
# enrolled	170

ADMISSIONS
Average GPA and MCAT scores

Overall GPA	3.57
MCAT Bio	10.45
MCAT Phys	10.09
MCAT Verbal	9.59
MCAT Essay	P

Application Information

Regular application	12/1
Regular notification	10/15
Early application	8/1
Early notification	10/1
Are transfers accepted?	Yes
Admissions may be deferred?	Yes
Interview required?	Yes
Application fee	$75

Academics

BASIC SCIENCES: During the first 2 years, small-group sessions and tutorials account for about one-third of scheduled sessions, with the remainder of class time used for lectures and labs. Students are paired with physicians in the community, working with them one afternoon each week as part of primary care preceptorships. Courses demand about 27 hours per week, in addition to individual study time. First-year courses are Biochemistry and Molecular Biology, Cell and Tissue Biology, Genetics, Gross and Developmental Anatomy, Neuroscience, Physiology, Problem-based Learning, Psychiatry, Public Health, and the Art of Medicine. Clinical skills, which focus on the physical examination, are also part of the first year. During the second year, topics are coordinated among courses and are organized around organ systems. Courses are Clinical Preventive Medicine and Nutrition, Immunology, Introduction to Clinical Sciences, Microbiology, Pathology, Pharmacology, and Psychiatry and the Clinical Interview. The Medical Sciences Building, where basic sciences are taught, is connected to the University Hospital and the George F. Smith Library, the latter of which houses 70,000 volumes and more than 2,000 periodicals. The proximity of clinical facilities to classrooms and labs encourages first- and second-year students' involvement in clinical activities. The Office of Student Affairs provides services ranging from personal counseling to guidance on elective and residency selection.

CLINICAL TRAINING

Required third-year clerkships are Internal Medicine (12 weeks), General Surgery (8 weeks), Pediatrics (8 weeks), Obstetrics/Gynecology (8 weeks), Psychiatry (6 weeks), and Family Medicine (6 weeks). During the fourth year, 16 weeks of electives are required in addition to Neurology (4 weeks); Emergency Medicine (4 weeks); Substance Abuse (2 weeks); Physical Medicine and Rehabilitation (2 weeks); Ophthalmology, Orthopedics, Otolaryngology, and Urology (1 week each); and an acting internship in medicine, family medicine, obstetrics, pediatrics, or surgery (4 weeks). Most clinical training takes place at the contiguous 518-bed University Hospital, which serves the needs of the immediate community and, with its specialized care units, attracts patients from around the state. Other affiliated teaching hospitals are Hackensack University Hospital, Morristown Memorial Hospital, Veterans Affairs Health Care System, East Orange, and Kessler Institute for Rehabilitation.

Campus Life

Eighty-four percent of the NJMS entering students are New Jersey residents. Underrepresented minorities account for 19 percent of the student body. The average age of students entering the class of 2005 was 26, ranging from 19 to 41, and the matriculated class size was 170.

STUDENT LIFE

Students are involved in intramural sports and organized student events. Each entering student is assigned to a peer group of first- and second-year students. Students initiate and develop service activities such as: AMA (American Medical Association), AMSA (American Medical Students Assoc.), AMWA (American Medical Women's Association), BLHO (Boricua Latino Health Organization), Center for Humanism and Medicine, Community 2000, which conducts clinical screening and health education with local churches, Early Start Mentoring Program, Family Medicine Interest Group, New Moms, Peer Support, Project Pediatrics (Border Babies), Students Health Advocates for Resources and Education (SHARE), Students are actively involved in community-service projects through the SHARE Center. Student Family Health Care Center (SFHCC) (Clinic), SNMA (Student National Assoc.), STATS (Students Teaching AIDS to Students), Student Council, and Unite for Site.

NJMS is located in University Heights. Newark offers many artistic and creative activities including the performing arts, jazz clubs, and diverse neighborhoods. It is home to the Newark Bears, the New Jersey Symphony Orchestra, the New Jersey State Opera, New Jersey Performing Arts Center, the Newark Museum, the Ballantine House, Newark Symphony Hall, the Newark Library, the Cathedral Basilica of the Sacred Heart and the Garden State Ballet and several institutions of Higher Education. New York City is an easy train ride and serves as a convenient distraction for medical students.

GRADUATES

Each year, graduates are successful in obtaining residencies at prestigious institutions such as Massachusetts General, Columbia Presbyterian, the Children's Hospital in Washington, DC, and New Haven Hospital at Yale. The alumni association is very enthusiastic, and among its activities is the provision of scholarships and research stipends to medical students.

Admissions

REQUIREMENTS

The minimum course requirements are 8 semester hours of biology; 8 semester hours of physics, 16 semester hours chemistry (general or inorganic chemistry and organic chemistry), all with associated labs; and 6 semester hours of English. Although math is not required it is strongly recommended. The MCAT is required; scores must be no more than 3 years old. There is no minimum GPA or MCAT requirement but intense competition tends to favor those with stronger credentials, as the average GPA of our accepted applicants is 3.6 with an average MCAT of 30. Approximately 19 percent of the 4,047 applicants are interviewed with interviews taking place between August and April. About one-third of interviewees are accepted. Wait listed candidates may send supplementary information to update their files.

Applicants are selected on the basis of academic excellence, leadership qualities, demonstrated compassion for others, and broad extracurricular experiences. The Admissions Committee considers related factors such as passion, motivation, perseverance, special aptitudes, and stamina (personal statement, letters of recommendation and the interview are also very important factors in evaluation). NJMS encourages nonresidents to apply but New Jersey residents will be given some preference.

SUGGESTIONS

Research or experience in a health care setting is useful. Personal traits, such as compassion, dedication, and interpersonal skills, are very important.

PROCESS

Once an application file is complete (AMCAS application, MCAT scores, letters of recommendation, supplemental application, and $75 fee) a Screening Committee reviews the applicant's file. If the Screening Committee determines that the applicant should be interviewed, the Office of Admissions notifies and formally invites the applicant for an interview. Applicants are interviewed by medical school faculty and administrators who will discuss personal and educational achievements, motivation, drive, ability, background, personality, long term goals, and extracurricular activities. Interviews vary in length but generally last about one hour.

Admissions Requirements (Required)

MCAT scores, science GPA, non-science GPA, letters of recommendation, interview, essay/personal statement, extracurricular activities

Admissions Requirements (Optional)

State residency, exposure to medical profession

COSTS AND AID

Tuition & Fees

In-state tuition	$22,246
Out-of-state tuition	$34,811
Fees	$885

Financial Aid

% students receiving aid	84

University of Medicine and Dentistry of New Jersey
Robert Wood Johnson Medical School

Office of Admissions, 675 Hoes Lane, Piscataway, NJ 08854 • Admission: 732-235-4576
Fax: 732-235-5078 • E-mail: RWJAPADM@UMDNJ.EDU • Website: WWW.RWJMS.UMDNJ.EDU

STUDENT BODY

Type	Public
Enrollment	642
% male/female	47/53
% minorities	16
# applied (total/out)	3,170/2,026
# accepted (total/out)	369/47
# enrolled (total/out)	165/4
Average age	23

FACULTY

Total faculty (number)	850
% female	35
% minority	23

ADMISSIONS
Average GPA and MCAT scores

Overall GPA	3.64
MCAT Bio	10.5
MCAT Phys	10.4
MCAT Verbal	9.7
MCAT Essay	P

Application Information

Regular application	12/1
Regular notification	Rolling
Early application	6/1–8/1
Early notification	10/1
Are transfers accepted?	Yes
Admissions may be deferred?	Yes
Interview required?	Yes
Application fee	$75

Academics

Students are encouraged to pursue a variety of educational opportunities. In addition to the traditional 4 year medical school curriculum, students may enroll in one of the dual degree options including MD/PhD, MD/JD, MD/MPH, MD/MBA, MS/MS biomedical informatics, and MD/MS jurisprudence. A MS in clinical and translational research is planned for 2007. The flexible curriculum allows the rearranging of certain courses to enable students to pursue the dual degrees, relevant projects, personal interests, research, or employment. Student scholars may take an additional year to pursue the basic science or clinical research or off-campus community health projects. Students who complete a thesis graduate with distinction in research. New distinction programs in service to the community and medical education have been established. The grading policy uses pass/fail in years 1 and 2, and honors/high pass/conditional pass/fail in years 3 and 4. Steps 1 and 2 of the USMLE are required for graduation. Research facilities include the Center for Advanced Biotechnology and Medicine, Child Health Institute, The Cancer Institute of New Jersey, Environmental and Occupational Health Science Institute, Stem Cell Institute, and Cardiovascular Institute.

BASIC SCIENCES: Curricular changes in the first 2 years have been implemented toward the following twofold mission: Better preparation of clinicians as lifelong learners and a shift toward self-directed learning. The changes include more small-group learning, a new course in patient-centered medicine structured as small clinic groups facilitated by a mentor, problem-based approaches, a reduction in lecture time in addition to a systems-based approach in the second year. Clinical correlation is emphasized in all first-year disciplines. First-year courses include the following: Basic Life Support I, Biological Chemistry, Cellular and Genetic Mechanisms and Histology, Epidemiology and Biostatistics, Gross and Developmental Anatomy, Medical Microbiology and Immunology, Medical Physiology, Neuroscience, Patient-Centered Medicine, Principles of Environmental and Community Medicine. Second-year courses include the following: Basic Life Support II, Behavorial Science and Psychiatry, Biochemical Basis of Nutrition, Clinical Pathophysiology, Clinical Prevention and Environmental Medicine, Pathology and Laboratory Medicine, Patient-Centered Medicine, Pharmacology, and Universal Precautions/Venipuncture. A vast array of noncredit pre-clinical electives enriches the experience during the first and second years. Courses include Alternative and Complementary Medicine, Business in Medicine Elective, Community and Child Health, Emergency Room Elective, Geriatric Issues, Humanities in Medicine, and Issues in Women's Health. The Medical Science Complex include 26 state-of-the-art multipurpose classrooms a clinical skills center, and anatomy laboratories for the educational programs.

CLINICAL TRAINING

Most clinical training takes place at the principal teaching hospitals, Robert Wood Johnson University Hospital on the New Brunswick Campus and Cooper University Hospital on the Camden Campus. A Clinical Skills Center with a standardized patient program is used to teach and assess the clinical skills of first, second, third and fourth year medical students. During the third year of medical school, students rotate through clerkships in family medicine, medicine, neurology, obstetrics/gynecology, pediatrics, psychiatry, and surgery. Additionally, there is a significant amount of elective work during the third year. During the fourth-year students are required to take rotations in emergency medicine, neurology, and critical care. A longitudinal care experience runs through the third and fourth years.

Campus Life

Approximately 80 percent of the students apply as New Jersey residents. There is great diversity among the student body. Fifty-one percent of students describe themselves as minorities, with 14 percent from underrepresented groups. Typically between 10–20 percent of the student body took some time off between undergraduate studies and medical school. The class size is 156. One-third of the class completes their clinical training on the Camden campus.

STUDENT LIFE

New Brunswick offers the many amenities of a university city. Princeton and New York City are short train rides away. Students who complete clinical training on the Camden campus enjoy the proximity of Philadelphia. The medical school does not have on-campus housing; however, the school helps students secure accomodations in the area. Medical students have access to Rutgers University athletic facilities which include golf, swimming pools, gyms, squash, racquetball, and volleyball courts. Rutgers also offers social, cultural, and recreational activities for medical students. There are many student organizations and interest groups, including chapters of the major national medical student associations. Many students participate in volunteer organizations including the student run HIPHOP (Homeless and Indigent Persons Health Outreach Project) and UHI (Urban Health Initiatives). Honor societies include Alpha Omega Alpha and the Humanism in Medicine Honor Society.

GRADUATES

Graduates have done particularly well in securing outstanding training positions throughout the country, as well as within the school's training programs. About one-half of the class chooses internal medicine, pediatrics, or family medicine, but all specialties are represented.

Admissions

REQUIREMENTS

Two semesters of biology, general chemistry, organic chemistry, and physics, with laboratory; two semesters of English or writing intensive courses; and one semester of college-level mathematics are required. The MCAT is required and must be no more than 4 years old. For applicants who have taken the exam more than once, all scores are considered, but the most recent score is given the most weight.

SUGGESTIONS

Course work in the behavioral sciences and humanities is recommended. Medically related experiences, research, and community service are all valued by the Admissions Committee.

PROCESS

As a state institution, preference is given to in-state residents; however, the importance of geographic diversity is recognized and out-of-state residents are encouraged to apply. Approximately one-half of New Jersey applicants and 5 percent of out-of-state applicants are interviewed on one of the three campuses: Piscataway, New Brunswick, or Camden. Generally students are interviewed by one faculty member. Some applicants are also interviewed by a student member of the Admissions Committee. All applicants have the opportunity to meet and tour with a current student. About one-third of those interviewed are accepted. Acceptances are offered on a rolling basis. Several alternative means of acceptance exist. There is a combined BA/MD program with Rutgers University. There is also an accelerated acceptance program for students completing post-baccalaureate studies at a number of institutions including the University of Pennsylvania, Columbia, Johns Hopkins, Rutgers, Drexel, NYU, Bryn Mawr, and LaSalle.

Admissions Requirements (Required)

MCAT scores, science GPA, non-science GPA, letters of recommendation, interview, essay/personal statement, extracurricular activities, exposure to medical profession

Admissions Requirement (Optional)

State residency

Overlap School

Rutgers, the State University of New Jersey.

COSTS AND AID
Tuition & Fees

In-state tuition	$22,246
Out-of-state tuition	$34,811
Room and board (off-campus)	$10,026
Cost of books	$1,768
Fees	$3,112

Financial Aid

% students receiving aid	78
Average grant	$5,000
Average loan	$25,000
Average debt	$102,000

UNIVERSITY OF MIAMI
MILLER SCHOOL OF MEDICINE

ADMISSIONS R-159, POB 016159 MIAMI, FL 33101 • ADMISSION: 305-243-6791 • FAX: 305-243-6548
E-MAIL: MED.ADMISSIONS@MIAMI.EDU • WEBSITE: WWW.MIAMI.EDU/MEDICAL-ADMISSIONS

STUDENT BODY

Type	Private
Enrollment	640
% male/female	50/50
% minorities	8
# applied (total/out)	4,551/2,963
# accepted (total/out)	360/133
# enrolled (total/out)	176/51
Average age	22

FACULTY

Total faculty	1,202
% female	12
% minority	7
% part-time	0
Student-faculty ratio	0:1

ADMISSIONS
Average GPA and MCAT Scores

Overall GPA	3.7
MCAT Bio	11
MCAT Phys	10
MCAT Verbal	11
MCAT Essay	P

Application Information

Regular application	12/1
Regular notification	10/15
Are transfers accepted?	No
Admissions may be deferred?	Yes
Interview required?	Yes
Application fee	$65

Academics

Most students follow a four-year curriculum, leading to the M.D. A number of students participate in a six-year B.S./M.D. program organized with Miami's undergraduate college. Up to six students each year enter a combined M.D./Ph.D. program, earning the doctorate degree in Biochemistry and Molecular Biology; Molecular, Cell, and Developmental Biology; Microbiology and Immunology; Molecular and Cellular Pharmacology; Neuroscience; or Physiology and Biophysics. Opportunities for summer research are also available to medical students. Students are graded with percentile scores during the first two years and with ratings of Honors, High Pass, Pass, and Fail during the second two years. Promotion to year three requires a passing score on the USMLE Step 1. Step 2 of the USMLE must be taken in order to graduate.

BASIC SCIENCES: The first year begins with a set of core modules designed to provide medical students with a sound working knowledge of the sciences basic to medicine. There are five modules that last for about five months: Molecular Basis of Life, Cellular Function and Regulation, Host Defenses and Pathogens, Human Structure and Adaptation to Disease, Introduction to Epidemiology and Infectious Diseases. The rest of the first two years are taught in integrated organ system modules. The second year ends with several problem-based, case-based learning sessions. Throughout the first two years, students work with practicing community physicians and learn about history-taking, how to do a physical examination and clinical diagnosis. The acquisition of clinical skills during the first two years is reinforced and broadened through interaction with clinical faculty in Academic Societies. Students are in the classroom about 20 hours per week. Lectures are the primary instructional modality, but small group discussions are also used, and are becoming more important. The basic sciences are taught in the Rosenstiel Medical Sciences Building, which houses newly renovated lecture halls, teaching labs, and a student computer system.

Clinical Sciences: The third and fourth years are actually a continuum in which students take both required clerkships and electives. Required clerkships include Internal Medicine, Surgery, Pediatrics, Generalist-Primary Care, OB/GYN, Family Medicine-Geriatrics, Psychiatry, neurology, Anesthesia, Neurology and Radiology. Some elective time is available in the third year and at the end of the fourth year. Students may choose from a variety of ward experiences and consultation services that provide more advanced training in their specific areas of interest. Up to three months may be spent at other institutions. Clnicial training takes place at Jackson Memorial Hospital (1,567 beds), Veterans Affairs Medical Center (900 beds), Ryder Trauma Center, Sylvester Comprehensive Cancer Center, The Miami Project to Cure Spinal Cord Paralysis, the Diabetes Research Institute and the Mailman Center for Child Development. Clinical opportunities are available at a large number of hospitals in the Miami area.

CLINICAL TRAINING

Required third-year clerkships are Introduction to Medicine (1 week); Radiology (1 week); Medicine (8 weeks); Surgery (8 weeks); Primary Care (8 weeks); Ob/Gyn (6 weeks); Psychiatry (6 weeks); Pediatrics (6 weeks); and Family Medicine (4 weeks). Fourth-year requirements are Geriatrics (2 weeks) and Neurology (4 weeks). The remainder of the fourth year is devoted to selectives, which must include at least eight weeks of Direct Patient Care, and electives which may be clinical or research-based. Clinical training takes place at: Jackson Memorial Hospital (1,567 beds); Veterans Affairs Medical Center (900 beds); Bascom Palmer/Anne Bates Leach Eye Hospital; Sylvester Comprehensive Cancer Center; Ryder Trauma Center; Diabetes Research Institute; and The Mailman Center for Child Development. Up to three months of the fourth year may be spent in clerkships at other institutions.

Students

A recently entering class had the following profile: age range, 18-37; women, 55 percent; underrepresented minorities, 10 percent; Florida residents, 97 percent; Science majors, 65 percent. Thirty-six colleges and universities were represented. Class size is 148.

STUDENT LIFE

Although the medical campus is separate from the main campus, medical students have access to extracurricular programs and events sponsored by the greater University. In addition, the medical campus has athletic and other recreational facilities of its own. Medical students are involved in student organizations and volunteer activities in areas such as AIDS prevention, general health education, and drug-abuse counseling. Students enjoy the good weather and multicultural environment of Miami. Medical students live off campus in various parts of Miami, and usually drive to school or take Metrorail.

GRADUATES

Graduates are successful in securing residency positions nationwide. A significant proportion enter programs at Jackson Memorial Hospital, which features at least 15 postgraduate training programs.

Admissions

REQUIREMENTS

Prerequisites are one year each of Biology, Chemistry, Organic Chemistry, Physics, Math, and English. Science courses should include associated labs. The MCAT is required and scores must be from within the past three years. For applicants who have taken the exam on multiple occasions, the best set of scores is weighed most heavily.

SUGGESTIONS

Florida residents are given preference, and only highly qualified out-of-state residents are encouraged to apply. Recommended coursework includes Biochemistry, Cell and Molecular Biology, Microbiology and Immunology, Genetics, Embryology, Mammalian Physiology, and Computer Science. Students should display achievement in the humanities and social sciences as well as in the natural sciences. Beyond academic credentials, the Committee on Admissions values interpersonal skills, leadership, maturity, motivation, and compassion. Meaningful patient-contact experience is essential.

PROCESS

About 75 percent of Florida residents and 20 percent of out-of-state residents are sent secondary applications. About 300 applicants are interviewed on campus. Interviews take place on Fridays, between August and April, and consist of one session with a faculty member. About 60 percent of interviewed candidates are accepted, with notification occurring on a rolling basis. Approximately 25 positions in each entering class are reserved for participants in the University of Miami Honors Program in Medicine, a six-year B.S./M.D. program.

Admissions Requirements (Required)

MCAT scores, Science GPA, Non-science GPA, Letters of recommendation, Interview, Essays/personal statement, Extracurricular activities, Exposure to medical profession

Admissions Requirements (Optional)

State residency

COSTS AND AID
Tuition & Fees

Tuition	$29,298
Room and board (off-campus)	$11,800
Cost of books	$1,630
Fees	$750

Financial Aid

% students receiving aid	85
Average grant	$9,100
Average loan	$35,300
Average debt	$143,000

UNIVERSITY OF MICHIGAN
MEDICAL SCHOOL

ADMISSIONS OFFICE, M4130 MEDICAL SCIENCE I BUILDING, ANN ARBOR, MI 48109 • ADMISSION: 313-764-6317
FAX: 313-936-3510 • E-MAIL: PIBS@UMICH.EDU • WEBSITE: WWW.MED.UMICH.EDU/MEDSCHOOL

STUDENT BODY	
Type	Public
Enrollment	177
% male/female	51/49
% minorities	15
# applied	4,931
# enrolled	177

ADMISSIONS	
Average GPA and MCAT Scores	
Overall GPA	3.72
Application Information	
Regular application	11/15
Regular notification	Rolling
Early application	6/1–8/1
Early notification	10/1
Are transfers accepted?	No
Admissions may be deferred?	Yes
Interview required?	No
Application fee	$50

Academics

Most students follow a 4 year program leading to the MD, although a growing number opt for combined degrees. A combined MD/PhD curriculum allows students to pursue graduate studies in numerous departments, including anatomy and cell biology, biological chemistry, cellular and molecular biology, human genetics, microbiology and immunology, neuroscience, pharmacology, and physiology. Some MD/PhD students are MSTP participants, while others are funded through institutional sources. For students who are interested in research, but who are not interested in earning an additional degree, summer and year-long research fellowships are available. In addition, combined programs with Public Health and Business Administration are available. Passing Step 1 of the USMLE is a requirement for promotion to year 3 and passing Step 2 is a requirement for graduation.

BASIC SCIENCES: During the first year, grading is strictly satisfactory/fail. This promotes student cooperation and allows for variation in the level of scientific knowledge among incoming students. Throughout the first and second years, students take Introduction to the Patient, which includes interdisciplinary perspectives and the use of simulated patients; and multidisciplinary conferences, which provides clinical correlations for basic science concepts. Other first year courses are Molecular and Cell Biology, Gross Anatomy, Human Genetics, Pathology, Embryology, Histology, Host Defenses, Microbiology, Pharmacology, and Physiology. Year 2 is organized around organ and body systems. These are cardiovascular, dermatology, endocrine, gastrointestinal, hematology, infectious diseases, musculoskeletal, neuroscience, oncology, renal, reproduction, and respiratory. The Medical School's basic science instructional facilities include recently renovated lecture halls with audiovisual and computer equipment. A Learning Resource Center is open 24 hours per day and has more than 50 computers for student use. The Taubman Medical Library is one of the largest in the United States in terms of the number of volumes, journals, and electronic resources that it holds. The Office of Academic Enrichment provides academic counseling and organizes study groups and tutoring services.

CLINICAL TRAINING

During the second, third, and fourth years, students are evaluated with honors/high pass/pass/fail. Third-year required rotations are Surgery (12 weeks), Internal Medicine (12 weeks), Obstetrics/Gynecology (6 weeks), Pediatrics (6 weeks), Family Practice (4 weeks), Neurology (4 weeks), and Psychiatry (4 weeks). Students attend weekly conferences and discuss a range of topics including the ethical, social, and economic issues related to practicing medicine. Fourth-year requirements are sub internship (8 weeks); Intensive Care Unit Experience (4 weeks); Advanced Basic Science Experience (4 weeks); and electives (12–20 weeks), which are selected from more than 300 subjects. Clinical training takes place at the University Hospital (888 beds), St. Joseph Mercy Hospital (522 beds), the Veterans Affairs Hospital (486 beds), and at other affiliated institutions. With approval, students may earn elective credits at other academic or clinical sites in the United States and overseas.

Campus Life

About 50 percent of students are Michigan residents, with the remainder of the student body coming from all regions of the country. Typically, at least 10 percent of entering students are older, having taken some time off after college. Approximately 15 percent of students are underrepresented minorities. Class size is 170.

STUDENT LIFE

Incoming medical students benefit from the support and advice of more senior medical students through a peer-counseling program called Big Sib, Little Sib. Students interact outside of the classroom through participation in organizations that focus on issues such as community service, support for minority and gay/lesbian students, and recreational and professional pursuits. The Furstenberg Student Study Center features a well-being room for information and activities related to student health, computer stations, lounges, and quiet study rooms. Expansive sports and recreation centers also enrich student life on campus. Ann Arbor is an academic and cultural center, attracting scholars from around the world. To serve the university community, the area around the campus is filled with coffee shops, bookstores, restaurants, bars, and shops. In addition to commercial districts, Ann Arbor offers parks, lakes, theaters, farmers markets, and attractive residential areas. Although some limited campus-owned housing is available to medical students, most opt to live in privately owned apartment complexes that are within walking distance of the Medical Center.

GRADUATES

Medical students consistently score above the national average on both steps of the USMLE, contributing to their success in securing top residency positions. Among graduates, popular choices for specialty areas were internal medicine (23 percent), pediatrics (12 percent), surgery (11 percent), family practice (10 percent), obstetrics/gynecology (7 percent), and emergency medicine (6 percent).

Admissions

REQUIREMENTS

Prerequisites are chemistry (8 semester hours, which includes both organic and inorganic); biology (6 semester hours); physics (6 semester hours); English composition and literature (6 semester hours); and biochemistry (3 semester hours). In addition, at least 18 semester hours must be completed in areas other than the natural sciences or math.

SUGGESTIONS

In addition to the required science courses, genetics and cell biology are considered useful preparation for medical school. Humanities and social sciences course work is also important.

PROCESS

All AMCAS applicants are sent supplementary applications. Of those returning secondaries, about 15 percent are interviewed between September and March. Interviews consist of two 30-minute sessions, each with a faculty member or medical student. Candidates are also given a group informational presentation, a campus tour, and lunch with medical students. About one-third of interviewees are accepted and are notified between November and May. Others are rejected or put on a wait list.

Admissions Requirements (Required)

MCAT scores, science GPA, non-science GPA, letters of recommendation, state residency, extracurricular activities, exposure to medical profession

Admissions Requirements (Optional)

Interview, essays/personal statement

COSTS AND AID
Tuition & Fees

In-state tuition	$22,694
Out-of-state tuition	$36,018
Fees	$871

University of Minnesota—Duluth

Medical School

180 Medicine, 1035 University Drive, Duluth, MN 55812 • Admission: 218-726-8511
Fax: 218-726-7057 • E-mail: medadmis@d.umn.edu • Website: www.med.umn.edu/duluth/

STUDENT BODY

Type	Public
Enrollment	114
% male/female	50/50
% minorities	15
# applied (total/out)	1,330/864
# accepted (total/out)	88/17
# enrolled (total/out)	58/5
Average age	24

FACULTY

Total faculty (number)	48
% female	31
% minority	4
% part-time	6
Student-faculty ratio	2:1

ADMISSIONS

Average GPA and MCAT Scores

Overall GPA	3.62
MCAT Bio	9.66
MCAT Phys	9.09
MCAT Verbal	9.45
MCAT Essay	Q

Application Information

Regular application	11/15
Regular notification	Rolling
Early application	8/1
Early notification	10/1
Are transfers accepted?	No
Admissions may be deferred?	Yes
Interview required?	Yes
Application fee	$75

Academics

The University of Minnesota Medical School Duluth is a two-year rural program of the University of Minnesota Medical School in the Twin Cities. The basic science curriculum features system-based courses with clinical correlations and applications. Additionally, early patient contact through the Preceptorship Program in Family Practice is a hallmark of the first two years. Evaluation of medical student performance uses outstanding, excellent, satisfactory, incomplete, and no pass. Passing Step 1 of the USMLE is a requirement for promotion to the Medical School Twin Cities.

BASIC SCIENCES: The 2 year curriculum is a unique blend of basic medical and behavioral sciences and clinical hands-on experiences. The basic sciences, presented using an organ systems approach that begins with Principles of Basic Science, extends to various aspects of the prevention and pathophysiology of organ system disease, and concludes with discussions of several presenting clinical symptoms and multisystems diseases. The behavioral sciences portion of the curriculum emphasizes knowledge about the psycho-social aspects of health and illness that are relevant to the clinical setting and is interwoven with the organ systems component. The clinical experience is directed by community specialists and is augmented by UMD's nationally recognized Family Practice Preceptorship program. In addition to classrooms and labs, the Learning Resource Center serves as a computer and multimedia instructional facility. It is open 24 hours per day. The Biomedical Library houses 496,000 volumes, and 113 online data bases.

CLINICAL TRAINING

After successfully completing the preclinical years, students transition to the Twin Cities campus for their clinical clerkships. Selected required and elective rotations can be completed in Duluth and in some rural communities in Minnesota. These are Medicine (12 weeks), Obstetrics/Gynecology (6 weeks), Surgery (6 weeks), Pediatrics (6 weeks), Psychiatry (6 weeks), Neurology (4 weeks), Surgical Specialty (4 weeks), Emergency Medicine (4 weeks), and Ambulatory Care (8 weeks). The remaining time is reserved for elective study. Clinical facilities include Abbott Northwestern Hospital, Children's Health Care, Fairview-University Medical Center, Hennepin County Medical Center, Regions Hospital, St. Luke's Hospital (Duluth), St. Mary's Medical Center, and other sites. Each year, through the Rural Physician Associate Program, up to 40 third-year medical students study primary health care in a 9 month elective in Minnesota rural communities under the supervision of local physicians. Up to 12 weeks of clinical electives may be fulfilled at nonaffiliated institutions in other parts of the country or abroad.

Campus Life

STUDENT LIFE

Small class size and students' shared interest in family medicine promotes a supportive and cohesive atmosphere. University recreational events, facilities, and activities are open to medical students, including the student center, the gym, intramural sports, and student organizations. Students also take advantage of the extracurricular opportunities afforded by the school's location. Activities such as cycling, running, skiing, hiking, and camping are easily accessible within or around Duluth. Duluth functions as a cultural center for Northern Minnesota and has a symphony, a ballet, theaters, and art museums. Affordable off-campus housing options in the immediate area are available.

GRADUATES

About 95 percent of students are Minnesota residents. About 15 percent of students are minorities, most of whom are Native American. Class size is 58. At least 70 percent of graduates enter primary care fields, and most go on to practice in rural areas.

Admissions

REQUIREMENTS

Priority consideration is given to Minnesota residents who wish to become family practice physicians in a rural Minnesota setting or Native American community. Applicants from other states who demonstrate a high potential and motivation for practicing medicine in rural Minnesota or an American Indian community will also be considered. Applicants must be U.S. citizens or permanent residents and must have completed all requirements for a baccalaureate degree by the time of possible matriculation. Prerequisites are one quarter or semester of biology with lab; one quarter or semester of chemistry with lab; four additional quarters or semesters of life sciences (biology, genetics, zoology, botany, parasitology, etc.), biochemistry, chemistry, or physics, including at least two upper level courses; and one quarter or semester of humanities or social sciences with an extensive writing requirement. The MCAT is required, and scores must be no more than 3 years old.

SUGGESTIONS

UMD looks for applicants who demonstrate interest in entering family practice and working with underserved rural or small town communities in Minnesota or American Indian communities.

PROCESS

Secondary applications are sent to all applicants who are U.S. citizens or permanent residents. Of those returning secondaries, about 22 percent are invited to interview between October and April. Interviews consist of two 1-hour sessions, each with a member of the Admissions Committee. Notification occurs on a rolling basis, and about 63 percent of interviewees are offered a place in the class.

Admissions Requirements (Required)

MCAT scores, science GPA, non-science GPA, letters of recommendation, interview, state residency, essays/personal statement

Admissions Requirements (Optional)

Extracurricular activities, exposure to medical profession

Overlap Schools

A.T. Still University of Health Sciences, Creighton University, Mayo Clinic College of Medicine, Medical College of Wisconsin, University of Minnesota, University of Wisconsin—Madison.

COSTS AND AID
Tuition & Fees

In-state tuition	$28,227
Out-of-state tuition	$35,541
Room and board (off-campus)	$13,838
Cost of books	$2,534
Fees	$2,861

Financial Aid

% students receiving aid	99
Average scholarship	$2,000
Average loan	$45,000

University of Minnesota—Twin Cities

Medical School

Office of Admissions, PO Box 293, 420 Delaware Street, Southeast, Minneapolis, MN 55455 • Admission: 612-625-7977
Fax: 612-625-8228 • E-mail: MEDED@UMN.EDU • Website: WWW.MED.UMN.EDU

STUDENT BODY	
Type	Public
Enrollment	910
# applied (total/out)	2,528/1,872
# accepted	260
# enrolled (total/out)	165/34

ADMISSIONS
Average GPA and MCAT scores

Overall GPA	3.67
MCAT Bio	10.8
MCAT Phys	10.3
MCAT Verbal	10.1
MCAT Essay	P

Application Information

Regular application	11/15
Regular notification	Rolling
Early application	6/1–8/1
Early notification	10/1
Are transfers accepted?	Yes
Admissions may be deferred?	Yes
Interview required?	Yes
Application fee	$75

Academics

In addition to a 4 year curriculum leading to the MD degree, Minnesota offers a combined degree MSTP MD/PhD program, leading to the doctorate degree in biochemistry, biomedical engineering, biophysics, cell biology, genetics, immunology, microbiology, molecular biology, neuroscience, pharmacology, and physiology. Dual degree programs are also offered— MD/MPH, MD/MBA, MD/MHI, MD/MS [BME], JD/MD. Evaluation of medical student performance in year 1 and year 2 is pass/fail/honors. Evaluation of performance in the year 3 and year 4 curriculum uses grades of honors/excellent/satisfactory/incomplete/fail. Passing both steps of the USMLE is a graduation requirement. Faculty members serve as advisors to medical students.

BASIC SCIENCES: Basic sciences are taught as part of an interdisciplinary curriculum that also includes behavioral, social, and ethical aspects of medicine in addition to introductory clinical instruction. On average, students are in class or other scheduled sessions for 24 hours per week. First-year courses are Gross Anatomy; Histology; Biochemistry; General Pathology; General Pharmacology; Human Behavior; Human Genetics; Human Sexuality; Microbiology; Molecular and Cellular Biology; Neuroscience; Nutrition; Physiology; Physician and Society; and Physician and Patient, the last of which focuses on history-taking and the physical examination. Second-year curriculum is systems-based. The courses are Pathology—Systemic, Pathophysiology, Pharmacology, Physician and Patient, and Physician and Society. Second-year students participate in four 6-week tutorials in family practice, internal medicine, pediatrics, and neurology. First and second year instruction takes place in the Moos Health Tower and other buildings in the basic science complex. The Biomedical Library contains more than 428,000 volumes, 4,393 journals, 1,194 audiovisual programs, and 223 computer programs. The reference department has more than 50 computers and has access to several online databases.

CLINICAL TRAINING

Students rotate through required clerkships during their third and fourth years: Medicine (12 weeks), Ambulatory Care (8 weeks), Obstetrics/Gynecology (6 weeks), Surgery (6 weeks), Pediatrics (6 weeks), Psychiatry (6 weeks), Neurology (4 weeks), Emergency Medicine (6 weeks), and Surgical Specialty (4 weeks). The remaining time is reserved for elective study. Clinical facilities include the Fairview-University Medical Center, Variety Club Heart and Research Center, Masonic Cancer Center, Veterans of Foreign Wars Cancer Research Center, Children's Rehabilitation Center, Paul F. Dwan Cardiovascular Research Center, Hennepine County Medical Center, Regions Hospital, Abbott Northwestern Hospital, Veteran's Administration Hospital, and other hospitals and ambulatory medical facilities in the Twin Cities area. Each year, through the Rural Physician Associate Program, up to 40 third-year medical students study primary health care in Minnesota communities under the supervision of local physicians. One-fourth of clinical electives may be fulfilled at non-affiliated institutions in other parts of the country or abroad.

Campus Life

Of the 165 students in last year's entering class, 79 percent were Minnesota residents and 21 percent were multicultural. About 10 percent were from underrepresented minority groups. Typically, the average age of incoming students is 24.

STUDENT LIFE

Some students work part-time as graduate research or teaching assistants while in medical school. These positions provide academic opportunities and a source of income or tuition reduction. The Medical Student Adytum (adytum is Greek for "innermost sanctuary") is a spacious, comfortable area reserved solely for medical students and their guests. Students use the facility for studying, socializing, eating, and relaxing. Medical students also have the opportunity to interact with other health sciences students at an alternate student center—Center for Health Interdisciplinary Participation. Organizations bring students together around common interests, allowing them to contribute to the community and providing extracurricular activities. Examples of student organizations are Healthy Moms, Happy Babies; Phillips Neighborhood Clinic; Medical Student Computer Group; CLARION; Confidential Peer Assistance Program; SNMA; Physicians for Human Rights; and Students' International Health Committee. The medical school is part of the greater university, and medical students have access to its athletic and recreational facilities. Beyond the campus, the cities of Minneapolis and St. Paul offer a wide variety of restaurants, shopping, cultural activities, and entertainment. Housing options include residence halls, medical fraternities, and privately-owned apartments that are adjacent to the medical center.

GRADUATES

In the 2007 graduating class, the most popular fields for residencies were internal medicine (22 percent), family practice (16.9 percent), emergency medicine (8.4 percent), surgery (4 percent), pediatrics (5.8 percent), obstetrics/gynecology (5 percent), and orthopaedic surgery (4.4 percent). Generally, at least half of graduates enter postgraduate programs in Minnesota.

Admissions

REQUIREMENTS

Prerequisites are biology (2 semesters/quarters), general chemistry (2 semesters/quarters), organic chemistry (2 semesters/quarters), physics (2 semesters/3 quarters), English composition and literature (2 semesters), calculus (1 course), and biochemistry (1 course). In addition, 4 semesters/6 quarters of social and behavioral sciences and humanities are required. This requirement includes one course in psychology, with remaining course work in at least two of the following areas: Anthropology, comparative studies, history, music or art, philosophy, and sociology. The MCAT is required, and scores must be no more than 3 years old.

SUGGESTIONS

Minnesota residents are given preference. As indicated by the social science/humanities requirement, breadth in undergraduate preparation is important. In addition to academic strength, applicants should demonstrate volunteer/community service activity, personal integrity, high ethical standards, motivation, intellectual curiosity, enthusiasm, dedication to lifelong learning, and the ability to work well with others. Consistent with the Medical Student Education Mission, the Medical School seeks to matriculate a diverse student body. Diversity benefits the education of all students and supports the Medical School's commitment to graduate physicians who will serve the health needs of a diverse society. In evaluating an applicant's potential contribution to diversity in the Medical School, disadvantaged background, race and ethnicity, evidence of outstanding leadership, creativity, unique work or service experience, community involvement, noneducational progression, and demonstrated commitment to working with diverse populations are considered.

PROCESS

Qualified applicants who submit AMCAS applications are sent secondaries. Of those returning secondaries, about 80 percent of Minnesota residents and 30 percent of out-of-state applicants are invited to interview. Interviews take place on campus from September through March and consist of one session with a faculty member. Of interviewed candidates, about 25 percent of Minnesota residents and 15 percent of out-of-state residents are offered a place in the class. Applicants are accepted on a rolling admission basis, October through April. Additional materials from wait listed candidates are not accepted.

Admissions Requirements (Required)

MCAT scores, science GPA, non-science GPA, letters of recommendation, interview, essay/personal statement, extracurricular activities, exposure to medical profession

Admissions Requirement (Optional)

Research

COSTS AND AID
Tuition & Fees

In-state tuition	$27,405
Out-of-state tuition	$34,506
Room and board (on-campus)	$10,200
Room and board (off-campus)	$13,398
Cost of books	$2,100

Financial Aid

% students receiving aid	93
Average grant	$2,000
Average loan	$40,500
Average debt	$134,500

UNIVERSITY OF MISSISSIPPI
MEDICAL CENTER

2500 NORTH STATE STREET JACKSON, MS 39216 • ADMISSION: 601-984-5010
FAX: 601-984-5008 • E-MAIL: ADMITMD@SOM.UMSMED.EDU • WEBSITE: WWW.SOM.UMC.EDU

STUDENT BODY

Type	Public
Enrollment	407
% male/female	49/51
% minorities	14
# applied (total)	295
# accepted (total)	155
# enrolled (total)	110
Average age	24

FACULTY

Total faculty (number)	590
% female	24
% minority	14
% part-time	19
Student-faculty ratio	1:1

ADMISSIONS
Average GPA and MCAT scores

Overall GPA	3.5
MCAT Bio	9.4
MCAT Phys	8.6
MCAT Verbal	9.4
MCAT Essay	0

Application Information

Regular application	10/15
Regular notification	3/15
Early application	8/1
Early notification	10/1
Are transfers accepted?	Yes
Admissions may be deferred?	Yes
Interview required?	Yes
Application fee	$50

Academics

While most medical students follow a 4-year curriculum leading to the MD, some take advantage of other schools within the Medical Center and pursue joint-degree programs such as the combined MD/PhD curriculum, which leads to the doctorate in anatomy, biochemistry, microbiology, neuroscience, pathology, and pharmacology. Medical students receive percent scores and a class rank and may be awarded honors at the time of graduation. To be eligible for promotion, a student must achieve at least a 70 in each course, have a weighted average of 75 or higher, and attend 80 percent of the lectures and classes. Passing the USMLE Step 1 is a requirement for promotion to year 3, and passing Step 2 is a requirement for graduation.

BASIC SCIENCES: The basic sciences are integrated with clinical science courses and are taught through a combination of lectures, small groups, labs, and hands-on clinical experiences. Students are in class or other scheduled activity for about 22 hours per week. First-year courses are Behavioral Science and Psychiatry, Biochemistry, Cardiopulmonary Resuscitation, Gross Anatomy, Histology, Medical Physiology, and Neurobiology. Second-year courses are Biostatistics, Clinical Psychiatry, General and Systemic Pathology, Introduction to Clinical Medicine (ICM), Medical Genetics, Medical Microbiology, Pharmacology, and Preventive Medicine and Public Health,. In the ICM course, students learn history-taking, examination, and diagnosis skills through classroom presentations and small group sessions. The ICM experience helps prepare students for the clinical phase of the curriculum. Basic science instruction facilities are central to the campus and include the Holmes Learning Resources Center, which houses the Rowland Medical Library. The library is impressive, with more than 160,000 volumes and 2,500 periodicals.

CLINICAL TRAINING

Required third-year rotations are Family Medicine (6 weeks), Medicine/Neurology (12 weeks), Obstetrics/Gynecology (6 weeks), Psychiatry (6 weeks), Pediatrics (6 weeks), and Surgery (12 weeks). The fourth year is organized into 8-month-long blocks of selectives. Students choose specialty areas from within internal medicine, obstetrics/gynecology, pediatrics, and surgery. Throughout the fourth year, students participate in a Senior Seminar, which provides a forum for interdisciplinary instruction and discussion of issues relevant to modern medical practice. Clinical training takes place at the Medical Mall Ambulatory Clinic, and State Health Department offices. E. Batson Hospital for Children, in the 722-bed university hospitals and clinics—which include four new hospitals, The University Hospital, The Wiser Hospital for Women and Infants, the Conerly Hospital for Critical Care, the Veterans Administration Hospital, McBryde Rehabilitation Center for the Blind, Jackson Medical Mall, and State Health Department Clinics.

Campus Life

In recent years, all students have been Mississippi residents. Approximately 10 percent of students are underrepresented minorities, most of whom are African Americans. The average age of incoming students is generally around 24. The class size is 110.

STUDENT LIFE

Medical students use the resources and facilities of the university in addition to those of the greater community. As the state capital of Mississippi, Jackson offers numerous cultural and recreational attractions. Beyond clinical-care provision, the medical school contributes directly to the community through activities such as the Base-Pair Mentorship Program, which pairs medical school researchers and high school students and encourages them to pursue jointly academic projects.

GRADUATES

Graduates are successful in securing positions in a range of specialty areas. At the university hospital in Jackson, there are more than 38 residency programs into which a number of graduates enter each year.

Admissions

REQUIREMENTS

Due to high competition in the admissions process, state residency is virtually a requirement. Required science courses are 8 semester hours each of biology, chemistry, organic chemistry, and physics, all with associated labs. Three semester hours of College-level Algebra and 3 of College-level Trigonometry or 3 semester hours of calculus satisfies the Math requirement. Six semester hours of English, and six semester hours of advanced Science or Mathematics are additional prerequisites. The MCAT is required.

SUGGESTIONS

The April, rather than August, MCAT should be taken by applicants. Beyond requirements, some advanced science course work in areas such as Advanced Physics, Anatomy, Biochemistry, Embryology, Genetics, Histology, Physiology, or Physical chemistry is recommended. Other suggested courses are Advanced Computer Science, English, Fine Arts, Foreign Language, Geography, History, Philosophy, Psychology, and Sociology. Math and science courses designed for non-science majors are not counted toward minimum requirements.

PROCESS

All Mississippi residents who submit AMCAS applications are sent secondary applications. About half of those returning secondary applications are interviewed between August and January. Candidates have 3 interview sessions, each with a faculty member or administrator. In addition, a tour of the campus and the opportunity to have lunch with a current medical student is provided. Among interviewees, about half are accepted with notification occurring throughout the application cycle. Wait listed candidates may send additional information to update their files.

Admissions Requirements (Required)

MCAT scores, science GPA, non-science GPA, letters of recommendation, faculty letters of evaluation, interview, state residency, essay/personal statement, extracurricular activities, exposure to medical profession

COSTS AND AID
Tuition & Fees

In-state tuition	$9,649
Out-of-state tuition	$20,482
Room and board (off-campus)	$14,211
Cost of books	$2,184

Financial Aid

% students receiving aid	96
Average grant	$7,000
Average loan	$20,500
Average debt	$23,000

UNIVERSITY OF MISSOURI—COLUMBIA
SCHOOL OF MEDICINE

MA215 MEDICAL SCIENCES BUILDING COLUMBIA, MO 65212 • ADMISSION: 573-882-9219
FAX: 573-884-2988 • E-MAIL: EASTONM@MISSOURI.EDU • WEBSITE: WWW.MUHEALTH.ORG/~MEDICINE

STUDENT BODY

Type	Public
Enrollment	375
% male/female	51/49
% minorities	7
# applied (total/out)	916/506
# accepted (total/out)	160/40
# enrolled (total/out)	95/5

FACULTY

Total faculty (number)	542
% female	30
% minority	14
% part-time	16
Student-faculty ratio	1:1

ADMISSIONS
Average GPA and MCAT scores

Overall GPA	3.77
MCAT Bio	10.5
MCAT Phys	10.1
MCAT Verbal	9.8
MCAT Essay	P

Application Information

Regular application	11/1
Regular notification	3/15
Early application	8/1
Early notification	10/1
Are transfers accepted?	Yes
Admissions may be deferred?	Yes
Interview required?	Yes
Application fee	$75

Academics

Although most students complete the MD curriculum in 4 years, some follow an extended program, leading to the MS or PhD along with the MD doctoral programs are available in diverse areas.

BASIC SCIENCES: Missouri is one of the leaders in the movement toward problem-based learning. Students learn in small groups and, with less than 20 hours per week in scheduled sessions, have ample time for self-study or individualized projects. The first 2 years are organized into eight 10-week blocks, each of which consists of 8 weeks of instruction followed by 1 week of evaluation and 1 week of vacation. Each block is divided into 2 general instructional components, Problem-based Learning and Introduction to Patient Care. Block one is devoted to the Structure and Function of the Human Body, covering biochemistry, anatomy, histology, embryology, and molecular biology and genetics. Blocks 2, 3, and 4 each focus on a set of body/organ systems,which include the following: cardiovascular, respiratory, renal, gastrointestinal, metabolism, endocrine, neuroscience, liver, pulmonary, hematology, reproductive, immune response, and pharmacokinetics. Year 2 is comprised of blocks 5–8, which concentrate on pathophysiology and clinical management. One of the main objectives of the second year is to prepare students for clinical rotations. Grading for the first year is satisfactory/unsatisfactory, and for the second year, it is honors/satisfactory/unsatisfactory. The medical library and computer facilities are comprehensive and serve as educational resources for faculty, students, and the medical community.

CLINICAL TRAINING

Year 3 is divided into 7 blocks of required clerkships, which are the following: Child Health, Family Medicine, Internal Medicine, Obstetrics/Gynecology, Psychiatry, Neurology, and Surgery. A separate rural track offers up to 6 months of clinical experience in a rural community during the third year in lieu of some of the required rotations. Year 4 consists of 12 weeks of general electives and three 4-week advanced clinical selectives—1 must be in a core medical specialty, and another must be in a core surgical specialty. Finally, fourth-year students must complete 8 weeks of advanced basic science selectives. The majority of clinical training is conducted at University Hospital and Clinic, a 288-bed tertiary care facility that draws patients from throughout Central Missouri. Other training sites include Children's Hospital, Ellis Fischel Cancer Center, Columbia Regional Hospital, Truman Veterans Affairs Hospital, and the Missouri Rehabilitation Center. In total, clinical training sites encompass over 1,000 patient beds. Grading for both of the clinical years is honors/letters of commendation/satisfactory/unsatisfactory. Students must pass Step 1 of the USMLE to be promoted to year 4 and Step 2 CK and Step 2 CS to graduate.

Campus Life

The University of Missouri—Columbia is a state school, and the vast majority of the 96 entering students are Missouri residents. A large percentage attended the various public undergraduate colleges and universities throughout the state. Among students in the 2006 entering class, 70 percent were science majors as undergraduates. Approximately 7 percent of the medical students are underrepresented minorities. The average age of incoming students is usually 24.

STUDENT LIFE

The School of Medicine is located in the heart of the University of Missouri's main campus, allowing students to take advantage of its recreational, athletic, and entertainment facilities. The curriculum gives students flexibility within their schedules, allowing them to explore both their academic and non-academic interests. Student organizations are active, particularly the local chapter of the American Student Medical Association, which coordinates academic, social, and cultural events and sponsors community-service projects. Columbia is located within a few hours of both Kansas City and St. Louis. Most medical students live in privately owned apartments, generally a short distance from campus.

GRADUATES

About half of the graduates enter residencies in one of the primary care fields. A limited number of students seeking primary care careers are selected for a program that integrates the senior year of medical school with residency training in family medicine, internal medicine, pediatrics, or psychiatry.

Admissions

REQUIREMENTS

The School of Medicine requires 8 credit hours each of the following courses, all of which must be taken with associated labs: biology, general chemistry, general physics, and organic chemistry. In addition to the traditional premedical courses, 1 semester of math and 2 semesters of English composition are also prerequisites. The MCAT is required. If a student has taken the MCAT more than once, the highest total set of MCAT scores is considered.

SUGGESTIONS

Course work in biology and chemistry beyond the requirements and biochemistry is strongly recommended. In addition, applicants are encouraged to study humanities and social sciences while in college.

PROCESS

All Missouri residents (and some residents of other states) who submit an AMCAS application receive a secondary application, which should be submitted as soon as possible. Almost 50 percent of the Missouri-resident applicants and at least 50 out-of-state applicants are invited to interview between October and April. Students are interviewed one-on-one by 2 members of the Admissions Committee. Current medical students give a short tour of the facilities and host a lunch. About a month after interviewing, applicants may be notified of the committee's decision. Approximately 40 percent of interviewed candidates are accepted. Wait listed candidates are not encouraged to send supplementary information.

Admissions Requirements (Required)

MCAT scores, science GPA, non-science GPA, letters of recommendation, interview, essay/personal statement, extracurricular activities, exposure to medical profession

Admissions Requirements (Optional)

State residency, required course work from an accredited college

COSTS AND AID
Tuition & Fees

In-state tuition	$22,987
Out-of-state tuition	$44,749
Room and board	$8,720
Cost of books	$2,305

Financial Aid

% students receiving aid	94
Average grant	$3,495
Average loan	$33,495
Average debt	$119,666

UNIVERSITY OF MISSOURI—KANSAS CITY
SCHOOL OF MEDICINE

COUNCIL ON SELECTION, 2411 HOLMES, KANSAS CITY, MO 64108-2792 • ADMISSION: 816-235-1870
FAX: 816-235-6579 • E-MAIL: MORGENEGGM@UMKC.EDU • WEBSITE: WWW.UMKC.EDU/MED

STUDENT BODY

Type	Public
Enrollment	630
% male/female	40/60
% minorities	9
# applied (total/out)	476/199
# accepted (total/out)	176/44
# enrolled (total/out)	118/21
Average age	18

FACULTY

Total faculty (number)	484
% female	32
% minority	14

ADMISSIONS
Average GPA and MCAT Scores

MCAT Essay	M

Application Information

Regular application	11/15
Regular notification	4/1
Are transfers accepted?	No
Admissions may be deferred?	No
Interview required?	Yes
Application fee (in/out)	$35/$50

Academics

Rather than distinguishing premedical course work, pre-clinical medical course work, and clinical instruction, the curriculum integrates liberal arts, didactic medical sciences, and clinical training. Grading is letter grade, honors/credit/no credit, and narrative, and students must pass both Steps of the USMLE to graduate.

BASIC SCIENCES: During the first 2 years, students focus most of their efforts on working toward a baccalaureate degree through arts and science course work. Seventy-five percent of classroom hours are devoted to liberal arts studies and 25 percent to introductory medical course work. Year 1 (35 weeks) consists of undergraduate-level courses in Biology, General Chemistry, Introduction to Medicine, Psychology, and Sociology. The Introduction to Medicine Course gives special attention to the effects of illness on the patient, family, and community. Students become acclimated to the hospital environment and are introduced to the medical vocabulary and to basic clinical skills such as patient interviews and simple data gathering. The second year (44 weeks) includes Biostatistics, Human Biochemistry, Life Cycles, Medical Physiology, Organic Chemistry, and ongoing introductory clinical experiences. In years 3 and 4 (both 48 weeks), students take courses in Anatomy, Microbiology, Pathology, and Pharmacology and participate in clinical rotations, including a weekly continuing care clinic and family medicine preceptorship. Throughout the first 4 years, additional liberal arts courses are included in the curriculum that are considered part of the BA. To assist with clinical training, a physician-scholar (or docent) instructs and advises groups of 11 or 12 students. The docent acts as a mentor, guide, and preceptor throughout the entire six years.

CLINICAL TRAINING

Students enter fifth- and sixth-year clerkships having already had significant clinical exposure. They continue their weekly continuing care clinic experience. Year 5 (48 weeks) is comprised of rotations in Obstetrics/Gynecology (2 months), Pediatrics (2 months), Surgery (2 months), Internal Medicine (2 months), Community Medicine/Family Practice (1 month), and Psychiatry (1 month). One month is reserved for electives. The sixth year (48 weeks) gives students ample opportunity to explore their specific areas of interest with 6 months of elective rotations. Required rotations include internal medicine (2 months) and emergency medicine (1 month). During the fifth or sixth year, students also take 1 month of liberal arts courses. Most training takes place at Truman Medical Center, one of the clinical facilities associated with UMKC.

Campus Life

Approximately 80 percent of students are Missouri residents. Others come from high schools in neighboring states and other regions of the country. Underrepresented minorities account for about 6 percent of the student body. As a result of the structure of the program, students within a class are all roughly the same age.

STUDENT LIFE

For the most part, classes run year-round. Although the atmosphere is intense, students are committed and supportive of one another particularly because of the junior-senior partnership program. Students enjoy the resources of both the undergraduate campus and Kansas City. All students live on campus during the first year, but most choose to live off campus for the remainder of their studies.

GRADUATES

Graduates are successful in securing residency positions in all fields. Approximately 25 percent enter programs affiliated with UMKC.

Admissions

REQUIREMENTS

Applicants for admission at the freshman level must take the American College Test (ACT) or the SAT (out-of-state applicants only). Applicants should have completed 4 years of high school English; 4 years of math; 3 years of science, including 1 year each of biology and chemistry; 3 years of social studies; 1 year of foreign language; and 1 year in the fine arts. In addition, 1 year of physics and 1 semester of computer science are highly recommended by the medical school. If Advanced Placement (AP) courses are available, these are recommended as well. A limited number of positions are available at the year 3 level. Applicants to year 3 must have completed the standard premedical requirements of 1 year each of biology, chemistry, and organic chemistry as well as other requirements. The MCAT is required of these applicants, and scores must be from within the past 3 years.

SUGGESTIONS

For applicants to the BA/MD program and for those applying after college, some medically related experience is considered useful. High school students are encouraged to volunteer or work in a hospital or other health care environment.

PROCESS

UMKC is not a part of AMCAS. Applications may be obtained from the address above and are due by November 15. Interviews take place between December and mid-March and consist of two sessions, each of which is one-on-one. In addition to the interview, students and their parents attend group orientation sessions that cover a range of topics including financial aid. Applicants tour the campus and have the opportunity to meet with current students. All candidates are notified of the Admissions Committee's decision on April 1. Some are accepted from a wait list later in the spring.

Admissions Requirements (Required)

Letters of recommendation, interview, essays/personal statement, performance on the Toledo Chemistry Assessment

Admissions Requirements (Optional)

MCAT scores, science GPA, non-science GPA, state residency, extracurricular activities, exposure to medical profession

COSTS AND AID

Tuition & Fees

In-state tuition	$26,933
Out-of-state tuition	$52,229
Room and board (on-campus)	$7,390
Cost of books	$800
Fees	$1,169

Financial Aid

Average loan	$27,000

University of Montreal
Faculté de Médecine

CP 6128, Succursale Centre-Ville, Montreal, QC H3C 3J7 • **Admission:** 514-343-6265
E-mail: FACMED@MEDDIR.UMONTREAL.CA • **Website:** WWW.MED.UMONTREAL.CA

STUDENT BODY	
Type	Public
# applied (total/out)	1,859/270

ADMISSIONS	
Application Information	
Regular application	3/1
Regular notification	3/31
Admissions may be deferred?	No
Interview required?	Yes
Application fee	$45

Academics

Type Public Instruction is solely in French. Some students enter a 1-year premedical program that curriculum leads into the 4 year MD curriculum, while others who qualify enter the medical directly. Although clinical exposure begins during the first year of premedical or medical training, intensive clinical training begins in the third year. The premedical program is taught through lectures. On the other hand, the majority of instruction for medical students takes place in a small-group setting. In addition to the 4 year MD curriculum, Application Information graduate degree programs are offered in all major medical science fields. Affiliated with the School of Medicine are other health science programs in areas such as health administration, public health, social and preventive medicine, nutrition, rehabilitation, and speech language therapy.

BASIC SCIENCES: Students who enter the premedical program take courses in Basic Concepts in Ethics, Biostatistics, Cell Biology and General Histology, Cell and Molecular Biology, Cell Physiology and Pharmacology, Clinical Immersion, Genetics and Embryology, General Microbiology and Virology, Introduction to Clinical Anatomy, Introduction to Physiology, Introduction to Sociology, Nutrition and Metabolism, Psychology and Human Behavior, and an elective. First-year medical school courses are Introduction to Medical Studies; Growth, Development, and Aging; General Pathology and Immunology; Infectious Diseases; Hematology; Neurological Sciences; Mind; Musculoskeletal System; Introduction to Clinical Medicine; History of Medicine; Epidemiology; and an elective. Second year studies are largely organized by anatomical systems. These are cardiovascular, digestion, endocrinology, multisystem, respiratory, and kidney. Second-year students also take an elective and continue with introduction to clinical medicine.

CLINICAL TRAINING

For clinical training, students complete a series of required clerkships held over two years (80 weeks) that provide hands-on experience in the major medical disciplines. During the third year, required clerkships are Medicine (8 weeks), Surgery (8 weeks), Pediatrics (8 weeks), Psychiatry (8 weeks), Obstetrics/Gynecology (8 weeks), and Family Medicine (4 weeks). Third-year students also have the opportunity for a 4 week clinical elective. Fourth-year clerkships are Emergency Medicine (4 weeks), Radiology (2 weeks), Geriatrics (4 weeks), Community Medicine (4 weeks), Anesthesiology (1 week), Ophthalmology (1 week), and an elective (4 weeks). Selectives are chosen from medical or pediatric subspecialties (8 weeks) and from surgical subspecialties (4 weeks). Clinical training takes place at more than 15 affiliated hospitals including Hôpital Maisonneuve-Rosemont, Hôpital Notre-Dame, Hôpital Riviere-des-Prairies, Hôpital du Sacre-Coeur de Montréal, Hôpital Louis-H Lafontaine, Hôpital Sainte-Justine, Hôpital Saint-Luc, Hôtel-Dieu de Montréal, Institute de Cardiologie de Montréal, Institut de Readaptation de Montréal, Centre Hospitalier de Verdun, Cite de la Sante de Laval, Institut de Recherches Clinique de Montréal, Institut Philippe-Pinel de Montréal, Centre Hospitalier Cote-des-Neiges, Centre Hospitalier Régional de Trois-Rivières and Centre Hospitalier de Shawinigan. Since 2004, a regional campus has been established in Mauricie (150 km from Montreal). Each year, 32 students are admitted to take the undergraduate or complete formation, wich includes the premedical year and four years of medecine. Moreover, the university also has several affiliations in foreign regions of the Québec province.

Campus Life

Entering class size is 259. In a recent class, all but four students were from the province of Quebec. About 60 percent of the students are women.

STUDENT LIFE

Medical students enjoy a good quality of life. The School of Medicine is committed to its students, providing academic and nonacademic support services. Outside of the classroom, medical students interact through student groups and organized social activities. The resources of the greater university, including athletic and recreational facilities, are available to medical students as well. Finally, the city of Montreal is an internationally recognized cultural center with a wealth of activities accessible to students.

GRADUATES

Graduates enter both academic and clinical medicine. At hospitals affiliated with the University of Montreal, postgraduate medical training is available in anesthesiology, family medicine, medicine, obstetrics/gynecology, ophthalmology, pediatrics, psychiatry, radiology, surgery, and many other postgraduate programs.

Admissions

REQUIREMENTS

Only Canadian citizens, landed immigrants, and highly qualified French-speaking applicants from the United States are considered for admission. Fluency in French is a requirement. Two years of college is the minimum requirement for admission to the School of Medicine. Prerequisites are behavioral sciences, biology, English, French, general chemistry, mathematics (through trigonometry), organic chemistry, philosophy, physics, social sciences.

SUGGESTIONS

Strong preference is given to applicants from the province of Quebec. Selection is based on both records of academic performance and interviews.

PROCESS

The absolute deadline for applications is March 1. About one-third of all applicants are asked to interview, with invitations based on the candidate's academic record. The strongest candidates are then selected from those interviewed. Admissions decisions are made in the spring, with the first acceptance notices given in May. Accepted applicants have 2 weeks in which to confirm their place in the entering class.

Admissions Requirements (Required)

Interview

COSTS AND AID
Tuition & Fees

In-state tuition	$2,575
Out-of-state tuition	$12,836
Fees	$30

UNIVERSITY OF NEBRASKA MEDICAL CENTER
COLLEGE OF MEDICINE

986585 NEBRASKA MEDICAL CENTER OMAHA, NE 68198-6585 • ADMISSION: 402-559-2259 • FAX: 402-559-6840
E-MAIL: GRROGERS@UNMC.EDU • WEBSITE: WWW.UNMC.EDU/UNCOM/

STUDENT BODY

Type	Public
Enrollment	476
% male/female	57/43
% minorities	11
# applied (total/out)	1,373/1,050
# accepted (total/out)	166/47
# enrolled (total/out)	121/22
Average age	24

FACULTY

Total faculty	672
% part-time	16

ADMISSIONS
Average GPA and MCAT Scores

Overall GPA	3.73
MCAT Bio	10
MCAT Phys	9.4
MCAT Verbal	9.7
MCAT Essay	0

Application Information

Regular application	11/1
Regular notification	Rolling
Early application	8/1
Early notification	10/1
Are transfers accepted?	Yes
Admissions may be deferred?	No
Interview required?	Yes
Application fee	$45

Academics

Most medical students complete the M.D. curriculum in four years, although some may take an additional year for research projects or other activities. A combined M.D./Ph.D. program is offered to qualified students, leading to the doctorate degree in a number of fields, including Cell Biology and Anatomy, Biochemistry and Molecular Biology, Physiology and Biophysics, Pathology and Microbiology, and Pharmacology. For medical students interested in discrete research projects, summer research stipends are available on a competitive basis. Passing the USMLE Step 1 is a requirement for promotion to year three, and all students must record a score on Step 2 in order to graduate.

BASIC SCIENCES: Throughout the first two years, basic sciences are integrated with introductory clinical instruction and topics are organized into blocks, referred to as Cores. Students are in class for about 32 hours per week, most of which is spent in lectures, small groups, or labs. During the first year, these are Structure and Development of the Human Body; Cellular Processes; Neuroscience; and Function of the Human Body. Throughout the first and second years, Integrated Clinical Experience (ICE) covers the history and physical examination, interviewing skills, behavioral sciences, ethics, preventive medicine, health care policy, and health care services research. Through ICE, students have the opportunity to work alongside primary care physicians in a longitudinal clinical experience and a summer preceptorship. Also spanning both years is Problem-Based Learning, in which students work in small groups and apply basic science concepts to clinical case studies. Second year Cores are Introduction to Disease Processes; Cardiology/Pulmonary/Endocrinology/Ear, Nose, and Throat; Neurology, Ophthalmology and Psychiatry; Hematology/Oncology/Musculoskeletal; Dermatology and Infectious Disease; and Genitourinary/Gastroenterology. The Leon S. McGoogan Library of Medicine holds over 200,000 volumes and 2,100 current journals. Multimedia materials for computer-assisted and self-instruction are available, as are online informational systems.

CLINICAL TRAINING

Required third-year clerkships are: Internal Medicine (12 weeks); Ob/Gyn (6 weeks); Pediatrics (8 weeks); Surgery (10 weeks); Psychiatry (6 weeks); Community Preceptorship (8 weeks); Basic Science Selective (4 weeks); and a mini-clerkship in an area of choice (2 weeks). During the fourth year, a basic science selective in addition to 28 weeks of electives are required. Clinical facilities at UNMC are Nebraska Health System (650 beds); University Medical Associates, which operates over 60 primary care and subspecialty clinics throughout the greater Omaha metropolitan area; Meyer Rehabilitation Institute; Omaha Veterans Affairs Medical Center; Children's Hospital; Immanuel Hospital; and Methodist Hospital.

Students

Most students in each class are Nebraska residents. Class size is 130.

STUDENT LIFE

Medical students are active in student organizations ranging from the Student Alliance for Global Health, to the Family Practice Club, to a group focused on alternative medicine. The local chapter of the American Medical Student Association is particularly active, organizing volunteer projects, film series, and opportunities for enhanced clinical exposure. Omaha is a city of 900,000, offering a symphony, theaters, art museums, shopping, restaurants, and parks, among other attractions. Students live off campus in the surrounding communities, where, for an urban area, housing is relatively inexpensive.

GRADUATES

Students are successful at securing residencies in both primary care and specialty areas. A significant percentage of graduates enter post-graduate programs at UNMC, which oversees 18 residency programs. In recent years, at least 60 percent of graduates have gone on to practice in the state of Nebraska.

Admissions

REQUIREMENTS

Prerequisites are Biology (8 semester hours); General Chemistry (8 hours); Organic Chemistry (8 hours); Physics (8 hours); Humanities and/or Social Sciences (12 hours); English Composition (3 hours); Calculus or Statistics (3 credits); Biochemistry (3 hours); and Genetics (3 hours). All science courses must include associated labs. The MCAT is required, and scores must be from 2006 or later.

SUGGESTIONS

State residents are given preference, but other highly qualified candidates are considered, particularly if they have ties to Nebraska and are interested in practicing in underserved communities in the state. Beyond required courses, the following are recommended: Molecular Biology, Immunology and Microbiology, Communications, Ethics, and Personnel Management.

PROCESS

All Nebraska residents who apply through AMCAS, and a small percentage of out-of-state applicants, are asked to submit supplementary materials and are interviewed. Interviews are conducted between October and January, and consist of a 30-minute session with a faculty member. On interview day, there is also a group information session and a campus tour. Typically, about 40 percent of Nebraska residents are accepted, with notification beginning in December.

Admissions Requirements (Required)

MCAT scores, Science GPA, Non-science GPA, Letters of recommendation, Interview, State residency, Essays/personal statement, Extracurricular activities, Exposure to medical profession

COSTS AND AID

Tuition & Fees

In-state Tuition	$21,988
Out-of-state Tuition	$51,560
Room and board	$14,400
Cost of books	$1,800
Fees	$2,346

Financial Aid

% students receiving aid	90
Average grant	$0
Average loan	$0
Average debt	$118,669

UNIVERSITY OF NEVADA
SCHOOL OF MEDICINE

OFFICE OF ADMISSIONS, MS#0357 RENO, NV 89557-0357 • ADMISSION: 702-784-6063 • FAX: 702-784-6194
E-MAIL: ASA@MED.UNR.EDU • WEBSITE: WWW.MEDICINE.NEVADA.EDU/

STUDENT BODY

Type	Public
Enrollment	224
# applied (total/out)	988/677
# accepted (total/out)	62/5
# enrolled (total/out)	62/5
Average age	23

FACULTY

Total faculty	170

ADMISSIONS
Average GPA and MCAT Scores

Overall GPA	3.6

Application Information

Regular application	11/1
Regular notification	1/15
Early application	06/01–08/01
Early notification	10/1
Are transfers accepted?	Yes
Admissions may be deferred?	Yes
Interview required?	Yes
Application fee	$45

Academics

The first two years provide a foundation in basic clinical sciences, significant preclinical training, and clerkships that take place statewide in community clinics as well as hospital settings. The School of Medicine applicants or current medical students may apply to jointly pursue a M.D./Ph.D. program in several areas including cell and molecular biology, pharmacology, and physiology. For students interested in research without undertaking a Ph.D., projects can be arranged with faculty members.

BASIC SCIENCES: The first two years at Nevada focus on the basic sciences , but also give considerable attention to community health and social issues. Additional scientific material is presented through lectures, labs, and small group formats at the Reno campus. Students apply scientific principles to clinical challenges through problem-solving courses using case study methods. This approach promotes the development of problem-solving skills in medical students. Concurrent with basic and behavioral science courses, students learn fundamental skills for doctor-patient relationships and physical exams through weekly sessions that are supervised by physicians and senior medical students. In this way, students learn not only from full-time faculty but also from knowledgeable and experienced clinical faculty physicians throughout the state. First-year coursework includes Human Biochemistry, Human Anatomy, Embryology, Histology, Neuroanatomy, Human Behavior, Medical Cell Biology, Neurosciences, Systems Physiology, Clinical Problem Solving, Nutrition, and Introduction to Patient Care. Year two courses include Human Genetics, Medical Mircobiology, Medical Pharmacology, Pathology, Laboratory Medicine, Psychiatric Medicine, Medical Ethics, Community Medicine, Introduction to Patient Care II, and Clinical Problem Solving II. Most courses are graded on a letter grade from A through F, and students must receive at least a C to be promoted. Students are evaluated on both cognitive and noncognitive factors. Two major medical libraries serve the medical students: the Savitt Medical Library on the Reno campus, containing more than 40,000 volumes, and the University Medical Center Library in Las Vegas, both of which maintain computer labs that feature an assortment of general and curriculum-based software. Additional learning resource labs are available in Las Vegas in the ambulatory care centers. Students have electronic access to all of Nevada's university and community college collections through terminals located throughout the teaching sites in the state. Students are issued computer accounts for email and Internet access. In addition, the USMLE Step 1 is required passage for promotion to year three.

CLINICAL TRAINING

Training takes place at affiliated hospitals, clinics, and ambulatory care centers throughout the state. Most students have required rotations including The Practice of Medicine, which is a 24-week integrated clerkship experience that includes Family Medicine (6 weeks), Internal Medicine (12 weeks) and Pediatrics (6 weeks). The Practice of Medicine also includes a core curriculum that runs throughout the state via distance education facilities. Medical students also complete required specialty rotations of Ob/Gyn (6 weeks), Psychiatry (6 weeks), and Surgery (12 weeks). There is an increased emphasis in all of the rotations to blend ambulatory and hospital-based practice to give the students a balanced educational experience. During the fourth year, students rotate through 32 weeks of elective clerkships and 4 weeks of a required rural clerkship. Elective study can take place in Reno, Las Vegas, rural Nevada, other states, or abroad. Although the obvious emphasis and strength of the program is primary care and rural medicine, hospitals in Reno and Las Vegas treat urban and often international populations. Evaluation of clinical performance is Honors/Pass/Fail. In addition, special awards and honors are granted to students who have made unique and outstanding achievements in clinical areas. Passing the USMLE Step 2 is required for graduation.

Students

Eighty-five percent of students majored in a science-related discipline in college. About 5 percent are underrepresented minorities, most of whom are Mexican or Native American. Almost all students are Nevada residents, although many attended college in other states. About one quarter of each class took some time off between college and medical school.

STUDENT LIFE

Small class size promotes cohesion among students. A designated lounge on campus gives medical students a place to relax and interact. Athletic facilities are available: Students in the Reno area use the Lombardi Recreational Facility and, in Las Vegas, the McDermott Physical Education Facility. Student organizations include AMWA & OSR medical specialty interest groups, the Significant Others Group for partners of medical students, and the University of Nevada Student Outreach Clinic, through which medical students, with supervision, volunteer to treat patients from underserved areas. Beyond campus, Lake Tahoe is just an hour from Reno and offers outstanding outdoor activities all year. Virtually all medical students live off campus, where housing is affordable and comfortable.

GRADUATES

The majority of graduates enter residency programs outside the state. Almost all graduates ultimately become practicing clinical physicians.

Admissions

REQUIREMENTS

Required coursework includes Biology (12 Semester hours); Chemistry (8 hours); Organic Chemistry (8 hours); Physics (8 hours); and Behavioral Science (6 hours). The Biology and Behavioral Science requirements specify that at least 3 semester hours be upper-division credit. GPA is used, along with MCAT scores, to screen for interview invitations. The most recent MCAT scores are used, and the exam must have been taken within the past 3 years.

SUGGESTIONS

Only applicants from Nevada, Wyoming, Alaska, Montana, and Idaho, and those who have close ties to Nevada are considered for admission. Nevada residents are given preference. Community-focused work and health care experience are considered important.

PROCESS

Interviews are held from September through January. The interview is composed of two 50-minute sessions, which may be with faculty, or medical students. Of interviewed candidates, about 25 percent of Nevada residents are offered a place in the class, and about 10 percent of out-of-state applicants are accepted. The first acceptances are sent in January. Wait-listed candidates are ranked.

Admissions Requirements (Required)

MCAT scores, Science GPA, Non-science GPA, Letters of recommendation, Interview, State residency, Essays/personal statement, Extracurricular activities, Exposure to medical profession

COSTS AND AID

Tuition & Fees

In-state Tuition	$13,075
Out-of-state Tuition	$32,931

Financial Aid

% students receiving aid	91

UNIVERSITY OF NEW MEXICO
SCHOOL OF MEDICINE

MSC 08 4690, BMSB ROOM 106, ALBUQUERQUE, NM 87131 • **ADMISSION:** 505-272-4766
FAX: 505-272-8239 • **E-MAIL:** SOMADMISSIONS@SALUD.UNM.EDU • **WEBSITE:** WWW.HSC.UNM.EDU/SOM

STUDENT BODY

Type	Public
Enrollment	324
% male/female	43/57
% minorities	43
# applied (total/out)	994/760
# accepted (total/out)	92/4
# enrolled (total/out)	75/4
Average age	28

FACULTY

Total faculty (number)	715
% part-time	14
Student-faculty ratio	2:1

ADMISSIONS
Average GPA and MCAT Scores

Overall GPA	3.59
MCAT Bio	9.8
MCAT Phys	9.1
MCAT Verbal	9.5

Application Information

Regular application	11/15
Regular notification	3/15
Early application	8/1
Early notification	10/1
Are transfers accepted?	Yes
Admissions may be deferred?	Yes
Interview required?	Yes
Application fee	$50

Academics

The 4 year curriculum is organized into 3 phases, all of which involve at least some basic science instruction and clinical training. In addition, all students conduct research projects under the guidance of a faculty mentor. The complete project consists of research, presentation, and a written paper. Applicants interested in pursuing a combined MD/PhD may apply to the graduate committee at the School of Medicine in addition to completing medical school admissions requirements. Medical students are evaluated as outstanding, good, satisfactory, marginal, and unsatisfactory. The USMLE Step 1 must be passed prior to graduation, and Step 2 must be taken to graduate.

BASIC SCIENCES: The first year and a half (phase I) is organized into discrete segments, most of which focus on an organ system. First-year subjects are cardiovascular/pulmonary, foundations, GI/nutrition/metabolism, musculoskeletal, Neuroscience, and renal/endocrine. During the summer following year 1, students take part in a 3-month practical immersion experience that involves hands-on clinical work in either a rural or urban setting. Phase I continues in the first semester of year 2 with Human Sex and Reproduction, Infectious Disease, Neoplasma, and Molecular Genetics. A range of learning methodologies are used, including lectures, labs, discussions, tutorials, and seminars. Concurrent to basic science instruction are weekly clinical experiences in both inpatient and ambulatory settings. Here, students learn interviewing and examination techniques, and are able to improve communication and personal interaction skills. Much of phase I and II take place in the Basic Medical Sciences Building. The nearby Health Sciences Center Library supports educational, research, and clinical activities. It houses 150,000 volumes in addition to audiovisuals, online search services, and computer software.

CLINICAL TRAINING

Phase II begins midway through year 2 with a 3-week pharmacology block and orientation to the hospital. Clinical rotations are accompanied by ongoing small-group sessions focused on problem solving and integrating information. Students rotate through required clerkships throughout the spring and summer of the second year and the fall and winter of the third year. Requirements are Internal Medicine (8 weeks), Surgery (8 weeks), Neurology/Psychiatry (8 weeks), Family Medicine Ambulatory (8 weeks), Pediatrics Ambulatory/Inpatient (8 weeks), and Obstetrics/Gynecology Ambulatory/Inpatient (8 weeks). Phase III begins in the spring of year 3 and is comprised entirely of selectives and electives. A one month-long, community-based preceptorship, in which students work alongside a primary care physician who serves as a mentor, is also required. Clinical training takes place at the University Hospital (370 beds) and at several affiliated sites, namely: Regional Federal Medical Center (429 beds); UNM Cancer Center; UNM Mental Health Center; UNM Children's Psychiatric Hospital (73 beds); and the Carrie Tingley Hospital for Children.

Campus Life

About 25 percent of students are underrepresented minorities, most of whom are Mexican Americans. At least 90 percent of students are New Mexico residents, and about half of each class graduated from UNM's undergraduate college. In a recent class, the average age of entering students was 25, and around one-third of students took time off after college. Class size is 73.

STUDENT LIFE

The medical school is located on the North campus of UNM, allowing students access to the resources and facilities of the university. The city also provides an outlet for students who need a break from studying. The greater Albuquerque metropolitan area is home to nearly one-third of the state's population and offers numerous cultural and recreational opportunities. Although no on-campus housing is available, off-campus options are convenient and comfortable.

GRADUATES

About 35 percent of graduates enter residencies at UNM, which offers programs in 12 different departments. The majority of graduates enter primary care fields.

Admissions

REQUIREMENTS

Prerequisites are general biology (8 semester hours), general chemistry (8 semester hours), organic chemistry (8 semester hours), physics (6 semester hours), and biochemistry (3 semester hours). Competency in English and the MCAT are additional requirements.

SUGGESTIONS

Knowledge of Spanish or a Native American language is an advantage. Course work in the humanities and social sciences is important. The April, rather than August, MCAT is advised. Students are selected on the basis of academic achievement, motivation for the study of medicine, problem-solving ability, self-appraisal, ability to relate to people, maturity, breadth of interest and achievements, professional goals, and the likelihood of serving the health care needs of the state following postgraduate training.

PROCESS

All New Mexico AMCAS applicants receive secondary applications and are invited to interview. Qualified WICHE and other out-of-state applicants who apply for early decision are also sent secondary materials and invited to interview. Interviews are conducted from June through March and consist of two sessions with members of the Admissions Committee, who are either full-time faculty members or community physicians. On interview day, lunch and a tour of the facilities are provided. Of interviewed candidates, about 20–25 percent are accepted. Wait listed candidates are ranked and notified of their position on the list.

Admissions Requirements (Required)

MCAT scores, letters of recommendation, interview, state residency, essays/personal statement, extracurricular activities, exposure to medical profession

Admissions Requirements (Optional)

Science GPA, non-science GPA

COSTS AND AID

Tuition & Fees

In-state tuition	$12,893
Out-of-state tuition	$37,032
Room and board (off-campus)	$9,976
Cost of books	$1,546
Fees	$1,749

Financial Aid

% students receiving aid	89
Average grant	$3,700
Average loan	$23,000
Average debt	$91,461

THE UNIVERSITY OF NORTH CAROLINA AT CHAPEL HILL

SCHOOL OF MEDICINE

121 MacNider Building, CB #9500, Chapel Hill, NC 27599 • Admission: 919-962-8331
Fax: 919-966-9930 • E-mail: ADMISSIONS@MED.UNC.EDU • Website: WWW.MED.UNC.EDU

STUDENT BODY	
Type	Public
% male/female	54/46

ADMISSIONS	
Average GPA and MCAT Scores	
Overall GPA	3.7
MCAT Bio	10.57
MCAT Phys	10.48
MCAT Verbal	10.25
Application Information	
Regular application	11/1
Early application	8/1

Academics

The core curriculum gives students the required comprehensive education needed before they embark on the next stage of their careers. In addition, many students pursue focused research training in the clinic or at the bench. Research stipends are available through training grants or individual research grants. Students with a particular interest in research may apply for the MSTP-supported MD/PhD program at UNC. Other students take the opportunity to combine an advanced degree in business, law, or public health with their medical studies. Grades of honors, pass, and fail are used to evaluate medical students in the first 2 years. Students must pass the USMLE Step 1 examination before promotion to the third year and pass Step 2 before graduation.

BASIC SCIENCES: The first 2 years are devoted primarily to studying the scientific basis of clinical practice, with emphasis on demonstrating clinical implications and correlation. Clinical instruction begins early in the first year with the 2 year course Introduction to Clinical Medicine (ICM), in which students have the opportunity to develop the clinical skills (such as history-taking, physical examination) and problem-solving abilities needed for the clinical years. ICM also serves as a forum for discussion of a wide range of cross-cutting topics such as substance abuse, domestic violence, and computing in medicine. Three months of both the first and second years are spent in a community working with a physician tutor. Other first-year courses are Biochemistry, Cell Biology, Gross Anatomy, Histology, Immunology, Introduction to Pathology, Medical Embryology, Medical Physiology, Medicine and Society, Microbiology, and Neurobiology. Many of the courses in the second year are organized around the pathophysiology of particular organ systems such as cardiovascular, endocrine, gastrointestinal, hematology/oncology, musculoskeletal, neurology and special senses, reproductive biology, respiratory, skin, and urinary. Closely integrated with the study of particular organ systems are courses in genetics, humanities, pathology, psychiatry, and social sciences. Throughout the first and second years, students participate in small-group discussions, lectures, labs, clinical practice sessions, and real clinical experiences. The needs of the curriculum are well served by continuous training in information technology coupled with the requirement that each student have a laptop computer. The Health Sciences Library serves the Schools of Dentistry, Medicine, Nursing, Pharmacy, and Public Health and the UNC Hospitals. The library has approximately 300,000 volumes, 4,000 serial titles, and 9,000 audiovisual and microcomputer software programs.

CLINICAL TRAINING

Students rotate through 6 major clinical disciplines during their third year. These are medicine (12 weeks), pediatrics (8 weeks), surgery (8 weeks), Family Medicine (6 weeks), Psychiatry (6 weeks), and Obstetrics/Gynecology (6 weeks). An additional requirement is life support skills (1 week). The purpose of the fourth-year program is to offer a flexible educational experience that can be tailored to the career goals and intellectual interests of each student. Requirements are an ambulatory care selective (4 weeks), an acting internship (4 weeks), a neuroscience selective (4 weeks), and a critical care/surgery selective. A total of 28 weeks of electives is required, some of which may be completed at other universities or clinical settings, either in the United States or overseas.

Campus Life

Approximately 90 percent of students are North Carolina residents. The School of Medicine is committed to admitting students who are representative of the diversity of the population of North Carolina. About one-third of entering students have pursued other interests or careers before applying to medical school.

STUDENT LIFE

The School of Medicine is responsive to students' needs and provides a range of support services. Faculty advisors are assigned to entering students and serve as mentors and academic counselors throughout all 4 years. The School of Medicine has 26 student organizations, including the student body government, student chapters of national medical professional organizations, community service groups, and special interest groups. Students are particularly active in outreach efforts such as Habitat for Humanity, the Domestic Violence Coalition, Physicians for Social Responsibility, and manage two community clinics. During the academic year, scheduled events bring faculty, students, families, and the community together. The university offers single room accommodations for some graduate students in a building near the medical center. Other students live off campus in surrounding neighborhoods.

GRADUATES

Among 2,000 graduates, 53 percent entered primary care fields, and 30.6 percent chose postgraduate training programs within North Carolina. Eighty-four percent of the class of 2000 matched with one of their top three choices for residency training.

Admissions

REQUIREMENTS

Prerequisites are under review and may be changed. Current prerequisites are 8 semester hours of biology, at least 4 hours of which must be accompanied by a lab. Students are strongly encouraged to have taken at least one course in molecular and cell biology. Eight semester hours of general chemistry, organic chemistry, and physics, all with lab, are also required, in addition to 6 semester hours of English. The MCAT is required.

SUGGESTIONS

Preference is given to residents of North Carolina. Thus, successful applicants who are not residents of North Carolina typically have outstanding qualifications.

PROCESS

Approximately 50 percent of AMCAS applicants who are North Carolina residents, and fewer than 10 percent of nonresidents, are sent secondary applications and are invited to interview. Interviews take place between August and March and consist of two sessions with faculty members and one member of the Admissions Committee. On interview day, candidates also have lunch with currently enrolled medical students and go on tours of the campus.

COSTS AND AID	
Tuition & Fees	
In-state tuition	$9,802
Out-of-state tuition	$33,468
Room and board	
(on-campus)	$12,128
Cost of books	$1,050
Fees	$1,616

UNIVERSITY OF NORTH DAKOTA
SCHOOL OF MEDICINE AND HEALTH SCIENCES

OFFICE OF ADMISSIONS, 501 N. COLUMBIA RD., STOP 9037 GRAND FORKS, ND 58202-9037 • ADMISSION: 701-777-4221
FAX: 701-777-4942 • E-MAIL: JDHEIT@MEDICINE.NODAK.EDU • WEBSITE: WWW.MED.UND.NODAK.EDU

STUDENT BODY

Type	Public
Enrollment	242
% male/female	50/50
% minorities	13
# applied (total/out)	261/129
# accepted (total/out)	84/28
# enrolled (total/out)	62/17
Average age	24

FACULTY

Total faculty (number)	1,489
% female	44
% minority	18
% part-time	91
Student-faculty ratio	2:1

ADMISSIONS
Average GPA and MCAT scores

Overall GPA	3.62
MCAT Bio	9.5
MCAT Phys	8.7
MCAT Verbal	9.2
MCAT Essay	O

Application Information

Regular application	11/1
Regular notification	1/15
Are transfers accepted?	No
Admissions may be deferred?	Yes
Interview required?	Yes
Application fee	$50

Academics

Pre-clinical instruction takes place at the University of North Dakota campus in Grand Forks, and clinical training takes place throughout the state. After students have been admitted to the MD program, they may apply to pursue a joint MD/PhD program in anatomy and cell biology; biochemistry and molecular biology; microbiology and immunology; and physiology, pharmacology, and therapeutics. Evaluation of students is with ratings of satisfactory/unsatisfactory during the first year and honors/satisfactory/unsatisfactory for the final 3 years. Step 1 and 2 of the USMLE must be passed to graduate.

BASIC SCIENCES: An interdisciplinary approach is utilized to teach the basic sciences. A combination of lectures, labs, and small-group sessions are used. The curriculum puts significant emphasis on active student participation and early clinical experience. Social science topics such as statistics, human behavorial patterns, and social issues that are relevant in North Dakota and other rural areas are integrated into the basic science and clinical curriculum throughout the first and second years. The first-year courses are organized into blocks, namely Biology of the Nervous System, Biology of Organ Systems I; Biology of Organ Systems II; and Functional Biology of Cells and Tissues. These blocks are offered in the morning. The afternoons are reserved for self-study or Introduction to Patient Care (IPC), which is the clinical component and is also organized into blocks, such as IPC Block I—Interviewing and Professionalism. The same format continues into the second year. Second-year blocks include: Introduction to Pathobiology and Pathobiology I, II, and III. The IPC component again is covered during afternoon sessions. Students also complete their first clinical rotation, Introduction to Inpatient and Ambulatory Practice of Medicine (3 weeks). Most instruction takes place in either the Medical Sciences Building, which houses administrative offices, classrooms, labs and the library or the nearby Clinical Education Center. The Harley E. French Library of the Health Sciences has over 80,000 books, periodicals, and audiovisual programs. It is fully automated and offers computers for informational and research purposes.

CLINICAL TRAINING

Third-year required clerkships include Family Medicine (8 weeks); Medicine (8 weeks); Pediatrics (8 weeks); Obstetrics/Gynecology (8 weeks); Psychiatry (8 weeks); and Surgery (8 weeks); and Clinical Epidemiology, which is taken throughout the year. Students are assigned to the Bismarck, Fargo, or Grand Forks campuses for the third year, or they may participate in the ROME (Rural Opportunities in Medical Education) program. ROME students are assigned to a rural practice site for 7 months of their third year and to their home campus for the balance of the year. During the fourth year, students train at regional sites in Bismarck, Fargo, Minot, and Grand Forks. Each campus is affiliated with 10–22 hospitals and provides health care services to 9–18 counties. The fourth year includes acting internships and electives. Clinical students train at sites throughout the state, including community hospitals, clinics that are part of the Indian Health Service, and physicians' offices. The University of North Dakota's Center for Rural Health focuses on policy analysis and research on rural health care delivery at the state, regional, and national levels.

Campus Life

Most students are North Dakota residents, though up to 11 students in each class may be from Minnesota, Montana, and Wyoming. Up to 7 students in each class (admitted as part of INMED) are Native American. In total, underrepresented minorities account for about 13 percent of the student body. About 20–25 percent of an entering class is composed of older students who took time off between college and medical school. The class size is 62.

STUDENT LIFE

Grand Forks is a community of 50,000 people, located in the Red River Valley on the border between North Dakota and Minnesota. The city is affordable and safe and offers the services that students need. Students have access to the facilities of the greater university and are encouraged to participate in student organizations, including the local chapters of national medical student organizations. On-campus housing is available, though many students opt to live off campus. Since clinical training takes place around the state, students will experience a variety of living situations throughout their 4 years.

GRADUATES

About one-half of the graduates enter residency programs in primary care fields, and a significant number go on to practice in North Dakota. Postgraduate training programs are offered at all the regional training sites.

Admissions

REQUIREMENTS

State residency is a requirement, with the exception of applicants certified by the Western Interstate Commission for Higher Education (WICHE) and Native Americans, admitted through the INMED Program, who must be enrolled members of a federally recognized tribe. Minnesota residents also are given some consideration. Prerequisite course work in the following areas is required: biology (8 hours), college algebra (3 hours), general chemistry (8 hours), language arts (6 hours) organic/biochemistry (8 hours), physics (8 hours), and psychology/sociology (3 hours). All science course work must be completed with the appropriate laboratory sessions. A minimum GPA of 3.0 is expected. The MCAT is required, and scores must be no more than 3 years old. For applicants who have retaken the test, the most recent set of scores is considered.

SUGGESTIONS

Preference is given to students who are broadly educated in the sciences and humanities. For students who have been out of college for a period of time, some recent course work is suggested. Computer literacy also is advised.

PROCESS

North Dakota does not participate in AMCAS. Applicants may apply either online or using the traditional paper application. Applications can be requested from the address listed above or at www.med.und.nodak.edu. About 40 percent of applicants are invited to interview in December or January. The committee consists of faculty, administrators, practicing physicians, and medical students. After interviewing, candidates are notified of the committee's decision within 4–6 weeks. About 40 percent of the interviewees are accepted. Wait listed candidates are not encouraged to send supplementary information.

Admissions Requirements (Required)

MCAT scores, science GPA, non-science GPA, letters of recommendation, interview, state residency, essay/personal statement, extracurricular activities, exposure to medical profession

COSTS AND AID
Tuition & Fees

In-state tuition	$18,908
Out-of-state tuition	$50,482
Room and board	$8,704
Cost of books	$2,250
Fees	$1,262

Financial Aid

% students receiving aid	98
Average grant	$1,250
Average loan	$35,380
Average debt	$123,520

UNIVERSITY OF OKLAHOMA
COLLEGE OF MEDICINE

PO Box 26901, OKLAHOMA CITY, OK 73190 • ADMISSION: 405-271-2331
FAX: 405-271-3032 • E-MAIL: ADMINMED@OUHSC.EDU • WEBSITE: WWW.MEDICINE.OUHSC.EDU/ADMISSIONS

STUDENT BODY

Type	Public
Enrollment	601
% male/female	61/39
% minorities	26
# applied (total/out)	1,288/884
# accepted (total/out)	221/46
# enrolled (total/out)	164/19
Average age	23

FACULTY

Total faculty (number)	856
% female	32
% part-time	20
Student-faculty ratio	1:1

ADMISSIONS
Average GPA and MCAT scores

Overall GPA	3.69
MCAT Bio	9.81
MCAT Phys	9.48
MCAT Verbal	9.90
MCAT Essay	O

Application Information

Regular application	10/15
Are transfers accepted?	Yes
Admissions may be deferred?	No
Interview required?	Yes
Application fee	$65

Academics

All students spend their first 2 years on the Oklahoma City campus. On completion of year 2, about 25 percent of the class enter clinical rotations at sites affiliated with the University of Oklahoma's Tulsa campus. Tulsa is particularly well-equipped for primary care and community-based medical instruction. Qualified students may pursue the joint MD/PhD degree from any graduate department. OUHSC also offers a joint-MD/MPH. Medical students are evaluated on an A–F scale. They must pass Step 1 of the USMLE to be promoted to year 3, and graduates must take, but not necessarily pass, Step 2 to earn their diploma.

BASIC SCIENCES: Basic sciences are taught through lectures, labs, computer-assisted instruction, problem-based learning, and small-group discussions. During the first 2 years, students are in class or other scheduled sessions for 20–25 hours per week, allowing ample time for self-directed study. First-year courses are Biochemistry/Molecular Biology, Embryology, Gross Anatomy, Histology, Human Behavior I, Integrated Medical Problem Solving, Medical Statistics, Neuroscience, Principles of Clinical Medicine I, and Physiology. Second-year courses are Human Behavior II, Integrated Medical Problem Solving, Introduction to Human Illness, Microbiology and Immunology, Principles of Clinical Medicine II, Pharmacology, and Professional Ethics and Professionalism. Basic sciences are taught in the Basic Sciences Education Building, which, in addition to class-rooms and labs, houses a study area. The Robert Bird Library contains more than 250,000 books, journals, and audiovisuals and has two special collections—the Indian Health Collection and the Rare Book Collection. Students can access a number of online catalogs and databases from the library.

CLINICAL TRAINING

Third-year rotations are Medicine (8 weeks), Surgery (8 weeks), Obstetrics/Gynecology (6 weeks), Psychiatry (6 weeks), Pediatrics (6 weeks), Family Medicine (4 weeks), Geriatrics (4 weeks), specialty selectives (6 weeks), and Neuroscience (2 weeks). Fourth-year clerkships are specialty selectives (6 weeks), Adult Ambulatory Medicine (4 weeks), a rural preceptorship (4 weeks), and clinical electives (24 weeks). Clinical affiliates and training sites are OU Medical Center, Department of Veterans Affairs Medical Center, Oklahoma Medical Research Foundation, Oklahoma City Clinic, Oklahoma Allergy Clinic, Dean A. McGee Eye Institute, Oklahoma Blood Institute, State Medical Examiner's Office, Department of Mental Health, and Oklahoma State Department of Health. Students may also do training at the Baptist Medical Center, St. Anthony Hospital, and Mercy Health Center in Oklahoma City. At the Tulsa campus, clinical facilities contain more than 2,000 patient beds, and additional rural training sites are currently being developed. The Oklahoma Telemedicine Network is among the largest medical communications systems in the world, successfully bringing information and expertise to rural physicians, clinics, and hospitals.

Campus Life

At least 85 percent of students must be Oklahoma residents, but generally only five or ten students are from out of state. There is a wide age range among incoming students, and students older than 35 are not unusual. About 26 percent of students are underrepresented minorities, most of whom are Native Americans. Class size is 162.

STUDENT LIFE

Students are cohesive, both inside and outside of the classroom. A student-run note service is one example of cooperation among students. The OUHSC Student Center facilitates both social and academic interaction. It features an exercise room, study areas, computers, a food service court, and common rooms. For a fee, medical students also have access to the recreational center at the nearby Healthy Living Center. Medical students are active in student organizations that offer support and focus on recreational pursuits, professional goals, and community service. Medical students are also involved in coed intramural football, basketball, and soccer. Students are eligible for intercollegiate athletic tickets and other university-wide events. Affordable and comfortable university-owned housing for married and single students is available. Downtown Oklahoma City is one mile from the OUHSC campus and offers a range of activities and attractions.

GRADUATES

Typically, about half of graduates enter residencies in Oklahoma. Others are successful in securing positions nationwide. There are seven OUHSC-affiliated postgraduate programs in Tulsa and more than 25 in Oklahoma City.

Admissions

REQUIREMENTS

Prerequisites are general zoology/biology with lab (1 semester); embryology, genetics, anatomy, cellular biology, or histology (1 semester); inorganic chemistry (1 year); organic chemistry (1 year); general physics (1 year); English (3 semesters); any combination of sociology, psychology, anthropology, humanities, philosophy, or foreign language (3 semesters). The MCAT is required. For applicants who have retaken the exam, the most recent set of scores is considered. Basic computer skills are required.

SUGGESTIONS

Strong preference is given to Oklahoma residents, making competition intense for out-of-state residents. Applicants are encouraged to take additional courses in computer sciences, English, fine arts, humanities, and social sciences. In addition to academic achievement, a candidate's personality, maturity, and character are evaluated. Admissions decisions are made with recognition of the importance of social and cultural diversity.

PROCESS

All AMCAS applicants receive supplemental Information Requests. Of those returning supplemental information, about 20 percent are interviewed. Interviews are conducted between September and February, and consist of one session with a panel of three members of the Admissions Committee. On interview day, applicants tour the campus and have the opportunity to meet informally with current students. Of interviewed candidates, about 80 percent (not including wait listed candidates) are accepted on a rolling basis. Wait listed candidates may send updated transcripts.

Admissions Requirements (Required)

MCAT scores, science GPA, non-science GPA, letters of recommendation, interview, essay/personal statement, extracurricular activities, exposure to medical profession

Admissions Requirement (Optional)

State residency

COSTS AND AID
Tuition & Fees

In-state tuition	$15,746
Out-of-state tuition	$39,402
Room and board (off-campus)	$17,416
Cost of books	$7,500
Fees	$3,304

Financial Aid

% students receiving aid	90
Average grant	$5,500
Average loan	$38,500
Average debt	$110,000

University of Ottawa

451 Smyth Road, Room 2046, Ottawa, ON K1H 8M5 • **Admission:** 613-562-5409 • **Fax:** 613-562-5651
E-mail: ADMISSMD@UOTTAWA.CA • **Website:** WWW.MEDICINE.UOTTAWA.CA/ENG/UNDERGRADUATE.HTML

STUDENT BODY

Type	Public
# applied	2,440
# accepted	191
# enrolled	136

ADMISSIONS

Average GPA Scores

Overall GPA	3.65

Application Information

Regular application	10/15
Regular notification	5/31
Are transfers accepted?	Yes
Admissions may be deferred?	Yes
Interview required?	Yes
Application fee	$175

Academics

During the 4 year MD program, students acquire the knowledge, skills, and attitudes they need to apply effective, efficient strategies for the prevention and management of health problems ranging from the most common to the most severe. The program integrates the basic and clinical sciences throughout the 4 years. It also emphasizes health promotion and disease prevention and is responsive to individual needs and abilities and to the changes occurring in society and the health care system. Instruction is available in both French and English. In addition to the MD, master's, and PhD, programs are offered in Biochemistry, epidemiology and cellular and molecular medicine, Microbiology and Immunology, and Neuroscience.

The program is scheduled over four calendar years and is divided into two stages. The first stage includes 70 weeks of study of essential biomedical principles and consists of 14 multidisciplinary blocks. Students learn communication and clinical skills in an integrated fashion with the study of body systems. The second stage lasts for two calendar years and is devoted to clinical clerkships; an extended period of 14 weeks is available for elective study. For more information on the undergraduate MD program at the University of Ottawa, visit the program website at www.medicine.uottawa.ca/eng/undergraduate.html.

Campus Life

For the 2004–2005 academic year there were 123 year 1 positions available. Additionally, there were eight positions made available through the Centre National de Formation en Sante program, and five positions available through the Canadian Department of National Defense. Typically, all but a few are residents of the province of Ontario. About 50 percent of members of the student body are women.

STUDENT LIFE

Medical students benefit from the resources and activities of a large university and an urban environment. Student clubs and organizations exist within the medical school and the greater university. Support services, such as counseling, child care, health care, and academic assistance are available to medical students. On-campus housing is offered.

GRADUATES

Graduates enter both clinical medicine and research-oriented careers. Graduate-level medical training is offered at Ottawa in most clinical fields.

Admissions

REQUIREMENTS

To be eligible for admissions, applicants must have successfully completed 3 years of full-time university studies in any undergraduate program leading to a bachelor's degree, including 1 year of general biology (with laboratory session); 1 year of humanities or social sciences; and 2 years of some combination of biochemistry, general chemistry, and organic chemistry (with laboratory sessions). Because the University of Ottawa does not require the submission of MCAT scores, an applicant's academic records will likely meet with increased scrutiny during the review process. Only Canadian citizens or permanent residents are accepted, with the exception of eligible children of the University of Ottawa alumni.

SUGGESTIONS

The Admissions Committee primarily considers those eligible candidates who have maintained a weighted average of at least a B-plus in the last 3 years of their undergraduate university studies. Priority is given in order to Franco-Ontarians, Aboriginal applicants, residents of underserviced areas, bona fide residents of the Ottawa-Outaouais region, Ontario residents, and residents of other provinces. In recent entering classes, about 8 percent of applicants were accepted.

PROCESS

After a written application is submitted, supporting materials and an interview will be requested of applicants with acceptable academic records. The interview is used to further screen applicants. Documents for application to the first year of medicine are available through the Faculty or through OMSAS (Ontario Medical School Application Service). Kits are available in July of the preceding year from: OMSAS, PO Box 1328, 650 Woodlawn Road, West, Block C, Guelph, Ontario N1H 7P4. Applications must be completed and returned by October 15.

Admissions Requirements (Required)

Interview

COSTS AND AID
Tuition & Fees

In-state tuition	$14,000
Fees	$552

UNIVERSITY OF PENNSYLVANIA
SCHOOL OF MEDICINE

DIRECTOR OF ADMISSIONS, EDWARD J. STEMMLER HALL, SUITE 100, PHILADELPHIA, PA 19104 • ADMISSION: 215-898-8001
FAX: 215-573-6645 • E-MAIL: ADMISS@MAIL.MED.UPENN.EDU • WEBSITE: WWW.MED.UPENN.EDU/ADMISS

STUDENT BODY	
Type	Private
Enrollment	720
% male/female	48/52
% minorities	15
# applied (total/out)	6,344/5,532
# accepted (total/out)	153
Average age	23

ADMISSIONS
Average GPA and MCAT scores

Overall GPA	3.8
MCAT Bio	12
MCAT Phys	12
MCAT Verbal	11
MCAT Essay	Q

Application Information

Regular application	10/15
Regular notification	3/15
Are transfers accepted?	No
Admissions may be deferred?	Yes
Interview required?	Yes
Application fee	$80

Academics

The 4 year curriculum is organized into six modules, some of which overlap. Patient contact begins on day 1, and clinical rotations begin midway through the second year. Research and scholarly projects are encouraged, and may be pursued in a wide range of areas including biomedical science, clinical medicine, Behavioral Science, and public-health related fields. For qualified students, combined MD/PhD, and MD/master's degree programs are available. Among other disciplines, graduate degrees may be earned in bioengineering, cell and molecular biology, chemical/structural biology and biophysics, epidemiology, health care systems, history and sociology of science, immunology, neuroscience, pharmacological sciences, philosophy, psychology, and public policy and management. Another option is a joint MD/MBA in conjunction with the Wharton School of Business. Grading is pass/fail during module 1 and honors/high pass/pass/fail during the remaining modules.

BASIC SCIENCES: Basic sciences are taught primarily through an integrated organ/disease system model, correlated with clinical examples and hands-on experiences. Module 1 occupies the first semester and is devoted to core principles. Courses are Cellular Physiology, Metabolism, and Pharmacological Processes; Developmental and Molecular Biology; Human Body Structure and Function; Host Defenses; and Pharmacological Responses. Module 2 spans the second semester of the first year and the first semester of the second year. It is entitled integrative systems and disease and is organized around body or organ systems. These are brain and behavior, cardiology/pulmonary, endocrinology and reproduction, gastrointestinal and nutrition, skin/connective tissue/musculoskeletal/hematology/oncology. Throughout the entire first year and a half, students are introduced to clinical medicine in Module 3, the technology, art, and practice of medicine. In addition to providing training in basic clinical techniques, Module 3 addresses ethics, technological issues, population-based medicine, public health, and humanistic perspectives. Classroom instruction is enhanced by various academic resources, including multimedia, video, and computerized instructional programs. The Biomedical Science Library houses more than 100,000 volumes and receives more than 2,000 periodicals.

CLINICAL TRAINING

Students rotate through required clerkships during Module 4, which covers the second semester of year 2 and the first semester of year 3. These are Internal Medicine (9 weeks), Surgery/Anesthesia (9 weeks), Obstetrics/Gynecology (6 weeks), Pediatrics (6 weeks), Psychiatry/Substance Abuse (6 weeks), Emergency Medicine (3 weeks), Family Medicine (3 weeks), Neurology (3 weeks), and Clinical Specialists (3 weeks). Module 5 begins in the second semester of year 3 and continues until graduation at the end of year 4. It includes a sub internship, advanced electives, and a required 3-month scholarly or research experience. A large portion of clinical training takes place at the Hospital of the University of Pennsylvania and also at the site of research institutions and labs. Other training sites are Children's Hospital of Philadelphia, Veterans Affairs of Philadelphia Hospitals, Penn Medicine at Radnor, Chestnut Hill Health Care, Chester County Hospital, Friends Hospital, Holy Redeemer Health System, and the Presbyterian-University of Pennsylvania Medical Center.

Campus Life

The student body at U. Penn is nationally represented. About 15 percent of students are underrepresented minorities, and about 35 percent of students took significant time off after college. Class size is 155.

STUDENT LIFE

Pass/fail grading in the first semester contributes to the high degree of cooperation among students. U. Penn, a comprehensive private university, offers a wide range of extracurricular activities on and around campus, and students are involved in both school and community organizations. Medical students have access to all recreational facilities, including athletic centers. Philadelphia is an important urban center and is also the home of a very large number of universities. The student community is vast, and the city serves the student community well. Other metropolitan areas such as New York, Baltimore, and Washington, DC, are easily accessible by train, and mountains and beaches are a short drive. The Graduate Towers and High Rise North is a university-owned graduate student apartment complex available to medical students. However, most students choose to live off campus.

GRADUATES

During a recent 3-year period, the most prevalent residency programs selected by graduates were primary care disciplines (41 percent), which included medicine (22 percent) and pediatrics (15 percent); surgical specialties (17 percent), which included ophthalmology (4 percent), orthopedics (4 percent), and neurosurgery (2 percent); radiology (8 percent); surgery (2 percent); psychiatry (4 percent); emergency medicine (3 percent); and obstetrics/gynecology (4 percent).

Admissions

REQUIREMENTS

Applicants must complete a course of study leading to a baccalaureate degree at an accredited college or university. No prerequisites are specified, although the MCAT is required, suggesting a comprehensive science preparation. Penn will accept MCAT scores from January–September for each admission season.

SUGGESTIONS

Recommended undergraduate preparation includes courses in English, biology, chemistry, economics, ethics, history, math, organic chemistry, physics, philosophy, and political science. For applicants who have taken time off after college, some recent course work is advised. Experience in hospitals, clinics, or community service projects is important.

PROCESS

All AMCAS applicants receive secondary applications. Of those returning secondaries, about 20 percent are interviewed between October and February. Interviews consist of two sessions, one with a student and one with a faculty member. On interview day, candidates tour the campus, attend group informational sessions, and have the opportunity to meet informally with students. Of interviewed candidates, about 20 percent are accepted. Wait listed candidates may send additional information to update their files.

Admissions Requirements (Required)

MCAT scores, science GPA, non-science GPA, letters of recommendation, extracurricular activities, exposure to medical profession

COSTS AND AID
Tuition & Fees

Tuition	$39,648
Room and board (on-campus)	$14,135
Cost of books	$700
Fees	$3,225

Financial Aid

% students receiving aid	80
Average debt	$113,000

University of Pittsburgh
School of Medicine

Office of Admissions, 518 Scaife Hall, 3550 Terrace Street Pittsburgh, PA 15261 • **Admission:** 412-648-9891

Fax: 412-648-8768 • **E-mail:** ADMISSIONS@MEDSCHOOL.PITT.EDU • **Website:** WWW.MEDSCHOOL.PITT.EDU

STUDENT BODY

Type	Public
Enrollment	589
% male/female	53/47
% minorities	10
# applied (total/out)	5,297/4,436
# accepted (total/out)	458/367
# enrolled (total/out)	147/102
Average age	24

FACULTY

Total faculty	1,881
% female	32
% minority	4
% part-time	3
Student-faculty ratio	0:1

ADMISSIONS
Average GPA and MCAT Scores

Overall GPA	3.68
MCAT Bio	11.66
MCAT Phys	11.43
MCAT Verbal	10.64
MCAT Essay	P

Application Information

Regular application	11/15
Regular notification	10/16
Are transfers accepted?	Yes
Admissions may be deferred?	Yes
Interview required?	Yes
Application fee	$75

Academics

We seek to train tomorrow's physician-scientists, academic leaders, and finest practicing physicians. To accomplish these goals, the curriculum combines a strong foundation in basic science with early introduction to patients, small-group learning, and an emphasis on critical thinking and problem solving. Each student participates in a mentored scholarly project.

Our four-year curriculum encourages sensitivity to patient concerns and communication that is supported by sound problem-solving skills and evidence-based decision-making. Extensive interaction among students and faculty fosters the development of habits of lifelong learning through curriculum, role-modeling, and individual mentoring in both formal and informal settings.

BASIC SCIENCES: During the first two years, students take classes that are grouped into blocks. Year one has five blocks: Fundamentals of Basic Science, covering the essentials of the sciences underlying physiology and medicine; Patient, Physician, and Society, covering ethical, behavioral, and sociological issues related to medicine; Introduction to Patient Care, introducing Physical Diagnosis and History-Taking; Scientific Reasoning in Medicine, focusing on analysis of medical literature; and Organ Systems, covering physiology, pharmacology, pathophysiology, and introduction to medicine, with Neuroscience and Introduction to Psychiatry in the first year. The latter four blocks continue into year two: Organ Systems includes Cardiovascular, Renal, and Pulmonary Medicine; Digestion; Hematology; Endocrine; and Reproduction/Development. The final segment of year two integrates all the organ systems in a problem-based learning format and, while doing so, revisits important points of the previous two years and challenges students to diagnose and treat clinical problems. Lectures, small-group sessions, conferences, labs, and simulations are the instructional methods used during the first two years, and students are in a structured learning environment for about 28 hours per week. Problem-based learning is used throughout the curriculum. An extensive simulation program using both mannequins and trained human patient simulators is integrated throughout the first two years. A number of elective, non-credit experiences are offered during the first two years, including Medical Journalism, the Natural History of Medicine, Concepts in Human Motion, and Pandemic Preparedness, among others. With the exception of clinical work, classes meet in Scaife Hall, which houses classrooms, labs, and a library, which has state-of-the-art access to extensive online medical information services. Grades during the first two years are Honors/Pass/Fail. The USMLE Steps 1, 2CS, and 2CK are required for graduation.

CLINICAL TRAINING

Patient contact begins in year one during the Physical Exam course and the Clinical Experiences course. Students interact with patients both in the hospital as well as in ambulatory settings in years one and two. Clinical clerkships begin in mid-May of second year. The eight clerkships are Medicine (8 weeks), Surgery (8 weeks), Pediatrics (4 weeks), Obstetrics and Gynecology (4 weeks), Family Medicine (4 weeks), Specialty Care (4 weeks), Combined Ambulatory Care (Medicine and Pediatrics, 8 weeks) and Clinical Neurosciences (Psychiatry and Neurology, 8 weeks). Selected electives may be taken during third year. Fourth year requirements are an acting internship (4 weeks) and an Integrated Life Science course (4 weeks). All other weeks in the fourth year are elective. Clinical training takes place in the many facilities of the internationally renowned University of Pittsburgh Medical Center (UPMC), which comprises numerous major teaching hospitals and centers including a site in Palermo, Italy.

Students

About 10 percent of students are underrepresented minorities, most of whom are African American. There is a large age range within the student body, and many students have taken some time off before entering medical school. Class size is 148.

STUDENT LIFE

The structure of the curriculum promotes student interaction and collegiality. In addition, medical students get to know each other through involvement in organizations and extracurricular activities. Some of the many student groups on campus are the American Medical Student Association, the American Medical Association, specialty interest groups in most areas of medicine, Pitt Women in Medicine, and the History of Medicine Society. Medical students have access to all facilities of the University of Pittsburgh, including athletic facilities. Pittsburgh is an accessible and exciting city, and, although on-campus housing is available, most medical students choose to live off campus.

GRADUATES

Graduates are successful in gaining admittance to the most prestigious residency programs in the country.

Admissions

REQUIREMENTS

Requirements are one year each of Biology, Physics, Chemistry, and Organic Chemistry (all with associated labs), and English. In assessing grades, consideration is given to the undergraduate institution attended and the course load taken. The MCAT is required and scores must be no more than three years old.

SUGGESTIONS

Competence in science and math is valued as is evidence of success in social science and humanities courses. The University of Pittsburgh School of Medicine assesses interpersonal skills and commitment to community service in applicants. For applicants who graduated college several years ago, some recent coursework is advised.

PROCESS

Secondary applications are sent to all AMCAS applicants. About 25 percent of Pennsylvania residents, and 20 percent of out-of-state residents, are interviewed. Interviews are conducted from September through February and consist of two sessions, one with a faculty member and one with a medical student. Notification occurs on a rolling basis. Wait-listed candidates may send additional information to strengthen their applications and to indicate interest in the school.

Admissions Requirements (Required)

MCAT scores, Science GPA, Non-science GPA, Letters of recommendation, Interview, Essays/personal statement, Extracurricular activities, Exposure to medical profession

Admissions Requirements (Optional)

State residency

COSTS AND AID

Tuition & Fees

In-state Tuition	$33,184
Out-of-state Tuition	$38,064
Room and board	$15,000
Cost of books	$4,350
Fees	$650

Financial Aid

% students receiving aid	87
Average grant	$17,602
Average loan	$35,000
Average debt	$129,152

UNIVERSITY OF PUERTO RICO
MEDICAL SCIENCES CAMPUS

A-878 MAIN BUILDING, PO BOX 365067, SAN JUAN, PR 00936-5067 • ADMISSION: 787-758-2525 EXT. 1800
FAX: 787-756-8475 • E-MAIL: MARRIVERA@RCM.UPR.EDU • WEBSITE: WWW.RCM.UPR.EDU

STUDENT BODY

Type	Public
Enrollment	1,716

FACULTY

Total faculty	189
Student-faculty ratio	9:1

ADMISSIONS

Application Information

Regular application	12/1
Regular notification	Rolling
Early application	6/1
Early notification	Rolling
Application fee	$15

Academics

Medical training is accomplished through a variety of educational experiences, both in the classroom and at multiple service settings in the public and private sectors of Puerto Rico. Medical students benefit from the resources of other health professional schools and from interaction with students at other schools. Through the Center for International Health, medical students gain exposure to the research and policy issues surrounding global health. Grading for all courses is on an A–F scale.

BASIC SCIENCES: Basic sciences are taught using a combination of lectures, small-group discussions, labs, and exposure to clinical correlates. Required first-year courses are Behavioral Sciences, Human Development I, Human Physiology, Introduction to Biochemistry, Introduction to Clinical Diagnosis, Integration Seminar I, Medical Embryology, Medical Gross Anatomy, Medical Histology, Medical Neuroscience, and Public Health and Preventive Medicine I. Second-year courses consist of Basic Clinical Clerkship, Fundamentals of Clinical Diagnosis, Human Development II, Infectious Diseases, Integration Seminar II, Mechanisms of Disease, Medical Pharmacology, Pathobiology—Introduction to Laboratory Medicine, Public Health and Preventive Medicine II, and Psychopathology. Outside of the classroom, students learn in the Learning Resources Center, the Standardized Patient Laboratory, and the Clinical Learning Laboratory.

CLINICAL TRAINING

The third year is comprised of clinical rotations. These are Medicine (12 weeks), Pediatrics (10 weeks), Surgery (10 weeks), Obstetrics/Gynecology (6 weeks), Psychiatry (4 weeks), Family Medicine (4 weeks), and Radiology (2 weeks). During year 4, clerkships are Public Health (3 weeks); Dermatology (1 week); Physical Medicine and Rehabilitation (1 week); Legal, Ethical, and Administrative Aspects in Medicine (1 week); and selective clerkships (8 weeks). In addition, 18 weeks are open for clinical and research electives. Clinical education uses a variety of settings including University Hospital, University Pediatric Hospital, San Juan City Hospital, Veterans Administration Hospital, and the Oncology Hospital. In addition, the school uses certain private hospitals, clinics, and public health facilities. Some electives may be taken at institutions other than those affiliated with the University of Puerto Rico, such as hospitals in other regions of Puerto Rico and in other countries.

Campus Life

Each entering class has about 100 students. Students come from foreign countries and the mainland United States as well as Puerto Rico. Fifty percent of students are women.

STUDENT LIFE

Recreational facilities on campus include the sports and gym center. The medical school promotes student health through its exercise/wellness program and by sponsoring a range of student activities and events. When they have free time, medical students enjoy the city of San Juan and its surroundings.

GRADUATES

The University of Puerto Rico and its affiliated hospitals offer residency programs in most major medical fields.

Admissions

REQUIREMENTS

With few exceptions, entering students must have completed their bachelor's degree. Prerequisite courses are 1 year each of biology, general chemistry, organic chemistry, and physics. The MCAT is required, and August in the year prior to admission is the latest acceptable test date.

SUGGESTIONS

Both residents of Puerto Rico and nonresidents are considered for admission. Grade point average and MCAT scores are important in admissions decisions. In addition to academic credentials, the University of Puerto Rico looks for integrity and motivation in its students.

PROCESS

All applicants are encouraged to visit the campus. Candidates for the MD program must submit an application by December 1. Those who qualify are invited to interview after their applications are reviewed. Final decisions and notifications are made throughout the year and are completed in the spring.

Admissions Requirements (Required)

MCAT scores, letters of recommendation, science GPA

Admissions Requirements (Optional)

State residency

COSTS AND AID
Tuition & Fees

In-state tuition	$6,965
Out-of-state tuition	$15,000
Fees	$1,600
Room and board (on-campus)	$4,840
Books and expenses	$7,893

UNIVERSITY OF ROCHESTER

SCHOOL OF MEDICINE AND DENTISTRY

MEDICAL CENTER, PO BOX 601A, ROCHESTER, NY 14642 • **ADMISSION:** 585-275-4539 • **FAX:** 585-756-5479
E-MAIL: MDADMISH@URMC.ROCHESTER.EDU • **WEBSITE:** WWW.URMC.ROCHESTER.EDU/SMD/ADMISS

STUDENT BODY	
Type	Private
Enrollment	433
% male/female	45/55
% minorities	14
# applied (total/out)	3,496/2,598
# accepted (total/out)	260/170
# enrolled (total/out)	100/63
Average age	24

FACULTY	
Total faculty (number)	1,317
% female	33
% minority	3
% part-time	10
Student-faculty ratio	3:1

ADMISSIONS	
Average GPA and MCAT Scores	
Overall GPA	3.68
MCAT Bio	11.0
MCAT Phys	10.8
MCAT Verbal	10.5
MCAT Essay	P
Application Information	
Regular application	10/15
Regular notification	11/1
Are transfers accepted?	No
Admissions may be deferred?	Yes
Interview required?	Yes
Application fee	$75

Academics

Special emphasis is placed on skills acquisition and use, with a commitment to lifelong learning. Sensitivity to the world of the patient is encompassed in the biopsychosocial integration of the curriculum and the learning experience, with mechanisms in place for continuous curricular improvement through the collaboration of students and faculty. By ensuring adequate and early electivity for students to enhance their special interests, along with rigorous training and assessment of all of the competencies demanded by modern medical practice, the curriculum generates a knowledge base characterized by depth, breadth, rigor, and flexibility. Students interested in careers in medical science may participate in the fully funded Medical Scientist Training Program (MD/PhD), or joint-degree programs including the MPH/MD and MBA/MD program in Health Care Management in conjunction with the William E. Simon Graduate School of Business Administration. Vacation and full-year fellowships facilitate student research or international medicine experiences. Evaluation of student performance uses satisfactory/fail, except in the required clerkships, where honors/high pass/pass/fail grades are used. Passing the USMLE is not required for promotion to the third year.

BASIC SCIENCES: An introductory module at the beginning of year 1 prepares students in the acquisition, management, and presentation of medical information. Students learn how to meet the challenges of active and independent learning by becoming competent in data management, information technology, and critical evaluation of the medical literature. Every course is interdisciplinary; basic sciences are integrated with one another and basic and clinical sciences are woven together as the strands of the Double Helix Curriculum throughout the 4 years. Clinical skills training from day 1 leads not to shadowing or preceptor experiences in clinics but to real clinical work as part of the health care team while still in the first year. Not just paper cases, but students' actual clinical cases drive the learning of science through the school-wide use of multidisciplinary Problem-Based Learning (PBL) cases. Three 2-hour PBL tutorials per week and an average of about 14 hours of lecture per week, with adequate time for self-study, and the use of labs, conferences, seminars, and computer-assisted learning—all these things characterize the classroom setting of the curriculum. Electives are available during all 4 years, including electives in medical humanities, international medicine, and community outreach programs. The Edward G. Miner Library holds more than 225,000 volumes and a modern, computer-based learning resource center.

CLINICAL TRAINING

Beginning in year 1, students complete their introduction to clinical medicine in the fall and then participate in an Ambulatory Clerkship Experience beginning in the spring. This experience, unlike any other in the country, includes all the ambulatory components of ambulatory surgery, family medicine, internal medicine, pediatrics, psychiatry, and women's health, and is completed by the end of the second year. Inpatient clerkships are completed by December of the fourth year and focus on acute illness experiences in adult medicine, women's and children's health, mind/brain/behavior, and urgent/emergent care. Strong Memorial Hospital (700 beds) is the principal site for clinical teaching, along with a newly completed ambulatory care center and four affiliated hospitals (2,000 beds), covering acute and chronic care.

Campus Life

Students come from all regions of the country. About 14 percent are underrepresented minorities. The average age of incoming students is 24; one-third have majored in areas outside the sciences, and 100 students are accepted each year.

STUDENT LIFE

Most medical students have active lives outside of the classroom. Many participate in community outreach programs, international medicine electives, and student organizations and events. Students have access to resources of the university campus and athletic facilities in the medical center. Located on the southern shore of Lake Ontario in the Finger Lakes wine-producing region of upstate New York, Rochester is a progressive, metropolitan community of more than 1 million people. Rochester has a rich cultural life and is an affordable and friendly city. It is a haven for boaters and other outdoor enthusiasts.

GRADUATES

Among the 2006 graduates, the most popular residencies were internal medicine (21 percent), pediatrics (13 percent), surgery (9 percent), neurology (7 percent), radiology (7 percent), med-peds (6 percent), emergency medicine (5 percent), anesthesiology (4 percent), obstetrics/gynecology (4 percent), orthopedics (4 percent), and psychiatry (4 percent).

Admissions

REQUIREMENTS

Prerequisite science courses are 1 year of biology, general chemistry, organic chemistry, and physics, all associated with labs. One semester of biochemistry may be substituted for one semester of organic. One year of English or expository writing is also required. Rochester belongs to AMCAS, and the MCAT exam is required; scores should be from the past 3 years. The best set of scores is considered.

SUGGESTIONS

In addition to required science courses, 12–16 credit hours in the humanities and/or social sciences are required. Experiences in research, clinical settings, and the community are strongly recommended. Rochester looks for evidence of leadership, excellent interpersonal skills, a love of learning, appreciation of diversity, and outstanding scholarship.

PROCESS

Rochester is an AMCAS school. About 19 percent of applicants are interviewed between September and February. Interviews consist of two sessions with faculty, and applicants have a tour, lunch with current students, and a financial aid presentation. About 40 percent of the interviewed applicants are offered acceptance, with notification beginning in November and continuing through May. About 15 positions in each class are reserved for students from several programs, such as the Rochester Early Medical Scholar Program and the Bryn Mawr or Johns Hopkins postbaccalaureate program.

Admissions Requirements (Required)

MCAT scores, science GPA, non-science GPA, letters of recommendation, interview, essays/personal statement, extracurricular activities, exposure to medical profession, exposure to research

Admissions Requirements (Optional)

State residency

Overlap Schools

Boston University, Case Western Reserve University, Cornell University, Dartmouth College, Harvard University, Mt. Sinai School of Medicine, New York University, Tufts University, University of Pittsburgh, University of Virginia.

COSTS AND AID

Tuition & Fees

Tuition	$35,800
Room and board (off-campus)	$9,500
Cost of books	$2,000
Fees	$1,911

Financial Aid

% students receiving aid	92
Average grant	$17,217
Average loan	$26,866
Average debt	$134,367

UNIVERSITY OF SASKATCHEWAN
COLLEGE OF MEDICINE

A204 HEALTH SCIENCE BUILDING, 107 WIGGINS ROAD SASKATOON, SK S7N 5E5 • **ADMISSION:** 306-966-8554
FAX: 306-966-2601 • **E-MAIL:** MED.ADMISSIONS@USASK.CA • **WEBSITE:** WWW.MEDICINE.USASK.CA / ADMISSIONS

STUDENT BODY

Type	Public
Enrollment	68
% male/female	57/43
% minorities	9
# applied	568
# accepted (total/out)	68/4
# enrolled (total/out)	68/4
Average age	23

FACULTY

Total faculty	245
% female	30

ADMISSIONS
Average GPA and MCAT Scores

MCAT Bio	9.64
MCAT Phys	9.14
MCAT Verbal	9.56
MCAT Essay	P

Application Information

Regular application	11/1
Regular notification	5/16
Are transfers accepted?	No
Admissions may be deferred?	Yes
Interview required?	Yes
Application fee	$50

Academics

The goal of the College of Medicine is to enable medical students to develop the knowledge, skills, values, and attitudes that will serve as a foundation for subsequent education in primary and specialty patient care and research. In its curriculum, the College promotes the integration of basic and clinical sciences. Independent learning, problem-solving, and early patient interaction are emphasized. The curriculum is divided into four phases. For the most part, basic science instruction occurs during the first three phases. However, basic science and clinical training are integrated throughout the four-year curriculum.

BASIC SCIENCES: Phase A (1 year) comprises 33 weeks and includes the introductory study of basic sciences, the History of Medicine, Professional Skills (includes two-week community experience), and Life Cycle and Humanities. Instruction in basic sciences is interdisciplinary, covering fundamental principles of Anatomy, Physiology, Biochemistry, and Microbiology. Instruction in the basic sciences continues into Phase B (1 year) which lasts 33 weeks. Subjects include Pathology, Microbiology, and Pharmacology. Also included in Phase B is Clinical Sciences, Systems, and Genetics. Phase C comprises 15 weeks only and is a continuation of Clinical Sciences and Systems, but also includes the Microbiology, and Community Health and Epidemiology.

CLINICAL TRAINING

Phase D (16 months) is a discipline-based rotation clerkship that builds on the clinical training and offers students the opportunity to study clinical electives (12 weeks) and specialty fields. Teaching Hospitals are Royal University Hospital, St. Paul's Hospital, Saskatoon City Hospital, Regina General Hospital, and Pasqua Hospital.

Students

The current size of the entering classes is 60. Typically, 90 percent of students are from the province of Saskatchewan. In general, about 50 percent of students are women.

STUDENT LIFE

With a relatively small student body and a curriculum that encourages interaction, students are generally cohesive. Between the medical school and the greater University, a wide range of extracurricular activities and events are offered. Medical students live both on and off campus.

GRADUATES

Though research is an increasingly important activity for the College of Medicine, a large number of graduates become practicing clinical physicians in the province of Saskatchewan.

Admissions

REQUIREMENTS

A minimum of two years of undergraduate work is required. In general, prerequisites are Biochemistry, Biology, Chemistry, Organic Chemistry, Physics, English, Social Sciences, and Humanities. Incoming students require an academic average of 70 percent in pre-requisite courses in order to be considered for admission. The competitive academic average is based on the best two full years of university and must be at least 78 percent. The MCAT must be taken within the last 5 years with minimum scores of 8 and N met although one 7 or an M will be accepted.

SUGGESTIONS

Criteria for selection are academic performance and personal qualities. Academic performance is based on applicants' two best full undergraduate years of study. Personal qualities are assessed primarily by interview. Realistically to be competitive academically, an overall two-year average of over 80 percent is required.

PROCESS

Application forms may be obtained from the Admissions Secretary after July 1 or from the Internet at the address above. Applications must be post-marked no later than December 1. Personal qualities are assessed through an interview process normally held during a weekend in March. Three letters of reference are also considered. All candidates are notified of their acceptance mid to late May.

Admissions Requirements (Required)

MCAT scores, Science GPA, Non-science GPA, Letters of recommendation, Interview, State residency

Admissions Requirements (Optional)

Essays/personal statement, Extracurricular activities, Exposure to medical profession

Overlap Schools

University of Alberta, University of Calgary, University of Manitoba.

COSTS AND AID
Tuition & Fees

Tuition	$11,460
Room and board (on-campus)	$7,200
Cost of books	$1,800

UNIVERSITY OF SHERBROOKE

2500 BOULEVARD DE L'UNIVERSITÉ, SHERBROOKE, QC J1K 2R1 • ADMISSION: 819-821-7686
E-MAIL: STIC-MED@USHERBROOKE.CA • WEBSITE: WWW.USHERBROOKE.CA/MEDECINE

STUDENT BODY

Type	Public

ADMISSIONS

Application Information

Regular application	3/1
Regular notification	Rolling
Admissions may be deferred?	No
Application fee	$30

Academics

Sherbrooke offers a 4 year curriculum leading to the MD degree. Educational methodology is based on small-group discussions, case studies, audiovisual and computer-assisted learning, and hands-on clinical experiences. Combined-degree programs, such as the MD/MSc program are open to highly qualified students who have an interest in research.

BASIC SCIENCES: The first academic period begins in late August and spans 39 weeks. In general, students are in class or other scheduled session for approximately 30 hours per week. Courses are Introduction to MD Program, Biological Medicine I and II, Clinical Immersion, Growth Development and Aging, Locomoter System, Nervous System, Psycho-social Sciences, Preventive Medicine and Community Health, Integration, and Clinical Skills. The second year is organized into blocks based on anatomical/physiological systems. These are cardiovascular system, endocrine system, gastrointestinal system, hemato-immunologic system, human sexuality, infectious disease, respiratory system, reproductive system, and urinary system. In addition, students take part in a rotation in community hospitals and a course in clinical skills.

CLINICAL TRAINING

The third and fourth years are organized into several components. These are required courses, required primary clerkships, rotations in community, elective programs, integration period, and final exam. Required courses are Clinical Skills, Interdisciplinary Concepts, and Introduction to Clerkships. The required primary clerkships are Medicine (10.5 weeks); Surgery (7 weeks); Pediatrics (7 weeks); Psychiatry (7 weeks); Obstetrics/Gynecology (7 weeks); and Multidisciplinary (3.5 weeks). Rotations in community include Family Medicine and Emergency (7 weeks) and Community Health (4 weeks). The elective program lasts 12 weeks, followed by the integration period (6 weeks) and the final exam period (1 week). Teaching hospitals are Cuse Fleurimont, Cuse Bowen, Hôpital Charles Le Moyne, and Hôpital Sainte-Croix.

Campus Life

Each entering class has approximately 105 students. About 80 percent of students are from the Province of Quebec. Women account for 60 percent of students.

STUDENT LIFE

The University of Sherbrooke is a large university with many social, recreational, and other extracurricular activities for medical students. Medical students have both on-campus and off-campus housing options.

GRADUATES

Many graduates enter one of the residency programs offered at hospitals affiliated with Sherbrooke.

Admissions

REQUIREMENTS

Fluency in French is required. The minimum requirement for admissions is 2 years of university or a BA degree. Prerequisites are general biology (1 year), general chemistry (1 year), organic chemistry (1 year), physics (3 semesters), and mathematics through calculus. The MCAT is not required.

SUGGESTIONS

In addition to prerequisite courses, students should complete course work in the humanities and in the social sciences. Priority is given to residents of Quebec, and 86 positions in each entering class are reserved for this group of applicants. Fifteen additional places are reserved for applicants from New Brunswick, one place is reserved for an applicant from Prince Edward Island, one from Nova Scotia, and two places are available for qualified foreign applicants. Overall, about 5 percent of applicants are admitted each year.

PROCESS

Applications are available from the Admissions Office at the address above. Following review of applications, qualified candidates are invited to a learning-skills test (THAMUS).

COSTS AND AID

Tuition & Fees

In-state tuition	$3,127
Out-of-state tuition	$15,127

UNIVERSITY OF SOUTH ALABAMA
COLLEGE OF MEDICINE

OFFICE OF ADMISSIONS, 241 CSAB, MOBILE, AL 36688 • ADMISSION: 251-460-7176
FAX: 251-460-6278 • E-MAIL: MSCOTT@USOUTHAL.EDU • WEBSITE: WWW.USOUTHAL.EDU/USA/DEPS-GRD.HTML

STUDENT BODY

Type	Public
Enrollment	280
% male/female	49/51
% minorities	11
# applied (total/out)	809/449
# accepted (total/out)	116/20
# enrolled (total/out)	70/8
Average age	24

FACULTY

Total faculty (number)	300
% female	30
% minority	10
% part-time	9
Student-faculty ratio	1:1

ADMISSIONS
Average GPA and MCAT Scores

Overall GPA	3.7
MCAT Bio	11.0
MCAT Phys	10.0
MCAT Verbal	10.0
MCAT Essay	O

Application Information

Regular application	11/15
Regular notification	Rolling
Early application	6/1–8/1
Early notification	10/1
Are transfers accepted?	Yes
Admissions may be deferred?	Yes
Interview required?	Yes
Application fee	$75

Academics

The curriculum is semi-traditional and uses a lecture format for most of the pre-clinical instruction. Although some early clinical exposure is offered, during the first 2 years, the program focuses on ensuring a solid understanding of the basic sciences. Combining medical and doctorate studies is possible if pursuing a PhD degree in a medically related discipline. About 10 percent of the class enters the School of Medicine via a combined undergraduate-medical school program that is open to both Alabama and out-of-state high school seniors.

BASIC SCIENCES: The school operates on a quarter system. During the first year, lecture courses are Biochemistry, Developmental Anatomy, Gross Anatomy, Histology, Neuroanatomy, and Physiology. Generally, students are in lecture for about 25 hours per week. The course Medical Ethics is taught by using both lecture and small-group format. Medical Practice and Society and Physical Diagnosis use lectures and a case-based approach. During the second year, traditional lecture/lab courses include Genetics, Microbiology, Pharmacology, and Pathology. Introduction to Behavioral Sciences and a course covering principles of public health are also part of the curriculum. In addition, students take part in weekly sessions in clinical settings, as part of an introductory course in clinical medicine. Basic sciences are taught in the Medical Sciences Building, which contains administrative offices, classrooms, and laboratories. The Biomedical Library houses 65,000 volumes and offers computer and online services. Grading is A–F for most courses, and promotions are based not only on grades but also on faculty evaluation of students' ethical and personal maturity. Medical students are involved in the schools' administrative affairs through an elected student governing body, which also participates in issues relating to the greater university. The schedule for the first 2 years is relatively firm, and students are encouraged to focus on their studies, rather than pursue employment or other activities during this period. The USMLE Step 1 is required following the basic-science portion of study.

CLINICAL TRAINING

Year 3 is composed entirely of required clerkships: Medicine (12 weeks), Surgery (8 weeks), Psychiatry/Neurology (8 weeks), Pediatrics (8 weeks), Obstetrics/Gynecology (6 weeks), and Family Practice (6 weeks). The fourth year is also 48 weeks but is composed of elective rather than required rotations. Students must select a 1 month rotation from each broad field: ambulatory care, neuroscience, surgical subspecialties, primary care, and in-house elective. Students train at university-affiliated hospitals that together constitute the largest medical complex along the Gulf Coast and that contain a total of 880 beds. All levels of trauma care and surgery are available, and patients come not only from around the state but from neighboring states as well. In downtown Mobile, the Children's and Women's Hospital offers clinical rotations in pediatric services and neonatal care. The hospital system serves managed care clients, among others, ensuring a client base. Cancer research and treatment, organic transplant, aeromedical transport, and preventative care are a few of the noteworthy services available through the university network. Students receive grades of A–F for clinical performance during required rotations and honors/pass/fail during elective rotations. The USMLE Step 2 is required for graduation. A large percentage of students take part in rotations at out-of-state institutions or overseas.

Campus Life

At least 80 percent of medical students must be Alabama residents. Reflecting the state's demographics, about 9 percent are underrepresented minorities, most of whom are African American. Each year, about 15 students enter who have taken time off after college. The student body is diverse in terms of undergraduate majors, and class size is relatively small, about 74 students.

STUDENT LIFE

Students take advantage of the university campus, with its recreational facilities and activities. Students also use nearby municipal recreational facilities, which include a golf course. The School of Medicine provides opportunities for students to participate in medically related projects and events, such as volunteer activities and special seminars. The majority of students live in a variety of apartment complexes that are in close proximity to the campus. Many students find buying a house a very viable option.

GRADUATES

Of the graduating class of 70, 50 percent chose primary care specialties, 20 percent went into internal medicine, 5 percent into family medicine, and 2 percent chose medicine/pediatrics. obstetrics/gynecology, pathology, radiology, and surgery were also popular choices.

Admissions

REQUIREMENTS

Requirements are 1 year each of biology, general chemistry, organic chemistry, and physics, all with associated labs; and 1 year each of English, math, and humanities. In total, 90 semester hours of undergraduate course work are required. The quality of the undergraduate institution is considered in evaluating GPA. Generally, courses taken abroad are not counted. The MCAT is required and should be no more than 3 years old. The most recent score is considered, and there is no preference for the April or August MCAT.

SUGGESTIONS

Preferably, the math requirement should be fulfilled with calculus. Nontraditional students who have taken time off after college are advised to demonstrate recent course work, particularly in the sciences. The goal of the Admissions Committee is to select candidates who have the potential to address the wide spectrum of needs faced by the medical profession, suggesting that diverse backgrounds are valued in addition to medically related experience. Because spots are few, out-of-state candidates should be competitive on a national level.

PROCESS

All Alabama residents receive a secondary application, which is sent upon receipt of the AMCAS application. About one-fourth of out-of-state residents receive a secondary. The secondary application is due on November 15, but the School of Medicine advises applicants to submit it as soon as possible. Fifty percent of Alabama residents and about 10 percent of out-of-state residents are interviewed. Interviews are held on campus from September through March. Students receive three half-hour interviews, which may vary in format. The interview day provides applicants and faculty an opportunity to become acquainted and is considered a two-way process. Of those interviewed, about 30 percent are accepted and 20 percent are placed on a ranked wait list. Candidates are accepted on a weekly basis, beginning in December.

UNIVERSITY OF SOUTH CAROLINA
SCHOOL OF MEDICINE

ADMISSIONS OFFICE, COLUMBIA, SC 29208 • ADMISSION: 803-733-3325
FAX: 803-733-3328 • E-MAIL: MILLS@GW.MED.SC.EDU • WEBSITE: WWW.MED.SC.EDU

STUDENT BODY

Type	Public
Enrollment	297
% male/female	53/47
% minorities	20
# applied (total/out)	1,047/715
# accepted (total/out)	133/19
# enrolled (total/out)	80/10
Average age	23

FACULTY

Student-faculty ratio	1:1

ADMISSIONS
Average GPA and MCAT Scores

Overall GPA	3.5
MCAT Bio	9.0
MCAT Phys	8.0
MCAT Verbal	9.0
MCAT Essay	0

Application Information

Regular application	12/1
Regular notification	10/15
Early application	6/1–8/1
Early notification	10/1
Are transfers accepted?	Yes
Admissions may be deferred?	Yes
Interview required?	Yes
Application fee	$45

Academics

In addition to the MD, the School of Medicine offers the MS and PhD degrees in biomedical science with specialization in anatomy, cell biology, experimental pathology, microbiology and immunology, pharmacology, and physiology. For qualified students, a combined MD/PhD program is possible. A combined MD/MPH program, offered in conjunction with the School of Public Health at USC, is available. Also offered is the MS in genetics counseling and biomedical science, with specialization in nurse anesthesia and rehabilitation counseling. The MD curriculum stresses psychological and social perspectives along with biological principles. Elective opportunities are available throughout all 4 years to assist students in pursuing individual interests and career goals. Medical students are evaluated with an A–F scale. Passing Step 1 of the USMLE is a requirement for promotion to year 3, and passing Step 2 is a graduation requirement.

BASIC SCIENCES: Throughout the first 2 years, clinical case studies are correlated with basic-science material. The 2 year introduction to clinical practice course emphasizes active, independent, and cooperative learning and uses a small-group format. Other first-year courses are Biochemistry, Gross Anatomy, Microscopic Anatomy, Neuroanatomy, and Physiology. Second-year courses are Microbiology, Pathology/Pathophysiology, and Pharmacology. An important resource is the USCSM Library, which has a collection of more than 90,0000 volumes. Medical students also use the USC Thomas Cooper Library, which has more than 2.5 million bound volumes.

CLINICAL TRAINING

Clerkship experiences in the third year include 8 week rotations in family medicine, medicine, obstetrics/gynecology, surgery, pediatrics, and psychiatry. During the fourth year, required clerkships are 4 weeks each in neurology, surgery, and medicine, and a 4-week acting internship. A 4-week multidisciplinary rotation concludes undergraduate clinical training and prepares students for the transition to residency and clinical practice. The remainder of the year is reserved for electives and selectives, many of which may be completed at locations around the state, at other medical schools, with federal and state agencies, and through an international elective program. While the majority of students complete core clinical training at the five affiliated hospitals in Columbia, about 15 students in each class train at the Greenville Hospital System in Greenville, South Carolina. In the Columbia area, teaching hospitals include Palmetto Richland Memorial Hospital (649 beds), Dorn Veterans Hospital (447 beds), and the William S. Hall Psychiatric Institute (270 beds).

Campus Life

Approximately 98 percent of students are South Carolina residents. About 10 percent of students are underrepresented minorities, most of whom are African American. Typically, about 20 percent of students in each entering class are nontraditional, having taken time off or pursued other careers or interests after college.

STUDENT LIFE

Because the School of Medicine is an important component of a comprehensive research university, medical students have many opportunities for interaction with students in other disciplines and can take advantage of the numerous student organizations, intramural sporting events, and social opportunities of the main university. Medical student organizations include chapters of the AMSA and the American Medical Women's Association, in addition to professionally focused groups such as the emergency medicine, family practice, internal medicine, and pediatrics clubs and the psychiatry/behavioral science society. Medical students have initiated a number of community service activities, including participation in the Columbia Free Medical Clinic, tutoring and social events at area children's homes, and the Health Education Leadership Program for primary school students. The School of Medicine has its own fitness center, but medical students also have access to all athletic facilities of the main campus. Columbia is a city with a population of almost 500,000, providing a wide variety of recreational and cultural activities. Both the ocean and the Great Smoky Mountains are within a few hours drive. On-campus housing is available for married couples, although most students live off campus in the area adjacent to the USC campus.

GRADUATES

Two-thirds of USCSM graduates go on to practice in primary care fields, making the School of Medicine a leader among U.S. medical schools in the percentage of graduates entering primary care. Although many graduates do enter primary care, USCSM grads match in all specialties all over the United States.

Admissions

REQUIREMENTS

Prerequisites are 8 semester hours each of general biology or zoology, inorganic chemistry, organic chemistry, and general physics, all with associated labs. In addition, 6 semester hours of college-level English and math are required. The MCAT is required, and scores must be no more than 5 years old. For applicants who have taken the exam more than once, the most recent set of scores is weighed most heavily.

SUGGESTIONS

A maximum of 6–8 positions in each class are open to residents of states other than South Carolina. Thus, nonresident applicants should be highly qualified. USCSM looks for applicants who are interested in primary care and who are likely to serve within the state.

PROCESS

All competitive AMCAS applicants who are South Carolina residents are sent secondary applications. About 40 percent of nonresident AMCAS applicants are sent secondaries. Of those returning secondaries, about 25 percent are interviewed between August and April. Interviews consist of two sessions, each with a member of the Admissions Committee. Candidates also have lunch with medical students and attend informational presentations. Notification of the Committee's decision occurs on a rolling basis, beginning in October. Approximately one-third of interviewed candidates are accepted. Others are rejected or put on hold and possibly accepted later in the year.

Admissions Requirements (Required)

MCAT scores, science GPA, non-science GPA, letters of recommendation, interview, essays/personal statement, extracurricular activities, exposure to medical profession

Admissions Requirements (Optional)

State residency

Overlap Schools

Medical University of South Carolina.

COSTS AND AID
Tuition & Fees

In-state tuition	$20,496
Out-of-state tuition	$59,268
Room and board (on-campus)	$10,050
Cost of books	$7,000
Fees	$50

Financial Aid

% students receiving aid	95
Average grant	$3,000
Average loan	$25,000
Average debt	$71,352

UNIVERSITY OF SOUTH DAKOTA
SANFORD SCHOOL OF MEDICINE

OFFICE OF MEDICAL STUDENT AFFAIRS, 414 EAST CLARK STREET VERMILLION, SD 57069 • ADMISSION: 605-677-6886
FAX: 605-677-5109 • E-MAIL: USDSMSA@.USD.EDU • WEBSITE: WWW.USD.EDU/MED/MD

STUDENT BODY

Type	Public
Enrollment	209
% male/female	52/48
% minorities	5
# applied (total/out)	744/605
# accepted (total/out)	75/7
# enrolled (total/out)	50/4
Average age	23

FACULTY

Total faculty	1,039
% female	26
% part-time	72
Student-faculty ratio	0:1

ADMISSIONS
Average GPA and MCAT Scores

Overall GPA	3.76
MCAT Bio	9.91
MCAT Phys	9.37
MCAT Verbal	9.57
MCAT Essay	0

Application Information

Regular application	11/15
Regular notification	Rolling
Are transfers accepted?	Yes
Admissions may be deferred?	Yes
Interview required?	Yes
Application fee	$35

Academics

Students complete 167 credits during their four-year M.D. program. They are evaluated with letter and numerical grades. Students must pass USMLE Step 1, Step CK and a school-administered OSCE, and must take USMLE step 2-CS to graduate. During the break between years one and two, medical students have the opportunity to undertake clinical or basic science research projects, arranged through the Summer Research Program. This program teams qualified students with physician/faculty mentors, and offers fellowship support.

BASIC SCIENCES: Basic biomedical sciences are taught in the Lee Memorial Medical Science Building on the USD campus in Vermillion. The Lommen Health Sciences Library is also on the Vermillion campus. The basic biomedical sciences are taught by lecture, lab, small-group discussions, and case-based presentations, all with an emphasis on clinical correlation. Students are in class or other scheduled sessions for about 30 hours per week. First-year courses are Biochemistry, Gross Anatomy, Embryology, Histology with Phisiology, Neuroscience, and Introduction to Clincical Medicine (ICM). The ICM course is an interdisciplinary sequence that continues into the second year. During the first year, the course is titled Introduction to the Patient: Personal and Professional Issues. The focus is on integrating biological, social, and psychological models and introducing the patient in all stages of the life cycle. Students also learn doctor/patient communication skills. Second-year courses are Advanced Behavorial Science, ICM, Pathology, Microbiology, Pharmacology, and Radiology-I. During year two, ICM provides students with experiences in performing comprehensive history and physical examinations on patients in a clinical setting. At the end of year two, students travel to a rural community within the state to take a four-week preceptorship with a Family Practice Physician.

CLINICAL TRAINING

During the third and fourth years, students rotate through hospitals and clinics in Sioux Falls, Rapid City, or Yankton. All students participate in three weeks of clinical colloquium. For the Sioux Falls and Rapid City campuses, the third year consists of six clerkships taken two at a time during three blocks of sixteen weeks. The clerkships are Family Medicine paired with General Internal Medicine, Pediatrics and Adolescent Medicine paired with Obstetrics and Gynecology, and General Surgery paired with Psychiatry and Neurology. In addition, students take Radiology and participate in a weekly Primary Care Ambulatory Clinic throughout the year. Alternatively, third-year students may enter a unique, primary care curriculum at the Yankton campus that emphasizes community involvement and self-directed learning. The entire 12 months is based in a multidisciplinary clinic, and students follow patients in each of the six specialties throughout the year. Fourth-year required clerkships for all students are Family Medicine (4 weeks), Emergency Room (2 weeks), Sub-Internship (4 weeks), and Surgical Specialties (6 weeks). An additional 22 weeks are reserved for electives. As a community-based medical school, the Sanford School of Medicine (SSOM) neither owns nor operates the clinical facilities utilized by SSOM for teaching. Rather, the school maintains strong affiliations with a range of health care providers throughout the state, including

Rapid City Regional Hospital; Stanford USD Medical Center in Sioux Falls, Avera McKennan Hospital, and University Health Center in Sioux Falls; Avera Sacred Heart Hospital and the Yankton Medical Clinic in Yankton; and Veterans Affairs Hospitals in Sioux Falls, Fort Meade, and Hot Springs.

Students

All admitted students are either South Dakota residents or have significant personal ties to South Dakota. About 5 percent of students are underrepresented minorities, most of whom are Native Americans. The average age of incoming students is about 24. Class size is 50.

STUDENT LIFE

The small class size encourages collaborations and interaction among students, as well as between faculty and students. Several student organizations give the students an opportunity to become involved in a variety of service and support activities. During years one and two, students have access to the recreational and athletic facilities of the University of South Dakota as well as on-campus residence halls. During years three and four, students have varied options, depending on where their clinical training takes place.

GRADUATES

Graduates are successful in securing residencies nationwide and typically choose 10-14 different specialties. Approximately one-third of graduates enter primary care fields.

Admissions

REQUIREMENTS

Prerequisites are one year each of Biology, Chemistry, Organic Chemistry, Physics, and college-level Math. Advanced Placement and CLEP courses may count for meeting prerequisites if granted on pre-medical transcript, and there is other evidence of appropriate knowledge in the subject area. The MCAT is required, and the exam must be within three years of the application deadline. For applicants who have retaken the exam, the most recent set of scores is compared to previous scores.

SUGGESTIONS

Residents of South Dakota, nonresidents with strong personal ties to the state (for example, they graduated from high school in South Dakota, or their parents live in-state) and applicants of Native American descent who can demonstrate enrollment in federally recognized tribes in South Dakota or in border states are invited to submit secondary applications. Beyond academic credentials, exposure to the medical profession, volunteer activities, and interest in practicing primary care medicine and working with underserved communities are all valued.

PROCESS

Qualified AMCAS applicants who meet residency criteria are sent secondary applications. These applicants are invited to interview with the admissions committee between October and February. Interviews consist of two one-to-one interviews with a faculty member who serves on the admissions committee. Of interviewed candidates, about 30 percent are accepted, with notification beginning in December. Several students are placed on an alternate list and are given a rank order for admission if vacancies occur. All accepted applicants must pass background checks prior to matriculation. SSOM does not consider applications for transfer with advanced standing from students at non-LCME accredited medical schools.

Admissions Requirements (Required)

MCAT scores, Science GPA, Non-science GPA, Letters of recommendation, Interview, Supplemental application

Admissions Requirements (Optional)

State residency, Essays/personal statement, Extracurricular activities, Exposure to medical profession

Overlap Schools

Creighton University, Mayo Clinic College of Medicine, The University of Iowa, University of Minnesota, University of Minnesota, Duluth, University of Nebraska Medical Center.

COSTS AND AID

Tuition & Fees

In-state Tuition	$14,314
Out-of-state Tuition	$34,287
Room and board	$18,280
Cost of books	$1,750
Fees	$4,122

Financial Aid

% students receiving aid	99
Average grant	$6,376
Average loan	$32,339
Average debt	$129,457

University of South Florida

College of Medicine

ADMISS./MDC-3, 12901 BRUCE B DOWNS BLVD TAMPA, FL 33612 • **ADMISSION:** 813-974-2229 • **FAX:** 813-974-4990
E-MAIL: MD-ADMISSIONS@LYRIS.HSC.USF.EDU • **WEBSITE:** WWW.HEALTH.USF.EDU/MEDICINE/MDADMISSIONS

Academics

The 4-year curriculum is designed to permit the student to learn the fundamental principles of medicine, to acquire skills of critical judgment based on evidence and experience, and to develop an ability to use principles and skills wisely in solving problems of health and disease. Medical students interested in careers in research may pursue a combined MD/PhD program, earning the doctorate in a number of biomedical fields. For students interested in public and community health issues, a combined MD/MPH program is offered in conjunction with the College of Public Health. A combined MD/MBA is available to students interested in the Business of Medicine. Medical students are evaluated with honors/pass with commendation/ pass/ fail. Passing Step 1 of the USMLE is a requirement for promotion to year 3, and passing Step 2 CK and CS exams is a graduation requirement.

BASIC SCIENCES: First-year students focus mainly on basic sciences and are instructed in a variety of ways including lectures, labs, small group conferences, and interdisciplinary methods; computers are an important educational resource. Students begin year 1 with an introduction to medicine in the Profession of Medicine course (3 weeks) before transitioning to science courses. First-year students investigate ethical and behavioral aspects of medicine in the courses Behavioral Medicine and Medical Ethics. They begin to learn patient-interaction skills through Longitudinal Clinical Experience (LCE) and Physical Diagnosis (PD) courses that extend into the second year. The LCE places the student with a clinical preceptor where the student participates in weekly hands-on clinical training with real patients in our community medical facilities. Other first-year courses are Human Anatomy, Medical Neuroscience, Molecular Medicine, and Physiology. The second year is an integrated presentation of basic and clinical sciences with year-long courses in Clinical Diagnosis and Reasoning, a problem-based learning course called Clinical Problem Solving, Evidence-Based Medicine, Immunology and Infectious Diseases, Pathology and Laboratory Medicine, Pharmacology, and Principles of Microbiology. Students are in class or other scheduled sessions for about 32 hours per week. In between the first and second year, there are opportunities for involvement in research. The pre-clinical curriculum provides a solid foundation for the transition to clinical medicine, whereby via the LCE, students will have had live (4 hours weekly) clinical experiences in three separate specialties of medicine before entering the third year.

CLINICAL TRAINING

Third-year required clinical rotations are arranged in 5 clinical areas including: Emergency Medicine/Urgent Care (4 weeks), Inpatient Medicine/Pediatrics (12 weeks), and Maternal/Newborn (4 weeks), Neuropsychiatry (8 weeks), Outpatient Primary Care/Special Populations (12 weeks), and Surgical Care (8 weeks). The fourth year is divided between 4 required clerkship blocks (2 in Critical Care, 1 in Dermatology/Musculosketal, and 1 in Oncology) and 5 electives, a portion of which may be taken at other academic or clinical institutions or locations around the state, country, or overseas. Most clinical training takes place at Tampa General Hospital (1,000 beds); H. Lee Moffitt Cancer Center and Research Institute (162 beds); James A. Haley Veterans Hospital (577 beds); the USF Psychiatry Center, USF Medical Clinic; All Children's Hospital (168 beds); USF Eye Institute; University Diagnostic Institute; Shriners Hospital for Crippled Children; Bayfront Medical Center (518 beds); and Bay Pines Veterans

Medical Center (520 beds). A number of community-based clinics are also used as clinical training.

Campus Life

Most students are Florida residents. About 13 percent of students are from those ethnic groups underrepresented in medicine; representing only a portion of the diverse cultures found among students. Although most students enter shortly after college graduation, there is a wide age range in each class. The class size is 120.

STUDENT LIFE

Students are cooperative, often studying together and interacting outside of the academic setting. The medical school sponsors student events and organizations and has a strong emphasis on involvement in school and community activities. The medical school is located on the main USF campus, giving students access to the amenities of a large university. Tampa has many cultural and recreational opportunities and is generally a popular city among students. Most students live off campus, where housing is relatively affordable and comfortable.

GRADUATES

Graduates are successful in securing residency positions in all specialty areas. At USF, postgraduate training programs are offered in more than 10 fields.

Admissions

REQUIREMENTS

Science requirements include 1 year each of basic introductory courses and laboratories in biological science, general chemistry, organic chemistry, and physics. One year of both English and mathematics is also required. The MCAT is required, and at least 1 score must be from within the past 3 years. For applicants who have taken the exam more than once, the best set of scores is weighed most heavily. Thus, there is no advantage in withholding scores.

SUGGESTIONS

State residency is given preference. Courses that are recommended, but not required, include physical chemistry or biological chemistry, biochemistry, embryology, cell biology comparative anatomy, genetics and statistics. Course work in communication arts, humanities, and natural sciences is encouraged. No specific requirement is set in the area of mathematics since, at most colleges; some mathematics is prerequisite to physics and chemistry. Some college level work in calculus is strongly recommended. Familiarity with the principles of statistics and their application to the analysis of data are important assets for any medical student. Consideration should be given by the student to participation in honors courses, independent study, and scientific research. These activities present opportunities for unstructured learning experiences. Noncognitive experiences (shadowing, health care experience [voluntary or paid], community service, leadership roles, and research) enhance an applicants' understanding of careers in medicine. All applicants are advised to apply as early as possible because the application process is rolling.

PROCESS

All AMCAS applicants who meet minimum standards are sent secondary applications. About 15 percent of those who return secondary applications are invited to interview between September and April. Interviews are one onone with 2 faculty members or a fourth-year medical student. On interview day, candidates have the opportunity to tour the campus and meet informally with current medical students. About 50 percent of interviewees are accepted with notification occurring on a rolling basis. Others are rejected or wait listed.

Admissions Requirements (Required)

MCAT scores, science GPA, non-science GPA, letters of recommendation, interview, essay/personal statement, extracurricular activities, exposure to medical profession

Admissions Requirement (Optional)

State residency

Overlap Schools

University of Florida, University of Miami.

COSTS AND AID

Tuition & Fees

In-state tuition	$17,272
Out-of-state tuition	$47,005
Room and board (off-campus)	$10,200
Cost of books	$8,722
In-state fees	$2,064
Out-of-state fees	$3,551

Financial Aid

% students receiving aid	88
Average grant	$7,000
Average loan	$35,000
Average debt	$103,453

University of Southern California

Keck School of Medicine

1975 Zonal Avenue, KAM 100-C, Los Angeles, CA 90089-9021 • Admission: 323-442-2552
Fax: 323-442-2433 • E-mail: MEDADMIT@HSC.USC.EDU • Website: WWW.USC.EDU/MEDICINE

STUDENT BODY

Type	Private
Enrollment	665
# applied (total/out)	6,391/2,799
# accepted	383
# enrolled (total/out)	162/46

FACULTY

Total faculty (number)	1,324
% part-time	3

ADMISSIONS
Average GPA and MCAT scores

Overall GPA	3.6

Application Information

Regular application	11/1
Early application	8/1
Early notification	9/1
Are transfers accepted?	Yes
Admissions may be deferred?	Yes
Interview required?	Yes
Application fee	$90

Academics

While the majority of students earn their MD in 4 years, USC offers a variety of joint-degree programs. The MD/PhD program is administered by the USC Graduate School and the School of Medicine, allowing students to earn the doctorate in anatomy, biochemistry, biomedical engineering, biophysics, cell biology, genetics, immunology, microbiology, molecular biology, neuroscience, pathology, pharmacology, and physiology. For those interested in more discrete research projects, the Research Scholar Program allows students to spend 1 year involved in research at USC or another approved institution. Students also have the option of entering a combined MD/MPH program.

BASIC SCIENCES: Lectures, labs, and periodic small-group discussions are the instructional modalities used during the first 2 years. Currently, the faculty and students are working together to design a revised curriculum, which may depend more on small-group sessions and problem-based learning. The first year (38 weeks) begins with an introductory review course entitled human biology, which is followed by a sequence of courses based on organ systems. They are cardiovascular, endocrine/reproduction, gastrointestinal/liver, renal/respiratory/skin, Neuroscience, and blood. Students benefit from patient contact from the very beginning in Introduction to Clinical Medicine. The second year (37 weeks) is also organized around body/organ systems and is dedicated to studying the mechanisms of disease. USC's library is comprehensive and has an ample supply of computers. Computers with course material, online resources, and other study aids are also available in individually assigned laboratory spaces, which serve as student study areas. Grading for the first 2 years is honors/satisfactory/unsatisfactory. Students must pass Step 1 of the USMLE to be promoted to year 3.

CLINICAL TRAINING

The clinical years are the hallmark of USC's education. The majority of teaching takes place in L.A. County and USC Medical Center. It is among the major public hospitals for Los Angeles and receives patients with every imaginable illness and injury. Students are allowed extensive patient contact. The curriculum of required courses and electives is continuous over the third and fourth years and is individually designed. Required clerkships are Family Medicine (6 weeks), Pediatrics (6 weeks), Obstetrics/Gynecology (6 weeks), General Surgery (6 weeks), Psychiatry (6 weeks), Neurology (4 weeks), Internal Medicine (two of 6 weeks each), Specialized Surgery (2–3 weeks), and a basic or clinical sciences clerkship (4 weeks). An additional 12 weeks of selectives are required. Students may take up to 16 weeks of electives at approved institutions throughout the nation. In addition to LAC and USC Medical Center, clinical facilities include Children's Hospital Los Angeles, USC University Hospital, and USC/Norris Comprehensive Cancer Center. Grading during the clinical years is honors/near honors/satisfactory/unsatisfactory. Students must record a score on the USMLE Step 2 to graduate.

Campus Life

Of the 168 students in each class, about 70% are California residents. About 18% of students are underrepresented minorities. The average age of incoming students is about 24, with a wide age range including significant numbers of students in their thirties.

STUDENT LIFE

Most students choose to live in one of the many exciting surrounding neighborhoods that Los Angeles has to offer such as Silverlake, Pasadena, Downtown Los Angeles, and Hollywood. Nonetheless, USC has a cohesive and cooperative student body. Many first-year students attend a camping retreat prior to the beginning of classes, during which they are introduced to each other and to returning students. During the academic year, students typically study in groups, and spend time together outside of school. The School of Medicine offers a wide range of extracurricular activities, including volunteer programs, intramural sports, and student clubs and organizations. USC's main campus is easily accessible by car, and medical students regularly use its extensive recreational facilities. University-sponsored activities, such as intercollegiate sporting events, films, and parties, are also popular with medical students.

GRADUATES

Graduates are successful in securing positions nationwide, in both specialty and primary care fields. Most enter residency programs in California.

Admissions

REQUIREMENTS

Prerequisites are 2 semesters each, with associated labs, in biology, general chemistry, organic chemistry, and physics. In addition, applicants must have completed a course in basic molecular biology and an additional 30 semester hours in a combination of English composition, humanities, and social sciences. The MCAT is required, and scores must be from within the previous 2 years.

SUGGESTIONS

The Admissions Committee looks very favorably upon hospital or other medical experience that involves patient care and demonstrates a commitment to service. Research experience is also helpful. USC strongly recommends additional course work in statistics and higher mathematics.

PROCESS

All AMCAS applicants are asked to submit a supplemental application. Of those students who return supplemental applications, approximately 600 are invited for interviews. The interview day consists of a tour, lunch with medical students, and one or two hour-long interviews with faculty and/or medical students. Initial acceptances are sent at the beginning of January, but most students are placed in a hold category, with the majority of acceptances offered in May. About 40 percent of interviewed candidates are accepted. Wait listed candidates may send additional information to update or strengthen their files.

Admissions Requirements (Required)

MCAT scores, science GPA, non-science GPA, letters of recommendation, interview, essay/personal statement, extracurricular activities, exposure to medical profession

COSTS AND AID
Tuition & Fees

Tuition	$45,536
Room and board (off-campus)	$15,842
Cost of books	$3,200
Fees	$4,358

Financial Aid

% students receiving aid	68
Average grant	$19,166
Average loan	$46,400
Average debt	$142,961

THE UNIVERSITY OF TENNESSEE—HEALTH SCIENCE CENTER
COLLEGE OF MEDICINE

ADMISSIONS OFFICE, 910 MADISON AVENUE, SUITE 500, MEMPHIS, TN 38163 • ADMISSION: 901-448-5559
FAX: 901-448-1740 • WEBSITE: WWW.UTMEM.EDU/MEDICINE

STUDENT BODY

Type	Public
Enrollment	600
% male/female	61/39
% minorities	12
# applied (total/out)	1,477/818
Average age	24

FACULTY

Total faculty (number)	854
% female	24
% minority	5
% part-time	2
Student-faculty ratio	2:1

ADMISSIONS

Application Information

Regular application	11/15
Regular notification	10/15–4/1
Are transfers accepted?	Yes
Admissions may be deferred?	Yes
Interview required?	Yes
Application fee	$50

Academics

Students follow a 4-year curriculum, leading to the MD. For students interested in intensive research, an MD/PhD program is available. Medical students generally receive percentage scores on exams and are evaluated with an A–F scale. Examinations in some courses are administered by computer. Passing both steps of the USMLE is a requirement for graduation.

The Faculty of the College of Medicine is committed to educating physicians whose primary responsibilities will be evaluating, treating, and preventing disease. The educational program is designed to prepare students to become knowledgeable, skillful, and compassionate physicians. Students are imbued with both the ideal that the study of medicine is a lifelong process and the sense of a physician's deep commitment to high moral and ethical standards regarding patients, colleagues, and society.

BASIC SCIENCE

Year 1 of the curriculum begins in August with Gross Anatomy; Prevention, Community and Culture (PCC); Doctoring: Recognizing Signs and Symptoms (DRS); Molecular Basis of Disease; and Physiology, and runs through March. In April and May of year 1, some concepts from the Pathophysiology, Microbiology, Pathology, and Pharmacology courses are presented. Year 2 begins in August with Pharmacology, Microbiology, Pathology, Pathophysiology, Neurosciences, PCC and DRS.

CLINICAL TRAINING

Students are introduced to clinical medicine in their first semester through PCC and DRS. These courses expose students to the practice of medicine by placing them in a community physician's office and emphasizing professionalism. The third-year clerkships focus on patient problem solving with an increasing level of responsibility. The fourth year is composed of six 4-week clerkships and four 4-week electives.

Campus Life

At least 90 percent of students are Tennessee residents. Others are usually from the eight states contiguous to Tennessee. These are Mississippi, Arkansas, Missouri, Kentucky, Virginia, North Carolina, Georgia, and Alabama. The average age of incoming students is typically about 24 with a wide age range among students. Underrepresented minorities account for about 12 percent of students. Class size is 150.

STUDENT LIFE

Medical students are cohesive and supportive of one another. As part of the Big Sib Program, incoming medical students are assigned to sophomore students as mentors. Typically, the Big Sibs will pass along their class notes to the new students to use as a guide during basic science lectures. Medical students are part of a larger community that includes students of all professional schools and programs. More than 35 campus-wide organizations are open to medical students. Students enjoy a fitness center that houses a multipurpose gym, a swimming pool, spa, racketball courts, and a weight room. An outdoor complex has playing fields, volleyball courts, tennis courts, golf-practice facilities, and a track. Intramural sports are popular, as is the Outdoor Adventures Program, which leads canoeing, hiking, rafting, and camping trips. Memphis is a festive city, renowned for its music scene. Other attractions include riverside areas, parks, restaurants, a lively arts community, and quiet residential neighborhoods. UT HSC offers facilities for single students.

GRADUATES

Among 2007 graduates, the most popular fields for residencies were the following: internal medicine (15 percent), pediatrics (12 percent), family practice (13 percent), obstetrics/gynecology (10 percent), surgery (10 percent), radiology (5 percent), and medicine/pediatrics (5 percent). A significant proportion of graduates remains in Tennessee for postgraduate training.

Admissions

REQUIREMENTS

Prerequisite course work is 8 semester hours each of biology, general chemistry, general physics, and organic chemistry, all taken with associated labs. In addition, 6 hours of English is required. The MCAT is required and scores must be no more than 5 years old. For applicants who have taken the exam more than once, all sets of scores are considered.

SUGGESTIONS

Residents of Tennessee are given preference. Children of UT alumni are also considered, regardless of their state of residence. As a state-supported institution, no more than 10 percent of students may be nonresidents. Thus, nonresident applicants should be highly qualified. Students are encouraged to take courses in the humanities, fine arts, and social sciences. Demonstration of analytic ability and independent thinking is important.

PROCESS

All AMCAS applicants who are considered competitive are sent supplemental applications. Of those returning supplementals, approximately 400 applicants are invited to interview between October and March. The interview gives insights into the applicant's character and how well he/she has formulated plans for the study of medicine. Interviews consist of two sessions, each with a faculty member or current medical student. On interview day, applicants have lunch, attend group informational sessions, sit in on classes, and tour the campus. Of interviewed candidates, about 60 percent are accepted on a rolling basis. Others are either rejected or placed on a wait list.

Admissions Requirements (Required)

MCAT scores, state residency, extracurricular activities, exposure to medical profession

Admissions Requirements (Optional)

Science GPA, non-science GPA, letters of recommendation, interview, essays/personal statement

COSTS AND AID
Tuition & Fees

In-state tuition	$18,050
Out-of-state tuition	$35,440
Room and board (on-campus)	$1,400
Room and board (off-campus)	$3,600
Cost of books	$1,600
Fees	$544

Financial Aid

% students receiving aid	85
Average grant	$5,569
Average loan	$22,000
Average debt	$123,485

THE UNIVERSITY OF TEXAS
MEDICAL BRANCH AT GALVESTON SCHOOL OF MEDICINE

OFFICE OF ADMISSIONS, SUITE 1204, ASHBEL SMITH BUILDING, GALVESTON, TX 77555-1317 • ADMISSION: 409-772-3517
FAX: 409-747-2909 • E-MAIL: TSILVA@UTMB.EDU • WEBSITE: WWW.UTMB.EDU

STUDENT BODY

Type	Public
Enrollment	861
% male/female	50/50
% minorities	25
# applied (total/out)	3,443/537
# accepted (total/out)	292/32
# enrolled (out-of-state)	228/12

ADMISSIONS

Application Information

Regular application	10/1
Regular notification	11/15
Are transfers accepted?	Yes
Admissions may be deferred?	Yes
Interview required?	Yes
Application fee (in-state)	$55
Application fee (out-of-state)	$100

Academics

UTMB is committed to educate and employ a health care work force whose diversity mirrors the population they serve. Therefore, our student body is culturally and ethnically diverse and our curriculum offers myriad educational approaches and geographic locations for study. The diversity in our student body is reflected in the high level of participation in global health opportunities and in providing health care to underserved populations. The diversity of educational approaches is exhibited in our commitment to problem based, small group learning an introduction of clinical experiences into the first 2 years of the curriculum. In addition, many students choose to do some or all of their and fourth year clinical clerkships at our Austin campus, or elective experience throughout Texas, the U.S., or internationally.

CLINICAL TRAINING

The third year begins with a week-long Clinical Skills Experience, followed by the required clerkships: Family Medicine, Internal Medicine, Obstetrics/Gynocology, Pediatrics, Psychiatry, and Surgery. Third year also includes one elective period. Year 4 includes required Senior Surgery, Emergency Medicine, and Neurology clerkships along with Basic Science and Humanities and Ambulatory Community Selectives. The fourth year required experiences also include Advanced Cardiac Life Support, an Autopsy Exercise, and the Integrated Clinical Evaluation Exercise. At least 20 weeks are reserved for elective study.

BASIC SCIENCE

The Integrated Medical Curriculum is designed to provide the student with multiple learning opportunities. The foundation of our year 1 and 2 courses is small group (8–9 students per group) problem-based learning (PBL) sessions highlighted by student-centered, active learning that is guided by faculty facilitators. Subsequent lectures, laboratories, clinical wrap-up sessions, and other faculty-generated activities are designed to reinforce the student's understanding and to fill in any knowledge gaps. Year 1 and 2 course run sequentially as modules of approximately 8 weeks in duration. The first 3 modules, Gross Anatomy and Radiology, Molecules Cells and Tissues, and Pathobiology and Host Defenses, comprise the basic science core. The remainder of the year 1 and 2 course are system based and include Neuroscience and Human Behavior, Cardiovascular and Pulmonary, Renal, Fluids and Electrolytes, Gastrointestinal/Nutrition, Endocrine/Reproduction, Derm/Heme/Musculoskeletal, and Great Syndromes. The Practice of Medicine is a comprehensive course that addresses the development of knowledge, skills, attitudes, and behaviors that are necessary to practice the art and science of medicine and runs concurrently with the basic science curriculum throughout the first 2 years.

Campus Life

At least 90 percent of students are Texas residents. Typically, about 10–15 percent of entering students are nontraditional, having taken significant time between college and medical school. Approximately 25 percent of students are underrepresented minorities. Class size is 228.

STUDENT LIFE

Students benefit from the resources and facilities of a large, modern campus. The Lee Hage Jamail Student Center serves as a meeting place for medical students. It has a cafeteria, meeting rooms, study areas, and recreational facilities. Coed medical fraternities located close to campus offer housing, meals, and social opportunities to medical students. The UTMB Alumni Field House features a variety of indoor and outdoor facilities, including tennis courts, baseball diamonds, volleyball courts, an outdoor basketball court, racquetball courts, fitness centers, spa facilities, an outdoor track, and an Olympic-size pool. UTMB has more than 60 student organizations that range from support groups for minority students, to community service oriented groups, to professional organizations. The university operates a small number of dormitories and apartments for single students.

GRADUATES

Graduates are successful in securing residencies at top institutions nationwide.

Admissions
PROCESS

Applications are submitted online through the Texas Medical and Dental Schools Application Service (TMDSAS, UTsystem.edu/TMDSAS). Applications must be submitted between May 1 and October 1. About 900 applicants are invited to interview from July through November. Candidates receive 2 interviews, each with a faculty member. On interview day, there are also orientation sessions, a campus tour, and several opportunities to meet informally with current medical students. Students are accepted on a rolling basis between November 15 and December 31 and the class is filled by the TMDSAS match held on February 1. Students who have interviewed but not been accepted may be put into the alternate pool. This pool is not ranked. When positions become available, the Admissions Committee will review all candidates in the pool for acceptance. The number taken from the pool varies from year to year, but is usually somewhere between 10 and 15.

REQUIREMENTS

A grade of at least a C must be earned in all of the prerequisite courses: English (1 year); biology (2 years); math (1 semester of calculus or statistics); physics (1 year); chemistry (1 year); and organic chemistry (1 year). All science courses must include laboratory work. The MCAT is required, and scores older than 5 years will not be considered. For applicants who have taken the exam on multiple occasions, the scores from the best testing are considered.

SUGGESTIONS

As a state-supported institution, UTMB gives preference to Texas residents. Applicants are encouraged to take the MCAT during the spring because late receipt of scores may delay application processing. The Admissions Committee, in determining an applicant's eligibility for admission, considers aspects such as the recommendation of the health professions advisor or advisory committee, personal qualifications, academic profile, undergraduate course work, grades, and MCAT scores. Academic and non-academic factors are of equal importance. Particular consideration is given to the applicant's maturity, motivation, and intellectual curiosity as reflected by academic honors, demonstrated leadership roles, research experiences, and participation in activities such as public or community service, athletics, performing arts, and social organizations. Also considered are interpersonal skills, oral and bilingual communication skills, and unique educational, career, or life experiences.

Admissions Requirements (Required)

MCAT scores, science GPA, non-science GPA, letters of recommendation, extracurricular activities, exposure to medical profession, interview, essays/personal statement

Admissions Requirements (Optional)

State residency

COSTS AND AID
Tuition & Fees

In-state tuition	$6,550
Out-of-state tuition	$19,650
Room and board	
(on-campus)	$8,076
(off-campus)	$12,240
Cost of books	$2,720
Fees	$4,400

Financial Aid

% students receiving aid	82
Average grant	$10
Average loan	$29,264
Average debt	$108,392

THE UNIVERSITY OF TEXAS HEALTH SCIENCE CENTER AT HOUSTON
MEDICAL SCHOOL AT HOUSTON

OFFICE OF ADMISSIONS, MSB G.420 HOUSTON, TX 77030 • ADMISSION: 713-500-5116
FAX: 713-500-0604 • E-MAIL: MSADMISSIONS@UTH.TMC.EDU • WEBSITE: WWW.MED.UTH.TMC.EDU

STUDENT BODY

Type	Public
Enrollment	868
% male/female	54/46
% minorities	27
# applied (total/out)	2,922/524
# accepted (total/out)	289/23
# enrolled (total/out)	213/13
Average age	24

FACULTY

Total faculty (number)	870
% female	37
% minority	31
% part-time	11
Student-faculty ratio	1:1

ADMISSIONS
Average GPA and MCAT scores

Overall GPA	3.67
MCAT Bio	9.7
MCAT Phys	9.2
MCAT Verbal	9.3
MCAT Essay	P

Application Information

Regular application	10/1
Regular notification	2/15
Early application	10/1
Early notification	12/15
Are transfers accepted?	No
Admissions may be deferred?	No
Interview required?	Yes
Application fee	$55

Academics

Although most medical students complete studies in four years, some follow an Alternate Pathway curriculum, which extends first-year courses over a two-year period and which leads to the MD degree in five years. Others follow a 7-year program leading to both the MD and the PhD degrees, while others earn a Master's in Public Health along with the MD in five years. Summer research opportunities are available, most of which are paid. Medical students are evaluated with honors/high pass/ pass/ marginal performance/ fail. All students must take the USMLE Steps 1 and 2.

CLINICAL TRAINING

Third-year required rotations are Medicine (12 weeks); Surgery (8 weeks); Obsterics/Gynecology (6 weeks); Pediatrics (8 weeks); Psychiatry (6 weeks); Neurology (4 weeks); and Family Medicine (4 weeks). During the fourth year, required rotations are Family Practice (1 month); Medicine (1 month); and Surgery (1 month) and a new Transition to Residency Month. Third and fourth-year students receive advanced technical skills training and radiology. Clinical training takes place primarily at the numerous hospitals, clinics, and care centers associated with the Texas Medical Center in Houston and in a city/county hospital in northeast Houston. There is flexibility in terms of where elective credits may be earned, and some students opt to study elsewhere in the country or at one of several international programs.

BASIC SCIENCE

First-year courses are Biochemistry, Gross Anatomy, Developmental Anatomy, Histology, Immunology, Introduction to Clinical Medicine (ICM), Microbiology, Neuroscience, Physiology and Radiology. The ICM course introduces students to interviewing, history-taking, and physical-examination skills, and offers the venue for early patient contact. Instructional methods used during the first year include videotaped lectures, small-group sessions, tutorials, and labs. The first year courses are all coordinated to integrate a systems-based approach overlaying the traditional topics. A problem-based learning curriculum links basic and clinical sciences and allows second-year students to begin addressing complex medical problems. Problem-based learning is an important part of the second-year curriculum, serving to integrate the various courses and provide clinical skills. Second-year courses are Behavioral Science, Genetics, Fundamentals of Clinical Medicine, Pathology, Pharmacology, Physical Diagnosis, and Reproductive Biology. During the first two years, students are in class or other scheduled sessions for about 22 hours per week. All lectures are videotaped for online review. The Learning Resource Center has textbooks, audiovisuals, anatomical models, audiotapes, and videotapes of lectures, computers, files of past exams, USMLE review materials, and other instructional aids. Networked computers with free access to computer-based services and instructional materials are also provided.

Campus Life

At least 90 percent of students are Texas residents. Most students are recent college graduates, although there is typically a wide age range among incoming students. In terms of ethnic backgrounds, students represent the diverse population of the state.

STUDENT LIFE

There are numerous student organizations, focusing on areas such as public service projects, professional interests, religious and ethnic interests, athletics, and recreation. Houston is an exciting city for students, with a wide range of entertainment, recreational attractions, restaurants, shopping areas, and facilities for outdoor activities. The university offers apartments a short distance from school and a free shuttle runs throughout the week from this and many other complexes.

GRADUATES

Of approximately 208 UT Houston Medical School graduates, about 61 percent go on to practice in Texas. Among the 2006 graduates, the most popular fields for residencies were pediatrics (13.5 percent), anesthesiology (12.9 percent), family practice (10.5 percent), internal medicine (9.6 percent), psychiatry (7 percent), obstetrics/gynecology (6 percent) and surgery (5.8 percent).

Admissions

PROCESS

The University of Texas does not participate in the AMCAS system. Applications may only be made online at the Texas Medical and Dental Schools Application Service website: UTSystem.edu/tmdsas. Applications must be submitted between May 1 and October 1. Additional information about the admissions process may be obtained from: Texas Medical and Dental Schools Application Service, 702 Colorado Street, Suite 6400, Austin, TX 78701, Phone: 512-499-4785. About 1,200 applicants are interviewed at UT Houston between August and January. Applicants generally receive 2 one on one interviews, each with a faculty member. On interview day, candidates also have lunch with medical students and faculty, tour the campus, and attend group orientation sessions. About one-fifth of interviewees are accepted, with notification occurring via the TMD-SAS website on February 1. Some wait listed candidates are accepted later in the spring and summer.

REQUIREMENTS

Prerequisites are one year of English, one year of physics with lab, two years of biology with lab, one year of general chemistry with lab, and one year of organic chemistry with lab. The MCAT is required, and scores should be from within the past 5 years. For applicants who have retaken the exam, the last three scores will be reviewed.

OTHER

The state legislature limits the student body to 10 percent nonresidents; thus, admission is very competitive for nonresidents. A strong liberal arts background is important and, as long as science requirements are fulfilled, students are encouraged to pursue a major in their area of interest, science or non-science, while in college. Criteria for evaluating applicants include intellectual capacity, interpersonal and communication skills, breadth and depth of premedical educational experience, potential for service to the State of Texas, motivation, and integrity.

Admissions Requirements (Required)

MCAT scores, science GPA, non-science GPA, letters of recommendation, interview, essay/personal statement, extracurricular activities, exposure to medical profession

Admissions Requirement (Optional)

State residency

Overlap Schools

Baylor College of Medicine, Texas A&M University System Health Science Center, Texas Tech University, University of North Texas, University of Texas Health Science Center—San Antonio, University of Texas Southwestern Medical Center, The University of Texas.

COSTS AND AID
Tuition & Fees

In-state tuition	$9,775
Out-of-state tuition	$22,875
Room and board (off-campus)	$13,360
Cost of books	$2,000
Fees	$1,908

Financial Aid

% students receiving aid	99
Average grant	$2,539
Average loan	$10,012
Average debt	$98,345

THE UNIVERSITY OF TEXAS HEALTH SCIENCE CENTER AT SAN ANTONIO
MEDICAL SCHOOL AT SAN ANTONIO

MEDICAL SCHOOL ADMISSIONS OFFICE, 7703 FLOYD CURL DRIVE, SAN ANTONIO, TX 78229 • ADMISSION: 210-567-2665
FAX: 210-567-2685 • E-MAIL: CHAPAB@UTHSCSA.EDU • WEBSITE: WWW.UTHSCSA.EDU

STUDENT BODY

Type	Public
Enrollment	814
% male/female	58/42
% minorities	16
# applied (total/out)	2,795/525
Average age	24

FACULTY

Total faculty (number)	678
% female	28
% part-time	5

ADMISSIONS

Application Information

Regular application	10/1
Regular notification	1/15
	until filled
Are transfers accepted?	Yes
Admissions may be deferred?	No
Interview required?	No
Application fee	$45

Academics

Almost all medical students follow a 4 year curriculum leading to the MD. A few students enter combined MD/PhD programs after their first year of medical school. Grading for most courses uses an A–F system. All students must pass Step 1 of the USMLE for promotion to year 3.

BASIC SCIENCES: Basic sciences are primarily covered during the first 2 years, although introductory clinical training also begins in year 1. San Antonio operates on a semester system, with a break scheduled around Christmas. First-year, first-semester courses are Biochemistry, Clinical Integration Course, Gross Anatomy and Embryology, Microscopic Anatomy, and Microbiology. Second semester courses are Neuroscience and Physiology. Other first-year courses use a combination of lectures, labs, and small-group sessions. Students are in class or other scheduled sessions for about 21 hours per week during year 1. During the second year, the curriculum is increasingly clinically oriented. First semester courses are Behavioral Sciences, Pathology, and Pharmacology. Second semester courses are Pathology and Psychopathology. During year 2, students are in class for about 19 hours per week, providing ample study time. An important resource for students, faculty, and the community is the Dolph Briscoe Library, which houses more than 200,000 books and journals.

CLINICAL TRAINING

The clinical integration course is an interdisciplinary program that starts with the first month of medical school and extends through the second year. Students learn basic clinical skills in the initial month of the program, spend time with community physicians, rotate with third-year students, and assume patient responsibilities to gain experience in continuity of care. The third and fourth years are devoted primarily to clinical clerkships. However, didactic instruction is also an important part of the curriculum. Topics covered are advanced cardiopulmonary resuscitation, basic cardiac life support, clinical orientation, clinical pathology, emergency medicine, epidemiology, genetics, infectious disease, medical humanities, medical jurisprudence, patient rehabilitation, and radiology. Third-year required rotations are Medicine (12 weeks), Surgery (12 weeks), Pediatrics (6 weeks), Psychiatry (6 weeks), Obstetrics/Gynecology (6 weeks), and Family Practice (6 weeks). Fourth-year requirements are medicine (8 weeks); surgery (4 weeks); a choice of pediatrics, obstetrics/gynecology, psychiatry, or family practice (4 weeks); and other selectives (16 weeks). An additional 8 weeks are reserved for electives. The primary teaching hospital is the University Hospital, which has 547 beds. Training also takes place at the facilities of the South Texas Veterans Health Care System and at other affiliates. University-affiliated patient care covers a geographical area from San Antonio to the Rio Grande Valley and is delivered in clinics, hospitals, traveling vans, as well as in sites in schools and churches. The Health Science Center serves the entire South Texas/Border region.

Campus Life

At least 90 percent of students are Texas residents. Underrepresented minorities account for 16 percent of the student population. Mexican Americans are particularly well represented. The student body is slightly older than at many other medical schools. The average age of incoming students is usually about 24, and about 15 percent of students in each class are in their thirties or older.

STUDENT LIFE

Medical students enjoy a collegial environment and appreciate the diversity within the student body. Mentoring and peer-support programs help incoming students with the transition to medical school, and special programs are available to assist underrepresented minority students. Students are very active in community-service programs and events. Activities range from volunteering at clinics to participating in health education programs in schools. All students live off campus. San Antonio offers affordable housing accessible to the Medical Center by public transportation.

GRADUATES

More than half of graduates enter primary care fields, and a significant number go on to practice in Texas.

Admissions

REQUIREMENTS

Required courses are 2 years of biology (1 of which may be biochemistry); 2 years of chemistry, which should include both organic and inorganic chemistry; 1 semester of calculus; and 1 year each of English and physics. The MCAT is required. For applicants who have taken the exam more than once, the best set of scores is weighed most heavily. Thus, there is no advantage in withholding scores.

SUGGESTIONS

In addition to academic requirements, personal traits and an applicant's background are considered. Some type of medically related experience or research is required.

PROCESS

The University of Texas medical schools do not participate in AMCAS. Rather, applications may be obtained from The Texas Medical and Dental Application Service, 702 Colorado, Suite 6400 Austin, Texas 78701. Applications must be completed by October 15. About one-third of applicants are interviewed between August and December. Interviews consist of two half-hour sessions with Admissions Committee members who may be faculty or senior students. On interview day, candidates also have lunch with students, attend group-orientation sessions, and tour the campus. The initial group of accepted candidates are notified in January. Others are notified later in the spring. An alternate pool of applicants is established and candidates are admitted as positions become available.

Admissions Requirements (Required)

MCAT scores, state residency, essays/personal statement, extracurricular activities, likelihood of serving in most urgently needed types of primary care

Admissions Requirements (Optional)

Science GPA, non-science GPA, letters of recommendation, interview, exposure to medical profession

UNIVERSITY OF TEXAS SOUTHWESTERN MEDICAL CENTER
MEDICAL CENTER AT DALLAS

5323 HARRY HINES BOULEVARD DALLAS, TX 75390-9162 • ADMISSION: 214-648-5617 • FAX: 214-648-3289
E-MAIL: ADMISSIONS@UTSOUTHWESTERN.EDU • WEBSITE: WWW.UTSOUTHWESTERN.EDU

STUDENT BODY

Type	Public
Enrollment	909
% male/female	54/46
% minorities	20
# applied (total/out)	3,376/546
# accepted (total/out)	219/30
# enrolled (total/out)	232/31
Average age	25

FACULTY

Total faculty	1,740
% female	33
% minority	16
% part-time	18
Student-faculty ratio	1:1

ADMISSIONS
Average GPA and MCAT Scores

Overall GPA	3.73
MCAT Bio	11.3
MCAT Phys	11.0
MCAT Verbal	10.15
MCAT Essay	Q

Application Information

Regular application	10/15
Regular notification	11/15
Are transfers accepted?	Yes
Admissions may be deferred?	Yes
Interview required?	Yes
Application fee	$100

Academics

The vast majority of students follow a four-year path leading to the M.D. degree. A small number of students each year enter a joint M.D./Ph.D. program in conjunction with the Southwestern Graduate School of Biomedical Sciences. For the most part, students are evaluated using an A-F scale in which a C is required to pass. Fourth-year courses are taken Pass/Fail.

BASIC SCIENCES: During the first two years, a variety of teaching/learning formats are used, including lectures, small-group, problem-based learning, computerized curriculum, and standardized patient interviews. First-year courses include Biology of Cells and Tissues; Human Anatomy and Embryology; Integrative Human Biology; Medical Biochemistry; Human Behavior; and Endocrinology and Human Reproduction. In addition, Clinical Ethics in Medicine exposes first-year students to the ethical, behavioral, and clinical perspectives of medicine in a problem-based learning format. During the 10-week period between the first and second years, numerous clinical and research opportunities are available for students who wish to participate. Clinical exposure continues in the second year through Clinical Medicine: Principles and Practice when students learn about the physical examination and experience direct, one-on-one, patient contact. Second-year courses also include Immunology and Medical Microbiology; Anatomic and Clinical Pathology; Medical Pharmacology; and Psychopathology. On average, students are in scheduled sessions for 25-30 hours per week. The campus where preclinical instruction takes place is also part of a large medical complex that includes several hospitals, research centers, and the medical school library, which holds more than 229,000 volumes and currently subscribes to almost 2,000 journals. Passing the USMLE Step 1 is required in order to progress to the fourth year.

CLINICAL TRAINING

Building upon the clinical experiences in the first two years, the third and fourth years offer intense clinical experiences involving medical students in direct patient care. Third-year required clinical rotations are Surgery (8 weeks); Pediatrics (8 weeks); Obstetrics and Gynecology (6 weeks); Internal Medicine (12 weeks); Psychiatry (6 weeks); and Family Practice (4 weeks). The fourth year is organized into 4-week periods filled with electives, selectives, and a few remaining required rotations. Requirements include Neurology (4 weeks); Internal Medicine (4 weeks of a subinternship and 4 weeks of ambulatory care); and Women's Health Care (4 weeks). Four 4-week periods remain, two of which are for selectives and two of which are reserved for electives. Clinical training takes place at University sites and affiliated institutions, including Parkland Memorial Hospital; the James Aston Ambulatory Care Center; Zale Lipshy University Hospital; Children's Medical Center; Dallas Veterans Affairs Medical Center; Southwestern Institute of Forensic Sciences; Baylor University Medical Center; Presbyterian Hospital of Dallas; Methodist Hospitals of Dallas; St. Paul Medical Center; Texas Scottish Rite Hospital for Children; and John Peter Smith Hospital in Fort Worth. Students may fulfill many of their senior rotations at academic or medical institutions in other parts of the state, the country, or the world.

Students

At least 90 percent of the student body are Texas residents. Underrepresented minorities account for about 10 percent of the population. The average age of incoming students is usually 24; the range of ages is typically 20 to 45. Incoming class size at UT Southwestern is 200 students.

STUDENT LIFE

The Bryan Williams, M.D. Student Center has exercise and recreational facilities and offers students a convenient place to relax and socialize. Dynamic campus activity programming includes intramural sports, special-interest organizations, recreational and cultural events, and parties. Students also join groups based on professional and academic interests or participate in community service projects. Dallas is an exciting city with a diverse population and many kinds of cultural, recreational, and entertainment activities. All students live off campus, and most students own cars.

GRADUATES

Graduates are successful in securing residencies at prestigious institutions all over the country. The majority of graduates go on to become practicing physicians, typically with a large percentage choosing primary care specialties. Some go into academic medicine or research.

Admissions

REQUIREMENTS

Prerequisite courses include one semester of Calculus or statistics, two semesters of English, two semesters of Physics (with lab), four semesters of Biology (two of which should be with lab and one of which may be Biochemistry), and four semesters of Chemistry (with lab), which should be equally divided between Organic and Inorganic Chemistry. The MCAT is required, and scores must be no more than five years old. For applicants who have retaken the exam, the best set of scores is used.

SUGGESTIONS

Admission for out-of-state applicants is highly competitive, as Texas law requires that no more than 10 percent of each class be nonresidents. In addition to academic credentials (GPA, MCAT score, relative rigor of the undergraduate curriculum, letters of recommendation), the Admissions Committee considers extracurricular activities, socioeconomic background, any time spent in outside employment, personal integrity and compassion for others, the ability to communicate in English, motivation for a career in medicine, and other personal qualities and individual factors such as leadership, insightful self-appraisal, determination, social/family support, and maturity/coping capabilities. Applicants are also evaluated for the demonstration of significant interest and experiences that parallel the mission of UT Southwestern.

PROCESS

UT Southwestern does not participate in the AMCAS system. A common application is available for the University of Texas System medical schools (Southwestern at Dallas, Galveston, Houston, and San Antonio), Texas A&M University College of Medicine, and Texas Tech University School of Medicine; and Texas Tech Health Science Center at El Paso. An online application is available at http://www.utsystem.edu/tmdsas. Applications must be submitted between May 1 and October 1. About one-quarter of the applicants are invited to interview, with interviews taking place between September and December. Interviews consist of two sessions with individual faculty members. About 40 percent of interviewed candidates are accepted, with notification beginning on February 1.

Admissions Requirements (Required)

MCAT scores, Science GPA, Non-science GPA, Letters of recommendation, Interview, Essays/personal statement, Extracurricular activities, Exposure to medical profession

Admissions Requirements (Optional)

State residency

Overlap Schools

Baylor College of Medicine, Duke University, Texas A&M University—College Station, Texas Tech University, The University of Texas HSC at Houston, University of Texas Health Science Center at San Antonio, Vanderbilt University.

COSTS AND AID

Tuition & Fees

In-state Tuition	$10,250
Out-of-state Tuition	$23,350
Cost of books	$1,940
Fees	$1,382

Financial Aid

% students receiving aid	82
Average grant	$4,500
Average loan	$18,700
Average debt	$90,000

THE UNIVERSITY OF TOLEDO
COLLEGE OF MEDICINE

2801 WEST BANCROFT, TOLEDO, OH 43606-3390 • ADMISSION: 419-381-4229
FAX: 419-381-4005 • E-MAIL: MEDADMISSIONS@UTNET.UTOLEDO.EDU • WEBSITE: HTTP://HSC.UTOLEDO.EDU/MED

STUDENT BODY

Type	Public
Enrollment	565
% male/female	70/30
% minorities	10
# applied (total/out)	2,848/945

FACULTY

Total faculty (number)	335
% female	23
% minority	15
% part-time	10
Student-faculty ratio	2:1

ADMISSIONS

Application Information

Regular application	11/1
Regular notification	10/15
	until filled
Early application	6/1–8/1
Early notification	10/1
Are transfers accepted?	Yes
Admissions may be deferred?	Yes
Interview required?	No
Application fee	$30

Academics

Although most students follow a 4 year program, some educationally disadvantaged students enter the Flexible Curriculum Program, which permits extension of the MD curriculum over a 5-year period. Joint-degree programs offered in conjunction with affiliated schools are available, including the MD/MS and MD/PhD through which a doctorate degree may be earned in the following areas: anatomy, biochemistry, microbiology, neuroscience, pathology, pharmacology, physiology, and numerous other fields. Medical students are evaluated with ratings of honors/high pass/pass/fail. Passing Step 1 of the USMLE is a requirement for promotion to year 3. In order to graduate, a score on Step 2 must be recorded.

BASIC SCIENCES: The first 2 years are devoted to an integrated approach to the basic sciences, behavioral sciences, primary care preceptorships, introductory clinical experiences, and problem-based learning (PBL) for all students. First-year courses are the following: Cellular and Molecular Biology; Human Structure and Development; Neuroscience and Behavioral Science; Integrated Pathophysiology I (PBL); and Physician, Patient, and Society I. During the first year, students are in class for about 30 hours per week, most of which is either lecture or lab periods. Second-year courses are Introduction to Primary Care; Immunity and Infection; Organ Systems; Integrated Pathophysiology II (PBL); and Physician, Patient, and Society II. Physician, Patient, and Society includes Introduction to Primary Care; Introduction to Clinical Medicine (ICM); and a series of courses that address topics in medical ethics, managed care, medical decision-making, nutrition, geriatrics, and substance abuse disorders. The ICM course covers practical skills such as taking patient histories and conducting physical examinations. It also serves as a forum for correlating basic science principles with clinical case studies and for discussing ethical issues related to practicing medicine. Second-year students are in class for about 20 hours per week. Basic science instruction takes place in the Health Sciences Teaching and Laboratory Building and the Health Education Building. The Mulford Library holds 125,000 volumes and 1,800 journals and, along with the Computer Learning Resource Center, provides educational and informational resources to students.

CLINICAL TRAINING

Third-year required clerkships are the following: Medicine (12 weeks), Surgery (12 weeks), Pediatrics (6 weeks), Psychiatry (6 weeks), Family Medicine (6 weeks), and Obstetrics/Gynecology (6 weeks). During the fourth year, one basic science selective (4 weeks) and one neurology clerkship (4 weeks) are required. The remaining 28 weeks are reserved for elective study. Three teaching hospitals operate on campus, the Medical College of Ohio Hospital (258 beds), Coghlin Rehabilitation Hospital (36 beds), and Lenore W. and Marvin S. Kobacker Center (25 beds, a children's psychiatric hospital). Other associated hospitals include St. Vincent Mercy Medical Center, The Toledo Hospital/Children's Medical Center of Northwest Ohio, Flower Hospital, and Northwestern Psychiatric Hospital. Through the Area Health Education Center clerkships, MCO students also have the opportunity to train in rural and inner-city communities.

Campus Life

At least 80 percent of students are Ohio residents although many attended undergraduate institutions outside of the state. Underrepresented minorities, mostly African Americans, account for approximately 10 percent of the student body. Among entrants, there are significant numbers of older individuals, some of whom are in their late thirties and early forties. Typically, about 80 percent of medical students were science majors in college.

STUDENT LIFE

In addition to providing academic resources, the Office of Student Affairs supports students inside and outside of the classroom, organizing events such as an annual orientation for incoming students. There are many student associations, ranging from one that administers a community care clinic to a student-to-student support group to organizations focused on personal, recreational, religious, cultural, and professional interests. MCO is situated on 475 acres of land, with ponds, streams, trees, and open areas. The campus offers extensive athletic and recreational facilities. Major attractions in Toledo are easily reached on public transportation and include riverside restaurants and bars, museums, parks with golf courses and other facilities, a zoo, theaters, and shopping areas. Further distraction is found in Detroit, Cincinnati, Pittsburgh, Cleveland, and Chicago, all of which are in driving distance of MCO. Students live off campus, usually in the surrounding residential neighborhood.

GRADUATES

About 40 percent of graduates go on to practice in Ohio. In recent years, about 60 percent of graduates have entered primary care fields.

Admissions

REQUIREMENTS

Prerequisites are 1 year each of biology, English, general chemistry, math, organic chemistry, and physics. All science courses must include labs. The MCAT is required. For applicants who have retaken the exam, the best set of scores is weighted most heavily. Thus, withholding scores is not advantageous.

SUGGESTIONS

As a state-supported institution, MCO gives preference to Ohio residents. Additional preparation in biology is recommended as are courses in the humanities and social sciences. For students who have been out of school for a significant period of time, some recent course work is advised. Community service and medically related experience involving patient contact are both considered valuable.

PROCESS

About 75 percent of AMCAS applicants are sent secondary applications. Of those returning secondaries, about 25 percent of Ohio residents and 10 percent of nonresidents are invited to interview. Interviews take place between October and April and consist of 2 hour-long sessions each with a faculty member, medical student, or school administrator. Also on interview day, candidates tour the campus, hear group informational sessions, and have the opportunity to meet informally with current students. About one-third of interviewees are accepted, with notification occurring throughout the year. Wait listed candidates may send additional information, such as transcripts and test scores, to update their files.

Admissions Requirements (Required)

MCAT scores, science GPA, non-science GPA, state residency, extracurricular activities, exposure to medical profession

Admissions Requirements (Optional)

Letters of recommendation, interview, essays/personal statement

COSTS AND AID

Tuition & Fees

In-state tuition	$21,412
Out-of-state tuition	$51,508
Cost of books	$2,054
Fees	$2,082

Financial Aid

% students receiving aid	90
Average grant	$6,000
Average loan	$18,500

University of Toronto
Faculty of Medicine

315 Bloor Street, West Toronto, ON M5S1A3 • **Admission:** 416-978-2190
Fax: 416-978-7022 • **Website:** WWW.UTORONTO.CA

STUDENT BODY	
Type	Public
# applied	1,731

ADMISSIONS

Application Information

Regular application	10/15
Regular notification	5/31
Are transfers accepted?	No
Admissions may be deferred?	Yes
Interview required?	Yes
Application fee	$75

Academics

The curriculum is based on four guidelines: Patient-centered learning, integrated and multidisciplinary content, student-motivated learning, and structured problem-based learning. In addition to the 4 year program leading to an MD, a 6 year MD/PhD program is offered jointly by the Faculty of Medicine and the School of Graduate Studies.

BASIC SCIENCES: The initial phase of the undergraduate medical program spans approximately 82 weeks. The curriculum consists of the following sequential blocks or units, which focus on principles of medicine: Art and Science of Clinical Medicine, Brain and Behavior, Foundations of Medical Practice, Metabolism and Nutrition, Determination of Community Health, Pathobiology of Disease, and Structure and Function. Students meet actual as well as simulated patients and are introduced to clinical medicine by faculty members in teaching hospitals. The emphasis is on student-centered, self-directed work, and small group tutorials. Students are in scheduled sessions for approximately 35 hours per week. Most learning takes place in small group settings. Independent study is also important.

CLINICAL TRAINING

The third and fourth academic periods are comprised mainly of 6-week clinical clerkships. These are ambulatory and community experience, emergency medicine and anesthesia, family and community medicine, medicine, obstetrics/gynecology, pediatrics, psychiatry, specialty medicine, specialty surgery, surgery, and three electives. Training takes place at a network of teaching hospitals and community-based health agencies. Affiliated hospitals include Baycrest Centre for Geriatric Care, Centre for Addiction and Mental Health (formerly Addiction Research Foundation and the Clarke Institute of Psychiatry), The Hospital for Sick Children, Mount Sinai Hospital, St. Michael's Hospital, Toronto Rehabilitation Institute (formerly Hillcrest Hospital and Queen Elizabeth Hospital), Sunnybrook and Women's College Health Science Centre, The Toronto Hospital (formerly the Toronto Hospital and the Ontario Cancer Institute/Princess Margaret Hospital). Students are also able to learn in the community through participation in settings such as teaching health units and physicians' offices.

Campus Life

About 15 percent of students are from outside of the province. Approximately 40 percent of students are women. Class size is 177.

STUDENT LIFE

One of the advantages of attending medical school at the University of Toronto is the city itself. The university campus is located within easy walking distance of the attractions and facilities of Toronto. Students enjoy clubs, concerts, museums, major league sporting events, and shopping. Just outside of the city, skiing and other outdoor sports are readily accessible. On-campus activities include pubs, concerts, special lectures, theaters, intramural sports, student government, special interest clubs, and the Medical Journal. Medical students benefit from the large campus of 55,000 students and its resources. Student support includes health services and a housing office that coordinates both on- and off-campus housing. Residence halls with meal plans are one of many housing options.

GRADUATES

A key aspect of the program is that it provides exposure to all medical career options. Graduates enter primary care fields, specialties, academic medicine, research, and leadership positions.

Admissions

REQUIREMENTS

Academic achievement is measured by grades and MCAT results. Prerequisite courses are at least two full course equivalents in life sciences and at least one full course equivalent in humanities, social sciences, or languages. These courses should provide applicants with an understanding of the basic principles and vocabulary of physics, chemistry, and biology, a working knowledge of statistics, and the ability to gather, interpret, and present information from complex texts both in writing and orally. Students must be in their third year or higher of university to be considered for admission.

SUGGESTIONS

Students from social sciences, humanities, and physical and life sciences are encouraged to apply. Demonstrated high-level proficiency in oral and written English is considered essential for success in the curriculum and in practice, and applicants are encouraged to have completed at least two full equivalents in a course that required expository writing. Generally, minimum requirements are an average grade point average of 3.6/4.0 and a minimum of 8 on each section of the MCAT. Desired personal characteristics include a perceptive nature, strong commitment, high personal standards, and a history of academic and personal achievement.

PROCESS

Applications for admission to the medical school must be submitted by October 15 to OMSAS, Ontario Universities Application Center, PO Box 1328, Guelph, Ontario N1H 7P4. The faculty will invite selected applicants for an interview. Notices of acceptance are sent to students in the spring or summer prior to the proposed date of enrollment.

Admissions Requirements (Required)

Interview

COSTS AND AID
Tuition & Fees

In-state tuition	$14,000
Out-of-state tuition	$23,750
In-state fees	$919
Out-of-state fees	$1,498

UNIVERSITY OF UTAH
SCHOOL OF MEDICINE

OFFICE OF ADMISSIONS, 30 NORTH 1900 EAST #1C029 SALT LAKE CITY, UT 84132-2101 • ADMISSION: 801-581-7498
FAX: 801-581-2931 • E-MAIL: DEANS.ADMISSIONS@HSC.UTAH.EDU • WEBSITE: HTTP://UUHSC.UTAH.EDU/SOM/ADMISSIONS

STUDENT BODY

Type	Public
Enrollment	404
# applied (total/out)	1,169/747
# accepted (total/out)	134/44
# enrolled (total/out)	102/27
Average age	26

ADMISSIONS
Average GPA and MCAT scores

Overall GPA	3.6
MCAT Bio	10
MCAT Phys	9
MCAT Verbal	10

Application Information

Regular application	11/1
Regular notification	10/15
Are transfers accepted?	Yes
Admissions may be deferred?	Yes
Interview required?	No
Application fee	$100

Academics

The curriculum of the University of Utah School of Medicine is designed to produce highly skilled physicians who are technically proficient, caring, compassionate, and capable of adapting to the changing health care demands of the twenty-first century. Active learning approaches, critical-thinking skills, and information management techniques are all a part of our educational environment. Our curriculum builds on the strengths of traditional learning methods and explores areas of study opened up by the explosion of biomedical knowledge and the transformation of America's health care delivery system.

In the first 2 years, students develop a solid foundation in the basic sciences. Courses also cover Biostatistics, Community and Public Health, Epidemiology, Health Care Financing and Delivery, and Research Methodology and Medical Literature Analysis. Patient evaluation skills are covered in depth. The third year centers on clinical clerkships in Family Practice, Internal Medicine, Obstetrics and Gynecology, Pediatrics, Psychiatry, and Surgery. A Public Health course, sub internship, Neurology clerkship, Medical Ethics course, and Health Care Delivery System course are required in the fourth year. Students pursue areas of particular interest during fourth-year electives.

Campus Life

The medical school is situated on the east bench of the Salt Lake Valley with the Wasatch Mountains as a backdrop. Public transportation connects the school with downtown Salt Lake City and surrounding areas. University Hospital is home to many centers and clinics that provide research and specialized patient care to patients from all over the world. Rotations are performed at University Hospital, VA and LDS hospitals, and Primary Children's Medical Center. Primary care rotations may be performed in community settings.

STUDENT LIFE

Medical students take advantage of the campus and the surrounding areas. The University of Utah is situated on a 1,500-acre campus that offers indoor and outdoor recreational activities. Salt Lake City is at the base of spectacular mountains and is only short drive from excellent skiing or hiking, depending on the season. Several national parks are accessible to the city. Housing is available on and off campus. Accessible housing is available through the following resources: University of Utah Office of Student Housing (Apartments.utah.edu) and University of Utah Office of Residential Living (ORL.utah.edu). Information about student interest groups can be found on the medical student website at http://umed.med.utah.edu.

Admissions

REQUIREMENTS

A bachelor's degree is required to enter the University of Utah School of Medicine. Applicants must complete their schooling in a United States or Canadian college or university accredited by 1 of the following: The Western Association of Schools and Colleges, Middle States Association of Colleges and Schools, New England Association of Schools and Colleges, North Central Association of Colleges and Schools, Northwest Association of Schools and Colleges, or Southern Association of Colleges and Schools.

The following course work from a fully accredited institution (see above) is required prior to matriculation to medical school. Advanced Placement, CLEP credit, independent study, and correspondence courses do not satisfy these requirements except as noted.

Chemistry: 2 years that should include both a general chemistry series including all applicable laboratories (incorporating both quantitative and qualitative analysis) and an organic chemistry series that includes all applicable laboratories. Advanced Placement credit earned with a score of 4 or 5 is acceptable toward fulfillment of this requirement. Physics: 1 year with all applicable laboratories. Writing/speech: 1 year of courses that emphasize written and/or verbal communication. Biology: 2 courses, one course must be in cellular biology or biochemistry. Social science: 1 course (history, economics, anthropology, or psychology). Humanities: 1 course (art, music, drama, or literature). Diversity: 1 course that focuses on the culture or current circumstances of a nondominant population group in the United States. Diversity course(s) taken to fulfill requirements of the degree-granting undergraduate institution are acceptable.

The minimum acceptable GPA is 3.0. Applicants with a science, non-science, or overall GPA below 3.0 will not be considered. To determine average criteria, the applicant's GPA is compared to the average GPA of students who have gone on to attend medical school from the institution granting the applicant's highest degree.

All applicants are required to take the MCAT within 3 years of their application. For the class entering medical school in 2008, scores will be accepted from tests taken in 2007, 2006, and 2005. Tests taken after August 2007 will not be considered for the 2008 application year. The minimum acceptable score for each section (physical science, biological science, and verbal reasoning) of the MCAT examination is 7. The average score for entering freshman is 10 in each section. If the test is taken more than once within 3 years of application, the best score for each section will be considered.

PROCESS

The University of Utah School of Medicine is a state-assisted institution. A minimum of 75 positions are offered to Utah residents. The School of Medicine has contracted with the State of Idaho to accept 8 Idaho residents each year. To be so considered, applicants must be certified as Idaho residents. Approximately 19 positions are offered to nonresidents. For consideration, nonresidents must meet one of the following requirements:

- Have significant ties to Utah. (e.g., lived in, own property in, or have family members who live in Utah). Documentation of ties to Utah will be required and will be considered by the Admissions Committee.

- Apply to the MD/PhD program. Applications are available for U.S. citizens or permanent U.S. residents only.

- Be specifically recognized as a member of a population group underrepresented in the physician workforce (i.e., Africans and African Americans; American Indians; Alaska Natives; Polynesians including Native Hawaiians, Tongans, Samoans, Filipinos, Tahitians, Maoris, Fijians, Niueans, Palauans; Chicanos/as and Latinos/as, including Puerto Ricans, Mexican Americans, Central Americans, and South Americans).

Admissions Requirements (Required)

MCAT scores, science GPA, non-science GPA, letters of recommendation, state residency, essay/personal statement, extracurricular activities, exposure to medical profession, research, volunteer, physician shadowing, leadership

Admissions Requirement (Optional)

Interview

COSTS AND AID

Tuition & Fees

In-state tuition	$18,577
Out-of-state tuition	$35,169
Room and board	$8,964
Cost of books	$2,100
Fees	$695

Financial Aid

% students receiving aid	94
Average grant	$4,000
Average loan	$22,500
Average debt	$110,000

UNIVERSITY OF VERMONT
COLLEGE OF MEDICINE

89 BEAUMONT AVENUE, E215 GIVEN BUILDING, BURLINGTON, VT 05405 • ADMISSION: 802-656-2154
FAX: 802-656-9663 • E-MAIL: MEDADMISSIONS@UVM.EDU • WEBSITE: WWW.MED.UVM.EDU

STUDENT BODY

Type	Public
Enrollment	400
% male/female	41/59
% minorities	20
# applied (total/out)	5,119/5,005
# accepted (total/out)	202/142
# enrolled (total/out)	101/58
Average age	24

FACULTY

Total faculty (number)	1,806
% female	30
% minority	10
% part-time	10

ADMISSIONS
Average GPA and MCAT scores

Overall GPA	3.6
MCAT Bio	10
MCAT Phys	10
MCAT Verbal	10
MCAT Essay	Q

Application Information

Regular application	11/1
Regular notification	10/15
Early application	8/1
Early notification	10/1
Are transfers accepted?	Yes
Admissions may be deferred?	Yes
Interview required?	Yes
Application fee	$85

Academics

The new integrated curriculum, fully launched in Fall 2003, progresses through 3 levels of increasing competency. Block courses in level I/foundations provide students with a fundamental understanding of the basic biology of health and illness within systems ranging from genes to organs to individuals to populations. A comprehensive assessment of integrated knowledge and skills takes place at the end of the first year and again at the completion of the level midway through the second year of school. Level II/clinical clerkships focuses on the student's development of clinical skills, decision-making skills, and application of foundational sciences. It consists of seven clerkships with a longitudinal bridge curriculum of advanced sciences and clinical skills over a period of 13 months. Clinical training takes place primarily at adjacent teaching hospital Fletcher Allen Health Care, an integrated health care delivery system located in Burlington, which serves the State of Vermont and beyond, attracting patients from New York and around New England. Students also have the opportunity to do some clerkship rotations at Maine Medical Center, located in Portland. The patient population is largely rural, and rural medicine is considered a strength of UVM. Students advance to level III/advanced integration after successful achievement on a clinical competency exam. During the final 15 months of advanced integration, the student gains an understanding of the impact of economic, social, and political systems on the health care environment. This level includes acting internships, an emergency medicine rotation, a teaching practicum, and scholarly project. During this section, there is flexibility in how students may earn elective credit. Many rotate to hospitals outside of the state, some work on Indian reservations, and others head overseas. Throughout the college's curriculum, complementary curricular themes aim to teach the student to take an integrated approach to patient care and responsibility for their own professional development. Student leadership groups provide the student with an opportunity to collaborate with classmates, a faculty facilitator, and various family faculty members from the community. These groups, which begin the first week and continue through the curriculum, support such efforts as public health research projects, individual scholarly projects, and teaching requirements and statewide health education and health delivery programs. The MD/PhD program is designed to train future physician-scientists through a curriculum that integrates clinical care with basic research. The MD-PhD degree is awarded by the joint efforts of The College of Medicine and the Graduate College. Award of the MD degree requires completion of the entire medical curriculum. Award of the PhD degree requires fulfillment of the requirements of any of the basic science graduate programs, which include anatomy and Neurobiology, Biochemistry, Microbiology and molecular Genetics, molecular Physiology and biophysics, and pharmacology, or those of the multidisciplinary program in cell and molecular biology. It is anticipated that a period of 7 years will be necessary to complete the combined program. Four students are chosen yearly for this program. Students enrolled in the program will receive financial support that includes full medical and graduate school tuition remission, as well as a stipend consistent with National Institutes of Health guidelines. A new ambulatory center opened adjacent to the campus in fall 2005. A student assessment center, built in 2002, is home to a well-established standardized patient program. The Academic Medical Center, along with the rest of the University of Vermont campus, is located in picturesque Burlington. The city is safe, affordable, and comfortable.

Campus Life

Approximately 40 percent of students are residents of Vermont, 10 percent are from Maine, and the remainder come from out of area. In the class entering in 2005, the average age was 24. Students came from 64 different universities, 6 countries, and a variety of academic backgrounds. Class size is 105.

STUDENT LIFE

Students have access to all of the university's athletic facilities. Burlington and the surrounding area offer excellent skiing, hiking, and mountain biking. The campus is integrated into the city, which is safe, friendly, and student-oriented. Housing options on- and off-campus are good. On-campus choices include UVM's married-student housing, about 4 miles from campus, and nearby apartments and residence halls.

GRADUATES

Graduates are successful in obtaining residencies at strong programs nationwide. In 2005, about half of the graduates entered primary care residencies. Favored specialties include internal medicine (23 percent), emergency medicine (12 percent), pediatrics (16 percent), and anesthesiology (10 percent).

Admissions

REQUIREMENTS

One year each of biology, chemistry, organic chemistry and physics, all with associated labs, are required. The MCAT is required, and all sets of scores are considered.

SUGGESTIONS

We recommend one course in biochemistry or molecular genetics be taken. We recommend that the MCAT be taken no later than April of the application year to facilitate timely review of the entire application file. We encourage students who have a broad and balanced educational background during their undergraduate years. In addition to prerequisite courses in the sciences, recommended areas of study include literature, mathematics, behavioral sciences, history, philosophy, and the arts. College work must demonstrate intellectual drive, independent thinking, curiosity, and self-discipline. A career in medicine calls for excellent oral and written communication skills. Applicants should seek out opportunities to develop such skills during their college years. Successful applicants often have a history of service to community. We encourage students who have a broad and balanced educational background during their undergraduate years. In addition to prerequisite courses in the sciences, recommended areas of study include behavioral sciences, history, literature, mathematics, philosophy and the arts. College work must demonstrate intellectual drive, independent thinking, curiosity, and self-discipline.

PROCESS

All AMCAS applicants receive a supplemental application. All well-qualified VT residents who apply are interviewed. Approximately 10 percent of out-of-state applicants are interviewed. Interviews take place from September through March and consist of a meeting with a faculty member of the admission committee. Decisions are made on a rolling basis, and applicants are notified of their status—accept, reject, or wait list— shortly after the interview. Wait listed candidates should indicate if UVM is their first choice.

UNIVERSITY OF VIRGINIA
SCHOOL OF MEDICINE

PO BOX 800725, CHARLOTTESVILLE, VA 22908 • **ADMISSION:** 804-924-5571
FAX: 804-982-2586 • **E-MAIL:** BAB7G@VIRGINIA.EDU • **WEBSITE:** WWW.MED.VIRGINIA.EDU/HOME.HTML

STUDENT BODY

Type	Public
Enrollment	556
% male/female	50/50
% minorities	8
# applied (total/out)	3,721/2,055
# accepted (total/out)	140/74
# enrolled (total/out)	140/74
Average age	24

FACULTY

Total faculty (number)	800
Student-faculty ratio	1:1

ADMISSIONS
Average GPA and MCAT scores

Overall GPA	3.74
MCAT Bio	11.33
MCAT Phys	11.11
MCAT Verbal	10.58
MCAT Essay	P

Application Information

Regular application	11/1
Regular notification	10/15
Are transfers accepted?	Yes
Admissions may be deferred?	Yes
Interview required?	Yes
Application fee	$80

Academics

Most medical students follow a 4 year, highly integrated curriculum leading to the MD. Each year 6 students enter a combined MD/PhD curriculum. Training for the PhD degree is usually in one of the biomedical science programs, which include anatomy, biochemistry, biophysics, microbiology, neuroscience, pharmacology, and physiology. A Generalist Scholars Program supplements the medical education of students with special opportunities in the area of primary care. Students who participate in this program work closely with a faculty mentor and complete a thesis as part of their graduation requirements. Medical students are evaluated in a variety of ways including both pass/fail and letter grades.

BASIC SCIENCES: First-year courses are Biochemistry; Cell and Tissue Structure; Genetics; Gross Anatomy; Human Behavior; Medical Ethics; Neuroscience; Physiology; Physical Diagnosis; and the Practice of Medicine, in which topics such as human behavior and medical ethics are discussed. Basic clinical skills such as the patient interview are also introduced. Second-year courses are Clinical Epidemiology, Community Preceptorship, Introduction to Clinical Medicine (ICM), Microbiology, Pathology, Pharmacology, Psychiatric Medicine, and Psychopathology. Basic-science concepts are coordinated with the ICM course, which involves discussion of clinical cases in small-group tutorials. In the spring of the second year, each student completes a 1 month community medicine preceptorship that provides hands-on primary care experience and serves as a transition to third-year clinical rotations. Instruction takes place at the Harvey E. Jordan Hall, a 7-story structure that houses lecture halls and laboratories. First- and second-year students also use the School of Medicine Learning Center, which contains conference rooms, tutorial rooms, and a student lounge. The Claude Moore Health Sciences Library is a modern, fully computerized facility with almost 79,000 books, 3,000 periodicals, and 4,000 audiovisual titles.

CLINICAL TRAINING

Third-year required rotations are medicine (12 weeks), surgery (12 weeks), pediatrics (8 weeks), obstetrics (6 weeks), psychiatry (6 weeks), family medicine (4 weeks), and neurology (4 weeks). Clinical training takes place primarily at the University of Virginia Medical Center University Hospital (552 beds), Kluge Children's Rehabilitation Center, and at 40 outpatient clinics associated with the Medical Center. Students also train at affiliated hospitals, which include The Community Hospital of Roanoke Valley (400 beds), Roanoke Memorial Hospital (677 beds), and the Veterans Affairs Medical Center (750 beds). Electives may be taken at other academic or clinical institutions in other parts of the country or abroad.

Campus Life

About 90 of the 139 students in each class are Virginia residents. Underrepresented minorities account for approximately 10 percent of the student body. There is typically a wide age range among incoming students, with at least a few students in their thirties.

STUDENT LIFE

Students are highly active in on-campus activities and events. Many are involved in community activities such as Service, Humanity, Action, Responsibility, Education (SHARE), which initiates health education projects and other service-oriented activities. Support groups for minority students are available, as are clubs focused on professional interests and recreational pursuits, such as singing. UVA also has local chapters of national medical student organizations. Medical students enjoy Charlottesville, a thriving tourist and cultural center located at the foot of the Blue Ridge Mountains and close to the Shenandoah Valley. The city of Richmond, Virginia, is a 1 hour drive, and Washington, DC, is just 2 hours away.

GRADUATES

Graduates are successful in securing top residency positions in all regions of the country. A significant number stay on to do postgraduate training at UVA-affiliated hospitals.

Admissions

REQUIREMENTS

Prerequisites are 1 year each of biology, general chemistry, organic chemistry, and physics, all with associated labs. The MCAT is required, and scores must be no more than 3 years old at the time of matriculation. For applicants who have taken the exam more than once, the best scores are considered. Thus, there is no advantage to withholding scores.

SUGGESTIONS

State residency is a factor in admissions decisions as about 65 percent of positions in a class are reserved for Virginia resident applicants. The Admissions Committee looks for students who will make significant contributions to society as members of the medical profession. Factors such as depth of motivation and commitment to medicine are evaluated. Some medically related experience that involves patient contact is considered important.

PROCESS

AMCAS applicants are sent secondary applications. About 25–30 percent of Virginia resident applicants are interviewed, while only about 10 percent of nonresidents make it to the interview stage. On interview day, applicants have two interviews, each with a member of the Admissions Committee. Candidates also attend a group orientation session, have the opportunity to tour the campus, and eat lunch with current medical students. Notification begins after October 15 and continues on a rolling basis until the class is filled. Wait listed candidates may send additional information to update their files.

Admissions Requirements (Required)

MCAT scores, science GPA, non-science GPA, letters of recommendation, interview, essay/personal statement, extracurricular activities, exposure to medical profession

Admissions Requirement (Optional)

State residency

Overlap Schools

Duke University, Johns Hopkins University, Vanderbilt University.

COSTS AND AID

Tuition & Fees

In-state tuition	$30,100
Out-of-state tuition	$40,100
Room and board (off-campus)	$12,000
Cost of books	$1,000

Financial Aid

% students receiving aid	85
Average grant	$12,000
Average loan	$18,000
Average debt	$82,000

UNIVERSITY OF WASHINGTON
SCHOOL OF MEDICINE

ADMISSIONS OFFICE, A-300 HEALTH SCIENCES, PO BOX 356340, SEATTLE, WA 98195 • ADMISSION: 206-543-7212
FAX: 206-616-3341 • E-MAIL: ASKUWSOM@U.WASHINGTON.EDU • WEBSITE: WWW.WASHINGTON.EDU/MEDICINE/SOM/

STUDENT BODY	
Type	Public
Enrollment	734
% male/female	52/48
% minorities	10
# applied (total/out)	3,124/2,203
# accepted (total/out)	229/39
# enrolled (total/out)	176/12

ADMISSIONS
Average GPA and MCAT Scores

Overall GPA	3.7
MCAT Bio	11.2
MCAT Phys	10.7
MCAT Verbal	10.3
MCAT Essay	Q

Application Information

Regular application	11/1
Regular notification	11/1
Are transfers accepted?	Yes
Admissions may be deferred?	Yes
Interview required?	Yes
Application fee	$35

Academics

Students who enter UW as residents of Wyoming, Alaska, Montana, and Idaho spend their first year at the university site in their home state. Twenty Washington students begin medical studies at Washington State University in Pullman and then transfer to the UW campus after completion of their first year. Other students complete a 4-year program based in Seattle. From 8–10 students each year enter the MSTP MD/PhD program. The doctorate degree may be earned in biochemistry, bioengineering, biomathematics/biostatistics, biological structure, epidemiology, environmental health, genetics, immunology, microbiology, molecular biotechnology, pathology, pharmacology, physiology, biophysics, and zoology. Medical students are evaluated with honors, satisfactory, and not satisfactory. Passing Step 1 of the USMLE is a requirement for promotion to year 3 and passing Step 2 is a requirement for graduation.

BASIC SCIENCES: First-year courses at the UW campus are Biochemistry; Cell and Tissue Response to Injury; Epidemiology; Gross Anatomy and Embryology; Introduction to Immunology; Mechanisms in Cell Physiology; Microscopic Anatomy; Natural History of Infectious Diseases and Chemotherapy; Nervous System; and Systems of Human Behavior, Head, Neck, Ear, Nose and Throat. Most second-year topics are organized around body/organ systems, which are cardiovascular, complementary medicine, endocrine, gastrointestinal, genetics, hematology, musculoskeletal, nutrition, pharmacology, reproduction, respiratory, skin, systemic pathology, and urinary. Other courses are Introduction to Clinical Medicine and Medicine, Health, and Society. The Rural/Underserved Opportunities Program enables first-year medical students to work with practicing physicians in small towns or inner-city neighborhoods and to learn first-hand about working with underserved communities.

CLINICAL TRAINING

The clinical curriculum covers the third and fourth years and includes clerkships in Medicine (12 weeks), Obstetrics/Gynecology (6 weeks), Pediatrics (6 weeks), Psychiatry (6 weeks), Surgery (6 weeks), Family Medicine (6 weeks), Emergency Medicine (4 weeks), and Rehabilitation (2 weeks). An additional 24 weeks of electives are required. Selected third-year students participate in an alternate, rural training program, which involves 6 months in a rural, primary care practice. In its teaching, patient care, and research programs, the School of Medicine is affiliated with Children's Hospital, Harborview Hospital (411 beds), UW Medical Center (450 beds), Seattle Veterans Affairs Hospital, Fred Hutchinson Cancer Research Center, Boise Veterans Affairs Hospital, Providence Hospital, Swedish Hospital, Madigan Hospital, and the Group Health Cooperative. Additional affiliations across the Pacific Northwest enable medical students to train in more than 75 communities in Washington, Alaska, Montana, and Idaho. The International Medical Education Office organizes a range of activities including exchange programs that allow UW medical students to participate in clinical electives overseas.

Campus Life

About 93 percent of the 176 students in each class are residents of Washington, Alaska, Montana, Wyoming, or Idaho. Out-of-region students, which includes a total of about 10 percent of the student body, are MD/PhD students. There is a wide age range among medical students, with significant numbers of entrants in their late 20s and 30s.

STUDENT LIFE

UW offers countless extracurricular opportunities and attractions, including cultural programs, student groups, intercollegiate sporting events, and social functions. Medical students take advantage of these opportunities and the tremendous resources afforded by UW and its student community. Seattle is an ideal city for students, offering outstanding daytime and outdoor activities and an excellent nightlife. Around the city are beautiful areas suitable for hiking, camping, mountain climbing, running, biking, swimming, and skiing. Most students live off campus.

GRADUATES

Of the roughly 5,000 UW School of Medicine alumni, about 50 percent are practicing or training in fields designated as physician-shortage specialties, which include family physicians, general internists, general pediatricians, psychiatrists, general surgeons, and general practitioners.

Admissions

REQUIREMENTS

Prerequisites are chemistry (12 semester hours, which can be satisfied by any combination of inorganic, organic, biochemistry, or molecular biology courses), biology (8 semester hours), and physics (4 semester hours). In addition, the understanding of basic biochemistry molecular biology concepts is required. An additional 8 semester hours of unspecified science course work is required. This requirement can be met by taking other courses in any of the above three categories. The MCAT is required, and scores must be from within 3 years of application.

SUGGESTIONS

Preference is given to legal residents of Washington, Wyoming, Alaska, Montana, and Idaho. Applicants from disadvantaged backgrounds or who are willing to serve the underserved are also considered. Candidates should be proficient in the use of the English language and in basic mathematics and are expected to have an understanding of personal computing and information technologies. Some biochemistry or molecular biology is also recommended.

PROCESS

All Washington residents and a limited number of highly qualified nonresidents are sent secondary applications and invited to interview. Interviews take place between October and April and consist of one session with a panel of interviewers. Also on interview day, candidates have the opportunity to meet with current students and tour the campus. About 30 percent of interviewed candidates are accepted. Others are rejected or put in a hold category.

Admissions Requirements (Required)

MCAT scores, letters of recommendation, interview, state residency, essays/personal statement

Admissions Requirements (Optional)

Science GPA, non-science GPA, extracurricular activities, exposure to medical profession

COSTS AND AID
Tuition & Fees

In-state tuition	$15,347
Out-of-state tuition	$37,169
Fees	$525

Financial Aid

% students receiving aid	83

UNIVERSITY OF WESTERN ONTARIO
ADMISSIONS AND STUDENT AFFAIRS

HEALTH SCIENCES BUILDING, LONDON, ONTARIO N6A 5C1 • ADMISSION: 519-661-3744
FAX: 519-661-3797 • E-MAIL: ADMISSIONS@SCHULICH.UWO.CA • WEBSITE: WWW.SCHULICH.UWO.CA

STUDENT BODY	
Type	Public
Enrollment	534
% male/female	55/45
# applied	1,872
# accepted	133
# enrolled	133
Average age	23

ADMISSIONS
Average GPA and MCAT Scores

Overall GPA	3.7
MCAT Bio	10.0
MCAT Phys	9.0
MCAT Verbal	10.0
MCAT Essay	P

Application Information

Regular application	10/15
Regular notification	5/15
Are transfers accepted?	No
Admissions may be deferred?	No
Interview required?	Yes
Application fee	$175

Academics

The Faculty of Medicine and Dentistry, along with the Faculty of Graduate Studies, has established a combined MD-PhD program in which the research curriculum of the graduate program is integrated into the MD program. Applicants must be accepted to the medical school as MD candidates before entering the combined program.

BASIC SCIENCES: During the third year integrated clerkship, the student will become an active member of clinical care teams in the following medical disciplines: family medicine, medicine, obstetrics and gynecology, pediatrics, psychiatry, and surgery. Under the supervision of faculty and more senior house staff, clerks will be given graded responsibility in the investigation, diagnosis, and management of patients in hospital and outpatient settings. The clerkship year incorporates rural experiences throughout Southwestern Ontario. Some students will be placed outside London for the entire clerkship year.

Beginning in year 4, clinical electives will be arranged by the student in any area of medicine, at UWO or other approved centers. For students wishing to arrange electives in developing countries, we have a medical electives overseas officer who advises and assists students in making their arrangements. After completion of the clinical electives, students will return to the UWO in February for the transition period, which includes advanced basic sciences (e.g., surgical anatomy, medical Physiology); advanced communication skills; general review; and health care systems. This will permit students to further integrate the basic and clinical aspects of medicine in light of their clinical experience.

CLINICAL TRAINING

The first 2 years of the new curriculum will provide students with a solid grounding in the basic and clinical sciences. These 2 years are each divided into a series of 6 blocks. Within each block various subject areas are presented which integrate the basic and clinical sciences. The blocks are Digestive Systems and Nutrition, Endocrine and Metabolism, Eye and Ear, Genitourinary System, Heart and Circulation, Immunology and Skin, Introduction to Medicine, Life Cycle, Musculoskeletal, Neurosciences, Psychiatry and Behavioral Sciences, Reproduction, and Respiration and Airways.

During each week or block, the case of a single patient will be discussed. A facilitator will help students determine the biological, behavorial, and population issues that are pertinent to the patient, and the objectives for the week's instruction will be described. Students will then receive instruction throughout the week relevant to the patient's case using a variety of teaching methods such as lectures, small-group sessions, and labs. Students will also be expected to obtain information pertinent to the case objectives. The faculty has excellent library and resource facilities to support self study. In the middle of the week, students will meet to review the instruction to date and relate it to the patient case. At the end of the week, the students will meet in a plenary session to discuss the case of the week. A particular strength of our program will be the opportunity for early patient contact. Patient-centered care recognizes the need to see the health concerns of a patient through the patient's eyes. The illness experience differs markedly from the traditional teaching in medical schools in which the emphasis has been on teaching about the disease only and not on the experiences of the patient with that disease. In the patient-centered approach, the emphasis is on defining the unique illness experience of the patient and his or her relation to family and community in economic, social, and environmental dimensions. The first 2 years of the program provide a variety of opportunities for students to better understand the relationship between health care and the community.

Campus Life

Class size is 133.

STUDENT LIFE

The University of Western Ontario offers students a rich lifestyle. School-sponsored events and countless clubs and organizations are offered on campus. London is a small city of about 300,000 with a range of cultural and recreational activities. Both on- and off-campus housing is available.

GRADUATES

The curriculum is designed to allow graduates to enter any clinical or medical research field. A significant portion of graduates enter residency programs at hospitals affiliated with the University of Western Ontario.

Admissions

REQUIREMENTS

Enrollment is limited to Canadian citizens and permanent residents of Canada. Those who are in the third year or have successfully completed 3 full years of study in any degree program at a recognized university are eligible to apply. A minimum of 5 full or equivalent courses must be included in the final undergraduate year (September to April only). Science prerequisites are 1 full course in biology, 1 full course in organic chemistry, and 1 additional full science course. Non-science prerequisites are 2 full non-science courses from different disciplines and 1 senior-level course in one of these 2 subjects. Interested applicants should contact the faculty for more detailed course requirements. The MCAT is required. The latest date that applicants should take the exam is August in the year of application. Only applicants who have achieved a certain GPA and MCAT scores will be considered for admission. Typically, the minimum GPA is 3.50 and minimum MCAT scores are a 9 on biological sciences, an 8 on physical sciences, a 9 on verbal reasoning, and a Q on the writing sample. English proficiency is a requirement.

SUGGESTIONS

For entrance in the Fall of 2005, there were 1,872 applicants for 133 positions. Thus, admission is competitive. Apart from science prerequisites, there is no prescribed premed program. Students at Western Ontario come from a variety of undergraduate programs and a wide range of disciplines. For those who have taken the MCAT more than once, only the most recent scores are used.

PROCESS

The deadline for application is October 15 for matriculation the following September. Applicants now apply online at: www.ouac.on.ca/omsas. Those applicants who satisfy the course load, GPA, and MCAT requirements will generally be invited for an interview. Letters indicating admissions decisions are sent to applicants beginning in the end of May and continuing until the class is full.

Admissions Requirements (Required)

MCAT scores, science GPA, non-science GPA, letters of recommendation, interview, state residency

Admissions Requirements (Optional)

Essays/personal statement, extracurricular activities, exposure to medical profession

COSTS AND AID
Tuition & Fees

Tuition	$14,566
Room and board (off-campus)	$13,000
Cost of books	$2,200
Fees	$863

UNIVERSITY OF WISCONSIN—MADISON
SCHOOL OF MEDICINE AND PUBLIC HEALTH

2130 HEALTH SCIENCES LEARNING CENTER, 750 HIGHLAND AVE MADISON, WI 53705 • ADMISSION: 608-263-4925
FAX: 608-262-4226 • E-MAIL: LWALL@WISC.EDU • WEBSITE: WWW.MED.WISC.EDU

STUDENT BODY

Type	Public
Enrollment	618
% male/female	48/52
% minorities	6
# applied (total/out)	1,138/631
# accepted (total/out)	255/99
# enrolled (total/out)	155/32
Average age	24

ADMISSIONS
Average GPA and MCAT Scores

Overall GPA	3.76
MCAT Bio	10.9
MCAT Phys	10.6
MCAT Verbal	9.8
MCAT Essay	P

Application Information

Regular application	11/1
Regular notification	Rolling
Early application	8/1 and 9/1
Early notification	10/1
Are transfers accepted?	Yes
Admissions may be deferred?	Yes
Interview required?	Yes
Application fee	$54

Academics

The UW School of Medicine and Public Health offers an M.D. degree and a dual degree (M.D. and Ph.D) option. In addition, flexibility exists to allow for combining training for the M.D. degree with earning a Master's Degree in Public Health. Medical students are evaluated with letter grades. Students must pass Step 1 of the USMLE for promotion to year three and Step 2 and 3 must be taken to graduate.

BASIC SCIENCES: First- and second-year courses provide an optimal balance between hands-on and didactic/independent learning, featuring a lively and varied educational experience through multiple teaching formats. These include lectures, small group discussions, labs, case-based learning, interdisciplinary approaches and adaptation of Web-based materials. An important component of the patient, doctor, society cause is the Generalist Partners Program (GPP) which matches first-year medical students with primary care physicians who practice in the community and who serve as teachers and mentors to students. Through GPP, students learn firsthand about generalist medicine, and enjoy early patient-care opportunities. Other first-year courses are Integrated Medical Anatomy, Biomolecular Chemistry, Genetics, Neuroscience, Psychiatry, Pathology, and Physiology. The second-year Pathophysiology courses are organized around body/organ systems, including Hematology, Cardiovascular, Renal, Respiratory, Neoplastic Disease, Endocrine, Gastrointestinal, and Hepatic. Other courses are Infection and Immunity, and Pharmacology. Population Medicine and Epidemiology is also a second-year course. The Ebling Medical Library is used by students for research and for studying. It houses more than 330,000 volumes and 3,000 publications.

CLINICAL TRAINING

The third- and fourth-year clerkships expose students to a wide variety of clinical settings (outpatient, inpatient, community based, rural, and inner city). Training takes place at University Hospitals in Madison as well as affiliated sites such as Milwaukee, La Crosse, and Marshfield. Third-year required clerkships are Medicine (8 weeks); Primary Care (8 weeks); Surgery (8 weeks); Pediatrics (6 weeks); Ob/Gyn (6 weeks); Anesthesia (2 weeks); Neuroscience (6 weeks); Psychiatry (4 weeks); and Radiology (2 weeks). During the fourth year, students complete an Acting Internship in Medicine (4 weeks); an advanced Surgery Clerkship (4 weeks); a Preceptorship (6 weeks); and 18 weeks of electives. A portion of electives may be taken at other academic and clinical institutions, both in the United States and overseas.

Students

Each class is comprised of 150 students, plus 5 students in the rural medicine program. Approximately 80 percent of students are Wisconsin residents, and during the past four years, about 50 percent of students attended UW for their undergraduate education. About 12 percent of students are underrepresented minorities. About 10 or more students in each class are in their late twenties or thirties.

STUDENT LIFE

The School of Medicine and Public Health benefits from the resources of one of the nation's top public universities. Medical students have access to the facilities of the large campus and enjoy the lively environment of a popular college city. Students are active in community service projects such as volunteering at homeless shelters and clinics, and organizing AIDS or other education projects. On-campus housing, including married-student facilities, is available. However, most students prefer to live in shared apartments off campus. Madison is a medium-sized city, organized around three lakes, which provide many opportunities for outdoor recreation.

GRADUATES

Graduates are successful in securing residency positions at prestigious institutions nationwide and within Wisconsin.

Admissions

REQUIREMENTS

Minimum science requirements are General Biology with lab (1 semester); Advanced Biology/Zoology with lab (1 semester); Biochemistry (1 semester); General Chemistry with lab (1 year); Organic Chemistry (1 semester); General Physics with lab (1 year); and Mathematics (2 semesters). The MCAT is required, and for the 2007 entering class, scores must be from 2004 or later. Where more than one MCAT has been taken, the higher values of the two most recent scores are used.

SUGGESTIONS

UW gives preference to residents of Wisconsin. Each incoming class consists of 15 to 20 percent nonresidents. A sound liberal arts education, including both humanities and social sciences, is considered important. While specific courses are not required, the applicant's preparation should include courses in those areas that prepare for the social, psychological, and economic aspects of medical practice. The Admissions Committee members rely heavily on the applicants' essays, letters of recommendation, and the personal interviews to assess motivation and personal character. Community service and exposure to medicine and patient care is needed.

PROCESS

Upon receipt of the AMCAS application, the UW Secondary Application, is sent to selected applicants who meet the minimal academic thresholds (GPA > 2.80, MCATS > 7,7,8). Further selection of applicants are invited to interview. Interviews take place between August and March and consist of one session with a faculty member and one with a small group of medical students and applicants. Interview-day activities include group informational sessions, tours, and lunch with medical students.

Admissions Requirements (Required)

MCAT scores, Science GPA, Non-science GPA, Letters of recommendation, Interview, Essays/personal statement, Extracurricular activities, Exposure to medical profession

Admissions Requirements (Optional)

State residency

Overlap Schools

Medical College of Wisconsin, Stanford University, University of California, Hastings, University of Michigan—Ann Arbor, University of Pittsburgh, University of Washington, Washington University in St. Louis (Olin).

COSTS AND AID

Tuition & Fees

In-state Tuition	$21,534
Out-of-state Tuition	$32,658
Room and board (on-campus)	$11,520
Room and board (off-campus)	$10,080
Cost of books	$2,000
Fees	$730

Financial Aid

% students receiving aid	72
Average grant	$6,334
Average loan	$32,638
Average debt	$130,000

VANDERBILT UNIVERSITY
SCHOOL OF MEDICINE

215 LIGHT HALL, NASHVILLE, TN 37232-0685 • ADMISSION: 615-322-2145 • FAX: 615-343-8397
E-MAIL: PAT.SAGEN@VANDERBILT.EDU • WEBSITE: WWW.MC.VANDERBILT.EDU/MEDSCHOOL/ADMISSIONS/INDEX.PHP

STUDENT BODY

Type	Private
Enrollment	417
% male/female	56/44
% minorities	13
# applied (total/out)	4,787/4,439
# accepted (total/out)	282/257
# enrolled (total/out)	105/85
Average age	22

FACULTY

Total faculty (number)	1/905
% female	34
% minority	19
% part-time	4
Student-faculty ratio	50:1

ADMISSIONS
Average GPA and MCAT scores

Overall GPA	3.80
MCAT Bio	12.01
MCAT Phys	11.82
MCAT Verbal	10.56
MCAT Essay	Q

Application Information

Regular application	11/15
Regular notification	Semi-rolling
Early application	6/1–8/1
Early notification	10/1
Are transfers accepted?	Yes
Admissions may be deferred?	Yes
Interview required?	Yes
Application fee	$50

Academics

Most students complete a 4-year curriculum leading to an MD degree. Some students opt to take an additional year for research or independent projects. A few students each year enter one of a series of combined degrees including MD/PhD, MD/JD, and MD/MBA. Grading is entirely pass/fail in the VMS I year. For students in the VMS II—IV years, an honors grade is also possible for those with exemplary performance in a particular course/clerkship. Students may also receive a high pass grade in the VMS III—IV year.

BASIC SCIENCES: During the first 2 years, students focus on the basic and social sciences, which are taught primarily through small group sessions, tutorials, individualized study, labs, and some lectures. Courses are the Emphasis Program; Foundations of the Profession; Microbiology and Immunology; Molecular Foundations of Medicine; Patient Profession and Society ; and Structure, Function, and Development. In addition, first-year students participate in 3 intercessions, week-long courses designed to provide comprehensive integration of basic science, clinical medicine, and the social and cultural aspects of medicine as they relate to a topic of public health importance. Several afternoons each week are reserved for electives, many of which are problem based. During the second year, students take courses in Physical Diagnosis; Disease, Diagnosis, and Therapeutics; Patient, Profession, and Society; and Neuroscience. During the first 2 years, students are in class of other scheduled sessions for about 32 hours per week. Additionally, all students participate in the Emphasis Program, which allows a student an opportunity to conduct independent study/research in any 1 of 9 different subject areas. Students are paired with a faculty mentor and have protected time throughout both the first and second years of medical school to conduct their work. The Emphasis Program is designed to encourage student scholarship and provide students with the freedom to explore an area of interest in great depth. Most instruction takes place in Light Hall, which is connected by tunnels to clinical and research facilities. For research and study purposes, students and faculty use the Eskind Biomedical Library, which houses more than 200,000 volumes and 2,000 periodicals, in addition to computer-based informational resources. The Vanderbilt University Computer Center provides a full range of computing services and resources to faculty, staff, and students.

CLINICAL TRAINING

Required third-year clerkships are Medicine (11 weeks), Obstetrics/Gynecology (5.5 weeks), Pediatrics (5.5 weeks), Psychiatry-Neurology (11 weeks), and Surgery (11 weeks). Students also participate in 4 week-long intercessions, which provide a review of the pertinent basic sciences and an in-depth exploration of interdisciplinary topics such communication skills and palliative care. During their fourth year, students must also complete 3 advanced clerkships selected from medical or surgical, primary care, and emergency medicine fields. All students are required to take a 4-week Capstone course, which will provide comprehensive reviews of the basic and social sciences related to major disease processes. Sixteen weeks of electives are also required. Most clinical training takes place at Vanderbilt University Hospital (660 beds), other VUMC institutions, and clinical affiliates such as Veterans Administration Medical Center (439 beds); Baptist Hospital; and Middle Tennessee Mental Health Institute. With permission, some elective requirements may be fulfilled at other academic or clinical institutions.

Campus Life

The 2007 entering class came from 30 states and 7 foreign countries. Fifty-one undergraduate institutions were represented. The age range was 21–30, 10 percent of students were underrepresented minorities, and 48 percent were females.

STUDENT LIFE

Vanderbilt's attractive campus provides a focal point for student life and promotes cohesiveness within the student body. Students interact in common areas, such as dining halls, cafes, study areas, and the student center. Athletic facilities include fitness centers; indoor and outdoor tracks; a tennis center; playing fields; a swimming pool; basketball, racquetball, and squash courts; and a rock-climbing wall. Medical students join other graduate and professional students for intramural sports, fitness classes, and recreational clubs. In addition to being a world-renowned hub for live music, Nashville offers many attractions including a historic riverfront district, restaurants, brew pubs, coffeehouses, nightclubs, bookstores, seasonal street fairs, farmers markets, museums, and a large performing arts center. Nashville is also an academic center and is home to more than a dozen colleges and universities. Conveniently located, university-owned apartments are available to single and partnered students and students with larger families. In addition, off-campus housing is readily available.

GRADUATES

Students perform exceptionally well on the USMLE, contributing to their success in securing residency positions at prestigious institutions nationwide.

Admissions

REQUIREMENTS

Prerequisites are 8 semester hours each (with labs) of biology, chemistry, organic chemistry, and physics. Six semester hours of English are also required. The MCAT is required, and scores should be from within the past 3 years. For applicants who have taken the exam on multiple occasions, the most recent set of scores is considered. Thus, there is no real advantage in withholding scores. No AP credit nor pass/fail or CLEP credit is accepted for any required course.

SUGGESTIONS

Students with strong backgrounds in both the sciences and liberal arts are sought. The spring, rather than fall, MCAT is advised. Extracurricular activities, particularly those that involve hospital and medical exposure, are important.

PROCESS

For 2007, secondary applications will be sent only to those granted an interview. Interviews are conducted between August and March and consist of 1 session with a faculty member or administrator. On interview day, applicants also take part in a group orientation session, lunch with students, and a tour of the campus. About 25 percent of interviewees are accepted with notification occurring on a rolling basis. Wait listed candidates may send supplementary information to update their files.

Admissions Requirements (Required)

MCAT scores, science GPA, non-science GPA, letters of recommendation, interview, essay/personal statement

Admissions Requirement (Optional)

State residency, extracurricular activities, exposure to medical profession

Overlap Schools

Northwestern University, Pittsburgh State University, Johns Hopkins University, Washington University in St. Louis, Yale University.

COSTS AND AID

Tuition & Fees

Tuition	$36,600
Room and board	$10,260
Cost of books	$540
Fees	$2,911

Financial Aid

% students receiving aid	85
Average grant	$30,500
Average loan	$33,700
Average debt	$111,300

VIRGINIA COMMONWEALTH UNIVERSITY

SCHOOL OF MEDICINE

PO BOX 980565, RICHMOND, VA 23298 • **ADMISSION:** 804-828-9629
FAX: 804-828-1246 • **E-MAIL:** SOMUME@HSC.VCU.EDU • **WEBSITE:** WWW.MEDSCHOOL.VCU.EDU

STUDENT BODY	
Type	Public
Enrollment	734
% male/female	52/48
% minorities	9
# applied (total/out)	5,664/4,887
# accepted (total/out)	410/205
# enrolled (total/out)	184/69
Average age	23

FACULTY	
Total faculty (number)	853
% female	33
% minority	4
% part-time	26
Student-faculty ratio	1:1

ADMISSIONS
Average GPA and MCAT Scores

Overall GPA	3.6
MCAT Bio	10.2
MCAT Phys	9.8
MCAT Verbal	9.5
MCAT Essay	P

Application Information

Regular application	10/15
Regular notification	10/15
Early application	6/1–8/1
Early notification	10/1
Are transfers accepted?	Yes
Admissions may be deferred?	Yes
Interview required?	Yes
Application fee	$80

Academics

The MD degree program is 4 years in length. A combined MD/PhD program is also offered and generally takes 7 years to complete. Medical students interested in public health can earn an MPH concurrently with the MD degree. Students can take a year off for research between the M3 and M4 years. Students with interest in health administration can earn a MD/MHA degree in 5 years. A fellowship program gives medical students the opportunity to participate in research projects, either during summers or throughout the school year. Medical students are graded with honors, high pass, pass, marginal, and fail.

BASIC SCIENCES: Although the emphasis is on the basic sciences, Behavioral Science, preventive medicine, epidemiology, and public health are also taught during the first 2 years. Laboratory and classroom time is supplemented by a longitudinal experience designed to give students early clinical exposure. First-year courses are the following: Anatomical Sciences; Behavioral Sciences; Biochemistry; Cell Biology; Ethics; Human Genetics; Immunology; Neuroscience; Physiology; Population Medicine/Biostatistics; Pathogenesis; and Foundations of Clinical Medicine, which meets two half-days per week, uses community physicians as mentors, and teaches the basics of patient interviewing and physical diagnosis. The second-year curriculum is organized largely by body/organ systems. Courses are the following: Autonomic Pharmacology, Behavioral Science, Cardiovascular, Central Nervous System, Endocrine, Gastroenterology, Hematology/Oncology, Microbiology/Infectious Diseases, Musculoskeletal/Dermatology, Preventive Medicine, Renal, Reproduction, Respiratory, and Continuation of Foundations of Clinical Medicine. Two libraries, the University Library and the Tompkins-McCaw Library, support the research needs of students and faculty. Another important educational resource is the computer-based instructional laboratory, which features computer workstations and audiovisual equipment.

CLINICAL TRAINING

Third-year required clerkships are the following: Medicine (12 weeks); Surgery (8 weeks), Psychiatry (6 weeks), Obstetrics/Gynecology (6 weeks), Pediatrics (8 weeks), Family Practice (4 weeks), and Neurology (4 weeks). An additional requirement is 1 week of a workshop that covers topics such as nutrition, ethics, legal medicine, health economics, and clinical pharmacology. Fourth-year requirements are an acting internship, a board review course, a clinical update course, and 24 weeks of electives. For training purposes, medical students have access to more than 1,050 beds at MCV hospitals. A level I trauma center, a transplant center, and one of the nation's most prominent head injury centers are among MCV's clinical facilities. Students also have contact with outpatients at McGuire Veterans Administration Medical Center. 24 M3 students elect to do the 3rd year clerkships and 4th year electives at the INOVA Fairfax campus, located in Northern Virginia. This hospital is also a Level 1 training center and does 10,000 deliveries per year.

Campus Life

Approximately 55 percent of students are Virginia residents. The average age of incoming students is usually 24, 85 students under 25 entered VCU, and each year about 30 students in their late twenties and thirties enter VCU. Underrepresented minorities account for about 10 percent of the student body. Class size is 192.

STUDENT LIFE

VCU has at least 20 student organizations. These include groups focused on professional pursuits, community service, and religious interests. A variety of facilities, services, and programs designed to meet the leisure and health needs of students are coordinated by the recreational sports staff. The Cary Street Recreation complex and the main VCU gym offer fitness facilities including a pool, weight rooms, areas for fitness classes and squash, tennis, and basketball courts. Students have the opportunity to interact outside of class in the new student lounge and in other common areas. Richmond offers many recreational attractions such as parks, museums, historical centers, and shopping areas. While some medical students live in campus residence halls, most live in nearby restored neighborhoods or in surrounding suburban areas.

GRADUATES

MCV students score above the national average on the USMLE, contributing to their success in obtaining postgraduate positions. About 25 percent of each graduating class enters residency programs administered by MCV Hospitals, while others are successful at securing positions in other parts of the state and country. VCU alumni sponsor a unique bed-and-breakfast program, whereby members of the alumni host medical students when they travel for residency interviews.

Admissions

REQUIREMENTS

Prerequisites are 8 semester hours each of biology, chemistry, organic chemistry, and physics all with associated labs. Two semesters of English and two semesters of college-level math are also required. The MCAT is required and must have been taken within 3 years of application. Significant medical experience is a very important part of the applicant's review.

SUGGESTIONS

Students are encouraged to pursue their own intellectual interests in college. VCU recognizes that studying medicine requires commitment, strong analytical abilities, good judgment, and sound communication skills. In addition to academic abilities, the Admissions Committee looks for important attributes of character and personality.

PROCESS

About 75 percent of AMCAS applicants who are Virginia residents are sent secondary applications, and about 40 percent of nonresidents are sent secondaries. Applicants returning secondary applications are further screened, and some are invited to interview on campus. Interviews take place between August and March, and consist of one session with a faculty member, medical student, or administrator committee member. On interview day, students also attend group informational sessions, have lunch with current medical students, and tour the campus. Notification occurs on October 15, in mid-December, February 1, and in mid-March.

Admissions Requirements (Required)

MCAT scores, science GPA, non-science GPA, letters of recommendation, interview, essays/personal statement, extracurricular activities, exposure to medical profession

Admissions Requirements (Optional)

State residency

Overlap Schools

Duke University, Eastern Virginia Medical School, Emory University, Georgetown University, Johns Hopkins University, The George Washington University, University of Virginia.

COSTS AND AID
Tuition & Fees

In-state tuition	$25,646
Out-of-state tuition	$39,281
Room and board (on-campus)	$8,630
Cost of books	$3,285
Fees	$2,112

Financial Aid

Average grant	$5,000
Average loan	$29,400
Average debt	$154,000

WAKE FOREST UNIVERSITY
SCHOOL OF MEDICINE

OFFICE OF ADMISSIONS, MEDICAL CENTER BOULEVARD WINSTON-SALEM, NC 27157-1090 • ADMISSION: 336-716-4264
FAX: 910-716-9593 • E-MAIL: MEDADMIT@WFUBMC.EDU • WEBSITE: WWW.WFUBMC.EDU

STUDENT BODY

Type	Private
Enrollment	446
% male/female	57/43
% minorities	30
# applied (total/out)	6,672/6,048
# accepted (total/out)	257/184
# enrolled (total/out)	114/69
Average age	23

FACULTY

Total faculty (number)	1,452
% female	26
% minority	16
% part-time	39
Student-faculty ratio	1:1

ADMISSIONS
Average GPA and MCAT scores

Overall GPA	3.59
MCAT Bio	10.4
MCAT Phys	10.3
MCAT Verbal	10
MCAT Essay	P

Application Information

Regular application	11/1
Regular notification	Rolling
Early application	6/1–8/1
Early notification	10/1
Are transfers accepted?	Yes
Admissions may be deferred?	Yes
Interview required?	Yes
Application fee	$55

Academics

The Wake Forest curriculum, which combines features of traditional and problem-based learning methodologies, was implemented in 1998. For details about the curriculum, contact the admissions office. Joint-degree programs include the MD/MBA in conjunction with The Babcock Graduate School of Management, the MD/MS in Health Sciences Research; and the MD/PhD in conjuction with the graduate school. The PhD is offered in the following fields: anatomy, biochemistry, genetics, immunology, microbiology, molecular biology, neuroscience, pathology, pharmacology, and physiology. Students are evaluated using a 0–3 scale, and both steps of the USMLE are required for graduation.

BASIC SCIENCES: The pre-clinical curriculum emphasizes self-directed and lifelong-learning skills, core biomedical science knowledge, problem solving/reasoning, interviewing and communication skills, information management, and professional attitudes and behavior. The course Foundations of Clinical Medicine is taken throughout years 1 and 2 and provides instruction in interviewing and physical examination skills. First-year courses provide a foundation in the core biomedical sciences, and second-year courses are organized around body/organ systems. The course Being a Physician develops the concept of medical professionalism into a clearly definded and utilitarian set of guiding principles assessed through observations of personal behaviors and attitudes. Most pre-clinical instruction takes place in the Hanes Research Building. The James A Gray Building houses the library, which contains more than 150,000 volumes and 2,300 medical and scientific journals, in addition to audiovisual and computer-based educational aids.

CLINICAL TRAINING

Third-year required rotations are Anesthesiology (1 week), Inpatient Medicine (8 weeks), Neurology/Rehibilitation Medicine (4 weeks), Obstetrics/Gynecology (6 weeks), Pediatrics (8 weeks), Radiology (1 week), and Surgery (8 weeks). Required outpatient clerkships are Family Medicine (4 weeks), Internal Medicine (4 weeks), and Obstetrics/Gynecology and Women's Health (6 weeks). During the fourth year, students fullfill the remaining requirements, which are Advancement Patient Management (8 weeks), Emergency Medicine (4 weeks), Intensive Care (4 weeks), and electives (24 weeks). Training takes place at North Carolina Baptist Hospital (806 beds), which includes a children's hospital and a rehabilitation unit, among other specialty facilities. Other sites used for instruction, located in both rural and urban areas include Forsyth Memorial Hospital and the Downtown Health Plaza.

Campus Life

Approximately 30–40 percent of each class is made up of North Carolina residents, and about 10 percent are from Wake Forest's undergraduate program. The remainder represent up to 100 different colleges. About 14 percent of students are underrepresented minorities, most of whom are African American. The class size is 120.

STUDENT LIFE

A Student Life and Fitness Center gives students the opportunity to work out, study, gather, or simply relax. The fitness center includes Nautilis equipment, free weights, showers, and a steam room. Other features are a quiet, 24-hour study area, vending machines, a TV lounge, and rooms suitable for small-group discussions. The School of Medicine is located on the Bowman Gray campus, about 4 miles from the Reynolda campus of Wake Forest, where many academic and cultural events take place. Two state parks are within an hour's drive of Wake Forest, and the Carolina beaches are about 4 hours away. There is no campus housing, but apartments and rooms are readily available in the surrounding area.

GRADUATES

Wake Forest's reputation, coupled with its students above-average scores on national boards, allows graduates to enter competitive residency programs all over the country.

Admissions

REQUIREMENTS

Ninety semestser hours (3 years) of undergraduate course work including 8 semester hours each of biology, chemistry, organic chemistry, and physics. The MCAT is required, and scores must be no more than 3 years old. For applicants who have retaken the exam, the best set of scores is considered.

SUGGESTIONS

A well-rounded academic experience, including courses in the Humanities, is strongly advised. For students who have taken significant time off after college, recent course work is suggested. The April, rather than August, MCAT is recommended, as it allows applicants to retake the exam if necessary. Medically related or community service experiences are considered valuable. Most entering students have 4-year degrees.

PROCESS

Approximately a third of AMCAS applicants are sent secondary application materials. About 10 percent of those returning secondary applications are invited to interview sometime between September and March. Interviews are one-on-one and consist of three 15–20 minute sessions with faculty and/or Admissions Committee members. On interview day, candidates also receive a tour and group orientation. Notification occurs on a rolling basis, the possible outcomes being accept, reject, or wait list. Wait listed candidates are generally not encouraged to submit supplementary materials. An alternate path to admissions is through an early assurance program, which accepts competitive college juniors without the MCAT. If successful, these students complete their senior year knowing that they have been admitted to medical school for the year following college graduation.

Admissions Requirements (Required)

MCAT scores, science GPA, non-science GPA, letters of recommendation, interview, essay/personal statement, extracurricular activities, exposure to medical profession

Admissions Requirement (Optional)

State residency

Overlap Schools

Duke University, Emory University, University of North Carolina at Chapel Hill, Vanderbilt University, Virginia Commonwealth University.

COSTS AND AID
Tuition & Fees

Tuition	$35,706
Room and board (off-campus)	$15,095
Cost of books	$2,007
Fees	$0

Financial Aid

% students receiving aid	85
Average grant	$13,177
Average loan	$35,437
Average debt	$119,475

WASHINGTON UNIVERSITY IN ST. LOUIS
SCHOOL OF MEDICINE

OFFICE OF ADMISSIONS, BOX 8107, 660 SOUTH EUCLID STREET, ST. LOUIS, MO 63110 • ADMISSION: 314-362-6848
FAX: 314-362-4658 • E-MAIL: WUMSCOA@MSNOTES.WUSTL.EDU • WEBSITE: WWW.MEDSCHOOL.WUSTL.EDU/ADMISSIONS

STUDENT BODY

Type	Private
Enrollment	578
% male/female	55/45
% minorities	40
# applied	3,733
# accepted	337
# enrolled	122
Average age	23

FACULTY

Total faculty (number)	2,787
% female	26
% minority	10
% part-time	41
Student-faculty ratio	2:1

ADMISSIONS
Average GPA and MCAT Scores

Overall GPA	3.8
MCAT Bio	12.5
MCAT Phys	12.6
MCAT Verbal	11.3
MCAT Essay	Q

Application Information

Regular application	12/1
Regular notification	Rolling
Are transfers accepted?	Yes
Admissions may be deferred?	Yes
Interview required?	Yes
Application fee	$50

Academics

In addition to the 4 year MD program, students may apply for a 5 year combined MA/MD program, which involves a year of funded research and the completion of a thesis. The MSTP-sponsored MD/PhD program is one of the largest in the country, with up to 23 positions available each year. During the first year, students are graded using a pass/fail system, but grades of honors/high pass/pass/fail are used from the second year onward.

BASIC SCIENCES: During the first 2 years, students are in class for about 20 hours per week. Scheduled sessions are divided among lectures, labs, and problem-based sessions conducted in small groups. Topics covered in lectures are documented by a transcript service, to which most students subscribe. Most first-year courses address normal human structure and function. They are Anatomy, Cell and Organ Systems Biology, Genetics, Immunology, Neuroscience, and the Molecular Foundations of Medicine. The course physicians, patients, and society offers first-year students a multidisciplinary perspective on practicing medicine and continues into the second year. Patient contact begins in the first year, in Introduction to Clinical Medicine. Second-year courses focus on the effects of disease and are organized into blocks, most of which are defined by body systems or physiological concepts. These are Cardiovascular, Clinical Epidemiology, Dermatology, ENT, Endocrinology and Metabolism, Nervous System, Gastrointestinal and Liver Disease/Nutrition, Hematology and Oncology, Infectious Disease, Nervous System, Obstetrics/Gynecology, Ophthalmology, Pathology, Pediatrics, Pulmonary, Renal and Genitourinary, and Rheumatology. Clinical experience is expanded and integrated into Pathology, Pathophysiology, and Pharmacology. Students have significant input in curriculum development and revision. The library is extensive, housing about 300,000 volumes and equipped with computer and Internet facilities. The gross anatomy lab is particularly renowned.

CLINICAL TRAINING

The third year is reserved for core, required clerkships, which are combined Obstetrics/Gynecology and Pediatrics (12 weeks); Ambulatory Care, which involves Emergency Medicine, Family Practice, and Psychiatric Consultation (12 weeks); Medicine (12 weeks); Surgery (12 weeks); Neurology (4 weeks); and Psychiatry (4 weeks). The fourth year (44 weeks) is reserved entirely for electives, which may be in clinical and/or basic science departments. Students are permitted to fulfill up to 12 weeks of clinical clerkships at nonaffiliated institutions. While many other academic health care institutions are struggling, Washington University's Medical Center and their other Barnes-Jewish associated hospitals and clinics are thriving and expanding. Children's Hospital ranks as one of the premier pediatric hospitals in the country. In total, affiliated hospitals provide more than 2,000 patient beds. Students are exposed to a local population in need of basic care and to patients who have come from around the world for the most advanced treatments. The School of Medicine expects students to play important roles in the provision of patient care.

Campus Life

The current student body represents 43 states and 21 foreign countries. Although most are recent college graduates with degrees in one of the hard sciences, there is tremendous diversity in terms of age and undergraduate background. Class size is 120.

STUDENT LIFE

Since most students come from out-of-state (and country), they are eager to get to know each other and tend to form a coherent group quickly. An extensive orientation session at the beginning of the year aids in this process. Student groups are extremely active and range from those that focus on community service projects, such as operating a free clinic on weekends to intramural sports clubs to Hot Docs (a musical group). Well-used, on-campus facilities include the Hilltop Campus Athletic Facility, which is a comprehensive gym and sports center. Social life often centers on the restaurants and bars of the Central West End and the tree-lined paths of Forest Park. Campus housing is available adjacent to the Medical School, but many students prefer to live in the surrounding areas, where housing is affordable and attractive.

GRADUATES

Graduates gain acceptance to the nation's most competitive residency programs. About half enter a primary care field.

Admissions

REQUIREMENTS

Washington University expects applicants to have completed 1 year each of biology, general chemistry, organic chemistry, and physics, in addition to math through the calculus level. The MCAT is required, and scores must be no more than 3 years old.

SUGGESTIONS

The Admissions Committee looks favorably on those who have pursued in-depth study of a particular subject, whether in the natural sciences, social sciences, or humanities. Successful applicants also demonstrate commitment and leadership through their extracurricular activities. Since the medical school offers rolling admissions beginning October 15, applicants should make every attempt to complete materials early.

PROCESS

About 20 percent of AMCAS applicants are interviewed, with interviews taking place between September and March. Interviews consist of one session with a member of the school's faculty or administration. Notification occurs on a rolling basis, and about one-third of interviewees are accepted. Wait listed candidates are not ranked and are generally not encouraged to send supplementary material.

Admissions Requirements (Required)

MCAT scores, science GPA, non-science GPA, letters of recommendation, interview, essays/personal statement

Admissions Requirements (Optional)

State residency, extracurricular activities, exposure to medical profession

COSTS AND AID

Tuition & Fees

Tuition	$41,910
Cost of books	$1,613

Financial Aid

% students receiving aid	72
Average grant	$27,192
Average loan	$25,264
Average debt	$49,905

WAYNE STATE UNIVERSITY
SCHOOL OF MEDICINE

ADMISSIONS, 540 EAST CANFIELD, SUITE 1310, DETROIT, MI 48201 • ADMISSION: 313-577-1466
FAX: 313-577-9420 • E-MAIL: ADMISSIONS@MED.WAYNE.EDU • WEBSITE: WWW.MED.WAYNE.EDU/ADMISSIONS

STUDENT BODY

Type	Public
% male/female	100/0
# applied (total/out)	2,722/1,640
# accepted (total/out)	504/102
# enrolled (total/out)	257/30
Average age	24

ADMISSIONS
Average GPA and MCAT Scores

Overall GPA	3.5
MCAT Bio	9.8
MCAT Phys	9.5
MCAT Verbal	8.8
MCAT Essay	O

Application Information

Regular application	12/15
Regular notification	10/15
Early application	6/1–8/1
Early notification	10/1
Are transfers accepted?	Yes
Admissions may be deferred?	Yes
Interview required?	Yes
Application fee	$50

Academics

The School of Medicine administers academic programs leading to the MD, MS, and PhD. Some medical students pursue a combined MD/PhD, leading to the doctorate degree in Anatomy and cell biology, cellular and clinical neurobiology, immunology/microbiology, medical physics, molecular biology and genetics, pathology, pharmacology, and physiology. Other students earn an MS in biomedical or behavioral sciences along with the MD. The standard medical curriculum consists of 2 years of basic sciences, a year of clinical clerkships, and a year of clinical electives. Evaluation of medical student performance uses honors, pass, and fail. Promotion to year 3 requires passing Step 1 of the USMLE. To graduate, all students must record a score on Step 2 of the USMLE.

BASIC SCIENCES: Basic-science courses are taught primarily in a lecture/lab format, with some use of small-group sessions. Students are in class for about 20 hours per week. This schedule gives students the time they need to study, pursue independent projects, and take part in community service or other extracurricular activities. During year 1, students learn about the normal functions of the human body. Courses are Anatomy, Behavioral Medicine, Biochemistry, Clinical Nutrition, Embryology, Evidence-Based Medicine, Genetics, Histology, Introduction to the Patient, Human Sexuality, Neuroscience, and Physiology. Second-year courses focus on the effects of disease and the principles of drug action and therapy. The Pathophysiology course is organized by body/organ systems, which are connective tissue, cardiovascular, endocrine, gastrointestinal, hematology, neuroscience, pulmonary, and renal. Other courses are Human Sexuality, Introduction to the Patient, Medical Ethics, Microbiology, Pathology, Pharmacology, Physical Diagnosis/Interviewing, Psychiatry, and Public Health and Preventive Medicine. The majority of first- and second-year classes are conducted in Scott Hall, a modern building that houses laboratories, lecture halls, and faculty offices. The Shiffman Medical Library has more than 150,000 volumes, computer facilities, and ample space for studying. Students can view recorded lectures and take advantage of other audiovisual study aids in the Self-Instruction Center.

CLINICAL TRAINING

During the third year, students complete 8-week, required clerkships in internal medicine, obstetrics/gynecology, pediatrics, and surgery. There are also 4-week clerkships in family medicine, neurology, and psychiatry. During the fourth year, selectives in ambulatory medicine (4 weeks) and emergency medicine (4 weeks), in addition to a sub internship (4 weeks), are required. Five months of electives are also required, a significant portion of which may be taken at other institutions. Clinical training takes place at the Detroit Medical Center (DMC), which is comprised of numerous hospitals, institutes, and care centers and has, in total, more than 2,400 beds. DMC includes Harper Hospital, Grace Hospital, Hutzel Hospital, Children's Hospital of Michigan, Rehabilitation Institute of Michigan, Detroit Receiving Hospital/University Health Center, Gershenson Radiation Oncology Center, Kresge Eye Institute, and Huron Valley Hospital. Medical students also rotate to affiliated hospitals in suburban areas.

Campus Life

About 90 percent of the 256 students in each class are Michigan residents. Approximately 12 percent of students are underrepresented minorities, most of whom are African American. Although a few students are older or nontraditional, most entering students are in their early twenties.

STUDENT LIFE

Medical students are involved in chapters of national organizations, such as the American Medical Student Association; professionally oriented groups, such as the Family Medicine Interest Group; production of a student newspaper; and numerous community-service projects. Volunteer activities involve working with the city's youth, elderly, and under- and noninsured populations. Medical students also enjoy the extensive extracurricular offerings of Wayne State University, as well as the diverse culture of Detroit. Students live off campus, usually in apartments in the Detroit metropolitan area or in surrounding suburbs. Parking is available on campus, and most students own cars.

GRADUATES

About 65 percent of graduates chose residency programs in Michigan hospitals, with more than 50 percent staying in the Detroit area. In recent years, more than half of graduates entered primary care fields.

Admissions

REQUIREMENTS

One year each of biology, chemistry, organic chemistry, and physics, all with associated labs, is required. The MCAT is required, and scores should be from the spring or fall of the year prior to entrance. For applicants who have retaken the exam, the most recent set of scores is weighed most heavily. Thus, there is no advantage in withholding scores.

SUGGESTIONS

Although most positions are reserved for Michigan residents, well-qualified nonresidents are also considered. In addition to academic credentials, the Admissions Committee is interested in extracurricular activities and work. Health-related volunteer work and research are valuable.

PROCESS

About 50 percent of AMCAS applicants are sent secondary applications. Of those returning secondaries, about 20 percent are interviewed between September and April. The interview consists of one session with a member of the Admissions Committee. Candidates also receive a tour and have the opportunity to meet with current students. About one-third of interviewed candidates are accepted and are notified shortly after the interview. Wait listed candidates are generally not encouraged to send additional information.

Admissions Requirements (Required)

MCAT scores, science GPA, nonscience GPA, letters of recommendation, interview, essays/personal statement, extracurricular activities, exposure to medical profession

Admissions Requirements (Optional)

State residency

Overlap Schools

Michigan State University, University of Michigan—Ann Arbor.

COSTS AND AID

Tuition & Fees

In-state tuition	$22,953
Out-of-state tuition	$47,765
Cost of books	$1,000
Fees	$1,651

Financial Aid

% students receiving aid	83
Average grant	$5,452
Average loan	$22,649
Average debt	$62,468

WEST VIRGINIA UNIVERSITY
SCHOOL OF MEDICINE

ROBERT C. BYRD HEALTH SCIENCES CENTER, PO BOX 9111, MORGANTOWN, WV 26506 • **ADMISSION:** 304-293-2408
FAX: 304-293-7814 • **E-MAIL:** MEDADMISSIONS@HSC.WVU.EDU • **WEBSITE:** WWW.HSC.WVU.EDU/SOM

STUDENT BODY

Type	Public
Enrollment	417
% male/female	60/40
% minorities	5
# applied	2,037
# accepted	170
# enrolled	110
Average age	26

FACULTY

Total faculty (number)	700
% female	35
% minority	15
% part-time	15
Student-faculty ratio	1:2

ADMISSIONS
Average GPA and MCAT scores

Overall GPA	3.65
MCAT Bio	9.6
MCAT Phys	9.2
MCAT Verbal	9.0
MCAT Essay	0

Application Information

Regular application	10/15
Regular notification	Rolling
Are transfers accepted?	Yes
Admissions may be deferred?	Yes
Interview required?	Yes
Application fee	$100

Academics

WVU has a traditional 4-year curriculum resulting in an MD degree. A number of students are selected to join our MD/PhD or MD/MPH programs. The first two years are conducted on the Morgantown campus with a new state-of-the art Learning Center. Unique to the school is a laptop computer program; in which all testing is conducted; 2 years of Physical Diagnosis, with early patient encounters; and an active PBL program. Years 3 and 4 are conducted on one of the three campuses (Morgantown, Charleston, or Eastern) and include an emphasis on rural medicine and an option for international travel. An international track certificate program is available to a limited number of qualified students. The grading system consists of honors/satisfactory/ unsatisfactory plus a narrative for all courses. Students must pass USMLE Step 1 for promotion into year 3. Passing both parts of Step 2 is a graduation requirement. In addition, all students must complete 100 hours of approved community service to graduate.

BASIC SCIENCES: Basic Sciences: All basic science education occurs on the Morgantown campus. First year courses include Human Function (biochemistry, physiology and genetics); Human Structure (gross anatomy, histology and embryology); Public Health (epidemiology, biostatistics and public health); Physical Diagnosis-Clinical Integration; Neurobiology; and Problem-based Learning. Second year courses include Immunity, Infection and Disease (microbiology and immunology); Mechanisms of Human Disease (pathology), Pharmacology; Physical Diagnosis-Clinical Integration; Behavioral Medicine and Psychopathology; and Health Care Ethics. Classes are conducted in the new Learning Center with state-of-the-art facilities and technology including a secure online environment.

CLINICAL TRAINING

Approximately 60 students remain in Morgantown, one-third go to Charleston and the remainder go to the Eastern campus for similar experiences. Third-year required clerkships include 8-week experiences each in Medicine, Surgery, Obstetrics and Gynecology, Behavioral Medicine and Psychiatry and Neurology; Pediatrics and Family Medicine (one month of which is a WV rural rotation). Fourth year requirements include 4 weeks Sub-internship in Family Medicine, Internal Medicine, Pediatrics or Surgery; 4 weeks Acute care rotation; 8 weeks WV Rural Medicine; 2 weeks USMLE prep, and 16 weeks of electives. Clinical training occurs at all three campuses and can be viewed at our website www.hsc.wvu.edu/som/students. In Morgantown, education occurs primarily at the Ruby Memorial Hospital (376 beds with Level 1 Trauma Center). The Robert C. Byrd Health Sciences Complex also contains Physicians Office Center (outpatient clinics), Mary Babb Randolph Cancer Center, Chestnut Ridge Psychiatric Hospital, HealthSouth Regional Rehabilitation Hospital and a National Institute of Occupational Safety and Health (NIOSH) facility. The Charleston Campus is the oldest branch campus in the U.S. The Charleston Area Medical Center encompasses three hospitals, the General, Memorial, and Women and Children's. Health care is provided to a population base of 500,000 with over 40,000 admissions/year and 200,000 outpatient visits. The Eastern Division provides community-based education in a 9-county area with an emphasis on Family Medicine, Primary Care, and Rural Health. Patient services are provided at City Hospital, Jefferson Memorial Hospital, and the Veterans Hospital as well as a variety of outpatient locations.

Campus Life

Approximately 70 percent of the students are West Virginia residents, and more than one-third attended WVU for undergraduate studies. About 60 other undergraduate institutions are represented in a typical class. Approximately 65 percent of the students were biology or chemistry majors in college. The typical class size is 110 students.

STUDENT LIFE

There are more than 1,900 students enrolled at the Robert C. Byrd Health Sciences Center studying in medicine, dentistry, pharmacy, research, nursing, physical or occupational therapy, medical technology, and exercise physiology. Within the medical school classes, a great camaraderie exists. There are a number of student interest groups and clubs and many opportunities for community service. There is an active outreach project for the local homeless and a student-run clinic for the uninsured. Morgantown is consistently rated as a top livable city by many nationwide surveys. Low crime and many social activities are available within the community. A modern student recreational center is near the campus. Its 177,000 square feet house weight and exercise equipment, multiple sports courts, two pools, an indoor jogging track, and a 50 foot climbing wall.

GRADUATES

A significant number of practicing physicians in the state of West Virginia are WVU graduates. Consistently, at least half of the graduates each year enter primary care fields in family medicine, pediatrics, internal medicine, and obstetrics/gynecology. The rest are successfully matched into all the other specialties.

Admissions

REQUIREMENTS

Ninety credit hours and three years of college through an accredited US or Canadian college/university are required for application. All requirements must be completed with a grade of C or higher by January 1 of the admission year. Courses required include biology/zoology, general chemistry, organic chemistry, physics and social/behavioral classes. All science courses must include labs. A recent MCAT and personal interview are required.

SUGGESTIONS

WVU gives strongest preference to competitive WV residents. Strong consideration is also given to non-residents with WV ties and documented interests in primary care or rural medicine. Courses in biochemistry and cellular and molecular biology are highly recommended in preparation for medical school. No particular major is recommended, but applicants with non-traditional majors should be aware that the minimum science courses required often do not fully prepare you for the rigors of medical school. Community service, medical experiences and physician shadowing are also strongly encouraged. An early decision program is offered for competitive residents and no-residents.

PROCESS

Each primary application is reviewed and only highly qualified applicants are sent a secondary application. The majority of those who return a secondary application are interviewed. The interviews are conducted between October and March, and general include a tour and lunch meeting with medical students prior to an interview with two Admissions Committee members. Limited accommodations may be available with one of our medical students as space allows. Applicants are accepted on a rolling basis throughout the interview season.

Admissions Requirements (Required)

MCAT scores, science GPA, letters of recommendation, interview, essay/personal statement, exposure to medical profession, minimum 90 semester hours

Admissions Requirements (Optional)

Nonscience GPA, state residency, extracurricular activities

COSTS AND AID

Tuition & Fees

In-state tuition	$18,278
Out-of-state tuition	$39,900
Room and board (off-campus)	$11,950
Cost of books	$4,114
Fees	$2,000

Financial Aid

% students receiving aid	92
Average grant	$8,348
Average loan	$26,225
Average debt	$153,679

WRIGHT STATE UNIVERSITY
BOONSHOFT SCHOOL OF MEDICINE

OFFICE OF STUDENT AFFAIRS/ADMISSIONS, P.O. BOX 1751 DAYTON, OH 45401-1751 • ADMISSION: 937-775-2934
FAX: 937-775-3322 • E-MAIL: SOM_SAA@DESIRE.WRIGHT.EDU • WEBSITE: WWW.MED.WRIGHT.EDU

STUDENT BODY

Type	Public
Enrollment	409
% male/female	44/56
% minorities	31
# applied (total/out)	3,237/2,157
# accepted (total/out)	220/18
# enrolled (total/out)	100/8
Average age	23

FACULTY

Total faculty	1,255
Student-faculty ratio	3:1

ADMISSIONS
Average GPA and MCAT Scores

Overall GPA	3.58
MCAT Bio	9.75
MCAT Phys	9.1
MCAT Verbal	9.54
MCAT Essay	0

Application Information

Regular application	11/15
Regular notification	10/15
Early application	8/1
Early notification	10/1
Are transfers accepted?	Yes
Admissions may be deferred?	Yes
Interview required?	Yes
Application fee	$45

Academics

Although most students complete the M.D. curriculum in four years, a few enter the M.D./Ph.D. program, which requires additional coursework. Graduate degrees are offered in most Biomedical Sciences including Anatomy, Physiology, Biochemistry, Pathology, and Pharmacology. Medical students are evaluated with percentile scores and ratings of Pass/Fail. Students take the USMLE Step 1 after completion of year two and Step 2 after the completion of year three.

BASIC SCIENCES: Basic-science instruction includes use of small groups, clinical case studies, team-based learning, and computer-aided instruction. First-year courses are Human Structure, Human Development, Introduction to Clinical Medicine I (ICM I), Molecular Basis of Medicine, Cellular, and Tissue Biology, Social and Ethical Issues in Medicine, Principles of Disease, and Evidence-Based Medicine. The second year is organized around organ/body systems. These are Pathobiology and Therapeutics, Blood, Cardiology, Endocrine, GI, Integument, Musculoskeletal, Neuroscience, Renal, Reproductive, and Respiratory. Students also learn about Infectious Diseases and continue clinical training in ICM II. The ICM course provides clinical contact from the very first week of class. In this series, students learn to take medical histories, conduct physical exams and identify common diseases. Two two-week elective periods during the first two years give students the opportunity to pursue intensive research or clinical projects. Students are also encouraged to participate in faculty-guided research during the summer between the first and second years. The Fordham Health Sciences Library is fully computerized and provides 106,000 volumes, in addition to journals and special collections. Students also study in the Student Lounge and the main university's libraries. The Interdisciplinary Teaching Laboratory enhances learning through the use of audio-visual equipment, hard-wired labs, and medical software. Audio recordings and Power Point slides from lectures are available from a password-protected website.

CLINICAL TRAINING

Third-year required rotations are: Family Medicine (6 weeks); Internal Medicine (12 weeks); Women's Health (8 weeks); Pediatrics (8 weeks); Psychiatry (6 weeks); and Surgery (8 weeks). Fourth-year requirements are Emergency Medicine (4 weeks), Neurology (4 weeks), and a variety of electives (6 months). Training takes place at Children's Medical Center (155 beds); Dayton Veterans Affairs Medical Center; Good Samaritan Hospital and Health Center (560 beds); Greene Memorial Hospital (210 beds); Kettering Medical Center (486 beds); Miami Valley Hospital (811 beds); and Wright-Patterson Air Force Base Medical Center (301 beds). Some students rotate overseas as part of individually designed or faculty-led experiences.

Students

About 90 percent of entering students are Ohio residents. From 20 to 25 percent of entering students are typically minorities. Typically, about 10 percent of entering students took significant time off between college and medical school. The class size is 100.

STUDENT LIFE

Medical students have active extracurricular lives, taking advantage of the offerings of the Medical School, the main University, and the greater community. Students are involved in community service organizations and projects such as the Center for Healthy Communities, which provides health education services to the Dayton community. Other student organizations are chapters of state and national medical organizations, honor societies, support groups, and clubs focused on professional or recreational interests. Athletic facilities on campus include racquetball, squash, basketball and tennis courts, indoor and outdoor tracks, and several fitness centers. The University's 200 acres of woods are used for walking and jogging. The University is located 12 miles northeast of Dayton, a city of nearly one million residents. Students live in privately owned apartments, condominiums, and homes which are generally affordable and conveniently located.

GRADUATES

Typically about 55 percent enter primary care residencies, which include Family Medicine, Internal Medicine, and Pediatrics. About 50 percent typically choose residency programs in Ohio.

Admissions

REQUIREMENTS

Prerequisites are one year each of Biology, Chemistry, Organic Chemistry, and Physics, all with associated labs. In addition, one year each of English and Mathematics are required. The MCAT is required, and scores should be from within the past three years. For applicants who have retaken the exam, all scores are considered.

SUGGESTIONS

Ohio residents are given strong preference, making admission for nonresidents very competitive. In addition to academic strength, selection is based on dedication to human concerns, communication skills, maturity, and motivation. Some hospital or other medically related experience is recommended.

PROCESS

All AMCAS applicants receive secondary applications. About 15 percent of those returning secondaries are invited to interview between September and March. Interviews consist of two sessions, each with a member of the admissions committee. On interview day, students also attend group information presentations, have lunch with students, and tour the campus. About 45 percent of interviewed candidates are accepted on a rolling basis. Others are rejected or put on a wait-list. Wait-listed candidates are not encouraged to send additional information.

Admissions Requirements (Required)

MCAT scores, Science GPA, Non-science GPA, Letters of recommendation, Interview, Essays/personal statement, Extracurricular activities, Exposure to medical profession

Admissions Requirements (Optional)

State residency

COSTS AND AID

Tuition & Fees

In-state Tuition	$24,220
Out-of-state Tuition	$34,288
Room and board (off-campus)	$11,946
Cost of books	$1,757
Fees	$2,078

Financial Aid

% students receiving aid	93
Average grant	$10,195
Average loan	$39,633
Average debt	$139,649

YALE UNIVERSITY
SCHOOL OF MEDICINE

OFFICE OF ADMISSIONS, 367 CEDAR STREET, NEW HAVEN, CT 06510 • ADMISSION: 203-785-2643 • FAX: 203-785-3234
E-MAIL: MEDICALSCHOOL.ADMISSIONS@QUICKMAIL.YALE.EDU • WEBSITE: WWW.INFO.MED.YALE.EDU/EDUCATION/ADMISSIONS/INDEX.HTML

STUDENT BODY

Type	Private
Enrollment	479
% male/female	51/49
% minorities	18
# applied (total/out)	3,093/3,472
Average age	24

ADMISSIONS

Application Information

Regular application	10/15
Regular notification	3/15
	until filled
Early application	6/1–8/1
Early notification	10/1
Are transfers accepted?	Yes
Admissions may be deferred?	Yes
Interview required?	No
Application fee	$60

Academics

Although most students complete courses, clerkships, and a thesis in 4 years, about 30–50 percent of students extend their studies over a 5 year period at no extra cost. Some students take an extra year to earn a MPH along with the MD. Other combined-degree programs offered are the MD/JD, MD/MDiv, and MD/PhD. Entering students are assigned a clinical tutor who serves as a mentor during all 4 years. Also throughout all 4 years, students take a series of lectures, workshops, and clinical discussion under the broad topic of medicine, society, and public health. Evaluation of students is strictly pass/fail. Passing Steps 1 and 2 of the USMLE is a graduation requirement.

BASIC SCIENCES: The first 2 years are spent building a foundation in the basic sciences, as well as learning skills and techniques for training in clinical responsibilities. Year 1 is devoted to understanding normal relevant biological form and function. Year 2 concentrates on the study of disease. Formats include lecture, small-group discussion, laboratories, demonstrations, and individual tutorials; many of these involve patients, both at the bedside and in the classroom. First-year students must pass the following courses: Aspects of Child and Adolescent Development, Biological Basis of Behavior, Cellular and Physiologic Basis of Medicine (Physiology and Cell Biology), Human Genetics, Human Anatomy and Development, Molecular Foundations of Medicine (Biochemistry), Neurobiology, and Psychological Basis of Medical Practice. In addition there is an umbrella course called Medicine, Society, and Public Health that includes related but distinct subcourses: Biostatistics, History of Medicine, Professional Responsibility, and Health Policy. Pre-clinical training is included in The Doctor/Patient Encounter. The major, second-year course is called Mechanisms of Disease and is organized into two segments. The initial offering, called Basic Principles, includes immunobiology, laboratory medicine, pathology, pharmacology, microbiology, and basics of diagnostic radiology. The second segment is called Mechanisms of Disease: Organs/Systems. Each integrated module, organized around body systems or organs, includes diagnostic radiology, laboratory medicine, pathology, pharmacology, pathophysiology, and prevention. The modules are Blood/Hematology; Cardiovascular System; Clinical Neuroscience; Digestive System; Endocrine Systems; Female Reproductive System; Musculoskeletal System; Neoplasias/Oncology; Psychiatry; Renal, Urinary Tract and Male Reproductive System; Respiratory System; and Skin. Medicine, Society, and Public Health continues, offering Epidemiology and Public Health in the first semester and relevant prevention during the modules. The Doctor/Patient Encounter course also continues, building as it progresses.

CLINICAL TRAINING

There are seven required clerkships in the third year, one of which may be completed early in the fourth year. These are Internal Medicine (12 weeks), General Surgery/Surgical Subspecialties (12 weeks), Pediatrics (8 weeks), Psychiatry (6 weeks), Obstetrics/Gynecology (6 weeks), and Clinical Neuroscience (4 weeks). During the fourth year, an integrated Clinical Medicine clerkship (3 weeks) and a Primary Care clerkship (4 weeks) are required. The primary care clerkship takes place in a variety of community- and practice-based sites. Most clinical rotations are completed at the Yale New Haven Hospital and the West Haven Veteran's Administration Hospital. Other affiliated hospitals are Bridgeport Hospital, Danbury Hospital, Greenwich Hospital, Griffin Hospital in Derby, Hospital of Saint Raphael, Lawrence and Memorial Hospital,

Norwalk Hospital, Saint Mary's Hospital in Waterbury, Saint Vincent's Medical Center in Bridgeport, and Waterbury Hospital. Several clinics and mental health centers are also used for training. Although some students begin working on their thesis early in medical school, the majority of research and writing takes from 4–7 months and is completed in the fourth year. Some students publish their work, while others continue developing their research post-graduation.

Campus Life

Yale attracts students from all regions of the country. Approximately 15–20 percent of entering students are underrepresented minorities. Class size is 100.

STUDENT LIFE

The School of Medicine is a short walk from the university's main campus. This gives medical students access to athletic facilities, student meeting areas, libraries, and university-sponsored events. Medical students participate in intramural sports, competing against other graduate and professional school teams. About three-quarters of medical students are involved in community service activities such as STATS (Students Teaching AIDS to Students), the Prenatal Care Project, and ASAP (the Adolescent Substance Abuse Prevention Project). The Office for Women in Medicine is the oldest of its kind in the nation and provides support, guidance, and special programs of interest for women medical students. The Office for Multicultural Affairs recruits and supports minority students, serves as a link between the school and its surrounding community, and sponsors various cultural events and centers. The Edward S. Harkness Memorial Hall is a residence hall for medical, physician associate, nursing, public health, and other graduate students. Both dormitory-style rooms and apartments are available.

GRADUATES

Among graduates, the most popular areas for residency training were internal medicine (40 percent), pediatrics (12 percent), orthopedics (8 percent), surgery (5 percent), otolaryngology (5 percent), plastic surgery (4 percent), dermatology (3 percent), and diagnostic radiology (1 percent).

Admissions

REQUIREMENTS

Prerequisites are 1 year each of general biology or zoology, general chemistry, organic chemistry, and general physics, all taken with associated labs. The MCAT is required, and scores should be from within the past 4 years. For applicants who have retaken the exam, the best set of scores is considered.

SUGGESTIONS

In addition to academic credentials, the Admissions Committee looks for intelligent, mature, and highly motivated students who possess integrity, common sense, personal stability, dedication to service, and the ability to inspire and maintain confidence.

PROCESS

Yale does not participate in AMCAS. Applications should be requested from the address above, or downloaded from info.med.yale.edu/medadmit. About 25 percent of applicants are interviewed between October and February. Interviews consist of two sessions, each with a faculty member or medical student committee member. Candidates attend group information sessions and have the opportunity to eat lunch and tour the campus with current medical students. About 15 percent of interviewed candidates are accepted. Notification occurs in mid-March.

Admissions Requirements (Required)

MCAT scores, state residency, essays/personal statement, extracurricular activities, exposure to medical profession

Admissions Requirements (Optional)

Science GPA, non-science GPA, letters of recommendation, interview

COSTS
Tuition & Fees

Tuition	$39,130
Room and board (on-campus)	$9,650
Cost of books	$1,700
Fees	$375

Yeshiva University

Albert Einstein College of Medicine

1300 Morris Park Avenue, 1300 Morris Park Avenue, Bronx, NY 10461 • Admission: 718-430-2106
Fax: 718-430-8825 • E-mail: ADMISSIONS@AECOM.YU.EDU • Website: WWW.AECOM.YU.EDU

STUDENT BODY

Type	Private
Enrollment	724
% male/female	51/49
% minorities	7
# applied (total/out)	5,943/4,522
# accepted (total/out)	521/336
# enrolled (total/out)	180/92
Average age	23

FACULTY

Total faculty (number)	3,510
% female	35
% part-time	42
Student-faculty ratio	1:1

ADMISSIONS
Average GPA and MCAT Scores

Overall GPA	3.6
MCAT Bio	10.6
MCAT Phys	10.5
MCAT Verbal	9.4
MCAT Essay	P

Application Information

Regular application	12/31
Regular notification	1/15
Early application	8/1
Early notification	10/1
Are transfers accepted?	No
Admissions may be deferred?	Yes
Interview required?	Yes
Application fee	$90

Academics

In addition to the requirements described below, all students conduct research projects through the Independent Scholars Program. Such research often leads to publication or to distinction at the time of graduation. Projects involve a faculty mentor and can be in traditional or nontraditional medical science fields. Students may apply for joint-PhD/MD programs at the time of initial application or while enrolled in the MD program. Those accepted into this program receive stipends, either through the MSTP program or from institutional sources. The PhD may be earned in the following fields: anatomy, biochemistry, biophysics, cell biology, genetics, immunology, microbiology, molecular biology, neuroscience, pathology, pharmacology, and physiology. Evaluation of student performance uses honors, pass, and fail. Passing the USMLE Steps 1 and 2 is a requirement for graduation.

BASIC SCIENCES: Throughout the first and second years, Introduction to Clinical Medicine complements the basic science curriculum by addressing practical and personal issues related to the patient interview and examination. About 40 entering students participate in a Generalist Mentorship Program, which involves shadowing a primary care physician. First-year courses, taught primarily with lectures and labs, are Anatomy, Cardiovascular Physiology, Disease Mechanisms, Histology, and Principles of Pharmacology. The course Molecular and Cellular Foundations of Medicine uses both lectures and small-group sessions. During the second part of year 1, and throughout all of year 2, instruction is organ-based, is carried out in small groups, and uses a case-based approach. Courses are Cardiovascular System, Endocrine System, Gastrointestinal System and Liver, Hematology, Nervous System and Behavior, Renal Physiology and Pathobiology, Reproductive System and Human Sexuality, Respiratory System, and Rheumatologic and Orthopedic Disease. Other second-year courses are Microbiology and Infectious Disease and Parasitology. On average, students spend about 20 hours per week in class. A Cognitive Skills Program offers reviews for the USMLE and tutoring for students who will benefit from it. Basic science instruction takes place in the Arthur B. and Diane Belfer Educational Center for Sciences, which is open 24 hours a day and contains classrooms, laboratories, study areas, a student bookstore, and computer rooms. The D. Samuel Gottesman Library has 250,000 volumes, 2,400 journal subscriptions, computer databases, and other informational technology. Electronic search mechanisms allow easy access to several large collections in the New York area.

CLINICAL TRAINING

Third-year required clerkships are Medicine (11 weeks), Pediatrics (7 weeks), Psychiatry (6 weeks), Obstetrics/Gynecology (6 weeks), Surgery (8 weeks), Family Medicine (6 weeks), Geriatrics (2 weeks), and Neurology (2 weeks). During the fourth year, 2 months of a sub internship in either medicine or pediatrics is required, as are 2 months in an ambulatory care program. For clinical training, Einstein students have access to six prominent hospitals in New York, comprising a total of 6,988 beds. These are Jacobi Medical Center (537 beds), Montefiore Medical Center (745 beds), Long Island Jewish Medical Center (829 beds), Beth Israel Medical Center (212 beds), and the Bronx-Lebanon Medical Center (two centers with 540 beds). Training also takes place at mental health facilities and long-term care centers primarily for older populations. Several nationally recognized research institutes are part of Einstein's resources and provide further opportunities for students. Fellowships are available for up to 20 fourth-year students, enabling them to fulfill elective requirements overseas. Numerous organized exchange programs also exist, with countries such as Germany, Sweden, Israel, France, Japan, and Cuba.

Campus Life

Students come from around the country. Undergraduate institutions that are particularly well represented are Yeshiva, State Universities of New York, private northeastern colleges and universities, and public universities in California. In a typical entering class, about 9 percent of students are minorities, most of whom are African American. Students who have taken time off after college account for about one-third of entering classes, and those over 30 years old account for about 5–10 percent. Class size is 180.

STUDENT LIFE

Central meeting areas, such as the Lubin Student Lounge and the Max and Sadie Friedman Lounge, feature music, food, television, and an opportunity for interaction outside of the academic environment. There are full athletic facilities for student use. School-sponsored activities include class parties, clubs focused on films or the outdoors, and organizations based on cultural, religious, or ethnic affiliations. Einstein has its own symphony orchestra. The beaches of Long Island and the culture, entertainment, and excitement of Manhattan are easily accessible by car or public transportation. Most students live on campus, in the Eastchester Road or Rhinelander Residences, where studios and 1- and 2-bedroom apartments are available.

GRADUATES

Among graduates, the predominant residency choices were internal medicine (45 percent), pediatrics (12 percent), surgery or general surgery (10 percent), obstetrics/gynecology (6 percent), emergency medicine (6 percent), psychiatry (5 percent), family practice (4 percent), and ophthalmology (3 percent). Einstein has the largest postgraduate training program in the country and is the destination of about 40 percent of Einstein School of Medicine graduates. Programs at other New York institutions, in the Philadelphia area, and in California are also popular choices.

Admissions

REQUIREMENTS

Requirements are biology (8 hours), chemistry (8 hours), English (8 hours), organic chemistry (8 hours), physics (8 hours), and college math (6 hours). The MCAT is required and should be no more than 3 years old. For those who have retaken the MCAT, the best score is counted. Thus, there is no advantage to withholding scores.

SUGGESTIONS

College students should pursue studies in their area of interest, as no particular major is considered more appropriate than the next. Course work in the humanities and social sciences is important. Statistics is useful, and computer literacy is necessary. Einstein looks closely at the personal interaction skills of its applicants and at their ability to work with people from diverse backgrounds.

PROCESS

All AMCAS applicants are sent secondary applications. Of those returning secondaries, about 20 percent are invited to interview. Interviews with faculty members last for about 1 hour and take place between August and May. On interview day, there is a tour of the campus and a lunch period with current Einstein students. Notification begins in January, during which applicants are accepted, wait listed, or rejected. Wait listed candidates may submit additional material.

Admissions Requirements (Required)

MCAT scores, science GPA, non-science GPA, letters of recommendation, interview, essays/personal statement, extracurricular activities, exposure to medical profession

Admissions Requirements (Optional)

State residency

Overlap Schools

New York University, State University of New York—Stony Brook University, State University of New York—Downstate Medical Center, UMDNJ.

COSTS AND AID

Tuition & Fees

Tuition	$39,450
Room and board (on-campus)	$4,000
Room and board (off-campus)	$7,000
Cost of books	$1,600
Fees	$2,250

Financial Aid

% students receiving aid	75
Average grant	$8,500
Average loan	$20,000
Average debt	$65,000

8 Naturopathic Profiles

BASTYR UNIVERSITY
SCHOOL OF NATUROPATHIC MEDICINE

14500 JUANITA DR NE KENMORE, WA 98028 • ADMISSION: 425-602-3330 • FAX: 425-602-3090
E-MAIL: ADMISSIONS@BASTYR.EDU • WEBSITE: WWW.BASTYR.EDU/SUB/ADTRACK.ASP?ADID=PR13

STUDENT BODY

Type	Private
Enrollment	478
% male/female	20/80
% minorities	34
# applied (total/out)	255/190
# accepted (total/out)	168/115
# enrolled (total/out)	109/75
Average age	29

FACULTY

Total faculty (number)	28
% female	60
% part-time	64
Student-faculty ratio	13:1

ADMISSIONS
Average GPA and MCAT Scores

Overall GPA	3.32

Application Information

Regular application	2/1
Regular notification	4/15
Early application	11/1
Early notification	2/1
Are transfers accepted?	Yes
Admissions may be deferred?	Yes
Interview required?	Yes
Application fee	$75

Academics

Bastyr's naturopathic doctoral (ND) program educates future physicians in the tradition of medical science and the art of natural healing. The school does this by providing a comprehensive understanding of the basic medical sciences, accurate diagnostic skills, and the ability to apply the natural and minimally invasive methods of whole-person health care characteristic of naturopathic medicine. Bastyr's Vision: Bastyr University will be the world's leading academic center for advancing knowledge in the natural health sciences. Bastyr's Mission: We educate future leaders in the natural health arts and sciences. Respecting the healing power of nature and recognizing that body, mind, and spirit are intrinsically inseperable. We model an integrated approach to education, research, and clinical service. Original research is conducted regularly and a research fellowship has been funded. Students are engaged in primary clinical research at the teaching clinic. The university maintains a library with current journals; special collections in alternative medicine, acupuncture, nutrition, midwifery, and naturopathic medicine; and audiovisual aids. Students also have access to the nearby University of Washington Health Sciences Libraries.

BASIC SCIENCES: During the first two years of the program, students receive a thorough foundation in the basic medical sciences along with instruction in naturopathic medicine, clinical and laboratory diagnosis, nutrition, and counseling. Basic science courses within the ND program emphasize anatomy, physiology, and biochemistry as the foundation for further basic science and all chemical courses. Further courses include pathology, immunology, infectious diseases, embryology, and research methods. Problem-solving, clinical cases, and examples are an integral part of the basic science curriculum.

CLINICAL TRAINING

The second two years of education at Bastyr University focus on clinical diagnosis and therapeutics, including clinical studies in nutrition, botanical medicine, homeopathy, obstetrics, pediatrics, geriatrics, and other specialty areas. Students receive their clinical education through supervised internships at the university's own teaching clinic, Bastyr Center for Natural Health (BCNH), as well as at numerous off-site clinic placements. All ND students are required to accrue 132 hours in preceptorships. These hours are spent observing and "shadowing" health-care professionals in their practices. Bastyr ND students receive a minimum of 1200 clinical training hours. Those hours must include a minimum of 350 direct patient contacts in order to graduate. Most of our students, however, average approximately 600 patient contacts by the time they earn their degree. Students in the ND/acupuncture and Oriental medicine (AOM) dual program are eligible to participate in clinical internships in China-either at Chengdu University of TCM or Shanghai University of TCM. Chengdu University has been Bastyr's sister college since 1993 and is one of the four colleges approved by the State Council in 1956.

Students

Bastyr University's natural health science campus is located in Kenmore, just north of Seattle in the beautiful Pacific Northwest. The 186,000-square-foot facility rests on 51 acres of fields and woodlands on the northeast shore of Lake Washington. Built in 1959 as a Catholic seminary, this building houses the university's classrooms and other facilities: Laboratories and research facilities; Library and reading room; University bookstore; Conference and seminar space; Administrative offices; Vegetarian cafeteria; Chapel; Dormitory space on campus. A variety of off-campus apartments and rental homes are available in the Juanita, Mountlake Terrace, Bothell and Kenmore areas. Bastyr students thrive in our close-knit and nurturing community, enjoying a campus surrounded by lush woodlands-a perfect setting for the study and celebration of nature. At Bastyr you will be part of a community that thrives on diversity and the free exchange of ideas-that understands the essential roles played by the mind, body, and spirit in the totality of human health.

STUDENT LIFE
Bastyr students find a wide variety of activities on campus to keep them busy. Students are involved in the governance system of the university through student and university councils, and board of trustees memberships. Other activities include service in the medicinal and culinary herb garden and various clubs and committees: other facilities; Bastyr Environmental Action Team (BEAT); Herbal Ways; Nutrition Advisory Committee; Cultural Awareness, Task Force; American Psychological Association; Aikido; African-American Support Group; Student Dietetics Association; Supper Club; Student Chapter of Physicians for Social Responsibility; Natural Products Student Reps; Various spiritual groups; Various athletic groups. Various special events help create a sense of school identity and a feeling of community. Bastyr students are involved in making the surrounding community a "well" place to live.

GRADUATES: Graduates of Bastyr's ND program are qualified primary health care practitioners who, as they diagnose and treat disease, are focused on treating the whole person and promoting optimal health. Their scope of practice includes all aspects of family care, from pediatrics to geriatrics, and relies on a broad spectrum of modalities, including: Botanical medicine; Nutrition; Homeopathy; Hydrotherapy; Naturopathic manipulation; Psychological counseling. Graduates leave Bastyr University qualified to pass professional licensure exams and prepared to set up and maintain private practices.

Admissions
REQUIREMENTS
Credentials to be submitted are all official transcripts, two letters of recommendation, a completed application form, and a $75 application fee. While a bachelor's degree is strongly recommended, exceptions are made for outstanding students who have completed at least 135 quarter credits or 90 semester credits (must include at least 45 quarter or 30 semester credits of upper-division course work). In recent years, more than 97 percent of entrants have held a bachelor's degree. Required minimum course work includes one course in college-level algebra or precalculus, four courses in chemistry (including a two-term sequence of organic with lab), three quarters or two semesters of biology with labs (must include work in cell biology and genetics), at least one course in physics (must include mechanics, optics, electricity, and magnetism), and one course in psychology. Additional requirements for those without a bachelor's degree include two courses in English and two courses in humanities. Courses earning a C- or below are not accepted for prerequisite consideration. Required chemistry and biology courses not taken within seven years of matriculation into the program are subject to review by the admissions committee. Additional course work may be required. Applicants who meet the basic admission standards may be invited to an interview.

SUGGESTIONS
For priority consideration, applications should be received by February 1 for admission the following fall, although late applications are considered on a space-available basis. When requesting an application or program information, please be sure to indicate the specific program of interest and what materials you would like sent.

PROCESS
Admission is based on academic achievement, personal and social development, relevant experience, and demonstrated humanistic qualities.

Admissions Requirements (Required)
Science GPA, Non-science GPA, Letters of recommendation, Interview, Essays/personal statement, Exposure to medical profession

Admissions Requirements (Optional)
MCAT scores, State residency, Extracurricular activities, Experience with CAM desired

COSTS AND AID
Tuition & Fees

Tuition	$23,515
Room and board (on-campus)	$4,100
Room and board (off-campus)	$9,200
Cost of books	$2,325

Financial Aid

% students receiving aid	80
Average grant	$3,000
Average loan	$33,500
Average debt	$185,000

BOUCHER INSTITUTE OF NATUROPATHIC MEDICINE

300-435 COLUMBIA STREET NEW WESTMINSTER, BC CANADA, V3L 5N8 • ADMISSION: 604-777-9981
FAX: 604-777-9982 • E-MAIL: SSPARLIN@BINM.ORG • WEBSITE: WWW.BINM.ORG

STUDENT BODY	
Type	Private
Enrollment	140
% male/female	20/80
# applied	76
# accepted	35
# enrolled	35
Average age	35

FACULTY	
Total faculty (number)	50
% female	50
Student-faculty ratio	12:1

ADMISSIONS
Average GPA and MCAT Scores

Overall GPA	3.0

Application Information

Regular application	11/30
Are transfers accepted	Yes
Admissions may be deferred	No
Interview required?	Yes
Application fee	$150

Academics

The academic philosophy as evidenced by the Institute's curriculum design, strives to incorporate principles of both proven conventional academic wisdom and a mentorship program. BINM's commitment to small class size allows maximum flexibility in the incorporation of various educational methodologies including hands-on situational learning. Thirty-five hundred hours of instruction are divided among the five basic categories of courses that constitute the Naturopathic Medical Program academic curriculum: Clinical Practice and Integration, Clinical Science, Biomedical Sciences, Naturopathic Therapeutic Modalities, and Professional Development.

CLINICAL TRAINING

Twelve hundred hours are spent on the clinical component of the student's education, with an additional 300 preceptorship hours spent in the offices of practicing physicians.

Campus Life

Boucher Institute is pleased to announce that it has acquired the 46,000 square-foot Columbia Centre building located at 435 Columbia Street in New Westminster, which also provides access to the Columbia Street Sky Train Station. This acquisition enables the institute to expand its campus by occupying more than half the building, to accommodate its growing enrollment of approximately 140 naturopathic medical students expected for the 2008/2009 academic year. Established in 2001, the Boucher Institute is Western Canada's only initially approved college of naturopathic medicine, offering a full-time four year and a part-time six year, 5,000-hour program of postgraduate training culminating in a Doctor of Naturopathic Medicine diploma. This new campus provides the Institute with more than 20,000 square-feet of contiguous newly-renovated space for modern classrooms, expanded library facilities, teaching labs, an expanded teaching clinic, administrative offices, and student activities.

Admissions
REQUIREMENTS

A university bachelor's degree is required from a recognized post-secondary institution or the equivalent (as listed by the Canadian Information Centre for International Credentials—www.bcit.ca/ices—or as listed by the U.S. Department of Education—www.ope.ed). For credentials earned outside of the United States and Canada, a comprehensive evaluation must be completed from ICES—www.bcit.ca/ices—or from WES—www.wes.org—and sent directly to the Admissions Committee prior to the admissions deadline. Applicants must have completed the following specific courses as part of, or in addition to a bachelor's degree: biochemistry (1 semester/3 credit hours), biology (1 full year/6 credit hours; this may be fulfilled by 1 year of general biology or 1 semester of cell biology plus 1 semester of an appropriate biology, such as anatomy, botany, genetics, microbiology, and zoology), English/humanities (1 full-year/6 credit hours; the course must include an essay component, and applicants may be required to write a short essay at the time of interview), general chemistry (1 full-year/6 credit hours), organic chemistry (1 semester/3 credit hours), and psychology (1 semester/ 3 credit hours). In addition, prospective students would benefit by completing additional courses in some or all of the following areas: anatomy, cell biology, genetics, human physiology, microbiology, physics, sociology, and statistics. A passing mark of 60 percent is the absolute minimum grade required for all prerequisites. It is recommended that an overall GPA of 3.0 on a 4.0 scale (i.e., 75 percent) be attained for the applicant to be competitive for the limited seats available. For more information, contact the Registrar's Office. Credit might not be given for courses completed more than 10 years prior to application for admission.

PROCESS

The Boucher Institute of Naturopathic Medicine evaluates all applicants in accordance with the constitutional guidelines that protect the rights of individuals. The primary objective of the applicant screening process is to assure that applicants accepted into the program have made an informed commitment to naturopathic medicine as a career and that there is a good match between the applicant's goals and expectations and what the Institute's unique program has to offer. Applicants must be temperamentally and morally suited to the profession and must have a reasonable probability of successfully completing the program and becoming licensed to practice in a regulated jurisdiction.

The successful applicant is expected to have demonstrated reasonable academic ability in previous educational endeavours; have reasonable knowledge of and realistic attitudes toward health and healing and toward naturopathic medicine in particular; understand the importance of self-care, demonstrate a reasonable understanding of holistic health care, and be able to discuss the role of the healer in the natural self-healing process; have some knowledge and personal experience of naturopathic medicine; recognize the ongoing responsibilities inherent in a life of service to the community as a naturopathic physician; understand that naturopathic medicine is a rapidly-advancing field in which there is a continuing need to update skills and knowledge by keeping current with journals and through continuing education; have realistic expectations regarding the income potential of naturopathic physicians; be aware of the potential for mental and emotional stress involved in this occupation, and have an understanding of the relationship of naturopathic medicine to other health care professions; have devoted sufficient time and energy to researching the naturopathic medicine profession and, considering personal goals and expectations, to be confident in this career choice; have an appreciation of the importance of diversity in society and show evidence of the maturity, emotional stability, and physical ability necessary to engage in the activities required for naturopathic training and practice; be able to demonstrate an ability for critical thinking and have good communication skills; be able to discuss professionalism as it applies to the provision of health care; be able to provide references as to the applicant's character and ability; and be able to demonstrate adequate financial resources to become a full-time student.

Applicants who meet the academic requirements specified and who have also satisfied the aforementioned criteria, as evidenced through their application, essay, and interview, are eligible for admission to the Institute at the discretion of the Admissions Committee.

Admissions Requirements (Required)

Letters of recommendation, interview, essay/personal statement, exposure to medical profession, BINM prerequisites

Overlap Schools

Bastyr University, Canadian College of Naturopathic Medicine, National College of Natural Medicine, Southwest College of Naturopathic Medicine

COSTS AND AID
Tuition & Fees

Tuition	$17,200
Room and board (off-campus)	$12,000
Cost of books	$2,500
Fees	$75

Financial Aid

Average loan	$9,000
from government sources	

THE CANADIAN COLLEGE OF NATUROPATHIC MEDICINE

1255 SHEPPARD AVENUE, TORONTO, ON M2K 1E2 • **ADMISSION:** 416-498-1255, EXT. 245 • **FAX:** 416-498-3197
E-MAIL: INFO@CCNM.EDU • **WEBSITE:** WWW.CCNM.EDU

STUDENT BODY	
Type	Private
Enrollment	489
% male/female	26/74
# applied	280
# accepted	200
# enrolled	154
Average age	27

FACULTY	
Total faculty (number)	117
% part-time	50

ADMISSIONS	
Average GPA and MCAT Scores	
Overall GPA	3.35
Application Information	
Regular application	1/31
Are transfers accepted	Yes
Admissions may be deferred	Yes
Interview required	Yes
Application fee	$150

Academics

The Canadian College of Naturopathic Medicine is Canada's premier institute for education and research in naturopathic medicine. CCNM brings new thinking, new research and new approaches to health care, harnessing science to unleash the healing power of nature. Graduates of its intensive 4-year postgraduate accredited medical program are recognized for regulation/licensure in all Canadian and most American jurisdictions in which naturopathic medicine is regulated.

CCNM's Doctor of Naturopathic Medicine program comprises more than 4,200 hours of classroom and clinical study. Fourth-year students take the role of senior clinicians in CCNM's Robert Schad Naturopathic Clinic (RSNC), Canada's largest naturopathic teaching clinic. The clinic cares for more than 100 patients a day, of all ages and with a wide range of health concerns. Experience is augmented by participation in pediatrics, sports medicine, and pain management shifts.

Campus Life

STUDENT LIFE

CCNM's location in Toronto offers a wealth of entertainment, leisure, and cultural activities for students to enjoy. Whether your tastes lead you to exotic cuisines, multicultural festivals, sports events, or the theater district, there's always something to capture your interest in Toronto.

Campus Facilities Include:

Student residence—conveniently located adjacent to the main campus building.

Offers coed accommodations on both a short-term and year-round basis. Two hundred single occupancy rooms include a single bed, desk and chair, wardrobe closet, and personal refrigerator. Residents are just steps away from such amenities as the Learning Resources Centre and the Robert Schad Naturopathic Clinic.

Security—24-hour security personnel as well as fully monitored security cameras are located on the campus grounds.

Student lounge—with satellite TV, games room, meditation room, and piano room. Also houses the student newspaper, extracurricular clubs, and the Naturopathic Students' Association offices.

Fitness center—equipped with change rooms, lockers, and saunas. A tennis/basketball court is located behind the building on the northwest corner. A variety of campus and intramural sports teams are organized by students each year, based on interest.

Courtyard and herb garden—a relaxing oasis for reflection and meditation, used as a teaching garden for CCNM students and visitors. Brick barbecues and picnic tables are available for student use.

The Green Life Café offers healthy foods at reasonable prices in a pleasant atmosphere. Open Monday to Friday from 7:30 A.M. to 6:00 P.M. during the regular academic year, excluding holidays. It operates on a limited basis in summer and reading weeks.

Recycling and composting—CCNM runs a comprehensive composting program. In addition to yard waste, food waste is recycled into compost used on campus lawns and gardens. Cans, bottles, and paper are collected throughout the campus. Food waste is collected in the student residence kitchens, staff, and student lounges and in the cafeteria. Used household batteries are also collected.

Public transit—in accordance with its environmental program, CCNM encourages the use of public transit. CCNM offers discounted transit passes and has direct access to Toronto's subway system.

Learning Resources Centre—with more than 11,000 resources on naturopathic and complementary health care.

Bookstore—Body Mind Science Resources sells textbooks, software, and medical equipment. Also serves the wider community of complementary health care professionals, carrying a complete line of clinic supplies. It stocks a range of organic foods and healthy snacks.

NATUROPATHIC STUDENTS' ASSOCIATION (NSA)

The Naturopathic Students' Association (NSA) includes all students in the ND program, and each year, 14 executive members are elected from the student body to represent the interests of the students in all aspects pertaining to their education, clinical experiences, and everyday life as a future naturopathic doctor.

Admissions

The Canadian College of Naturopathic Medicine is committed to excellence in naturopathic education and to the success of our graduates. All candidates for admission are evaluated based on their academic history as well as their motivation for becoming a naturopathic doctor, leadership skills, problem solving- and critical-thinking skills, and specific personal qualities and characteristics.

Applicants seeking entry into the 2008–2009 academic year will must have completed a baccalaureate degree prior to entry. Competitive applications should have a cumulative grade point average of at least 3.3 on a 4-point scale (equivalent to B-plus). A lower grade point average may be acceptable, depending on the applicant's academic history, interview, essay, references. and autobiographical sketch.

Credit will not be given for the completion of prerequisites unless a grade of C-minus (60 percent) or better is earned. Required courses include general biology (6 credit hours/1.0 unit), general chemistry (6 credit hours/1.0 unit with lab), organic chemsitry (3 credit hours/0.5 unit with lab), biochemistry (3 credit hours/0.5 unit), psychology (6 credit hours/1.0 unit), and humanities (6 credit hours/1.0 unit). Some prerequisite sciences courses can be completed at CCNM through continuing education.

Applicants are required to complete a personal statement/essay. Details of the personal statement /essay are outlined in the application package, contains two confidential reference forms. These forms must be completed by independent referees and mailed by the referee directly to CCNM. We recommend the applicant receive references from a naturopathic doctor, a professor, or an employer. The application package contains an autobiographical sketch form. Applicants are asked to provide, in chronological order, a brief description of their most significant activities and achievements over the past 10 years. A resume may be submitted in addition to but not as a replacement for an autobiographical sketch.)

Admissions Requirements (Required)

Science GPA, letters of recommendation, interview, essay/personal statement

Admissions Requirements (Optional)

Non-science GPA, state residency, extracurricular activities, exposure to medical profession

Overlap Schools

Bastyr University, Boucher Institute of Naturopathic Medicine, National College of Natural Medicine, Southwest College of Naturopathic Medicine, University of Bridgeport.

COSTS AND AID
Tuition & Fees

Tuition	$17,239
Room and board (on-campus)	$395
Room and board (off-campus)	$700
Cost of books	$1,800
Fees	$455

Financial Aid

% students receiving aid	70
Average grant	$1,000
Average loan	$11,000
Average debt	$65,000

NATIONAL COLLEGE OF NATURAL MEDICINE

049 SW PORTER STREET PORTLAND, OR 97201 • ADMISSION: (503) 552-1660 • FAX: 503-499-0027
E-MAIL: ADMISSIONS@NCNM.EDU • WEBSITE: WWW.NCNM.EDU

STUDENT BODY

Type	Private
Enrollment	505
% male/female	24/76
% minorities	12
# applied (total/out)	268/174
# accepted (total/out)	164/106
# enrolled (total/out)	135/88
Average age	27

FACULTY

Total faculty (number)	104
% female	49
% minority	15
% part-time	75
Student-faculty ratio	4:1

ADMISSIONS
Average GPA and MCAT Scores

Overall GPA	3.31

Application Information

Regular application	2/1
Are transfers accepted?	Yes
Admissions may be deferred?	Yes
Interview required?	Yes
Application fee	$75

Academics

National College of Natural Medicine's mission is clear: To educate and train physicians and practitioners in the art and science of natural medicine. Naturopathic medicine is a patient centered primary care approach that uses natural means to restore and optimize health. It is a distinct system of health care—an art, science, philosophy, and practice of diagnosing, treating, and preventing disease. Methods of treatment respect the natural healing process and emphasize maintaining wellness over suppressing symptoms. Modalities include nutrition, botanical medicine, physical medicine, counseling, homeopathy, hydrotherapy, and pharmacotherapy. Established in June of 2003 at the National College of Natural Medicine, the Helfgott Research Institute (Helfgott) has a state of the art basic science laboratory, as well as the resources to foster clinical research focused on Chinese medicine, naturopathic medicine, and energy medicine. Helfgott has recruited several leading investigators to head research projects and provide mentorship for NCNM faculty, students, and residents who wish to conduct clinical studies. Helfgott is well positioned to study natural therapeutics as our faculty members specialize in their clinical use.

BASIC SCIENCES: The basic sciences are the primary focus of the first two years of instruction. First year students will study anatomy, physiology, cellular biology, palpation and histology. In the second year, emphasis shifts to pathology, pharmacology, homeopathy, nutrition, and clinical diagnosis. The curriculum is structured to provide a solid scientific understanding of the body while never losing the philosophies inherent to naturopathic medicine.

CLINICAL TRAINING

Naturopathic Clinical Sciences: these courses present the naturopathic perspective on diagnosis, prevention, and treatment of disease by system and region. They integrate multiple treatment forms with the principles of naturopathic philosophy into case management, along with criteria for referral. NCNM prides itself on offering the most complete and integrated clinical experience available. In addition to the two teaching clinics, NCNM, in conjunction with other agencies and as a member of the Coalition of Community Clinics, offers free and low-cost naturopathic and Chinese medicine health care at 14 sites around the Portland metropolitan area. These community clinics offer students the opportunity to work with a broad range of medical conditions from mental and women's health to acute care for the homeless and migrant farm workers.

Students

A haven for those seeking well-being, community, culture, and an environment steeped in natural beauty, Portland, Oregon, is an ideal place for studying natural medicine. Life in Portland often reflects life on campus. The city offers an eclectic mix of people and ideas with a common thread of sustainability and social justice. Portland is home to a wide variety of medical programs including naturopathic medicine, classical Chinese medicine, traditional Chinese medicine, allopathic medicine, and chiropractic medicine; making it unique in its perspective on health and healing.

STUDENT LIFE

NCNM students promote natural medicine with the American Association of Naturopathic Physicians and the Naturopathic Medical Student Association. On campus there are groups for a broad range of interests. The Environmental Action Committee is dedicated to sustainability on campus, AWARE promotes and supports diversity on campus, and Queers and Allies advocates for LGBT students, faculty, staff, and patients. In addition to these groups NCNM has soccer, ultimate Frisbee and dragon boat teams.

GRADUATES

NCNM graduates leave school with the knowledge and skills required to succeed in their licensing exams. Graduates also receive institutional support through extensive continuing education and a vast network of alumni. The college is alma mater to over 1,700 alumni who practice world wide. In addition to private practice, many NCNM graduates go on to publish books about natural health, conduct research, speak at national conferences, and teach.

Admissions

REQUIREMENTS

Applicants must have a bachelor's degree (or its equivalent) from a regionally accredited college or university. There is no advantage to holding a BS rather than a BA, as long as you have completed the program's prerequisites. Credit will only be given for prerequisite coursework earning a C or better. Applicants may apply with coursework still in progress; however, the Office of Admissions must receive all official transcripts showing completed coursework prior to matriculation. For the purpose of prerequisites, the Office of Admissions defines a "course" as either a quarter or semester term. Prerequisites are as follows: Mathematics (1 course), General Chemistry with lab (2 courses), Organic Chemistry (2 courses), General Biology with lab (2 courses), Physics (1 course), Social Science (2 courses, at least one course must be in general psychology), Humanities (2 courses at least one course must be English composition).

SUGGESTIONS

Strongly recommended courses biochemistry or cellular biology anatomy physiology statistics business and/or marketing Other suggested courses biomedical ethics philosophy of science public speaking microbiology immunology, and public health

PROCESS

Applicants must submit the following items, which are required to complete an application:

1. Application Form

2. $75 Application Fee.

3. Transcripts: Students need to mail transcripts of all colleges or universities attended to National College of Natural Medicine (NCNM)

4. Personal Essay: The personal essay/statement should tell us about an applicant's background, abilities, interests, and experiences, and how these will make them good candidates for medicine school at NCNM.

5. Two Letters of Recommendation: We require two letters of recommendation (academic preferred or professional), but will take up to three.

6. Resume: The resume should include work experience, activities, community service, and any honors/awards received.

7. Supplemental materials: These include statements regarding academic dismissal, criminal charges, scholarship statements, diversity statements, and/or an addendum with any additional info the applicant wishes to share with the committee.

Applicants are selected regardless of race, gender, age, religion, national or ethnic origin, sexual orientation, marital status, disabilities, or any other protected class under local, state, or federal law.

Admissions Requirements (Required)

Science GPA, Non-science GPA, Letters of recommendation, Interview, Essays/personal statement

Admissions Requirements (Optional)

MCAT scores, State residency, Extracurricular activities, Exposure to medical profession

Overlap Schools

Bastyr University, Southwest College of Naturopathic Medicine.

COSTS AND AID
Tuition & Fees

Tuition	$20,000
Room and board (off-campus)	$19,500
Cost of books	$2,250
Fees	$750

SOUTHWEST COLLEGE OF NATUROPATHIC MEDICINE

2140 EAST BROADWAY ROAD TEMPE, AZ 85282 • ADMISSION: 888-882-7266
FAX: 480-858-9116 • E-MAIL: ADMISSIONS@SSNM.EDU • WEBSITE: WWW.SCNM.EDU

STUDENT BODY

Type	Private
Enrollment	315
% male/female	28/72
% minorities	23
# applied (total/out)	171/119
# accepted (total/out)	81/60
# enrolled (total/out)	62/43
Average age	31

FACULTY

Total faculty (number)	21
% female	25
% part-time	65
Student-faculty ratio	14:1

ADMISSIONS

Average GPA and MCAT Scores

Overall GPA	3.4

Application Information

Regular application	2/1
Regular notification	3/1
Early application	12/15
Early notification	1/15
Are transfers accepted?	Yes
Admissions may be deferred?	Yes
Interview required?	Yes
Application fee	$65

Academics

Founded in 1992, SCNM offers a 4-year professional medical degree in naturopathic medicine accredited by the Council on Naturopathic Medical Education (CNME) and The Higher Learning Commission of the North Central Association of Colleges and Schools. Students are educated in the same basic sciences as MDs, including natural therapeutics and nontoxic approaches to therapy with an emphasis on disease prevention and optimizing wellness. Naturopathic physicians are primary care practitioners, trained as specialists in preventative medicine and natural therapies. We combine and individualize a wide variety of therapies based on a philosophy that acknowledges and encourages patients to be active participates in their own health care as well treat and deal with their physical, psychological, and emotional aspects and barriers. Graduates are trained in the use of natural therapies such as nutrition, botanical medicine, homeopathy, acupuncture, oriental medicine, counseling and hydrotherapy to treat disease and combine these therapies with conventional medical treatments when appropriate.

BASIC SCIENCES: SCNM's curriculum features several required courses in every naturopathic modality. Students are educated in all modalities and methods of treatment, including botanical medicine and homeopathic medicine, nutrition, acupuncture, physical manipulation, and mind/body medicine. Therefore, a student is educated to be a manager of total integrated naturopathic medical care.

CLINICAL TRAINING

The clinical training program at SCNM is a key part of your medical education. As students under the supervision of attending physicians, they apply the scientific knowledge acquired in the academies study to real-life clinical cases and develop the skills and confidences necessary to deliver patient-oriented are. Clinical rotations with NDs, MDs, and DOs are available through the college's medical center or affiliated extended and off-site clinics and treatment centers. This combination of clinical training opportunities makes the clinical education at SCNM a unique experience—one that is committed to excellence in clinical education leading to superior health care that empowers the individual and the community.

Campus Life

The campus is set on 15 acres in the college town of Tempe, Arizona, home to Arizona State University. Campus grounds offer students beautiful and tranquil outdoor spaces to study, relax, and play—all, of course, in the generously sunny and warm climate of Arizona.

STUDENT LIFE

The Southwest College campus culture is easy to sense, yet difficult to describe in words. Once you walk onto our campus, you'll feel the energy. This is a place for meaningful discovery, academic challenge, real-life experience, and lasting friendships. Student enroll at Southwest College and quickly realize they share a common bond in their passion for naturopathic medicine and a unified goal in making an impact in medicine and health care. More than 15 student clubs and organizations provide unlimited leadership, educational, social, and cultural opportunities, as well as terrific resume-building material and networking opportunities for students. SCNM encourages student involvement in professional and community organizations that range in variation. Here are just a few of the organization that are here on campus.

SGA is the official voice of the SCNM student body. SGA representatives work closely with students and college administrators to work on policies and identify ways to best serve the campus and its students. SGA also sponsors several services and events, such as New Student Welcome Dinners, student activities, and student club/organizations.

The American Association of Naturopathic Physicians (AANP) is the national professional society representing naturopathic physicians who are licensed or eligible for licensing as primary care providers.

The Arizona Naturopathic Medical Association is the state professional society representing naturopathic physicians who are licensed or eligible for licensure in the state of Arizona.

The purpose of the Homeopathic Society is to broaden and strengthen knowledge of homeopathy through readings and discussions of the Organon of Medicine, Materia Medica, and guest lectures.

Imhotep Circle's Mission is to encourage and develop programs that promote unity and contribute to the education, welfare, and growth of underserved communities and the students of SCNM. This organization's goals are to raise funds for local programs, volunteer our time to benefit the underserved communities, and establish programs within the SCNM community that promote our mission.

Naturopathic Public Awareness Campaign is dedicated to furthering and supporting current and future public awareness efforts for naturopathic medicine in the United States and Canada. In coordination with the AANP and the accredited naturopathic medical schools, we strive to expand public awareness of naturopathic medicine as a viable, affordable option for quality health care. As a strong naturopathic student organization, NPAC is an extremely effective vehicle for public health education and community outreach.

Naturopathic Society International provides educational opportunities and resources concerning Naturopathic Philosophy for physicians and students of naturopathic medicine.

Admissions
REQUIREMENTS
Application, application fee, professional essay, 3 letters of reference, official transcripts, professional resume, and an in-personal interview are required.

SUGGESTIONS
Visit our website for more information on our program and admission requirements. Please do not hesitate to contact us by phone 480-858-9100, toll free 1-888-882-SCNM (7266), or by e-mail at admissions@scnm.edu with any questions you may have regarding application, naturopathic medicine, relocation, naturopathic career opportunities, and so on.

PROCESS
The college has two intakes a year (spring and fall). Application deadlines are February 1 for the fall intake and December 1 for the spring intake.

Admissions Requirements (Required)
Science GPA, non-science GPA, letters of recommendation, interview, essay/personal statement, professional resume

Admissions Requirements (Optional)
MCAT scores, state residency, extracurricular activities, exposure to medical profession

Overlap Schools
Bastyr University, National College of Natural Medicine.

COSTS AND AID
Tuition & Fees

Tuition	$21,824
Room and board (off-campus)	$8,400
Cost of books	$3,332
Fees	$2,100

Financial Aid

% students receiving aid	92
Average grant	$1,000
Average loan	$36,500
Average debt	$150,000

University of Bridgeport
College of Naturopathic Medicine

126 Park Avenue, Bridgeport, CT 06604 • Admission: 203-576-4108 • Fax: 203-576-4941
E-mail: NATMED@BRIDGEPORT.EDU • Website: WWW.BRIDGEPORT.EDU

STUDENT BODY	
Type	Private
Enrollment	126
% male/female	30/70
# applied	96
# accepted	58
# enrolled	40
Average age	31

FACULTY	
Total faculty (number)	32
% female	38
% part-time	78
Student-faculty ratio	4:1

ADMISSIONS	
Average GPA	
Overall GPA	3.16

Application Information	
Are transfers accepted?	Yes
Admissions may be deferred?	Yes
Interview required?	Yes
Application fee	$75

Academics

University of Bridgeport College of Naturopathic Medicine provides an educational program for the training of generalist naturopathic physicians able to competently provide comprehensive natural health care. The college's mission is to provide appropriate educational experiences to prepare candidates to become doctors of naturopathic medicine. UBCNM's mission is to train the next generation of physicians as competent and caring clinicians; as insightful scholars and researchers; and as courageous leaders in the integration of natural medicine into the health care system. The school provides comprehensive natural health care through the Integrated Health Science Center and in conjunction with a variety of community agencies. Students are involved with the research department, which conducts basic and clinical research on natural and alternative therapeutics. Joint-degree programs such as ND/MS in Acupuncture and ND/MS in Nutrition are offered. The University of Bridgeport library supports student/faculty research with over 272,000 volumes of classified books and bound journals/indexes, over 1,128,000 microforms, and subscriptions to more than 1,100 periodicals.

BASIC SCIENCES: The first 2 years of the program focus on basic science courses such as anatomy, physiology, biochemistry, histology, microbiology, embryology, pathology, research methods, public health, clinical and laboratory diagnosis, counseling, nutrition, and history and philosophy of naturopathic medicine. These basic science courses are the foundation of clinical education and training at UBCNM.

CLINICAL TRAINING

The third and fourth year of ND education at UBCNM focuses on clinical education the focus of which is diagnosis and therapeutics which includes botanical medicine, homeopathy, clinical nutrition, physical medicine, obstetrics and gynecology, pediatrics, geriatrics, cardiology, gastroenterology, eye and ENT, diagnostic imaging, pharmacology, environmental medicine, endocrinology, neurology, urology/proctology, oncology, dermatology, and hydrotherapy. Students receive their clinical training at the university's own Health Science Center and at various off-site clinics through supervised internships.

Campus Life

University of Bridgeport was founded in 1927 as the Junior College of Connecticut—the first junior college chartered by any legislature in the Northeastern states. The Junior College of Connecticut became the University of Bridgeport in 1947. The university is located on the 86-acre, picturesque Long Island Sound 50 miles north of New York City. The architectural diversity of UB's 75 buildings, from stately homes as well as newer structures of modern design, reflects the origins and progress of the university and also embodies its twofold commitment to solidity and change. University of Bridgeport offers a wide range of opportunities for students to learn about other cultures and to understand American culture. Students from approximately 80 countries attend the university. The College of Naturopathic Medicine was founded in 1997, and is an integral part of the University of Bridgeport. It is the only college of naturopathic medicine in the Eastern United States. The main Magnus Wahlstrom Library occupies 5 floors in the centrally located Wahlstrom Building, and supports student/faculty research with over 272,000 volumes of classified books. UB has a large dining hall, café, and recreation center. The university supports a wide range of clubs, organizations, and special interest groups that expand and cultivate the academic, professional, and cultural interests of the students.

STUDENT LIFE

Being a part of the large university, naturopathic students at the University of Bridgeport are always involved in activities with other programs within UB or within the Division of Health Sciences programs which includes naturopathic medicine, chiropractic, the Acupuncture Institute, human nutrition, and dental hygiene. Students are involved in the decision-making process of the university as well as that of the College of Naturopathic Medicine through various committees. The Naturopathic Student Government Association and college administration work very closely.

GRADUATES

Graduates of University of Bridgeport College of Naturopathic Medicine are trained and qualified primary health care professionals who are qualified to pass professional licensure exams and are prepared to set up and maintain private practices. Some of UB's graduates have joined group practices and are part of research teams in various medical universities. Depending on the state laws, their scope of practice varies but includes all aspects of family care.

Admissions

REQUIREMENTS

Applicants must submit a completed application with $75 application fee, personal statement, three letters of recommendation—one must be from a health care provider—and official transcripts from all colleges/universities attended. A bachelors degree is required with 6 semester hours of biology with lab (2 courses), 6 semester hours of general chemistry with lab, 6 semester hours of organic chemistry with lab, 3 semester hours of physics with lab, 3 semester hours of psychology, 6 semester hours (2 courses) of communication/language skills, 3 semester hours of social science, 3 semester hours of humanities, and 9 semester hours of elective courses. Earned grades of C-minus or below are not accepted. All science courses must be completed within the last 7 years. Applicants meeting all the requirements are invited for an interview.

SUGGESTIONS

For the fall semester, applications should be received by February 1. The school does have rolling admissions, but it is better to apply early. Late applications are considered on a space available basis.

PROCESS

Acceptance decision is made by the admission committee and is based on academic achievement, relevant experience, knowledge of naturopathic philosophy, personal standard of ethics, financial planning, demonstrated verbal communication ability, and personal attitude.

Admissions Requirements (Required)

Science GPA, non-science GPA, letters of recommendation, interview, essays/personal statement

Admissions Requirements (Optional)

State residency, extracurricular activities, exposure to medical profession

COSTS AND AID

Tuition & Fees

Tuition $18,000

9 Osteopathic Profiles

A.T. STILL UNIVERSITY OF HEALTH SCIENCES

KIRKSVILLE COLLEGE OF OSTEOPATHIC MEDICINE

800 WEST JEFFERSON KIRKSVILLE, MO 63501 • ADMISSION: 660-626-2237 • FAX: 660-626-2969
E-MAIL: ADMISSIONS@ATSU.EDU • WEBSITE: WWW.ATSU.EDU

STUDENT BODY

Type	Private
Enrollment	697
% male/female	60/40
% minorities	4
# applied (total/out)	3,103/2,919
# accepted (total/out)	386/341
# enrolled (total/out)	172/143
Average age	25

FACULTY

Total faculty	87
Student-faculty ratio	3:1

ADMISSIONS

Average GPA and MCAT Scores

Overall GPA	3.42
MCAT Bio	8.95
MCAT Phys	8.25
MCAT Verbal	8.74
MCAT Essay	O

Application Information

Regular application	2/1
Regular notification	Rolling
Early application	8/1
Early notification	10/15
Are transfers accepted?	Yes
Admissions may be deferred?	Yes
Interview required?	Yes
Application fee	$60

Academics

The Kirksville College of Osteopathic Medicine is the founding school of osteopathic medicine, and is distinguished by offering an education firmly based on holistic care, wellness, and academic excellence. Kirksville has a reputation for training physicians in primary care areas, as well as providing a strong clinical and basic science education for specialization. Though the first two years are reserved for basic science instruction, a clerkship with a primary care physician is included in the first-year curriculum. Traditional tenets of osteopathic medicine are coupled with the use of all modern technology, thus providing a well-rounded, comprehensive education. Problem solving and critical thinking are emphasized in both the basic science courses and clinical training. Clinical rotations currently take place in one of the following areas: Arizona, Michigan, Missouri, Ohio, Utah, Colorado, Pennsylvania/New Jersey, and Florida. Kirksville is a community of approximately 20,000 residents. With a 2005 class size of 172, the average age is 25 with a composite MCAT of 26 and an overall GPA of 3.40.

Admissions

REQUIREMENTS

As a private institution, no preference is given to Missouri residents, and almost all states are represented in the student body. Course requirements are Biology (8 semester hours); Chemistry (8 hours); Organic Chemistry (8 hours); Physics (8 hours); and English (6 hours). To be considered for admission, applicants should have a minimum GPA of 2.5 in both the sciences and overall. The MCAT is required and scores must be no more than three years old. About 10 percent of AACOMAS applicants are interviewed, with interviews consisting of two sessions with faculty or administrators. Financial aid, both merit- and need-based, is available in the form of grants and loans.

PROCESS

The Kirksville College of Osteopathic Mediicine participates with other osteopathic colleges in a centralized application processing service called the American Association of Colleges of Osteopathic Medicine Application Service (AACOMAS).

An application may be submitted online at www.AACOM.org

Applicants meeting the minimum 2.5 cumulative and science grade point average requirement will receive a KCOM Secondary Application. A non-refundable application fee of $60 and letters of evaluation from the preprofessional college and a physician or employer are required at the time the additional information is submitted.

Applications should be submitted no later than February 1 of the academic year prior to which admission is sought. Applicants are encouraged to apply far in advance of the February 1 deadline. As "The National College of Osteopathic Medicine," KCOM seeks students from all parts of the United States who are interested in a career in osteopathic medicine. The college also actively seeks and encourages underrepresented minority students to apply.

Admissions Requirements (Required)

MCAT scores, Science GPA, Non-science GPA, Letters of recommendation, Interview, Essays/personal statement, Extracurricular activities, Exposure to medical profession

Admissions Requirements (Optional)

Exposure to Osteopathic Medicine

COSTS AND AID

Tuition & Fees

Tuition	$37,275
Room and board (off-campus)	$10,593
Cost of books	$2,813
Fees	$725

Financial Aid

% students receiving aid	94
Average grant	$9,880
Average loan	$43,627
Average debt	$143,952

DES MOINES UNIVERSITY
COLLEGE OF OSTEOPATHIC MEDICINE

3200 GRAND AVENUE DES MOINES, IA 50312-4198 • ADMISSION: 515-271-1451 • FAX: 515-271-7163
E-MAIL: DOADMIT@DMU.EDU • WEBSITE: WWW.DMU.EDU

STUDENT BODY

Type	Private
Enrollment	814
% male/female	53/47
% minorities	15
# applied (total/out)	2,674/2,227
# accepted (total/out)	409/359
# enrolled (total/out)	215/156
Average age	24

FACULTY

Total faculty	62
% female	32
% minority	1
% part-time	35
Student-faculty ratio	13:1

ADMISSIONS
Average GPA and MCAT Scores

Overall GPA	3.64
MCAT Bio	9.12
MCAT Phys	8.47
MCAT Verbal	8.33
MCAT Essay	0

Application Information

Regular application	2/1
Regular notification	Rolling
Early application	Rolling
Early notification	3/1
Are transfers accepted?	Yes
Admissions may be deferred?	Yes
Interview required?	Yes
Application fee	$50

Academics

At the Des Moines University College of Osteopathic Medicine, students learn within a supportive environment. This includes a solid basic sciences education, extensive practical experience in the clinical setting, and one-on-one interaction with seasoned educators and clinicians. The curriculum emphasizes state-of-the-art standardized patient assessment laboratories and problem-based learning opportunities which emphasize critical thinking and problem solving. The college is the second-oldest osteopathic school. Located in a safe metropolitan setting, the campus offers proximity to affordable housing. A new 143,000-square-foot Student Education Center provides students with modern facilities and a location to exercise, relax, and learn. Other distinguishing features of DMU include a wireless campus, laptop and hand-held computers for incoming students, and a dual master's degree program in Health Care Administration or Public Health. The College of Osteopathic Medicine provides a flexible program which allows students to explore a range of professional goals. Students learn to consider the overall needs of the patient rather than an isolated medical problem. During the first two years, basic science lectures and laboratory studies are combined with experience in hospitals, clinics, and community service agencies. This pre-clinical phase features a systems approach and the innovative use of simulated patients. The last two years of the four-year program involve clinical training. Third- and fourth-year rotations in hospitals and clinics may be selected from sites across the country.

BASIC SCIENCES: The College of Osteopathic Medicine provides a flexible program which allows students to explore a range of professional goals. Students learn to consider the overall needs of the patient rather than an isolated medical problem. During the first two years, basic science lectures and laboratory studies are combined with experience in hospitals, clinics, and community service agencies. This pre-clinical phase features a systems approach and the innovative use of simulated patients. The last two years of the four-year program involve clinical training. Third- and fourth-year rotations in hospitals and clinics may be selected from sites across the country.

CLINICAL TRAINING

The College of Osteopathic Medicine provides a flexible program which allows students to explore a range of professional goals. Students learn to consider the overall needs of the patient rather than an isolated medical problem. During the first two years, basic science lectures and laboratory studies are combined with experience in hospitals, clinics, and community service agencies. This pre-clinical phase features a systems approach and the innovative use of simulated patients. The last two years of the four-year program involve clinical training. Third- and fourth-year rotations in hospitals and clinics may be selected from sites across the country.

Students

STUDENT LIFE

The College of Osteopathic Medicine provides a flexible program which allows students to explore a range of professional goals. Students learn to consider the overall needs of the patient rather than an isolated medical problem. During the first two years, basic science lectures and laboratory studies are combined with experience in hospitals, clinics, and community service agencies. This pre-clinical phase features a systems approach and the innovative use of simulated patients. The last two years of the four-year program involve clinical training. Third- and fourth-year rotations in hospitals and clinics may be selected from sites across the country. Each entering class has about 200 students. A wide variety of undergraduate majors are represented, ranging from biology to the humanities. Though the average age of incoming students is 25, student ages range from the early 20s to the 50s. Beyond classes and labs, students have numerous opportunities to get involved and meet others through community service, clubs, and social events. From the beginning, first-year students are paired up with second-year students as part of Big Brother/Little Sister. DMU also offers peer tutoring. Over 30 professional clubs and organizations invite students to become part of a larger community of students and student concerns. Many students also get involved in community outreach. Through La Clinica they provide free medical care. The Literacy Army tutors reading and other subjects to elementary schools. At various local races and marathons DMU students have provided free OMM to the involved athletes.

GRADUATES

Graduates may enter residency programs in any specialty or subspecialty area. Des Moines University has over 8,600 alumni in virtually every state in the nation.

Admissions

REQUIREMENTS

Eight semester hours (with lab) each in biology, chemistry, organic chemistry, and physics are required. In addition, applicants must have taken six semester hours of English. We accept students without regard to legal state of residence. Usually 75 percent of students are from states other than Iowa. You can apply while working on your undergraduate degree but you should have plans to receive it by the time you register with the College. The MCAT (taken within the last two years) is required. Those AACOMAS applicants who meet the minimum requirements for GPA and MCAT are sent secondary applications and about half of those who return secondary applications are invited for an interview. Notification occurs on a rolling basis.

PROCESS

The College of Osteopathic Medicine provides a flexible program which allows students to explore a range of professional goals. Students learn to consider the overall needs of the patient rather than an isolated medical problem. During the first two years, basic science lectures and laboratory studies are combined with experience in hospitals, clinics, and community service agencies. This pre-clinical phase features a systems approach and the innovative use of simulated patients. The last two years of the four-year program involve clinical training. Third- and fourth-year rotations in hospitals and clinics may be selected from sites across the country.

Admissions Requirements (Required)

MCAT scores, Science GPA, Non-science GPA, Letters of recommendation, Interview, Essays/personal statement, Extracurricular activities, Exposure to medical profession

Admissions Requirements (Optional)

State residency

Overlap Schools

A.T. Still University of Health Sciences, Kansas City University of Medicine and Biosciences, Michigan State University, Midwestern University, New York Institute of Technology.

COSTS AND AID

Tuition & Fees

Tuition	$32,830
Room and board (on-campus)	$0
Room and board (off-campus)	$12,690
Cost of books	$3,050
Fees	$0

Financial Aid

% students receiving aid	96
Average grant	$22,287
Average loan	$37,426
Average debt	$138,000

Edward Via Virginia College of Osteopathic Medicine

Office of Admissions, VCOM, 2265 Kraft Drive Blacksburg, VA 24060 • Admission: (540) 231-6138
Fax: 540-231-5252 • E-mail: ADMISSIONS@VCOM.VT.EDU • Website: WWW.VCOM.VT.EDU

STUDENT BODY

Type	Private
Enrollment	615
% male/female	47/53
% minorities	25
# applied (total/out)	2,364/2,141
# accepted (total/out)	250/169
# enrolled (total/out)	162/106
Average age	25

FACULTY

Total faculty	636
% female	51
% minority	10
% part-time	93
Student-faculty ratio	5:1

ADMISSIONS

Average GPA and MCAT Scores

Overall GPA	3.53
MCAT Bio	8
MCAT Phys	8
MCAT Verbal	8
MCAT Essay	P

Application Information

Regular application	2/9
Regular notification	12/8
Early application	8/8
Early notification	10/8
Are transfers accepted?	Yes
Admissions may be deferred?	Yes
Interview required?	Yes
Application fee	$85

Academics

The curriculum for students enrolled in VCOM is modern and innovative. The basic science and clinical content are interwoven throughout the four years. In the first two years students learn about the normal state of homeostasis of the human body, the propensity for health and ability of the human body to heal, the clinical conditions that most often affect the human body and the presentations of those conditions. The curriculum is "patient-centered" and integrates patient cases throughout the four years that focus on physical health (the body), mental health (the mind), and spiritual health. The curriculum also emphasizes the community-centered approach to health care.

The curriculum is based upon a learner-centered approach. Students are given the opportunity to learn relevant material through clinical systems organized approach. Students attend lectures and labs that are interwoven with small group conferences, self-directed learning computer tutorials and clinical experiences. Students are given patient-centered cases to integrate biomedical and clinical curriculum. Students must employ problem solving through third-year clinical-based modules that require literature searches, group analysis, and collaboration. Students develop lifelong learning skills that foster the team approach to medicine as well as independent study. Students must assume the responsibility to participate and learn in this environment where a base of medical knowledge and dutiful approach to learning is expected. Assessment of knowledge occurs often to assure students are meeting the educational objectives.

The Principles of Primary Care Clinical Course in the first year emphasizes patient communication, the patient-doctor relationship, physical exam skills, professionalism and ethics, preventive medicine, community health, diversity issues, social issues, and clinical problem solving. Each month the principles learned in this course are reinforced and assessed by primary care physicians in the ambulatory office setting, public health and community settings, and the hospital. VCOM has a predominance of primary care physician faculty who accept the responsibility to teach, mentor and assess the students. In addition to the traditional medical physical exam, diagnosis and treatment skills, students are taught osteopathic principles, the art of palpation and manipulation as primary care management tools.

Comprehensive Examinations are given at the end of the Foundations of Medicine courses, and each systems block. Students must pass each course as well as the comprehensive block final exams in some courses.

Integrated exams are given at the end of years one and two. The curriculum is spiral where the understanding of the second year curriculum is dependent on knowledge gained in the first year and the clinical curriculum in the third year is dependent on the knowledge gained within the first two years. Clinical comprehensive exams are also given at the end of years two and three. Comprehensive exams allow the college to assess the student and the student to assess his/her preparedness for boards.

BASIC SCIENCES: The first academic block of the medical curriculum is designated for the "Foundations of Medicine." Courses within this block include such courses as: 1) Biochemistry, 2) Genetics, Reproduction and, Embryology, 3) Immunology, 4) Microbiology, 5) Medical Ethics and 6) Primary Care (including Professionalism and

Ethics). Students must pass the Foundations block to continue in school.

Following the Foundations of Medicine, students enter a sequence of systems-based, clinical-based blocks. The curriculum in each block is presented by faculty from the disciplines of anatomy, physiology, histology, pathology, pharmacology, principles of primary care, OMM, physical diagnosis and clinical case presentations. The clinical content is reinforced in each block with clinical experiences where many of the same professors who teach on campus provide clinical training and assessment, maintaining continuity between the classroom and the clinical setting.

Third-year and fourth-year students train primarily in the clinical setting. Student return to campus periodically during the third year Core Rotations for advanced clinical Conferences. The conferences are taught in both the lecture format and through small group assignments. Students are assigned to groups according to their clinical training sites. Online cases are an essential part of the second-year curriculum. Cases are focused along lines of clinical practice and are: Internal Medicine and the medical subspecialties, Psychiatry, Surgery and the surgical subspecialties, Emergency Medicine, Obstetrics and Gynecology, Orthopedics and Sports Medicine, Family Practice and Osteopathic Manipulative Medicine. Clinical faculty prepare cases and basic scientists often present a pertinent review of integrated subject matter.

CLINICAL TRAINING

Clinical experiences are found throughout the four years at VCOM. Students begin with eight hours per month in a curriculum-focused clinical experience. Clinical experience time gradually progresses to 16 hours per month in the second year. By OMS-III, students spend a minimum of four days per week in the clinical setting and in the fourth year students spend five days per week in the clinical setting. Students returning to campus or educational sites for clinical case conferences in the third year and online modules provide curriculum to the student at their clinical site.

During primary care experiences, students train predominately in the rural and underserved clinical settings where a relationship is developed with the physician as both a teacher and mentor. Longitudinal experiences also occur throughout the first two years within a primary care setting. Students also learn the role of the physician in the community and the rewards of rural life, primary care, and caring for the underserved.

Students

Tuition includes activity fees for VCOM-sponsored programs and for activities purchased through a collaborative agreement with Virginia Tech.

Via Wellness - VCOM sponsors social, fitness, spiritual, cultural, and vocational activities throughout the year. "Via Wellness" strives to promote balance in the busy lives of medical students and provides incentives for participation in a spectrum of activities. Information and a schedule of activities sponsored through "Via Wellness" are available from the VCOM Office of Student Services and are listed on the Activities Calendar.

The VCOM Passport provides first- and second-year osteopathic medical students full access to recreational and athletic facilities on the Virginia Tech campus, admittance to social and cultural events, use of the library and bus transportation to the main campus and the bus routes. In instances where Virginia Tech assesses a fee for its students for activities (e.g., rental of equipment, admittance fees to special events, etc.), VCOM students are typically required to pay the same fee as a Virginia Tech student. Following are a partial list of activities and services available to VCOM students through the collaborative agreement with Virginia Tech.

Hokie Sports - Tickets for Hokie Varsity Sports are available to VCOM students in the same manner they are available to Virginia Tech students. Visit www.HOKIESPORTS.com or call 1-800-VATECH4 for more information.

Admissions Requirements (Required)
Science GPA, overall GPA, MCAT score, clinical experience, community outreach, academic and clinical letter of recommendation (must be from an osteopathic physician), interview, personal statement

Admissions Requirements (Optional)
State residency

Overlap Schools
Eastern Virginia Medical School, Nova Southeastern University, Ohio University, Philadelphia College of Osteopathic Medicine, Virginia Commonwealth University, West Virginia School of Osteopathic Medicine.

COSTS AND AID
Tuition & Fees

Tuition	$32,900
Room and board (off-campus)	$22,600
Cost of books	$2,700
Fees	$750

Financial Aid

% students receiving aid	97
Average grant	$22,928
Average loan	$45,608
Average debt	$158,866

KANSAS CITY UNIVERSITY OF MEDICINE AND BIOSCIENCES
COLLEGE OF OSTEOPATHIC MEDICINE

OFFICE OF ADMISSIONS, 1750 INDEPENDENCE AVENUE, KANSAS CITY, MO 64106-1453 • ADMISSION: 800-234-4847
FAX: 816-460-0566 • E-MAIL: ADMISSIONS@KCUMB.EDU • WEBSITE: WWW.KCUMB.EDU

STUDENT BODY

Type	Private
Enrollment	960
% male/female	50/50
% minorities	2
# applied (total/out)	2,850/2,639
# accepted (total/out)	485/418
# enrolled (total/out)	250/199
Average age	24

FACULTY

Total faculty (number)	436
% female	29
% minority	12
% part-time	85
Student-faculty ratio	8:1

ADMISSIONS
Average GPA and MCAT Scores

Overall GPA	3.55
MCAT Bio	9.10
MCAT Phys	8.36
MCAT Verbal	8.84
MCAT Essay	Q

Application Information

Regular application	4/8
Regular notification	Rolling
Early application	Fall
Early notification	11/7
Are transfers accepted?	No
Admissions may be deferred?	Yes
Interview required?	Yes
Application fee	$50

Academics

Kansas City University of Medicine and Biosciences is both the largest medical school in the state of Missouri and the oldest in Kansas City, Missouri. The university's core values are leadership, humility, faith and positivity, integrity, compassion and service. These core values, coupled with exemplary basic sciences and clinical training, are at the heart of the KCUMB educational process from a student's first day on campus to the end of post-doctoral training and beyond.

During their years at KCUMB, students build on that foundation by learning from a progressive and innovative twenty-first century curriculum that emphasizes early clinical experience and an integrated, patient-centered approach to medicine. An outstanding faculty, who are dedicated to helping students achieve their goals, and state-of-the-art facilities, provide unparalleled educational opportunities.

KCUMB medical students consistently perform well above national averages on board examinations. Ninety-two percent of KCUMB medical students match with their first choice for residency programs. More than half of all incoming students cite our unique curriculum as one of their top reasons for choosing to attend KCUMB.

KCUMB's College of Osteopathic Medicine students also can pursue unique dual-degree programs, earning a Master of Business Administration in Healthcare leadership or a Master of Arts in Bioethics concurrently with their Doctor of Osteopathic Medicine.

CLINICAL TRAINING

Through the integrated, patient-centered Genesis curriculum, medical students develop clinical decision-making skills from day 1. A variety of teaching and learning methods are used in the first 2 years, including classroom lectures, laboratory exercises, small-group discussions, computer-assisted instruction, and specialized workshops, as well as standardized patients and human patient simulators.

The new Kesselheim Center for Clinical Competence significantly enhances this early clinical education. By linking 8 high-tech human patient simulators with the KCUMB's Standardized Patient Program, medical students are provided opportunities to evaluate, diagnose and treat hundreds of "patients" in a realistic, yet risk-free environment.

KCUMB's sports medicine program and the Score 1 for Health program, both of which combine medical education and service, also give students hands-on clinical training while still in medical school. Score 1 for Health, which utilizes second-year KCUMB medical students to provide free health screenings to urban-core, elementary-age children, will serve more than 16,000 children in 2007-2008.

Student spend the last 2 years of medical school in clerkships at any of more than 40 sites throughout the U. S. Students complete clerkships in eight core areas and any number of specialties ranging from neurosurgery to toxicology.

Campus Life

While the Kansas City area might be best known for its smooth jazz, beautiful fountains, and superior barbecue, the area has much to offer, from upscale shopping districts and world-class entertainment, to ample recreational activities and thrilling professional sporting events. Located at the junction of the Missouri and Kansas rivers, Kansas City sits in the middle of the United States, about 1,900 miles from each coast. Approximately 1.8 million people live in the Kansas City metro area, which includes more than 135 cities in 11 counties on both sides of the state line.

While students come to KCUMB to earn a first-class education, they can take advantage of opportunities to meet new people, participate in professional organizations and find time for rest and relaxation through one of the many clubs and organizations represented on campus. Whether they are interested in an intramural pick-up game of basketball, singing in the Osteopera or serving in student government, there are many opportunities to represent explore interests on campus.

Admissions

REQUIREMENTS

The minimum academic requirements for admission to the first-year class are as follows: The Medical College Admissions Test (MCAT) is required for entrance into KCUMB. The average MCAT score is 26. A baccalaureate degree or commendable completion of at least 90 semester hours or 135 term credit hours of the required credits for a baccalaureate degree, from a regionally accredited college or university. The baccalaureate degree is preferred and preference is given to those candidates who will have earned the degree prior to matriculation in the medical school program. Satisfactory completion, with a grade of C or higher, of the following college courses, including laboratory work: Biological sciences (12 semester hours), biochemistry (3 hours in addition to chemistry hours), chemistry (13 semester hours), English composition/literature (six semester hours), genetics (3 semester hours in addition to biological sciences), physics (eight semester hours). Total number of semester hours equals 45.

SUGGESTIONS

Applicants are encouraged to begin the application process a year prior to matriculation. The following represents a monthly guide for application preparation:

- May: Contact all colleges and universities attended and have official transcripts forwarded directly from the educational institution to AACOMAS. Submit AACOMAS application. Supplemental application or materials are mailed to qualified applicants immediately upon receipt of the AACOMAS application in the Admissions Office.

- September: Personal interviews begin.

- February 1: Application deadline (AACOMAS). Supplemental applications are accepted and processed until all interview positions have been filled.

- February 15: Transcript deadline to AACOMAS.

- April 1: KCUMB application deadline.

PROCESS

AACOMAS online is available in early May 2006 for the 2007 entering class. All application materials, including detailed instructions, can be accessed through the AACOM website, AACOM.org.

AACOMAS gathers all the necessary material about each applicant and transmits the information in a standardized format to the college(s) of osteopathic medicine selected by the applicant. AACOMAS has no participation in the selection process.

The applicant will receive a computer-generated applicant profile with a calculation of GPA and MCAT averages from AACOMAS. KCUMB will also receive the applicant profile, accompanied by a photocopy of the AACOMAS application and personal statement. KCUMB conducts an initial review of the transmitted AACOMAS application, MCAT scores, and academic record to determine which applications will be further processed.

Applicants meeting the initial review criteria will receive a KCUMB supplemental application. A supplemental application may be forwarded to an applicant under some circumstances when specific information is not available or will be submitted later. These circumstances generally relate to applicants who have not taken the MCAT and/or are registered to take the next scheduled MCAT exam. Applicants are encouraged to include the scheduled MCAT test dates on the AACOMAS application to indicate the intent of taking or retaking the exam.

Admissions Requirements (Required)

MCAT scores, science GPA, non-science GPA, letters of recommendation, interview, essays/personal statement, extracurricular activities, exposure to medical profession, community service/volunteer work

COSTS AND AID

Tuition & Fees

Tuition	$37,920
Room and board (off-campus)	$16,038
Cost of books	$1,400
Fees	$60

Financial Aid

% students receiving aid	96
Average grant	$1,100
Average loan	$40,500
Average debt	$175,000

LAKE ERIE COLLEGE OF OSTEOPATHIC MEDICINE

OFFICE OF ADMISSIONS, 1858 WEST GRANDVIEW BOULEVARD ERIE, PA 16509 • ADMISSION: 814-866-6641
FAX: 814-866-8123 • E-MAIL: ADMISSIONS@LECOM.EDU • WEBSITE: WWW.LECOM.EDU

STUDENT BODY

Type	Private
Enrollment	1,567
% male/female	53/47
% minorities	8
# applied (total/out)	5,292/4,720
# accepted (total/out)	531/349
# enrolled (total/out)	389/238
Average age	25

FACULTY

Total faculty (number)	1,675
% part-time	92
Student-faculty ratio	1:1

ADMISSIONS

Average GPA and MCAT Scores

Overall GPA	3.4
MCAT Bio	9.0
MCAT Phys	8.2
MCAT Verbal	9.0
MCAT Essay	0

Application Information

Regular application	3/1
Regular notification	Rolling
Are transfers accepted?	No
Admissions may be deferred?	No
Interview required?	Yes
Application fee	$50

Academics

Lake Erie College of Osteopathic Medicine located in Erie, Pennsylvania with a branch campus in Bradenton, Florida, is the nation's largest medical college. Its mission is to train physicians to meet the country's growing demand for health care professionals. The majority of LECOM graduates become primary care physicians. LECOM has introduced a new Primary Care Scholars Pathway that condenses 4 years of medical education into 3 years by concentrating on specific courses and clinical training required to become a family physician.

LECOM recognizes student-centered learning styles by offering 3 curriculum pathways. The traditional, lecture-discussion curriculum begins with core basic science and pre-clinical courses and progresses with a systems-based curriculum in year 2. Problem-based learning offers small group training following patient cases, and independent study allows qualified students to use educational modules based on the core and systems curricula.

BASIC SCIENCES: All students are required to complete 12 weeks of Gross Anatomy in the first semester. Biochemistry; Genetics; Health Care Management; Immunology; Microbiology; Pathology; Pharmacology; Physiology; and Spirituality, Medicine, and Ethics are the core of the lecture-discussion and independent study pathways and integrated into the cases of the problem-based learning pathway.

CLINICAL TRAINING

Clinical training at LECOM begins in the first year as students spend time with standardized patients, and clinical office training in the second year. LECOM has affiliations with more than 100 hospitals in a dozen states where third-year and fourth-year students complete their clinical rotations.

Campus Life

LECOM's main campus is located in Pennsylvania's fourth largest city and overlooks Lake Erie. The city is a resort community with a large number of tourist, entertainment, and recreational facilities. Erie County has 5 colleges and supports several professional minor league teams in baseball, football, and hockey. LECOM—Bradenton is located in a master-planned community in one of the fastest growing regions of Florida.

STUDENT LIFE

LECOM encourages students to participate in community service and extracurricular activities. LECOM clubs offer social activities and opportunities to become involved in local events. LECOM students have organized mentoring programs for underserved children and Boy Scout and Girl Scout troops and provided health care screenings and other related services to local citizens.

GRADUATES

While the majority of LECOM graduates become primary care physicians, many alumni have completed residencies and fellowships in other medical specialties. LECOM has developed postgraduate training at 30 hospitals. Graduates have matched for residencies at major hospitals around the country. LECOM offers a master of science in medical education for medical college graduates who want to become teaching physicians.

Admissions

REQUIREMENTS

LECOM is a private college and a majority of students come from out of state. Students are required to apply through AACOMAS, the central processor for osteopathic colleges. Applicants may access the LECOM supplemental application from the college website or it will be mailed upon receipt of the AACOMAS application. LECOM schedules interviews between October and March. Acceptance notification occurs on a rolling basis.

The MCAT is required, and scores must be no more than 3 years old. The mean MCAT score for successful candidates is 24, and their science GPA is a 3.2 or higher. The college requires 2 letters of recommendation and a letter from an osteopathic physician. Science course requirements are 8 semester hours of biology, chemistry, organic chemistry, and physics. In addition, 6 semester hours of behavioral science and English are required.

SUGGESTIONS

LECOM encourages applicants to learn more about the profession by getting to know an osteopathic physician to enhance awareness of the osteopathic medical philosophy and prepare for the admissions interview. The college looks for students who exemplify the osteopathic philosophy of compassionate, total person health care.

Admissions Requirements (Required)

MCAT scores, science GPA, non-science GPA, letters of recommendation, interview, essay/personal statement, exposure to medical profession, letter of recommendation from an osteopathic physician

Admissions Requirements (Optional)

State residency, extracurricular activities

COSTS AND AID

Tuition & Fees

In-state tuition	$25,900
Out-of-state tuition	$27,250
Room and board (off-campus)	$10,500
Cost of books	$1,000
Fees	$750

Financial Aid

% students receiving aid	92
Average grant	$16,500
Average loan	$35,000
Average debt	$154,000

MICHIGAN STATE UNIVERSITY
COLLEGE OF OSTEOPATHIC MEDICINE

C110 EAST FEE HALL, MSUCOM, EAST LANSING, MI 48824-1316 • **ADMISSION:** 517-353-7740
FAX: 517-355-3296 • **E-MAIL:** COMADM@COM.MSU.EDU • **WEBSITE:** WWW.COM.MSU.EDU

STUDENT BODY

Type	Public
Enrollment	556
% male/female	54/46
% minorities	6
# applied (total/out)	1,621/1,224
# accepted (total/out)	194/24
# enrolled (total/out)	124/5
Average age	25

FACULTY

Total faculty (number)	177
% female	37
% minority	19
% part-time	11
Student-faculty ratio	3:1

ADMISSIONS
Average GPA and MCAT Scores

Overall GPA	3.5
MCAT Bio	8.7
MCAT Phys	8.0
MCAT Verbal	8.2
MCAT Essay	O

Application Information

Regular application	12/1
Regular notification	rolling
Early application	8/15
Early notification	10/15
Are transfers accepted?	yes
Admissions may be deferred?	yes
Interview required?	yes
Application fee	$75

Academics

The Michigan State University College of Osteopathic Medicine (MSUCOM) was created by the Michigan legislature in 1971 to provide osteopathic physicians to meet the health care needs of the state's population. Educating primary care and specialty care osteopathic physicians occurs in a spectrum that includes premedical programs, osteopathic medical college, internships, residencies, and fellowships. The college has partnerships for clinical education with 20 osteopathic hospitals in Michigan in its Statewide Campus System, and it also occurs in private clinics and other environments. Medical research is a high priority of the college, and MSUCOM provides educational opportunities for physician/scientists, especially in its joint DO/PhD curriculum, the Medical Scientist Training Program. The curriculum, based on a study of the body's organ systems, emphasizes osteopathic principles and practices, early patient care, behavioral and diversity aspects of medicine, lifelong learning, and use of technology. The smallest college in university with nearly 45,000 students, MSUCOM is a close-knit community known for compassionate care and its volunteer work in the communities. For further information, see www.com.msu.edu.

The Michigan State University College of Osteopathic Medicine (MSUCOM) provides a full continuum of education—premedical programs, osteopathic medical school, internships, residencies, fellowships, and continuing medical education. The college has partnerships for clinical education with 25 hospitals in its Statewide Campus System and with nearly 2,000 clinical faculty practicing in communities.

Students learn from a faculty of top-flight educators in the heart of one of the premier scientific and research institutions in the nation. The curriculum emphasizes patient-centered care, osteopathic principles and practices, early exposure to the clinical setting, behavioral and diversity aspects of medicine, lifelong learning, and the use of technology.

The college offers the nation's first DO/PhD program; the MA in bioethics, humanities, and society; a joint DO/MPH; and the Osteopathic Medical Scholars Program for undergraduate students.

BASIC SCIENCES: Unit I is a four-semester sequence of basic science courses including anatomy, biochemistry, molecular biology/genetics, neuroscience, radiology, microbiology, histology, cell biology/physiology, pathology, and pharmacology. Students are introduced to physical examination, doctor-patient interactions, and the principles of osteopathic palpatory diagnosis and manipulative therapy.

Unit II is a three-semester sequence with an emphasis on body systems: integumentary, neuromusculoskeletal, hematopoietic, cardiovascular, respiratory, gastrointestinal, endocrine, genitourinary, reproductive, growth and development, and behavioral systems. These courses provide integrated presentations of basic and behavioral science and clinical aspects of each system. Students are required to master clinical skills associated with each system and to observe and selectively participate in patient care and office management under the direct supervision of a physician.

Unit III, the clerkship curriculum is a 76–84-week program designed to equip osteopathic physicians with skills necessary to enter primary care practice or pursue further specialty training. There is an emphasis on preparing for practice in ambulatory settings, with continuity in training and experience in working with allied health professionals in a team approach.

Students

Located on one of largest and most beautiful campuses in the nation, MSUCOM offers all the benefits of a fine university—from world-class arts and entertainment to Big Ten sports, from daily seminars and performances to research that spans hundreds of disciplines. Nearly 45,000 students from all over the world attend MSU, offering diversity and a rich cultural exposure.

STUDENT LIFE

Because academic life is so rigorous at MSUCOM, students must be highly motivated and organized to maintain a healthy life balance. The college maintains an active array of events, social options, extracurricular learning opportunities, and student support services. MSUCOM has a strong reputation as an institution that values the individual, cooperation, compassion, excellence, and community service.

GRADUATES

Wherever MSUCOM graduates live and work, their caring and commitment have made an impact on the communities they serve. Among our alumni are medical school deans, nationally recognized researchers in areas such as cardiovascular disease and genomics, a former surgeon general of the U.S. Coast Guard, the head of the largest U.S. study concerning women's health, the forensic psychiatrist who worked on the Jon Benet Ramsey, Columbine High School, and Kobe Bryant cases, and a physician who has received international attention for her decades of work with the poor in Mississippi.

Admissions

REQUIREMENTS

To satisfy the requirements, students must achieve a 2.0 grade in the required number of credit hours for each subject area. Students are required to have at least 8 credits of biology, but preferably 16–20 advanced level credits (biology, physiology, microbiology, anatomy, neuroscience, etc.)—AP credits are not accepted; 8 credits of physics; 6 credits of English; 6 credits of behavioral science, and a minimum total of 90 completed credit hours. There are prerequisite changes pending; please see the website for additional information.

The average for each entering class has consistently been 3.5. Most important are your grades in upper level science classes. The average MCAT for each entering class has ranged from 26–27. Community service is a heavily weighted factor. You must have experience in a clinical setting to be considered, but this can also include paid employment, shadowing, or other voluntarism. We require two recommendations (the individuals should know you well).

For additional information on other admission factors, see our website. We also suggest starting admissions counseling early in your admissions process: Call us at 517-353-7740 to schedule your appointment.

PROCESS

MSUCOM employs an aggressive rolling admission process with the goal of filling the class by early December.

* The AACOMAS Application Service website (www.aacom.org) begins taking applications May 15. For MSUCOM, December 1 is the last day AACOMAS accepts applications and December 15 is the last day AACOMAS accepts transcripts. However, September 1 is the last day you should be submitting your AACOMAS application if you are serious about applying to MSUCOM.

Admissions Requirements (Required)

MCAT scores, science GPA, non-science GPA, letters of recommendation, interview, essays/personal statement, extracurricular activities, exposure to medical profession

Admissions Requirements (Optional)

State residency

COSTS AND AID
Tuition & Fees

In-state Tuition	$21,951
Out-of-state Tuition	$47,751
Room and board (on-campus)	$10,656
Cost of books	$2,605
Fees	$85

Financial Aid

% students receiving aid	93
Average grant	$2,720
Average loan	$25,455
Average debt	$117,220

MIDWESTERN UNIVERSITY
ARIZONA COLLEGE OF OSTEOPATHIC MEDICINE

OFFICE OF ADMISSIONS, 19555 NORTH FIFTY-NINTH AVENUE, GLENDALE, AZ 85308 • ADMISSION: 623-572-3275
FAX: 623-572-3229 • E-MAIL: ADMISSAZ@ARIZONA.MIDWESTERN.EDU • WEBSITE: WWW.MIDWESTERN.EDU

STUDENT BODY

Type	Private
Enrollment	690
% male/female	45/55
% minorities	29
# applied (total/out)	2,934/2,586
# accepted(total/out)	429/286
# enrolled(total/out)	167/72
Average age	24

FACULTY

Total faculty (number)	345
% female	24
% minority	12
% part-time	22
Student-faculty ratio	2:1

ADMISSIONS
Average GPA and MCAT Scores

Overall GPA	3.52
MCAT Bio	9.13
MCAT Phys	8.45
MCAT Verbal	8.64
MCAT Essay	0

Application Information

Regular application	1/1
Regular notification	Rolling
Are transfers accepted?	Yes
Admissions may be deferred?	Yes
Interview required?	Yes
Application fee	$50

Academics

The Arizona College of Osteopathic Medicine (AZCOM) was founded in 1995. The college, along with its sister college, the Chicago College of Osteopathic Medicine (CCOM), is part of Midwestern University. In addition to the Colleges of Osteopathic Medicine, Midwestern University also includes a college of pharmacy and a college of health sciences. The school is located on a 124-acre site in scenic Glendale, Arizona, a suburb of Phoenix. Facilities include three main academic centers housing lecture halls; conference rooms; a student services facility; numerous lecture and laboratory classrooms boasting the finest in educational equipment; cadavers for anatomy laboratories rather than plastic models; on-campus housing, which features one- and two-bedroom student apartments and a heated pool; a comprehensive library with computer resources and study rooms; a research facility; a clinic; and a student clubhouse. The mission of Arizona College of Osteopathic Medicine of Midewestern University responds to the contemporary societal need for physicians by emphasizing primary care and education experiences needed to serve in rural and underserved urban communities.

Admissions
REQUIREMENTS

As a private institution, the college attracts a national applicant pool, and out-of-state residents account for over 80 percent of the group. Only 145 positions are available in each class, and in recent years there have been over 3,000 applicants. The average GPA of successful applicants is about 3.4 in both sciences and overall. Minimum course work includes six semester hours in English and eight semester hours in each of the following: biology, inorganic chemistry, organic chemistry, and physics. The MCAT is required and must be no more than 3 years old. In addition to the AACOMAS application, applicants must submit a supplemental application (provided by the AZCOM after the AACOMAS application has been received and the student meets the GPA criteria of 2.75 in both science and overall).

PROCESS

To be considered for admission within our competitive selection process, an applicant should:

1. Possess both a science and a total GPA over 3.0 on a 4.0 scale as well as a bachelor's degree. A minimum science and overall GPA of 2.75 on a 4.00 scale is required to receive a supplemental application.

2. Complete a bachelor's degree at an accredited college or university prior to matriculation. Applicants participating in special affiliated programs with the college and other exceptions to this policy will be considered on an individual basis.

3. Submit competitive scores on the Medical College Admissions Test (MCAT). Students who entered AZCOM in 2005 had an average MCAT score of 27. The MCAT test must have been taken no more than 3 years prior to application. To register for the exam contact the MCAT Program Office at 319-337-1357, or visit AAMC.org/students/mcat. The exam is offered each April and August.

4. Two letters of recommendation are required. One must be from either the premedical advisory committee or science professor; the other must be from either a DO or an MD. Letters from osteopathic physicians are strongly recommended. Letters written by immediate family members will not be accepted. All letters of evaluation must be submitted by the evaluators. The Office of Admissions does not accept letters submitted by students.

5. Demonstrate a sincere understanding of and interest in osteopathic medicine.

6. Reflect a people/service orientation through community service or extracurricular activities.

7. Reflect proper motivation for and commitment to health care as demonstrated by previous work, volunteer, or other life experiences.

8. Possess the oral and written communication skills necessary to interact with patients and colleagues.

9. Pass a criminal background check.

10. Agree to abide by Midwestern University Drug-Free Workplace and Substance Abuse Policy.

Admissions Requirements (Required)

MCAT scores, science GPA, non-science GPA, letters of recommendation, interview, essay/personal statement, extracurricular activities, exposure to medical profession, demonstration of strong oral and written communication skills

Admissions Requirement (Optional)

State residency

COSTS AND AID

Tuition & Fees

Tuition	$36,391
Room and board (on-campus)	$10,107
Room and board (off-campus)	$11,925
Cost of books	$2,000
Fees	$412

Financial Aid

% students receiving aid	90
Average loan	$50,000
Average debt	$151,270

MIDWESTERN UNIVERSITY
CHICAGO COLLEGE OF OSTEOPATHIC MEDICINE

OFFICE OF ADMISSIONS, 555 THIRTY-FIRST STREET, DOWNERS GROVE, IL 60515 • **ADMISSION:** 800-458-6253
FAX: 630-971-6086 • E-MAIL: ADMISSIL@MIDWESTERN.EDU • WEBSITE: WWW.MIDWESTERN.EDU

STUDENT BODY

Type	Private
Enrollment	690
% male/female	47/53
% minorities	28
# applied	3,200
# accepted	380
# enrolled	173
Average age	24

FACULTY

Total faculty (number)	294
% female	23
% minority	11
% part-time	50
Student-faculty ratio	2:1

ADMISSIONS
Average GPA and MCAT Scores

Overall GPA	3.5
MCAT Bio	9.0
MCAT Phys	8.3
MCAT Verbal	8.5
MCAT Essay	O

Application Information

Regular application	1/1
Regular notification	Rolling
Are transfers accepted?	Yes
Admissions may be deferred?	Yes
Interview required?	Yes
Application fee	$50

Academics

Midwestern University administers the Chicago College of Osteopathic Medicine (CCOM), the Chicago College of Pharmacy, and the College of Health Sciences, in addition to related programs in Glendale, Arizona. The MWU campus is located in Downers Grove, which is a western suburb of Chicago, Illinois. Clinical training takes place at various sites around the city and throughout the Midwest region. Students enjoy early clinical exposure through volunteering, preceptor programs, and formal patient contact in the second quarter of year one. Research is also important at CCOM, which offers a combined DO/PhD program and has summer research awards for medical students. The Downers Grove campus offers modern academic and recreational facilities, in addition to on-campus housing. In Fall 2005, the Downers Grove campus enrolled a total of 1,884 students in its various professional degree seeking programs.

BASIC SCIENCE: CCOM has developed and continues to refine a 4-year curriculum that educates students in the biopsychosocial approach to patient care, as well as the basic medical arts and sciences. Within this curricular format, CCOM students spend their first 2 years both completing a rigorous basic science curriculum and preparing for their clinical studies. During their third and fourth years, students rotate through a variety of clinical training sites accruing an impressive 92 weeks of direct patient care experience

CLINICAL TRAINING

Students begin obtaining hands-on experience during their first year through the Introduction to clinical medicine courses that are taught within the program. Students must complete and successfully pass required clinical rotations in the following disciplines: family medicine, internal medicine, surgery, pediatrics, psychiatry, osteopathic manipulative medicine, obstetrics/gynecology, and emergency medicine. These rotations cannot be done at out-of-system sites. Students must also complete elective rotations in recognized fields of medicine that include the following areas: anesthesiology, cardiology, family medicine (division of community medicine), osteopathic manipulative medicine (additional rotation), dermatology, emergency medicine (additional rotation), gastroenterology, hematology/oncology, infectious disease, nephrology, neurology, neurosurgery, nuclear medicine/endocrinology/metabolism, obstetrics/gynecology (clinical and/or elective at Olympia Fields), ophthalmology, orthopedic surgery, otorhinolaryngology, pathology, rheumatology/immunology, general surgery (additional rotation), cardiovascular/thoracic surgery, and urology. Students can pursue clinical rotations at other osteopathic, allopathic, or military institutions; however, they must plan their elective program with the Office of Clinical Education in order to obtain academic credit for these rotations. In the past, students have also had an opportunity to complete one international rotation as an elective rotation.

Student Life

Believing that well-rounded individuals make more caring health care professionals, we offer our students a variety of social, academic, and personal enrichment activities. Midwestern University offers a few different housing options for students through traditional style residence halls and one bedroom apartments. Most of the facilities are designed to be single occupancy. MWU provides a variety of student services outside of the classroom for students. Our website highlights the student organizations, intramural sports, wellness center, tutoring services, and counseling services that are available for students. Please refer to Midwestern.edu for additional information.

GRADUATES

CCOM's class of 2004 matched into 72 programs in 19 states. The graduates' match rate was 87.8 percent into a first or second residency choice, far surpassing the national match rate of 61.9 percent.

Admissions

REQUIREMENTS

Minimum overall and science GPAs of 2.75 on 4.00 scale, MCAT scores, AACOMAS application, secondary application materials, letters of recommendation, and an interview are required. Additional admission requirements can be found on our website at Midwestern.edu.

PROCESS

Students may begin the application process through AACOMAS and must submit the AACOMAS application with all required materials by January 1 of a given year. Midwestern University will distribute a secondary application to those applicants meeting the minimum GPA requirements. The secondary application must be submitted to the Office of Admissions with all required materials by March 1 of a given year. Midwestern University operates on a rolling admissions basis. As completed applications are submitted, they are reviewed and considered for admission into the program. Competitive applicants will be invited on campus to participate in the interview process. The admissions committee for the Chicago College of Osteopathic Medicine meets approximately once a month to make final admissions decisions.

Admissions Requirements (Required)

MCAT scores, science GPA, nonscience GPA, letters of recommendation, interview, essays/personal statement, extracurricular activities, exposure to medical profession, oral and written communication skills

Admissions Requirements (Optional)

State residency

COSTS AND AID

Tuition & Fees

Tuition	$31,838
Room and board (on-campus)	$9,400
Cost of books	$2,300
Fees	$412

Financial Aid

% students receiving aid	85
Average grant	$12,000
Average loan	$40,500
Average debt	$150,000

NEW YORK INSTITUTE OF TECHNOLOGY
NEW YORK COLLEGE OF OSTEOPATHIC MEDICINE

OFFICE OF ADMISSIONS, NYCOM/NYIT, PO BOX 8000, OLD WESTBURY, NY 11568 • **ADMISSION:** 516-686-3747
FAX: 516-686-3831 **E-MAIL:** ADMISSIONS@NYIT.EDU • **WEBSITE:** WWW.NYIT.EDU

STUDENT BODY

Type	Private
% male/female	60/40
% minorities	16

ADMISSIONS

Application Information

Regular application	2/1
Are transfers accepted?	No
Admissions may be deferred?	No
Interview required?	Yes

Academics

The New York College of Osteopathic Medicine is committed to educating primary care physicians and the focus is on the health care problems of the inner city and rural communities. NYCOM allows incoming students to select one of 2 educational tracks: The Lecture-Discussion Based (LDB) track integrates the biomedical and clinical sciences through a systems-based approach, while the Doctor Patient Continuum (DPC) employs a problem-based curriculum whose cornerstone is small-group, case-based learning. The 2 tracks converge after completion of the second year, when clerkships in the third and fourth years provide students with a variety of clinical experiences. In addition to the 4-year DO degree, combined DO/MBA and DO/MS programs are also open to qualified students.

BASIC SCIENCES: Depending on the track they select, the first- and second-year curriculum in basic and clinical sciences will differ for students.

(LDB) track: Here, the courses in the first 2 years are organized in a systems-based format. The systems are preceded by a fundamentals course, and the fundamentals course is composed of 3 components (threads): The cellular and molecular basis of medicine; the structural and functional basis of medicine; and the practice of medicine. The cellular and molecular basis of medicine thread discusses the scientific principles specific to each organ system as it relates to wellness and disease and includes content material from the following disciplines: biochemistry, genetics, histology, microbiology, neuroscience, pathology, pharmacology, and physiology. The structural and functional basis of medicine thread uses a systems-specific approach to discuss the interrelationship between structure and function in wellness and disease, and incorporates extensive didactic and laboratory experiences in applied anatomy and osteopathic principles and practices. In year 2 students take the practice of medicine, a systems-based introduction to the essentials of clinical medicine. It presents the principles of patient-centered health care, emphasizing primary care in the pediatric, adult, and geriatric patient populations. It includes didactic and practical experiences in the doctor-patient relationship, as well as simulated clinical exercises.

(DPC) Track: This problem-based curriculum is founded on "continuum" education principles and instruction is set in the context of clinical-case scenarios. The cases function as an interface between the patient and the physician, in which the skills, knowledge, and attitudes of the practicing clinician will later be applied. The curricular content is rooted in evidence-based medicine and students are expected to explore aspects of health and disease pertinent to the clinical case at seven levels: molecular; cellular; tissue; organ; integrated organ system; whole person; and family, society, and environment. The DPC curriculum is highly student-centered and promotes the development of critical thinking and clinical problem-solving skills. Course work in the DPC curriculum during the first two years includes: Introduction to the fundamentals of osteopathic medicine; cellular and molecular; structure and function; the practice of medicine; and a series of courses in biomedical and clinical sciences. Second-year courses in the clinical sciences include didactic and laboratory experiences in osteopathic manipulative medicine and physical diagnosis, as well as experiences with standardized and simulated patients.

CLINICAL TRAINING

NYCOM students spend most of their third and fourth years doing clinical clerkships. An equitable lottery system determines how the students are assigned to clerkships. Required third-year clinical clerkships include Family Medicine (6 weeks); Medicine (12 weeks); Obstetrics/Gynecology (6 weeks); Pediatrics (6 weeks); Psychiatry (6 weeks); and Surgery (12 weeks). Fourth-year students complete a set of clinical clerkships including: 2 sub-internships in medicine, pediatrics, surgery, obstetrics/gynecology, psychiatry, or family medicine (4 weeks each); emergency medicine (4 weeks); Radiology (4 weeks); a preceptorship with a board-certified DO (4 weeks); 2 selectives in medicine, pediatrics, surgery, or obstetrics/gynecology (4 weeks each); and 3 electives (4 weeks each). Students often use the fourth-year clerkships to highlight their competencies to potential postgraduate training institutions. Students are encouraged to integrate structural evaluations and osteopathic manipulative medicine throughout all clerkships.

CAMPUS LIFE

NYCOM offers a great education in one of the world's largest cultural centers. New York City provides students with an exciting life outside of the classroom, from world-renowned arts and entertainment, to exciting sports teams, great dining, and an incredible colloquium of educational resources across all disciplines.

STUDENT LIFE

The numerous student associations on campus include the American Medical Woman's Association, the Christian Student Fellowship, and Project for Latino Health and provide an invaluable support network for student-physicians and their families.

GRADUATES

NYCOM graduates make an impact on the communities they serve. Historically, NYCOM students have matched well before graduation and are ready and able to meet professional challenges.

ADMISSIONS

REQUIREMENTS

Applicants for admission into the 4 year medical program must first meet the following academic requirements prior to matriculation: Obtained a baccalaureate degree from an accredited college or university; achieved a pre-professional science grade point average of at least 2.75/4.0 and an overall grade point average of at least 2.75/4.0; completed 8 semester hours of biology, chemistry, organic chemistry, and physics, in addition to 6 semester hours of English. The MCAT is required and scores must not be more than 3 years old.

SUGGESTIONS

In assessing an applicant for admission, NYCOM evaluates the whole record, environment, initiative, and circumstances of each applicant. Applicants are encouraged to take additional courses such as calculus, comparative anatomy, genetics, physical chemistry, biochemistry, and behavioral and neurosciences. Volunteer or professional work is another way students can express their commitment to the healing profession. The educational process at NYCOM relies heavily on modern educational technologies as well as good study and organizational skills of the students. Therefore, all potential students are expected to prepare themselves well on these fronts.

PROCESS

The New York College of Osteopathic Medicine participates with other colleges of osteopathic medicine in the American Association of Colleges of Osteopathic Medicine Application Service (AACOMAS). About 20 percent of AACOMAS applicants are interviewed, with interviews taking place between November and May. The supplementary application is given to candidates at the time of the interview. Interviews are conducted with basic science faculty and/or osteopathic physicians from the community. Preference is given to New York residents and to residents of states in the northeastern United States.

Admissions Requirements (Required)

Science GPA, non-science GPA, letters of recommendation, interview, state residency, extracurricular activities, exposure to medical profession

Admissions Requirements (Optional)

MCAT scores, essays/personal statement

COSTS AND AID
Tuition & Fees

Tuition	$34,984
Fee	$60

Nova Southeastern University
College of Osteopathic Medicine

3200 South University Drive, Fort Lauderdale, FL 33328 • Admission: 954-262-1101 • Fax: 954-262-2282
E-mail: com@nova.edu • Website: www.medicine.nova.edu

STUDENT BODY	
Type	Private
Enrollment	822
% male/female	50/50
% minorities	32
# applied (total/out)	2,800/2,277
# accepted (total/out)	430/256
# enrolled (total/out)	236/112
Average age	25

FACULTY	
Total faculty (number)	956
% female	19
% minority	26

ADMISSIONS
Average GPA and MCAT Scores

Overall GPA	3.4
MCAT Bio	8.56
MCAT Phys	8.00
MCAT Verbal	8.45
MCAT Essay	O

Application Information

Regular application	1/15
Regular notification	Rolling
Are transfers accepted?	Yes
Admissions may be deferred?	Yes
Interview required?	Yes
Application fee	$50

Academics

Our innovative curriculum is designed to fulfill our mission of training primary-care physicians. The design of the curriculum is based on successful academic models— carefully developed and integrated. It emphasizes interdisciplinary collaboration, guiding students to develop a holistic, and more importantly, an osteopathic approach to medicine. Basic scientific information is continually correlated with fundamental clinical application. Students are exposed to clinical settings in their first semester, which gives them an opportunity to prepare for the "real world" of medicine. This clinical exposure continues into the second year when students have increased opportunity to interact with standardized patients on campus as well as be involved, under physician supervision, with real patients in the office and hospital setting. A notable aspect of the clinical program is a required 3 month rotation in a rural practice setting. In rural clinics throughout Florida, our students provide health care to medically underserved and indigent patients. Our students learn to treat various patients whose lifestyles, practices, and attitudes toward health care differ from those in more traditional training sites. This enriching educational experience cannot be taught in the classroom.

BASIC SCIENCES: Basic Sciences are covered during the first 2 years of medical school. Courses such as Medical Histology, Gross Anatomy, Medical Biochemistry, Medical Physiology, Neuroanatomy, Medical Microbiology, Principles of Pharmacology, and Principles of Pathology are completed.

CLINICAL TRAINING

The Interdisciplinary Generalist Curriculum (IGC) Program exposes medical students to primary care clinical settings from the beginning of their first year, with the long term goal of increasing the numbers of graduates who will pursue careers in family medicine, general internal medicine and general pediatrics. The premise of the program is that exposure to professional role models is a significant determinant of medical students' career choices, and that an early clinical experience is an essential learning component for medical students to begin to correlate classroom knowledge with actual patient encounters.

During the third and fourth year, students complete the core clinical rotations. These include Psychiatry, Geriatrics, Family Medicine, Internal Medicine, Obstetrics/Gynecology, Pediatrics, General Surgery, Emergency Medicine, and Rural Medicine. Students complete their electives in their fourth year.

Student Life

The College of Osteopathic Medicine Student Council is the official voice of all osteopathic medical students. Its meetings are open to all students of the college and it welcomes proposals and participation from the entire student body. A variety of student clubs and organizations that address various professional and practice-related interests are also open for student membership.

Admissions

REQUIREMENTS

Nova Southeastern University receives over 3,000 applications each year to fill a class of 230 students. All AACOMAS applicants receive a secondary application, but not everyone that applies is granted an interview. Interviews begin in August and consist of a session with a panel of health professionals including a DO. Science prerequisites must include 8 hours of each (with labs) in biology, chemistry, organic chemistry, and physics. In addition, 3 semester hours of English Literature and 3 hours of English composition are required. The MCAT is required and should be no more than 3 years old. The best set of scores will be used.

SUGGESTIONS

Because of the time it takes for AACOMAS to provide all of the student information, and the fact that NSU is on rolling admissions, making application early is advisable.

PROCESS

Preference will be given to students with a cumulative grade point average (GPA) of 3.0 or higher. However, the dean is empowered to evaluate the total qualifications of every student and to modify requirements in unusual circumstances.

The college participates in the American Association of Colleges of Osteopathic Medicine Application Service (AACOMAS) for the receipt and processing of all applications. AACOMAS takes no part in the selection of students.

Admissions Requirements (Required)

MCAT scores, science GPA, non-science GPA, letters of recommendation, interview, state residency, essays/personal statement, extracurricular activities, exposure to medical profession, DO recommendation

Overlap Schools

Des Moines University, New York Medical College, Philadelphia College of Osteopathic Medicine

COSTS AND AID

Tuition & Fees

Tuition	$25,785
Room and board (off-campus)	$12,040
Cost of books	$2,000
Fees	$925

Financial Aid

% students receiving aid	96
Average loan	$42,944
Average debt	$225,000

OHIO UNIVERSITY
COLLEGE OF OSTEOPATHIC MEDICINE

102 GROSVENOR HALL ATHENS, OH 45701 • ADMISSION: 800-345-1560 • FAX: 740-593-2256
E-MAIL: ADMISSIONS@EXCHANGE.OUCOM.OHIOU.EDU • WEBSITE: WWW.OUCOM.OHIOU.EDU

STUDENT BODY

Type	Public
Enrollment	433
% male/female	44/56
% minorities	24
# applied (total/out)	3,173/2,684
# accepted (total/out)	156/14
# enrolled (total/out)	108/14
Average age	24

FACULTY

Total faculty	115
% female	30
% minority	15
% part-time	33
Student-faculty ratio	4:1

ADMISSIONS

Average GPA and MCAT Scores

Overall GPA	3.51
MCAT Bio	8.4
MCAT Phys	7.55
MCAT Verbal	8.4
MCAT Essay	P

Application Information

Regular application	2/8
Regular notification	Rolling
Are transfers accepted?	Yes
Admissions may be deferred?	Yes
Interview required?	Yes
Application fee	$40

Academics

The Ohio University College of Osteopathic Medicine (OU-COM) is dedicated to preparing well-rounded primary care and specialty physicians for service to the state of Ohio as well as the nation. Students begin their first two years of training in Athens while the final two years take place at one of 13 hospitals in our Centers for Osteopathic Research and Education (CORE). The learning environment at OU-COM and the CORE is constructed based on the principles of adult learning, which include student empowerment and clinical relevance. Students will enroll in one of two tracks-the Patient-Centered Continuum (PCC) curriculum or the Clinical Presentation Continuum (CPC) curriculum. Both curricula view medical education as an organized building process that extends from the first day of medical school through residency training and beyond. Students in both curricula begin interacting with real patients in the first weeks of their medical education. The PCC curriculum is a student-directed approach that uses a problem-based learning environment and places emphasis on small group discussions, case analysis, collaborative learning, and problem solving as its primary educational tools. The CPC curriculum provides students with opportunities to learn the biomedical science fundamentals of medicine in an integrated, clinically relevant environment. This faculty-directed curriculum uses the most common and/or important symptoms that patients present to primary care providers as its organizing focus. Demographic information includes a first-year student body that is 59 percent female, 30 percent underrepresented minority, 87 percent Ohio residents and ranges in age from 21-45.

Demographic information includes a first year student body that is 56 percent female, 17 percent underrepresented minority, 83 percent Ohio residents and ranges in age from 21-45.

CLINICAL TRAINING

In order to become a patient-centered osteopathic physician, we feel that it is extremely important to have patient contact from the very beginning of your undergraduate medical education. As part of the OU-COM curricula, you will receive patient contact within the first week of your first year through our Clinical and Community Experience (CCE) program. Students are able to see firsthand the roles of other health-care professionals and become aware of cultural, economic and social issues that can affect health status and health-care delivery. Through OU-COM's pioneering Simulated Patient Program, students begin to hone their history taking, psychosocial and physical examination skills. One of the first in the country, this program -in place for over 25 years- features "patient actors" who role play a variety of conditions. Whenever possible, patients with actual symptoms or illnesses such as diabetes or rheumatoid arthritis are used as part of the simulated patient experience. Students are also able to get involved in health-care initiatives and community health service programs related to rural Southeastern Ohio. The Childhood Immunization Program and the Breast and Cervical Cancer Screening Clinic are both delivered through one of the college's two Mobile Health Units. Opportunities for clinical service also abound at University Medical Associates-an ambulatory health-care facility in Athens-and in OU-COM's satellite clinics in the outlying rural areas. Clinical rotations at one of our thirteen CORE hospitals will take place in the third and fourth years of study.

Clinical rotations at one of our 12 CORE hospitals will take place in the third and fourth years of study.

Students

Being part of a major university has its advantages! From cultural and athletic events to phenomenal student recreation opportunities, OU-COM students enjoy it all. Located within minutes of Strouds Run State Park, students can relax by hiking, swimming, or fishing, or, they can blade, walk, bike, or jog our 19-mile, paved fitness path that extends from Athens to Nelsonville. Even more outdoor adventure is available in nearby Wayne National Forest. Ohio University also provides a nine-hole golf course, a natatorium, ice arena as well as indoor and outdoor tennis courts all within walking distance of the OU-COM campus. Intramural sports are also very popular. OU-COM has produced championship teams in both basketball and broomball over the past two years.

STUDENT LIFE

While it is no surprise that most of a med student's day is spent studying, there is still time for fun. Students can enjoy the many amenities offered by the university or get involved in OU-COM student government or other medically related student organizations. The environment at OU-COM is one of collegiality and cooperativeness. Students are often seen studying together, having a meal together or even living in close proximity to one another. The quality of life for an OU-COM student is high. Support from caring and dedicated faculty and staff alongside the beauty and history of Ohio University make OU-COM an extraordinary place to obtain a medical education.

The environment at OU-COM is one of collegiality and cooperativeness. Students are often seen studying together, having a meal together or even living in close proximity to one another. The quality of life for an OU-COM student is high. Support from caring and dedicated faculty and staff alongside the beauty and history of Ohio University make OU-COM an extraordinary place to obtain a medical education.

GRADUATES

OU-COM was founded for the express purpose of providing outstanding primary care physicians for the state of Ohio. Since our first graduating class in 1980 we have accomplished that and more. Fifty-six percent of our graduates do go on to specialize in family medicine, internal medicine or pediatrics, with 50 percent going specifically into family medicine. The remaining 40 percent are pursuing specialties such as orthopedic surgery, neurology, nephrology, psychiatry, anesthesiology, and ophthalmology just to name a few.

Admissions

REQUIREMENTS

Eight semester hours each in Biology, Chemistry, Organic Chemistry, and Physics are required. In addition, applicants must have taken six semester hours of English and Behavioral Science. As a state-affiliated institution, the college gives preference to Ohio residents, who make up about 80 percent of the student body. About 80 percent of AACOMAS applicants are sent supplemental applications. About 16 percent of those who submit supplemental applications are invited to interview. Interviews take place from October through April, and consist of three 30-minute sessions with members of the faculty and administration. Approximately half of interviewees are accepted, with notification occurring on a rolling basis. In the past, successful candidates have had a mean GPA of 3.5 and an average of at least 8 on each section of the MCAT.

SUGGESTIONS

Additional coursework in biochemistry, histology, gross anatomy, and immunology is recommended but not required.

OKLAHOMA STATE UNIVERSITY
COLLEGE OF OSTEOPATHIC MEDICINE

1111 WEST SEVENTEENTH STREET, OFFICE OF STUDENT AFFAIRS TULSA, OK 74107 • ADMISSION: 918-561-8421
FAX: 918-561-8243 • E-MAIL: AMANDA.GUTIERREZ@OKSTATE.EDU • WEBSITE: WWW.HEALTHSCIENCES.OKSTATE.EDU

STUDENT BODY

Type	Public
Enrollment	351
% male/female	52/48
% minorities	19
# applied (total/out)	486/280
# accepted(total/out)	144/36
# enrolled(total/out)	88/10
Average age	24

FACULTY

Total faculty (number)	536
% female	20
% minority	10
% part-time	84
Student-faculty ratio	2:1

ADMISSIONS
Average GPA and MCAT Scores

Overall GPA	3.62
MCAT Bio	9
MCAT Phys	8
MCAT Verbal	9
MCAT Essay	0

Application Information

Regular application	2/1
Regular notification	Rolling
Are transfers accepted?	Yes
Admissions may be deferred?	No
Interview required?	Yes
Application fee	$40

Academics

The curriculum at OSU College of Osteopathic Medicine includes hands-on clinical experiences, student-centered and problem-based methods of instruction, as well as frequent consultation with faculty and community-based physicians. The first year focuses on biomedical sciences, and the second year emphasizes case-based learning and problem solving as it relates to conditions seen in primary care environments. The third and fourth years are composed of clinical rotations, most of which take place at OSU Medical Center, the country's largest osteopathic hospital (521 beds). Students also rotate to adjacent rural areas, and they may fulfill requirements at various medical institutions across the country. Although 64 percent of graduates enter primary care, they are prepared to enter residencies in all medical specialty fields. The medical school, a college of Oklahoma State University, is located in Tulsa, a very livable city of of 386,000.

Admissions

REQUIREMENTS

Of the 88 positions in a class, 68 are reserved for Oklahoma residents. Prerequisites for application are 8–10 semester hours of biology, chemistry, organic chemistry, and physics, with labs, in addition to 6–8 hours of English and at least 1 upper-division science course. The minimum overall undergraduate GPA is 3.0, with a minimum science GPA of 2.75. An average score of 7 (21 total) on the MCAT is required. Approximately 10 percent of all qualified applicants are interviewed. Interviews begin in October and continue through April. Applicants are interviewed simultaneously by 2 faculty members (1 DO and 1 PhD) for 35–40 minutes. Notification of admission occurs on a rolling basis, and about 35–40 percent of interviewees are accepted.

Admissions Requirements (Required)

MCAT scores, science GPA, non-science GPA, letters of recommendation, interview, essay/personal statement, extracurricular activities, exposure to medical profession, Familiarity with osteopathic physician

Admissions Requirement (Optional)

State residency

Overlap School

University of Oklahoma.

COSTS AND AID

Tuition & Fees

In-state tuition	$16,045
Out-of-state tuition	$31,265
Room and board (off-campus)	$7,200
Cost of books	$3,500
Fees	$893

Financial Aid

% students receiving aid	96
Average grant	$2,500
Average loan	$30,000
Average debt	$150,000

PHILADELPHIA COLLEGE OF OSTEOPATHIC MEDICINE

OFFICE OF ADMISSIONS, 4170 CITY AVENUE PHILADELPHIA, PA 19131 • ADMISSION: 800-999-6998
FAX: 215-871-6719 • E-MAIL: ADMISSIONS@PCOM.EDU • WEBSITE: WWW.PCOM.EDU

STUDENT BODY

Type	Private
Enrollment	2,090
% male/female	39/61
% minorities	29
# applied (total/out)	3,484/2,901
# accepted (total/out)	375/116
# enrolled (total/out)	268/96
Average age	26

FACULTY

Total faculty	1,508
% female	16
% minority	5
% part-time	4
Student-faculty ratio	1:1

ADMISSIONS

Average GPA and MCAT Scores

Overall GPA	3.4
MCAT Bio	8.56
MCAT Phys	8.03
MCAT Verbal	8.0
MCAT Essay	P

Application Information

Regular application	2/1
Regular notification	Rolling
Are transfers accepted?	No
Admissions may be deferred?	No
Interview required?	Yes
Application fee	$50

Academics

Established in 1899, Philadelphia College of Osteopathic Medicine (PCOM) is a private, not for profit institution built on over 100 years' tradition of excellence in medical education. Students find the educational program at PCOM is an optimal blend of classroom teaching, clinical experience and research. From the first day of medical school, PCOM students begin learning the osteopathic approach to health care: treating the whole person, not just the symptoms. Early clinical exposure through community service activities and formal course work implement basic science instruction. The curriculum is interdisciplinary and includes topics such as medical ethics and medical law, and emphasizes primary care and prevention. Clinical training takes place at 37 affiliated institutions in and around Philadelphia. In addition, students may arrange to fulfill elective requirements in other states or in other countries. Joint degree programs lead to the D.O. /M.B.A., D.O. /M.P.H. and D.O. /PhD. PCOM is committed to helping each of its students choose a career that matches their specific talents and interest. The entering class of 2007 in Philadelphia included 268 students from 26 states. The male/female ratio was 48/52 and the average age was 26.

Georgia Campus—PCOM proudly welcomed its first class of 85 students in August, 2005. The College is dedicated to educating osteopathic medical students and serving the health care need of the people in Georgia and the Southeast by providing a program of medical study guided by osteopathic medical tradition, concept and practice. Contact information for Georgia Campus—PCOM is Office of Admissions, 625 Old Peachtree Road NW, Suwanee, Georgia 30024; the telephone number is 678-225-7509. The Georgia Campus—PCOM Admissions Office email is gaadmissions@pcom.edu.

Admissions

REQUIREMENTS

Admission to PCOM is competitive and selective. Acceptance by the Faculty Committee on Admissions is based on the applicant's fulfillment of undergraduate course requirements, grade point average, Medical College Admissions Test (MCAT) scores and a personal interview with the committee. We seek well rounded, achievement oriented persons whose character, maturity and sense of dedication point to a productive life as an osteopathic physician. The Admissions Committee is looking for applicants who bring passion, leadership, compassion and service to the filed of osteopathic medicine and have demonstrated these qualities in their background and preparation for medical school.

PROCESS

As a private institution, PCOM accepts applicants from all over the country and does show preference for Pennsylvania residents. Science preparation must include eight semester hours (including lab) each in Biology, Inorganic Chemistry, Organic Chemistry and Physics. In addition, six hours of English Literature and Composition are required. The MCAT is required and must be taken within three years of desired matriculation. All AACOMAS applicants receive secondary applications. Of the approximately 5,000 applicants returning secondary applications, approximately sixteen percent are invited (via email) to interview on campus, with interviews beginning in September. The interview consists of one session with a panel that could include faculty, students and administrators. Notification of committee decision occurs on a rolling basis until the class is filled.

Admissions Requirements (Required)

MCAT scores, Science GPA, Non-science GPA, Letters of recommendation, Interview, Essays/personal statement

Admissions Requirements (Optional)

State residency, Extracurricular activities, Exposure to medical profession, D.O. letters of reference recommended

Overlap Schools

Drexel University, Lake Erie College of Osteopathic Medicine, New York Institute of Technology, Penn State University, Temple University, UMDNJ-School of Osteopathic Medicine, University of Medicine and Dentistry of New Jersey.

COSTS AND AID

Tuition & Fees

Tuition	$37,509
Cost of books	$1,800
Fees	$1,050

Financial Aid

% students receiving aid	91
Average grant	$7,578
Average debt	$173,467

PIKEVILLE COLLEGE
SCHOOL OF OSTEOPATHIC MEDICINE

147 SYCAMORE STREET, PIKEVILLE, KY 41501 • ADMISSION: 606-218-5406 • FAX: 606-218-5405
E-MAIL: AHAMILTO@PC.EDU • WEBSITE: WWW.PCSOM.EDU

STUDENT BODY

Type	Private
Enrollment	301
% male/female	56/44
% minorities	10
# applied (total/out)	1,770/1,671
# accepted(total/out)	133/86
# enrolled(total/out)	80/39
Average age	26

FACULTY

Total faculty (number)	29
% female	33
% part-time	0
Student-faculty ratio	6:1

ADMISSIONS
Average GPA and MCAT Scores

Overall GPA	3.3
MCAT Bio	7.4
MCAT Phys	6.9
MCAT Verbal	7.7
MCAT Essay	0

Application Information

Regular application	2/7
Regular notification	Rolling
Are transfers accepted?	Yes
Admissions may be deferred?	Yes
Interview required?	Yes
Application fee	$75

Academics

The Pikeville College School of Osteopathic Medicine (PCSOM) is the nineteenth school of osteopathic medicine in the country. PCSOM offers a 4-year program that leads to the degree of Doctor of Osteopathic Medicine (DO). The first 2 years of the curriculum focus on basic sciences, and the third and fourth years emphasize clinical work. Osteopathic principles are integrated throughout the 4-year curriculum, and students learn osteopathic manipulative treatment for prevention, diagnosis, and treatment of disease. Pikeville College's Board of Trustees has decided that no student should be organizationally or academically disadvantaged because of a lack of adequate personal funding. To this end, PCSOM provides each student with a state-of-the art Pentium laptop computer; all required texts and workbooks; all anatomy dissection equipment; a new portable OP&P table; stethoscope; opthalmoscope; otoscope; lab coats; scrub suits; outside board review; and the cost of taking Part I and Part II of the NBOME certification exam once.

BASIC SCIENCES: During the first 2 years, students take lecture-based courses with labs covering the typical medical school disciplines with special emphasis in the following areas: manual medicine; community and behavior medicine; and ambulatory care. Friday afternoons are spent in doctors' offices, where students learn to take patient histories and conduct physical exams. First-year courses include Osteopathic Principles and Practice; Gross Anatomy; Radiology; Clinical Skills; Neuroscience; Opthalmology; Immunology; and Medical Ethics. Second-year courses include Pathology; Pharmacology; Pediatrics; Community and Behavioral Medicine; and Psychiatry. During the summer of their second year, students take medicine and surgery, 2 intensive, full-time courses that will prepare students to fully interact at the bedside or in an ambulatory care setting during the final 2 years of their medical school education.

CLINICAL TRAINING

During the third and fourth years students enter their clinical training, rotating through urban, suburban, and rural settings, while gaining exposure to all areas of medicine. Rotations occur on a monthly basis, starting on the first day of each calendar month and ending the last day of the month. The following rotations are required and assigned: Family Medicine (2 months); Emergency Medicine (2 months); General Internal Medicine (2 months); Pediatrics (2 months); General Surgery (2 months); Osteopathic Principles and Practice (1 month); Women's Health (1 month); Psychiatry (1 month); Radiology (2 weeks); Anesthesiology (2 weeks); 2 selective rotations in a clinical subspecialty (1 month each). In addition, students complete elective rotations in medicine and surgery (1 month each) and an additional 2 months in the elective of their choice.

CAMPUS LIFE

The Admissions Office seeks to recruit students who will help Pikeville fulfill its mission to provide men and women with an osteopathic medical education that emphasizes primary care, and produce graduates who are committed to serving the health care needs of communities in the Appalachian regions.

STUDENT LIFE

PCSOM offers students a variety of professional and social clubs and organizations on campus. The PCSOM Emergency Medicine Student Club is a new organization that focuses on emergency medicine and aims to foster professional growth and interest in emergency medicine by providing relevant educational programs and service projects to the PCSOM community.

The Student Government Association (SGA) is the official voice for students, and is responsible for dispersing funds for student activities; acting as liaison for the student body; and working to improve the quality of life for all PCSOM students.

Other clubs of note include the Student Osteopathic Surgical Association (SOSA) for students who want to learn more about careers in surgery, and the Student Osteopathic Medical Association (SOMA) which works to improve the quality of health care delivery, contribute to the education of osteopathic medical students, and promote the ideals of osteopathic medicine. SOMA is recognized by the American Osteopathic Association (AOA) and the American Medical Association (AMA) as the National Professional Society of Osteopathic Medical Students. Membership in SOMA offers students a legitimate voice in shaping the future of their chosen profession. It also provides a means of communication among the students of the 19 colleges of osteopathic medicine. All students of osteopathic medicine are eligible for membership in SOMA, which comes with an extensive student benefits package, including discounts on books and equipment.

GRADUATES

After graduation, students complete one year of a rotating internship and 2–5 years of residency, depending upon which specialty is selected. PCSOM continues to form affiliations with hospitals in the Appalachian region to ensure that adequate postgraduate training sites are available for PCSOM graduates so that they can and will stay in the area.

ADMISSIONS

REQUIREMENTS

The minimum requirements for admission are: Completion of at least 90 semester hours of the required credits for a baccalaureate degree from a regionally accredited college or university; MCAT scores from an MCAT exam not taken more than three years ago; 12 semester hours of biology (with labs); 8 semester hours each of chemistry, organic chemistry, and physics (with labs); and 6 semester hours of English.

SUGGESTED

The baccalaureate degree is preferred, and preference is given to those candidates who will have earned the degree prior to starting the medical school program. The ability to use a personal or network computer is an important skill that will assist students with PCSOM course work. Therefore, each entering student should have a good working knowledge of common PC use and applications.

PROCESS

Pikeville participates in the AACOMAS application process.

Admissions Requirements (Required)

MCAT scores, science GPA, non-science GPA, letters of recommendation, interview, essay/personal statement, extracurricular activities, exposure to medical profession

Admissions Requirement (Optional)

State residency

Overlap Schools

Marshall University, Ohio University, University of Kentucky, University of Louisville, West Virginia School of Osteopathic Medicine.

COSTS AND AID

Tuition & Fees

Tuition	$29,250
Room and board (off-campus)	$9,000
Cost of books	$0
Fees	$0

Financial Aid

% students receiving aid	96
Average grant	$11,110
Average loan	$28,000
Average debt	$106,000

TOURO UNIVERSITY—CALIFORNIA
COLLEGE OF OSTEOPATHIC MEDICINE

OFFICE OF ADMISSIONS, 1310 JOHNSON LANE, VALLEJO, CA 94592 • ADMISSION: 707-638-5270
FAX: 707-638-5250 • E-MAIL: SDAVIS@TOURO.EDU • WEBSITE: WWW.TU.EDU

STUDENT BODY

Type	Private
Enrollment	540
% male/female	52/48
% minorities	5
# applied	3,317
# accepted	135
# enrolled	135
Average age	26

ADMISSIONS
Average GPA and MCAT Scores

Overall GPA	3.35
MCAT Bio	9.13
MCAT Phys	8.72
MCAT Verbal	8.31

Application Information

Regular application	4/15
Regular notification	Rolling
Early application	8/15
Early notification	9/15
Are transfers accepted?	Yes
Admissions may be deferred?	Yes
Interview required?	Yes
Application fee	$100

Academics

The Touro University College of Osteopathic Medicine (TUCOM), California, is located in the northeast part of San Francisco Bay on Mare Island. The mission of the TUCOM is to train osteopathic, family practice physicians to help meet the need for primary care practitioners in California and throughout the country. Though preventative medicine and primary care are emphasized, graduates are also prepared to enter residency programs that train osteopathic specialists. Patient contact begins in the first year, and clinical training takes place at sites throughout the greater Bay Area including hospitals, clinics, and physicians' offices. Students have the opportunity to experience both urban and rural patient populations.

TUCOM prepares students to become outstanding osteopathic physicians who uphold the values, philosophy, and practice of osteopathic medicine and who are committed to primary care and the holistic approach to the patient. The college advances the profession and serves its students and society through innovative education, research, and community service.

BASIC SCIENCES: TUCOM students take courses in all of the subject areas one would expect any physician to master, including anatomy, pathology, histology, osteopathic principles and practices, pharmacology, clinical skills, etc. Our goal is to prepare students for the realities of medicine as it presently exists, as well as how it is likely to be in the future. Practice in problem-solving is part of the daily classroom clinic experience as we strive to deliver a curriculum consistent with emerging directions of health care.

Student Life

Touro University—California occupies a spectacular 44-acre site on Mare Island, located in the Northeastern part of the San Francisco Bay Area. In addition to the College of Osteopathic Medicine, the university is home to the College of Education, College of Health Sciences, and the College of Pharmacy. The campus enjoys wireless Internet access, state of the art lecture halls, breakout rooms, and an anatomy lab.

TUCOM students participate in several organizations, including the Student Osteopathic Medical Association, and a variety of student organized clubs. With a campus that is centrally located in the San Francisco Bay Area, students are within an hour's drive of Napa Valley, Sacramento, and San Francisco.

Admissions
REQUIREMENTS

Candidates are required to obtain a bachelor's degree prior to matriculating into the College of Osteopathic Medicine. A qualifying MCAT score is also required and must have been taken within the last three years. In addition, candidates are required to obtain 8 semester units (with lab) of the following: biology/zoology, general (inorganic) chemistry, organic chemistry, and physics. Successful candidates typically have cumulative and science GPAs of 3.0 or above and MCAT scores of 23 and higher.

PROCESS

What follows is a brief summary of the admissions procedures to apply to TUCOM. Further details should be reviewed by going to TU.edu, and clicking on Prospective Students, followed by College of Osteopathic Medicine.

- Complete the primary application with AACOMAS. This can be accomplished by clicking on the AACOMAS link on our website or by going to AACOM.org. TUCOM's school number is 618.

- Qualified applicants will be invited to complete a supplemental application. This application is available online but should not be completed or submitted until eligibility is determined.

- If eligible for a supplemental application, submit an evaluation from a pre-professional advisory committee, or letters from two science faculty familiar with your work.

- Submit a physician (DO or MD) letter of recommendation.

- If invited to do so, schedule a formal interview with the Admissions and Standards Committee.

Admissions Requirements (Required)

MCAT scores, science GPA, non-science GPA, letters of recommendation, interview, essay/personal statement, extracurricular activities, exposure to medical profession

COSTS AND AID
Tuition & Fees

Tuition	$35,500
Cost of books	$1,784

Financial Aid

% students receiving aid	97
Average grant	$0
Average loan	$0

UNIVERSITY OF MEDICINE AND DENTISTRY OF NEW JERSEY
SCHOOL OF OSTEOPATHIC MEDICINE

ONE MEDICAL CENTER DRIVE, SUITE 210, STRATFORD, NJ 08084 • ADMISSION: 856-566-7050 • FAX: 856-566-6895
E-MAIL: SOMADM@UMDNJ.EDU • WEBSITE: SOM.UMDNJ.EDU

STUDENT BODY

Type	Public
Enrollment	413
% male/female	41/59
% minorities	26
# applied	3,386
# accepted	174
# enrolled	108
Average age	24

FACULTY

Total faculty (number)	187
% female	39
% minority	18
% part-time	19

ADMISSIONS
Average GPA and MCAT Scores

Overall GPA	3.5
MCAT Bio	9.33
MCAT Phys	8.75
MCAT Verbal	8.59
MCAT Essay	Q

Application Information

Regular application	2/1
Regular notification	Rolling
Are transfers accepted?	Yes
Admissions may be deferred?	Yes
Interview required?	Yes
Application fee	$90

Academics

All applicants are processed and reviewed without regard to state of residence. The minimum course requirements are 8 semester hours of biology, physics, chemistry and organic chemistry, all with associated labs, and 6 semester hours each of English, math, and social sciences. Applicants should have at least a 3.0 GPA in both sciences and overall, as the average GPA of successful applicants is 3.50. The MCAT is required and must be no more than 5 years old. The average MCAT of successful applicants is in the 89 range. Just over 15 percent of approximately 2,000 applicants are interviewed, with interviews taking place between August and April. About half of interviewees are accepted. Wait list candidates may send supplementary information to update their files.

The instructional program at the UMDNJ—School of Osteopathic Medicine reflects the essence of the holistic philosophy of osteopathic medicine which regards the human body as an integrated whole. The curriculum provides comprehensive instruction in the basic and clinical sciences, emphasizing the primary care of the patient. The ultimate goal of the curriculum is to develop in students the lifelong learning skills of a physician.

The primary focus of the first year of medical school is the development of a solid foundation in the basic sciences. The study of the history and conceptual framework of osteopathic medicine, including the basic techniques of osteopathic manipulative therapy, is also included. The second year is devoted to the integration of the basic sciences and clinical medicine. Using a modularized design based on body system, the information is taught through a coordinated effort of basic science and clinical faculty. Instruction is provided by a combination of lectures, independent reading, and problem-oriented group discussions which enable students to acquire, assimilate, and analyze clinical knowledge. Additionally, students receive instruction and practice in the basic clinical skills of history-taking and physical examination as well as in the more complex techniques of osteopathic manipulative therapy.

The third and fourth years are devoted to the development of clinical competence through directly supervised patient care activities. Through didactic instruction and "hands-on" education, students increase the scope and depth of their clinical knowledge and skills. These clinical experiences permit students to apply their skills to solving patient problems, as well as to develop strategies which promote wellness and the prevention of disease. A unique feature of the clinical curriculum is the participation in a longitudinal community-based health care program. A variety of settings are utilized for the clinical education, including the three Kennedy Memorial Hospital—University Medical Center site, Our Lady of Lourdes Hospital, Christ Hospital, Barnert Hospital, ambulatory health care centers, private offices, nursing homes, and community-based clinics.

The Problem Based Learning Curriculum

The Problem Based Learning Curriculum (PBLC) is an alternative curricular track available to 7 students. The PBLC was established to meet the needs of those applicants who find problem-based learning an attractive option. It is a 2-year program, and with the start of the clerkships in the third year, PBLC students join the rest of their classmates.

Admissions

The Admissions Committee requires that every applicant submit results from the Medical College Admissions Test, as well as a premedical committee letter. All accepted students must have earned a baccalaureate degree upon matriculation at UMDNJ—SOM. Other requirements include 8 hours of biology, 8 hours of organic chemistry, 8 hours of inorganic chemistry and 8 hours of physics, all with laboratories. Additionally, 3 hours of English composition are required, as well as 3 hours from the English department; 6 hours of college level mathematics are required, three hours of which may be satisfied by computer science or statistics and six hours of behavioral science (psychology, sociology or cultural anthropology). UMDNJ—SOM strongly recommends that applicants take 6 additional semester hours of science courses. Biochemistry, genetics, physiology, and anatomy are strongly suggested.

Those applicants whose credentials are judged to be most competitive will be invited for an interview; interviews are not granted at an applicant's request. Applicants who are not considered for the first round of interviews will be held for further review. Candidates whose credentials are considered noncompetitive will receive a rejection notice at an early date.

Applicants may complete an online application through the American Association of Colleges of Osteopathic Medicine Application Service (AACOMAS) by logging onto their WEBSITE: AACOM.org. Applications are available in early May and may be completed and submitted between June 1 of that year and February 1 of the year of the desired admission. All applications are considered without regard to state of residence. Applicants must be U.S. citizens or permanent residents at the time the application is filed.

Combined Degree Programs

DO/PhD

The joint DO/PhD program is a unique interdepartmental program between the Departments of Cell Biology and Molecular Biology intended to prepare future physicians anticipating careers in biomedical research or teaching. All DO/PhD candidates receive an annual stipend and a tuition waiver for each year of participation in the combined-degree programs.

DO/JD

The joint DO/JD program is offered in cooperation with Rutgers University—School of Law, Camden Campus. The program is designed to prepare future physicians for joint careers in medicine and law.

DO/MPH

The joint DO/MPH program is offered in cooperation with the UMDNJ—School of Public Health. The Masters in Public Health degree is designed to prepare future physicians to address a multitude of health issues within our society.

DO/MS

The Joint DO/MS program is offered in cooperation with the UMDNJ—Graduate School of Biomedical Sciences. The program is designed to prepare future physicians with strong research orientation in the Biomedical Sciences.

DO/MBA

The joint DO/MBA is offered in cooperation with Rowan University. The Master of Business Administration is designed to prepare future physicians to establish business and medical practices and/or other business endeavor and assume leadership positions within for-profit and not-for-profit organizations.

Admissions Requirements (Required)

MCAT scores, science GPA, non-science GPA, letters of recommendation, interview, essays/personal statement, extracurricular activities, exposure to medical profession

Admissions Requirements (Optional)

State residency

COSTS AND AID
Tuition & Fees

In-state tuition	$23,136
Out-of-state tuition	$36,208
Room and board (off-campus)	$10,000
Cost of books	$8,536
Fees	$2,587

Financial Aid

% students receiving aid	92
Average grant	$4,500
Average loan	$32,759
Average debt	$122,661

UNIVERSITY OF NEW ENGLAND
COLLEGE OF OSTEOPATHIC MEDICINE

UNECOM OFFICE OF RECRUITMENT, STUDENT AND ALUMNI SERVICES, 11 HILLS BEACH ROAD, BIDDEFORD, ME 04005
ADMISSION: 207-602-2329 • FAX: 207-602-5967 • E-MAIL: UNECOMADMISSIONS@UNE.EDU
WEBSITE: WWW.UNE.EDU/COM

STUDENT BODY

Type	Private
Enrollment	501
% male/female	45/55
% minorities	13
# applied (total/out)	3,250/3,190
# accepted (total/out)	232/204
# enrolled (total/out)	124/100
Average age	27

FACULTY

Total faculty	518
% female	5
% minority	1
% part-time	90
Student-faculty ratio	10:1

ADMISSIONS
Average GPA and MCAT Scores

Overall GPA	3.43
MCAT Bio	8.8
MCAT Phys	8
MCAT Verbal	8.8
MCAT Essay	Q

Application Information

Regular application	2/1
Regular notification	Rolling
Are transfers accepted?	Yes
Admissions may be deferred?	No
Interview required?	Yes

Academics

The University of New England College of Osteopathic Medicine (UNECOM) is a private, nonprofit institution with a mission to provide for the education of osteopathic physicians and other health professionals for the people of New England and the nation. The curriculum focuses on three areas of excellence: primary care, osteopathic principles and practice, and geriatrics. The academic environment is one of collaboration and support among the student body and with faculty members. The typical class size is 117-124 students, who come from a wide variety of educational and professional backgrounds. While approximately 60 percent of the class is from New England, there are students from around the country. Some come directly from undergraduate studies, while others have completed master's and professional degrees. The male/female ratio is about 45/55 and the average age of entering students is 27 years old.

BASIC SCIENCES: The modified systems-based curriculum begins with a focus on developing a solid preparation in the basic sciences and an exposure to the physician-patient relationship through early clinical experiences in the Essentials of Osteopathic Medicine course. The Gross Anatomy course is one of the most comprehensive in the country, providing for the full dissection of a cadaver with just three other students, and the incorporation of radiographic anatomy and live (palpatory) anatomy in the overall course. Building on the first year, the systems-based modules of the second year are taught by a cadre of practicing clinicians and basic scientists who bring the real world into the classroom. Students' clinical skills are enhanced in the Experiences in Doctoring course, with community placements and practice with standardized patients at the Clinical Skills Assessment Center, as well as the differential diagnosis classes.

CLINICAL TRAINING

The third year is devoted to clerkships in core disciplines of internal medicine, pediatrics, surgery, psychiatry, obstetrics, and family medicine at clinical training centers (CTCs) in the Northeast. Students are involved in patient care and didactic sessions in ambulatory, hospital, and rural settings. The third year concludes with a student colloquium for the assessment of acquired skills in the simulated patient program. Year four requires clerkships in internal medicine, surgery, emergency medicine, osteopathic manipulative medicine, and rural medicine and community health while providing an opportunity for electives throughout the United States and overseas as the student completes their preparation for residency.

Students

The College of Osteopathic Medicine is one of four colleges of the University of New England. The medical school and the College of Arts and Sciences are located on the waterfront campus in Biddeford, Maine; the Westbrook College Campus in Portland is home to the College of Health Professions and the new College of Pharmacy. Osteopathic medical students have access to a full range of student services on both campuses. Most students live less than six miles from campus in the cities of Biddeford (21,000) and Saco (17,000).

STUDENT LIFE

With an active student government, class officers, and more than 30 clubs and organizations, there are many opportunities for first- and second-year students to be involved on campus and assume leadership positions. First- and second-year students also serve the Biddeford community through various programs including the Biddeford Free Clinic, local soup kitchen, and mentoring program with one of the elementary schools. Students maintain a health balance in their lives by utilizing the Campus Center (including the fitness room, racquetball court, gym, indoor track, pool and hydro-spa, and saunas) and participating in the University's intramural leagues. The campus sits at the mouth of the Saco River where it meets the Atlantic Ocean, and the southern coastal Maine area is ideal for jogging and running, cycling, mountain biking, kayaking, and canoeing. Hiking, backpacking, camping, climbing, skiing, and snowboarding opportunities are less than two hours away in the White Mountains. Portland, Maine's largest city, is only a half hour to the north and Boston is an hour and a half to the south.

GRADUATES

UNECOM has more than 2,200 graduates working in primary care and specialty fields around the country. Approximately sixty-five percent of each class pursues residency programs in family practice, general internal medicine, pediatrics and obstetrics. Others choose to bring a patient-centered approach to a wide variety of specialties including emergency medicine, anesthesiology, general and orthopedic surgery, sports medicine, and physical medicine and rehabilitation, to name a few. Others will specialize in neuro-muscular medicine (NMM). Graduates continue to serve the osteopathic community by serving in leadership positions in state societies and specialty colleges.

Admissions

REQUIREMENTS

Specific academic requirements include eight semester hours of biology and physics, and six hours of English composition or literature. Four semesters of chemistry are also required, one of which must be biochemistry. Appropriate labs are required for all science courses with the exception of biochemistry. The minimum GPA is 2.7 in both the sciences and overall, while the class average is in the 3.3-3.6 range. The MCAT is required and must be no more than two years old at time of application. The minimum MCAT is 18 with M on the writing sample, but the class average is in the 24-27 range (8s and 9s in each of the three sections). In addition to the requirements noted above, the following non-academic achievements are important in the evaluation process: leadership experience and organizational involvement; healthcare experience, whether volunteer or paid employment; community service and volunteer experience. Passion and commitment to working with and serving others is important to the Admissions Committee. There is some preference for candidates from the six New England states, but approximately 40 percent of the class is from the rest of the country.

PROCESS

The primary application to the University of New England College of Osteopathic Medicine (UNECOM) is through the American Association of Colleges of Osteopathic Medicine Application Service (AACOMAS). More than 3,360 AACOMAS applications were received during the 2007-2008 application cycle. Applicants who meet all prerequisites are invited to submit a UNECOM-specific online supplemental application and letters of recommendation. A letter from an osteopathic physician is not required, but strongly encouraged. Once all materials have been received, applicant's files are reviewed for possible interview. On-campus interviews are conducted from September through April. Interview teams are often comprised of a basic science faculty member, practicing clinician, and a second-year student. Qualified candidates are offered acceptance on a modified rolling admissions basis.

Admissions Requirements (Required)

MCAT scores, Science GPA, Non-science GPA, Letters of recommendation, Interview, Essays/personal statement, Extracurricular activities, Exposure to medical profession, Volunteerism/community service

Admissions Requirements (Optional)

State residency

Overlap Schools

A.T. Still University of Health Sciences, Dartmouth College, New York Institute of Technology, Nova Southeastern University, Philadelphia College of Osteopathic Medicine, UMDNJ-School of Osteopathic Medicine, University of Vermont.

COSTS AND AID

Tuition & Fees

Tuition	$38,930
Room and board (off-campus)	$11,500
Cost of books	$2,400
Fees	$590

Financial Aid

% students receiving aid	91
Average grant	$9,500
Average loan	$50,000
Average debt	$180,730

University of North Texas Health Science Center
Texas College of Osteopathic Medicine

Office of Admissions and Outreach, EAD-248, 3500 Camp Bowie Boulevard, Fort Worth, TX 76107-2699
Admission: 817-735-2204 • Fax: 817-735-2225 • E-mail: TCOMAdmissions@hsc.unt.edu
Website: www.hsc.unt.edu/education/tcom/admissions.cfm

STUDENT BODY

Type	Public
Enrollment	492
% male/female	48/52
% minorities	9
# applied (total/out)	1,350/97
# accepted (total/out)	155/16
# enrolled (total/out)	127/7
Average age	25

FACULTY

Total faculty	198
% female	22
% minority	8

ADMISSIONS
Average GPA and MCAT Scores

Overall GPA	3.6
MCAT Bio	9.2
MCAT Phys	8.72
MCAT Verbal	8.49
MCAT Essay	O

Application Information

Regular application	11/1
Regular notification	2/1
Early application	8/1
Early notification	10/1
Are transfers accepted?	Yes
Admissions may be deferred?	Yes
Interview required?	Yes
Application fee	$0

Academics

The University of North Texas Health Science Center at Fort Worth trains osteopathic physicians, physician assistants, biomedical scientists, and public health professionals. Its academic components are the Texas College of Osteopathic Medicine, the Graduate School of Biomedical Sciences, and the School of Public Health. Dual-degree programs combine medical training with research and public health. U.S. News & World Report and the Texas Academy of Family Physicians have both recognized TCOM's commitment to primary care.

BASIC SCIENCES: The first portion of the curriculum is designed to help students integrate the basic and clinical sciences, further develop their ability to diagnose illness, and increase their understanding of the context within which medicine is practiced. The integrated systems approach is built on the same strong foundation of scientific and clinical knowledge that has long characterized TCOM's outstanding academic program.

CLINICAL TRAINING

During the third and fourth years of study, students pursue a number of clinical training programs throughout the state at university sites, clinics, and affiliated teaching hospitals. A rural medicine track provides extensive preparation for those who wish to practice in small communities.

Students

UNT Health Science Center is located on a 17-acre, $107-million medical care complex in Fort Worth, Texas, in the city's beautiful Cultural District. Downtown Fort Worth, major thoroughfares, parks, museums, theaters, restaurants, shops, and affordable housing are all within minutes of campus.

STUDENT LIFE

The campus is located in the midst of a world-renowned cultural district, near parks and a variety of arts and entertainment facilities. The DFW Metroplex is home to several major and minor league sports teams, including the Dallas Cowboys, Texas Rangers, and Dallas Stars. A variety of student organizations bring a sense of community and camaraderie to campus. The health science center does not provide on-campus student housing, but a variety of affordable housing options are available in the area. Every student is responsible for making his or her own housing arrangements.

GRADUATES

Named as one of the nation's top 50 medical schools for primary care medicine by U.S. News & World Report, TCOM is a leader in training physicians skilled in comprehensive primary care. Approximately 65 percent of TCOM's graduates practice primary care medicine (family practice, general internal medicine, pediatrics, obstetrics and gynecology). One of the distinct advantages of an osteopathic medical education is that it prepares students to enter all three of the nation's residency programs: allopathic, military, and osteopathic. Our graduates have been placed in residency and internship positions throughout the United States. UNT Health Science Center offers residency programs through the Texas Osteopathic Postdoctoral Training Institutions (OPTI) in the following areas: Family Medicine, Internal Medicine, Obstetrics & Gynecology, Orthopedics, Radiology, Surgery and Manipulative Medicine. The Health Science Center also offers fellowship programs in Osteopathic Manipulative Therapy, Geriatric Medicine, Sports Medicine, and Vascular Surgery.

Admissions

REQUIREMENTS

At least 90 percent of the positions in each class of 150 are reserved for Texas residents. Traditional pre-medical science training at an accredited undergraduate institution is necessary to prepare for matriculation. In addition, applicants are required to submit MCAT scores, test results must be from within the past three years. Applications are accepted through the Texas Medical and Dental Schools Application Service (TMDSAS). Selected applicants are invited to interview between August and December. Initial offers of acceptance are sent on February 1 and continue until the incoming class is full. Applications are accepted through the Texas Medical and Dental Schools Application Service (TMDSAS). Selected applicants are invited to interview between August and December. Initial offers of acceptance are sent on February 1 and continue until the incoming class is full.

SUGGESTIONS

In addition to the required science course work, it is recommended that students take advanced course work in Bio-chemistry and Genetics in order to prepare for the rigors of medical education.

Admissions Requirements (Required)

MCAT scores, Science GPA, Non-science GPA, Letters of recommendation, Interview, Essays/personal statement, Exposure to medical profession, Secondary Application

Admissions Requirements (Optional)

State residency, Extracurricular activities

Overlap Schools

Baylor College of Medicine, Texas A&M University—College Station, Texas Tech University, The University of Texas HSC at Houston, University of Texas Health Science Center at San Antonio, University of Texas Southwestern Medical Center, University of Texas.

COSTS AND AID

Tuition & Fees

In-state Tuition	$6,550
Out-of-state Tuition	$19,650
Room and board (off-campus)	$10,098
Cost of books	$2,426
Fees	$2,480

Financial Aid

% students receiving aid	91
Average grant	$5,000
Average loan	$24,418
Average debt	$86,000

WEST VIRGINIA SCHOOL OF OSTEOPATHIC MEDICINE

DIRECTOR OF ADMISSIONS, 400 NORTH LEE STREET, LEWISBURG, WV 24901 • ADMISSION: 800-356-7836
FAX: 304-645-4859 • E-MAIL: ADMISSIONS@WVSOM.EDU • WEBSITE: WWW.WVSOM.EDU

STUDENT BODY

Type	Public
Enrollment	598
% male/female	51/49
% minorities	17
# applied (total/out)	2,770/2,634
# accepted (total/out)	518/456
# enrolled (total/out)	198/145
Average age	27

FACULTY

Total faculty (number)	150
% female	41
% minority	5
% part-time	19
Student-faculty ratio	6:1

ADMISSIONS
Average GPA and MCAT Scores

Overall GPA	3.44
MCAT Bio	7.7
MCAT Phys	7.1
MCAT Verbal	8.0
MCAT Essay	N

Application Information

Regular application	2/15
Regular notification	Rolling
Are transfers accepted?	Yes
Admissions may be deferred?	Yes
Interview required?	Yes
Application fee	$155

Academics

The West Virginia School of Osteopathic Medicine is part of the West Virginia State System of Higher Education. As a state school located in Lewisburg, West Virginia, it is geared toward meeting the primary care needs of West Virginia's significantly rural population. This curriculum includes a systems-based and problem-based approach to learning basic sciences and clinical training at community sites. Average student age is 26.

The West Virginia School of Osteopathic Medicine's curriculum, leading to the degree Doctor of Osteopathic Medicine, is both demanding and enriching. Full participation in required classroom, small group, laboratory, and clinical training experiences is essential. The curriculum reflects WVSOM's interrelated education, service, and research mission, and is designed to produce osteopathic physicians who are confident in rural settings.

BASIC SCIENCES: In the first year the systems-based learning curriculum includes courses in the basic and clinical sciences that provide the foundation for the study of the organ systems that follow. The problem-based curriculum is an innovative curriculum that relies heavily on small group and student-directed learning to provide the foundation for further studies. Throughout the second year, basic science and clinical instruction are focused on individual organ systems. Integration of osteopathic principles with basic and clinical sciences is maintained throughout both years.

CLINICAL TRAINING

Introduction to the clinical aspects of medical education occurs early in the student's studies, in the correlated organ systems instruction. Clinical education is designed to accomplish 4 objectives: provide ambulatory care training; provide hospital-based training; consolidate and apply clinical knowledge and skills in a family medicine setting; and allow students, through electives, to augment their training in those areas of medicine that are of special interest. The majority of years 3 and 4 of a student's medical education takes place in clinical settings including physician offices, health centers, medical center, and hospitals.

Campus Life

WVSOM students come to Lewisburg with diverse academic and professional backgrounds. Each class is composed of individuals with different levels of previous exposure to sciences and humanities.

GRADUATES

For those students who fulfill the degree requirements, graduation exercises are held the last Saturday in May.

STUDENT LIFE

There are numerous campus organizations available to students. Many involve community service projects calling for student volunteers.

Admissions

WVSOM uses the American Association of Colleges of Osteopathic Medicine Application Service (AACOMAS) to process its applications. WVSOM makes admissions decisions on a rolling basis; we review applications, conduct interviews, and make decisions throughout the admissions cycle.

REQUIREMENTS

The minimum course requirements are eight semester hours of biology, physics, general chemistry, and organic chemistry, all with associated labs, and six semester hours of English. The MCAT is required and the test must be taken no later than the fall prior to the entering class year. Average MCAT or successful applicants is in the 7–8 range. Interviews take place between August and April. Evaluation letters are required from a DO and a premed advisor, premed committee, or an approved science faculty member.

SUGGESTIONS

It is strongly recommended that prospective students take additional upper-level science courses, shadow physicians, and volunteer in health-related settings.

Admissions Requirements (Required)

MCAT scores, science GPA, letters of recommendation, interview, essay/personal statement, exposure to medical profession, minimum 90 semester hours

Admissions Requirements (Optional)

Non-science GPA, proof of West Virginia residency, extracurricular activities

COSTS AND AID
Tuition & Fees

In-state tuition	$18,886
Out-of-state tuition	$46,736
Room and board (off-campus)	$11,950
Cost of books	$8,140
Fees	$0

Financial Aid

% students receiving aid	96
Average grant	$1,000
Average loan	$55,000
Average debt	$153,679

WESTERN UNIVERSITY OF HEALTH SCIENCES
COLLEGE OF OSTEOPATHIC MEDICINE OF THE PACIFIC

OFFICE OF ADMISSIONS POMONA, CA 91766-1854 • ADMISSION: 909-469-5335
FAX: 909-469-5570 • E-MAIL: ADMISSIONS@WESTERNU.EDU • WEBSITE: WWW.WESTERNU.EDU

STUDENT BODY

Type	Private
Enrollment	829
% male/female	50/50
% minorities	17
# applied (total/out)	2,223/2,160
# accepted (total/out)	511/298
# enrolled (total/out)	220/89
Average age	27

FACULTY

Total faculty (number)	44
% female	23
% minority	32
% part-time	20
Student-faculty ratio	18:1

ADMISSIONS
Average GPA and MCAT Scores

Overall GPA	3.55
MCAT Bio	9.73
MCAT Phys	9.17
MCAT Verbal	5.72
MCAT Essay	B

Application Information

Regular application	4/15
Regular notification	Rolling
Are transfers accepted?	Yes
Admissions may be deferred?	Yes
Interview required?	Yes
Application fee	$65

Academics

Founded in 1977, Western University of Health Sciences is a nonprofit, graduate university for the health professions located next to Southern California's historic downtown Pomona. With 5 colleges and 1,885 students studying toward advanced degrees in osteopathic medicine, pharmacy, graduate nursing, physical therapy, physician assistant studies, health professions education, and veterinary medicine, Western University is one of the largest graduate schools for the health professions in California.

BASIC SCIENCES: The educational program is centered on the basic concepts of osteopathic medicine. The College of Osteopathic Medicine of the Pacific identifies and develops the knowledge, cognitive and psychomotor skills, and the personal and professional behaviors required of an osteopathic physician to provide competent and comprehensive health care to all members of a family, on a continuing basis. The first semester of the first year is designed to introduce the students to the basic concepts of anatomy (gross, embryology, and histology), biochemistry, microbiology, pathology, pharmacology, and physiology. Interwoven throughout the curriculum are osteopathic principles and practice.

The second phase begins in the second semester of the first year and continues throughout the year 2. The basic and clinical sciences concerned with one particular organ system of the body are integrated in classroom instruction. This approach emphasizes the relevance of basic sciences to clinical practice. The osteopathic approach is continually emphasized by lecture and laboratory demonstration, including manipulative techniques.

CLINICAL TRAINING

Clinical training via rotation through each of the major medical disciplines (Family Practice, Internal Medicine, Surgery, Pediatrics, Obstetrics/Gynecology, Pathology, Psychiatry, Emergency Medicine, and Radiology) is accomplished in the third and fourth years of training. Twenty-two rotations of 4 weeks each provide an opportunity for clinical skill development in primary care medicine. Several elective options are also offered during this 2-year period. The goal of the clinical curriculum is to prepare each and every student with the knowledge, attitudes, and skills to excel in his or her chosen postdoctoral-training program.

Campus Life

The main campus of Western University is in Pomona, a city of approximately 150,000, located about 35 miles east of Los Angeles near the foothills of the San Gabriel Mountains.

STUDENT LIFE

Western University provides YMCA or designated fitness club individual memberships for students at a minimal cost. The YMCA is within walking distance of the Pomona campus and offers coeducational facilities for swimming, racquetball, basketball, exercise programs, and so on.

GRADUATES

The College of Osteopathic Medicine of the Pacific supports Western University of Health Sciences (WesternU) in its mission to increase the availability of physicians to serve the needs of the people living in the western region of the United States. The College of Osteopathic Medicine provides the educational basis for internship and residencies in all medical specialties.

Admissions

REQUIREMENTS

Applicants applying for admission to the DO program must meet the following minimum academic requirements at the time of application: a minimum of 90 semester hours at a regionally accredited college or university; a completed application, which can be submitted prior to taking the MCAT; scores from the MCAT, which must be taken prior to January of the entering year; 8 semester units each of biology, inorganic chemistry (with a lab), organic chemistry (with a lab), physics; and 6 semester units of English and behavioral science.

PROCESS

Prospective applicants must submit a primary application through AACOMAS. Applications can be submitted electronically by accessing http://AACOMAS.AACOM.org, or a request for application material can be made by mail at the following address: AACOMAS, 550 Friendship Boulevard, Suite 310, Chevy Chase, MD 20815-7231, 301-968-4190. The AACOMAS deadline is April 15.

Once the AACOMAS application is received, selected applicants are contacted by postcard or e-mail with instructions on how to submit the supplementary application. At this time, applicants are instructed to complete the supplementary application online. The supplementary application and all supporting documents should be received by the Admissions Office within 30 days of the date we contact you regarding the supplementary application. The AACOMAS application, together with the supplemental application, letters of recommendation, and official MCAT score constitutes an application ready for evaluation. Once the interview process begins, students are admitted to the program on a rolling basis; therefore, students are encouraged to apply early.

As part of the application process, you are required to submit letters of recommendation from a pre-health professions committee (or the committee on your campus responsible for writing recommendations) and 1 physician. If such a committee does not exist at your college, you are required to submit 2 evaluations from science professors (i.e., biology, chemistry, or physics), 1 evaluation from a non-science professor, and 1 evaluation from a physician, DO, or MD who you have worked with or observed in a clinical setting. A recommendation letter from a DO is preferred. The science/non-science letters must be from professors who have instructed you, and the recommender should specify the course(s). All recommendations must be on the Western University form provided or on college or professional letterhead. Applicants who wish to use course work completed outside the United States must submit the transcripts for evaluation to one of the following services: World Education Services, PO Box 745, Old Chelsea Station, New York, New York, 10113-0745, 212-966-6311, WES.org; Josef Silny & Associates, 7101 SW 102 Avenue, Miami, Florida, 33173, 305-273-1616, JSilny.com; Educational Credential Evaluators, Inc., PO Box 514070, Milwaukee, Wisconsin, 53203-3470, 414-289-3400, ECE.org; International Educational Research Foundation, Inc., PO Box 3665, Culver City, California, 90231-3665, IERF.org.

A course-by-course evaluation is required, and all course work must be designated as undergraduate, graduate, or professional. Western University will only honor evaluations from one of these services. The evaluation must be included with the application.

10 Post-baccalaureate Premedical Programs

Colleges and universities offer organized post-baccalaureate premedical programs. Although this list is quite comprehensive, it may be incomplete because many schools have just recently adopted post-bacc programs. In addition, many undergraduate institutions that do not offer formal programs have flexible enrollment policies that facilitate post-bacc studies.

For further listings of post-bacc programs, Syracuse University Health Professions Advisory Program (315-443-2321) has an online compilation at: http://services.aamc.org/postbac/.

AGNES SCOTT COLLEGE: POST-BACCALAUREATE PREMEDICAL PROGRAM

Dr. Nancy Devino
Program Director
141 East College Avenue
Decatur, GA 30030
404-471-5395
E-mail: post-bacc@agnesscott.edu

AMERICAN UNIVERSITY

Post-baccalaureate Premedical Certificate
Program
Dr. Christopher Tudge, Premedical
Programs Coordinator
Department of Chemistry
American University
4400 Massachusetts Avenue Northwest
Washington, DC 20016-8014
202-885-2033
Fax: 202-885-1752
E-mail: ctudge@american.edu

ARMSTRONG ATLANTIC STATE UNIVERSITY: POST-BACCALAUREATE PREMEDICAL PROGRAM

Dr. W. C. Zipperer
Program Director
11935 Abercorn Street
Savannah, GA 31419
912-921-5660
Fax: 912-961-3226
E-mail: zipperwc@mail.armstrong.edu

ASSUMPTION COLLEGE

Heather Wilkins, PhD
Biology Department, Assumption College
Program Director
500 Salisbury Street
Worcester, MA 01609-0005
508-767-7657
E-mail: hwilkins@assumption.edu

AVILA UNIVERSITY: POST-BACCALAUREATE PREMEDICAL PROGRAM

Dr. C. Larry Sullivan,
Prehealth Professors Advisor
11901 Wornall Road
Kansas City, MO 64145
816-501-3655
Fax: 816-501-2457
E-mail: Larry.Sullivan@avila.edu

BARRY UNIVERSITY: BIOMEDICAL SCIENCES

Dr. Ralph Lauden, Associate Dean and
Director
School of Natural & Health Sciences
11300 Northeast Second Avenue
Miami Shores, FL 33161-6695
305-899-3227 or 800-756-6000, ext. 3379
Fax: 305-899-3225
Program Contact: Mrs. Denise Deen
E-mail: healthsciences@mail.barry.edu

BENNINGTON COLLEGE: POST-BACCALAUREATE PREMEDICAL PROGRAM

Dr. Janet Foley, Program Director
Office of Admissions
Bennington College
One College Drive
Bennington, VT 05201
800-833-4885
Fax: 802-440-4320
Program Contact: Jane Cary
E-mail: jcary@bennington.edu

BOSTON UNIVERSITY
Post-baccalaureate Certificate in
Premedical Studies
PMC Program Coordinator
725 Commonwealth Avenue, Room 102
Boston, MA 02215
617-353-2980
Fax: 617-353-4190
E-mail: metuss@bu.edu

BRANDEIS UNIVERSITY
Post-baccalaureate Certificate Program
Kate Fukawa-Connelly, Program Director
Office of Undergraduate Academic
Affairs
Kutz 108/MS 001
Waltham, MA 02454-9110
781-736-3470
E-mail: Kfconnelly@brandeis.edu

BRYN MAWR COLLEGE
Post-baccalaureate Premedical Program
Bryn Mawr College Canwyll House
101 North Merion Ave.
Bryn Mawr, PA 19010-2899
610-526-7350
E-mail: postbac@brynmawr.edu

CARSON-NEWMAN COLLEGE
Dr. Frank Pinkerton
Program Director
Carson-Newman College
Box 71992, Russell Avenue
Jefferson City, TN 37760
865-471-3257
Fax: 865-471-3578
E-mail: fpinkerton@cn.edu

CHAPMAN UNIVERSITY
Dr. Virginia Carson, PhD
Post-baccalaureate Premedical Program
One University Drive
Orange, CA 92866
714-997-6696
Fax: 714-532-6048
E-mail: carson@chapman.edu

CITY UNIVERSITY OF NEW YORK—
CITY COLLEGE
Belinda Smith
J-529 Program in Premedical Studies
138th Street at Convent Avenue
New York, NY 10031
212-650-7845
Fax: 212-650-7816
Program Contacts: Mr. B. Jinadu and Ms.
Y. Scott
E-mail: bsmith@sci.ccny.cuny.edu

CREIGHTON UNIVERSITY
Premedical Post-bacculaureate
Dr. Sade Kosoko-Lasaki
Program Director
2500 California Plaza
Omaha, NE 68178
402-280-2124
Program Contact: Channing Bunch
E-mail: cbunch@creighton.edu

DOMINICAN UNIVERSITY
Post-baccalaureate Premedical Program
Dr. Louis Scannichio, Program Director
7900 West Division Street
River Forest, IL 60305-1066
708-524-6901
E-mail: lscann@email.dom.edu

DREXEL UNIVERSITY
Medical Science Preparatory Program
Drexel University College of Medicine
245 North Fifteenth Street, MS 344,
Room 4-104 NCB
Philadelphia, PA 19102
215-762-4692
Fax: 215-762-8651
Program Contact: Joy Henderson
E-mail: postbac@drexelmed.edu

DREXEL UNIVERSITY
Drexel Pathway to Medical School
Drexel University College of Medicine
Dr. Loretta Walker, Program Director
245 North 15th Street,
MS 344, Room 4122 NCB
Philadelphia, PA 19102
215-762-4692
E-mail: imsinfo@drexel.edu

DREXEL UNIVERSITY
Evening Post-baccalaureate Premedical
Program
Drexel University College of Medicine
Dr. Laura Mangano, Program Director
245 North 15th Street,
MS 344, Room 4122 NCB
Philadephia, PA 19102
215-762-4692
E-mail: imsinfo@drexel.edu

DREXEL UNIVERSITY
Interdepartmental Medical Science
Program
Drexel University College of Medicine
245 North 15th Street,
MS 344, Room 4122 NCB
Philadelphia, PA 19102
Program Contact: Dr. Laura Mangano
215-762-4692
E-mail: imsinfo@drexel.edu

DUQUESNE UNIVERSITY
Post-baccalaureate Premedical Program
Dr. Kyle Selcer, Program Director
B101 Bayer Learning Center
600 Forbes Avenue
Pittsburgh, PA 15282
412-396-6335
Fax: 412-396-5587
Program Contact: Amy Whittington
MSW/LSW, Associate Director
E-mail: whitting@dug.edu

EAST TENNESSEE STATE UNVERSITY
FasTrack Program
Dr. Lattie Collins, Program Director
PO Box 70592—ETSU
East Tennessee State University
Johnson City, TN 37614
423-439-5602
Fax: 423-439-4840
E-mail: premed@etsu.edu

EASTERN VIRGINIA MEDICAL SCHOOL
Medical Master's Program
Nicole Priest, Administrator
700 West Olney Road
Norfolk, VA 23507
757-446-8480
Fax: 757-446-8449
Priestnl2@evms.edu

GEORGETOWN UNIVERSITY

Post-baccalaureate Premedical Certificate
Program
Dr. Mark Esrick, Program Director
37th O Street, Northwest,
Reiss Building, Room 506
Washington, DC 20057
202-687-6039
E-mail: esrickm@georgetown.edu

GEORGETOWN UNIVERSITY

Adam Myers, Program Director
Special Master's Program, Department of
Physiology
Georgetown University, Box 571460
Washington, DC 20057-1460
Program Contact: Ms. Aureller Cabiness
202-687-1179
Fax: 202-687-7407
E-mail: physio@georgetown

HARVARD UNIVERSITY

Health Careers Program
Dr. William Fixsen, Program Director
51 Brattle Street
Cambridge, MA 02138
617-495-2926
Program Contact: Owen Peterson
E-mail: hcp@dcemail.harvard.edu

HOFSTRA UNIVERSITY

Post-baccalaureate Premedical Program
Ellen Davolio, Program Director
Hofstra University, 250 University
College Hall
Hempstead, NY 11549
516-463-7600
Program Contact: Jennifer Jokinen
E-mail: uccelibarts@hofstra.edu

HUNTER COLLEGE—CITY UNIVERSITY OF NEW YORK

Post-baccalaureate Pre-health Professions
Program
695 Park Avenue
New York, NY 10021
212-772-5244
Program Contact: Woldine Guerrier
E-mail:
woldine.guerrier@hunter.cuny.edu

GOUCHER COLLEGE

Liza Thompson, Program Director
Post-baccalaureate Premedical Program
1201 Dulaney Valley Road
Baltimore, MD 21204-2794
800-414-3437
Fax: 410-337-6461
E-mail: lthompso@goucher.edu

INDIANA UNIVERSITY SCHOOL OF MEDICINE

Master of Science in Medical Science
Program
Indiana University School of Medicine
Dr. William Agbor Baiyee, Program
Director
Medical Science Building 207
635 Barnhill Drive
Indianapolis, IN 46202
317-278-1724
Fax: 317-278-5211
E-mail: msms@iupui.edu

INDIANA UNIVERSITY SCHOOL OF MEDICINE
Dr. Stephen Kempson, Program Director
MS in Health Sciences
635 Barnhill Drive
Physiology—MS 309
Indianapolis, IN 46202-5120
317-274-7772
Program Contact: Marlene Brown
E-mail: msphysio@iupui.edu

JOHNS HOPKINS UNIVERSITY
Post-baccalaureate Premedical Program
David Trabilsy, Program Director
3400 N. Charles Street
Wyman Park Building, Suite G1
Baltimore, MD 21218
410-516-7748
Fax: 410-516-6017
Program Contact: Kristin Schulze, Coordinator
E-mail: postbac@jhu.edu

LAKE ERIE COLLEGE OF OSTEOPATHIC MEDICINE (LECOM)
Dr. R. Nassiri, Program Director, Dean of Health Sciences
LECOM
1858 West Grandview Boulevard
Erie, PA 16509
814-866-8146
Fax: 814-886-8411
E-mail: rnassiri@lecom.edu

LAMAR UNIVERSITY
Dr. Oney Fitzpatrick, Program Director
College of Arts and Sciences
PO Box 10058
Beaumont, TX 77710
409-880-8508
Fax: 409-880-8007
E-mail: oney.fitzpatrick@lamar.edu

LOMA LINDA UNIVERSITY
Biomedical Sciences Certificate
Kenneth Wright, Program Director
Shryock Hall, Room 214
Loma Linda, CA 92350
909-558-7602
Fax: 909-558-0119
E-mail: kwright@llu.edu

LOYOLA MARYMOUNT UNIVERSITY
Post-baccalaureate Premedical Program
Dr. Rebecca Pazdral, Program Director
1 LMU Drive
MS 8225
Los Angeles, CA 90045-2659
310-338-7350
Fax: 310-338-7339
E-mail: rebecca.pazdral@lmu.edu

LOYOLA UNIVERSITY OF CHICAGO
Master of Arts in Medical Sciences
Dr. Diane Suter, Graduate
Program Director
Department of Biology
6525 North Sheridan Road
Chicago, IL 60626
773-508-3285
E-mail: dsuter@luc.edu

MANHATTANVILLE COLLEGE
Post-baccalaureate Pre-health Professions
Program
Academic Advising Office
2900 Purchase Street
Purchase, NY 10577
914-798-5353
Fax: 914-323-5338
Program Contact: Jennifer Talbot
E-mail: talbotj@mville.edu

MEDICAL UNIVERSITY OF OHIO
Post-baccalaureate Premedical Program
Carol Bennett-Clarke, PhD, Program
Director
3045 Arlington Avenue
Toledo, OH 43614-5805
419-383-4903
E-mail: carol.bennett-clarke@utoledo.edu

MIDWESTERN UNIVERSITY
Master of Biomedical Services
Leonard Bell
19555 N. 59th Ave.
Glendale, AZ 85308
623-572-3622
E-mail: lbell@midwestern.edu

MILLS COLLEGE
Post-baccalaureate Program
5000 MacArthur Boulevard
Oakland, CA 94613
510-430-2317
Fax: 510-430-3314
Program Contact: Jo Sullivan
E-mail: jscullio@mills.edu

MONTANA STATE UNIVERSITY
Post-baccalaureate Premedical Certificate
Program
MSU Division of Health Sciences, 308
Leon Johnson Hall
Bozeman, MT 59717-3080
406-994-1670
Program Contact: Jane Cary
E-mail:hpa@montana.edu

MOUNT HOLYOKE
Frances Perkins Post-baccalaureate
Studies Program
Kay Althoff
Newhall Center
50 College Street
South Hadley, MA 01075
413-538-2077
Fax: 413-538-3013
E-mail: psotbac@mtholyoke.edu

NEW YORK MEDICAL COLLEGE
Graduate School of Basic Medical
Sciences
Dr. Norman Levine, Program Director
Basic Sciences Building, Room A-41
Valhalla, NY 10595
Program Contact: Marge Riley
914-594-4110
Fax: 914-594-4944
E-mail: marge_riley@nymc.edu

NEW YORK UNIVERSITY
Post-baccalaureate/Pre-health Studies
Ms. Soomie Han, Program Director
Silver Professional Center
100 Washington Square East, #901
New York, NY 10003-6699
212-998-8160
Fax: 212-995-4549
E-mail: postbac@nyu.edu

NORTHWESTERN UNIVERSITY SCHOOL OF CONTINUING STUDIES
Premedical Professional Health Careers
Program
Admissions Coordinator
405 Church Street
Evanston, IL 60208-2650
847-491-0990
Fax: 491-3660
E-mail: scadmissions@northwestern.edu

OKLAHOMA STATE UNIVERSITY
OSU Center for Health Sciences College
of Osteopathic Medicine
Leah Haines, Program Director
1111 West 17th Street
Tulsa, OK 74107-1898
918-561-8468
Program Contact: Amanda Gutierrez
E-mail: amanda.gutierrez@okstate.edu

PENNSYLVANIA STATE UNIVERSITY
Post-baccalaureate Premedical Certificate
Program
Dr. Rodriguez, Program Director
213 Whitmore Lab
University Park, PA 16802
814-865-7620
Fax: 814-865-7214
E-mail: mxr22@psu.edu

PHILADELPHIA COLLEGE OF OSTEOPATHIC MEDICINE
Biomedical Sciences Program
Office of Admissions
4170 City Avenue
Philadelphia, PA 19131
800-999-6998
Fax: 215-871-6719
E-mail: gradadmissions@pcom.edu

RICHARD STOCKTON COLLEGE OF NEW JERSEY
Post-baccalaureate Certificate Program in
Health Professions
Dr. Ralph Werner, Program Director
Jim Leeds Road
Pomona, NJ 08240
609-652-4462
E-mail: ralph.werner@stockton.edu

RIDER UNIVERSITY
Premedical Studies Program
Dr. James Riggs, Program Director
2083 Lawrenceville Road
Lawrenceville, NJ 08648
609-895-5426
Fax: 609-895-5782
E-mail: riggs@rider.edu

ROCKHURST UNIVERSITY
Post-baccalaureate Premedical Program
Dr. James Wheeler, Program Director
Department of Chemistry
1100 Rockhurst Road
Kansas City, MO 64110
816-501-4068
Fax: 816-501-4802
E-mail: james.wheeler@rockhurst.edu

RUTGERS UNIVERSITY—NEWARK
Post-baccalaureate Pre-health Program
Dr. Victoria Ukachukwu
54 Joyce Kilmer Ave.
Piscataway, NJ 08854
732-445-4181 x164
E-mail:
vukachuck@andromeda.rutgers.edu

SAN DIEGO STATE UNIVERSITY
Pre-professional Health Advising Office
Barbara Huntington
5500 Campanile Drive
MC-1017
San Diego, CA 92182-1017
619-594-6638
Fax: 619-594-0244
E-mail: healthpr@sciences.sdsu.edu

SAN FRANCISCO STATE UNIVERSITY
Barry Rothman, Program Director
Department of Biology,
1600 Holloway Avenue
San Francisco, CA 94132
415-338-2418
E-mail: brothman@sfsu.edu

SAN FRANCISCO STATE UNIVERSITY
Health Professions Prep and
Re-applicant Program
Dr. Barry Rothman, Program Director
1600 Holloway Avenue
San Francisco, CA 94132
415-338-2418
Fax: 415-338-2295
E-mail: brothman@sfsu.edu

SCRIPPS COLLEGE
Post-baccalaureate Premedical Program
Ms. Jodi Olson, Program Director
W. M. Keck Science Center
925 North Mills Avenue
Claremont, CA 91711
909-621-8764
Fax: 909-8588
E-mail: jodi.olson@scrippscollege.edu

SEATTLE UNIVERSITY
Post-baccalaureate Premedical Program
Dr. Margaret Hudson, Program Director
Biology Department Seattle University
901 Twelfth Avenue, PO Box 22200
Seattle, WA 98122
206-296-5486
Fax: 206-296-5634
E-mail: mhudson@seattleu.edu

SOUTHERN ILLINOIS UNIVERSITY SCHOOL OF MEDICINE
Medical/Dental Education Preparatory
Program (MEDPREP)
Dr. Harold Bardo, Program Director
Wheeler Hall
Carbondale, IL 62901-4323
618-453-1554
Fax: 618-453-1919
Program Contact: Vera Felts
E-mail:
MedPrepAdmissions@siumed.edu

STATE UNIVERSITY OF NEW YORK— STONY BROOK UNIVERSITY
Post-baccalaureate Premedical Program
Dr. Harvard Lyman
Room E2360
Stony Brook, NY 11704-3353
631-632-8534
E-mail: prehealth@notes.cc.sunysb.edu

TOWSON UNIVERSITY
Post-baccalaureate Premedical and Pre-dental Program
Dr. Erik Silldorff, Program Director
Dept. of Biology
8000 York Road
Towson, MD 21252-0002
410-704-3120
Fax: 410-704-2604
E-mail: esilldorff@towson.edu

TUFTS UNIVERSITY
Post-baccalaureate Premedical Program
Carol Baffi-Dugan, Program Director
419 Boston Avenue
Dowling Hall
Medford, MA 02155
Program Contact: Liz Regan
617-627-2321
Fax: 617-627-3907
E-mail: liz.regan@tufts.edu

TULANE UNIVERSITY
Hayward Genetics Center One-year
Master's Degree Program
Dr. Mona Hoyle
1430 Tulane Avenue
New Orleans, LA 70112
504-988-6242
Fax: 504-988-3684
E-mail: hgcedprg@tulane.edu

UNIVERSITY AT BUFFALO—ROSWELL PARK CANCER INSTITUTE
Interdisciplinary Biomed/Oncology MS Program
Craig Johnson, Program Director
Roswell Park Cancer Institute
408 Research Studies Center
Buffalo, NY 14263-0001
716-845-8134
Fax: 716-845-8178
E-mail: craig.johnson@roswellpark.org

UNIVERSITY OF CALIFORNIA—IRVINE COLLEGE OF MEDICINE
Post-baccalaureate Reapplicant Program
Ms. Ellen Munoz
Medical Education Building 802
PO Box 4089
Irvine, CA 92697-4089
949-824-8930
E-mail: pbreapp@uci.edu

UNIVERSITY OF CALIFORNIA—LOS ANGELES, DAVID GEFFEN SCHOOL· OF MEDICINE
UCLA Premedical Predental
Enhancement Program
Louise Howard, Program Director
13-154 CHS Office of Academic Enrichment
10833 Le Conte Avenue
Los Angeles, CA 90095
310-825-3575
Fax: 310-206-7180
E-mail: aeotemp2@mednet.ucla.edu

UNIVERSITY OF CALIFORNIA—
SAN DIEGO SCHOOL OF MEDICINE

Re-applicant Post-baccalaureate Program
Saundra Kirk
Student Outreach Services
Date Building, Room 105, 9500 Gilman
Ave.
La Jolla, CA 92093-0655
858-534-4171
Fax: 858-534-5293
E-mail: sjkirk@ucsd.edu

UNIVERSITY OF CALIFORNIA—
SAN FRANCISCO

UCSF Post-baccalaureate Programs
Valerie Margol, Program Director
1855 Folsom Street
Room 305, Box 0409
San Francisco, CA 94143-0409
Program Contact: Felicia Tripp
415-514-1390
Fax: 415-502-1680
E-mail: tripp@medsch.ucsf.edu

UNIVERSITY OF CINCINNATI

Master of Science in Physiology
(12 Month Premedical Program)
Dr. Robert Banks, Program Director
231 Albert B. Sabin Way
PO Box 670576
Cincinnati, OH 45267-0576
513-558-3104
Fax: 513-558-5738
Program Contact: Karen Coleman
E-mail: Karen.Coleman@uc.edu

UNIVERSITY OF CONNECTICUT
SCHOOL OF MEDICINE

Post-baccalaureate Program
Keat Sanford, Program Director
Admissions Center
263 Farmington Avenue
Farmington, CT 06030-3906
Program Contact: Tricia Avolt
860-679-4306
Fax: 860-679-1899
E-mail: robertson@nso2.uchc.edu

UNIVERSITY OF MARYLAND—
COLLEGE PARK

College of Chemical and Life Sciences
Dr. Joelle Presson, Program Director
1322 Symons Hall
University of Maryland
College Park, MD 20742
301-405-6892
E-mail: jpresson@umd.edu

UNIVERSITY OF MASSACHUSETTS—
BOSTON

Post-baccalaureate Premedical Program
Grace McSorley
University Career Services
100 Morrissey Boulevard
Boston, MA 02125
617-287-5500
Fax: 617-287-5525
E-mail: grace.mcsorley@umb.edu

UMDNJ-GRADUATE SCHOOL OF BIOMEDICAL SCIENCES AT NEW JERSEY MEDICAL SCHOOL

Master's in Biomedical Sciences
Dr. B.J. Wagner, Program Director
ADMC 1, Suite 110
Newark, NJ 07103
973-972-4511
Fax: 973-972-5656
E-mail: Wagner@umdnj.edu

UNIVERSITY OF MIAMI

Pre-medical Post-baccalaureate Program
Linette Aguiar, Program Director
205 Ashe Building
Coral Gables, FL 33124-4622
Program Contact: Alisa Rodriguez
305-284-5176
Fax: 305-284-4686
E-mail: premed@miami.edu

UNIVERSITY OF NORTH CAROLINA—GREENSBORO

Premedical Program
Robert E. Cannon, PhD
Post-Baccalaureate Premed Program,
UNC—Greensboro
Department of Biology, PO Box 26170
Greensboro, NC 27402-6170
336-256-0071
Fax: 336-334-5839
E-mail: Robert_Cannon@uncg.edu

UNIVERSITY OF NORTH FLORIDA

Post-baccalaureate Premedical Program
Dr. Michael Lentz, Program Director
4567 St. Johns Bluff Road South
Jacksonville, FL 32224
904-620-2608
E-mail: mlentz@unf.edu

UNIVERSITY OF NORTH TEXAS

Post-baccalaureate Pre-certification in
Medical Science
Carla Lee, Program Director
3500 Camp Bowie Boulevard,
Suite EAD-816
Fort Worth, TX 76107
817-735-2560 or 800-511-4723
Program Contact: Amanda Griffith
E-mail: gsbs@hsc.unt.edu

UNIVERSITY OF OREGON

Post-baccalaureate Premedical Program
Office of Academic Advising
University of Oregon
Eugene, OR 97403-5217
541-346-3211
Fax: 541-346-6048
Program Contact: Karen Cooper
E-mail: karenc@uoregon.edu

UNIVERSITY OF PENNSYLVANIA

Post-baccalaureate Pre-health Program
Grace Hershman, Program Director
3440 Market Street, Suite 100
College of General Studies
Philadelphia, PA 19104-3335
215-898-3110
Fax: 215-573-2053
E-mail: gracemh@sas.upenn.edu

UNIVERSITY OF PITTSBURGH

Arts and Sciences Post-baccalaureate
Program
Donna Walker, Program Director
201 Thackeray Hall
University of Pittsburgh
Pittsburgh, PA 15260
412-624-6444
Fax: 412-624-3707
E-mail: walker@as.pitt.edu

UNIVERSITY OF SOUTH FLORIDA
Biomedical Sciences
4202 East Fowler Ave.
SCA 400
Tampa, FL 33620
813-974-2144
Fax: 813-974-5314
E-mail: chemadvising@cas.usf.edu

UNIVERSITY OF SOUTHERN CALIFORNIA
Post-baccalaureate Premedical Program
Admissions Coordinator
CAS 120, USC College
Los Angeles, CA 90089-0151
213-821-2354
Fax: 213-740-3664
E-mail: postbacc@usc.edu

UNIVERSITY OF VERMONT
Post-baccalaureate Premedical Program
Polly Allen
1322 South Prospect Street
Burlington, VT 05401
802-656-2085
Fax: 802-656-3891
E-mail: profdev@uvm.edu

VIRGINIA COMMONWEALTH UNIVERSITY
Premedical Basic Sciences
Dr. Jan Chlebowski, Program Director
Office of Graduate Education VCU
School of Medicine
1101 East Marshall Street Box 980565
Richmond, VA 23298-9565
804-828-0641
Fax: 804-827-1469
E-mail: jfchlebo@vcu.edu

WASHINGTON UNIVERSITY IN ST. LOUIS
Post-baccalaureate Premedical Program
Dr. Steven Ehrlich, Program Director
One Brookings Drive, Campus Box 1064
St. Louis, MO 63130-4899
314-935-4320
E-mail: ehrlich@wustl.edu

WAKE FOREST UNIVERSITY SCHOOL OF MEDICINE
Post-baccalaureate Premedical Program
Brenda Latham-Sadler, Program Director
Medical Center Boulevard
Office of Student Services
Winston-Salem, NC 27157
Program Contact: Nicole Henry
336-716-4271
Fax: 336-716-5807
E-mail: nhenry@wfubmc.edu

WEST CHESTER UNIVERSITY
Premedical Program
Dr. Stephen Zimniski, Program Director
117 Schmucker Science Center South
West Chester, PA 19383
610-436-2978
Fax: 610-436-3277
E-mail: pmed@wcupa.edu

WORCESTER STATE COLLEGE
Post-baccalaureate Premedical Program
Dr. Allan Cooper, Program Director
486 Chandler Street
Worcester, MA 01602
508-929-8600
E-mail: acooper@worcester.edu

ALPHABETICAL INDEX

INDEX BY LOCATION

INDEX BY COST

LESS THAN $30,000

$30,000–$40,000

MORE THAN $40,000

ABOUT THE AUTHOR

Malaika Stoll is a recent graduate of Stanford Medical School. She grew up in Berkeley, California, and graduated from Dartmouth College. After college she worked for two years as a Health Educator with the Peace Corps in Zaire. She earned a master's degree in public affairs from Princeton University, and went on to work in international health and development for the World Bank and the United States Agency for International Development. She completed her science requirements at Goucher College's Post-bacc Premedical Program. She is about to begin her family practice residency at Lehigh Valley Hospital in Pennsylvania.

Paying For Graduate School 101

You've been to college. You've got the degree (and the student loans) to show for it. So you might be thinking, "Hey, I did this once, do I really need to go over it all again?" In a word, yes.

More Grad School Tips from The Princeton Review
Graduate School Companion

You're not going to grad school to study the exact same things you've already spent four years learning, are you? So why assume that you don't need to learn anything new about paying for grad school?

While you might understand the basics about how federal loans work and how scholarships, grants, and fellowships can reduce the final bill, there are lesser-known and fairly new options out there. After all, laying down $100,000—possibly more—in loans, cash, and other funds in exchange for a top-notch education requires just as much research and planning as deciding which school gets all that dough!

The good news is that you still have a little time before you have to really worry about signing on the dotted line for any type of financial assistance. Take a moment right now and let us show you what it takes to afford an excellent postgraduate education.

YOU'RE NOT AN UNDERGRAD ANYMORE...

Graduate school is not College 2.0. Not only are you not going to be studying the same things this time around, but your circumstances aren't the same either. Maybe you're coming back to school after a few years in the professional world, maybe you've got a family now, maybe you want a higher degree to give you an edge over others in your field. Whatever the changes, you're going to have to take them into account when considering how to pay for school and when applying for financial aid.

One important difference to keep in mind is that this time, at least with respect to government-sponsored loans, you'll be considered independent. Lenders will not take into account your parents' income and assets—just yours. Your credit history will also be important. When you started college as an undergrad, you probably had little or no credit history to speak of. By now, however, you've no doubt accumulated some, most likely through your undergraduate student loans and/or some high-interest credit card debt. If your credit history is less than positive, lenders may require you to have a co-signer.

Your enrollment status will also affect just how much grad school will end up costing you. If you're going to grad school full-time, you may have to forgo the earned income that part-time students can take home from a paycheck; but part-time students don't get some of the financial aid options that full-time students are eligible for. Therefore, it's in your best interest to figure out your financial aid eligibility in each scenario.

If you have no credit history or a creditworthy co-borrower, you should consider Preprime™: an underwriting methodology pioneered by MyRichUncle. It takes into account your academic performance and student behavior to see if you will be a responsible borrower. www.myrichuncle.com/PreprimeLoans.aspx

Employer-Financed Opportunities

Some employers will offer tuition reimbursement or a limited financial sum for employees to attend graduate school part time. Employers expect the advanced degree to enhance your performance on the job or to make you eligible for a different job within the company. Some employers expect you to commit to staying with the company for a certain length of time after receiving your degree. Be sure you understand all aspects of your employer's tuition reimbursement program before you sign on.

Check out the Scholarship Search page at: PrincetonReview. com/college/finance

Scholarships and Grants

These are the best form of financial aid because you don't have to pay them back. Remember, though, that most scholarships require a minimum GPA and that some grants are good for only one year. When evaluating your payment options, make sure there is a reasonable expectation that the financial aid package being offered will be available for the length of time you expect it will take to get your degree.

Fellowships, Stipends, and Assistantships

Fellowships, stipends and assistantships are other options available to graduate school students. Professional degree programs (law, business, medicine, and so on) typically do not offer them to students.

Fellowships come in many different forms. Sometimes partial tuition scholarships are called fellowships. These university-sponsored fellowships consist of a cash award that is promptly subtracted from your tuition bill. You can earn the amount of the award by teaching for a department or by completing research for a faculty member. The percentage of students who receive this type of fellowship and the amount paid to each will vary depending on the intended degree and field, enrollment status (full- or part-time), and years of enrollment.

It's important to note that survival on a fellowship alone is unlikely. Fellowships are taxable income—federal, state, county, and city—and you may be expected to pay for school fees, supplies, and books out of your fellowship, as well as tuition. If the fellowship doesn't cover the full cost of your attendance, you'll have to explore other financing options.

LOAN OPTIONS

When scholarships, grants, and fellowships don't cover the full cost of attendance, many students take out loans to help out with the rest. The federal government and private commercial lenders offer educational loans to graduate students. As with undergraduate student loans, federal loans are usually the "first choice" for borrowers because some are subsidized by the federal government and offer lower interest rates. Private loans, on the other hand, have fewer restrictions on borrowing limits, but may have higher interest rates and more stringent credit qualification criteria.

Federal Loans

Stafford Loans

For many students seeking financial aid, the Stafford loan is the typical place to start. The Stafford loan program features a fixed interest rate and yearly caps on the maximum amount a student can borrow. Stafford loans can either be subsidized (the government pays the interest while the student is in school) or unsubsidized (the student is responsible for the interest that accrues while in school). Starting July 1, 2007, the maximum amount a student can borrow is $20,500, of which $8,500 can be subsidized.

For either program, the borrower submits a federal application known as the Free Application for Federal Student Aid (FAFSA). The application is available online at www.fafsa.ed.gov.

Many people assume that the government sets the rate on student loans, and that this rate is locked in stone. That's not true. The government merely sets the maximum rate lenders can charge (which is fixed at 6.8% as of 2007). Lenders are free to charge less than that if they want to.

Historically, however, most lenders have charged the maximum rate because Stafford loans are distributed via colleges' financial aid offices, which maintained preferred lender lists of a select number of lenders to choose from. Reduced numbers of lenders meant little competition for borrowers, which gave lenders very little incentive to offer more competitive rates.

Federal Stafford loans also have cumulative or "aggregate" limits: graduate students may, in certain cases, borrow up to $138,500 inclusive of their undergraduate aggregate limit. Some medical students can borrow up to $40,500 a year and $189,125 in total during the course of their medical education.

GradPLUS Loans

The GradPLUS loan is a federal loan that is an alternative for graduate and professional students. Getting approved for one might be easier than getting approved for a private loan (as long as your credit history is good). Grad-PLUS loans have a fixed interest rate.

GradPLUS loans have no yearly limit. Graduate and professional students can borrow up to the full cost of education minus any financial aid received. The school must certify an applicant's eligibility for this loan.

In order to receive a federally sponsored student loan, you must not owe a refund on a federal grant or already be in default on a federal student loan.

For help filling out the FAFSA, check out MyRichUncle's easy-to-use FAFSA-Assistant tool at MyRichUncle.com/TPR

According to federal law, students denied a GradPLUS loan, unlike the ParentPLUS loan program, are NOT eligible for increased Stafford loan limits.

Private Loans

Private student loans can make it possible to cover the costs of higher education when other sources of funding have been exhausted. Additionally, private loans can pay expenses that federal loans can't, such as application and testing fees, room and board expenses, and the cost of transportation and books. When you apply for a private loan, the lending institution will check your credit score and determine your capacity to pay back the money you borrow. While private loans do not have annual borrowing limits, they can have higher variable interest rates and are not protected under interest caps.

Borrow the minimum
Just because someone is offering to lend you thousands upon thousands of dollars doesn't mean you should necessarily take them up on that offer. At some point, you'll be responsible for repaying the debt. Wouldn't it be better to put more money toward retirement, rather than student loan interest repayment? Think about it.

KNOW WHAT YOU WANT

When it's all said and done, you will have to take a variety of factors into account in order to choose the best school for you and for your future. You shouldn't have to mortgage your future to follow a dream, but you also shouldn't downgrade this opportunity just to save a few bucks. Visit the schools on your short list and try to meet faculty and students. The right program—at the right price—will challenge you and provide you with the skills necessary to make the business venture of business school worth the calculated risk.

KNOW YOUR RIGHTS

You have the right to shop for and secure the best rates possible for your student loans. You have the right to choose the lending institution you prefer. You do not have to use the lenders recommended by your school. All your school must do—and all it is legally allowed to do—is to show the lending institution of your choice that you are indeed enrolled and the amount you are eligible to receive.

DO YOUR RESEARCH

All student loan lenders are not created equal, so investigate all your options, and look for lenders that are offering loans at rates less than the federally mandated maximum (remember, that's 6.0% for subsidized Staffords, and 6.8% for unsubsidized Staffords as of July 2008).

One lending institution that's been in the news lately is MyRichUncle. MyRichUncle offers federal loans, including subsidized and unsubsidized Stafford loans and private loans. However, MyRichUncle has remembered that the government sets the maximum interest rate for Stafford loans, and has chosen to discount the rate upon repayment. Those discounts will not disappear, like they may with other lenders, unless you default on the loan. Remember, maximize your lowest cost funds first.

SO, WHY MY RICH UNCLE?

Well, we here at The Princeton Review think it's important that you have all the information when you're figuring out how to pay for grad school, and we think MyRichUncle is doing something different—and helpful—with their approach to student loans.

They know that paying for postgraduate education can be a complicated and intimidating process. They believe, as does The Princeton Review, that students should have access to the best education possible. They also believe student loan debt can be a serious problem, so your loans should be about getting the tools necessary for the best education that will position you for the most opportunities when you graduate.

Something else to remember: Your student loan is solidly your responsibility.

When you enter into a loan agreement, you're entering into a long-term relationship with your lender—10 to 15 years, on average. The right student loan, from the right lender, can help you avoid years of unnecessary fees and payments.

MyRichUncle was featured in *FastCompany* magazine's Fast 50 and *BusinessWeek*'s Top Tech Entrepreneurs. MyRichUncle and its parent company, MRU Holdings, are financed by a number of leading investment banks and venture capitalists, including subsidiaries of Merrill Lynch, Lehman Brothers, and Battery Ventures.

For more information, check out

Notes

Notes

Notes

Notes

Notes

Notes

Notes

ST. GEORGE'S UNIVERSITY
School of Medicine

INTRODUCTION

Founded in 1977, St. George's University (SGU) is an international center of education located in Grenada, West Indies. St. George's gives students a global educational experience unlike that of any other university.

With the core mission of providing an international education, St. George's University actively explores and initiates worldwide partnerships, and draws faculty and students from more than 90 countries. With this international focus, students are given the opportunity to develop the distinct social and professional skills they need to practice medicine on a global scale.

CURRICULUM

Students can enter SGU's seven-year Bachelor of Science/Doctor of Medicine (BS/MD) program following high school; however, the majority of students from North America who hold a bachelor's degree with the appropriate premedical courses enter directly into the MD program, delivered over four calendar years. A medical student will begin studying traditional basic science disciplines on Grenada's True Blue campus. St. George's University also offers an alternate option for medical students to spend the first year of the program on the campus of Northumbria University in the United Kingdom as part of the Keith B. Taylor Global Scholars Program.

The clinical program takes place in the final two years, and students are placed at Clinical Centers and affiliated hospitals in the United States and the United Kingdom. St. George's University's highly integrated system of affiliated ACGME-approved hospitals and Clinical Centers offers students the ability to train in both the US and UK systems.

St. George's University students also have access to the Windward Islands Research and Education Foundation (WINDREF). WINDREF draws researchers from around the world, and works in collaboration with The Rockefeller University, Harvard University, Johns Hopkins University and other American and British institutions.

Additionally, medical students can advance their knowledge in specific areas of medical study with dual degree programs within the School of Medicine. The Doctor of Medicine/Master of Science (MD/MSc) dual degree program is designed for medical students who desire to become involved in original, thesis-oriented research. Also offered is the Doctor of Medicine/Master of Public Health (MD/MPH) dual degree program. MD/MPH students specialize in Biomedical Public Health, which expands on areas relevant to the mental and physical health of and preventative measures for communities.

GRENADA CAMPUS

The stunning True Blue campus is the heart of the University. This wireless-enhanced, state-of-the-art university campus is located on the southwestern corner of Grenada, on a peninsula overlooking the Caribbean Sea. The campus has recently seen the construction of more than 50 new buildings including a library, anatomy labs, dormitories, lecture halls and a research institute.

STUDENTS

Student support services are deeply ingrained into the culture of the St. George's University community. Virtually all students take advantage of SGU's comprehensive Student Success Division, operated by the Dean of Students and the Department of Educational Services, that helps students adapt learning styles to various teaching methods with course tutorials, personal evaluations, and seminars in time management, study skills and note-taking.

Students enjoy a rich student life, with almost 50 diverse student organizations and a wide variety of organized athletic programs. In addition, all students have access to the 17,000-square-foot Student Center, which houses a cafeteria, food court, offices for student organizations, a fitness center, lockers, showers and many more amenities.

FACULTY

One of the most impressive features of St. George's University is the outstanding international faculty numbering more than 800. Many have taught at St. George's for decades, some from its inception over 30 years ago. The student to faculty ratio is 9 to 1 in the Basic Sciences years.

Each year there are more than 120 visiting scholars in the School of Medicine coming from institutions such as Cambridge University, Georgetown University and Emory University. The Visiting Scholar Program gives students exposure to a variety of experts in various fields within carefully structured curricula. This ongoing program gives students the luxury of a controlled academic program that features a continuous stream of international experts who become a lifelong network of colleagues.

AFFILIATED HOSPITALS AND UNIVERSITIES

St. George's University has affiliated hospitals in New York, New Jersey, Maryland, Michigan, Connecticut, California, Florida and 18 hospitals in the United Kingdom. In addition to the Keith B. Taylor Global Scholars Program, St. George's University has partnerships with other universities in the United Kingdom, Bermuda and the British Virgin Islands.

GRADUATES

Approximately 99% of eligible US graduates who applied obtained ACGME-approved residency positions.

More than 7,000 School of Medicine graduates are currently practicing medicine in over 35 countries. They work in virtually every specialty and subspecialty, and frequently hold academic positions in other medical schools around the world.

St. George's University students have a ten-year average pass rate of 90% for US and Canadian first-time USMLE Step I examinees.

FINANCIAL AID

Approximately 80% of St. George's University School of Medicine students utilize financial aid to pay for all or part of their educational expenses. The School of Medicine has been approved by the US Department of Education to participate in the US government-sponsored student loan program.

CONTACT

To learn more about St. George's University School of Medicine, call 1 (800) 899-6337, extension 280, or visit www.sgu.edu.

*See St. George's University's ad on the inside-back cover of this book.

More expert advice from The Princeton Review

If you want to give yourself the best chance for getting into the medical school of your choice, we can help you get the highest test scores, make the most informed choices, and make the most of your experience once you get there. Whether you want to be an M.D., a nurse, or any other kind of health care professional, we can even help you ace the tests and make a career move that will let you use your skills and education to their best advantage.

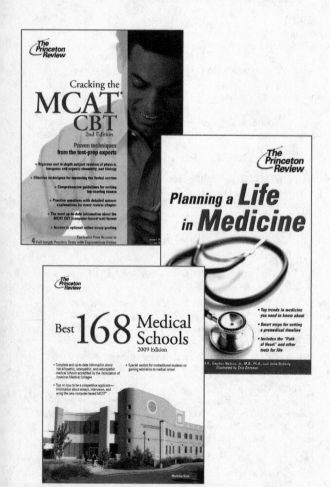

Cracking the MCAT CBT, 2nd Edition
978-0-375-76597-1 • $59.95/C$77.00

MCAT Workout
978-0-375-76631-2 • $22.95/C$29.95

Cracking the NCLEX-RN with Sample Tests on CD-ROM, 8th Edition
978-0-375-76542-1 • $34.95/C$44.00

Anatomy Coloring Workbook, 2nd Edition
978-0-375-76342-7 • $19.95/C$27.95

Biology Coloring Workbook
978-0-679-77884-4 • $18.00/C$27.00

Human Brain Coloring Workbook
978-0-679-77885-1 • $17.00/C$25.00

Physiology Coloring Workbook
978-0-679-77850-9 • $18.00/C$27.00

Best 168 Medical Schools, 2009 Edition
978-0-375-42881-4 • $22.95/C$25.95

Planning a Life in Medicine
978-0-375-76460-8 • $16.95/C$23.95

 Available at Bookstores Everywhere
www.PrincetonReview.com